BUDGETING FOR MODERN GOVERNMENT

Second Edition

BUDGETING FOR MODERN GOVERNMENT

Second Edition

DONALD AXELROD

Professor Emeritus of Public Administration
Nelson A. Rockefeller College of Public Affairs and Policy
State University of New York at Albany

St. Martin's Press, Inc.

New York

Executive editor: Don Reisman
Manager, publishing services: Emily Berleth
Editor, publishing services: Doug Bell
Project management: Publication Services, Inc.
Production supervisor: Joe Ford

Library of Congress Catalog Card Number: 94-65237

Manufactured in the United States of America.
9 8 7 6 5
f e d c b

For information, write:
St. Martin's Press, Inc.
175 Fifth Avenue
New York, NY 10010

ISBN: 0-312-08417-X

To Rosemary and Jonathan

CONTENTS

PREFACE

The preface to the first edition of this book emphasized that "budgeting at all levels of government commands the headlines as never before." In subsequent years these words have proved to be an understatement. Budgeting now dominates almost the entire political agenda. The big questions are: What shall we do? Can we afford it? How shall we pay for it? Deficits, debt, taxes, and expenditures have become household words, indeed fighting words. Federal, state, and local election campaigns turn on issues of fiscal policy once left to political insiders and technocrats.

Yet, for all the debate, greater public understanding of budget issues has not led to a meeting of the minds on budget priorities, the means of financing them, the expansion of entitlement programs such as social security and Medicare, deficit and debt reduction, and the role of the budget in stimulating an ailing economy. Instead, gridlock paralyzes nearly every aspect of budgeting at all levels of government. It has become increasingly difficult to achieve a political consensus on budget policy and the budget process itself.

In sheer frustration at their inability to cope with the complexities of budgeting, political leaders turn to mechanical formulas to limit expenditures, control deficits, and reduce debt, such as constitutional amendments to balance the budget, five-year schedules to cut deficits, automatic budget cuts when expenditures exceed a preset limit, and caps on revenue increases. The effect is to put government on automatic pilot. A knowledgeable observer of the federal budget process has proclaimed that the capacity to govern is the capacity to budget. Considering current developments, he doubts that the latter exists.

Similarly, voters are cynical, disenchanted with the budget process, and susceptible to glib panaceas. So distrustful are they that they have taken matters in their own hands and, bypassing legislatures, have approved referenda that set limits on taxes, expenditures, and debt. Increasingly, the 1990s have become the era of "budgeting by ballot."

Such is the environment of budgeting today. Is this bleak outlook justified? Has American budgeting failed as a political decision-making process? Or are the problems exaggerated? Is a stagnant economy responsible for the sharp budget conflicts, which in time may ease as the economy rebounds? Or can we expect budgetary combat well past the year 2000? What can be done to revitalize the budget process even in periods of slow economic growth? How far can we go in controlling hitherto uncontrollable expenditures, deficits, and debt? Or are these problems less perilous than many lurid accounts suggest? Is budgeting as it is practiced today suffering from a unique American malaise or do other countries experience similar conflicts? Can any budget system cope with a complex global economy that is beset by recessions?

These controversial issues, the increasing complexity of budgeting, and the fast-moving changes in the last ten years have called for an updating and revision of this book. Comprehensive in scope, the book deals with the processes, problems, policies, theories, and controversies of budgeting at all levels of government in the United States in the last decade of the twentieth century. While the book is not a comparative study, it highlights several practices in other countries that may be relevant for the United States.

Budgeting for Modern Government assumes no previous knowledge of budgeting on the part of the reader, who could be a graduate student in public administration, political science, economics, health administration, criminal justice administration, or welfare administration; an advanced undergraduate student in these fields; a program administrator; a practitioner; or an interested citizen who would like to understand some of the seemingly intractable issues of the day. It covers in detail every significant phase of budgeting in simple, nontechnical language and is replete with many examples from the "real world."

The book looks at all facets of budgeting: budget formulation and implementation; capital budgeting, with an emphasis on financing the reconstruction of a decaying infrastructure; the proliferation of off-budget budgets that befuddle voters and politicians alike; two information systems that make budgeting possible (governmental accounting systems and measurement of the agency performance); the linkages between the budget and economic policy against a backdrop of deficits and debt and the political appeal of balanced budgets; the revival of budgeting as a tool to "reinvent government" and cut expenditures; and the pervasive impact of the courts on budget decisions.

Since budgeting appears to be in disarray everywhere, the book examines fifteen major reforms designed to improve government's capacity to budget. In so doing, it focuses on budget theories that have surfaced over the years, and identifies those that have met the test of time and those that have turned out to be irrelevant or exercises in fantasy.

While the primary focus of the book is not the politics of budgeting, which has been dealt with ably by several writers, it emphasizes that no phase of budgeting, no matter how seemingly technical, escapes political pressures. From the beginning to the end of the budget process, political values determine budget decisions. If budgeting is conflict ridden, it is because it mirrors the lack of consensus on the size, functions, and financing of government.

The thirteen chapters in the book encompass the following dominant themes that pervade the budget process:

Chapter 1 focuses on budgeting as the nerve center of federal, state, and local governments and describes the eight major functions of budgeting and their linkages with the political process.

Chapter 2 shows how the stage is set for the budget process even before agencies submit budget requests; describes top-down fiscal and policy guidance that agencies receive from chief executives and central budget offices before the official beginning of the budget season; and identifies the extent of agency flexibility, if any, under these and other constraints.

Chapter 3 probes the ways in which individual agencies prepare their budget requests; analyzes their systems, or nonsystems, for reaching a consensus; and portrays their strategies, ploys, and frustrations.

Chapter 4 lays out the policies and steps leading to the preparation of the government's budget by the chief executive and the central budget office; emphasizes the constraints, successes, and failures that attend this process; and stresses the importance of forecasts of revenue and expenditures, which frequently lead to flawed decisions.

Chapter 5 underscores the fact that capital budgeting is an integral part of budgeting, but "different"; develops the pros and cons of capital budgets; and analyzes the complexities of financing and rehabilitating a decaying infrastructure.

Chapter 6 points out the paradox of "off-budget budgets," which don't appear in budget documents or appropriations bills; explains the reasons for their explosive growth, especially in the form of government corporations, public authorities, and special districts; and raises issues of accountability and control.

Chapter 7 links budget, fiscal, and economic policy at all levels of government; explores the impact of the economy on the budget and the budget on the economy; identifies the forces that propel tax, expenditure, and debt policy; and probes the issues surrounding deficits, debt, and balanced budgets.

Chapter 8 describes and evaluates the role of federal, state, and local legislative bodies in formulating and implementing budgets; explores their frequently tortured relationships with chief executives; raises the question of whether expanded legislative staffs result in better budgets; and considers abortive congressional efforts to reform internal budgetary procedures, suggesting that in many respects state legislatures can show them the way.

Chapter 9 stresses the fact that the "real" budget is not the one proposed by chief executives and embodied in appropriations bills, but rather the budget implemented by the end of the year; identifies and accounts for the differences between the proposed budget and the implemented budget; and demonstrates that budget implementation is equally as significant as budget formulation.

Chapter 10 argues that budgeting is no better than the information systems that support it—accounting systems and performance measurement systems; describes the concepts and practices of both systems; and points out that the "database" of budgeting comprising the two systems is one of the fastest-moving developments in budgeting.

Chapter 11 examines the fifteen major reforms designed to improve government's capacity to budget, weighs their successes and failures and lasting imprint on the budget process and analyzes their impact on budget decision making.

Chapter 12 spotlights the role of the courts in budget decisions; demonstrates that budgeting is no longer just a legislative and executive "show"; notes the dramatic impact of judicial decisions on financing education, health and mental health, corrections, and welfare; and lays out the pros and cons of judicial intervention.

Chapter 13 accents the symbiotic relationship of budgeting and management improvement since the earliest days of budgeting; traces the ups and downs of management improvement programs over a sixty-year span; explains the low priority given to them during the last two decades; and explains that there are new opportunities for such programs because of pressures of deficits and the current fad of "reinventing government."

Like the first edition, this book has grown out of many years of first-hand experience with budgeting as a practitioner, a teacher, a writer, and a consultant in the United States and other countries. It draws heavily on published and unpublished data of governments; interviews with budget officials at all levels of government; professional organizations of budgeteers, public administrators, and academics; and organizations representing states, municipalities, and international agencies. It also owes much to many gifted writers on budgeting whose works are recognized in the bibliography and the endnotes.

Budgeteers have been especially generous with their advice and assistance. Brian M. Roherty, Executive Director of the National Association of State Budget Officers, provided current data on state budget practices. So did various officials of the National Conference of State Legislatures. At least twenty state and local budget officers either shared internal documents with me or critically reviewed my assessment of various phases of budgeting. Especially helpful were Rudy F. Runko, Budget Director of New York State; Mike Marsh, former Administrator of the Budget and Management Division of the state of Oregon; and Richard F. Keevey, former Director of the Office of Management and Budget in New Jersey, and now Chief Financial Officer in the Department of Defense. Steven D. Gold, Director of the Center for the Study of the States of the Rockefeller Institute of Government, State University of New York, gave me access to significant data on state and local governments and particularly on state–local fiscal relations.

At the federal level, the Office of Management and Budget, the General Accounting Office, the Congressional Budget Office, the Bureau of the Census, the Joint Financial Management Improvement Program, and the Senate and House Budget Committees continued to be invaluable sources of information and analysis. Among international agencies, I should like to acknowledge the unfailing assistance of A. Premchand, Assistant Director of Financial Affairs of the International Monetary Fund, and Digambar Bhouraskar, former director of the Development Administration Division of the United Nations.

Several colleagues reviewed parts of the manuscript and, in some cases, all of it. Their many helpful suggestions proved to be invaluable. Among them are Richard F. Fenno, Jr., Professor of Political Science, the University of Rochester; Martin Ives, Director of Research of the Governmental Accounting Standards Board; Naomi Caiden, Professor of Political Science, California State University, Los Angeles; Harry C. Bredemeier, Professor Emeritus of Sociology, Rutgers University; Raymond Frost, former director of the Institute of Economic Development of the World Bank; the late Albert J. Abrams, former Secretary of the New York State Senate; Herbert Persil, Director of the Office of Budget, Housing, and Urban Development Department,

Washington, D.C.; Anne Khademian, Professor, Robert La Follette Institute of Public Affairs, University of Wisconsin; Krishna K. Tummala, Professor of Political Science, Kansas State University; Earle Klay, Professor of Public Administration and Policy, Florida State Universtiy; Nicholas Alozie, Professor of Political Science and Public Affairs, Arizona State University; Thomas P. Lauth, Professor of Political Science, University of Georgia; Gloria A. Grizzle, Director, School of Public Administration and Policy, Florida State University; and Michael E. Meyer, Professor, Department of Criminal Justice, University of North Dakota.

In exploring the vast literature on budgeting and in tapping several computerized databases for information and citations, I owe much to Richard D. Irving of the Thomas E. Dewey Graduate Library of Rockefeller College of the State University of New York in Albany.

This revision also reflects the continuing influence of three individuals who guided me in the preparation of the first edition: the late Frederick C. Mosher of the University of Virginia, who over the years had been a leader in advancing the art and science of budgeting; Michael J. White, formerly of the University of Southern California and now in private law practice, who proved to be a superb budgeteer and extraordinary editor; and T. N. Hurd, former budget director and secretary to the governor of New York State, who originally encouraged me in shaping this book.

Above all, I owe much to the support and sharp editorial eye of my wife Selma. It was not always easy to meet her high standards of simplicity, clarity, and relevance. I hope I did at least in part.

I should also like to add the usual disclaimer that any errors of fact and misinterpretation of data are mine and mine alone despite the help I got along the way. The strong views in the book, many of them controversial, are also my own, which my colleagues may or may not share.

Finally, I should like to express my gratitude to Lori Saba, who typed and retyped several drafts of this book. How she was able to decipher my illegible scrawl and convert it into the presentable copy that flowed from the word processor remains a mystery to me.

Donald Axelrod

ABOUT THE AUTHOR

Donald Axelrod is one of the leading experts on government budgeting and management. As a practitioner, consultant, writer, and teacher in these fields, he has consulted widely with state and local governments in the United States and, through the United Nations and USAID, has advised some twenty-five governments struggling with budget crises and inefficient and costly state-owned enterprises. Among his clients have been Egypt, Indonesia, Nigeria, Sudan, Thailand, Turkey, Malaysia, the Philippines and Brazil.

Axelrod is Professor Emeritus of Public Administration at the Rockefeller College of the State University of New York at Albany and former chair of the Department of Public Administration. Among his prior assignments he served as assistant budget director of New York State; interregional adviser on government budgeting in the United Nations; consultant to the U.S. Agency for International Development (State Department); and staff director of the New York State Little Hoover Commission. He has written numerous journal articles and authored and co-authored several books. His most recent books are *Shadow Government* (Wiley and Sons, 1992); *A Budget Quartet* (St. Martin's Press, 1989).

Axelrod has a doctorate in political science (Maxwell School, Syracuse University) and has been the recipient of a Fulbright senior research fellowship and an award of the American Society for Public Administration for leadership in governmental budgeting and management.

BUDGETING
FOR MODERN GOVERNMENT

Second Edition

CHAPTER 1

BUDGETING AS THE NERVE CENTER OF GOVERNMENT
An Overview

Budgeting: One of the Chief Political Decision-Making Systems

Budgeting is the nerve center of government. It is a decision-making system for allocating funds and tapping resources in order to achieve governmental priorities and objectives efficiently, economically, and effectively. Always significant, budget decision making has never been more urgent than it is today. Some leading policy issues now and in the foreseeable future are the size, scope, and composition of budgets at all levels of government and the means of financing them. Going further, Schick argues that budgeting is central: the "capacity to govern is the capacity to budget."[1]

This preoccupation with budgeting has its roots in the seemingly inexorable climb of public expenditures, taxes, deficits, and debt and the near paralysis of government in dealing with this rise. Despite cutbacks induced by the recessions of the early 1980s and early 1990s, government budgets continue to consume an ever-growing proportion of the gross domestic product (GDP). This is but one rough indicator of current developments. At the national level, government debt and deficits have reached unprecedented heights while taxes have increased moderately. Among state and local governments, fiscal distress has been a trauma for much of the last ten years. These trends are apparent in all countries.

Consequently, budgetary decisions dominate public debate and presidential, gubernatorial, and local elections as never before. The stakes are high, for the budget process comes to grips with the big questions of politics: Who gets how much for what purpose and who pays? The decisions influence what proportions of national resources go to the public and private sectors, public priorities, the goals and objectives of thousands of programs and projects, and other claims that various groups in society make on the public purse. As a result, the budget reflects the aspirations, values, social and economic policies, and services of government.

Budgeting has therefore become one of the chief political decision-making systems, if not the major one. Although many major policy decisions are indeed made outside the budget process, virtually every decision entails budgetary considerations. Overshadowing policymaking is the umbrella of fiscal constraints. The key questions are "What shall we do?" and "Can we afford it?" They are inseparable. The budget is a financial and political plan designed to implement such decisions. It comprises both expenditures and the means of funding them: taxes, other sources of revenue, and borrowed funds.

The executive budget system is nearly seventy-five years old in the United States and about twice old in several European countries. Today it thrusts upon the chief executive at each level of government the task of formulating coherent budgets sensitive to the needs of national and subnational economies.

The end product of budget decision making is captured in highly oversimplified and graphic form in Figure 1.1 and Table 1.1, which show the distribution of revenues and expenditures in President Clinton's proposed executive budget for the federal government for fiscal year (FY) 1995. The figure and table synthesize thousands of large and small policy and fiscal decisions emerging from the budget process.

Figure 1.2 provides a quick view of the results of budget decision making in a state government. It displays proposed revenues and expenditures for the state of New Jersey, a state in the throes of a fiscal crisis, for 1992–1993. Figure 1.2 embodies program priorities in New Jersey and political decisions to increase the funding for some programs while cutting back others.

Trends in Vital Statistics

By any measure the financial stakes are high in budget decision making when we consider the separate components of fiscal policy: expenditures, revenue, and debt. All are controversial and little consensus exists as to the appropriate levels of each component. These are the trends that baffle policymakers.

Expenditures

By 1993 total government expenditures in the United States approximated $2.1 trillion and consumed 33.3 percent of the gross domestic product, a ratio that has prevailed with some ups and downs since 1975. Accounting for about 67 percent of all expenditures, the federal government was the chief spender. State and local governments accounted for about 33 percent of expenditures in 1993. The ratios were about the same in 1965—the beginning of President Johnson's Great Society programs—when all governmental expenditures totaled $176 billion. The shares were distributed as follows: the federal government 67 percent and state and local governments 33 percent.[2]

Over a twenty-eight-year period (1965–1993) governmental expenditures increased nearly twelvefold in current dollars. At the same time, the economy

FIGURE 1.1 THE FEDERAL GOVERNMENT DOLLAR: Fiscal Year 1995, Estimates

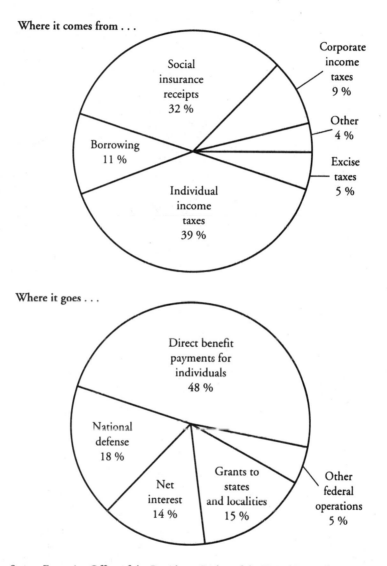

Where it comes from . . .

Social insurance receipts 32 %

Corporate income taxes 9 %

Other 4 %

Borrowing 11 %

Excise taxes 5 %

Individual income taxes 39 %

Where it goes . . .

Direct benefit payments for individuals 48 %

National defense 18 %

Net interest 14 %

Grants to states and localities 15 %

Other federal operations 5 %

Source: Executive Office of the President, *Budget of the United States of Government*, Fiscal Year 1995 (Washington, D.C., 1994), Introduction.

grew over eightfold, from a GDP of $702.7 billion in 1965 to about $6 trillion in 1993.[3] In constant dollars (i.e., adjusted for inflation) the increase would have been less dramatic, but still a sizable increase.

The major forces behind the sharp growth in expenditures were inflation; defense expenditures (now tapering off); recessions; federal and state grants; the

TABLE 1.1

An overview of the federal budget for fiscal year 1995

Outlays, Receipts, and Deficit Summary
(dollar amounts in billions)

	1993	1994	1995	1996	1997	1998	1999
Outlays:							
Discretionary	542.5	550.1	542.4	543.9	544.3	548.1	554.4
Mandatory:							
Deposit insurance	-28.0	-3.3	-11.1	-11.3	-6.1	-4.9	-3.3
Other mandatory	694.9	733.7	774.0	826.1	887.5	949.9	1,023.8
Subtotal, mandatory	666.9	730.4	762.9	814.9	881.4	945.0	1,020.5
Net interest	198.8	203.4	213.1	224.8	234.6	245.0	255.2
Total outlays	1,408.2	1,484.0	1,518.3	1,583.5	1,660.3	1,738.2	1,830.2
Receipts	1,153.5	1,249.2	1,342.2	1,410.4	1,479.5	1,550.8	1,629.0
Deficit	254.7	234.8	176.1	173.1	180.8	187.4	201.2
Totals as a percent of GDP:							
Outlays	22.4%	22.3%	21.6%	21.3%	21.2%	21.0%	20.9%
Receipts	18.3%	18.8%	19.1%	19.0%	18.9%	18.7%	18.6%
Deficit	4.0%	3.5%	2.5%	2.3%	2.3%	2.3%	2.3%
Memorandum—Totals with health reform:							
Deficit	254.7	234.8	165.1	169.6	186.4	190.5	181.1
Deficit as a percentage of GDP	4.0%	3.5%	2.4%	2.3%	2.4%	2.3%	2.1%

Source: Executive Office of the President, *Budget of the United States Government, Fiscal Year 1995* (Washington, D.C., 1994), p. 13.

Note: Chapters 7 and 8 cover discretionary and mandatory expenditures.

FIGURE 1.2 NEW JERSEY BUDGET: Resources and Recommendations for Fiscal Year 1993, All State Funds

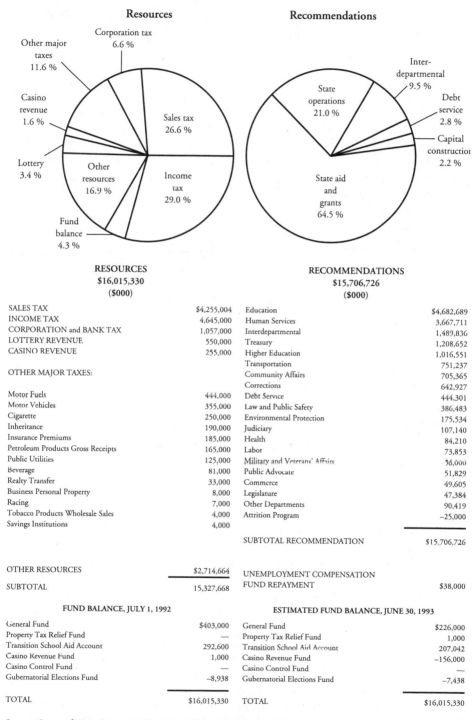

Resources

Recommendations

RESOURCES
$16,015,330
($000)

RECOMMENDATIONS
$15,706,726
($000)

SALES TAX	$4,255,004	Education	$4,682,689
INCOME TAX	4,645,000	Human Services	3,667,711
CORPORATION and BANK TAX	1,057,000	Interdepartmental	1,489,836
LOTTERY REVENUE	550,000	Treasury	1,208,652
CASINO REVENUE	255,000	Higher Education	1,016,551
		Transportation	751,237
OTHER MAJOR TAXES:		Community Affairs	705,365
		Corrections	642,927
Motor Fuels	444,000	Debt Service	444,301
Motor Vehicles	355,000	Law and Public Safety	386,483
Cigarette	250,000	Environmental Protection	175,534
Inheritance	190,000	Judiciary	107,140
Insurance Premiums	185,000	Health	84,210
Petroleum Products Gross Receipts	165,000	Labor	73,853
Public Utilities	125,000	Military and Veterans' Affairs	36,000
Beverage	81,000	Public Advocate	51,829
Realty Transfer	33,000	Commerce	49,605
Business Personal Property	8,000	Legislature	47,384
Racing	7,000	Other Departments	90,419
Tobacco Products Wholesale Sales	4,000	Attrition Program	−25,000
Savings Institutions	4,000		
		SUBTOTAL RECOMMENDATION	$15,706,726

OTHER RESOURCES	$2,714,664	UNEMPLOYMENT COMPENSATION
SUBTOTAL	15,327,668	FUND REPAYMENT $38,000

FUND BALANCE, JULY 1, 1992

ESTIMATED FUND BALANCE, JUNE 30, 1993

General Fund	$403,000	General Fund	$226,000
Property Tax Relief Fund	—	Property Tax Relief Fund	1,000
Transition School Aid Account	292,600	Transition School Aid Account	207,042
Casino Revenue Fund	1,000	Casino Revenue Fund	−156,000
Casino Control Fund	—	Casino Control Fund	—
Gubernatorial Elections Fund	−8,938	Gubernatorial Elections Fund	−7,438
TOTAL	$16,015,330	TOTAL	$16,015,330

Source: State of New Jersey, *Budget Fiscal Years 1992–1993* (Trenton, 1992) p. B21.

expansion of social programs such as social security, Medicare, and Medicaid; and a variety of health, welfare, and education programs.

Revenue

All governments in the United States raised $1,846.7 trillion in taxes in 1993, consuming 29.3 percent of the GDP. Federal deficits largely accounted for the gap of 4.0 percent between expenditures, which represented 33.3 percent of GDP, and revenues. The lion's share of revenue in 1993 went to the federal government: 62.5 percent in contrast to approximately 37.5 percent collected by state and local governments. The federal government virtually preempts the big moneymakers: personal income, payroll, and corporation taxes. State and local governments, how-ever, collect most sales and excise taxes, and local governments virtually monopolize property taxation.[4]

State and local governments also depend heavily on federal grants, their largest single source of revenue. In 1992 such aid totaled $178 billion, funded 22.0 percent of state and local expenditures, and accounted for 12.9 percent of all federal outlays. While federal aid as a percentage of state–local expenditures declined steadily from 1980 to 1989, it has begun to pick up in recent years and still represents a financial lifeline for fiscally strapped state and local govern-ments.[5] Local governments, in their turn, look to the states for additional assis-tance. In 1992 (the last year for which data were available) such aid amounted to $197.7 billion, exceeding federal assistance. It also represented about 30 percent of local budgets.[6]

Debt Financing

With few exceptions, expenditures outpaced revenues in the early 1990s in nearly all governments, leaving sizable deficits. Increasingly, governments have therefore resorted to debt financing to close the gap. For a variety of political, social, and economic reasons, this course of action has been preferable to sharp cuts in expenditures and tax increases. In the United States the federal govern-ment in particular has run up unprecedented deficits. By 1994 the federal budget was in deficit for the twenty-seventh straight year with the deficit in that year reaching $234.8 billion, and high deficits, though trimmed somewhat, were fore-cast for the rest of the 1990s. The national debt had increased to over $4 trillion.[7]

In theory, state and local governments cannot incur deficits because of consti-tutional requirements for a balanced budget. Nevertheless, hit hard by the reces-sions of the early 1990s, state governments moved from a surplus of $23.3 billion in 1980 to a negligible surplus of $3.4 billion in 1993, a figure comparable with trends during the Great Depression.[8] During the same period the majority of large cities experienced unprecedented deficits (see Chapter 7). State and local long-term debt, incurred mainly for capital construction, rose to $915.7 billion in 1991. At the same time a short-term debt of $21.7 billion helped to bail out state and local governments with deficits, although it was used for other purposes as well.[9]

Eight Interrelated Major Functions of Budgeting

Against this backdrop it is the responsibility of the budget process to cope with the unprecedented problems of priorities, expenditures, revenue, and debt financing. In doing so, it encompasses eight interrelated functions:

1. Allocating resources to programs and projects designed to achieve governmental priorities, goals, and policies.
2. Raising funds through taxes, fees, and loans to finance the budget.
3. Stabilizing the economy through fiscal policy (the mix of expenditures, taxes, and debt financing) in tandem with monetary policy (control over the money supply and interest rates). (This is primarily a national function, with state and local governments playing only a minor role.)
4. Holding operating agencies accountable for the efficient and effective use of resources provided in the budget.
5. Controlling expenditures to make certain they are legal, accurate, and compatible with the policies of political decision makers.
6. Transferring funds from one level of government to another.
7. Serving (in many countries) as a mechanism for achieving planned social and economic goals.
8. Providing leverage through the power of the purse to pressure agencies to manage their programs and projects more efficiently and effectively (management improvement, or "reinventing government").

These themes run through every segment of the budget process from budget formulation to legislative authorization of funds to budget implementation, and from tax policies to loans and loan guarantees to debt financing. Although succeeding chapters dwell in detail on these and related issues, it will be helpful at this point to discuss briefly the various budget functions. It is important to stress that budgeting does not stand by itself but rests on constitutional and statutory foundations. Therefore, an understanding of the legal and political framework of budgeting at all levels of government is essential. These are the formal rules of the game within which chief executives and legislatures plan their budget strategies.

Allocating Resources to Achieve Governmental Priorities, Goals, and Policies

Budgeting furnishes a framework for debate and decision about the size, allocation, and financing of limited resources to achieve policy and program goals. The determination of these goals and the proportion of resources committed to their fulfillment are the very stuff of politics. As a result, budgeting is conflict ridden every step of the way, either openly or not, depending on the nature of the society. And the slimmer the resources, the more intense will be the conflict.

For all its seemingly aseptic, technical, and (to some) dreary appearance, the budget is therefore a supremely political document. The figures tell the tale of claimants on the public purse who won, lost, or stayed even in the contest for available resources. The budget also synthesizes the total work program of government. Agency by agency, program by program, and project by project, the budget incorporates thousands of decisions on what will be done and at what cost. Such allocations result from a highly routinized and ritualized decision-making system at the executive and legislative levels.

The budget process itself is essentially neutral, although several budget watchers dispute this view, arguing that the the process determines outcomes and that all process changes have political implications. However, the experience of the last four decades suggests that political necessity determines the process. Whatever process works is what decision makers favor. In the relative affluence of the late 1950s and 1960s, budgeting was a mechanism for initiating new programs and expanding existing ones. In recent years it has served as a tool to redeploy limited funds and to cut back programs and projects, federal aid, and subsidies to hitherto favored groups in society. Given more favorable economic and political circumstances, the budget process will take new directions at the behest of its political masters.

Raising Funds through Taxes and Loans to Finance the Budget

Budgets are also financial plans that lay out not only proposed expenditures but also the revenues and loans necessary to support them. They can be simple as in the case of small local governments or complex as in Table 1.1, which summarizes the financial plan of the United States government for FY 1995. The financing of the budget raises a host of issues of fair play, equity, and economic and fiscal policy. What proportion of personal and corporate income should taxes consume? Who should bear the tax burden? What impact will raising or lowering taxes have on the economy in terms of economic growth, price stability, and employment? How much of the budget should be supported by taxes? By loans? To what extent, if at all, are deficits tolerable? What, if any, are the danger points in soaring deficits? Should tax limits be set? Should taxation be directed to social ends such as redistribution of income from high-income to low-income groups? To economic ends such as easing taxes for favored industries? What is the appropriate mix of taxes, including personal income taxes, payroll taxes, business taxes, real and personal property taxes, sales and gross receipts taxes, user fees and charges, excise taxes, customs duties, inheritance taxes, and export taxes? What is the ideal mix, if any? What percentage of revenue should each tax generate? What social and economic criteria should govern decisions as to the relative amount of taxes that should be levied on individuals and businesses? Should the tax system be progressive so that those with the ability to pay contribute a relatively higher proportion of income? Or should it be regressive, with taxes consuming a high percentage of the income of low-income groups? Or should it be a combination of both?

Other fiscal tools, though less obvious than taxes, expenditures, and debt financing, are also significant. In hundreds of programs the federal government in particular provides loans and loan guarantees to various groups in society such as small businesses, farmers, home owners, students, and exporters. In other programs it resorts to "tax expenditures," or tax breaks, for favored groups such as home owners and investors in municipal bonds. At times governments achieve their aims through regulation that imposes costs on the private sector without increasing governmental budgets.

Just to list these issues is to identify a divisive and controversial budgetary agenda. Ultimately, political preferences, shaped by economic and noneconomic values, determine the outcome, although rational economic analyses and forecasts abound to assist the decision makers and bolster their positions.

Stabilizing the Economy through Fiscal Policy and Monetary Policy

The economy has always shaped budget policy at all levels of government and, conversely, budget policy affects the economy. A recession results in lower personal income and corporate profits and hence in declining revenue. At the same time expenditures for unemployment insurance and other welfare programs rise and deficits mushroom. As the economy recovers, taxes increase, expenditures decline, and deficits shrink.

What is relatively new, at least during the last sixty years, is the attempt of national governments through fiscal and monetary policy to promote economic growth and employment, control inflation, and alter interest rates. This approach has taken several forms. In recessions governments cut taxes, increase expenditures, borrow funds extensively, and through the central bank (in the United States, the Federal Reserve Board) reduce interest rates. The aim is to stimulate the demand for goods and services by individuals and businesses so that the economy will revive. Conversely, in a booming economy with full employment, maximum utilization of resources, and a sharp demand for goods and services, the danger of inflation arises as money chases scarce goods. In this situation governments have tried to dampen the overheated economy through expenditure cuts, tax increases, and rises in interest rates. Whether the budget process can or should manage the economy in this fashion is one of the major controversial issues in budgeting.

Only the national government can cope with major economic problems. It has the resources and the necessary fiscal and monetary tools. On the other hand, state and local governments, taken together, account for a significant proportion of taxes and expenditures, as already noted. They have a marked impact on regional and local economies. The tax and expenditure policies they follow may or may not harmonize with national policies. In times of economic contraction, state and local governments, hemmed in by legal constraints, cut expenditures and raise taxes. To stimulate the economy, however, the federal government takes the opposite course of action. With different levels of government on a collision course, it becomes increasingly difficult to develop a coherent economic policy for the entire nation.[10]

Holding Operating Agencies Accountable
for the Use of Budgeted Resources

The annual (or biennial) budget cycle offers the executive and legislative branches of government a periodic means of taking stock of the performance of programs and projects and the use that agencies make of available resources. In requesting funds for the ensuing fiscal year, agencies must account through the budget system for the efficiency and cost effectiveness of their programs; their claims for funds may otherwise be given short shrift. In theory, then, the budget process enforces accountability.

Over the years the chief executive and the legislature have institutionalized budgeting and other systems of accountability to control the bureaucracy. Since the 1920s governments in the United States have developed increasingly powerful executive budget systems and established strong central and departmental budget offices. Equally well staffed in many governments, legislatures rely on the appropriation and oversight processes to exercise control. Through program authorization, spending, and revenue bills they can authorize, curtail, or limit programs; specify administrative powers and functions; determine funding levels; give or withhold discretion in the use of funds; and raise necessary revenues.

Unfortunately, control over and accountability of the bureaucracy is not enough. As Frederick C. Mosher reminded us, governments increasingly depend on third parties to perform major activities: contractors, other levels of government, public authorities that function outside of the governmental structure, nonprofit agencies, and quasipublic bodies. What the federal government does for itself directly amounts to less than one-fifth of the federal budget. In view of government's dependence on outsiders, accountability for results has become exceedingly murky. Unless governments devise appropriate tools for measuring the efficiency and effectiveness of third-party activities, accountability for the use of public funds will atrophy.[11]

Controlling Expenditures

Of the many roles served by the budgetary system, the most traditional and fundamental function is control of expenditures to make certain that they are legal, valid, appropriate, accurate, and honest. Such basic control is the bedrock of budgeting. Without it no other budgetary functions can develop successfully. Budget offices exercise their control through two powerful instruments: the allotment process and the accounting system.

The Allotment Process.   In most governments money does not flow automatically to agencies after the legislature approves appropriations. It is apportioned or allotted monthly, quarterly, or at other intervals by the central budget office for at least three reasons: (1) to avoid premature exhaustion of appropriations, necessitating supplemental appropriations; (2) to keep the rate of expenditures in line with the flow of revenue; and (3) to provide the funds agencies actually need in the course of budget implementation and no more.

The Accounting System.   The accounting system controls actual expenditures from appropriations and allotments. Every proposed expenditure must run the gamut of the accounting system to make certain that it complies with the terms of the appropriation bill, the allotment, and the financial laws of the government. Purchase orders, payrolls, vouchers, and contracts that fail to meet this test are turned down. In addition, the accounting system provides essential data for budgeting. It sets up an account for each appropriation and allotment and accumulates all the expenditures and obligations against the appropriations. Thus, it is in position to signal periodically the status of the appropriations, the amounts spent and obligated, and the unexpended and unobligated balances. This early warning alerts budget offices to the possible dangers of overspending and enables them to take corrective action.

Transferring Funds from One Level of Government to Another

With major revenue sources preempted by the national government, state and local governments rely on a tax base that is inadequate to finance their own programs. As a result, they need a larger share of national revenue. Similarly, local governments seek assistance from the states. Over the years intergovernmental grants and transfer payments soared dramatically, and then tapered off at the national level in the 1980s only to resume a climb in the late 1980s and early 1990s. As noted earlier, they still remain the largest single source of revenue for state and local governments. So dependent are these governments on federal grants that cutbacks of recent years, compounded by state and local tax and spending limits, have complicated budget making as never before.

As a result of intergovernmental financing, all levels of government share, in varying degree, the costs of major domestic programs such as welfare, education, health, and transportation. On the surface the intricate financial arrangements resemble a bewildering patchwork quilt. For all the untidiness and seeming lack of pattern, however, the intergovernmental grant system serves some major purposes in addition to shoring up the finances of state and local governments. It enables the national government to delegate the implementation of major programs to state and local governments by holding out the lure of extensive funding. But he who pays the piper calls the tune. To receive these funds the recipients must pursue national objectives and follow national policies, mandates, and guidelines. Similarly, state governments exact compliance with numerous fiscal and programmatic requirements as a condition for grants to local governments.

Grants and transfer payments assume various forms: revenue sharing, block grants, and categorical (or project) grants. The overwhelming favorite of state and local governments is revenue sharing, because it has few strings attached to it. The federal government, however, dropped revenue sharing for state governments in

FY 1980 and for local governments in FY 1987. Somewhat more numerous constraints at the federal level govern block, or broad-based, grants, which are lump sums dedicated to major program areas such as community development, health, education, law enforcement, and other functions. Recipients must comply with an array of planning, policy, fiscal matching, and reporting requirements.

The most restrictive grants are categorical grants, whereby the federal government transfers funds to state and local governments for specific programs and projects and attaches numerous conditions to their use. Of 557 federally aided programs, categorical grants are the favorite, constituting approximately 85 percent of transfer payments. Most of the funds go to health (e.g., Medicaid) and income security programs.[12] The popularity of categorical grants is no accident. They enjoy wide support among interest groups, legislative committees, and professional groups because they fund specific programs favored by this coalition. By the very nature of categorical grants, chief executives and legislatures of state and local governments have little discretion in allocating funds.

Political pressure and controversy surround transfer payments every step of the way. Each state and local government wants to be sure of getting its fair share. Interest groups compete with each other for grants. Poor governments request more grants, arguing that resources among governments should be equalized. Wealthier governments resist any equalization that takes from the rich and gives to the poor. Although subnational governments are eager to receive grants, they nevertheless resent the controls attached to their use. Broader budgetary issues surface periodically: What taxes should remain the sole preserve of the national, state, and local governments? What taxes should they share? What functions should the various levels of government assume? To what extent should the federal government devolve more domestic functions to the states? How should the functions be funded?[13]

Serving As a Mechanism for Achieving Planned Social and Economic Development

Once limited to the former Communist bloc and other "socialist" countries and viewed with suspicion in the United States and several other market economy countries, medium-term (usually five years) and long-term (over five years) social and economic planning serves as a framework for budgeting in most countries, despite skepticism about the effectiveness of such planning.[14] France, Japan, and India have been leaders in developing medium-term plans and using the budget process to implement the plans. The plans laid out targets for the public sector and desirable social and economic goals for the private sector, with the latter coaxed, subsidized, or regulated to move in the right direction. In the late 1980s enthusiasm for this type of planning cooled, as few plans seemed capable of dealing with a stubborn recession.

Despite a strong ideological bias in the United States against it, going back to opposition to FDR's New Deal, planning persists in various forms in the public sector. One mechanism for five-year planning was PPBS (Planning, Programming, Budgeting System) in the federal government and among several states during the 1960s. The aim was to translate the goals in the five-year plan into the annual budget. Although the system failed for a variety of reasons discussed in Chapter 11, multiyear planning coupled with budgeting continues in such major functional areas of government as transportation, health and mental health, education, housing, agriculture, and energy at all levels of government. In 1993 Congress and the president revived interest in planning by approving the Performance and Results Act, which requires agencies to develop five-year strategic plans, long-term goals, and performance reports—all tied in with the budget process.[15]

Because of the long lead time required for construction, most governments in the United States also develop multiyear capital construction plans. In addition, chief executives and legislatures in the United States (and elsewhere in the world) increasingly engage in medium-term financial planning to cut expenditures and shrink deficits. Both types of planning influence annual budgetary decisions.

Providing Leverage to Improve Management in Operating Agencies

From its earliest days, the budget process has offered a singular opportunity to examine systematically the efficiency, productivity, and effectiveness of all programs and projects and, through the power of the purse, to initiate appropriate remedial action where needed. In making a case for continued or additional funding, agencies attempt to demonstrate the positive impact of their programs and the efficiency of their organizational structure, operating systems, policies, staff utilization, and resource management. It is the task of budget analysis to challenge all these claims and, on the basis of a searching review, to recommend higher or lower funding levels and means of achieving improved program management. The leverage of budgeting to effect management improvement is powerful if the political leadership and central budget offices have the will to exercise it.

In the United States the central budget office at all levels of government has spearheaded management improvement programs. Whether it should assume responsibility for management and program analysis in addition to its other functions is a controversial issue in budgeting.

Simplifying the Many Tasks of Budgeting: How, in Practice, the Tasks are Reduced from Paralyzing to Merely Staggering Complexity

Given the eight major tasks of budgeting, it is small wonder that budgeting is probably the most complex decision-making system in government. Furthermore, by its very nature it is a decision-forcing process. No matter what, a government must meet a statutory deadline for submitting a budget to the legislature. At that time all debate and equivocation on large and small issues temporarily cease. The search for options ends. Choices must be made in the face of uncertainty. It is in

this environment that thousands of decisions are made by all levels in the bureaucracy and the political leadership. The workload in developing and synthesizing
the decisions is so large, and the participants so many, that the decision-making
process is tortuous and protracted. To cope with it, the participants follow a
highly routinized system and a detailed timetable, or budget cycle.

The only saving grace under these enormous pressures is that the system does
not start from scratch each year, contrary to some popular impressions. In fact, if
this were the case, and the allocation of all funds an annual ritual de novo, the
participants would be crushed by the sheer weight of decision making, and political combat would intensify. Fortunately, several safety valves, good and bad, ease
budgetary pressures: calculation of the base budget; marginal adjustments in the
base, up or down; the uncontrollability of the greater part of the budget, which
cannot be changed without altering basic legislation; the off-budget status of programs not funded through the budget process; the use of special funds; and multiyear appropriations. Although various chapters of the book deal with these issues
in some detail, they merit emphasis in this overview of budgeting.

The Base Budget: The Reference Point in Budgeting

Every budget carries forward the legacy of the past. At any one time the budget is the total of past decisions on programs, policies, projects, tax structures,
staffing levels, and resource requirements. Budgeting therefore hinges essentially
on the answers to three questions: What is the cost of carrying forward last year's
budget into the next fiscal year? How much should we add to it? How much
should we cut from it? The starting point for the budgetary conflict, then, is a calculation of the cost of continuing existing programs and policies without change
and adjusting the cost solely to reflect shifts in workload and the impact of inflation and other economic conditions. This estimate is variously termed the base
budget, the current services budget, the continuing services budget, the core budget, and the recurrent budget. It is the baseline against which all budgetary
changes are measured.

By no means do governments agree on the components of the base budgets.
In the U.S. federal government the base budget is the cost of continuing existing
policies, not last year's appropriations. Conversely, state and local governments
regard last year's appropriations as the base, adjusted for price and workload
changes. Some change the base, to keep it within 80 percent or 90 percent of last
year's appropriations.

However defined, the base budget is not sacrosanct. Yet even with cuts, the
overwhelming part of the base budget successfully survives attacks. All the contestants in the budget battle understand this. They therefore direct the conflict at
small and large adjustments of the base budget. Without this focus the budget
process would not be manageable, as Wildavksy reminded readers in his early
writings on the federal budget system.[16]

During the affluent period spanning the 1950s and 1960s, the base budget
was taken for granted. At the very least agencies expected to get what they

received the year before in real dollars (that is, taking inflation into account; without an adjustment for inflation, they would have experienced a cutback). For example, in the face of a price increase of 10 percent, an agency with a $1 million budget would need $1.1 million just to stand still. Few if any political leaders challenged in any significant way the base budget until President Reagan in 1981, with the help of a compliant Congress, successfully mounted a massive attack on several domestic programs. Additional cutbacks in base budgets took place at the state and local levels in the early 1980s and in the early 1990s.

Adjusting the Base Budget: Incrementalism versus Decrementalism

In the years of economic growth, the tax structure in the United States and other industrialized countries generated enough revenue to take care of the base budget and still leave some tidy sums for increments to that budget. Agencies typically scrambled to get their fair share of this bonanza and cried "foul" when their share, though an increase, was less than that of a competing agency or program. For the most part the budget process focused on sorting out increments to the base budget for special attention. This was by no means an unusual phenomenon; from the earliest days of budgeting, decision makers, as a practical matter, have concentrated mainly on marginal adjustments to the base budget. In the 1960s, however, the increments were dramatically larger, permitting the initiation of new programs and projects and the expansion of existing ones. This led Wildavsky and other observers to overemphasize the role of incremental budgeting as the key to budget decision making and to minimize significant changes in the composition of the budget over a multiyear period, the selective use of zero-base budgeting, and budget changes that occur in the course of the fiscal year after appropriations are approved.[17]

Now that the growth in resources proceeds at a slower rate, the accent in budgeting is on decrements rather than increments. If incrementalism was the watchword of the 1960s, decrementalism, with some exceptions, is the budget policy of the 1990s. Budgeting has tended to become a zero-sum game, with nearly every winner offset by a loser. To increase the funding for one program, agencies must sacrifice other programs. To be sure, politically protected sanctuaries still exist and are relatively immune to cuts.

The Uncontrollability of the Budget

In the United States, presidents and legislative leaders lament the fact that about two-thirds to three-fourths of federal budgetary outlays (depending on how they are counted) are uncontrollable because statutes mandate most of the expenditures.[18] This is due primarily to an explosion of open-ended entitlement programs such as social security, Medicare, Medicaid, food stamps, unemployment insurance and other welfare programs, interest payments, contractual obligations, pensions, and farm price supports. Individuals are entitled to the benefits conferred by these programs so long as they meet statutory criteria for eligibility. Like it or not, once the legislation is on the books, the president and Congress must provide necessary funds for these programs. (They are, of course, free to change the legislation in the unlikely event they can muster enough political support.) The combined effect of these programs, interest on debt, and the payment of contractual obligations effectively puts the overwhelming part of the budget beyond the reach of the budget process. The budgetary decision makers control only the one-third to one-fourth of the budget that is discretionary.

State governments also find themselves in a similar self-imposed legal bind, with over one-third of the budget for all funds dictated by statutory formulas governing aid to individuals and grants to local governments, primarily for education, welfare, health, and transportation programs. The cutbacks of the early 1980s and early 1990s have had a relatively minor effect on these programs. In fact, aid to education, which constitutes the single largest component in state budgets, continues to increase.

Even control over discretionary parts of the budget has its limits. Presumably, it is possible to cut the budget by slashing defense expenditures at the federal level and laying off prison guards, mental health attendants, police, firemen, and teachers at the state and local levels—these categories of employment represent a major part of discretionary expenditures. In practice, some programs are virtually untouchable because of public support or union and other political pressures. The result is that until recently major parts of the discretionary budgets were only marginally controllable. However, the recession of 1990–1992 led to cuts in discretionary programs at all levels of government.

Between de jure and de facto uncontrollability, budget makers have little room for maneuver. Such budgetary inflexibility may be a cause of anguish, but, together with base budgets and marginal adjustments, it serves to cut down the number of budgetary decisions.

"Off-Budget" Budgets and Special Funds Lighten the Budgetary Burden

Off-Budget Budgets.   For various fiscal, political, economic, and administrative reasons discussed in Chapter 6, many significant governmental functions are off-budget; that is, they do not appear in budget totals. In the main these are functions performed by entities variously termed public enterprises, public authorities, special districts, or government corporations. Public enterprises engage in nearly every facet of governmental, financial, and economic activity: construction of public works, transportation, insurance, housing, medical care, operation of utilities, and a host of other functions. What they have in common in most cases are the autonomy and flexibility of business-type organizations, the power to raise and use their own revenue, and freedom from central budgeting, civil service, and purchasing controls.

Nearly all public enterprises in the United States are off-budget even though they are creatures of the government and instruments of government policy. They often get their startup capital from the government, sell tax-exempt bonds in the financial markets, and count on the government to guarantee their loans and cover their operating deficits. Yet they are in large part exempt from the budget controls that apply to operating agencies. (They do have their own internal budget systems, some of them quite admirable.) To be sure, other controls may exist: broad policy direction by government leaders, executive and legislative oversight, review and approval of overall financial policies, and governmental audits. These controls, however, operate outside of the budget process, relieving budget decision makers of still another burden but raising major questions of control over and accountability of public enterprises.

Special Funds. The use of statutory special funds further narrows the scope of budgetary decisions. Most revenues flow into a general, or consolidated, fund and can, without restriction, be used to support any governmental activities. Many programs, however, are financed by special, or earmarked, funds. Revenues in these funds can be used solely for special purposes and cannot be transferred to any other programs. Among the major earmarked funds at the federal level are the Highway Trust Fund and the Old Age Survivors and Disability Insurance Trust Funds (social security). The former uses taxes on motor fuel, tires, and the like primarily for grants to the states, which use them for highway design and construction, and to a limited extent for mass transportation. The latter is funded by payroll taxes and supports social security and Medicare payments.

State and local governments in the United States are especially restricted by a bewildering array of special funds that stifle budget flexibility and confine the budgetary battle to the general fund. The earmarked special funds cover a variety of programs, projects, and activities such as highway maintenance and construction, conservation, higher education, grants to local governments, unemployment insurance, and pension payments. Some funds may enjoy surpluses, whereas others may be forced to cut back programs. No transfers between the special funds can take place, with two exceptions: governments can (1) shift money from the general fund to special funds in financial difficulty, and (2) borrow from special funds but repay the loans at prevailing interest rates.

This elaborate and often bewildering fund structure does not represent the machinations of governmental accountants run amok; it serves two major purposes. First, it protects funds held in trust for pension, social security, and unemployment insurance payments. Second, it insulates programs supported by various interest groups from the political stresses and strains of the budget process by providing a sure source of revenue. Expenditures from the special funds are generally subject to legislative appropriations. This assures some control over their use.

Multiyear Appropriations Reduce Some Budgetary Pressures

The extensive use of multiyear appropriations eases the budgetary workload of chief executives and legislative leaders. Although annual appropriations draw most attention at the federal level in the United States, several programs are funded by multiyear and indefinite appropriations. Ten state governments engage in biennial budgeting, and eleven combine annual and biennial budgets. Nearly all governments approve multiyear appropriations for capital construction.

The Myth of the One Budget and the Political Necessity of Multiple Budgets

Public attention focuses on the budget that the chief executive presents to the legislature as if, apart from legislative changes, it were the be-all and end-all of budget decision making. Alas, budgetary life is not simple. The government budget that is presented to meet a constitutional or statutory deadline is a transitory snapshot of a confluence of forces and pressures at one point in time. It will never be the same again. It will be succeeded by other budgets that shift with changing social and economic conditions. After the legislature leaves its mark on the budget, further changes will take place through supplemental and deficiency appropriations. As appropriated funds are allotted, still more revisions will take place. The approved budget can be cut back because of revenue shortfalls. Conversely, emergency funds may supplement it. The result is that, at the end of the fiscal year, the budget that has been actually implemented departs significantly from the original budget.

  To some budget watchers, changing budgets are a sign of instability and a particular weakness of poor countries, whose resources do not match the aspirations in the budget. In contrast, budgets in affluent countries are supposed to be relatively stable.[19] This view hardly squares with the rapid succession of changing budgets in both rich and poor countries. Budgeting is not a once and for all decision-making system. It is a continuing, year-round process that spawns many budgets to cope with the uncertainty and instability of our day.

The Participants in Budgeting—The Biggest Game in Town

With so much at stake and so many claimants on the public purse, budgeting is the biggest game in town, with thousands of participants. The players vary with the institutional framework of each country. On the executive side the chief players are in the executive management cluster: the office of the chief executive, the budget office, the ministry of finance or the treasury (and in various countries the planning office, the civil service agency, and the administrative reform agency).

  Given top or lesser billing, depending on a country's governmental system, is the legislative cluster. In the United States the legislative chiefs and fiscal committees and their attendant bureaucracy are coequal with the executive management cluster in budgeting. In other countries legislators have only a minor role in budget formulation and implementation. In the wings, with varying impact on the budget process, are the chief accountants, the independent auditors-general, and the central bank.

  Numerous contestants for public funds participate vigorously in budgeting: operating agencies; state, local, and regional governments; public enterprises; and assorted interest groups. Their participation in the budget drama varies with the acceptable norms and legal systems in each country. The operating agencies and public enterprises have their own staffs for budget, management, program analysis, and accounting and auditing. Some are extraordinarily competent and exceedingly influential in formulating budgets; others are of negligible importance. But all are budgetary entrepreneurs.

In the United States nearly every bidder for a significant share of the budget, except possibly the poor, is represented in the federal and state capitals and is ready to intervene in every stage of the budget process. During the budget season the capitals are jammed with lobbyists for industry, agriculture, subnational governments, public employee unions, good-government groups, and pleaders for special causes. Even governors and mayors maintain "ambassadors" in Washington, D.C., to make sure they get their fair share of federal largesse.

Much of the dynamism of budgeting comes from the interplay of the many participants, with each one attempting to further a variety of goals—institutional, programmatic, career, political, social, ethnic, racial, regional, or economic. This friction produces a good deal of heat—and sometimes light.

Frustration with the Budget Process Leads to Numerous Proposals for Drastic Change

So significant yet frustrating is the budget process that the system is under continual attack by critics who have their own nostrums for allocating public funds. The result is that over the last fifty years budget reforms have followed on the heels of other reforms: for example, program and performance budgeting; PPBS (Planning, Programming, Budgeting System); MBO (management by objectives); ZBB (zero-based budgeting); and, most recently, target budgeting. Each of the systems searches for rational criteria (rational at least to the promoters) to allocate scarce funds in a political environment rent by economic and social tensions. Chapter 11 evaluates these proposals to change the rules of the game.

* * *

This chapter has attempted to give an overview of the budget process and to lay out the agenda for the rest of the book. Within this framework the critical steps of budget formulation take place. The next three chapters cover this phase of budget decision making.

Points for Discussion

1. How do you define budgeting? To what extent do you agree with the definition in the chapter?
2. Some critics charge that the budget process is out of control because of entitlement programs, mounting expenditures, deficits, and debt. To what extent do you agree with this view?

3. How many of the eight budget functions are essential? Which ones, if any, can be changed? In what way?
4. The chapter cites six safety valves that ease budgetary pressures. Which ones strengthen or undermine the budget process? How can we best control these safety valves?
5. No one budget suffices to meet the needs of government. Instead we have multiple and ever-changing budgets. To what extent is this a sign of a strong or weak budget process?
6. What are the best ways to cope with the decrementalism of the 1990s?
7. How can the budget process best accommodate the needs of the many participants in budgeting? How can we prevent undue pressures by "insiders?"
8. Review a recent budget of a state or local government to determine the extent to which it reflects the eight budgetary functions.
9. The budget has been called the "work program" of government. What evidence do you find in budgets that this indeed is the case?
10. Review a recent appropriations bill to ascertain the impact of the legislative body on budgeting.
11. Compare the annual report of a state or local comptroller to pinpoint the differences between the original budget and the budget implemented by the end of the fiscal year. How do you account for these differences?
12. The chapter cites different definitions of "base budgets." Develop examples that highlight the differences.
13. Review a multiyear plan that is integrated with the annual budget process. Discuss the differences and similarities.
14. What evidence is there that the budget process is an occasion for annual stocktaking of the performance of government programs?
15. Review a financial plan of the federal, state, and local governments and determine the extent to which it is the synthesis of budget decisions.

CHAPTER 2

SETTING THE STAGE FOR ANNUAL BUDGETING
The First Step

Budget formulation, or the proposed allocation of resources for the next fiscal year, comes in three phases. At the outset the chief executive and central staff agencies—primarily the budget office—send a long list of do's and don'ts to the operating agencies to guide them in the preparation of their budget requests. These admonitions and exhortations cover a wide variety of predetermined policies and procedures, large and small: fiscal and economic policy, expenditure ceilings and other constraints, program priorities and cutbacks, and detailed instructions on the preparation of the budget.

In the second stage, the operating agencies take over and, in conformity with "top-down" guidance, prepare their budget requests for submission to the central budget office by a fixed date. The third stage begins when the central budget office receives the massive tomes containing these thousands of budget requests. That office analyzes them and recommends appropriate action to the political leadership of the government, which, of course, has the final word. Equally important, the central budget office must balance proposed expenditures against estimated revenues in order to come up with a financial plan that either results in a balanced budget or limits the size of the deficit.

None of these three processes are mutually exclusive. In developing budgetary guidelines, the central budget office consults widely with the operating agencies (in effect, "bottom-up" participation). Nor do operating agencies begin budgeting the instant they receive instructions from the budget office. Knowing generally what's expected, many agencies (at least the better-managed ones) start the process earlier to provide adequate time for analysis and internal debates. Similarly, the central budget office anticipates many of the problems that will arise and begins working on them long before the requests arrive.

The three steps, though overlapping, are nevertheless distinct enough to warrant special attention in each of three chapters. This chapter focuses on budgetary guidance from the center, or "Setting the Stage for Annual Budgeting." Chapter 3 dwells on the role of operating agencies in budgeting. Chapter 4, "Budgeting at the Center," describes budgetary decision making by the central budget office and the political leadership.

The Budget's Own Calendar: The Fiscal Year

The entire thrust of the budget formulation process is to produce and enact a budget before the beginning of the fiscal year. For this purpose budgeting has its own calendar, which differs in many cases from the January to December calendar of the Western world. For example, note the fiscal years of the following sampling of governments:[1]

Government	Fiscal Year Beginning
United States:	
Federal government	October 1
State governments	July 1 (46 states)
	September 1 (1 state)
	October 1 (2 states)
	April 1 (1 state)
Local governments	Variously January, July, September, October
Other governments:	
Australia	July 1
Brazil	January 1
Britain	April 1
Egypt	January 1
France	January 1
Indonesia	January 1
Japan	April 1
Kenya	July 1
Russia	January 1

Complicating the budget calendar still further, fiscal years in the relatively few state governments that prepare biennial budgets span a two-year period, although in most of these states annual adjustments to the budget are made. Nearly sixty years ago, in a simpler era, the majority of state governments practiced biennial budgeting.

Practical Factors in Choosing the Fiscal Year

Confusing as the diverse budgeting calendars may be, several practical factors influence their choice. For one, legislatures in the United States generally convene in January. Under these circumstances the fiscal year obviously cannot begin in January because the legislature requires several months to act on the budget presented by the chief executive. When should the fiscal year begin? How much time does the legislative body require to analyze the proposed budget and appropriate necessary funds? In each government the political, legal, and institutional systems shape the budgetary calendar. In the United States the majority of governments prefer a fiscal year that begins on July 1 because it usually gives them adequate lead time to reach budgetary decisions. For Congress, however, the July 1 date has turned out to be impractical, so in 1974 it shifted to a fiscal year beginning on October 1. Two states—Alabama and Michigan—also opted for October.

Even with the expansion of the period between the submission of the budget and legislative appropriation of funds, some legislative bodies regularly fail to meet the deadline for acting on the budget prior to the beginning of the fiscal year. So complex has budgetary decision making become, so devastating the fiscal crunch of recent recessions, and so intense the political controversies surrounding budgeting that necessary solutions and compromises cannot always be reached on time. This has been a characteristic feature of congressional budgeting and of the budget practices of several states, including Illinois, Georgia, Pennsylvania, New Jersey, New York, and California.[2] When an impasse occurs, legislatures, by a special resolution, provide for continued funding of agencies and programs at more or less the same levels as those in effect during the previous fiscal year. Some occasionally issue IOUs, as in California in 1992, and scrip money until real dollars begin to flow from appropriations.

Other factors that shape the fiscal year are the electoral cycle, cash flows in the government, and programmatic requirements.

The Fiscal Year and the Electoral Cycle. In the United States, legislators who are elected in November, especially for the first time, and assume office in January are hardly in a position to penetrate budget mysteries quickly. At least three months are needed to get an approximate fix on the budget.

The Fiscal Year and Cash Flow. Cash flow is an extremely important consideration. Ideally, the beginning of the fiscal year should coincide with a heavy flow of revenue into the treasury so that enough cash will be on hand to meet obligations without the need for temporary borrowing. To a limited extent this is the case in the United States. Corporate and personal income taxes are due in April and provide a comfortable fiscal cushion for fiscal years beginning in April, July, and October. Unfortunately, during the rest of the year, even with the payment of withholding taxes for the following year, expenditures and revenues are not synchronized, with the former often outpacing the latter. At this point governments usually resort to temporary borrowing. To overcome the fiscal squeeze, governments on occasion change the fiscal year, the collection dates for miscellaneous taxes and receipts, or both.

The Fiscal Year and Programmatic Requirements. Expenditures for several programs peak at predetermined intervals. For example, intergovernmental grants for welfare, education, transportation, and general aid are due every quarter or at other fixed intervals. For education, the program year begins in September. This has led many school districts to adopt a fiscal year beginning in September.

The number of local governments in the United States and foreign governments with fiscal years beginning in January is surprising. In some governments, the effect is to compress the budget formulation process into a short period of time, which leaves limited opportunities for analysis in the operating agencies, the central budget office, and legislative staffs.[3] Otherwise it is necessary to begin the budget process at an earlier date than is customary in most governments in the United States. This is the practice in Germany and France, for example. In Germany budgeting begins almost a year before the start of the fiscal year in January, so that the Bundestag (the parliament) can act on the budget in the fall. The critical factor is the block of time devoted to budget analysis and formulation. Dates by themselves are meaningless.

Working with Differing Fiscal Years

State and local governments, which depend heavily on intergovernmental grants for about one-fourth to about one-third of their revenue, must also contend with the fiscal years of other governments. For example, California's fiscal year runs from July 1 through June 30. During this period it receives grants from the federal government, which operates on an October 1 through September 30 fiscal year. Straddling two federal fiscal years, California gets one-fourth of its grants in one federal fiscal year and three-fourths in the next. Another example is the state of New York. With a fiscal year starting April 1, it receives half of its annual federal grants in each of two federal fiscal years.

For local governments, juggling with fiscal years is even more complex. For example, on a July 1 through June 30 fiscal year, New York City must adjust both to the federal fiscal year and to the fiscal year of the state of New York. From each government, New York City receives one-fourth of its annual grants in one fiscal year and three-fourths in the following fiscal year.

Figure 2.1 shows the interrelationships of the fiscal years among these governments. No state or local government is shortchanged by the lack of identical fiscal years among governmental levels, but the present overlapping fiscal years complicate the preparation of the budget for both the donors and the recipients of grants. Were concurrent fiscal years for all levels of government in effect, as in Germany and France, budgeting timetables would be greatly simplified.

FIGURE 2.1 OVERLAPPING FISCAL YEARS OF FOUR GOVERNMENTS (MONTH AND QUARTER)

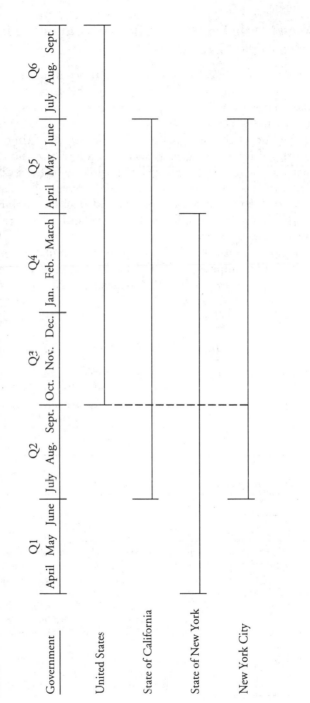

The Budget Cycle Forces Most Decisions to Be Made by the Beginning of the Fiscal Year

No budget will meet a constitutional or statutory deadline and no appropriations will be enacted prior to the beginning of the fiscal year without a rigorous timetable that covers every step in the process of budget formulation. This timetable, or budget cycle, often begins one to two years before the chief executive submits the budget to the legislature. To that period of time add another three to nine months or more for legislative action. So intricate and detailed is the budget cycle that it will not work unless all participants in the budget process accept a common sequence of action, comply with numerous deadlines, and assume responsibility for their share of analysis and decision making. In this sense the budget cycle is a mechanism for orchestrating and forcing most of the significant decisions at all levels of government.

Every government has its own timetable for formulating and approving the budget. For illustrative purposes it will be helpful to examine the time-consuming steps in the budgeting processes in effect in the federal government of the United States and the state government of Kansas.

A Budget Cycle Built for Two—U.S. Style

The budget cycle of the federal government of the United States is undoubtedly the most complex in the world. As Table 2.1 indicates, two sets of budget processes must dovetail: presidential and congressional budgeting. The formal

TABLE 2.1

Budget cycle in the U.S. government for fiscal year beginning October 1

Timing	Action
	Executive Action on the Budget
April–June	OMB (Office of Management and Budget) conducts reviews to establish presidential policy for the upcoming budget.
July–August	OMB sends presidential budget and fiscal policy guidelines to the agencies.
January–September 1	Budget preparation by operating agencies.[a]
September–October	Agencies and other branches of government submit initial budget requests to OMB.
September–January	OMB and presidential review of budget requests. Budget hearing with agencies.
November–December	OMB decisions sent to agencies. Appeals from decisions. Revision of budget requests based on president's decisions.
January–February	President transmits budget no later than first Monday in February.
February–March	Allowance letters spelling out president's requests sent to agencies.
July 15	Presidential midseason review updating budget estimates.

(continued)

TABLE 2.1 *(continued)*

Timing	Action
	Congressional Action on the Budget[b]
January–February	Congressional review of budget begins.
February	Committees and joint committees submit tentative estimates and requirements to Budget Committee in each house.
February	CBO (Congressional Budget Office) submits analysis of president's budget to Budget Committees.
April 1	Budget Committees report concurrent resolution on budget (establishing expenditure ceilings by broad function, revenue targets, and deficits or surplus).
April 15	Congress acts on concurrent resolution.
June 15	Congress completes action on reconciliation bill effecting legislative changes to make statutes compatible with resolution.
June 30	House passes annual appropriation bills.
September	Congress completes action on appropriation bills.
October 1	Fiscal year begins.

Source: Adapted from U.S. Office of Management and Budget Circular No. A-11 (Rev.): "Preparation and Submission of Budget Estimates" (Washington, D.C., 1992).

[a] The initial steps of budget preparation actually begin before OMB guidance.

[b] The congressional calendar is based on the Budget Act of 1974 as modified by the Balanced Budget and Deficit Control Act of 1985, subsequent amendments in 1987, and the Budget Enforcement Act of 1990.

process begins in April, when the Office of Management and Budget (OMB) takes the lead in developing budget policy for the forthcoming fiscal year. This is eighteen months before the start of the fiscal year and thirty months prior to its close. For example, in getting ready for the FY 1994–1995 budget beginning in October 1994, OMB has developed tentative guidelines during April–June 1993. Budgetary planning for the upcoming fiscal years takes place even earlier, usually in January. In effect, then, budgeting begins some twenty-one months prior to the start of the fiscal year and thirty-three months before its end. This is "normal" procedure. When a new president assumes office, deadlines change and improvisations begin.

Complicating what is at best an arduous schedule, agencies must also submit a multiyear budget that covers the four years following the budget year to aid in planning and deficit control. The budget requests, therefore, span six years: the current year, the budget year, and the four subsequent years.

While setting the stage for the 1994–1995 budget the president and Congress still had to act on the 1993–1994 budget. At the same time, the budget for 1992–1993 was in effect until September 30, 1993. Planning, approving, and implementing the budgets for three fiscal years simultaneously calls for a precise juggling act. The following sketch illustrates how budgeting straddled three fiscal years during 1993:

1993 Calendar Year	
Implementation of remainder of 1992–1993 budget	(started October 1, 1992, and ended September 30, 1993)
Implementation of 1993–1994 budget	(started October 1, 1993, and ended September 30, 1994)
Formulating 1994–1995 budget	(started January–April 1993 and ended September 30, 1994)

Under the best of circumstances it's difficult to maintain a tight budget schedule. Inevitable slippages occur for a variety of technical and political reasons. OMB, however, cannot afford to brook any delays. Come what may, the president's budget must be in the hands of Congress no later than the first Monday in February. OMB therefore controls the budget process carefully on the executive side. The significant delays occur in Congress, which has the problem of achieving consensus among its own members and working out compromises with the president. In recent years such problems have become particularly acute as a divided Congress has rejected much of the president's budget and developed what is essentially a congressional budget.

Budget Cycling in Kansas

State governments also follow a tight budget timetable. For example, the budget cycle in Kansas is akin to that in most states with annual budgets. As Table 2.2 demonstrates, the official timetable begins in April, fifteen months before the start and twenty-seven months before the end of the fiscal year. In practice, as is true in the federal government, preliminary budget planning begins even earlier. Although Kansas's budget cycle is not as protracted as the federal timetable, it has at times, in periods of fiscal stress, become difficult to manage. Delays have occurred primarily in the legislature because of sharp differences with the governor.

Other Government Systems for Cycling Budgets

Nineteen state governments have biennial budgets. Their budget schedules are similar to those of the other states, but during the same period of time they must make budgetary decisions covering a two-year period. This means that budgeting begins about a year in advance of the start of the fiscal year and three years prior to its end. For example, the Department of Administration in Wisconsin issued budgetary guidelines to the operating agencies in April 1992 for a biennial fiscal year beginning on July 1, 1993, and ending on June 30, 1995.[4]

How Administrations Guide Operating Agencies through the Budget Cycle

The budget process begins officially when, early in the budget cycle, the administration sounds the call to begin preparation of the budget for the upcoming fiscal

TABLE 2.2

Budget timetable in the state of Kansas

April–June	Budget Division develops revenue and expenditure estimates and proposes allocations for agencies to Governor.
June 1	Agencies submit to Budget Division any proposed revisions of program structure.
Mid-June–Mid-July	Budget Division distributes allocations for preparation of budget requests. (This is an advance ceiling on expenditures.)
July 1 ,	Agencies submit budget estimates for capital improvement projects and five-year capital improvement plans.
July 1	Agencies submit five-year office and storage space needs plan.
September 15	Agencies submit budget requests.
September–November	Budget Division reviews requests.
November 10	Recommendations of Budget Division transmitted to agencies.
November	Appeals of budget decisions to Secretary of Administration.
December	Final budget decisions by Governor.
No later than eighth day in January	Governor's budget and proposed appropriations bills sent to legislature.
No later than July 1	Legislative action on appropriations bills

Source: Budget Division, State of Kansas, *Budget Instructions* (Topeka, 1992).

year. At that point it issues a series of policy directives and instructions affecting every phase of budgeting. This is in addition to a formidable body of continually updated manuals on budget preparation and execution issued by the central budget office. The nature of the budget call varies enormously among governments in and outside of the United States. It can range from broad guidance on program priorities, expenditure ceilings, and fiscal and economic policy to specific restrictions on travel, staffing, and the purchase of cars and typewriters. In other governments the advice from the top is nothing more than stale cliches on the need to practice efficiency and economy with some instructions on the mechanical preparation of budget requests.

Nearly all state governors provide overall policy guidance in the budget letter, and about half of them lay out specific dollar and policy ceilings (e.g., size of program).[5] The same practice holds for presidents and most mayors.

Figure 2.2 shows a budget policy summary and accompanying letter sent by Governor Barbara Roberts of Oregon to all agencies. It typifies the top-down guidance that is a characteristic feature of modern budgeting.[6]

Developing Tentative Budget Policies

For such broad guidance to work, an administration must obviously first develop its own preliminary position on budget policy. The guidance must be tentative because it is bound to change as conditions, priorities, political necessities, and data change during the evolving and dynamic process of formulating the budget. It is difficult to synthesize a typical process from the many practices followed by governments in developing advance budget policies, but some common

FIGURE 2.2 TOP-DOWN GUIDANCE IN BUDGETING

March 3, 1992

To: All State Agencies

Subject: 1993-95 Budget Instructions

The budget instructions in this manual will require all of us to take a new approach to our programs and the use of public resources. The State of Oregon's fiscal constraints will have different impacts on each of us, and we all have different perspectives on the challenge. But we must all realize that when we are done, state government will be different.

Every state program -- not just General Fund agencies -- must tackle strategies to deliver services to the public with the greatest efficiency possible. I am asking all employees to use their talents to solve problems with creativity and commitment within available funds. Will it be easy? No, it won't. But it has to be done.

The budgets you are preparing must show you are improving efficiency, restructuring programs to deliver services better, and setting clear priorities. They must state the reductions you will need to make given our fiscal reality. We must be clear and explain the choices we face. These budgets will be a road map for the Legislature and the public to use and understand as we look to the future. We need to work with the public and our employees to develop our plans and to ensure wide understanding of our goals.

This manual offers instructions for reductions, but it does not ignore our vision for Oregon's future. The Oregon Progress Board has developed lead benchmarks to measure our progress as a state. As I prepare my 1993-95 budget proposal, I will use those benchmarks to decide where Oregon should invest using our limited resources. Only the highest priority programs that clearly help Oregon achieve its goals will meet my test. Clear measurements of that progress and of programs' preformance will help us show Oregonians what they get for their money.

As you construct your budget, please remember the urgent need to take care of our investments. We must maintain facilities, train a diverse group of employees, and emphasize customer service.

I appreciate the hard work each of you face as you begin the budget process. Thank you for your dedication and your willingness to meet this challenge together.

Sincerely,

Barbara Roberts
Governor

(continued)

FIGURE 2.2 *(continued)*

1993–95 Budget Instructions

EXECUTIVE SUMMARY

The budget process for 1993–95 requires state agencies to address directly the budget realities now facing state government. State agencies will prepare substantially constrained budget requests and increase only those programs that contribute to Oregon's progress. Unlike past biennia:

— General Fund <u>base budget</u> requests will be reduced to <u>80 percent</u> of the current service level. This will be referred to as the *reduced level budget*.

— An agency's <u>General Fund total request</u> including decision packages will not exceed 90 percent of the current service level.

— <u>Other Funds and Federal Funds Reduced Level Budgets</u> will be <u>90 percent</u> of the curent service level.

— An agency's <u>Other Funds and Federal Funds total agency request</u> including decision packages will not exceed <u>100 percent</u> of the current service level.

— The *current service level* will include phase-in costs, inflation, Emergency Board actions through April 1992, caseload increases, and approved budget exceptions. One-time expenditures, phased-out programs, and pilot programs will be excluded.

— *Personal Services* budgets will include the equivalent of one salary step increase for the 1993–95 biennium.

— *Decision packages* (both positive and negative) will be used to transfer or eliminate programs to reflect the Governor's policy decisions.

— A *Benchmarks Special Program* will be developed separate from the agency budget request by the Benchmarks leaders from proposals submitted by agencies. The Benchmarks Special Program may recommend General Fund packages of up to 10 percent of current service level, and Other Funds and Federal Funds increases above the current service level.

— Agencies will prepare *special reports* outlining progress in workforce diversity, training, and use of new technology

— *Performance measures* will begin to be used in budgets to measure the effectiveness and efficiency of programs.

— The 1993–95 Reduced Level Budget will reflect the general priorities of the program review process and the savings from eliminating over 4,000 positions during the 1991–93 biennium.

patterns are discernible. Most administrations will size up their fiscal position based on the latest data on revenues, expenditures, and debt; analyze the impact on the budget of such basic economic trends as the rate of economic growth, employment, price levels, trade balances, and the like; monitor conformity with tax and spending limits; and take a current reading of the performance of a few major programs close to the heart of the administration.

In governments with reasonably modern budget systems, the central budget office obtains this information routinely, using computerized systems that are now commonplace in nearly all governments. With a new fiscal year looming ahead, however, the tempo of analysis of this data must be accelerated in order to provide the chief executive with two basic estimates: the likely outcome of the current year's budget and a very rough approximation of budgetary requirements and revenues for the next fiscal year, based on existing policy and economic trends. Updated frequently, these estimates become the foundation on which an administration builds its tentative budget policy.

This overview is the "big picture"—it is the first rough approximation of the overall, or macro-, budget. It highlights the problems faced by the administration and influences the development of such specific policies as expenditure ceilings, program cutbacks or expansion, the legislative program, and changes in the revenue structure.

The practices of the federal government of the United States illustrate, on a large scale, the approach followed in macrobudgeting and the formulation of budgetary guidelines. In close and continuing consultation with the operating agencies, the Office of Management and Budget develops expenditure estimates in major program areas. Clearly, such bottom-up participation is essential for top-down guidance to work.[7] For revenue estimates OMB turns to the Treasury Department, and for the economic outlook it depends in large part on projections prepared jointly for the president by the Council of Economic Advisers, the Department of Labor, and the Department of Commerce. It also develops its own independent forecasts, which may or may not jibe with those of the other agencies.

In the next critical step OMB holds an annual "spring review" with the heads and senior staffs of the agencies, although not all budget directors have followed this practice in recent years. The participants assess the validity of the expenditure projections, evaluate the efficiency and effectiveness of selected programs, consider congressional reactions to specific items in the budget, identify major policy issues, and consider changes in and alternatives to existing programs.[8] (At times the exercise seems pointless to agency heads when they are given expenditure ceilings in advance.) Throughout this process OMB is in touch with the White House staff to alert them to the emerging issues and to get some early indication of presidential priorities. After this review, OMB is ready to develop budgetary options for the president and to seek direction on the formulation of budgetary guidelines. Figure 2.3 outlines this early phase of the budget process.

State and local governments follow their own variations of this approach. The smaller size of these governments makes it possible for central budget offices to

FIGURE 2.3 EXECUTIVE BUDGET PROCESS

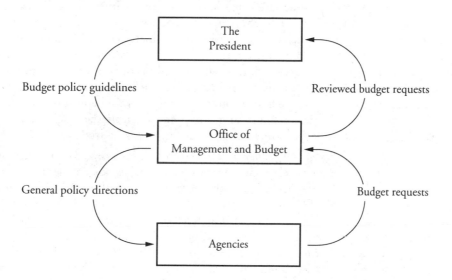

Source: Joint Finance Management Improvement Program, *Financial Handbook for Federal Executives and Managers* (Washington, D.C., August 1991), p. 8.

keep in close touch with the operating agencies, almost on a day-to-day basis, and to identify early in the budget cycle priorities for next year's budget. The emphasis is nevertheless on macrobudgeting.

Early macrobudgeting is common in virtually all industrialized countries. The Canadian system is probably one of the most comprehensive in this respect. Prior to the preparation of budget estimates by agencies, cabinet committees develop fiscal and program priorities and set expenditure limits for the major functions of government.

Factors That Influence the Shaping of Budgetary Guidelines

No central budget office starts with a clean slate when proposing budgetary guidelines to the chief executive. It must take into account a variety of constraints, problems, pre-existing policies, and past budget decisions that limit its flexibility. The following factors are probably the most significant:

1. *Commitments of the chief executive.* In the budget guidelines the budget office attempts to incorporate prior commitments of the administration. A list of these commitments can be gleaned from previous decisions, public statements, internal memoranda, legislative programs, and campaign promises of the chief executive. In the absence of explicit statements of an administration's objectives, this can be a frustrating exercise. Even the administration may not be certain of its own goals early in the budget process.

2. *The effect of constraints on agency budget making.* Too many constraints and prohibitions in budgetary guidelines may stifle an agency's initiative and severely limit its choices and options. The effect may be counterproductive, for the chief executive counts on his or her cabinet to prepare estimates reflecting their expertise and best professional judgment. On the other hand, it would be folly to invite freewheeling budgeting by agency heads without fiscal constraints when new or expanded programs cannot possibly be financed. Somehow, in budgetary guidance the administration and the budget office must find a middle ground between these two extremes. This increasingly common practice emphasizes tight controls on base budgets and yet leaves some safety valves for new initiatives.

3. *The uncontrollability of the greater part of the budget.* As previously noted, the greater part of the budget is relatively uncontrollable because of entitlement programs, statutory grants, fixed charges, and the political invulnerability of some discretionary programs. The staggeringly high ratio of uncontrollable expenditures ranges from about 75 percent in the federal government to over 80 percent in some state governments.[9] A determined administration and legislature can attempt to control the uncontrollables by changes in legislation and policy, but budgetary guidelines rarely touch on such drastic measures. They concentrate mainly on discretionary programs and aspects of entitlement programs that can be more easily controlled, such as workload and criteria for eligibility.

4. *Limits on expenditures and revenues.* Statutory and constitutional limits on revenues and expenditures beset every government and are key factors in shaping the budget. As a result of the Budget Enforcement Act of 1990 and the Reconciliation Act of 1993, the federal government must reckon with ceilings on discretionary expenditures. So must state and local governments, which face a variety of constitutional and statutory constraints on spending and taxing. All states but one must develop balanced budgets and some forty states have restrictions on the amount of debt they can incur. The effect of caps on spending, revenue, and debt is to limit budget options severely and they thus shape the guidelines issued by executives and the central budget office.[10]

5. *The necessity for further cuts in expenditures.* In recent years budget policy has focused on trying to arrest the growth of expenditures and shrink programs. State and local governments in the United States, in particular, have borne the brunt of these changes in the wake of the 1981–1982 and 1990–1992 recessions. In developing budget policy they confront the difficult choices of determining the programs, organizations, and activities that should be cut and the impact of these cuts on government employees and the clientele of various agencies.[11]

6. *Conformity of annual budget policy with multiyear expenditure plans.* Significant budgetary changes to control expenditures and deficits rarely take effect all at once. It takes time to develop a political consensus on the more sensitive issues in government. For this reason many governments have turned to three-to-five-year budget plans with expenditures, revenue, and deficit reduction targets set for each year of the multiyear period. Within the context of a longer-range planning horizon, they attempt to frame annual budget policy.[12]

7. *Conformity of annual budgets with multiyear social and economic development plans.* With the exception of the United States and several other countries, nearly all countries formulate comprehensive multiyear social and economic development plans and attempt to use the annual budget as a vehicle for implementing many of the targets in the plan. In the recent recessionary climate this has been a frustrating exercise.

8. *The fund structure.* As the previous chapter emphasized, the multiple funds in governments in the United States limit flexibility in developing budget policy. Between uncontrollable and earmarked funds, the range of discretion in advance budgetary planning is narrowed considerably.

9. *Concentration on a few big issues.* In any one year governments focus on only a few carefully selected priorities and controversial issues in their budgetary guidelines. To attempt more would strain the political process and result in continuing legislative–executive confrontation. In the U.S. government, the "hot" issues are health and welfare programs, crime, social entitlements, defense, agricultural support programs, and interest on the national debt. The agenda changes with each passing year.

10. *Compliance with legislative intent.* Legislative bodies in the United States spell out the intent of their budget policies in statutes and reports accompanying proposed appropriation acts. The reports issued by the fiscal committees recommend numerous restrictions on expenditures. Although these recommendations do not have the force and effect of law, prudent administrations attempt to comply with them in setting budget policy. Otherwise, they run the risk of intensifying legislative opposition to their budgets.

The Issuance of Budgetary Policy

These constraints, together with preliminary macrobudgeting and program evaluation, govern the development of budgetary policy and its issuance to the operating agencies. Budgetary guidelines take various forms: tentative overall expenditure ceilings, alternative expenditure levels, adjustments based on changes in price levels, and broad policy guidance, as follows:

Developing the Base Budget and Alternative Budgetary Levels. Budgetary guidelines in virtually all governments require agencies to come up with two sets of estimates: the base budget for the next fiscal year and proposed changes in the base budget. As we have noted, the base budget comes under different labels, such as the "baseline budget," the "current services budget," the "core budget," or the "recurrent budget." It is a forecast of estimated revenues and expenditures and is based on the assumption that present policies will remain unchanged and that the figures will be adjusted solely for changes in workloads, price levels, and other economic trends. These estimates are usually the starting point of budget analysis.

Adjusting Budgets for Changes in Price Levels. Should agencies be compensated for inflation? This is a major issue in budget policy. Without adjustment of their budgets to reflect changes in price levels, agencies, in effect, suffer a budget cut—the same money buys less. In the uncontrollable programs, national governments in the United States and other countries have virtually no discretion. To maintain the income of recipients, they are mandated by law to index payments to the Consumer Price Index (CPI), the most commonly used measure of inflation. In the United States several major government budgetary outlays such as social security payments are indexed to the CPI, so these automatically rise with inflation.[13] For discretionary programs, central budget offices face the problem of determining how far they should go in accommodating price changes. Most administrations at all levels of government issue explicit budgetary directives that address this problem. They advise the agencies on the measures that should be used in making adjustments (e.g., the CPI, the GNP (gross national product) deflator, or the Wholesale Price Index) and the allowable percentage increase for programs, supplies, and services.[14] Agencies are sometimes expected to absorb some of the price increases, in effect reducing the size of their budgets in real terms.

Providing Broad Policy Guidance. Preliminary policy guidance ranges from broad guidelines covering all programs, such as policies designed to help children, to instructions for specific programs, such as shelter and health care for the homeless. Among the guidelines issued by governments, those developed by the states of Texas, Ohio, Kansas, Oregon, and Pennsylvania and the government of Canada are undoubtedly the most explicit. They lay out significant social, economic, and fiscal trends; specify major programmatic and fiscal priorities and targets; urge agencies to change selected programs; emphasize the need for cutbacks in some program areas; and call for specific objectives and measures of performance for major programs as a basis for further policy development.[15]

How Budgetary Instructions and Forms Carry Out Budget Policy

Budget guidance to the agencies comes in two packages: the communication of budget policy and specific instructions for the preparation of budget requests. Governments resort to a variety of methods to advise agencies of budgetary guidelines, for example, letters, memoranda, and comprehensive directives. The head of the government typically issues a statement in broad terms, and this is followed by explicit instructions from the budget director or minister of finance. While some guidelines may be merely meaningless rhetoric, many governments regard the development of guidelines as an opportunity to articulate their social and economic policies for the benefit of the bureaucracy. However it is done, the issuance of the guidelines signals the beginning of another budget season.

Broad guidelines are not enough. To put them into effect, agencies must complete a variety of budget forms by specified dates and forward them to the central budget office. Completion of these forms is one of the mainsprings of the budget process, and the data required for budget decision making can be no better than the data called for by the instructions and the forms. Stated another way, the information that is presented on budget forms influences in varying degree the decisions that are made.[16] It establishes the framework for debate and negotiation. For this reason, budget forms and instructions assume an importance that is not readily appreciated by some administrators, who are indifferent to what appear to be mere mechanical details.

The forms are the basic building blocks of budgeting, and the data they call for vary with the nature of the budget system. So complex, standardized, and technical are the forms that most budget offices issue comprehensive manuals and examples of completed forms to guide agencies in the step-by-step preparation of the budget requests. Among the governments that regularly turn out model and frequently updated manuals are the federal government of the United States; the states of Texas, Pennsylvania, New York, Kansas, Washington, North Carolina, Wisconsin, and California; and the governments of the Philippines, France, and Sweden. These manuals may not make the pulse race, but administrators can ignore them only at the peril of their own programs.

The Scope of Budget Forms

To what extent should budget forms and instructions reflect all expenditures and revenue in the public sector regardless of source? This depends entirely on the type of budget chosen by the government. No budget comes down from on high like the Ten Commandments. It is fallible human product. It can be comprehensive and cover all expenditures, including those of special funds, public authorities, special districts, loan programs, and other levels of government or it can have a more limited scope. It can be fragmentary, with significant revenues and expenditures excluded. Each type of budget discloses certain types of information and conceals others. The extent of disclosure depends on the budget-making powers of the chief executive and legislature; the political will to reveal all budget transactions; and the emphasis on oversight, accountability, and expenditure control. Budgeteers strongly support comprehensiveness as a matter of principle for all agencies under the direct control of the government.

The federal budget of the United States has varied in its comprehensiveness over the years. In 1968 the president submitted for the first time a "unified budget," as a result of recommendations by the President's Commission on Budget Concepts.[17] The unified or comprehensive budget consolidated the conventional administrative budget and the receipts and outlays of trust funds, such as those for social security and highway construction. In later years it eroded as off-budget government corporations proliferated.[18] Finally, with the passage of the Balanced Budget and Emergency Deficit Control Act of 1985, the budget became less comprehensive. As a result of a political compromise, it included government corporations, but excluded the massive social security program.

In the past, state and local budgets in the United States concentrated mainly on the general fund.[19] A major shift, however, is now under way. Budgets are beginning to encompass all state and federal funds as well as funds of public enterprises. In this respect, the states of California and New York are each something of a model since they show the total spending plan regardless of the source of funds—state tax funds, special funds, bond funds, or federal grants.[20]

Still further fragmentation of the budget occurs in some governments when dual budgets exist—capital and operating budgets. Nearly all governments have capital budgets. For the most part they are integrated with the operating budget in the main budget document. Several developing countries, however, maintain separate capital and operating budgets. Where this is the case, the minister of finance prepares the operating budget and the central planning agency, the capital budget. Each office frequently follows different classification systems and budget instructions, resulting in predictable confusion in the operating agencies.[21]

Forming the Budget

The scope and comprehensiveness of the budget determine the number and complexity of forms used in budgeting. The more comprehensive the budget, the more varied and numerous are the forms and the systems for classifying data. The reverse is also true. Among a bewildering multiplicity of forms and classification systems, the following stand out and are indeed basic:

Traditional Forms and Classification Systems: Objects of Expense. Nearly all governments follow uniform classification systems to analyze and prepare their budgets. The most traditional classification of data, with roots in the earliest days of budgeting, calls as a minimum for the following basic information for the last completed fiscal year, the current year, and the forthcoming fiscal year: fund, organizational unit, and objects of expense. The "objects of expense" classification identifies the nature of the goods or services purchased (e.g., salaries, supplies, travel materials, or equipment). The federal government of the United States uses the following breakdown for objects of expense:[22]

Personnel compensation and benefits

Travel

Transportation of things

Rent, communications, and utilities

Printing and reproduction

Other services

Supplies and materials

Equipment

Land and structures

Investments and loans

Grants, subsidies, and contributions

Insurance claims and indemnities

Interest and dividends

Refunds

Undistributed

Each category encompasses subobjects and even sub-subobjects. No one classification system of objects of expense holds for all governments, although all classification schemes have common elements. Each government follows the breakdown of objects of expense most suitable to its needs. The rationale behind this oldest and most persistent type of budget classification is clear. It is an attempt to identify and control the resources required by each segment of government. In the zeal to implement budgetary reforms in recent years, it has been fashionable at times to downgrade the importance of the traditional classification of expenditures as mere inputs, in contrast with other systems that focus on the costs of outputs, or results. While both types of data are essential, the segregation of expenditures by object of expense and organization continues to be the very bedrock of budgeting. Without such data, it is impossible to manage resources, control expenditures, exert fiscal discipline, and pinpoint managerial responsibility for the use of funds. With them, a foundation exists for further improvement.

Personal Service. Regardless of budgetary classification schemes, traditional or nontraditional, the category that attracts most attention is personal service costs. This is the largest single item in the operating budget, approximating 60 to 80 percent of operating expenditures. As a result, numerous budget forms deal only with this area; they focus on staffing patterns, the methodology for determining staffing needs, tables of organization, salaries, position classifications, vacancy rates, and assorted fringe benefits (pensions, health insurance, unemployment insurance, etc.).

Organizational Unit. Budgeting by organizational unit raises the question of how far down the hierarchy an agency should go in developing its requirements. Should it be the smallest identifiable operational unit or a consolidation of such units? Should agencies budget by section, branch, office, bureau, division, institution, department, or some other appropriate organizational category? This is no trivial technical matter. It brings up a significant policy issue: Should budgeting proceed from the bottom up, with broad participation by all units in the agency, or mainly from the top down, with expenditure ceilings imposed by the central budget office or agency heads? Governments differ as to the level of detail they require from departments and agencies. Because of the growth and complexity of government, central budget offices tend to call for data by broad subdivisions within each agency, such as divisions, bureaus, large field offices, schools, and institutions. They leave it up to the agency to require additional data from other echelons in the organization for its internal purposes.

Effect of Changes in the Traditional Budgetary System on Forms and Instructions

During the last fifty years budget systems have changed significantly, and the forms and instructions reflect these changes. Superimposed on the basic budgetary data are requirements for still further information: the distinction between the base budget and increments and decrements, expenditures by function and program, measures of performance, multiyear projections, alternative funding levels, special data required by budgetary reforms, supporting data for capital construction, nonconventional expenditures, and revenue estimates.

The Base Budget and Changes to It. The aim of the forms and instructions is to identify and define the base budget and to separate it from proposed new programs and cuts in and expansion of existing programs. Most governments in the United States and several other countries now follow this approach.

Classification of Expenditures by Function. The functional classification of expenditures (sometimes called the sectoral classification) is standard practice in most countries. It aggregates expenditures in broad categories such as agriculture, health, education, and transportation to give decision makers an overall view of the purpose of expenditures. (See Chapter 11 on the significance of the functional classification.)

Classification by Programs. Program budgeting, one of the oldest and most durable of budgetary reforms, has profoundly affected the nature of budget instructions and the forms used in developing budget requests. It is practiced in the federal government, most state governments, many local governments, and many foreign governments. It requires a further breakdown of expenditures by program and by the components of a program: subprogram and activity. (A program is a network of related subprograms and activities designed to achieve one or more specific objectives.) The federal government of the United States has identified some 5,000 programs and many more subprograms and activities.[23]

In the budget forms the program costs are broken down still further by object of expense, in order to identify the personal and non–personal service costs of running, say, a community mental health care program. This type of budget presentation, combining object of expense and program classifications, is in wide use. The following example from the budget of the state of Wisconsin illustrates the use of the program structure coupled with the object of expense classification:

Function: Agriculture

Program: Food and Trade Regulation

Subprogram: Food Inspection

Activity (or program element):   Meat and poultry inspection

Measures of Performance. An integral part of program budgeting is the requirement imposed on operating agencies to identify the objectives of programs and to develop quantitative and qualitative measures of performance: workload, efficiency, and effectiveness. Virtually all governments in the United States require such data in varying degree, with especially comprehensive requirements in effect in the states of California, Texas, Wisconsin, Colorado, Washington, and New York.

Multiyear Projections and Alternative Funding Levels. In contrast to the standard three-year comparison (past, current, and upcoming budget year) many governments in the United States and elsewhere, as we have noted, call for projections for a five-year period (the upcoming budget year plus four). The projections may envisage two scenarios: receipts and expenditures based on existing policy and legislation, and estimates based on proposed changes in programs and policies.

Budget Reforms and Budget Requests. Every budget reform imposes new requirements for information on the operating agencies. ZBB (zero-based budgeting) led to alternative funding levels. Program budgeting, as noted, generated numerous special forms and instructions. The most comprehensive and controversial reform of all, PPBS (Planning, Programming, Budgeting System), resulted in even more drastic changes in budget requirements. Target budgeting has focused on caps on expenditures. (See Chapter 11 for a discussion of these budget reforms.)

Capital Construction. Some formidable-looking forms focus on capital construction and seek to elicit information on long-range capital programs and the physical progress and cost of each project, from the time it's on the drawing board until the time it becomes operational. Depending on the size of the government, thousands of projects may be under way at any one time. Other forms require agencies to justify requests for new capital projects by developing data on estimated costs and benefits, the compatibility of the projects with multiyear capital development plans, and the probable impact of the project on operating budgets (the cost of maintaining a completed project).

Some Major Miscellaneous Requirements. Equally complex forms deal with intergovernmental grants and transfer payments in such programs as health, transportation, welfare, and unemployment insurance. Other highly specialized forms relate to government corporations and public enterprises, debt service, special funds, and various nooks and crannies of the government that are not easily covered by conventional treatment.

Nonconventional Expenditures. Governments also attempt to achieve policy objectives through loans, loan guarantees, and tax expenditures (special tax abatements, credits, and deductions). There are forms to cover what Schick calls "nonconventional expenditures."[24]

Forms for Estimating Revenue. Instructions and forms for preparing revenue estimates are also important in budgeting. Governments look to agencies that collect taxes and other revenue to specify the amount of revenue collected in recent years and to forecast revenue collections for the current and upcoming fiscal years, based on trends in the economy as a whole and in individual sectors of the economy. This is done for each tax (personal, income, sales, corporation, real estate, etc.) and each source of nontax revenue such as customs duties and license fees. On the basis of this information, the central budget office, in cooperation with tax agencies, councils of economic advisers, and central planning offices, develops independent estimates.

The Necessity of Budget Guidelines, Forms, and Instructions

The amount of data required for modern budgeting is indeed staggering, even though much of it is processed by computerized budget systems. At first blush, the array of budget forms and instructions conjures up images of paperwork jungles and paper blizzards. Such descriptions may be colorful, but they miss the point. In a complex decision-making system, budget forms convey information and insights for action by the various levels in the government hierarchy. They ultimately affect, in varying degree, the decisions that are made, as Grizzle noted in a memorable article.[25] Since this is the case, forms *are* substance. The test of any budget system is not the number of forms and instructions, but their adequacy and relevance. Everything else is secondary.

So significant are budget guidelines and instructions in developing budgets that they merit more emphasis than they get in some governments and in budgetary literature. In 1979 the legislature of the State of California came to this conclusion when, in an unprecedented move, it required the Department of Finance to report annually on the methods and procedures it used in developing budget guidance and instructions. It was especially interested in the processes employed by the department to establish budget targets and priorities, to determine levels of service for programs supported by the base budget, and to identify the need for new and expanded programs. This pioneering move unfortunately withered in California and never caught on elsewhere.

The Language of Budgeting

As in other specialized fields, budgeting has its own language, a mixture of technical terms and jargon. Many of the key words and phrases that may illuminate your understanding of the budgeting process appear in the glossary at the end of this book.

Inundated by an increasing flow of budget guidelines and instructions, the operating agencies are now presumably ready to prepare their budget requests. The next chapter covers their policies, systems, ploys, and frustrations in budget formulation.

Points for Discussion

1. What are the relative advantages and disadvantages of "top-down" and "bottom-up" budget guidance?
2. What factors should determine the selection of a fiscal year by a government?
3. To what extent do you agree with the observation that the budget cycle is a coordinating and decision-forcing mechanism?
4. How explicit should budget guidelines be?
5. What major factors influence the development of budget guidelines?
6. How far should an administration go in imposing on operating agencies such financial guidelines as expenditure ceilings, alternative funding levels, and adjustments for inflation?
7. How far should it go in imposing broad policy and programmatic directives on agencies?
8. To what extent should budgets be comprehensive—covering the entire public sector under the control of the government?
9. What budget forms and instructions merit the highest priority? Why?
10. What are the major differences between traditional and nontraditional budget forms and instructions?
11. To what extent do you support legislative requirements in California requiring an annual report from the governor on the processes employed to provide budget guidance to agencies?
12. Review and discuss budget guidelines and instructions issued by a nearby state or local government.
13. Compare the budget forms with the format of the budget document to determine their usefulness and relevance.
14. Analyze the forms generated by specific budget reforms such as program budgeting, ZBB, PPBS, and target budgeting.
15. Compare the definition and treatment of the base budget in three different states or cities.

CHAPTER 3

DEVELOPING DEPARTMENTAL BUDGET REQUESTS
Strategies, Ploys, and Frustrations

In preparing departmental budget requests the head of each agency faces the challenge of producing a budget that will be compatible with the policies, guidelines, cash ceilings, and instructions of the chief executive and the central budget office. At the same time the budget must be sensitive to the needs of the major programs in the agency and responsive to the phalanx of interest groups, legislators, and bureaucracies that support these programs. It must also take into account the many constraints that burden budgeting—legal restrictions, relatively uncontrollable costs, spending caps, judicial decisions, legislative intent, legislative investigations, fund structures, and the requirements imposed by other levels of government. These assorted pressures complicate budget decision making in every agency. Hence, many agencies attempt to design custom-tailored budget systems that will meet their needs and facilitate decisions.

The quest for the ideal system never ceases. What internal budget procedures are most appropriate? What are the best ways and means of developing an overall budget strategy that will enhance the accomplishment of an agency's objectives and priorities? In what specific ways should the budget reflect the administration's policies and political positions? What budget controls will ensure prompt attention to the critical issues in budgeting? What are the best ways to overcome vulnerable policies and cost overruns? How far down the organization should budgeting take place? How adequate are performance and cost data? To what extent will the budget system flush out realistic options for decision by the agency head? These are some of the key issues in departmental budgeting that affect every agency.

Developing Custom-Tailored Budgeting Systems

Guidance from the central budget office provides the overall framework for budgeting and establishes common government-wide categories for aggregating necessary data. It is up to each department, however, to develop a budgetary system that meets its own unique requirements. No one best system of departmental budgeting exists; what works in one agency may be burdensome and irrelevant elsewhere. Each agency has the task of translating the policies and instructions of the administration and the central budget office into terms that are meaningful to each one of its subdivisions, field offices, institutions, and facilities. The way this is done varies with the managerial competence and sophistication of the agency. Some departmental heads merely provide routine instructions to their constituent units and pass along the requirements of the central budget office. As a result, budgeting becomes a humdrum, pro forma process with merely marginal adjustments of last year's budget. This is all too often the state of affairs in many agencies, unless cutbacks shake up the normal way of doing business.

Some departments, especially in local governments, lack professional staff resources for budgeting and must rely on the central budget office.

Most large operating agencies and well-managed smaller ones, however, recognize the importance of the budget process as a tool of internal managerial planning and control, and develop their own custom-tailored budget guidelines, policy statements, targets, instructions, forms, and manuals. This is true of many federal agencies and of large departments in state and local governments:

The Department of Health and Human Services (HHS) relies on an integrated Budget Information and Analysis System (BIAS) that in large part shapes its budget requests.

The Department of the Treasury provides a Budget Manual that covers the detailed steps of budget formulation, justification, and execution.

The Department of Transportation issues programming guidelines as a backdrop for budget requests.[1]

The New York State Department of Transportation has prepared a comprehensive manual that covers all phases of budgeting for highway and bridge design, construction, and maintenance.

Participants in Departmental Budgeting

The participants in budget decision making in the operating agencies vary with the size and location of the agency, the professional background of key officials, and the management style of the administrator. At the very least one would expect the head of the agency, the immediate deputies, and the chiefs of the major operating divisions to play a major role in budgeting. In some cases, however, administrators, indifferent to the potentialities in the budget process, are content to turn over the responsibility for assembling budget requests to their budget or finance offices, consulting only routinely with the bureau and division heads. Where agencies lack experienced budget staffs, as is true in many developing countries and various local governments, administrators often rely on the central budget office to dictate the preparation of budget requests.

Should All Levels in an Agency Participate in Budgeting?

A chronic issue in all agencies is the extent of participation by the various operating units in budget making. In the United States government and the various state governments, the agency organizational structures may include many divisions, bureaus, regional offices, institutions, and facilities. To what extent should this far-flung bureaucracy take part in budget formulation? How far down the organizational ladder should budgeting go—should bureaus and institutions involve lower levels such as branches, sections, and units? In short, should budgeting be top-down, bottom-up, or a combination of the two? And where exactly is the bottom?

What occurs in practice depends on the organizational values and management systems of an agency. Ideally, participation should be widespread and without limits. If budgeting is a tool for the systematic planning, financing, implementation, control, and evaluation of activities, then organizational units, no matter how small, must engage in budgeting to be effective. This is quite different from the demands of the central budget office and the head of the operating agency. When budgeting is an integral part of its management system, each organizational unit can contribute significantly to the development of an agency's annual budget. As budget requests and data from all segments of the organization move up the organizational hierarchy, they are bound to shape and influence budget decisions at each level. In fact, it is difficult to see how an agency can budget meaningfully without full-scale involvement of all its constituent units.

Reality differs significantly from this ideal prescription. In many cases the lower levels of an organization are shut out of the budget process entirely. By fiat they are told what to do and how much to spend. Some agencies involve field offices and institutions. Others do not. Where agencies invite bottom-up participation in budgeting, they may fail to provide guidance on the agency's policies, goals, and targets. At times they merely prescribe dollar ceilings and require the units to submit budget requests within these limits. Under these circumstances budget submissions from the lower units are often fragmentary and inadequate.[2]

The Role of Departmental Staff Units

A minimum essential for departmental budgeting is a strong agency budget office with a skilled professional staff, analytical capability, and an understanding of the interrelationships of budgeting, program evaluation, and management analysis. In more complex agencies, even this is not enough and it becomes necessary, as in the federal government of the United States and various state agencies, to establish budget offices in large bureaus, divisions, and institutions.

The role of the budget office in the agency varies with the overall organizational structure and the agency head's perception of the nature of the budget system. For years the prevailing mode was to have the budget office report directly to the head of the agency or the head's immediate deputy, as did other staff offices such as those responsible for personnel administration, accounting, organization and management, and program evaluation. This is still the case in many state and local agencies, with the budget office the first among equals.

During the last thirty years, however, the organizational pattern has changed as agency heads have found it increasingly difficult to coordinate the efforts of separate staff units. One approach followed by many state and local governments is to expand the scope of responsibility of the budget office by adding management analysis and program evaluation to its functions. On the other hand, some agencies are fearful of overloading the budget office or doubt its capability to undertake broader tasks. Another variation, then, is to make an assistant secretary or commissioner of administration responsible for the entire array of staff services including budgeting, program planning and evaluation, accounting, personnel administration, organization and management, property management, and procurement. This practice has been adopted in the New York State Department of Labor, the California Department of Transportation, and the Florida Department of Human Resources, to cite but a few examples.

Because of their sheer size, federal agencies in the United States are reluctant at times to place all staff services under one senior official. They have therefore tried various other organizational arrangements. One pattern, followed by the Department of Health and Human Services, is to set up an Office of Management and Budget, an Office of Planning and Evaluation, and an Office of Legislation, each under an assistant secretary. All participated actively in the departmental budget process.[3] In the 1980s the Department of Interior, however, preferred to lodge several staff functions in the Office of the Assistant Secretary for Policy, Budget, and Administration.[4] In whatever way the agencies structure their staff services, the intent is to draw on a variety of skills and expertise in making budget decisions.

Budget Making in the Operating Departments: Six Separate Paths

No matter how simple or complex an agency may be, budget making requires it to pull apart its entire budget, to disaggregate it, and to examine the needs of each program, project, activity, and organizational unit. The review can be cursory or detailed, superficial or searching. At the end of the review the agency must somehow reconcile its internal differences and pull together the separate bits and pieces of the budget into a coherent whole that will be compatible with the administration's policies. Were the agency to compress budgeting into a few short months, the task would be staggering. So onerous, however, are the demands of modern budgeting that it has become a year-round exercise. Budget decision making, performed in a short period of time, intensifies and accelerates what is an on-going process.

In well-managed agencies budgeting proceeds on six different analytical paths that ultimately converge at the top in time for the decisions to be made:

1. Determining the staffing and other resources required to achieve program goals.

2. Determining the need for new, expanded, or rehabilitated capital facilities to achieve program goals.

3. Developing new or revised policies and legislative proposals to implement them.

4. Identifying the need for management improvements to enhance the efficiency, effectiveness, and productivity of operations.

5. Evaluating costs and expenditure trends.

6. Taking into account external studies and investigations that affect the agency.

Determining the Resources Required to Achieve Program Goals

To determine staffing requirements that in some agencies preempt the greater part of the budget, it is necessary to develop an operating budget, or a work program, for each segment of the organization. This process starts at the lowest levels in the agency and works its way up through the successive layers of the hierarchy. Conceptually, the approach is relatively simple. In practice, however, it turns out to be complex and time consuming. Hence, program managers tend to resist it while endorsing it in principle, and top management is frequently indifferent. The minimum essentials for an operating budget, or work program (using the terms interchangeably), are identifying the activities; estimating the work to be performed or the outputs to be produced; developing unit costs and unit times for each output; and determining the resources needed to produce the outputs—staff, equipment, supplies, space, and other resources.[5]

Estimating Staffing Requirements. Of all the resources, staffing is the most expensive because most agencies are labor intensive. Excluding the military, which alone employs nearly 2 million people, 18.6 million employees staffed the federal, state, and local governments in 1991 (federal government—3.1 million; state and local governments—15.5 million).[6] Total civilian wages approximated $450 billion.[7] Table 3.1, though highly simplified, shows the applicability of work-programming techniques in estimating staffing requirements. While the work program approach is generally associated with program and performance budgeting, it stands by itself as a major tool for planning, costing, and controlling activities.

Still another example is Table 3.2, which shows how one Texas agency translated the work program into budget requests.

The workload factor. One of the key elements in operating budgets is the estimated workload. Some workloads fluctuate with only minor variations from year to year, such as the number of students in colleges and universities, the number of tax returns, or the number of miles of highway maintained. Even then,

TABLE 3.1

Work program for program X in organizational unit Y to determine staffing requirements

Activity	Unit of measurement (Output)	Volume of workload or proposed outputs	Staff-hours per unit	Staff-hours needed	Estimated staff-years	Number of positions	Average cost per position	Estimated cost
Investigation	Investigation by type	10,000	2	5,000	3	3	$26,000	$78,000
Laboratory tests	Test by type	250,000	1	250,000	152	152	30,100	4.6 million
Welfare clients	Client by type	100,000	85 per yr.	8.5 million	5,152	5,152	30,000	154 million
Tax audits	Tax audit	175,000	5	875,000	530	530	35,000	18.6 million

Note: All examples are hypothetical. Excluding vacation, holidays, and sick leave, it is assumed employees work 1,650 hours a year. The figures vary among governments.

49

TABLE 3.2

Priority allocations of the State of Texas Department of Environmental Quality

Strategy	1994 requested		Cumulative percent of 1993 state funds	1995 requested		Cumulative percent of 1993 state funds
	Total funds	State funds		Total funds	State funds	
Strategy Option 01-03-01-01						
Conduct ongoing studies of toxic chemical exposure	$500,000	$500,000	3.6	$500,000	$500,000	3.6
Percent of potential exposure cases analyzed	30.0%			35.0%		
Number of studies conducted	10			10		
Number of study participants	2,000			2,000		
Strategy Option 01-02-01-01						
Implement comprehen: Air Toxics Program	$4,000,000	$3,000,000	25.4	$4,000,000	$3,000,000	25.4
Percent reduction of toxic chemical discharges from 1990 levels	12.0%			15.0%		
Number of toxic sites undergoing emissions inventory	10			10		
Number of discharges inventoried	100			100		
Strategy 04-01-02						
Enforce NEPA guidelines on development projects	$1,400,000	$350,000	27.9	$1,500,000	$350,000	27.9
Percent of projects in compliance	75.0%			77.0%		
Number of development projects inspected	280			280		
Strategy 02-01-01						
Enforce water quality standards	$4,000,000	$3,000,000	49.7	$4,000,000	$3,000,000	49.7
Percent of industrial sites in compliance	80.0%			83.0%		
Number of industrial sites inspected	500			500		
Number of penalties assessed	200			200		

Source: State of Texas, Governor's Office of Budget and Planning and Legislative Budget Office, "Detailed Instructions for Preparing and Submitting Requests for Legislative" (Austin, 1993).

policy changes (e.g., enlarged opportunities in higher education or cutbacks in services because of a budget crisis) can result in abrupt shifts in workloads. Other workloads are sensitive to changing economic and social conditions or natural disasters and fluctuate from year to year. Among obvious examples are unemployment insurance claims; welfare benefits; loans to farmers and small businesses; and loans to communities battered by floods, fires, hurricanes, earthquakes, and civil disorder.

Unit times and costs. Another key measure is the staff-hours per output. Such units of measurement, and staffing ratios based on their application, are used extensively, and their use continues to grow. Among hundreds of ratios now in use are the number of tax examiners per 100,000 tax returns, the number of faculty required in the major disciplines in a university on the basis of accepted student–faculty ratios, the number of welfare clients per case worker, and the staffing of highway maintenance per mile of road.

As an unavoidable cost, administration in all activities is frequently denounced as excessive overhead. How does an agency determine how much administrative and related operating costs are required? One way is to develop a rough rule of thumb, specifying that administration of a given program or organizational unit may, on the basis of past experience, range from 7 to 10 percent of staff time and costs. A tougher and more analytical approach is to disaggregate administration into its component parts and develop a work program for each part. In 1993 the federal government took the easier course in Executive Order 12837 of prescribing across-the-board reductions of administrative expenses.

The Quantity vs. Quality Issue. A few words of caution are necessary about using time-per-output and staffing ratios as a basis for budgeting. The mere calculation of the time and cost per output gives no clue as to the quality of the activity and furnishes no basis for determining whether the unit time and cost is standard or substandard. Essentially, it is a measure based on a statistical analysis of past experience. To establish bona fide standards, it would be necessary to develop so-called engineered standards. This requires a step-by-step analysis of the work processes in each activity to simplify and improve them and, in consultation with supervisors and employees, to establish standard times for each of the many tasks comprising the activity. The overall time becomes the standard for the activity. It is not fixed, but changes as policies and procedures change. So difficult and time consuming is the development of performance standards for each activity that most operating agencies shy away from them. At best they rely on past experience with work and performance measurement.

Converting Labor-Hours into Positions. The critical task is converting estimated staff-hours and staff-years into positions. To do this, it is necessary to ascertain how many days and hours employees are actually available for work. Excluding weekends, holidays, vacations, sick leave, and even approved coffee breaks, it turns out that in many governments employees actually work about

1,600 hours, or 214 days, per year. Dividing these figures into the estimated staff-hours or staff-days required for the activity yields the estimated number of positions. In the hypothetical example of work programming in Table 3.1, it was assumed, based on the experience of several states, that employees work about 1,650 hours a year.

The U.S. government uses an even tougher, and possibly unrealistic, standard to arrive at the estimated number of full-time equivalent positions. It assumes that employees work 260 compensable days and 2080 compensable hours a year, and uses these figures in its formula for staffing.[8]

$$\frac{\text{Estimated number of required labor-hours}}{\text{Number of compensable hours per employee}} = \text{Number of full-time equivalent positions}$$

It is not enough to determine the gross number of positions for each activity. Every agency usually has an organization and staffing pattern. Within this framework, in accordance with a position classification plan, it must assign each position to an appropriate slot in the organizational hierarchy, for example, assistant director, principal statistician, senior clerk, laboratory assistant, and so on.

To arrive at the budget for personal service the operating agency multiplies the number of positions by the applicable salary. Most governments have a salary classification plan for all positions, based on studies by the central personnel office. The salary assigned for each position (showing the range from minimum to maximum) varies with the experience and seniority of the incumbent. The salary plan may also provide for automatic annual increments and merit increases based on the uncertain art of performance evaluation. In addition, governments may approve cost-of-living adjustments of salaries to keep pace with inflation in whole or in part. Still other adjustments include overtime, supervisory differentials, holiday pay, night work differential, and hazardous duty pay.

The "Perks" of Office. The total salary dollars don't tell the whole story. Overlaying them is the cost of a series of so-called fringe benefits, or "perks," such as pension plans, social security, health insurance, worker's compensation, family allowances, assorted leaves of all kinds, special post allowances, training, government-paid tuition, and housing. So significant are these perks that they hardly constitute "fringes" any longer. In some governments they account for one-third or more of the entire budget for personal services. Concerned about the growing impact of these fixed costs on the budget, many governments in recent years have either capped fringe benefits or slowed down their rise.

Analyzing Labor Utilization. This type of analysis not only results in building the personal service budget, but also makes it possible for the bureaus, the divisions, and the agency budget office to review labor utilization. A comparison of the approved budget with actual experience may reveal that several bureaus had failed to produce the estimated outputs. This may point up understaffing, inefficiency, or both. The time and cost per output may be unacceptably high or higher than planned. The application of performance standards may reveal obvious examples of overstaffing in relation to actual workload. Ferreting out such examples of the misuse of expensive resources may not win popularity contests, but it is an essential function of the agency budget office and should also be a major concern of the operating bureaus and divisions.

Does Analysis of Staffing Needs Make a Difference? The use of work programs in developing staffing needs has run into two major problems: the seeming futility of this type of analysis in an era of cutbacks and personnel ceilings, and the resistance of professional groups and unions to measurement and performance standards. In recent years work programming has appeared to be a rather sterile exercise, as agencies have experienced vacancy freezes, arbitrary cuts across the board, and the suspension of agreed-upon staffing ratios. Objective analysis of staffing requirements still has some advantages, though. It limits the amount of budgetary damage, highlights the adverse impact of cuts on the objectives of programs, and enables agencies to rid themselves of redundant staff in bureaus hitherto regarded as sacred cows. It also justifies the promise of more adequate funding as the economy picks up.

Professional, subprofessional, and technical groups frequently argue that it is difficult, if not impossible, to measure their work, report the time devoted to different activities, and set performance standards. It may be feasible, in their view, to measure clerical and blue-collar operations, but not activities involving judgment, creativity, and highly technical skills. As a result, they often propose staffing patterns based solely on their best professional judgment.

This position is somewhat shaky. The fact is that most governmental activities can be measured by employing varying methodologies. For example, time-reporting systems are in effect for engineers, architects, lawyers, researchers, and management consultants in the public and private sectors. The data serve as a basis for developing staffing needs. Physicians and dentists have developed time units of service as a basis for costing. Over the years staffing ratios such as student–faculty ratios, nurse–patient ratios, and caseloads per social worker have been established for various professional activities. All of these are essential for budgeting personal service.

Estimating Costs for Resources Other than Personal Service. Objects of expense other than personal service also represent significant cost elements, especially in capital-intensive programs such as computer services and transportation. In some agencies they may account for one-fifth to one-half of the budget. Senior officials nevertheless often display only a marginal interest in the non–personal service part of the budget other than travel (a frequent target of budget cuts), automatic data-processing systems, cars, and some heavy equipment. They are all too frequently indifferent to the costs of printing, reproduction, communications, utilities, space, supplies, furniture, and equipment. Compared to the heady issues of policy development, such miscellaneous costs appear to be trivial.

Lack of attention to all objects of expense can result in a slow hemorrhage of substantial sums of money. It is essential, therefore, to develop a rationale for these expenditures, just as it is for the personal services budget. Central budget offices and many operating agencies concur with this view and have established various criteria for determining resource requirements other than personal service. Among them are space standards, the complement of furniture for each position, the operating cost of a government vehicle per mile, the amount of miscellaneous supplies per position, the cost per square foot of maintaining buildings, estimated travel time and cost based on the number of travel days for each activity, the number of telephone units per 100 employees, the printing and reproduction needs of each program and activity, per capita food costs in hospitals based on the nutritional needs of various types of patients, and standards for acquiring computer systems.

None of these standards and criteria emerge spontaneously; they result from comprehensive studies that may take two to three years and involve collaboration on the part of the operating agency, the central budget office, the central supply or procurement agency, and the public works agency. Once developed, the criteria are not immutable. They require continuing adjustment to changing conditions.

The Indispensability of Operating Budgets. Operating budgets developed in this fashion, with personal service and non–personal service components, become indispensable tools for planning, costing, controlling, and evaluating programs and activities. They make it possible for operating agencies to pinpoint organizational responsibility for activities, to estimate required resources, and to hold organizational units responsible for results.[9]

Determining the Need for Improvements in Capital Facilities

In addition to funds provided by the operating budget, agencies require capital facilities to achieve program goals. These facilities encompass a wide range of projects: roads, streets, bridges, tunnels, dams, waste treatment plants, water supply systems, power generating and transmission systems, schools and universities, hospitals, nursing homes, housing, community health and mental health care centers, prisons, and a variety of other structures. In several respects budgeting for capital projects is akin to budgeting for programs and agencies, yet it is also significantly different. Chapter 5 discusses capital budgeting in detail.

Policy Development and Legislative Planning

Concurrent with the formulation of the operating and capital budgets, agencies step up the tempo of policy studies aimed at evaluating, initiating, expanding, revising, or cutting back programs. To be relevant, the studies should result in plans that can be used in formulating the budget. Several planning processes that affect policy development are often under way at any one time: systematic multiyear planning of priorities and program objectives, program evaluation, ad hoc policy studies, and legislative planning.

Multiyear Planning. Many agencies at all levels of government continue to link multiyear planning and budgeting (as in transportation, higher education, health, and mental health) despite the difficulties of the process and disenchantment with elaborate schemes to combine the two. They realize that it takes several years to achieve specific targets. Even in the face of uncertain budget policy, it is important to plan the targets in advance and to see to it that the annual budget provides the necessary resources for year-by-year progression toward the target.

After examining the process of budget formulation in ten major federal programs, the United States General Accounting Office still held fast to this position in the 1980s despite mixed experience in the agencies:

> Budget formulation should be part of a planning process that, based upon an adequate assessment of needs and congressional actions, identifies for a multiyear period annual program priorities and realistic program objectives ... Systematic planning is a key to sound budget formulation. Without adequate planning and program evaluation budget development may become a haphazard exercise that directs funds to areas of lesser need or programs of lesser effectiveness.[10]

In 1993 Congress finally endorsed this position by unanimously passing the Performance and Results Act. Approved by President Clinton on August 3, the Act requires federal agencies to develop five-year strategic plans with measurable long-term goals, annual performance plans, and annual performance reports comparing goals set to those actually achieved. After initial experimentation with selected agencies, the plans were to be integrated with performance-based budgeting.[11]

Program Evaluation. Program evaluation is an integral part of policy planning. As an agency contemplates new or revised programs, it must take into account the results of existing programs. Without evaluating the performance of programs and projects continuously in quantitative and qualitative terms, an agency is hardly in a position to adjust them and develop meaningful budget estimates. The nub of program evaluation is an assessment of the effectiveness of programs and projects. The term "effectiveness" is used here to mean the extent to which a program or activity meets predetermined objectives. If a program satisfies its objectives at acceptable or low costs, it is considered *cost* effective. Examples of measures of effectiveness include reductions in the prevalence and incidence of specified diseases; job placements resulting from a training or rehabilitation program; reduction of road accidents because of stepped-up law enforcement, improved highway engineering, or both; and the reduction of recidivism in parole supervision programs.

Ad Hoc Policy Studies. Agencies occasionally conduct internal studies of major policy issues by program managers, the planning office of the agency, and task forces composed of representatives of staff and line officers. These studies serve as a basis for policy development and budgeting within the agency. Whether initiated internally or requested by the administration, they represent important links with the budget process.

Legislative Planning. Policy planning and legislative planning are inseparable. If an agency plans to continue existing programs, change them, or add new programs, it must get the necessary statutory authorization through legislation and appropriation acts. For this reason the agency's legal staff participates actively in developing policy and drafting the statutes designed to implement it. The agency must also take into account judicial decisions that affect its programs and make certain that policies and budgets are compatible with those decisions.

Identifying the Need for Management Improvements

Management analysis also influences the preparation of the budget, especially with the current emphasis on "reinventing government" and "total quality management." Most large agencies and some of their major subdivisions have organization and management units that analyze continuously operating systems, organizational structures, productivity, and administrative policies and procedures. To be effective, their studies must be available in time for budget formulation. Frequently ignored in periods of affluence, they serve to rationalize budget cuts in a fiscal crunch. (See Chapter 13 for a discussion of management improvement programs.)

Evaluating Costs and Expenditure Trends

The analysis of expenditure trends is central in budgeting. It covers such categories as appropriations, allotments, funds, organizational units, objects of expense, programs, and activities. To get such data continuously, the operating agency depends on a central accounting system (in effect in many state and local governments in the United States) or on its own decentralized system (as is the case in the federal government and foreign governments). By the time the agency is ready to make its budget decisions, it should have, at least, monthly and cumulative expenditure reports for every relevant category in the budget and comparisons between projected and actual expenditures. Such data identify overspending and underspending by programs, facilitate expenditure control, and provide a baseline for estimating expenditures for the next fiscal year. Without a timely, accurate, and comprehensive accounting system, budgeting in the operating agencies becomes a rather meaningless exercise. (See Chapter 10 on information systems that support budgeting.)

Taking into Account External Studies and Investigations

Occasionally, external groups investigate an agency's management, programs, and policies. These groups include independent auditors and comptrollers; central budget offices; legislative committees; special investigating bodies, such as "blue-ribbon" commissions in Britain and the Moreland Commissions in New York State; "national performance reviews," such as the study headed by Vice President Gore in 1993; and earlier commissions, such as the Hoover and Grace Commissions in the United States and the Glassco Commission in Canada, which were charged with the monumental task of reviewing all governmental programs. The studies may be routine management audits or they may be major investigations triggered by shortcomings in departmental operations or the perception of widespread waste. Whether these investigations are welcome or not, the agencies must consider the recommendations in arriving at budget decisions. If they don't, the central budget office or the legislature certainly will.

At the Top: The Six Separate Paths Converge

Some months before an agency's budget requests are due in the central budget office, the six different budgetary paths converge: resource requirements for the operating budget; projects for the capital budget; policy development; management studies; expenditure analysis; and the results of external studies. Now comes the critical phase of synthesizing this information, developing recommendations and suitable alternatives, determining their impact on the agency's programs, and getting the head of the agency to make the necessary budgetary decisions. How this is done depends on the agency head's managerial style, her understanding of the budget process, her concept of her role as an advocate or overseer of departmental programs, the extent of her independence from the entrenched bureaucracy, and her standing in the administration.

The Dominant Role of the Agency Head

Budgeting is an agency head's most critical task. It is an unusual opportunity to take stock of past and current performance, identify problems and weaknesses, lay out possible corrective measures, determine needs, specify priorities and objectives in the light of shrinking resources, learn from the perspectives of program managers and interest groups associated with the programs, and debate available options. Should she choose to play it, the agency head can have the dominant role in what could be a grand annual debate. Only she can determine the agenda and the amount of time devoted to budgeting, although she is influenced heavily by the political necessities of the administration.

Reporting to the Agency Head

No matter what budget policies she adopts, the agency head must have at hand the results of the detailed analyses that have taken so many months to prepare at all levels in the hierarchy. Depending on the organizational framework of the agency, the first deputy, or the assistant commissioner for administration, or the budget officer will be responsible for bringing all the data together. It's a staggering task to compose a pithy summary of critical information for a busy agency head, who may have been in office only a short time, but this is what is done in agencies with strong budget systems. Though it is difficult to make broad general-izations, it is possible to synthesize the better practices, based on the experience of agency budget offices in the United States and elsewhere.[12]

For every major subdivision, program, and project in the agency the budget office, in collaboration with other staff units, usually prepares a short summary (illuminated, if possible, by charts and graphs) that concisely conveys to the agency head the following information:

1. Expenditure by organizational unit, object of expense, program, and project for both the last completed fiscal year and the current fiscal year; each operating unit's request for the next fiscal year; and the recommendations of the budget office and other staff offices.

2. The existing and proposed number of positions for the same periods.

3. Major expenditures and requests for non–personal service items.

4. The pros and cons of the operating units' requests, including an indication of those that will be favored and those disadvantaged by the request.

5. Key data on needs, workloads, outputs, efficiency, and results (effectiveness of pro-grams).

6. Some background information on the compatibility of the requests with the policies of the chief executive, legislative intent, approved short- and long-term plans, past budget decisions, court decisions, statutes, and views of powerful politicians and interest groups.

7. Summaries of internal and external studies on the efficiency, effectiveness, and impact of selected programs and projects.

8. Realistic options.

9. A summary of required legislation.

10. Major questions the head of the agency may wish to take up with the program direc-tors and bureau and division chiefs.

Try to do all this in a few pages! No matter how difficult, brevity is the soul of budgetary communication as well as wit. But even short memoranda mount up and take time to absorb; hence, budget officers and program managers frequently make it a point throughout the year to alert agency heads to emerging issues and problems. When the budget requests come in, they should therefore contain few major surprises. Surprises occur only to uninterested and inept agency heads and in agencies with mediocre management and budget systems.

Holding Internal Budget Hearings on the Requests

Once they are armed with comprehensive information and are in a position to raise searching questions, most heads of departments hold a series of budget hearings with representatives of bureaus, institutions, and divisions. Other partici-pants are generally the agency "cabinet," composed of key deputy and assistant commissioners; the chiefs of the staff offices (budget, program planning, law, accounting and finance, organization and management, and, where necessary, engineering and architecture); and, as needed, special technical advisers. In this conclave the agency budget director is but one voice among many, even though it is a voice that supposedly speaks to agencywide concerns and not to the parochial interests of particular programs and projects. However, this is not always the voice that catches the ear of the agency head.

At the hearings all issues relating to the policies, costs, efficiency, and effectiveness of programs should be fair game for discussion. The agency head is in a position to plumb the strengths and weaknesses of the case made by each component part of the agency, and should have a clear understanding of budgetary options by the time the hearing is over.

The Aftermath of the Hearings

The agency head is rarely in a position to make decisions on major issues at budget hearings. Each of these issues often has important fiscal, political, social, administrative, and economic implications that should be weighed carefully. The many competing and plausible claims for funds require sorting out. At the hearings and in budgetary analyses, the head of the agency concentrates on segments of the organization. Before final decisions are made, it is necessary to determine the interrelationships of the various segments and the effect of budgetary changes on each segment and on the departmental budget as a whole. In short, the time has come to pull together what the various analyses have torn apart.

In many agencies, the head of the department meets with the cabinet and advisers after the hearings and arrives at tentative budget decisions. This makes it possible for the budget office to prepare a draft of the budget, which gives the agency head the first clear view of the effect of the many decisions on the entire department and of the proposed level of expenditures. It reveals how the various subdivisions and programs of the agency will fare; which will hold steady, which will lose, and which will gain.

With this information at hand, the agency head can sound out key officials in and out of the agency, reconcile conflicting views, and negotiate differences with senior officials. He may attempt to get preliminary reactions from outside of the department: from the central budget office, officials attached to the office of the chief executive, leaders of constituencies supporting the agency's programs, and heads of other agencies that may be affected. From these soundings, the agency head gets a sense of how far it is prudent to go in the budget requests.

After these extensive consultations, and sometimes confrontations, the agency head at long last makes the final decisions on the size and composition of the budget and approves the specific requests that go to the central budget office. However painful the decisions may be, they represent just one stage in a protracted process that will produce the government's budget. At any point they are subject to change.

Packaging and Selling the Agency Budget

Depending on the size of the agency and the multiplicity of the forms in use, the budget requests may constitute a bulky package, approximating two to twelve inches in height and about five pounds in weight. To make certain that the sheer weight of the materials does not obscure the major points they would like to make, agency heads may prepare a comprehensive memorandum—the agency budget message, in effect—to accompany the estimates. Some of these memoranda are admirable in their scope, clarity, precision, and vivid use of illustrations. They are often first-class political papers that attempt to "sell" the budget. In too many cases, however, agency heads merely send routine letters of transmittal.

Budgetary Games

In their budgetary presentation, agency heads often rely on various ploys, strategies, and tactics to win over skeptics in the central budget office, the administration, and the legislature. The objective is at least to maintain the budget base and at most to expand it. Wildavsky anatomizes some favorite strategies from the 1960s: cutting popular programs, knowing full well they will be restored; asking for all or nothing on the grounds that the program will not be viable with further cuts; merging new or challenged programs with popular programs so that they will be less susceptible to attack; claiming new activities are really "old stuff" and part of the base; maintaining appropriations for a program at present levels while using the funds for other purposes; starting new programs with small sums, hoping the opening wedge will be enlarged in later years; claiming some expenditures are only temporary; using workload data to build up the budget base; arguing that a program will pay for itself through user charges; demonstrating that increasing expenditures now will result in later savings; and capitalizing on a crisis to initiate new activities.[13]

In budgetary folklore it is almost an article of faith that still other ploys work. Some program managers are convinced that the budget requests should deliberately contain "fat" so that the central budget office, as guardian of the public purse, can make a show of extracting it while still giving the agency what it wanted in the first instance. Still another strategy is to claim that a controversial budget request merely implements the administration's commitments and previously approved plans. In a case of old wine in new bottles, a faltering program may be given new labels and popular objectives in the hope of attracting support. Another tactic is to point out that a program or project is relatively free since most of the money comes from another level of government.

The agency may appeal to the pride of the central administration. It may argue in proposed budgets for health, education, and correctional services that a cut would result in lower standards than those prevailing in governments of comparable stature. It may play on fears by dramatizing dire economic consequences to the community if funds are not approved. It may cite overwhelming public demand for a program. It may agree in principle with the need for a cut, but plead temporary extenuating circumstances that make it unwise "at this time." If the central budget office is still unconvinced, the agency may make much of its professional expertise and argue that it alone has the know-how to determine budgetary needs in highly complex and scientific programs and projects.

Do These Ploys Work?

In simpler and more affluent days these and other seemingly plausible diversions may have worked, but their effectiveness today is doubtful. With a large and sophisticated budget bureaucracy in the executive and legislative branches hovering over the activities of the agency, only a straightforward and candid presentation of the needs and problems of the agency, supported by objective data, is likely to have a positive effect on decision makers. Anything less, however artfully presented, may jeopardize the credibility of the agency. The experience of many agencies suggests that the use of candor and objectivity is the best budgetary practice, especially in an era of budget cutbacks and often mindless "meat-ax budgeting."

To mask the truth about an agency's performance is to put the agency head in a morally ambiguous position. As an advocate of the agency's programs, she is understandably eager to report only successes and to minimize failures. This may appear to be smart politics and shrewd budgetary practice. It also serves to placate the mandarins in the agency who manage the major programs and their supportive constituencies. Sooner or later, however, the facts on program failures will out and may undermine the credibility of the agency head to the point where even justifiable programs are challenged.

Ultimately, the best strategy is a comprehensive budget decision-making system comprising the six major components discussed in this chapter. It will produce the data, policies, guidelines, standards, and criteria essential to budget making. To the extent that the criteria are accepted by the central budget office and the legislature, they will mitigate the effects of cutbacks. At least no one will have illusions about the impact of slashes on budget requests.

More anecdotage and myths than objective research are available on strategies to sell the budget. Whether they work remains a fruitful field for investigation.

Confidentiality of Budget Requests

Should an agency head make budget requests public at the time they go to the central budget office, send copies to the legislature, or leak them to the press? Actual practice depends on the budgetary norms in effect in the various governments. In the U.S. government the policy is to keep the budget requests confidential until the president releases the proposed budget:

> The nature and amounts of the President's decisions are confidential and will not be released until the budget is transmitted formally to Congress. The executive branch communications that have led to the budget will not be disclosed either by the agencies or by those who have prepared the budget.[14]

Only when Congress specifically asks for a copy of an agency budget request is the agency head free to release the information. This is rarely done.

States follow different practices. By law or informal practice, legislatures get copies of agency budget requests in states such as New York, Colorado, California, and Texas. Several states make it a point to include departmental budget requests in the governor's budget. For example, the New Jersey budget for FY 1992–1993 compares the requests of the Health Department with the Governor's recommendations:[15]

Department of Health, State of New Jersey
Summary of appropriations by program (thousands of dollars)

	Year ending June 30, 1993		
	1992 adjusted appropriation	Requested by agency	Recommended by governor
Health Services			
Vital Statistics	$ 1,039	$ 1,034	$ 1,034
Family Health Services	2,340	2,382	2,340
Epidemiology and Disease Control	7,000	7,580	7,580
Alcoholism, Drug Abuse, and Addiction Services	1,601	2,847	2,480
Laboratory Services	5,434	5,416	5,416
Occupational and Environmental Health	6,152	6,170	6,170
AIDS Services	5,502	5,594	4,610
Subtotal:	29,069	31,023	29,630
Health Planning and Evaluation			
Health Facilities Evaluation	2,169	2,151	2,151
Health Planning and Resource Development	5,028	4,588	4,588
Health Facilities Inspection Services	4,011	4,011	4,011
Subtotal:	11,208	10,750	10,750
Health Administration			
Office of Health Policy and Research	849	860	820
Management and Administrative Services	5,242	6,023	5,136
Subtotal:	6,091	6,883	5,956
Total Appropriations:	$46,368	$48,656	$46,336

Claiming autonomy, governing boards of higher education and occasionally state departments of education publicize their budget requests before the central budget office has had a chance to review them.

Those in the United States who support the confidentiality of budget requests argue that it is essential to the viability of the executive budget system. Without disclosure, no premature public debate will take place, and the chief executive will have the time and flexibility to deliberately consider available alternatives, priorities, and policies. Premature release of agency budget requests, on the other hand, with resulting public clamor, may complicate the task of preparing an overall, unified budget.[16] Furthermore, only the chief executive, and not the operating agencies, has the responsibility of formulating the executive budget. This is the only budget that counts and the chief executive stands or falls by it.

The time has come to question whether this position is still valid, at least in the United States. Considering the complexity and constraints of budgeting and the many participants in the budget process, more information rather than less may facilitate choice without necessarily eroding the executive budget process. In the United States the revelation of agency budget requests in several governments has not led to any known governmental crisis or paralysis in decision making. In fact, the quality of budget debate has improved.[17]

* * *

However they are prepared, justified, and publicized, agency budget requests go to the central budget office on the appointed day, or reasonably close to it. It is now the administration's turn at analysis, bargaining, combat, and decision making.

Points for Discussion

1. What are the major differences between government-wide budgetary guidelines and custom-tailored departmental budgetary instructions?
2. What are the desirable components of a system of departmental budgetary guidelines?
3. How would you organize an operating agency to ensure the availability of an effective budget system?
4. To what extent should all organizational units in an agency participate in budget making?
5. How would you determine staffing needs in a mental health agency; a public works agency; a correctional institution? In this connection review and analyze a departmental budget request from a state or local agency.
6. How would you measure the time spent in professional activities as a basis for staffing?
7. As an agency head, how would you coordinate policy development and management analysis with budgeting?
8. What steps should be taken to improve the quality of departmental budget analysis and budget hearings?
9. To what extent should an agency head advise the heads of bureaus and divisions of budget recommendations that go to the central budget office?
10. This chapter raises some reservations about the ploys and strategies used to justify departmental budgets. To what extent do you agree or disagree with this position?
11. How far should an agency head go in reporting program failures in the budget requests?
12. How would you sell the agency budget to the public and the central budget office?
13. To what extent, if at all, should agency budget requests be made public?
14. In an era of tax and expenditure limits, personnel ceilings, and unexpected budget cuts, how useful or wasteful is the comprehensive budget process outlined in this chapter?
15. What are the likely effects of strategic five-year plans on budgets as approved by Congress and the president in 1993?

CHAPTER 4

BUDGETING AT THE CENTER
How Presidents, Governors, and Mayors Budget

As reams of budget requests reach the central budget office, that agency has the responsibility of orchestrating thousands of large and small decisions in a few short months. Many of the decisions result directly from the budget process or are mandated by legislation. Others, especially some major ones, are made outside of the budget decision-making system by the chief executive. Any policy of consequence, however initiated, leaves its imprint on the budget.

Ordinarily, the task of compressing budget decision making at the center into such a short time span would be unmanageable. What makes the process feasible is, as we have stressed, the year-round nature of budgeting, which allows the budget staff time to become acquainted with the major programmatic, policy, fiscal, and economic issues and controversies. Furthermore, the annual exercise of developing budgetary guidelines enables an administration to formulate tentative budget policies.

Invaluable as these steps are, however, they are no substitute for a detailed and thorough analysis of budget requests in the light of the most current information. This takes place during a brief but hectic period when work weeks in the central budget office average seventy to ninety hours. It is the time for determining the latest expenditure trends; estimating revenue; weighing the soundness and validity of each budget request; bringing to a climax policy, management, and fiscal studies started earlier in the year; developing the latest economic assumptions and forecasts; and formulating alternative budget plans and fiscal policies for consideration by government leaders.

These are heavy responsibilities and they are central to decision making. Indeed, it is difficult to understand the budget process without a full appreciation of the role and functions of the central budget office, the nature of its internal decision-making process, and its relationship with the administration in facilitating budget decisions. This is the focus of this chapter.

Expanded Functions of Central Budget Offices

Modern budget offices cover a range of functions that would have startled budget directors and ministers of finance in the first thirty years of the twentieth century: fiscal policy, economic management, organization and management, policy development, multiyear planning, program evaluation, and intergovernmental financing. All this on top of the more conventional activities of reviewing estimates, forecasting revenue, and financial planning. These are the accepted norms in budgeting. Not all central budget offices perform all of the relatively new functions, but enough perform many of them so that the term "central budget office" is almost a misnomer. Many budget offices have become general managerial and fiscal arms of the government, not just guardians of the treasury. To cite a few examples, this is the case in the United States, Britain, Canada, France, Japan, Sweden, India, Brazil, and Mexico.

The comprehensive functions of central budget offices did not develop overnight. They evolved slowly in response to proliferating social, economic, and political problems; the growth in the size of the budget; and the rise in civilian employment in government. How each government defines the role of its budget office varies with its institutional and legal framework, fiscal structure, political values, and bureaucratic norms. While differences among budget offices exist, the trend is toward comprehensive offices.

Comprehensive Central Budget Offices

In the United States, central budget offices have developed a broad range of fiscal, managerial, and planning functions. Most pronounced at the federal and state government levels, this trend is increasingly evident among local governments as well. The aim in increasing responsibility is to serve and strengthen the office of the chief executive.

By the early 1990s, for example, the United States Office of Management and Budget (OMB) was responsible for the following functions in addition to the preparation and execution of the budget:

Participating in the development of fiscal and economic policy.

Monitoring, evaluating, and redesigning programs and policies.

Fostering interagency and intergovernmental cooperation and coordination.

Reviewing and coordinating legislative proposals by the executive branch, proposed testimony before congressional committees, and statutes enacted by Congress to determine compatibility with the administration's policies.

Reviewing departmental regulations to determine their impact on the economy and developing proposals for regulatory reform.

Improving management and organizational structures.

Providing leadership and direction in all aspects of financial management.

Simplifying and reducing paperwork by reviewing all governmental forms affecting businesses and individuals and coordinating the development and use of computer technology.

Developing procurement policies to effect economies in acquiring property, equipment, and services.

Keeping the President informed of agency performance and problems.[1]

All of these functions are vital, although not all administrations give them equal emphasis. The Roosevelt, Truman, and Clinton administrations prized administrative management whereas other administrations downplayed it. The Johnson and Carter administrations attempted to strengthen program planning and evaluation. In contrast, the Reagan administration was bent on cutbacks in domestic programs, and moved toward more narrow functions in OMB: tight fiscal management; the search for waste, fraud, and inefficiency; and lifting of governmental regulations regarded as onerous by the private sector.

Like fashions, various budgetary functions have their day in the sun, then recede. At any given time, the emphasis on some functions over others reflects such factors as (1) the managerial style, interests, and political, social, and economic values of chief executives and budget directors; (2) bureaucratic competition by such staff units attached to the office of the chief executive as the Council of Economic Advisers and policy advisers in the White House; and (3) the state of the economy. Despite the changing fortunes of some functions, the centerpiece of OMB and other budget offices remains budget formulation and implementation. This is the bedrock of budgeting.

Some 600 employees work for OMB. Most of the staff is concentrated in four functional areas: (1) human resources, veterans, and labor; (2) economics and government; (3) natural resources, energy, and science; and (4) national security and international affairs. Their major responsibilities are budget preparation and implementation and the conduct of special studies. In addition, specialized staffs direct OMB's programs in management improvement, financial management, procurement policy, oversight of regulations, and paperwork.[2]

State Budget Offices

The National Association of State Budget Officers sees budgeting as comprising six broad functions, perhaps not as many as at the federal level, but still a formidable list:

1. Program planning and evaluation
2. Management improvement
3. Financial planning
4. Budget management, execution, and expenditure control
5. Coordination of intergovernmental fiscal relations
6. Fiscal advice to the governor.[3]

State budget offices perform these functions in varying degree, regardless of the size of the office: All of these functions are carried out by Oregon's Budget and Management Division with a staff of forty; New Jersey's Office of Manage-ment and Budget with a staff of ninety; the New York State Budget Division with a staff of 350; and the California Department of Finance with a staff of 375. The organizational pattern for budgeting in each state varies. In New York State the Budget Division, which reports directly to the governor, is solely responsible for the broad array of budgeting functions. The state of Wisconsin, on the other hand, parcels out these functions among several co-equal units that are part of the Department of Administration. Similarly, the Department of Finance in California allocates budgetary functions to various subdivisions. In the case of the latter two superagencies, the office responsible for budget formulation and execution is the first among equals.[4]

Local Budget Offices

Many local governments in the United States have developed strong central budget offices with broad functions, which include capital planning, program evaluation, and management improvement. Toward the end of the 1980s, 451 municipalities with a population ranging from 25,000 to 1 million reported in a survey that they were committed to performance assessment and improved efficiency and effectiveness of programs.[5]

Agencies versus Central Budget Offices

The last chapter focused on a model of comprehensive budgeting in the best-run operating agencies. Under these circumstances, what can a central budget office, staffed primarily by generalists with a background in public administration, economics, financial management, and political science, contribute to the budget process? This question persistently troubles agencies with expertise in highly specialized fields. They are quite prepared to accept fiscal and policy constraints from the chief executive and his surrogate, the budget office, but within this restrictive framework they seek maximum flexibility in the details and financing of their programs, projects, and policies. From their perspective, much that goes on in the central budget office seems at best to duplicate at a more superficial level the intensive budgeting in the agency and at worst to represent sheer negativism and petty control. Agencies often regard the budgeteers at the center as well-meaning generalists who lack the understanding and sophistication of the specialists in the agency.

Central budget offices predictably take a different stand. They argue that budgeting in many agencies is far from satisfactory because of lack of data and objective analysis and frequent turnover of cabinet officers and other political appointees. Only the budget office can fill the vacuum left by instability or ineptitude in such agencies. Even where agencies have strong and comprehensive budget systems, the perspectives of the agency heads often differ significantly from the outlook of the chief executive and the chief staff agency, the budget office; their budget requests frequently reflect the pressures of special constituencies outside the agency and dominant groups in the agency.

As central budget offices see it, agencies tend to minimize or explain away data that points out deficiencies in their programs and projects. The agencies' emphasis is on promoting departmental programs and on getting a fair share of limited funds. What counts is their segment of government, not government-wide concerns. This is not surprising; the administration looks to the operating agencies to make the best case they can for their needs and requirements. Only the budget office, with an across-the-board point of view, is in a position to offset the special pleaders in the agencies.

Central budget offices see themselves as bastions of objectivity, rising above the parochial concerns of agencies. They pride themselves on sensitivity to the needs of an entire country or state and not just to special segments of the public. What seems like negativism and sheer cussedness to agencies is, to central budget offices, justifiable skepticism of the many claims made on the public purse, often without adequate justification. Only the central budget office, in its view, ferrets out inefficiency and ineffectiveness in programs and makes sure that the public gets appropriate value for the money invested in the budget. With a unique understanding of the complexity of government, the central budget office is aware of the interrelationships of programs. Virtually every major program cuts across departmental and intergovernmental lines. Hence, the budget office argues that it is in the best position to see how the bits and pieces of programs fit together.

In performing their functions, central budget offices are the eyes and ears as well as the right arm, of the chief executive. This is their self-image and for the most part, it is accurate. Their highest priority is to carry out and defend the policies and programs of the chief executive and to make certain that budget requests are in line with these policies. Where agencies falter, the central budget office provides an early warning of potentially significant problems through a steady stream of management intelligence on activities in the executive branch. They serve as a conduit for the transmission of directives from the chief executive to individual agencies and as an enforcer of these directives. Rising above narrow concerns, they take the necessary government-wide actions to improve management and decision making.[6]

In serving a political administration in this fashion, senior civil service officials in the central budget office grapple with some tormenting questions: Is it possible to be politically responsive to the administration without being partisan? How does one reconcile objectivity and political sensitivity? How can senior officials avoid the suspicion of future administrations if they are closely associated with the policies of prior administrations? In an operating agency these are critical issues. In a budget office, close to the center of political power, they are even more sensitive.

Political Neutrality versus Politicization of the Central Budget Office

During the first fifty years of the existence of the United States Bureau of the Budget (1921–1971), these issues were present, but mute. The Bureau (BOB) was noted for its political neutrality, even as it provided advice and analysis on sensitive and political issues to the Office of the President.[7] Only three or four senior officials were presidential appointees: the director, a deputy, and one or two assistant directors.[8] Career civil service officials headed the various program and technical units and reported directly to the director of the budget or the deputy director. Administrations came and went, but the career officials remained in their posts. In Heclo's memorable phrase, they and their staffs exemplified "neutral competence."[9] Uncommitted to the administration in power, they provided their best independent judgment to their partisan bosses. Budget watchers in and out of the United States regarded BOB as a place where the

> ethic was admired and defended, [a place where] you were both a representative for the President's particular view and the top objective resource for the continuing institution of the Presidency.[10]

This was and is the orthodox view in classic public administration and management theory. To a large extent it has also been the practice in many governments whose experience parallels that of the United States. In most of the advanced industrialized countries and many of the developing countries, senior career officials are the mainstay of the budget office and other central staff agencies. They serve their transient political masters responsibly, expertly, and objectively and are a highly respected elite corps. In state and local governments in the United States, career officials are also the backbone of central budget offices, serving in some cases as budget directors.

The Political Shadow Falls

In the United States the early assumptions about political neutrality have been challenged in the last twenty-five years by what some regard as the growing politicization of the Office of Management and Budget (formerly the Bureau of the Budget) in Washington, D.C., and of central budget offices in state and local government. Some presidents regarded BOB's neutrality as something of a myth and were wary of the staff's close association with the policies of previous administrations and the lack of responsiveness to their own initiatives. Presidents Eisenhower and Kennedy were downright suspicious of the loyalty of BOB and Presidents Kennedy and Johnson depended more on the White House staff and task forces for policy development than on BOB.[11] The Eisenhower, Kennedy, and Johnson administrations added several noncareer assistant directors to the BOB staff without, however, giving them line responsibilities to supervise the career employees.[12] From these beginnings the more overt politicization of the central budget office began.

Placing the "President's Men" in OMB

Equally suspicious of the BOB staff, President Nixon took the first direct steps to change the role of BOB and to put the "President's men" in key spots. In 1971 (with the approval of Congress) he changed the name of BOB to OMB to emphasize its role in managing and implementing programs rather than in developing policy; created a domestic council in the White House to formulate policy; and appointed noncareer associate directors in OMB to head program divisions and superintend the career staff. None of these were patronage appointments in the conventional sense of the term. Most of them had the necessary background, education, and experience for their posts. They served as a link between the career staff and the political leadership in OMB and between the White House and the operating agencies. What the Nixon administration started, the Carter, Reagan, Bush, and Clinton administrations continued. Instead of reporting directly to the head or deputy head of OMB, the top career officials were now insulated by two hierarchical levels of mostly short-term political appointees whose tenure was subject to the vagaries of politics. Furthermore, the White House staff intervened continuously in budget policy.

Reacting to an increasingly politicized OMB, an irate Congress in 1974 enacted legislation requiring the Senate to confirm future appointments of the director and deputy director of OMB, just as it does for the heads of operating agencies (PL 93-250, 1974). This effectively wiped out the special status of the budget director as the President's own personal appointment, which had been in effect since the Budget and Accounting Act of 1921.[13]

Political Neutrality of the Budget Office: An Illusion?

These developments have led several practitioners and students of the budget process to decry what they regard as the growing politicization of OMB and the loss of its vaunted neutral competence. Remembering the role of BOB in the "golden" 1950s, they concluded that the agency had lost its effectiveness as the conscience of the President.[14] If this could happen to the world's model budget agency, it could happen anywhere.

In reality, the political neutrality of OMB or any other central budget office is something of an illusion. At the federal level, the budget office has worked closely with the White House staff and various presidential task forces since the early 1950s. A self-study group in BOB in 1967 actually concluded that any distinction between loyalty to the President and loyalty to the presidency as an institution was unrealistic.[15] So involved is the central budget office in major social, fiscal, and economic issues that good policy reasons exist "for increasing political control over the agency and agency identification with the President."[16] If anything, the pressure on the budget office to implement the policies of the chief executive has intensified. It is more visible than in the past, with OMB actively participating in legislative hearings and meetings with legislative staffers and representatives of interest groups such as education lobbies and health and insurance organizations.[17]

This poses an acute dilemma for senior career officials. When the distinction between political and civil service erodes, two values are at stake. One is the need to draw upon the unique resources of the budget office and to provide the chief executive with objective, no-holds-barred analyses and an impartial perspective on the performance of programs. The other is the need for political sensitivity so that the budget office can advance the priorities and commitments of the administration. Both values can best be maintained by a viable mix of career and noncareer staff. The latter gets the political exposure and takes the political heat. The former avoids the risks of becoming a partisan instrument of the administration.[18] In practice, these neat distinctions do not always hold up. Some administrations do not take kindly to candid, objective, and unbiased appraisals of their pet schemes by the career staff, and attempt to make short shrift of messengers who bring bad news. Another problem is that senior budget officials may find that the views of the administration conflict so fundamentally with strongly held personal values that they have no choice but to resign. This is the American budget dilemma at the center.

Eight Paths to Decisions in Budget Making

Budget making in the central budget office brings together thousands of analyses, calculations, and arguments in time for budget decisions. It proceeds concurrently on what we will arbitrarily call eight decision paths, which eventually converge in the office of the budget director (or minister of finance) and the chief executive: budget analysis; program analysis; management analysis; legislative review; coordination of intergovernmental fiscal relations; and the triad that underpins budgeting from beginning to end: development of economic assumptions, expenditure estimation, and revenue estimation. This appears to be mechanical and tidy, but the journey is hazardous every step of the way.

Budget Analysis

What Budget Analysis Covers, or Should Cover. Budget analysis should cover all expenditure requirements of operating agencies regardless of the source of funds—general fund, special funds, grants from other levels of government, and short- and long-term loans. In several governments it also extends to the expenditures of autonomous public enterprises (government corporations, special districts, and public authorities), but this is not the case in every government. In some governments, analysis focuses primarily on the general fund, which is financed by income, sales, and property taxes and a variety of fees.

As budget examiners screen requests, they are mindful of the administration's budgetary guidelines, in which they had a hand. They also receive informal and formal guidance from the office of the budget director and, through that office, from the head of the government. Informal guidance also comes from campaign pledges, political commitments, prior decisions made outside of the budget process to fund programs, and pet peeves of the administration with regard to certain programs and projects. Some of these understandings are, in effect, directives, which leave little latitude to the budget examiners. For example, if the administration has committed itself in specific terms to build a bridge or support a questionable manpower training program, the examiner has no choice but to include these items in the budget.

Other directives may take fairly specific forms, such as predetermined expenditure and personnel ceilings, multiyear expenditure targets, "no increase" budgets with minor adjustments for inflation, vacancy freezes, onslaughts on uncontrollable funding through statutory and budget changes, limits on deficit spending, and selective increases for certain programs. For example, note the tough stand taken by the New York State Budget Division in 1988 (and reaffirmed in later years):

> The continued shortfall in tax revenues threatens our ability to submit a balanced budget for next year and makes it necessary to curtail spending for the remainder of the current year. Additional action at this time will also reduce the need for layoffs next year.
>
> Accordingly, effective immediately, the following types of transactions are frozen unless specifically exempted by the Division of the Budget (DOB):
>
> — Hiring in all permanent and temporary positions in *all* Funds;
>
> — All position reclassifications and reallocations;
>
> — All equipment acquisitions;
>
> — All new contracts for outside services (except in Local Assistance or Federal accounts pending agency analysis of discretionary spending);
>
> — Interchange of funds between Personal Service and Nonpersonal Service;
>
> — All State Operations expenditures from all unencumbered non-Federal reappropriations;
>
> — All acquisition of property;
>
> — Design of all discretionary capital projects; and
>
> — All approvals to bid capital projects.
>
> To ensure that savings are captured from these freezes, personnel targets must be reduced to reflect continuation of current vacancies and anticipated attrition caused by the hiring freeze. These actions must be taken in addition to the deficit reduction steps imposed earlier this year. Budget examiners will work with each agency to project attrition savings and to make corresponding permanent reductions in personnel targets.[19]

Guidance, however, is not a mechanical process, nor should it be. The chief executive is primarily interested in broad budget aggregates and leaves large and small details to the budget office.

The Critical Stages of Budget Analysis

Rough screening. In this climate budget examiners go through a number of critical stages in their analysis. First, they size up the budget requests preliminarily to compare proposed funding for the next fiscal year with the current year; to separate requests for new, expanded, or downsized programs and projects from the base budget; to note changes in staffing and in major non–personal service categories; and to identify gaps in information. This rough screening serves two purposes. It enables the budget examiners to send to the office of the budget director, as quickly as possible, data on the total amount of an agency's budget request in order to give the director the first overall view of the requests of all agencies. In addition, the examiners are in a position to request supplementary information from the agencies before beginning their review in earnest.

Detailed analysis. The detailed analysis covers every type of budget: operating, capital, intergovernmental grants (transfer payments), and public enterprises. Each budget requires a different analytical approach:

1. *The operating budget.* In reviewing the operating budget, examiners delve into the efficiency and effectiveness of departmental programs and the justification for staffing and other objects of expense. Literally hundreds of questions arise. For example, a health program for the poor may be swamped by delays and turn out to be unnecessarily costly. Without a drastic improvement in systems and policies, continued funding at existing levels would result in throwing good money after bad. Other examples include a reorganization of a major department, culminating in an expensive, top-heavy structure without any appreciable impact on the performance of programs; proposed staffing ratios for nurses, teachers, librarians, parole officers, and highway maintenance personnel that bear little relation to the efficiency and effectiveness of programs; and improved staffing of a police highway patrol that has shown no significant effect on the number of road accidents and deaths. What changes, if any, are appropriate?

In probing the justification for staffing and other objects of expense, examiners analyze estimated workloads and proposed work programs along the lines previously discussed. Wherever possible, they attempt to apply or develop performance standards.

2. *The capital budget.* Both policy and technical issues arise in analyzing budget requests for the construction and rehabilitation of capital facilities. The central question is, of course, the need for a facility or road. If a valid need exists, to what extent can it be met by refurbishing or intensifying the use of existing facilities? Are there other alternatives to construction? Chapter 5 covers capital budgeting in detail.

3. *The budget for intergovernmental grants.* Intergovernmental grants and transfer payments represent a major part of the budget in most countries and, among American states, the largest part of the budget. Complex statutory formulas govern the allocation of grants for education, health, mental health, welfare, transportation,

general aid, and other programs. Despite the use of formulas, budgeting for the grants is not a mechanical exercise. Numerous variables affect the size of the grants: economic trends, criteria for eligibility, the estimated number of individuals affected (students, patients, welfare clients, etc.), and demographic trends. Each one requires a searching analysis, which may disclose abuses in the implementation of policies and formulas. For example, a significant number of individuals who receive payments for education, unemployment insurance, or welfare may turn out to be ineligible, or examiners may find glaring examples of inequity in the allocation of funds among governments and individuals. The need for changes in laws, policies, and financing may become apparent through this analysis.

4. *The budget for public enterprises.* Budgeting for public enterprises (government corporations, public authorities, special districts, etc.) is highly specialized and, in many respects, significantly different from budgeting for conventional government departments and agencies. Chapter 6 covers this controversial process.

Informal budget hearings. By the time budget examiners conclude their initial review of agency budget requests, they will have a list of major issues of policy, program management, performance, and financing that require resolution. Any budget examination unit worth its salt will also have some tentative recommendations in mind that take into account the strengths and weaknesses of the budget submissions of the operating agencies. In most budget offices the next critical step is a full exploration of all these issues in a series of informal and off-the-record budget hearings with representatives of the operating agency.

The informal budget hearing is one of the most significant stages in budgeting. It offers an opportunity to call for more detailed justification of budget requests and gives the agency a chance to explain its poor performance in some programs and projects and to suggest possible corrective measures. It can be a testing ground for launching tentative recommendations and getting a feel for the minimum asking price of the agency head. It provides an opportunity to reach consensus, at least on smaller requests, and even, in some governments, results in a negotiation of differences on the size of and need for some major budget requests without involving higher levels in the government.

However amiable the informal hearing may be, it is essentially an adversarial proceeding that brings together the promoters (the agencies) and the skeptics (the central budget office). Both parties in the contest understand this. Whatever the results, informal hearings, when conducted professionally and objectively, satisfy the agency that it has at last had its day in court. In lieu of seemingly unilateral and arbitrary judgments by the budget staff, informal hearings, as well as later formal hearings, assure a kind of budgetary due process.

⍻ Program and Management Analysis

Although a goal of budgeting is to combine fiscal, program, and management analysis, the daily pressures of budgeting are so onerous as to leave little time for extended studies of the efficiency and effectiveness of programs and projects. As a result, specialized units have developed over the years in the central budget office at all levels of government: administrative management units in the 1930s and 1940s, program evaluation units in the 1960s, and performance review units in the 1990s. All are interrelated. What they do and their impact on budget decisions are covered in Chapter 13. For the present, it is important to stress that they probe major issues and formulate recommendations designed to influence budgetary decisions.

Legislative Review

An integral part of budget formulation is the review of two types of proposed legislation: drafts of departmental bills and bills either before or already approved by the legislature. While departmental bills are relatively few in number, they deal with major issues of the day and often will be part of the administration's legislative program. The budget office concentrates on the fiscal and policy implications of the proposed legislation and its compatibility with the views of the administration. Only departmental bills cleared in this fashion and approved by the office of the chief executive can be submitted to the legislature by the administration. Similarly, the budget office analyzes other bills considered by the legislature and solicits the comments of the agencies on the legislation. Before agency representatives testify at legislative hearings, the budget office also frequently clears their formal statements.[20]

As practiced in the budget office, legislative review is not a legal function, but an extension of budgeting. The budget office does what it is best equipped to do: point out the fiscal, programmatic, policy, and management implications of the legislation, leaving the actual drafting of bills and interpretation of statutes to lawyers. The rest is up to the office of the chief executive, which for policy or political reasons may not go along with the views of the budget office.

A related activity is the review and approval of regulations promulgated by operating agencies. These regulations have the force and effect of law, and can affect the economy, the environment, and the health and safety of individuals. They call for an extraordinary amount of paperwork and impose heavy costs on business and industry. Because of the far-reaching nature of federal regulations, the analysis of proposed and actual regulations has become a significant activity of OMB as well as in some state budget offices.

Coordination of Intergovernmental Fiscal Relations

So significant has the role of intergovernmental grants become that they command special attention by the donor governments and the receiving governments. For this reason, federal, state, and local budget offices have established special units to monitor grants, assess their utility, and propose necessary changes.

Forecasting Revenues and Expenditures and the Effect of the Economy on the Budget

Revenue and expenditure estimates begin the budget process, provide the framework for budget decision making, and trigger critical actions throughout the year that are designed to keep expenditures in line with revenue and to control deficits. They are central and indispensable in budget formulation and implementation. Because of their impact, it is important to determine the methods employed to develop the estimates and thus the reliability of the estimates. The estimates are no better than the underlying economic and other assumptions on which they are based. No matter the complexity and sophistication of the methodology that leads to them, the estimates will be grossly inaccurate if the assumptions are faulty.

The most critical variables are (1) the rate of economic growth (GNP and GDP), (2) price levels, (3) the unemployment rate, and (4) interest rates. (See the Glossary for definitions.) A forecast that assumes a growing economy, high employment, low inflation, and low interest rates will project higher revenues and lower expenditures. Conversely, a forecast that anticipates a stagnant, inflation-ridden economy or a recession will produce a gloomy scenario of revenue shortfalls, rising expenditures, and increasing deficits. For the federal government, these assumptions cover the national economy; for state governments, the state economy; and for local governments, the local or regional economy.

So sensitive are budget outcomes to economic assumptions that a mere 1 percent change, up or down, in the four major economic factors can raise or lower revenues and expenditures by billions of dollars at the federal level, and by hundreds of millions at the state level. For example, a sustained 1 percent drop in real economic growth (GDP adjusted for inflation) beginning in 1994 would have the following estimated budgetary consequences for the federal government by 1998: revenues down $93.0 billion, expenditures up $22 billion, and deficits up $115 billion. A 1 percent increase in unemployment during the same period would cut revenue by $54 billion, raise outlays by $20 billion, and increase the deficit by $74 billion. A 1 percent rise in interest rates would have little effect on revenue, but increase outlays by $35.0 billion and raise the deficit by $35.0 billion. Were a 1 percent rise in inflation to take place, receipts would go up by $68 billion, outlays up by $66.0 billion, and the deficit down by $1.0 billion.[21]

At best, the development of economic assumptions is a voyage into the relative unknown. It is necessary to estimate the impact on the four major variables of such interrelated factors as oil and food prices, international trade balances, the value of the dollar, monetary policy, domestic and international debt, the size of inventories at all levels of production and distribution, the level of domestic savings, and regional wars and natural disasters. How will probable developments specifically affect economic growth, unemployment, inflation, and interest rates? Such exercises can be a humbling experience even for the most professional and objective forecasters. For example, neither the Congressional Budget Office (CBO) nor OMB forecast the severe recessions of 1982–1983 and 1990–1993. In fact, they actually predicted an economic recovery beginning in 1982 and modest economic growth in the early 1990s. As a result, the revenue and spending estimates based on the economic assumptions turned out to be seriously inaccurate and budgets became exercises in unreality.

To hedge against the uncertainties of economic forecasting, CBO prepares several estimates and analyzes their effect on budget outcomes. One is a baseline estimate, which represents CBO's economic outlook. This is developed by the CBO staff in consultation with a Panel of Economic Advisors outside of the agency and compared with the "blue chip" consensus of private forecasters. CBO also forecasts high-growth and low-growth alternatives. Each scenario has a different effect on revenues, expenditures, and debt.[22]

Economic forecasting can be as much a political ploy as a technical exercise. To gain maximum political advantage, chief executives have a penchant for rosy estimates. A favorable economic outlook makes the budget politically appealing because of higher revenues and lower expenditures. If carried to an extreme, the politicization of economic forecasts undermines the estimating process. As CBO put it in 1993, "Erroneous economic assumptions have been a chronic source of error in past budget estimates. . . . In every year but one [of the last thirteen years] policymakers chose economic assumptions that proved to be overly optimistic."[23]

Even though administrations and legislatures differ on fiscal and budget policy, one would hope they could concur on a common set of economic assumptions, right or wrong, about the rate of growth and unemployment, inflation, and interest rates. Yet such assumptions and their accompanying revenue and expenditure estimates have become as controversial as the budget itself. To extricate themselves from this impasse at least seventeen state governments, including those in Florida, California, and Texas, develop a consensus on economic assumptions and revenue and expenditure estimates. In other states the executive and legislative branches formulate independent estimates.[24] Where a consensus exists, both the administration and the legislature can begin their budget debates with the same frame of reference. The federal government and other state governments might well emulate this approach.

Revenue Estimates

Revenue estimating is more of a complex art than a science. It is based on a series of economic assumptions and assorted methodologies. Different assumptions and methodologies lead to different estimates and, possibly, different fiscal policies. Even if the methodology is the same, the use of differing assumptions will lead to wide gaps between estimates. The critical phase in revenue estimating is calculating the effect of the economic assumptions on the tax base for each tax. For the income tax, this means estimating the three major components of taxable income: wages and salaries, corporate profits, and taxable nonwage income (rents, profits from unincorporated businesses and farms, dividends, and interest). Analysts apply the appropriate tax rates, including proposed changes, to the estimated tax base to arrive at projected revenue. They then adjust the data for deductions, exemptions, tax delinquency, and refunds.[25]

For sales, excise, and other consumption taxes, it is necessary to estimate, tax by tax, the effect of economic activity on wholesale and retail sales. After deducting exemptions, analysts come up with a new tax base to which they apply the tax rates. Property taxes are determined by the assessed value of property and the appropriate tax rates and adjusted to reflect exemptions, deductions, and statutory tax limits.

The methodology employed in estimating revenue ranges from simple projections based on an analysis of historical trends to the use of complex statistical and econometric models. Used cautiously in combination with other techniques, and with reservations about their predictive value, these models can be helpful in gauging the revenue effect of changes in the tax laws. Figure 4.1, based on the experience of the state of California, sketches the development of revenue estimates along the lines discussed above. Even with consensus, none of this guarantees accurate forecasts.

Given the fallibility of revenue estimating, it is small wonder that estimates frequently miss their targets, whether it be the result of poor economic forecasts, questionable assumptions about tax policy, or errors in technical analysis. In 1991 the U.S. Budget forecast total revenues of $1,156.3 billion, but actual receipts were $1,054.2 billion—an error of over 9 percent.[26] In FY 1992 state tax collections fell 3.6 percent short of original estimates, forcing states to reduce their enacted budgets to make up for the revenue shortfall.[27] The deepening recession was largely responsible for the drop in receipts.

Thus, fiscal policy rests in large part on a pillar of shaky revenue estimates. The way out may be more consensus estimates (on the theory that two or more heads are better than one) and fewer overly optimistic revenue estimates designed to make an administration look good.

Expenditure Estimates

In contrast with the emphasis on revenue estimating in budgetary literature, relatively little attention has focused on expenditure estimating. Budget analysis is an exercise in expenditure planning. It is different from expenditure estimating, which is a forecast of expenditures. The fact that the budget includes planned expenditures does not necessarily mean that the forecast expenditure will actually take place; for a variety of reasons under-spending or over-spending may occur.

FIGURE 4.1 DESCRIPTION OF REVENUE ESTIMATING PROCEDURES AND SOURCES OF REVENUE FORECASTING ERRORS

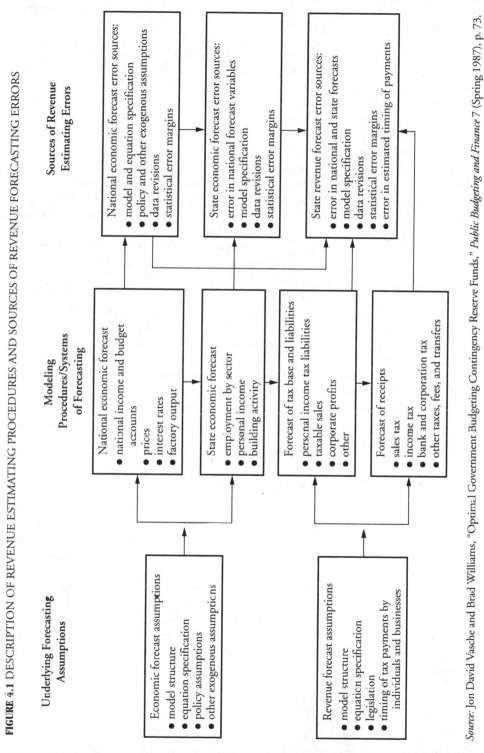

Source: Jon David Vasche and Brad Williams, "Optimal Government Budgeting Contingency Reserve Funds," *Public Budgeting and Finance* 7 (Spring 1987), p. 73.

Expenditure estimating is every bit as complex as revenue estimating. Admittedly, some certainties exist: debt service, fixed charges for fringe benefits, contract payments, and grants to state and local governments. Beyond these, it is necessary to engage in a detailed review of every program and project. Service demands, workloads, policies, and procedures change. Demographic patterns shift. Some activities meet their objectives; others fall behind. The rate of spending differs among programs. Inflation affects costs. The effects of collective bargaining on labor costs must be considered. Some of the most significant expenditures are especially sensitive to economic assumptions; for example, health, unemployment insurance, and welfare programs. Complicating expenditure estimating even further is the need to estimate the costs of programs funded by current, previous, and indefinite appropriations.

As in revenue estimates, marked differences exist among analysts with regard to economic assumptions affecting expenditures and the implementation of programs and projects. On this point CBO and OMB frequently differ. So do state and local administrations and legislatures.

The rate of spending is also a critical factor in developing expenditure estimates. Operating agencies base their budget estimates on their assumed ability to obligate and spend appropriations granted by the legislative body. Yet in many instances they misjudge their capacity to do this. As a result, especially at the federal level, they end the fiscal year with large unobligated and unexpended balances. This is no problem if uncommitted funds lapse at the end of the fiscal year and, unless they are reappropriated, revert to the treasury. This is the policy in most governments in the United States. Where funds carry over, they complicate expenditure estimating enormously.

Convergence of the Eight Paths of Analysis

Ultimately, the eight separate decision-making paths, including the latest estimates of revenue and expenditures, converge formally or informally in the office of the budget director. It is now the responsibility of the budget examination units and the specialized units to familiarize the budget director and other senior officials with the requests of the operating agencies, the results of their analyses, and their recommendations. By no means does the budget director come cold to these discussions. For some months she will have received the changing totals of budget requests, forecasts on revenues and expenditures, the most current reading of economic trends, and the evolving views of the administration on policies and priorities. No one has a better panoramic view of the big picture. What the director lacks are the details and a full understanding of available options.

Briefing Budget Directors

For a briefing on the details, the budget director and his top staff depend on the budget examination units. In a few short pages, which frequently take the

form of an issue paper, budget examiners have the formidable task of summarizing the following information for each agency: the agency's budget requests; their
recommendations; their views on the performance of the agency program by program and project by project; key data on agency performance; the compatibility
of the examiner's recommendations with the administration's plans, policies, and
commitments; an indication of which groups might be bloodied or favored by the
recommendations; options that might be considered if the going gets rough; the
implications of actions taken and not taken; and pointed questions to raise with
the heads of operating agencies.

Given the severe time constraints of budgeting, budget examiners cannot
overwhelm their superiors by covering in detail all the requests submitted by the
agencies. They must pick and choose and give the budget director an analysis of
only those requests that are urgent and merit priority. What they leave out, then,
becomes a matter of judgment and choice. This means that budget examiners, at
middle levels in the hierarchy, take action on many budget requests without refer-
ring them to the office of the budget director. If the examiners guess wrong, their
professional necks may be on the block. If they guess right (and most examiners
have a keen instinct for survival), they augment their already formidable decision-
making powers.

Following the analysis by the budget staff, the budget director and deputy
directors hold a series of meetings with the budget examiners to gain better
insight into the issues and to arrive at tentative recommendations. At this critical
moment the budget director needs the best and most comprehensive staff advice
she can get. To be limited solely to input from deputies and budget examiners
responsible for an agency's budget is too restrictive. Even at the risk of tense internal disputes, many budget directors recognize that it is wise to get the views of
other specialists in the budget office: management specialists, program analysts,
fiscal policy specialists, economic analysts, construction analysts, and other staff
advisers. This has the effect of flushing out all significant issues rather than
obscuring them. It also gets around the tendency of some budget examination
units to become advocates of a particular agency's programs and to protect the
interests of "their" agencies. The availability of specialized skills as an aid in decision making is no assurance that a budget director will use them, however; it takes
skill to use skills.

Holding Formal Budget Hearings

As part of the analysis of budget requests, budget directors in most governments also hold formal budget hearings with agency heads and their deputies. In
an elaborate scenario managed by the budget office, the budget director takes the
lead in questioning the agency head, brings up the touchy issues raised by the
budget requests, and gives the agency a chance to make its case.

For the most part, the formal budget hearings are a show arranged for the edi-
fication of the agency head. Rarely do the budget director and the central budget

staff gain additional insights and information from the hearings. After the informal hearings the formal hearings are often mere window dressing required by law or practice. A complication arises, however, when chairs of legislative fiscal committees and members of their staffs attend the executive budget hearings as observers, as is the practice in several state governments. It then becomes necessary for budget directors to exercise subtle but careful control over the hearings to make certain that the legislature does not get damaging information that it can use against the administration. Under these circumstances, the hearings may be carefully orchestrated to make the operating agency look good. When the legislative fiscal committees later hold their own hearings with agency heads, they will have an opportunity to take up critical questions that might have been glossed over at the budget director's hearings.

Options for Final Budget Decisions

Following the many analyses, discussions, and hearings, the budget director must now "make budget" if she is to meet the deadlines pressing in on her and get recommendations to the chief executive. How the budget directors and their deputies do this varies with the institutional arrangement and policies of the government and the director's personal style in decision making. Budget directors must simultaneously consider the needs of each agency, the economic outlook, and the latest revenue and expenditure estimates.

At best this is a trying decision-making exercise. Realistically, the budget director can only make decisions for each agency separately. After determining the overall fiscal effect of all these decisions, it may turn out that the approved requests of all agencies are greater than the government can afford. Under these circumstances it may become necessary to change some decisions in the light of evolving fiscal and economic trends.

Grim Options for Cutting the Budget

The options facing budget directors in the 1990s are grim. An engine of expansion in the 1960s, the budget has become a mechanism for budget cuts in the 1990s. What budget directors ultimately decide to recommend, then, depends on the most current and refined estimates of revenues, expenditures, and deficits or surpluses. In the event of surpluses that appear only rarely among some state and local governments, a budget director can toy with a series of pleasant alternatives such as cutting taxes, reducing borrowing, allocating more resources to agencies for new or expanded programs, increasing grants for other levels of government, stepping up construction, building up reserves against inevitable rainy days, and awarding pay increases and fringe benefits to the bureaucracy. For most budget directors this would be a unique and heady experience.

The more likely scenario is one that foreshadows revenue shortfalls, unexpected expenditures, and rising deficits. What can the hapless budget director do?

Nearly all the options are gloomy. Some obvious choices are to skewer new programs or proposed changes in existing programs unless they are part of the administration's agenda. The next less painful course of action is to choose one or more of the following options: slow down the planned rate of construction; enforce across-the-board percentage costs in the proposed budgets of all agencies; establish expenditure ceilings; defer preventive maintenance of buildings and roads and the purchase of equipment; freeze all positions vacated by resignations, retirements, transfers, and deaths; transfer responsibilities to other levels of government; curb official travel; look to other levels of government for help; or switch the financing of a program to another fund that may have ample revenue.

More Complex Ploys

The options in the preceding list are relatively easy ways to make major cuts, and are labeled "meat-ax budgeting" by cynics. More complex ploys follow:

1. *Debasing the budget base.* Previously immune to attack, the base budget, representing the cost of continuing current policies adjusted for workload and inflation, has become an annual target. Instead of getting the funds approximating last year's budget, operating agencies may get anywhere from 80 percent to 90 percent of that amount.

2. *Dismantling the work force.* Civil service tenure is no longer a protective cloak; in the late 1980s and early 1990s thousands of employees at all levels of government lost their jobs, as in the federal government and the governments of New York, New Jersey, California, Philadelphia, Bridgeport, and Yonkers. From 1991 to 1993 state employment dropped from 2,384,049 positions financed by the general fund to 2,091,885 jobs.[28] In addition, furloughs, paycuts, and pay freezes were widespread

3. *Shifting priorities.* Belying outdated theories of incrementalism in budgeting, major shifts of priorities occurred in the early 1990s. Among the states, elementary and secondary education, Medicaid, and correction services (jails) dominated budgeting. Funding for higher education, mental health, and local assistance lost out in this competition. At the federal level, savings in defense expenditures were diverted to domestic programs and deficit reduction. A consensus emerged on cutting funds for Medicaid and Medicare. With fewer functions, local governments backpedaled from existing responsibilities and attempted to free funds for law enforcement and welfare.

4. *Selling the family jewels.* To raise cash quickly, several governments sold some of their assets and then leased them back. For example, New York and New Jersey sold sections of highways to public authorities. New York took one further step and sold Attica prison for some $200 million to the Urban Development Corporation, a public authority. These transactions had the effect of forcing taxpayers to pay twice for the same facilities: the original payment plus debt service

paid to the public authorities for bonds they had issued to purchase the roads and jail.[29]

5. *Raiding pension funds.* By adopting actuarial assumptions that differ from the conservative estimates of fund managers, state and local governments have sharply cut their contributions to pension funds. This can be extremely lucrative: 201 state retirement systems and 2,213 local retirement systems operated in the United States in 1990. An innovator in this area, New York State cut its pension contributions from 20 percent of the payroll in 1980 to about 5 percent in 1990. This resulted in a savings of $600 million in 1990 and $429 million in 1991. At least eighteen other state and local governments took this step. California topped them all with a savings of $1.6 billion in 1991. Some states deliberately under-fund their pension systems in amounts ranging up to 50 percent of their liabilities: Illinois, Maine, Massachusetts, West Virginia, and Louisiana. Both of these tactics have the effect of shifting costs to future taxpayers. They have also been attacked in the courts as illegal. For example, New York State and its local governments have been ordered by the state's highest court to return $4 billion to the pension funds.[30]

6. *Early retirements.* As an alternative to layoffs, several governments offer seductive pension benefits to employees in their fifties and sixties who agree to take early retirement. By replacing such highly paid employees with low-paid beginners or freezing the positions altogether, governments can save hundreds of millions of dollars.

7. *Playing the public authority game.* Federal, state, and local governments can create the illusion of budget savings by transferring functions to public authorities, special districts, and government corporations. As Chapter 6 explains, this is a growing and expensive phenomenon.

8. *Enhancing revenues.* With "taxes" a fighting word, governments are seeking to "enhance" their revenues by imposing hundreds of new fees and charges. They are remarkably successful in this new venture, and fees have become one of the fastest-growing sources of revenue. (See Chapter 7.)

9. *Privatizing operations.* Although many activities of federal, state, and local governments are farmed out to private for-profit and nonprofit contractors (for example, nearly all construction, waste management, and management of specialized facilities), "privatization" is still a commanding word in the 1990s. For selected operations, federal agencies go through the annual exercise of comparing their costs with those of private firms. The winner takes all. Mental health facilities, social services, and transportation were likely candidates in most states for privatization in 1994 according to the Council of State Governments. A good deal of anecdotage surrounds privatization and occasional useful studies have been conducted, but comprehensive analyses of costs, benefits, and savings have yet to emerge.

10. *Practicing budget gimmickry.* Ingenious budget offices have come up with dubious devices to make the budget look smaller than it is: paying bills late (Illinois), delaying the payment of grants to local governments (New York

and California), tapping special funds to meet expenses and repaying them the following year, raiding surpluses of special funds, and accelerating the payment of taxes and fees. These are one-time measures that only delay the day of reckoning.

None of these ploys are cost free. Deferring capital construction and maintenance of facilities results in dangerous backlogs and ultimately in higher costs. Exploiting staff attrition leads to major inequities. Critical programs may experience staff turnovers and are cut, in effect, because vacant positions cannot be filled. Conversely, questionable programs may coast along from year to year with minimum staff changes. Through sheer happenstance they remain relatively untouched.

The crunch comes when these expedients are not enough and the choice narrows down to cutting continuing programs, slowing the growth of hitherto uncontrollable programs, raising taxes, or borrowing money. Each option has different effects. Budget cuts may adversely affect low-income groups and the economy in general. So may other components of fiscal policy. Taxes and deficit financing adversely affect individuals and businesses. Chapter 7 discusses the implications of these different moves.

Deciding What to Recommend to the Administration

Considering all the complexities, the pressures, the problems, and the uncertainties, how does a budget director put a budget together? How does he decide what to recommend to the chief executive? So complex is policy formulation of this nature that only detailed case histories can shed light on the process. It is only possible in the space allowed to make some broad generalizations based on the experiences of several governments.

Above all, the approach taken by the budget director is pragmatic and in tune with political reality. In a tightly compressed period of time the director runs through a series of financial plans that encompass proposed expenditures, revenue, and debt financing, and appraises each one searchingly. In this iterative process, many plans fall by the wayside. Finally, when time has just about run out, the budget director endorses the least damaging of the lot, one that generally is in line with the administration's ideological values and economic, fiscal, and social policies. It is intended to enhance the political fortunes of the party in power, or at least to limit any potential damage. It focuses on the priorities that dominate any administration at any one time. Throughout the decision-making process the budget director does not operate in a vacuum. He is in close touch with the chief executive and he gets a steady stream of signals from legislators and interest groups that enables him to know roughly whether he is on course.

The Stockman Affair

In a memorable and revealing interview with an editor of the *Washington Post*, David A. Stockman, director of the Office of Management and Budget in the Reagan administration, described candidly how the administration developed its first budget in 1981 and his own reservations about it. He termed the budget cuts enacted by Congress at the administration's prodding "illusory and inadequate." He regarded as "naively optimistic" the doctrine of supply-side economics, which the President "had embraced as justification for his across-the-board tax reductions." The defense budget was "bloated with waste." New legislation that cut business taxes "represented out-of-control greed and special interest favors." In making recommendations, Stockman admitted, he "did not fully grasp all the budget numbers." They were out of control and the chances of regaining control were slim. He foresaw enormous deficits because of the simultaneous effect of tax cuts and increases in defense expenditures. Only revisions of the tax program and deep cuts in entitlement and other domestic programs would result in controlling the deficits.[31]

Explaining how the Reagan plans went awry, Stockman stated with unusual candor:

> The reason we did it wrong—not wrong but less than the optimum—was that we said, Hey we have to get a program out fast. And when you decide to put a program of this breadth and depth out fast, you can only do so much. We were working in a twenty or twenty-five day time frame, and we didn't think it all the way through. We didn't add up all the numbers. We didn't make all the thorough, comprehensive calculations about where we really needed to come out and how much to put on the plate the first time, and so forth. In other words, we ended up with a list that I'd always been carrying of things to be done rather than starting the other way and asking what is the overall fiscal policy required to reach the target.[32]

As a direct consequence of this unaccustomed candor, especially about the questionable estimates, Stockman lost his credibility with Congress and demands arose for his resignation. Stockman's experience may be extraordinary and may not typify the annual ordeal of budget directors, for he was on the cutting edge of an administration determined to roll back the Roosevelt–Truman–Kennedy–Johnson welfare state.

Thirteen years later, in 1994, director of OMB Leon Panetta took a dramatically different position. In defending President Clinton's budget for FY 1994-1995, he claimed in his customary forthright style, "We need to basically be honest about what we're presenting to the American people. The numbers here do not present any rosy scenarios. . . . We have presented no gimmicks here. There are no smoke and mirrors. The numbers that you see here are the numbers that are there, and what you see is what you get in the budget."[33]

In 1989 Robert Mandeville, a long-time budget director in Illinois, agreed that he was more sensitive to dollars than to people and programs. He said, in effect, "That's my job":

> You will never get consensus on allocation of resources. I do care about programs, I have preferences like everyone else, but in the end I can't allow myself as director to become a strong advocate for any one program. There are plenty of other people who will speak for the programs. I see my prime job as the bottom line, to

keep the state solvent, to keep the credit rating high and to get the bills paid as quickly as possible. . . . I have learned that it is prudent to keep a reasonable [cash] balance, but having learned it I haven't been able to sell it. I advise others to keep a balance equal to four to five percent of the budget—at least three percent—but we have been getting along at two percent. What happens then, of course, is that if you have a dip in revenues, you just hold bills.[34]

Nearly all budget directors experience doubts about the soundness of some of an administration's pet programs, build their budgets on vulnerable forecasts, swallow unpalatable political decisions, and base major decisions on imprecise figures and "guesstimates." Greider puts the dilemma of budget directors this way:

That is the experience of government, repeated again and again of those mortals chosen to manage the complexities of the technocratic state. If one could administer truth serum to the budget directors who served under Johnson, Nixon, Ford, and Carter, they would be compelled to relate similar nightmares of confusion: runaway numbers that refused to conform to their predictions, bad guesses and wishful thinking that shaped major policy decisions, unforeseen events that wiped out their theoretical premises or sometimes rescued them from disasters.[35]

Budgeting during Transitional and Pre-Election Periods

Even more complex is the preparation of the budget in the United States during two difficult periods: the weeks following an election before an administration assumes office and the months preceding an election. Once an incumbent administration is defeated, it is the informal practice at virtually all levels of government in the United States for the victor to be invited to send representatives to the central budget office to observe the budget process. This occurs early in November while the outgoing chief executive is still legally required to submit a budget to the legislature in January, knowing that his successor will change it on the advice of the transitional team. The period is a trying one for all participants. The central budget office shares information with the transitional team, but it does not solicit its views on decisions. The demand for information by the newcomers conflicts with a tight budget schedule. Particularly difficult is the lot of senior civil servants, who in effect serve two masters for different purposes and in the process are often regarded suspiciously by both.

With an election pending, an administration in the United States plays its budgetary hand warily. Fearful of premature leaks on expenditure cuts and tax increases, it defers major decisions on budget policy until after the election, to the consternation of budget directors. This has the effect of almost paralyzing the budget process.

Budget Making with the Chief Executive

At the last possible moment, in a hectic environment of changing estimates and calculations, the budget director submits a draft of what he hopes will be a viable budget to the chief executive. The draft focuses only on the big issues and the big changes. The tacit understanding is that the budget director, with a minimum of damage to the administration, will decide or negotiate everything else.

No clearcut pattern of decision making holds for all governments in the United States. At the local level, a budget director either makes budget with a city manager (in council–city manager governments), an elected mayor, or an elected county executive. At the state level, the budget director works either directly with the governor or through a director of administration or director of finance who reports to the governor. In the federal government, the budget director is part of the Executive Office of the President and deals directly with the president and the White House staff on the budget.

Ultimately, the effectiveness of the budget director depends on his personal relationships with his political superiors. As a former director of the United States Bureau of the Budget noted, "Unless the budget director is tuned-in on the president's wave length, his desk will only become a temporary resting place for problems on their way to the president."[36]

Advising the Chief Executive

Other participants join the chief executive and the budget director in decision making. At the elbow of the chief executive are his valued official and unofficial advisers: the makeup of this group changes in accordance with his decision-making style and the subject under consideration. The President of the United States generally counts on the advice of key officials on the White House staff, the chairman of the Council of Economic Advisers (sometimes), the secretary of the treasury, other cabinet officials, business and labor leaders, political party leaders, influential friends, and, at times, legislative leaders.

The chief executive and the budget director run through several budget scenarios until final decisions are made. Often this process continues until the last possible moment for printing the budget. Even then, chief executives may change their minds after the budget is "put to bed." This requires destruction of the printed budget and publication of a new one in time to meet the statutory deadline. With modern computers this is no longer a traumatic problem. In fact, computer systems in nearly all budget offices have expedited budget decisions and introduced unprecedented flexibility in the budget process.

Appealing Budgetary Decisions

Through their budget directors, most chief executives in the United States advise agency heads of their budget decisions and give them an opportunity to appeal the decision either directly to them or to a review panel composed of the budget director and the executive's chief of staff. The right of appeal is sometimes illusory. It can be exercised only at the eleventh hour, when the budget is usually in the hands of the printer. This process presents the agency head with an acute dilemma. Even if he regards many of the decisions as unwise and indefensible, he cannot, as a practical matter, appeal all of them and ask the chief executive to reopen the entire budget-making process. Reluctantly, then, he may settle for a review of no more than two or three decisions. This enhances the power of the budget office, because even its questionable decisions may go unchallenged.

"Putting the Budget to Bed"

In the wake of final budget decisions, the herculean task of assembling the budget begins. This involves three major steps: the drafting of the budget message, or budget speech, which as a major state paper attracts most attention; the preparation of the detailed budget documents; and the drafting of the appropriation, budget, or finance bills (the terms are synonymous) necessary to carry out the budget. As noted, modern computer systems have expedited these three processes. An example is OMB's Control Budget Management System (CBMS). Figure 4.2 sketches the OMB process.

FIGURE 4.2 OMB'S CONTROL BUDGET MANAGEMENT SYSTEM (CBMS)

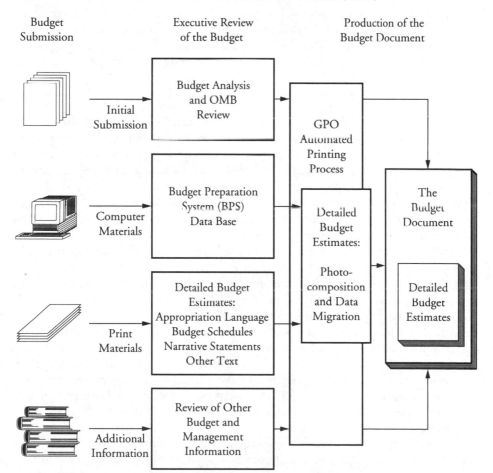

Source: OMB, Circular All (1992).

The Budget Message

Overarching the entire budget is the budget message delivered by presidents, governors, and mayors. It can be part of the budget document, a separate message, or both. In parliamentary systems the closest counterpart is the budget speech by the minister of finance. A major political document, the budget message lays out and defends the administration's policies; points with pride to past and current accomplishments; analyzes economic conditions; and summarizes the major proposals on programs, projects, revenues, expenditures, and debt. In many governments in the United States, a detailed appendix, replete with narratives, graphs, and tables, elaborates on the themes in the message. For the media and most citizens, the budget message is the budget; they rarely concern themselves with other parts of the budget. Hence, the administration takes more than ordinary care in couching the message in memorable and stirring rhetoric, even, at times, invoking the aid of the deity. In times of widespread fiscal distress, help from all quarters is welcome.

With budgets dominating public policy, chief executives in the United States have also increasingly used the occasion of their annual "state of the union," "state of the state," and "state of the city" messages to lay out fiscal and budget policies in broad terms, in effect foreshadowing their own budget document.

The Budget Document

Supporting the budget message is the budget document or documents. Embodying thousands of decisions, large and small, the budget often consists of one or more weighty volumes. In its text and many tables it is the centerpiece of a government's fiscal, programmatic, and economic policies. It is the reference point for popular and legislative debate, the record of how claimants on the public purse fared in the budgetary squabble, the baseline for later and never-ending changes, and the synthesis of the multiple purposes served by the budget process. Above all, it is and always has been an instrument of financial control.

While most budget documents throughout the world have common elements, there are still marked differences in their scope, format, and methods of classification. These variations are not mere technical distinctions, but spring from the political, legal, decision-making, and financial systems of governments. What appears in the budget document tells us much about the openness or secrecy of the budget process; who decides what; who needs what information for what purpose regarding what type of program, activity, or project; who is accountable to whom for what; the different audiences to whom the budget is directed; and the overriding purposes of the administration in power. For these reasons no one budgetary structure can satisfy all governments. Each government develops a budgetary format, suitable for its own unique requirements, and experiments continuously with variations.

In their comprehensiveness and clarity, budget documents differ markedly. At one extreme, the budgets of the United States government, many state and local governments, and several foreign governments cover nearly all revenues and expenditures in the public sector. (The weak link in some of these governments is the exclusion of the budgets for social security systems and public enterprises). At the other extreme, some budgets are fairly flimsy affairs with only a sketchy summary of expenditures and revenues in traditional classifications with little, if any, explanation. This is the case in a minority of local governments in the United States and in several governments in Asia, Africa, and Latin America.

Budget documents come in many forms and sizes. While generalizations are difficult, it is possible to discern two types of budget formats among a diversity of budget documents: "bare bone," or basic, budgets and enhanced, or comprehensive, budgets. Taken together, the two comprise adequate budgets. Supplementing them is a series of nonbudget documents that influence budget decisions. Examples of these are economic reports, multiyear and annual social and economic development plans, and year-end audit reports.

Bare Bone, or Basic, Budget Documents. The bare bone budget has roots going back to the earliest days of budgeting. It includes at a minimum the budget message; the proposed financial plan, including revenues, expenditures, and deficits or surpluses; the breakdown of expenditures by fund, organizational unit, and objects of expense; revenue estimates; economic assumptions underlying the proposed budget; proposed capital expenditures; intergovernmental grants; and a narrative highlighting and justifying major budgetary themes.

The financial plan. Appearing at the beginning of the budget document, the financial plan is the crown jewel of the budget, though lately a rather tarnished one. Deceptively simple, it is the quintessence of all decisions, policies, and priorities. It summarizes proposed expenditures and revenues for all funds and usually compares the proposed financial plan for the next fiscal year with the actual experience of the current and past fiscal years. The focus in the financial plan is on the bottom line—the difference between revenues and expenditures. In the United States and most other countries, this is the figure that attracts the most attention because it highlights probable surpluses or deficits. If deficits loom ahead, the financial plan can summarize the means of financing them. (For an example of the financial plans of the United States federal government and a state government, see Chapter 1.)

The traditional triad: Classification of expenditures by fund, character, object of expense, and organizational unit. Budget documents change in accordance with passing fads and in response to new needs, but one component rarely changes and that is the traditional classification of expenditures by fund, organizational unit, and character and object of expense. Historically and politically these classifications have facilitated legal control and accountability. However, such data tell us little about the purposes of expenditures and, by themselves, are patently inadequate for evaluating the results of programs and projects. Nevertheless, they have the important but frequently overlooked value of getting operating agencies to account for the management of the resources entrusted to them.

The data also facilitate economic analysis by showing the nature of the goods and services purchased by governments, and serve as input to broad aggregate measures such as GNP (Gross National Product), GDP (Gross Domestic Product), and National Income Accounts.[37]

Revenue estimates and the economic assumptions on which they are based. Virtually every budget document lays out the revenue estimates for the next fiscal year, or the biennium, as the case may be. Few documents, however, explain in detail the basis for the estimates. The data are available either behind the scenes or in separate documents such as economic reports or annual plans for economic development. One of the most informative explanations of revenue estimates appears in the annual budget document of the government of New York State. This is due not so much to an inordinate zeal for public disclosure as to an unusual constitutional requirement that mandates the inclusion of such data in the budget (New York State Constitution, Article VII, Section 2). After specifying the economic assumptions behind revenue estimates, this budget document goes on to justify the estimates for each separate tax.

The economic outlook is central in estimating revenues and expenditures because the ups and downs of the economy directly affect revenues and expenditures, as well as budget policy generally. For this reason budget documents frequently contain forecasts of the economic outlook that were used to frame the budget.

Capital budgets and debt service. Whether governments have separate capital and operating budgets or combine the two in one document, they specify in detail projects under way and projects proposed for the next fiscal year, the methods of financing the projects for at least the next four years, the total long- and short-term debt incurred by the government, and the funds required in the upcoming year to repay the principal and interest on the debt.

Grants and transfer payments. Transfer payments and intergovernmental grants, particularly federal and state aid, loom large in the budget documents of all governments. For state governments in the United States they are vital, and for local governments, critical. Hence, governments often devote a major segment of the budget document to such assistance.

The size of the government bureaucracy. With staffing and related fringe benefits accounting for the greater part of the operating budget, decision makers have a keen interest in the size of the bureaucracy. Consequently, budget documents typically summarize the number and types of staff positions in the government.

The budget time frame. The bare bone budget document usually has a three-year time frame. It compares proposed expenditures and revenue for the upcoming fiscal year with estimates for the current year and actual experience of the past year. What draws most attention and and is emphasized in the budget document is the difference, plus or minus, between estimated expenditures and revenue for the current year and the proposed budget. Where governments have a biennial budget, the comparative tables cover a six-year period.

Legislatures also look for the difference between current and proposed appropriations. The appropriations shown in the budget document often bear little resemblance to the original appropriations approved by the legislature at the last session. Subsequent to that action, a variety of changes may have taken place: supplemental appropriations, reappropriations, transfers between appropriations, or supplements from emergency or "rainy day" funds in effect in many governments. Added to the original appropriations, these adjustments show the actual total funds available to an agency, program, or project during the current year. This becomes the basis for comparison with the appropriation recommended for the next fiscal year.

The narrative that weaves the parts together. In most budget documents a narrative, supplemented by summary tables, charts, and graphs, weaves together the separate parts of the budget. The first part of the narrative usually sketches the big picture. A government uses it to highlight its major policies, to call attention to major changes, and to rationalize any significant shifts in fiscal policy and programs. On the heels of the overall narrative comes a discussion of the budget estimates for each agency. Depending on the government, the commentary can range from banal cliches that tell nothing to explicit analyses of the needs of each agency. Some governments omit the discussion altogether, merely presenting budgetary tables for each agency.

Enhanced Budget Documents. Such is the state of the art of budgeting that some governments fall short of even this "bare bone" approach that fails to serve the multiple purposes of budgeting. Thus it has become increasingly necessary to enhance the basic budget document by organizing information in different ways and adding new classifications and supplements to it. The principal new components of the enhanced budget are classifications by function and program; the use of performance data; multiyear projections of expenditures and revenues; an analysis of the relationship between medium-term plans and budgets; a focus on off-budget entities such as public authorities; an emphasis on management improvement; an analysis of "tax expenditures" (tax breaks); a discussion of credit and loan guarantee programs; and, in some countries, a foreign exchange budget.

Structuring Budgets to Gain Public Understanding. Even with bare bone budgeting, the problem of conveying all the relevant information in budget documents to decision makers, operating agencies, and the general public is complex. With comprehensive, or enhanced, budgets it is staggering. In size and sheer weight, budgets in one- or multi-volume editions vie with the Manhattan telephone directory and, pound for pound, often top it. To appreciate this point, one merely has to look at the budget documents produced by the United States government and the governments of Wisconsin, Pennsylvania, California, Massachu-setts, New York State, Ohio, and Florida. For example, during fiscal years 1991, 1992, and 1993 the Bush Administration turned out a massive U.S. budget in one volume totaling over 1,000 pages. Previously, six or seven publications had covered the budget: *Budget of the United States Government, Budget in Brief,* an *Appendix* covering detailed appropriations and financing, *Special Analyses, Historical Tables, Major Policy Initiatives,* and at times, a management report. Beginning in 1993, the Clinton administration reverted to the use of a multi-volume edition. In FY 1993–1994 New York State shifted from a weighty budget volume plus a small popular version to five documents: *Executive Budget 1993–1994, Annual Message, Briefing Book, Tax Expenditure Report,* and an abstract, the *Governor's Budget Presentation.* During the same year Massachusetts also produced five volumes; Illinois, three; and Kansas, three. To implement the budget, central budget offices also prepare appropriation bills, usually in separate documents, for action by the legislature.

Governments must somehow strike a balance between encyclopedic budgets and meaningful ways of presenting data to those who are not insiders, specialists, or technicians. For the latter, who thrive on complexity, massive budgets are no problem. Nor does the budget overwhelm the operating agencies and the many interest groups. They are well served by representatives who analyze in detail those parts of the budget that affect their vital interests. Only the general public, legislators who are not members of fiscal committees, and the media experience frustration in trying to understand the intricacies of the budget.

In selling the budget, governments increasingly realize that they must somehow reach this larger public. They attempt to do this in the following ways:

1. *The budget in brief.* In a relatively short version of the budget, governments summarize the main themes and proposals in the main budget document in non-technical language. Liberally interspersed with graphic and tabular displays, the budget in brief is essentially a self-serving public relations document. Especially informative in dealing with budget complexity were popular versions of the budget issued by the governors in Texas and Michigan for FY 1994–1995: *Working for Texas: The Governor's Policy Budget* and the state of Michigan's *Executive Budget.*

2. *The budget message.* Governments frequently publish the budget message separately. More comprehensive than the budget in brief, it presents in some detail the economic outlook and budgetary highlights. It is sometimes supplemented by an appendix containing summary data on revenue, expenditures, capital construction, intergovernmental financing, and off-budget entities.

3. *The budget summary.* Several governments in the United States, especially at the state level, issue budget summaries. These are not budgets in brief, but analyses of the budget from the perspective of the administration. Such summaries are

standard practices in the states of Washington, New Jersey, and California. Running up to 150 pages, these summaries capture in narrative and tabular form the essence of the budget document.

4. *Policy papers affecting the budget.* To focus attention on the major policy issues affecting the budget, several governments publish a separate document to identify these issues and explain the government's position. For example, policy papers prepared by the state of Wisconsin deal with dozens of urgent issues. On each issue the governor takes a stand that is reflected in the budget, defines the problem, gives the background, and explains the basis for the recommendation.[38]

5. *Supplementary volumes.* In a growing trend, governments have pruned the size of the main budget document to reduce it to manageable proportions, and have issued one or more appendices designed to cover in detail various segments of the budget. This is the practice in the United States government, the French government, and several state governments.

6. *The multiyear capital budget.* As noted earlier, governments follow varying procedures with regard to the capital budget, either incorporating it in the main budget or presenting it in a separate document, as do Illinois and New York State.

7. *Multiyear revenue and expenditure projections.* While many budget documents contain such projections, several governments publish them separately.

8. *Economic and demographic reports.* Several states, including Kansas and New Jersey, issue separate reports on the state and regional economies and demographic trends.

9. *Budget lexicon.* Budgetary language and jargon have become so specialized that many governments make it a point to include a glossary of terms in the main budget document or in a separate publication. With the aid of this lexicon, the reader, in theory, can probe the mysteries of "apportionments," "allotments," "backdoor spending," and other arcane, polysyllabic terms. The appendix includes critical budget, economic, and accounting terms in use in the United States government.

Publishing Documents on Other Phases of Budgeting. The publication of the budget documents is but the beginning of a dynamic process that will result in many changes in the estimates and proposals. At various strategic points in the budget process, governments attempt to summarize the changes by issuing still other budget documents, as follows:

1. *Budget revisions.* After releasing the budget document, chief executives may have some second thoughts in the light of changing conditions. In the federal government of the United States and in several state governments, they have the option of revising their budgets in about thirty days.

2. *Updating the budget after legislative action.* After the legislature has acted on the budget, it is no longer the same document submitted by the chief executive.

Many governments issue a summary of the adjusted budget, variously dubbed "post-legislative summary of appropriations," "final budget summary," or "legislative action on the governor's budget." These documents can be neutral or intensely political in nature.[39]

3. *Periodic review of the status of the budget.* In the United States government, OMB is required to submit a "Midyear Review of the Budget" by July 15 (approximately six months after the release of the executive budget). It is intended to update program revisions, economic assumptions, and spending and revenue totals. It is something of a partisan document. More highly regarded is the report, "Current Budget Estimates," which in April of each year updates the budget in light of the latest economic and programmatic trends. Nearly all state governments and many local governments update estimates of revenues, expenditures, and surpluses or deficits either quarterly or semiannually, based on the latest economic forecast.

4. *Year-end report on budget performance.* Many governments issue year-end reports comparing actual performance with the original budget as adjusted by the legislature. For the most part, these reports deal solely with expenditures and revenues and not with the performance of programs and projects.[40] This points up one of the major weaknesses in budget reporting. Relatively few governments attempt to report how programs fared compared with the original objectives and estimated outputs. Among the exceptions are Oregon and New Jersey.

5. *Combination of old and new budgets.* Some countries try still other gambits in issuing budget documents. For example, after India and Malaysia release budgets in the traditional format, they follow this up by issuing program and performance budgets, solely for information purposes. Recapitulating the data in the main budgets by program and activity, the supplemental budgets provide comprehensive data on the workload, efficiency, and effectiveness of programs and projects. To make these supplements especially informative, the Ministry of Finance in India publishes separate program and performance budgets for each major ministry and even for large subdivisions of ministries.[41]

6. *Supplemental and deficiency budgets.* When governments amend their main budgets by preparing supplemental and deficiency budgets, they submit these either as separate budget documents, or budget bills, or both. The supplemental budget covers changes in estimated expenditures and revenues for the *forthcoming* fiscal year while the deficiency budget provides additional funds to agencies during the *current* fiscal year. Otherwise, for various reasons, they would run out of funds before the year is over.

Do Comprehensive Budget Documents Result in Better Decisions? Except in those governments with a passion for secrecy or a dearth of data, it is apparent that budget documents, in all their variants, provide unprecedented and revealing information on budget policy to all the participants in the budget process.

Unfortunately, comprehensive data do not necessarily result in sound policies. No amount of budget documentation can substitute for sound value judgments and economic and political judgment. At best it provides ammunition to all contestants and, in a close call, may make the ultimate decision more rational than it might have been with less data available.

Selling the Budget

Even before the release of the budget documents, presidents, governors, and mayors begin an active selling campaign to gain maximum political advantage and public understanding. Their customary ploy is to leak parts of the budget to favored reporters without attribution or to hold off-the-record press conferences.

Since the mere size of the budget staggers even the most sophisticated budget watchers, some chief executives hold "budget schools" for media executives and reporters. A few days before such a conference, reporters receive copies of the budget message and the budget documents, with the understanding that they cannot release the information before a specified date. While little time is available for detailed analysis, the preview of the budget at least enables them to raise broad questions with the chief executive, the budget director, and other senior economic and program advisers.

Safety Valves in Budget Making

A government may guess wrong in releasing its budget. Changing conditions may require major revisions. New data and pressures may call for a modification of budget policies. Gross errors may be brought to light. Revenue and expenditure estimates may change. At least three safety valves for coping with these situations exist: revision of the main budget one month after its appearance, supplemental budgets, and deficiency budgets.

*   *   *

With the submission of the executive budget the key actors reach a milestone in budget decision making. But a long road still lies ahead as the legislature grapples with the budget and the chief executive implements appropriation bills.

Points for Discussion

1. To what extent are modern comprehensive central budget offices overloaded with functions? To what extent should other central staff agencies assume some of these responsibilities?
2. What, if any, are the unique functions of a central budget office, which cannot be performed by budget offices in the spending departments?

3. How "political" should a central budget office be in view of its intimate connection with an administration's policies?

4. What are the eight major decision-making paths in budgeting? How can they best be brought together to produce a coherent and coordinated budget?

5. What limits, if any, would you place on the powers of budget examiners in central budget offices? Would you restrict them solely to a review of proposed expenditures, or broaden their responsibilities to include program analysis, management analysis, review of intergovernmental relations, and review of legislation?

6. What are the major differences between budgeting planned expenditures and estimating expenditures?

7. In making recommendations to chief executives, how can budget directors guard against poor revenue and expenditure forecasts, lack of data, unpredictable crises, and questionable economic and programmatic assumptions?

8. If the right of agency heads to appeal budget decisions is illusory, how far would you go in broadening and strengthening the appeals process?

9. To what extent are the Stockman confessions, the Panetta self-congratulations, and the Mandeville outlook typical of the decision-making process?

10. What safety valves are available to an administration when the budget submitted by the chief executive to the legislature turns out to be inadequate, inaccurate, or politically vulnerable? Evaluate the usefulness of each of these safety valves.

11. What are the major differences between "bare bone" and enhanced budget documents? Review recent budget documents of federal, state, and local governments and evaluate their comprehensiveness.

12. Given a government that still follows traditional budget formats, what specific steps would you recommend to move it toward enhanced budget documents?

13. What are the best means of gaining public understanding of proposed budgets?

14. To what extent do you agree with the suggestion that governments should prepare a year-end budget report comparing actual results with the approved budget?

CHAPTER 5

THE SPECIAL CASE OF CAPITAL BUDGETING
Policy, Financial, and Technical Issues

Although capital budgeting is, or should be, an integral part of the overall budget process, it is sufficiently unique to merit special emphasis. Like major operating programs such as social security, mental health, and Medicaid, large-scale capital projects (roads, bridges, hospitals, schools, water systems, waste disposal plants, etc.) are costly. Once started, they become long-term financial commitments, and cannot easily be turned on and off without serious delays and irretrievable costs. By its very nature a major capital project is long-range. From the time the need for the project arises until it becomes an operating reality, five to ten or more years may elapse.

In most governments the financing of capital projects differs from the funding of operating programs. Current revenues and intergovernmental grants simply are not sufficient to pay for large capital costs. To "pay as you go" is not feasible. Hence, most governments are forced to borrow extensively to support their capital programs, just as individuals take out mortgages on their homes. This means that for a period of twenty to thirty years (depending on the duration of the loans) budgets must include enough funds to pay for debt service (principal and interest). To the extent that current revenues are available, the need for borrowing diminishes. In addition, it becomes necessary to provide funds in the operating budget for the maintenance, operation, and repairs of capital facilities.

Unlike operating programs, capital programs, especially in state and local governments in the United States, are hemmed in by numerous constitutional and statutory restrictions on borrowing. Several factors account for such constraints: the heavy fiscal burden imposed by capital projects; the reliance on debt financing; the imprudent fiscal behavior of several governments that defaulted on payment of their debt; and the chicanery, corruption, and political "pork barrels" associated with some capital projects.

Capital investments serve a number of vital purposes. They are obviously essential to the goals of such operating programs as health, education, correctional services, and housing. They are the underpinnings of economic development and, in a global economy, bolster national economic competitiveness. Without the infrastructure of roads, bridges, waste disposal plants, mass transportation, water supply systems, airports, communications systems, and power generating plants, local and regional economies would deteriorate. For advanced industrialized countries, capital projects are mainstays of economic development. For developing countries, they are also instruments of modernization.

Always important, capital facilities are especially critical today because of the neglect and decay of the infrastructure in the 1980s. Up to $3 trillion will be needed by the year 2000 at all levels of government to repair and modernize capital structures.

For these reasons capital budgeting is complex, difficult, and controversial, with much of the debate centering on the following issues:

The definition of a capital project. Sounds easy—it isn't.

The need for a capital budget. Some governments find they can do without it. Most can't.

Capital planning. This rather frayed process spots the need for projects and attempts to select them for inclusion in the budget. Four types of planning influence the formulation of the capital budget.

Criteria for selecting projects for the capital budget. These are a blend of objective, rational, intangible, and political factors.

Budgeting for capital projects. Still tough despite advance planning.

Financing capital construction. The policies, strategies, and ploys of decision makers.

The emphasis on borrowing as a major source of funding capital construction. For state and local governments in the United States, many legal constraints restrict borrowing, yet they manage to get around them.

Implementing the capital budget. This raises problems of managing debt and the costs of projects.

This chapter focuses on each of these themes.

Defining Capital Expenditures and Why the Definition Is Important

No agreement exists among governments as to what constitutes a capital expenditure. This has important implications for capital and operating budgets. At one extreme, only long-term tangible assets such as capital facilities and major pieces of equipment qualify as capital items. At the other extreme, several governments broaden the definition of capital investments to include not only tangible assets but also investments in human capital such as education and training programs.

Other factors such as the life and value of a facility or equipment also influence the definition of capital items.[1]

Some varying definitions highlight the similarities and differences among governments in classifying capital expenditures. The United States Bureau of the Census defines capital outlays as follows:

> Capital Outlay—Direct expenditure for contract or force-account [using government employees] construction, for purchase of equipment (including replacements), of land, and existing structures. Includes amounts for additions, replacements, and major alterations to fixed works and structures. However, expenditure for repairs to such works and structures is classified as current operation expenditure.[2]

For the United States General Accounting Office an asset qualifies as a capital item if it has a service life longer than two years, is tangible, costs $25,000 or more, provides services and benefits, and represents a nonrecurring expenditure.[3] Similarly, the Government Finance Officers Association classifies a capital asset as one "that has a useful life that extends for more than one year" and can be either "land, buildings, improvements other than buildings, and equipment or furniture."[4]

Practices vary among the fifty states. For Virginia capital expenditures subsume real property acquisition, improvements valued at over $250,000, new construction costing at least $250,000, and "stand-alone" equipment. California includes facilities improvements, fixed equipment costs, and related planning. Texas includes renovation, major repairs, rehabilitation, land acquisition, new construction, and equipment purchases.[5] The Government Accounting Standards Board (GASB), which sets accounting standards for state and local governments, focuses on tangible fixed and immovable assets such as roads, bridges, buildings, machinery, and equipment.

Taking a broader point of view, the United States Office of Management and Budget includes physical and nonphysical components in its definition of capital outlays:

> Capital outlays are outlays that yield long-term benefits. They take several forms and are made for many purposes. They are in the form of grants to State and local governments and direct Federal outlays. They can be for physical capital, which yields a stream of services over a period of years; or for research, development, education, and training, which are less tangible but also provide long-term benefits. They can also be for loans, which yield monetary returns, although the loans usually provide subsidies to the borrowers as well and therefore the face amount of the loans overstates the value of these assets.[6]

What difference do these technical distinctions make? A great deal, especially among state and local governments in the United States. To label an expenditure a capital item means that it belongs in the capital budget. As such, it is purchased largely with borrowed money. For example, a typewriter worth $500 costs just that if the funds come from the operating budget. Once the capital budget finances the purchase of the typewriter, it may cost up to $1500, because a government in effect pays for it on the installment plan, at high interest charges, over many years. Long after the typewriter reaches the end of its useful life, the payments go on inexorably. Notwithstanding the high costs, state and local governments have included supplies, library books, and minor equipment in their capital budgets. Are there abuses? Definitely.

Considered politically, these seemingly perverse actions are understandable. Take an item out of the operating budget, and it becomes easier to balance the budget. Of course the capital budget expands. But the sharp increase in expenditures is not immediately apparent, because the debt is spread out over a period of twenty to thirty years. Possibly the chief offender in this respect in the 1970s was New York City, which had manipulated its capital budget to include expenditures for programs and items that ordinarily belong in the operating budget. By 1975 these expenditures exceeded 50 percent of the capital budget and were a major factor in precipitating the city's fiscal crisis, which had national repercussions.[7]

Ultimately, labeling an item as a capital expenditure becomes a policy choice. To keep the capital budget free of manipulation, administrations and legislatures must agree on precise and consistent definitions of capital outlays. The Governmental Accounting Standards Board (GASB) is gradually steering state and local governments toward the use of common terminology. The Federal Accounting Standards Advisory Board is doing the same for the federal bureaucracy.

Necessity of Separate Capital Budgets for Most Governments

Relationship between Capital Budgets and Other Budgets

Most governments have a capital budget that brings together in one place a diverse array of capital items and classifies them by type (facilities, land, equipment, construction, rehabilitation, etc.), broad function, program, agency, cost, and source of funds. The capital budget is a distinctive part of the overall budget, the other major components being the operating budget and, where it exists, the transfer payments budget, which provides for grants and other aid to lower-level governments. In effect, then, governments can have dual or triple budgets or even more. They differ, however, in the policies and methods of linking the separate budgets. Most tend to link them closely. Some, however, segregate the capital budget from the other budgets and merely include capital costs in the budget totals.

Magnitude of Capital Budgets

Capital outlays by governments in the United States totaled $227.4 billion in 1991, with state and local governments accounting for $131.6 billion, or 58 percent, of the total and the federal government $95.8 billion, or 42 percent. In contrast to the federal government, which allocated over two-thirds of its capital outlays to defense, state and local governments spent their funds largely for the construction of highways, education facilities, utilities, housing, hospitals, and waste disposal systems.[8]

Governments with and without Capital Budgets

Because of their importance, governments single out capital expenditures for special attention, whether through capital budgets or other documents. The use of capital budgets is especially widespread, as the following sampling suggests:

1. *United States*

   a. *State governments.* Virtually all fifty state governments have a separate capital budget; of forty-seven states that responded to a questionnaire in 1991 by the National Association of State Budget Officers, forty-five reported that they had a distinct capital budget, which they displayed separately within an overall budget or issued in various other documents. Only twenty of the fifty states, however, combined capital and operating expenditures to arrive at unified budget totals.[9]

   b. *Local governments.* Among the first to develop capital budgets in the 1920s, local governments use them extensively. Large cities, in particular, have formulated comprehensive capital budgets.[10]

   c. *The federal government.* Unlike state and local governments and private business, the federal government still has no separate capital budget. It relies on a unified budget that combines operating and capital expenses and treats the acquisition of capital assets like any current operating expenditures. However, in a special analysis that is part of the annual budget, the Office of Management and Budget classifies and analyzes capital investments.[11]

2. *Other advanced industrialized countries.* While it is difficult to generalize from the practices of other advanced industrialized countries, it is apparent that most of them provide detailed information on capital investments, although they do not necessarily have a separate capital budget. Some examples follow:[12]

   a. *France.* In the French budgetary system the distinction between current and capital expenditures is basic. Both the main budget document and appendices to it highlight capital expenditures, although France has no capital budget per se. An important mechanism for allocating capital outlays is the Fund for Economic and Social Development.

   b. *Britain.* While Britain has no formal capital budget, it distinguishes in budgetary accounts between above-the-line expenditures (current outlays) and below-the-line expenditures (capital outlays). In an economic analysis of the budget, the government highlights expenditures for consumption and capital formation.

   c. *Sweden.* In 1937 Sweden introduced the capital budget as a countercyclical tool to combat the depression. Beginning with the 1980–1981 budget, it abandoned dual budgets in favor of a unified budget. Nevertheless, it still singles out for special attention in budget documents those capital assets with a life of three years or more and a predetermined monetary value.

Pros and Cons of Capital Budgeting

Pros. The proponents of separate capital budgets emphasize these major points about them:

1. *Uniqueness.* A public sector capital budget is markedly different from an operating budget. It results in the creation of public capital assets "whose benefits are spread over future generations."[13]

2. *Focus on capital investment needs.* A separate capital budget facilitates an analysis of the long-term investment needs of a government, the establishment of government-wide priorities, and the consideration of the costs and benefits of competing projects. By focusing on a specific area of policy, the capital budget makes it possible to avoid haphazard, ad hoc, and contradictory decisions. It thus becomes a useful framework for political decision making.[14]

3. *Vehicle of debt financing.* While debt financing is not the sole method of acquiring capital assets, it is a major means of doing so. Since the 1930s, the prevailing policy in most governments has been to finance the operating budget by taxes and the capital budget primarily by borrowing. The capital budget has thus become a vehicle of debt financing. By identifying proposed projects and the resources required to complete them, it facilitates choices in fiscal policy—the proportion of funding by taxes, grants, and loans.

4. *Instrument of expenditure control.* At the state and local levels of government in the United States, capital budgets are instruments of expenditure control. Governed by constitutional and statutory limits on debt, they provide some assurance to buyers of governmental bonds that governments have the legal and fiscal capacity to repay the debt. As noted later, this is not always the case.

5. *Equity in debt financing.* Debt financing for capital projects spreads the burden of paying the debt for long-term projects over several generations. This is equitable because those who use the facilities over the years should pay for them; the burden should not fall solely on the generation that initiated the project. Long-term debt financing thus enhances intergenerational equity. Stated another way, "Pay as you use" is preferable to "Pay as you go."

6. *Balancing the budget.* By shifting investment costs to the capital budget, which is financed mainly by borrowing, governments frequently find it possible to balance their operating budgets. This is the case in those state and local governments in the United States where a balanced budget is a legal mandate. The use of capital budgets as balancing mechanisms is defended on the grounds that the costs are one-time and extraordinary and should not come out of current revenues any more than the costs for a house or a manufacturing facility should come out

of the current income of an individual or a business. Had the federal government shifted capital items from the unified budget to a capital budget in fiscal years 1979 through 1982, actual deficits, depending on the assumptions used, would have been reduced sharply.[15]

7. *Visible capital formation.* Capital expenditures generally result in the creation of capital assets. Hence, every liability (debt) is matched by a valuable asset. Capital funds are not merely consumed; they result in the production of visible dams, roads, water systems, and mass transportation systems. A capital budget highlights the assets bequeathed to the future.

8. *Countercyclical tool.* In a period of depression or recession, a capital budget could be a powerful tool, together with other fiscal and economic measures, to offset the effects of a downturn in the business cycle. The evidence on this score is mixed, however, because of the late startup of capital projects—often too late to have an impact on the recession during which they were planned.

9. *Economic development.* An identifiable capital investment program stimulates economic development by attracting business to the states.

10. *Highlighting government investment.* In treating all expenditures alike, the budget "obscures the long-term investment characters of some federal activities. These activities, unlike spending for current consumption, produce assets that can generate future benefits to the economy as a whole. Differences between investment and consumption activities should be taken into account in allocating federal revenues."[16]

Cons. Those who oppose separate capital budgets raise several economic, financial, and management issues:

1. *Unsuitable for development of effective fiscal and macroeconomic policy.* While capital budgets may meet the unique needs of state and local governments and the private sector, they are not suitable for national governments. At any given time a national government must look at the effect of total spending—current *and* capital—on the economy. Only in this way can it develop an appropriate fiscal and macroeconomic policy encompassing levels of spending, taxing, and borrowing. It can't assume that borrowing is appropriate solely for capital outlays. In order to stimulate the economy, governments also borrow to cover current outlays, which represent the greater part of the budget, and to deliberately incur deficits.

2. *Not necessary for focusing on capital investments.* A separate analysis appended to a unified budget can identify the needs for capital investments and present all investment-type activities financed by the budget. The federal government of the United States has actually done this since 1951. On a more formal basis the Federal Capital Investment Program Information Act of 1984 requires the budget to assess the needs for nondefense capital expenditures and to project outlays for a ten-year period.

3. *Lack of capital budget does not impair budget process.* Meaningful analyses of the priorities and costs and benefits of capital projects take place whether or not a formal capital budget document exists.

4. *Impede trade-offs and priority setting.* In setting priorities, budget decisions should be based on trade-offs between capital investments and operating expenditures. With a unified budget the executive and the legislature can weigh the relative merits of, say, constructing dams and other facilities to irrigate farmland or allocating more funds for research and training so that farmers can use existing resources more efficiently. A capital budget creates a bias in favor of "bricks and mortar" rather than operating programs.

5. *Can be used as loopholes to evade budget discipline.* As the experience of New York City and several other governments has demonstrated, a capital budget lends itself to fiscal manipulation. It becomes a means of evading budget discipline by creating an incentive to make capital decisions on the basis of their usefulness in balancing the budget and not on the merits of the case.

6. *Ignore impact of borrowing on economy.* A capital budget rationalizes extensive borrowing by governments. The cumulative effect may be to reduce the availability of credit to the private sector and, because of the competition for funds, to raise interest rates.

7. *Focus exclusively on tangible assets.* By focusing on tangible assets, capital budgets obscure the fact that other types of investments such as family planning, research and development, and training can contribute to economic development.

8. *Limit budget flexibility.* To pay for capital facilities governments rely on a variety of taxes and fees earmarked specifically for this purpose, such as fuel taxes and highway tolls. This limits budgetary flexibility.

9. *Not necessary for determining economic impact of capital formation.* Governments don't need capital budgets to determine the economic impact of capital investments and the worth of their tangible assets. Economic analyses such as national income and product accounts (NIPA) measure aggregate economic activity and governmental expenditures, including those for capital formation. Many governments, including the United States, provide such data in the budget or in appendices to the budget.

10. *Obscure size of deficit.* By focusing on the operating budget, governments may obscure the impact of capital budgets on deficits.

The Target of the Debate: The U.S. Government

Much of the debate on capital budgets has centered on the federal government of the United States, which is the largest government in the world without a capital budget. During the last sixty years, various groups and individuals have urged the adoption of such a budget. In fact, the federal government came close to it in 1933 when President Roosevelt introduced a dual budget separating ordinary expenditures, financed by tax receipts, from extraordinary expenditures, supported by borrowing, which were designed to combat the Great Depression.[17]

The fifty-year debate finally led to the Federal Capital Investment Act of 1984 (PL 98-501), which adopted a two-prong approach toward capital budgeting:

1. *Inclusion in budget.* Beginning in January 1985, the legislation required that the President's budget include projections for major capital investment programs, an assessment of the needs for capital investment, and estimates of expenditures by state and local governments for capital facilities.

2. *Report on infrastructure.* Not later than February 15 in 1986, 1987, and 1988, a National Council on Public Works Improvements was required to report to the President and Congress on the age and condition of public works at all levels of government, methods of financing public works improvements, priorities in the development of infrastructure to sustain economic development, and maintenance needs and expenditures.

Both requirements have been met, but they produced no firm agreement on the need for a federal capital budget. In the most penetrating analysis of public works in the history of the country, the National Council on Public Works Improvement in 1988 rated all parts of the nation's infrastructure as substandard on a scale from A to D:

Highways	C+
Mass Transit	C–
Airports	B
Water resources	B–
Wastewater treatment	C
Solid waste treatment	D
Hazardous waste treatment	D

The culprit was lack of investment. The Council noted that fixed capital investment in the United States had sunk to the lowest level in three decades. Before 1988, gross fixed capital investment, public and private, had never fallen below 17 percent of the gross domestic product (GDP). From 1985 to 1988 it had declined to the point where it hovered around the unprecedented low of 16 percent of GDP. During the same period Japan invested 33 percent of its GDP in capital investment, and France, Germany, and Canada only 21 percent.

The Council estimated it would cost about $1 trillion by the year 2000 to repair the ravages of years of neglect. Estimates by other groups ranged from $1 trillion to $3 trillion.[18]

Considering the enormity of the problem and the need for large-scale capital investment, the GAO proposed highlighting the issues by splitting the unified budget into an operating and capital budget.[19] For each government function (e.g., national defense, transportation, energy, etc.) the annual budget would show operating and capital outlays.

Selecting Projects for the Capital Budget: Planning Processes

The capital budget has its roots in a planning process that most governments more or less follow. In particular, four types of planning influence the preparation of capital budgets: comprehensive planning, functional planning (also termed sectoral or program planning), multiyear programming, and facility planning.

Comprehensive Planning

Comprehensive planning, as the term suggests, is the broadest in scope of the four types of planning. Through this process, governments attempt to identify the social and economic needs of a country, a region, a state, a province, or a locality. This far-reaching analysis results in a blueprint for action with these features: short- and long-term goals; objectives and targets for the public sector and, in many countries, for the private sector as well; proposed policies, programs, and projects essential to the attainment of the objectives; and recommended fiscal and economic measures to finance the programs and projects. In this context capital planning is part of an overall planning process, and the capital projects specified in the plans are designed to further social and economic ends.

The coverage, complexity, and specificity of comprehensive plans vary from government to government. At the federal level in the United States, planning has been a capricious stop-and-go exercise in the face of a strong ideological bias against social and economic planning. At the state level in the United States, some forty states have planning bodies that develop comprehensive plans from time to time. Many local governments in the United States and elsewhere have long pioneered in urban planning, which, among other things, encompasses the construction and rehabilitation of capital projects to strengthen the local economy and make the city a more attractive place in which to live and work.[20]

The type of comprehensive planning described here as a framework for capital budgeting suggests a tidy and rational process. In practice, comprehensive plans fail or fall short of their targets. Numerous fiscal and economic barriers arise. Piecemeal and ad hoc decisions are often made without reference to comprehensive plans. Political, bureaucratic, and social forces may and do have the deciding voice on capital projects. Many plans are merely uncosted wish lists, and hardly the basis for action. However imperfect and vulnerable the plans may be, though, they still serve as a bridge between the needs of society and the capital plans and budgets intended to meet those needs.

Functional Planning

Less ambitious than comprehensive plans, functional plans deal with major functions and programs of government such as agriculture, health, education, correctional services, housing, and transportation. (The comprehensive plan attempts to pull together those separate functional plans into a balanced and coordinated blueprint for action.) In many governments, especially in the United States, multiyear functional plans carry more weight than overall plans in shaping capital budgets. A typical functional plan among state governments analyzes the needs and problems of a program, lays out the program targets for the next several years, specifies necessary operating programs and capital projects in some order of priority, and estimates the probable costs.

The approval of a capital project in the functional plan does not necessarily mean that the budget will finance it. Nevertheless, it is a prerequisite for funding should resources be available. Used this way, the functional plans are not mandates but rough guides for developing capital budgets.

Multiyear Programming

A multiyear capital investment program is an indispensable link between comprehensive and functional plans and the capital budget. In contrast to the plans, it is more of an action document. Covering at least five years in many governments and updated annually, the capital investment program (CIP) is a timetable that specifies the projects selected for improvement or construction; the target dates for every phase of the project: design, land acquisition, contract letting, construction, installation of equipment, and operation; the estimated costs; and the methods of financing.[21] It embodies a government's capital priorities and choices and fiscal strategies. It therefore directly influences the preparation of the annual capital budget.

Virtually every effective public, quasi-public, and private organization has rolling multiyear capital plans. States have been far more aggressive than the federal government in formulating annually updated CIPs. In most cases the capital-programming process is mandated by statute with specific guidelines promulgated by the central budget office. At least twenty-nine states prepare rolling, long-range capital plans and budgets for five or more years.[22]

California is among the states that prepare multiyear capital plans. The following table summarizes its capital needs for the five-year period ending 1994–1995:[23]

Projected capital needs for the State and K–12, 1990–91 through 1994–95 (in millions of dollars)	
	5-Year Total
Legislative, Judicial, Executive	$ 60
State, Consumer affairs	650
Business, Transportation, Housing	4,990
Resources	470
Health, Welfare	160
Youth, Adult Corrections	3,970
Education,	8,560
General government	30
TOTAL	$18,890

Paralleling the practices of the states, many local governments develop multi-year capital plans. In a sampling of larger municipalities in the 1980s, the Urban Institute found that 84 percent of the cities have a rolling five- or six-year capital improvement plan and that in many of the cities the first year of the plan becomes the annual capital budget.[24] For example, the Illinois Department of Commerce and Community Affairs urges local governments to adopt such plans by assessing the existing infrastructure, determining capital facility needs, setting priorities, encouraging public participation, and preparing a financial forecast. The outcome of the exercise is a rolling five-year capital improvement plan that ties in specific projects with sources of funding.[25]

As in other phases of budgeting, a wide gap exists between the theory and the practice of capital programming. The inherent political nature of the process often forces a shift in priorities and, in fact, determines priorities. To keep political peace and gain support for a capital program, it is frequently necessary to spread projects around geographically as visible reminders to the local voters of the beneficence of their legislators. Surely, in most governments a high correlation exists between the location of major projects and the residences of political leaders. Less dramatic, but still telling, are deficiencies in the capital-planning process noted in several state and local governments: the tendency to turn the capital program into a wish list; the lack of adequate criteria for the selection of proposed projects; a fragmentary program that omits many projects; inadequate attention to the financing of projects; poor cost estimating; the sacrifice of capital projects in a budget crunch; little consideration of possible alternatives to proposed projects; and a skewing of priorities in favor of projects supported by grants from other levels of government. In 1992, forty-eight of the larger cities separated capital and operating budgets with little attempt at integrating both. At best the budget process was fragmentary.[26]

Clearly, some governments have a long way to go to improve their capital-programming process. In no way, however, does this critique invalidate the obvious merits of a multiyear capital investment program: an orderly decision-making system for the acquisition, repair, and replacement of capital facilities and equipment; a tool to develop priorities in a political milieu; a financial-planning mechanism that relates costs to sources of funding; and a means of looking ahead to provide valuable lead time for major projects.[27]

Facility Planning

The selection of a project does not automatically assure that engineering and architectural design and budgeting can begin. Prior to these steps, the vital and often overlooked process of facility planning must take place. Facility planning focuses on the cost, scope, size, uses, and relationships of the spaces of a proposed project. It therefore springs from program planning. For example, facility planning for a mental hospital encompasses such factors as the projected population and staff; the functions and activities of the complex of buildings; approved space standards for each activity, such as the amount of square feet per patient for hospital treatment, housing, feeding, occupational therapy, and recreation; the total amount of required space; needed supplies and equipment; the most appropriate layout of the rooms from the standpoint of patient care, treatment, and cost; the juxtaposition of rooms and the separate buildings; road networks and utilities; and the flexibility of space arrangements in the event of program changes. Such analyses serve as a basis for designing, costing, and budgeting the project.[28] For nearly every governmental function, states have developed or followed space, engineering, and cost standards.

Factors in Selecting Projects for the Capital Budget

A multiyear capital program frequently embodies hundreds of projects. What criteria do governments use in selecting individual projects for the program? How do they assign priorities? How do they balance budgetary, programmatic, technical, economic, and political considerations in arriving at decisions? Several interrelated factors influence their decisions, for example, the deteriorating infrastructure, to which most governments have accorded the highest priority; the condition of other capital facilities; studies assessing the costs and benefits of proposed projects; the financial capacity to mount projects; and the need to stimulate economic development.

The Deteriorating Infrastructure

At all levels of government in the United States, a consensus has emerged to repair, improve, and replace the nation's deteriorating infrastructure: its highways, bridges, mass transportation systems, airports, water supply systems, and waste treatment facilities. Years of neglect have taken their toll; many of the systems and facilities fail to meet minimal levels of service and are technologically and dangerously obsolete. Not only do they pose risks to public health and safety, but they have also become a drag on economic development. Of 577,710 bridges in the United States, 42 percent are structurally deficient or functionally obsolete. Highways have also deteriorated seriously. Of 1.2 million miles of principal highways, 11 percent fail to meet accepted engineering and safety standards. The major 532 airports that handle commercial aviation are seriously congested and their access roads are clogged. Of 210,000 public water systems, nearly 40,000 fail to meet the standards of the Safe Drinking Water Act. According to the U.S. Environmental Protection Agency, 400 cities and towns cannot meet federal standards for waste-water treatment. Add to these thousands of inadequate solid waste disposal facilities, at least 890 hazardous waste sites, substandard light- and heavy-rail systems, deteriorating hospitals, poorly maintained government buildings, and obsolete school buildings.[29]

The breakdown in the nation's infrastructure is a direct result of inflation, uneven maintenance, recessions, tax and spending limits, misplaced priorities, and budget cuts. Just to catch up on the needs of the infrastructure would require, as noted above, expenditures ranging from $1 billion to $3 trillion for the rest of the century, depending on which studies one finds persuasive.

Condition of Existing Capital Facilities

Before any decisions are made to improve, replace, or acquire capital plants and equipment, it is essential to inventory all existing facilities, assess their condition, and determine their capacity to meet current and future needs. To be useful, this should be an ongoing, formal, systematic, comprehensive, and explicit process. In practice, inventories and analyses of the adequacy of facilities often take place on a spotty basis and, in some governments, only under the pressure of a crisis such as the collapse of a bridge or breakdowns in water supply systems. Nevertheless, useful standards and evaluation criteria have been developed for virtually every type of capital facility. They serve as a basis for determining capital investment needs and priorities for decisions to maintain, improve, or replace existing structures.[30] For example, the State of Connecticut and the New York State Thruway rate the conditions of their roads and bridges on a scale of 1–10 so as to estimate the cost of repairs and/or replacement to bring them back to an acceptable level of sufficiency.

Costs and Benefits of Proposed Projects

In selecting projects for the capital program and assigning priorities to them, decision makers must obviously reckon with the costs and benefits of proposed facilities and major equipment acquisitions. A variety of preproject studies purport to provide such analyses. Some are crude and simplistic—others, comprehensive and sophisticated. Among the more prominent analytical techniques are explicit and formal cost–benefit analysis (CBA); cost–effectiveness analysis (CEA); life-cycle costing; value-engineering analysis; and feasibility studies. All are interrelated and all represent attempts to apply economic analysis in project selection. This chapter merely sketches these analytical techniques in highly oversimplified terms.

Cost–Benefit Analysis (CBA). Cost–benefit analysis is a systematic means of estimating the costs and benefits of projects over their life. In theory, the least costly projects with the greatest benefits according to such analysis would get priority in the allocation of scarce funds. Conversely, expensive projects with minimal benefits would get short shrift. CBA involves such factors as placing a present value on project benefits and on costs that will take place in the future. A complex, highly quantitative, sophisticated technique, it has long occupied a prominent place in economic theory.[31] It was not, however, applied formally in decision making in governments in the United States until the passage of the Flood Control Act of 1936. This legislation mandated the selection of only those water resource projects whose estimated benefits exceed their costs. For every dollar invested in a project, more than a dollar in benefits has to be returned. Thus did the cost–benefit ratio become a major factor in decision making. A ratio of .9 (90 cents return on the dollar) was unacceptable; 1.5 was fine; 3.0 even better. For example, President Carter deleted from his 1977–1978 budget nineteen water resource projects with a ratio under 1.0.[32] From a concentration on water resources, CBA expanded to the point where it influenced decision making in operating programs and projects such as manpower training, health, highway safety, and transportation. Nevertheless, in the view of GAO, not enough agencies (not even the Office of Management and Budget) use this powerful analytical tool in decision making.[33]

Often oversold, CBA is a useful tool with some marked limitations. For one, it is difficult to quantify the costs and benefits of complex projects. Illustrative of this problem are the attempts to estimate the benefits and costs of air and water pollution control. Analysts who have struggled with this issue have run into numerous conceptual and methodological snags such as putting a price tag on damages resulting from pollution and on the benefits from clean air and water. Hard data simply don't exist and the state of the art of measurement is somewhat crude. The cost of fast-moving technology cannot be identified with any assurance. And prediction of future effects is always a hazardous exercise because of unanticipated consequences.

By its very nature CBA lends itself to bureaucratic and political manipulation. To make a project look attractive it is merely necessary to reduce anticipated costs and project enormous (though questionable) benefits some twenty or thirty years hence. With such assumptions the cost–benefit ratio will soar. Over the years expenditure estimates have proved to be vulnerable, as is apparent from numerous examples of cost overruns. This results from a combination of inflationary pressures, poor estimating techniques, lack of data, and flawed engineering and architectural plans that necessitate frequent changes in design.

Even with defensible data, CBA is but one factor among many, and not necessarily the most persuasive one, in selecting capital projects with social objectives. In public housing, mass transportation, and training facilities, costs may exceed quantifiable benefits with a CBA ratio below 1. Nevertheless, decision makers often place a higher value on equity and redistribution of resources to low-income groups than on a simplistic ratio that ignores these considerations. The old saw about the hazards of knowing the cost of everything and the value of nothing may still be apt.

CBA is at best a practical aid in decision making, not a prescription for decisions. It provides an analytic framework for defining problems; identifying needs; arraying alternatives; estimating costs and results; laying out the assumptions behind the estimates; spelling out gaps in data and areas of uncertainty; forecasting the possible consequences of a capital project, both good and bad; highlighting policy issues; and suggesting, in the light of limited data, the projects that merit priority. CBA can sharpen the insights of decision makers, but it is no substitute for seasoned judgment and sensitivity to social, economic, and political values.

Cost–Effectiveness Analysis (CEA). While cost–benefit analysis focuses on the selection of preferred projects among a welter of competing projects with similar objectives, cost-effectiveness analysis (CEA) is more limited in its application. CEA is a technique for examining several options designed to attain an agreed-upon objective and selecting the option that yields maximum benefits for a given cost. Alternatively, the emphasis might be on selecting projects that provide a fixed level of benefits at minimum cost.[34] Cost–effectiveness analysis is useful in arriving at decisions with regard to both capital and operating programs. Among numerous applications are policy choices such as developing community mental health centers rather than expanding hospital facilities for specified groups of patients; whether to resurface an existing road or build a new road in a given area; whether to replace a coal-fired plant with an oil-fired or gas-fired plant; and whether to rent or build a laboratory on a college campus. The accent is on optimizing the allocation of resources. The quantitative techniques are similar to those used in cost–benefit analysis.

Life-Cycle Costing. In capital budgeting, what counts is the total cost of a facility or major piece of equipment over its estimated useful life, not just the acquisition costs or the cost of design and construction. Besides these cost factors, other significant costs are research and development, preproject planning, packaging bonds for sale, debt service, operation and maintenance, and the salvage value of discontinued equipment or facilities. Labeled "life-cycle costing," this analysis gives a far better insight into the commitment a government undertakes in approving a capital facility than a more limited appraisal of design and construction costs. When all costs are considered, a project with a high construction cost may, in the end, turn out to be more economical than one built at a lower cost. Several states, including Florida, California, and Washington, have adopted life-cycle costing for these reasons, and OMB requires it for federal agencies.[35]

Value-Engineering Analysis. Value-engineering analysis is a "method of analyzing a product, [capital facility], or service so that its function can be performed at the lowest possible overall cost without sacrificing quality."[36] It is not a mindless hunt for economy no matter what. Rather, it is an explicit effort to seek the best design, the best materials, the best equipment, and the best techniques for operation and maintenance at the lowest possible cost. In a formal process, an interdisciplinary team that includes budgeteers, program specialists, engineers, architects, management specialists, and other technicians investigates every phase of the planning, design, construction, and supply process. It checks all options at every point and recommends those that meet predetermined criteria of efficiency, economy, and quality.

Feasibility Studies. "Feasibility studies" is an umbrella term that covers all the analytic techniques discussed above and more. Through such studies, governments seek to determine the feasibility of a proposed capital project or major piece of

equipment from several standpoints: economic, technical, technological, administrative, and environmental.

Some Other Criteria for Selecting Projects

In addition to formal studies, state and local governments rely on a variety of
criteria to develop priorities and select projects. For example, the state of Texas
uses some of the following categories to reflect the degree of urgency or relative
merits of projects.[37]

> *Hazards.* Projects designed to eliminate definite and immediate health and safety
> hazards.
>
> *Project completion.* Uncompleted projects to which the government has already com-
> mitted significant funds.
>
> *Major repairs that save money.* Repairs to reduce operating costs or to avoid further
> costly damage and deterioration.
>
> *Payoff from upgrading and converting existing facilities.* Projects resulting in new or high-
> priority use or leading to more efficient space utilization.
>
> *Needs assessment.* New construction that eliminates overcrowded conditions, accom-
> modates continuing growth, and meets accepted standards.
>
> *Meeting program objectives.* Projects necessary to implement new or expanded pro-
> grams.
>
> *Barriers to the handicapped.* Projects designed to remove current constructional bar-
> riers to the handicapped.
>
> *Effect on future operating costs.* Rationale for capital and operating cost estimates.

The Financial Capacity to Undertake Projects

Without cash, the foregoing analyses are but empty exercises. The financial
capacity to mount projects is necessarily the critical factor in project selection.
Three interrelated considerations are involved here: (1) the revenue that can be
raised directly by the government itself from taxes and fees, (2) grants from other
governments, and (3) the need to borrow funds if available resources are insufficient. Before a government commits itself to funding a project from its own revenue sources, it must review its revenue projections, its current level of
indebtedness, its cash position, its backlog of unimplemented projects, the impact
of a new project on its future fiscal status, and constitutional and legal limits on
debt. Only then can it proceed with any confidence to launch a new project.

Especially alluring to hard-pressed governments is aid from other governments,
even at the expense of its priorities. For example, it is difficult for state and local
governments to resist federal financing that supports most of the costs, under varying formulas, for interstate highways and other parts of the 150,000-mile national
highway system; federal aid for bridge replacement and rehabilitation (again,
the lion's share paid by the federal government); federal grants that pay up to

80 percent of capital projects for mass transit; federal subsidies for wastewater treatment plants; and airport grants that pay over half the cost of airport improvements.

The Six Pillars of Capital Budgeting

Capital budgeting thus rests on six pillars: comprehensive planning, functional planning, multiyear programming, facility planning, project selection criteria, and financial planning. All this seems rational and logical. Yet at any point, even approved plans can be upset by ad hoc decisions made outside of the planning process; shifts in programs and policies; political pressures to allocate projects evenhandedly to various areas, regardless of need or priority; changed conditions; revenue shortfalls; delays in borrowing funds; or problems in implementing projects. For these reasons annual (or biennial) capital budgeting is not an automatic exercise. One does not merely transfer mechanically approved projects from a five-year capital program to the capital budget and pin on them an appropriate price tag. Budgeting calls for a fresh look at and updating of each project, even at the risk of repetition. Plans provide a framework for decision making. Annual budgeting *is* decision making.

On the basis of its analysis of new and continuing projects, the central budget office recommends appropriations for the life of the project and appropriations covering estimated costs for only the next fiscal year. What affects agencies in particular is what they get each year. For example, at the request of the administration, the legislative body may authorize a seven-year project estimated to cost $100 million. To get the project started next year only $1 million may be needed this year for planning studies; in the second year $10 million may be required for land acquisition. And so it goes. Since the money authorized for the project is rarely spent in one year, the unspent balances are customarily reappropriated from year to year. This is generally the practice at state and local levels in the United States. In contrast, the federal government frequently resorts to indefinite and continuing appropriations for capital construction.

Capital Financing: Policies, Strategies, and Ploys

The financing of capital projects is one of the most complex and arcane arts in budgeting because funds come from a variety of sources. Only rarely do governments rely on current revenues (taxes, fees, and charges), which under the best of circumstances may cover up to a third of capital costs. Though still significant, the general fund is a declining source of capital financing. Dedicated funds such as motor fuel taxes for highway construction and sales taxes for mass transit have increased sharply, but above all, state and local governments depend largely on intergovernmental grants and borrowed funds. Borrowing, in particular, has become the chief source of capital financing in most states. In determining the appropriate mix of financing, several controversial issues are encountered: issues of fiscal policy, financial strategies, economic policy, and interpretations of constitutions and statutes governing borrowing limits.

Capital financing decisions are especially onerous because they are not made for one year, but for the life of the project. Reliance on loans now may reduce fiscal capacity to borrow in the future. Debt service increases, thus diverting funds from operating programs. The future revenue flow must be sure and certain, not only to support increased debt service for current and proposed capital projects, but also to continue to fund operating programs without incurring the risk of deficits.

To get a handle on these problems many governments develop multiyear revenue and expenditure plans and multiyear borrowing plans. Considering the significance of loans in financing capital construction, the latter is especially significant. For example, in Hawaii the budget office annually analyzes for each of the next seven years the total bonded debt, commitments to pay debt service, unused revenue from authorized bond sales, and unused fiscal capacity for additional borrowing.[38] The state of Maryland similarly, through a Capital Debt Affordability Committee, analyzes the impact of a growing debt on the state's capacity to both service that debt and retain its creditworthiness in the capital markets. The Committee aims to keep state tax–supported debt under 3.2 percent of state personal income and to keep debt service under 8 percent of available revenue. California, Texas, and Kentucky also undertake comprehensive debt capacity studies before launching new bond issues.[39]

Borrowing: A Major Source of Funding for Capital Outlays

In the United States, state and local governments thus continue to rely on borrowing as a major source of funding for capital outlays, and the federal government resorts to borrowing to fund its mounting deficit, only a small part of which is attributed to capital outlays. These three levels of government together issue more securities (bonds and notes) than any other country in the world. From 1950 to 1991 outstanding short- and long-term state and local debt, primarily for capital construction, soared from $24 billion to $911 billion (the greater portion being local debt).[40] The growing debt is reflected by the sharp rise in the annual volume of municipal bonds sold by the state and local governments.

Constraints on Loans for Capital Outlays

When Polonius advised Hamlet, "neither a borrower nor a lender be," he may have anticipated with unusual clairvoyance the problems and constraints that bedevil governments intent on borrowing funds for capital construction and other purposes. For the federal government in the United States the constraints are serious. For state and local governments they would be overwhelming were it not for the considerable ingenuity displayed in circumventing them. The major hurdles are economic constraints, intergovernmental financing, the dubious credit standing of some governmental entities, and legal and constitutional restrictions.

Economic Constraints. For much of the 1970s and early 1980s, recessions, inflation, and a tight money policy on the part of the Federal Reserve Board in the United States affected budgets, the capital market, and the level of borrowing. As noted earlier, capital facilities quickly became a casualty of the budgetary cutbacks of the early 1980s and 1990s. In the competition for scarce funds, proposed capital outlays at all governmental levels lost out to current and uncontrollable outlays.[41] When governments launched bond issues for capital construction, they ran into high interest rates induced by monetary policy, inflation, and the large demands for credit on the part of the federal government.

Volatile interest rates and unsettled credit conditions led several governments to cancel or delay the sale of bonds in the hope that interest rates would decline, as they eventually did by the mid-1980s. By the early 1990s tax-exempt bond interest for long-term bonds plummeted to about 6 percent, in contrast to rates that exceeded 10 percent in the early 1980s. Reversing previous trends, state and local governments went on a borrowing spree to refinance high-interest bonds sold in the 1980s and to undertake new ventures.

Intergovernmental Constraints. Through intergovernmental grants, the federal government in the United States influences the nature and amount of capital outlays by state and local governments. After a steady growth over thirty years, federal grants-in-aid peaked in 1981, then dropped during the next decade. In the early 1990s federal aid picked up again to the point where grants to state and local governments for capital construction in FY 1993 totaled about $30 billion. More than half of the funds went to highways and mass transportation.[42] Local governments also depend on state aid for public works; of $186.5 billion in state aid in 1991, less than 10 percent was allocated to capital construction.

The Complexities and Hazards of Tax-Exempt Bonds. On their face, tax-exempt bonds (municipal bonds) issued by state and local governments and their public authorities for capital construction have an irresistible appeal for governments and investors. Only the federal government is the loser. For example, in 1991 the government "lost" about $26 billion in revenue, representing tax-exempt interest on a variety of municipal bonds. The roots of tax exemption are in the shaky constitutional doctrine of reciprocal immunity, whereby state and local governments don't tax the federal government and the latter doesn't tax them. In 1988 the U.S. Supreme Court effectively demolished this doctrine.[43] Nevertheless, interest on such bonds has been tax-exempt since the passage of the federal income tax law of 1913. Over the years Congress has defeated attempts to eliminate tax-exempt bonds, but in 1982, 1984, and 1986 it limited tax-exemption for special types of bonds, especially so-called private purpose bonds for housing, industrial development, pollution control, and student loans.

Despite recent restrictions, tax-exempt bonds are still an attractive tax shelter for affluent individuals. Backed by state and local governments, the bonds appear to be gilt edged. As with any other investment, however, the buyer must be wary.

The bonds can decline in value as interest rates change, and governments may default on the payment of principal and interest. From 1920 to 1969 state and local governments and their entities such as public authorities defaulted on 5,440 separate occasions, with about 88 percent of the defaults occurring during the Depression of the 1930s. During the 1980s some $9 billion in defaults occurred in about 300 bond issues. In 1991 defaults totaled about $5 billion.[44]

Considering the size of the outstanding debt of state and local governments, relatively small sums were involved in each jurisdiction and, in time, investors recouped some of their principal and interest. But these defaults, which mainly affected bonds for industrial development, nursing homes, and retirement centers, were minor peccadilloes compared to three defaults in the 1970s and 1980s that undermined the confidence of investors in the creditworthiness of tax-exempt bonds: by New York City in 1975; the Urban Development Corporation, a public authority of New York State, also in 1975; and the Washington Public Power Supply System ("Whoops") in the State of Washington in 1983.

Only unprecedented measures overcame the financial crises of New York City and the Urban Development Corporation, and in the State of Washington investors received less than fifty cents on each dollar invested.[45]

The impact of these events on the municipal bond market of the United States cannot be exaggerated. They led to more thorough credit and economic analysis by bond rating agencies, banks, and brokerage firms; fuller disclosure of the financial condition of state and local governments eager to sell bonds; the revamping of state and local budgeting and accounting systems; more state oversight of the borrowing practices of local governments and public authorities; and the development of assorted guarantees to minimize investors' risks, such as bond insurance against default.[46]

Getting Around Legal Limits on Borrowing. More than the rest of the world, nearly all state and local governments in the United States face a bewildering array of constitutional and statutory limits on the amount of debt they can incur for capital construction and on the processes employed to authorize such debt. This is in addition to tax and spending limits for the operating budget in effect in twenty-four states, and combined tax and spending limits that restrict nearly all local governments. In national governments, however, including the federal government of the United States, it is economic and fiscal policy rather than legal restrictions that determine the amount of borrowing.

Many of the legal restrictions on state and local government borrowing in the United States came in the wake of widespread abuses and corruption in capital construction in the nineteenth century, and defaults and taxpayer revolts in the twentieth century. So varied are the limitations on borrowing that they almost defy succinct summarization, and hard-pressed governments may face more than one restriction.[47]

All fifty state constitutions contain severe constraints on borrowing. Nineteen require direct voter approval to go into debt or to override debt limits (usually spelled out in dollar terms or as a percent of revenue collections or property values). Eleven state constitutions impose tight borrowing limits, but don't require a voter referendum. Ten constitutions bar debt altogether, except in specified emergencies. The remaining ten constitutions call for super majority votes of the legislature (usually two-thirds) or apply other, less painful, brakes on borrowing.[48]

There are even tighter constitutional and statutory restrictions on the powers of local governments, including school districts and special districts (such as water supply, sewer, and lighting districts), to issue long-term bonds. In most cases, total debt cannot exceed a specified percent of the assessed value of property. In a minority of instances, debt is restricted to a multiple of tax receipts (for example, in Connecticut 2.25 times the latest tax receipts). Other than by amending state constitutions or statutes, debt limits cannot be exceeded in most local governments. Some minor legal flexibility exists to adjust limits, providing certain specified conditions are met.

Bonds approved by the voters that comply with constitutional restrictions are termed *general obligation bonds, full faith and credit bonds,* or *guaranteed bonds.* Having met all the constitutional requirements, they have behind them the full faith and credit of the government and the guarantee of the government to use its general taxing powers to pay the principal and interest on the debt, no matter what. This is the ultimate cachet. With repayment of the debt guaranteed by the constitution, in a fiscal crisis debt payments have priority over other claims on the government. As a consequence, general obligation bonds enjoy lower interest rates than other types of bonds. In some instances, voter approval is required to back up revenue bonds secured not by the general taxing power, but by the revenue of public enterprises such as toll roads and bridges. These, too, have a preferential ranking, because they carry with them the promise of state assistance should revenues prove to be inadequate. In effect, they enjoy a ranking similar to that of obligation bonds.

Another major category of bonds are *revenue bonds* authorized by statute, not by constitution, and issued without voter approval. Since the 1920s they have been the means of financing such diverse facilities as waste treatment systems, water supply systems, highways, housing, bridges, airports, power systems, and sports stadiums. The charges, fees, and rents paid by the users of the facilities are used to repay the debt. Without guarantees of the full faith and credit of the government behind them, revenue bonds usually carry higher interest rates than do general obligation bonds.

Circumventing Legal Limitations on Borrowing

By the 1960s legal constraints on debt proved to be especially irksome to state governors and legislatures intent on developing university systems, low- and middle-income housing, mental health facilities, pollution control systems, commercial and industrial facilities designed to assist the private sector, mass transportation systems, power plants, and public buildings for the burgeoning state bureaucracy.

Voter reaction to proposed general obligation bond issues was erratic, with the approval rate in the 1960s and 1970s ranging from 29 percent to 63 percent.[49] In addition, tax and spending limits curtailed the amount of funds available for both capital and operating budgets.

As a result of these barriers, the states, followed by local governments, increasingly began to bypass constitutional restrictions by resorting to a series of "creative" funding mechanisms to borrow money. All were approved by legislatures and governors, but not by popular referenda. Hence, none of the new debt was guaranteed by the full faith and credit provisions of state constitutions. Nevertheless, nonguaranteed debt soared. In 1949 it represented only 15 percent of the long-term debt of states. By 1991 it had reached 70 percent. Similarly, local nonguaranteed debt rose dramatically, moving from negligible beginnings to about 68 percent. The principal debt instrument for raising the new funds was revenue bonds, rather than general obligation bonds, which became the principal means of funding capital projects. Lacking constitutional guarantees, however, they carried lower credit ratings and bore the brunt of higher interest charges. Though the bonds were seemingly vulnerable to legal attacks because of circumvention of constitutional controls, the courts, for the most part, went along with these schemes.[50]

The most popular methods for surmounting constitutional obstacles are the following:

1. *Proliferation of public authorities and government corporations.* A favorite device for evading state constitutional restrictions is to establish a public authority/government corporation/special district (the terms are synonymous) and give it the power to issue its own nonguaranteed debt. In the 1960s and in subsequent years, public authorities proliferated among state and local governments as never before. Chapter 6 covers their unique role and unorthodox financing methods.[51]

2. *Expanded use of revenue bonds.* Revenue bonds are backed up by revenue generated by a capital facility and/or federal grants. So dramatic has been the swing from general obligation to revenue bonds that in the early 1990s the latter accounted for about 70 percent of all long-term bonds issued. Only twenty years before, in 1970, they represented only 34.5 percent of the new bonds.

3. *Moral obligation bonds.* Starting in New York State in 1960, a hybrid and controversial bond, the "moral obligation" bond, developed. Lacking voter approval and hence not backed by the state's full faith and credit, this new bond was sanctioned solely by the legislature and the governor. The authorizing legislation directed the state to replenish, if necessary, debt service reserve funds to pay the principal and interest on the debt. In fact, New York State did that in 1975 when the Urban Development Corporation floundered. At best the bonds are a moral obligation of the state. They are not legally enforceable. To default on their repayment would, however, jeopardize the credit standing of the state.

4. *Lease-purchase schemes.* Many public authorities engage in lease-purchase financing and are merely "shell authorities." They operate nothing and manage

nothing. They exist solely to sell revenue bonds to finance construction of public buildings, schools, universities, hospitals, and jails. The authority leases the new facility to the government and the grateful government pays "rent" out of regular appropriations for 20–30 years. At the end of the period the government owns the building. According to the fiction of this transaction, this is not debt, but merely rent money that comes out of the regular operating budget. Hundreds of such shell authorities exist in forty-one states, among them the New Jersey Building Authority, the New York State Urban Development Corporation, the Michigan State Building Authority, and over 700 school construction authorities in Pennsylvania.

5. *Nontraditional revenue bonds.* With a cornucopia of tax-exempt moral obligation, lease-purchase, and other revenue bonds available to them, state and local governments tapped this rich source of funds for a variety of nontraditional uses, not just for the public infrastructure. In the 1970s they began using revenue bonds for such unprecedented ventures as industrial development, single and multifamily housing, pollution control, hospitals, nursing homes, and student loans. From a small start in 1970, when bonds issued for nontraditional activities totaled less than $1 billion, these bonds soon outpaced debt for traditional activities and in 1990 accounted for about two-thirds of all bond issues.[52] This ratio will drop sharply, however, because of new federal controls.

6. *Certificates of participation (COPs).* Pioneered in California as a way of getting around Proposition 13 and other debt limits, COPs are sweeping the country and are firmly entrenched in eleven states. Some $50 billion worth were outstanding in 1990. They are but another form of lease financing. Frequently acting through a public authority, a state or local government invites a private firm to construct a jail, hospital, or convention center or to sell it major pieces of equipment such as computer systems. A bank acts as the broker between the lessor (the private firm) and the lessee (the public authority or government). The bank parcels out the lease into "certificates of participation," usually in units of $5,000. Investors who buy the certificates get tax-free rental payments from the bank. The funds come from regular annual appropriations and are called "operating expenses," not debt.

In the future, it seems clear that financially and constitutionally hard-pressed state and local governments will continue to rely on such "innovations" for capital financing because they do not count as part of their guaranteed debt or, at times, as part of their budget totals. Nothing stands in their way, least of all chief executives, legislatures, and courts.

The A, B, Cs of Credit Ratings

Credit ratings by private organizations affect nearly every aspect of governmental debt financing for capital construction in the United States, just as they influence financing in the private sector. Except for small issues, virtually all general obligation and revenue bonds authorized by states, local governments, public authorities, and special districts in the United States are rated as to their credit-worthiness by private rating organizations. Similarly, these services rate private corporate securities as well. Three organizations dominate the field: Moody's Investment Service, Standard & Poor's Inc., and Fitch Investment Service. None of the ratings are done automatically. Governments issuing the bonds must request a rating and pay a fee for the analysis of their credit standing and the safety of the bonds. The rating is continually updated until the bond is redeemed.

Actually, governments have little discretion as to whether or not to request ratings. Faced by a bewildering array of thousands of bond issues, investors are reluctant to part with their money without an objective analysis by a third party advising them as to the relative safety and risks of their investments. What counts most in the rating is the probability of the timely repayment of the principal and interest of a bond issue. Other factors that affect the ratings are the financial strength of the government; the risks of default; the opportunity to sell the bonds at a fair price in the secondary market prior to maturity; and the sensitivity of the value of the bonds to economic conditions. What's good for the investors also helps the taxpayer. The type of credit analysis and risk assessment reflected in the ratings alerts voters and decision makers to imprudent financial schemes.[53]

Credit ratings usually take the form of combined letter grades as the following oversimplified summary of Moody's ratings indicates:

Rating	Definition
Aaa	Best quality: carry the smallest degree of investment risk.
Aa1, Aa	High quality: margins of protection not quite as large as the Aaa bonds.
A1, A	Upper medium grade: security adequate but could be susceptible to impairment.
Baa1, Baa	Medium grades: neither highly protected not poorly secured; lack outstanding investment characteristics and sensitive to changes in economic circumstances.
Ba1, Ba	Speculative: protection is very moderate.
B1, B	Not desirable investment: sensitive to day-to-day economic circumstances.
Caa	Poor standing: may be in default with a workout plan.
Ca	Highly speculative: may be in default with nominal workout plan.
C	Lowest rated class of bonds: extremely poor prospects of ever attaining any real investment standing.

Sources: Moody's Investors Service and *The Municipal Bond Handbook*; United States General Accounting Office, *State and Local Finances* (Washington, D.C., 1993), p. 121.

Rating organizations also rate short-term notes. Moody's ratings vary from MIG1 (the best) to MIG4 (adequate with some element of risk). Ratings from Standard and Poor's run from SP-1 (strong) to SP-3 (speculative).

These ratings directly affect the borrowing costs of a government and are a significant factor in shaping budgets. Most coveted of all, a triple "A" rating results in interest rates that are below those in effect for a bond with a triple "B" rating. Such ratings result in savings running into millions of dollars. Conversely, low ratings may effectively bar a government from the capital market by raising its borrowing costs sharply. Moreover, laws and regulations permit commercial banks, insurance companies, and pension funds to invest only in well-rated securities.

Toward the end of 1992, only fifteen states had Standard and Poor's cherished AAA rating for some of their bond issues: California, Connecticut, Delaware, Illinois, Iowa, Maryland, Missouri, New Jersey, North Carolina, Pennsylvania, South Carolina, Texas, Utah, Virginia, and Wisconsin. At the bottom of the list were Massachusetts, New York, and Louisiana, with BBB, A– and A ratings. Among the cities, low ratings were in effect in Philadelphia, Bridgeport, Detroit, St. Louis, Yonkers, and New York City.

So formidable are the powers of the rating services that they have become involuntary participants in the political process. Their pursuit of full and reliable data has resulted in sweeping changes in budgetary, accounting, and auditing policies and systems. The threat of a lowered rating can move balky chief executives and legislatures to approve balanced budgets, pass appropriation bills on time, raise taxes, and exercise more control over the finances of hitherto autonomous public authorities. In this environment, budget offices have belatedly developed a sophistication in credit analysis and risk assessment so as to match the analytical weapons of the rating services.

Implementing the Capital Budget

Debt Management

Considering the heavy dependence on borrowing for capital construction, the role of autonomous public authorities and special districts, and the pitfalls and hazards associated with debt financing, several states have created special bodies in and outside of the central budget office to oversee and monitor debt. Among the most noteworthy are the following:

- *California.* A Debt Advisory Commission in the Department of Treasury collects and analyzes data on debt issued by all public agencies, including public authorities. Although it has no enforcement powers, it influences decisions by the governor, the director of finance and the legislature.

- *Florida.* The Bureau of Bond Finance in the Department of Banking and Finance structures, finances and sells both GO [general obligation] bonds and revenue bonds. No public authorities can issue bonds without the approval of that office that also monitors the repayment of debt.

- *Kentucky.* The Office of Investment and Debt Management reviews and approves all state bond issues; coordinates the marketing of issues; reviews the debt capacity of the state; monitors the financing of public authorities.

- *New Jersey.* The Treasurer's Office reviews and approves all GO bonds and advises the Governor on revenue bonds issued by public authorities.

- *New York.* The Public Authority Control Board, staffed primarily by the central budget office, monitors revenue bond issuances and approves bonds of selected public authorities.

- *North Carolina.* The Treasurer's Office controls and approves all GO and revenue bonds, including bonds of public authorities.

- *Texas.* No GO or revenue bonds can be issued without the approval of the Texas Bond Board. The Board's control also extends to public authorities.[54]

Integrating Capital and Operating Budgets

Within the broad and complex framework just described, the central budget office develops and implements the capital and operating budget for each agency. The focus is not on capital construction per se, but rather on capital facilities as a major means of attaining the objectives of programs, the other instruments being operating budgets and state aid to local government. To highlight these interrelationships, most state governments combine all funds in their budget presentation. New York State does so, as in the following example of the Department of Mental Hygiene for 1992–1993, which appears in the executive budget for that year:

State operations (operating budget)	$1,296,533,800
Aid to localities	440,579,300
Capital projects	392,198,000
TOTAL	$2,129,331,100

Because of the long term fiscal implications of debt financing, the budget also includes a summary of funding and debt service for capital projects. Nineteen states prefer to present a capital construction budget as such without relating it to operating programs in the budget document.

In funding capital facilities, the operating agency and the central budget office must simultaneously weigh the needs and objectives of the program, the case for a capital project in terms of costs and benefits and demonstrated need, the alternative methods of financing the project, the impact on operating programs, the effect on debt service, and the impact of the facility on such components of the operating budget as staffing, supplies, and maintenance.

Project Management

Once funds are appropriated, it becomes essential in the course of budget implementation to track the progress of the project every step of the way. So critical is this step that several states have formal monitoring systems. It is necessary to spot delays before they hold up the opening of hospitals, schools, power plants, and roads. Such delays, as well as unnecessary design changes, can result in major cost overruns. Other unforeseen problems can raise havoc with the project, such as deviations from approved plans, mismanagement, inferior construction, changed priorities, recessionary and inflationary pressures, and problems in raising funds in capital markets. All of these necessitate continuing adjustments in the capital budget. Capital budgeting is not a once-for-all exercise.

Considering the complexity of capital budgeting, the National Association of State Budget Officers has crystallized what it calls "good practices in capital budgeting."[55]

- Establish a clear definition of expenditures within the capital budget.
- Define maintenance expenditures and provide for adequate funding of maintenance in statute.
- Include specific operating costs for each capital project.
- Ensure that effective legislative involvement occurs throughout the capital budgeting process.
- Strengthen the review of the years beyond the budget year in long-range capital plans.
- Identify the criteria used in selecting capital projects.
- Define all program outcomes for capital investments.
- Evaluate cost-estimating methods to measure their validity.
- Establish a tracking system to keep projects on schedule and within budget.
- Define the factors to consider in decisions to own or lease.
- Develop a clear debt policy.
- Review cost–benefit comparisons for private sector participation in capital projects.
- Maintain an updated inventory system of capital assets.

Points for Discussion

1. To what extent would you go along with proposals to establish a separate capital budget for the federal government of the United States, similar to capital budgets in state and local governments?
2. Why is the definition of a capital item significant from fiscal and political standpoints?
3. In capital budgeting, what are the relationships between comprehensive plans, functional plans, multiyear programs, and facility plans? How do they influence the preparation of the capital budget?
4. What analytical techniques facilitate the selection of projects for the capital program? Discuss their strengths and weaknesses.
5. In financing capital projects, governments rely on a mix of taxes, intergovernmental grants, and loans. What are the relative merits of each type of financing? What ideal mix, if any, exists?
6. What are the major constitutional and legal restrictions on incurring debt for capital construction? What methods are employed to get around these constraints? To what extent do you support these methods? Cite examples from several state constitutions.
7. What are the major differences between guaranteed and nonguaranteed bonds; general obligation, revenue, and moral obligation bonds; traditional and nontraditional bonds? Why do the differences matter? How far would you go in controlling the issuance of the so-called nontraditional bonds?
8. What brought about the "creative financing" of capital construction by state and local governments in the late 1970s and early 1980s? What are the unique characteristics of creative debt instruments? To what extent do you support their issuance today?

9. Over the years various proposals have been made in Congress to eliminate tax-exempt bonds or to limit the annual volume of such bonds. To what extent do you support or oppose these positions?

10. Why are bond ratings by private rating services significant? What factors influence these ratings?

11. In the implementation of the capital budget, debt management and project management are vital controls. Discuss the features of each type of control and their advantages and disadvantages.

12. Review a current official statement, the bond prospectus issued by a government contemplating the sale of bonds. Analyze it in the light of the major themes of this chapter.

13. Review a multiyear capital plan of a state or local government. Discuss its strengths and weaknesses in the light of the criteria in this chapter.

14. Review the proposed capital budget and appropriation bill for selected governmental functions. What changes, if any, would you propose?

15. How far would you go in implementing or changing what the National Association of State Budget Officers calls "good practices in capital budgeting?"

CHAPTER 6

THE PARADOX OF OFF-BUDGET BUDGETS
Budgeting for Public Enterprises

What budgets contain is essential, but what they leave out is vital. This raises a controversial issue that runs through modern American budgeting. Why exclude any public expenditures, revenue, and debt from what is supposed to be a comprehensive budget? Indeed, why go "off budget" at all to fund governmental programs? Paradoxically, federal, state, and local governments have it both ways. The regular budget encompasses most expenditures of governments for operating and capital programs. For many other programs governments depend on a host of off-budget, quasi-governmental entities variously termed government corporations, public authorities, special districts, and public benefit corporations. Another preferred general term is "public enterprises." To the extent that budgets omit public enterprises, they understate the size, growth, and cost of the public sector.

This is no piddling affair. The fastest-growing part of the public sector in the United States and other countries is public enterprises. In the United States the better known enterprises include Amtrak, the Postal Service, and the Tennessee Valley Authority at the federal level; the Port Authority of New York and New Jersey, the Massachusetts Water Resources Authority, the Washington Public Power Supply System, and the New York State Housing Finance Agency at the state level; and thousands of housing, water, waste disposal, and transportation authorities at the local level. For the most part public enterprises are autonomous corporate bodies outside of the regular governmental structure. Also, with some exceptions, they are off-budget—they do not appear in budget totals or in budget documents. Yet they account for a significant share (in some governments a major share) of public expenditures, revenue, debt, and employment.

Created by special or general statutes, public enterprises engage for the most part in commercial-type, revenue-producing activities and are intended to be substantially self-sustaining. They are generally free to use their own revenue for operating expenses and capital investment, to borrow funds in capital markets, and to control their own assets. To give them the flexibility and autonomy of business enterprises, governments have set them up as corporate bodies with the power of self-governance through boards of directors or, occasionally, single administrators. As such, they are frequently exempt in whole or in part from central controls over staff appointments and procurement as well as budgets.

Despite their autonomous corporate status, public enterprises are fundamentally instruments of public policy. To carry out these policies governments could have turned to regular operating agencies or to the private sector instead of creating public enterprises. Yet for a variety of reasons discussed below, they have chosen to rely on public enterprises.

Owned in whole or in large part by governments, public enterprises depend on governments for their start-up capital in the form of advances, loans, grants, or the purchase of shares of equity (if they issue stock). They count on governments to guarantee loans directly or indirectly from investors in domestic and foreign capital markets. Where public enterprises issue bonds for the construction of capital facilities, investors look to governments to back up the payment of principal and interest. Should public enterprises fail to be self-supporting, governments assist them with subsidies for operating and capital expenses or bail them out if they default in paying their obligations. Conversely, in a minority of cases, public enterprises actually contribute to public revenue.

Notwithstanding the importance of public enterprises, only sketchy information exists on their activities, financing, and performance. No precise data are even available on the actual number of public enterprises. In effect, they are the "shadow government," the terra incognita of public administration. Except for a few studies cited in this chapter, most budgetary literature is surprisingly silent on the linkages of budgets and public enterprises.[1]

Public Enterprises in the Federal Government

The federal government and state and local governments diverge in the creation and handling of public enterprises, although similarities exist. In 1969 the U.S. government adopted a unified, or consolidated, budget that would include all governmental activities and fiscal transactions, on and off budget. This step implemented the major recommendations of the President's Commission on Budget Concepts in 1967. Budgetary rectitude, however, lasted only briefly. Since 1971 the number of off-budget entities increased as some existing enterprises were removed from the budget and new ones were created outside of the budget. As the U.S. Budget for FY 1993 explained,

> Off-budget Federal entities are federally owned and controlled, but their transactions are excluded from the budget totals by law. When a Federal entity is off-budget, its receipts, outlays, and deficit or surplus are not included in budget

receipts, budget outlays, or the budget deficit; and its budget authority is not included in the totals of budget authority for the budget.[2]

By 1993 federal off-budget public enterprises included the U.S. Postal Service, the social security trust funds (legally not a government corporation), and some thirty-five government corporations, including the Tennessee Valley Authority, the Federal Deposit Insurance Corporation, AMTRAK, the Pension Benefit Guaranty Corporation, the Federal Crop Insurance Corporation, the Corporation for Public Broadcasting, the Resolution Trust Corporation, and the Export-Import Bank. Of estimated FY 1993 outlays of $1.5 trillion, the OBEs (off-budget enterprises) accounted for $264 billion, or about 18 percent. Of total revenue of nearly $1.2 trillion during the same year, OBEs contributed about $326 billion, or 28 percent. Unlike the regular government, which was plagued by deficits, the OBEs enjoyed nothing but surpluses.[3]

Government corporations loom large in the economic life of the nation. They support housing, agriculture, banking, higher education, commerce, cooperatives, the export industry, and other sectors of the economy by purchasing mortgages and providing loans, loan guarantees, and insurance. They run revenue-producing enterprises and, in a few instances, dispense grants (e.g., Corporation for Public Broading and Legal Services Corporation).

As a consequence of credit and insurance programs of government corporations and other federal agencies, the U.S. government had $5.5 trillion in loans and insurance outstanding at the end of 1992, as follows:[4]

	Billions
Direct loans	$157
Guaranteed loans	587
Deposit insurance (commercial and saving banks, thrifts, credit unions)	2,779
Pension Benefit Guarantee Corporation (insurance)	850
Other insurance	1,080
	$5,453

This is quite apart from over $1.1 trillion loaned and borrowed by government-sponsored enterprises (GSEs), which are federally chartered but privately owned. (GSEs are discussed later in this chapter.) Combining credit and insurance programs of GSEs, government corporations, and other federal agencies, the face amount of federal and federally assisted credit and insurance was about $6.6 trillion by the end of 1991, the size of a year's GNP. The budget costs are real and immediate. In the event of defaults in the payment of loans, or the failure of insurance to cover liabilities, the federal government rushes to rescue the failing programs. In 1992 loan write-offs for defaults totaled $17.5 billion. Over the twenty-five-year period from 1969 to 1994, defaults on student loans alone totaled $22 billion.[5] The ultimate cost of bailing out savings and loan associations that are covered by federal deposit insurance will range upward of $150 billion.

The Rationale for Creating Off-Budget Government Corporations

No overarching theory of public ownership explains the rise of government corporations in the United States as it does in some other countries. For a variety of pragmatic, fiscal, and nonideological reasons the federal government has chosen to use government corporations to carry out public policy instead of relying on conventional organizational structures, the marketplace, regulation, tax incentives, and the budget system to fund additional expenditures.

1. *Flexibility of corporate structures.* Since the 1920s and 1930s, governments in the United States have relied on government corporations and state and local public authorities to deal with complex issues that could not be readily handled by conventional operating agencies or easily funded by the budget. The models for the proliferation of the public enterprises were the creation of the Port Authority of New York and New Jersey in 1921 and the New York State Power Authority in 1931. With these vivid examples before him, President Roosevelt turned to government corporations in 1933, during the Great Depression, to cope with failing businesses, mass unemployment, bankrupt farms, home foreclosures, and closed banks. In short order the New Deal created dozens of government corporations, for example, the Federal Deposit Insurance (FDIC) and the Federal Savings and Loan Insurance Corporation (FSLIC) to insure bank deposits; the Home Owners Loan Corporation (HOLC) to stave off home foreclosures; the Commodity Credit Corporation (CCC) and the Farm Mortgage Corporation (FMC) to lend money to hard-pressed farmers; the Government National Mortgage Association (GNMA) to insure mortgages; the refurbished Reconstruction Finance Corporation (RFC) to channel loans to businesses; and the Tennessee Valley Authority (TVA) to provide electricity, improve navigable waterways, and manufacture fertilizer in one of the most depressed regions of the country.[6]

Features of government corporations that appealed to the authors of the New Deal and to later proponents were the flexibility of the corporate structure; the freedom from red tape; the authority to finance programs through fees and charges without relying on the budget; adaptability to changing conditions in the marketplace; business-like practices; and legal separation from the regular government.

2. *Failings of the marketplace.* With the market unable to provide affordable housing to low- and moderate-income groups, public enterprises loan funds at below-market interest rates; construct and operate public housing; guarantee loans for housing; insure mortgages; subsidize housing costs; and purchase mortgages from commercial lenders to provide additional funds to build single-family

and multiunit apartments. Gaps and imperfections in the market have also resulted in the establishment of public enterprises to subsidize and guarantee loans to college students; operate and subsidize mass transportation systems; support the prices paid to farmers; provide electricity to rural areas; and protect bank depositors.

All of these programs have a direct and indirect impact on the budget. Subsidies increase operating costs. Should borrowers fail to repay loans, the defaults also increase expenditures. All guaranteed and insured loans and deposit insurance constitute a contingent liability for government. If the loans are not repaid, governments are legally obligated to pay the creditors. Thus, a loan guarantee shifts the risk of default from the lender to the government.[7]

3. *Aversion of private sector to risky and unprofitable ventures.* Without government loans, grants, and loan guarantees, private entrepreneurs are reluctant to undertake possibly risky, uncertain, and unprofitable ventures and to provide credit to marginal borrowers. Hence, in the energy crunch of the late 1970s the federal government established the Synthetic Fuels Corporation (later eliminated) to underwrite the commercial production of synthetic fuels through various forms of financial assistance and price guarantees. The Small Business Administration was created to guarantee loans to small businesses that had no ready access to commercial credit. Several government corporations exist to provide credit to homeowners, farmers, and students who otherwise might be turned down by private lenders.

4. *Rescuing ailing industries.* Unlike governments in other industrialized countries, which frequently take over ailing firms in key economic sectors, governments in the United States have generally limited their rescue efforts to railroads, buslines, and port terminals. For example, through Conrail (privatized in 1986) and AMTRAK, the federal government acquired defunct railroads. Going beyond public enterprises, the government also bailed out the Chrysler Corporation through loans and loan guarantees.

5. *Beating the system.* The federal government has also set up many government corporations to "beat the system" by exempting them from central controls over personnel ceilings, civil service salaries, budgets, audits, procurement, construction, and other red tape. Frequently, this motivation goes hand in hand with the impetus to finance the activities of the public enterprises outside of the regular budget. It is argued that the traditional bureaucracy is slow, slothful, sluggish, rigid, and ill-equipped to administer high-priority and novel programs. In contrast, autonomous public enterprises are regarded as fast moving, flexible, and creative and therefore in a position to assemble a specialized and talented staff quickly.[8]

6. *"Cutting" the budget.* To give the illusion of cutting budgets and deficits, administrations, with the consent of Congress and state legislatures, have transferred functions from the regular budget to off-budget government corporations. This has become a standard form of budget gimmickry.

7. *Regional and economic development.* In theory, virtually all forms of public enterprise stimulate regional and economic development. For some public enterprises this is their main mission, as is true of the Tennessee Valley Authority, the Delaware River Basin Commission, and the Bonneville Power Administration (not legally an autonomous public corporation).

Controlling Federal Off-Budget Expenditures and Credit Programs of Government Corporations

From the start, most corporations were exempt from controls of the Budget Bureau. The rationale was that corporations are self-sustaining and require no appropriations. Hence, there was no need for a central review of their fiscal needs. However, since the end of World War II the federal government has shifted its course several times in its attempts, through the budget process, to control public enterprises responsible for off-budget expenditures and credit programs. The first ambitious attempt to oversee public enterprises was the Government Corporation Control Act (GCCA) of 1945 (59 Stat. 597; 31 U.S.C. 841). The Act differentiated "wholly owned" and "mixed-ownership" corporations (the latter include some private funds). For wholly owned corporations, the legislation required the annual submission to the Bureau of the Budget (later OMB) of a "business-type budget" including "a statement of income and expense, an analysis of surplus or deficit, a statement of sources and applications of funds, estimates of operations by major types of activities together with estimates of administrative expenses, estimates of borrowings, and estimates of the amount of Government capital funds which shall be returned to the Treasury during the fiscal year or the appropriations required to provide for the restoration of capital impairment." After review and, where appropriate, revisions of the budget, the president was to transmit it to Congress as part of the annual budget of the federal government.

While mixed-ownership corporations were not subject to central budget review, the president was required to include in his budget any recommendations with regard to the return to the treasury of capital given to these entities. In this connection, the legislation required the secretary of the treasury to approve the terms and conditions of all bonds, notes, and other financial instruments issued by wholly owned and mixed-ownership corporations. The Act also required GAO to conduct commercial-type audits of all government corporations covering financial management, compliance with the law, and internal controls.[9]

The implementation of the Government Corporation Control Act fell far short of expectations. It turned out to be an inadequate instrument for controlling mixed-ownership corporations that relied on federal funds and did not apply to off-budget corporations at all. Hence, more government corporations went off-budget.

In 1981 OMB asked the National Academy of Public Administration (NAPA) to review the status of government corporations. Recognizing the need for flexible

instruments like government corporations, NAPA made the following recommendations:[10]

1. All government enterprises and corporations should be agencies of the
   United States.

2. All administrative and operational functions of the federal government
   should be performed by agencies of the United States located in the executive
   branch.

3. Although different organizational forms and powers and administrative flexibility are required for the effective performance of different governmental
   functions, all executive organizations should be accountable to the President,
   duly appointed officials and the Congress.

4. The officers and employees of government enterprises and corporations
   (other than mixed-ownership corporations intended for eventual private
   ownership) should be employees of the United States.

5. A government corporation should normally be placed under the head of an
   existing department or agency rather than established as an independent
   executive agency.

6. No government corporation should create a subsidiary without the approval
   of Congress.

7. Financial transactions of all government corporations should be included in
   the Federal Budget.

8. Corporations expected to be profit-making should be established in the private sector, and government corporations should be self-sustaining or potentially self-sustaining.

The next major change came with the Federal Credit Reform Act of 1990.
This was designed to identify in the budget the cost to the government of direct
loans and federally guaranteed private loans. Most federal credit programs subsidize loans through low interest rates and free guarantees of loans (no charges to
borrowers). Prior to the Federal Credit Reform Act the budget rarely captured
the costs of the subsidies, the probability of future losses from loan defaults, or
the administrative cost of originating and servicing loans and collecting debts.
Consequently, it was difficult to compare costs among credit programs and
between credit and noncredit programs as a basis for budget decisions. Beginning
in FY 1992, the value of expected future costs of interest subsidies and defaults
was incorporated in budget outlays and budget authority. Thus, the FY 1994
budget showed the present value (1993) of expected future costs ranging from
$203 to $293 billion. Estimated subsidy costs for 1993–1998 ranged from $63
billion to $129 billion. Because of technical and conceptual problems, adminis-
trative costs were excluded.[11]

That sweeping controls over public enterprises were long overdue was evident
from the failure of the Federal Savings and Loan Insurance Corporation (FSLIC),
a government corporation whose functions were later taken over by the Federal

Deposit Insurance Corporation (FDIC), and the Farm Credit System, a GSE (privately owned but covered by implied federal guarantees). By any standard the collapse of FSLIC, in the words of the Congressional Budget Office, was a "debacle, a disaster and a mess." Because of lax regulation and a budget system that concealed vital data, hundreds of "thrifts," or savings and loan associations, failed in the 1980s, making the government responsible for protecting bank deposits at a cost of over $150 billion (the final figures are not in as yet). These losses loomed suddenly "in a program that for decades had appeared to be an efficient, self-financing means of providing a safe haven for the savings of millions of Americans and for avoiding banking panics."[12]

While less spectacular, the failure of the Farm Credit System (FCS) was equally traumatic. When the farm economy fell apart in the mid-1980s and farmers defaulted on their loans from FCS, its losses climbed to at least $5 billion. Although the federal government had not guaranteed FCS loans, it nevertheless bailed out the System and nourished it until the fortunes of agriculture improved in the late 1980s.[13]

Loans by Government-Sponsored Enterprises (GSEs)

As a class, GSEs lend more and borrow more than government corporations and other federal agencies. By 1992 their outstanding loans totaled slightly over $1.1 trillion, in contrast to direct federal loans of $157 billion and loan guarantees of $587 billion.[14] The Congressional Budget Office defines a GSE as "a corporation chartered by the federal government to achieve public purposes that has nongovernmental status, is excluded from the federal budget, and is exempt from most, if not all, laws and regulations applicable to federal agencies, officers and employees . . . [It is] a privately owned, federally chartered financial institution that has nationwide operations and specialized lending powers and benefits from an implicit federal guarantee that enhances its ability to borrow."[15] Not subject to budget controls or the Federal Credit Reform Act of 1990, GSEs appear in the budget solely for information purposes.

Created by Congress, the seven major GSEs channel credit on favorable terms to farmers, homeowners, colleges, and students. Table 6.1 highlights their features. Three GSEs facilitate the flow of credit to agriculture: Farm Credit Banks, Banks for Cooperatives, and the Federal Agriculture Mortgage Corporation ("Farmer Mac"). Three promote lending for home ownership: Federal Home Loan Banks, the Federal National Mortgage Association ("Fannie Mae"), and the Federal Home Loan Mortgage Corporations ("Freddie Mac"). One GSE underpins higher education lending, the Student Loan Marketing Association ("Sallie Mae"). Among recently created GSEs are the Farm Credit System Financial Assistance Corporation (FAC), which raises funds for failing Farm Credit System institutions; the Financing Corporation (FICO) and the Resolution Funding Corporation (REF CORP), which are fund raisers for defunct "thrifts"; and the College Construction Loan Insurance Association ("Connie Lee"), which lends funds to colleges and universities.[16]

TABLE 6.1

Characteristics of government-sponsored enterprises

Enterprise	Assets financed	Organizational structure	Operations
Farm Credit system Farm Credit Banks and affiliated associations	Agricultural operating, production, supply, and real estate loans	11 regional banks, 262 associations; all are borrower-owned cooperatives	Lender
Banks for Cooperatives	Loans and leases to agricultural cooperatives, rural utilities, and others	3 national borrower-owned cooperatives	Lender
Federal Agricultural Mortgage Corporation (Farmer MAC)	Agricultural real estate and rural housing loans, and loans guaranteed by the Farmers Home Administration	Unitary firm	Guarantor
Federal National Mortgage Association (Fannie Mae)	Residential mortgage loans	Unitary firm	Guarantor and lender (about 28 percent of assets)
Federal Home Loan Mortgage Corporation (Freddie MAC)	Residential mortgage loans	Unitary firm	Guarantor and lender (about 6 percent of assets)
Federal Home Loan Bank system	Advances secured by residential mortgages or federal agency securities	12 district banks	Lender
Student Loan Marketing Assocation (Sallie Mae)	Federally guaranteed student loans and advances secured by them	Unitary firm	Lender

Source: Congressional Budget Office, *Public Purposes and Risks of GSEs,* (Washington, D.C., 1991), p. 5.

Like other private corporations, the GSEs borrow funds in the capital markets, buy mortgages and loans from banks to enlarge the lending pool, sell shares in their enterprises, and pay dividends in profitable years. Where they differ is the implicit guarantee they have from the federal government to pay their debt. Consequently, they enjoy low interest rates on their debt, only slightly higher than the rates commanded by the U.S. Treasury. The implicit federal guarantee of their obligations also transfers to the government "a large portion of the risk that creditors normally bear."[17] Because of their special relationship with the federal government, they enjoy other benefits as well: lines of credit from the treasury; exemption from the corporate income tax (two GSEs); exemption of investor interest income from state and local taxes (three GSEs); exemption from SEC registration and state regulation; and only perfunctory federal supervision of risky undertakings.[18]

Overall, the GSEs have stimulated home and farm ownership on a vast scale, and have made it possible for millions of students to attend colleges and universities. In so doing, the two largest, Fannie Mae and Freddie Mac, pose only "a low level of risk of loss to the government," and the FHLBs and Sallie Mae "pose a minimal risk of loss," according to the Congressional Budget Office. While the Farm Credit System has improved since the government bailed it out in 1987, it "remains quite vulnerable and continues to expose the government to more risk than any other enterprise."[19]

Because of the government's large stake in the GSEs, various proposals have been advanced to protect it against a possible contingent liability of over $1 trillion, especially against the background of the large losses of the thrift industry.

1. *Privatize the GSEs completely.* This would sever the "special relationship" between the GSEs and the federal government. On the other hand, it might curb the flow of credit to homeowners, farmers, and students.

2. *Strengthen federal supervision of GSEs.* This could be done through appropriate federal agencies such as the Department of Housing and Urban Development (HUD), Education, and Agriculture, or by creating a Federal Enterprise Regulatory Board, as proposed by the General Accounting Office.

3. *Protect the government against excessive risks.* Three possible strategies would be to increase the capital requirements of GSEs; to develop standards for acceptable lending risks; and to make shareholders liable for most risks.

4. *Make federal guarantees of loans explicit.* Rather than relying on ambiguous, implied guarantees of GSE obligations, new legislation might specify explicitly the nature and extent of the government's guarantees.

In 1992 Congress adopted the second proposal in part and created an Office of Federal Housing Enterprise Oversight in HUD to regulate Fannie Mae and Freddie MAC. This step foreshadows a power struggle between two independent, investor-owned corporations and HUD. According to Stanton, the outcome is uncertain:

> There is also a basic political question: does the federal government have the ability to impose fair but effective financial supervision upon financial institutions that use a federal guarantee to amass overwhelming financial and political leverage? That question was placed into perspective by the expensive collapse of the thrift industry, abetted by the dominance of the thrifts and their powerful trade associations over the relevant congressional committees. The same question now remains to be answered for the GSEs.[20]

State and Local Public Authorities and Special Districts

While not as large as GSEs and federal government corporations, some 40,000 off-budget and frequently autonomous state and local public authorities and special districts control some of the most vital services of the country: transportation, economic development, low- and moderate-income housing, water supply, sewage and waste disposal, power generation and distribution, urban redevelopment, higher education loans, and the construction of universities, schools, hospitals, prisons, and government buildings.[21]

Defining Public Authorities

The estimate of 40,000 public authorities and special districts is based on a variety of sources—no precise data are available anywhere. Only the United States Bureau of the Census attempts to compile data on the number of public enterprises in the United States, primarily at the state and local government levels. Yet at best, census information is limited. It comes out every five years (the latest data cover 1992) and lumps some, but not all, state and local public enterprises with special districts, which it defines as "limited purpose governmental units (other than school district governments) which exist as separate entities with substantial administrative and fiscal independence from general purpose local governments."[22] The bureau is often inconsistent in applying this definition and excludes from its compilation many of the largest and richest public authorities, such as power authorities, housing finance agencies, economic development authorities, and transportation authorities.[23]

These estimates are the best we have, however, of the number of public authorities in the United States. In its 1992 census of government, the Bureau identified 33,131 special districts. Accepting this as a base and supplementing this figure with an estimated 8,000 to 10,000 state and local public authorities excluded from the Bureau's count because of definitional problems, we can conservatively arrive at an estimate of 40,000 public authorities and special districts.[24]

Leading all other states in the Bureau's compilation in 1992 were Illinois, with 2,995 special districts; California, with 2,897; Texas, with 2,392; and Pennsylvania, with 2,244. According to state data, the figures are significantly understated.[25]

Part of the problem is semantic. Not all state and local public enterprises call themselves public authorities or districts. Some bear such labels as "agency" (the Texas Housing Agency); "system" (State of Washington Public Power Supply System); "fund" (the Economic Revitalization Fund of Pennsylvania); "bank" (Vermont Bond Bank); "trust" (New Jersey Wastewater Treatment Trust); "board" (Kansas City Board of Public Utilities); "commission" (Washington Suburban Sanitary Commission); "company" (Massachusetts Municipal Wholesale Electric Company); "corporation" (New York State Urban Development Corporation); and miscellaneous titles such as "BART" (Bay Area Rapid Transit) and "Metro Rail" (Southern California Rapid Transit District).

Regardless of labels, the public authorities display these features:[26]

- A public-benefit corporation created by a special law or a general law.
- A distinct corporate entity legally separated from the state or local government.

- A corporate management that includes a board appointed by a governor, mayor, or local government council (at times elected by local voters) and a chief executive officer and staff responsible to the board.

- Power to issue tax-exempt bonds and notes to finance its operations.

- Authority to finance, construct, and operate capital projects.

- Freedom to perform all authorized functions to carry out its mission.

- Power to set fees, charges, rents, and tolls for its services, but no power to tax unless the legislature permits assessments for its services.

- Freedom to enter into contracts and to own and dispose of property, to sue and be sued.

- Exemption (in most cases) from state and local government control over staff appointments, salaries, budgets, contracts, and procurement of supplies.

- Flexibility to create subsidiaries.

- Power to contract with federal, state, and local government and other public authorities.

Some exceptions exist. Not all public authorities enjoy freedom from the operating controls applicable to government agencies. They may get partial exemption. Not all public authorities and special districts are self-financed. Some, especially in housing, transportation, and education, are heavily subsidized. About two-fifths of the special districts can impose property and sales taxes if the voters approve. Most revenue, however, comes from user fees and charges. A public authority often collects its funds from a variety of sources: fees, charges, rent, subsidies, taxes, loans, and grants. Differences among public authorities aside, what they have in common is legal autonomy, independence from state and local government, and off-budget status.

As Axelrod points out in *Shadow Government*, "in power, affluence and assets public authorities rival the largest state and local governments and commercial banks in the United States. They borrow more billions of dollars than state and local governments combined. They have run up a debt that is second only to that of the U.S. government itself." In 1990 the outstanding long-term debt of state and local governments was $894 billion. Nearly two-thirds represented the debt of public authorities.[27]

No precise data are available on the expenditures of state and local public authorities. One estimate suggests that off-budget spending by state public authorities represents about one-third of total state outlays.[28] This estimate will have to do because it is not currently possible to combine on- and off-budget expenditures except on a selective basis in individual states. In several states such as New York, Massachusetts, Illinois, and New Jersey, the combined annual operating expenditures of public authorities exceed the budgets of many states and most countries of the world. Dozens of public authorities are multibillion dollar firms. Among them are the Municipal Electric Authority of Georgia, the New Jersey Economic Development Authority, the State of Washington Public Power

Supply System, the New York State Municipal Assistance Corporation, and the California Housing Finance Agency.[29]

Reasons for Creating Public Authorities

Why create public authorities and special districts, give them off-budget status, and grant them a large measure of autonomy? Both good and dubious reasons have prompted these moves. On the positive side, public authorities are indispensable in managing interstate, interregional, and intraregional functions. No viable substitute exists for the bistate Port Authority of New York and New Jersey; the Texas Housing Agency; the Bay Area Rapid Transit, which provides mass transportation in the San Francisco area; the Delaware Solid Waste Authority, with statewide jurisdiction; the Arizona Salt River Project; or the Massachusetts Water Resources Authority, which serves forty-three communities. They vault over outmoded political boundaries to attack problems that transcend such artificial borders.

Also straightforward and positive is the creation of public authorities to operate roads, bridges, utilities, ports, water and sewer systems, airports, and transportation systems. They have a corporate structure that facilitates decision making; follow business-like practices; charge fees for these services; and are largely self-sustaining. Housing and transportation authorities also benefit from a corporate structure, even though they require heavy subsidies from the state and federal governments to stay in business.

Political motives prompt the creation of thousands of other public authorities. They are devices to evade constitutional limits on debt and to con the voters by making state and local budgets look smaller than they actually are. As is emphasized in Chapter 5, on capital budgeting, nearly all state constitutions prohibit borrowing without a public referendum, or limit the amount of debt that can be incurred. Since the 1960s governors, mayors, and legislatures have surmounted these hurdles by creating public authorities outside of the regular governmental structure and empowering them to borrow funds by issuing tax-exempt revenue bonds as well as a variety of "creative" financial instruments such as moral obligation bonds, lease-purchase plans, certificates of participation, "contractual obligations," and the like. Concocted on Wall Street, these bonds are transparent devices to bypass constitutions. So far most state courts, regrettably, have gone along with these schemes.[30]

Most of the public authorities designed to circumvent constitutions are nothing but shells, as noted in Chapter 5. Their sole purpose is to sell revenue bonds to construct public buildings, schools, universities, hospitals, and jails. Once they raise the money, they turn it over to the state or local government, which then pays "rent" to the shell authorities for twenty to thirty years. The shells in turn pay interest to the bondholders. When the bonds are paid off the government owns the facility. In the fiction of this transaction, this is not constitutional debt—just rent money that comes out of the regular operating budget and is paid for by taxes. Thus do elected officials finance buildings without voter approval and even in the face of voter rejection of bond issues.[31]

Nearly all states practice this form of fiscal inventiveness, with Pennsylvania, New York, Illinois, Florida, California, and Texas the leaders among them. At the local level, Pennsylvania tops the list. To get around state constitutions and voter resistance to bond issues, local governments and school districts sponsored some 738 paper authorities for school construction in the early 1990s. These were part of a network of over 2,600 local public authorities created for a variety of purposes. All participate enthusiastically in lease-purchase financing.

In recent years political leaders have begun to use public authorities as tools to "cut" the budget. Just transfer a function such as water supply or waste disposal to a public authority or special district, and the size of the budget decreases. Of course the voters now pay fees and charges to the authority instead of supporting it through their taxes. So befuddled are they by the complexity of these moves that frequently they don't realize they are paying more than they did before. This, too, is part of the shell game.

Despite the impressive accomplishments of many public authorities, voters pay a heavy price for the creation of autonomous and unaccountable public authorities. Annmarie Hauck Walsh in *The Public's Business* (1978), Diana B. Henriques in *The Machinery of Greed* (1986), and Donald Axelrod in *Shadow Government* (1992) document the consequences of creating public authorities insulated from voter control: multibillion-dollar defaults; monumental spending sprees; the bailout of failed and bankrupt authorities; outright corruption, theft, and political patronage; manipulation of funds from various sources to confuse the voters; subversion of statutory missions by some public authorities; regressive fees that hit the poor; misuse of industrial bonds designed to create jobs; evasion of constitutions and laws; fragmentation of government; failure to monitor the performance and costs of public authorities; erosion of budget control; and a bonanza for brokers, bond attorneys, and financial advisers.[32]

Reluctance of Governors and Legislatures to Control Public Authorities

Despite the impact of off-budget public enterprises on state and local finances and economies, governors and legislatures are generally reluctant to control them unless scandals or fiscal crises erupt. In the first place, they created them to reduce or limit the size of the budget; to circumvent constitutional and statutory restrictions on expenditures, taxes, and debt; and to override controls over budgets, procurement, and staff appointments and salaries.[33] Hence, in most states they rarely turn against their own statutory creations by subjecting them to routine and detailed oversight and review of their financial performance, programmatic results, and budgets.

Yet this was the case in New York State, where the default of the Urban Development Corporation in 1975, heavy losses by the Dormitory Authority in 1982, and the problems of other public authorities led to a massive state intervention in the fiscal affairs of authorities. As a result, the state established for the first time the following unprecedented and sweeping controls over public authorities (unmatched by any other state). After more than ten years, however, the effectiveness of these controls has yet to be determined.

1. *Creating a State Public Authorities Control Board (PACB)*. Composed of a chair, who is selected by the governor (usually the director of the budget); the chairs of the two legislative fiscal committees; and two nonvoting members recommended by the minority leaders in each house, the board reviews and controls proposed financing and construction commitments for a selected number of authorities. (The law authorized the governor to select the chair.)

2. *Capping moral obligation debt*. With one exception the state capped all moral obligation debt. Only PACB can exceed the ceiling.

3. *Coordinating the sale of securities*. A State Securities Coordinating Committee controls the timing of bonds and notes issued by the state and the major public authorities.

4. *Requiring submission of annual reports*. The authorities were compelled to prepare more comprehensive and meaningful annual reports, covering operations, accomplishments, revenues, expenditures, assets and liabilities, outstanding bonds and notes, and obligations issued and redeemed in the course of the year.

5. *Requiring report of external audit results*. In addition to comprehensive audits by the state comptroller, public authorities are also required to report the results of any additional external examinations by private audit firms and other groups.

6. *Centralizing review of authorities in the budget office*. The patent need for intensified oversight by the budget office led to the creation of a special unit, which is responsible for monitoring authorities continuously and preparing detailed analyses of their operations and finances on behalf of the governor and the legislature.

7. *Establishing investment guidelines*. Public authorities must submit guidelines on investment standards and policies to the Division of the Budget, the comptroller, and the legislative fiscal committee.

8. *Requiring rolling five-year capital plans*. Every public authority must annually develop and send to the governor a rolling five-year capital plan that identifies the estimated costs of projects and the sources of funding.

Controls of this type are useful, but don't go far enough. Several states, the federal government, and some foreign governments have employed other workable mechanisms to oversee public authorities: a broad veto power by the governor over actions of authorities as in New Jersey; central agencies to monitor debt as in Texas, California, and Kentucky; full disclosure of the finances of the public authorities in budget documents as in New York; performance contracts between governments and public corporations as in France; full-scale audits of public authorities as in Illinois; restrictions on the growth of authorities as in Wisconsin and Massachusetts; and adoption of criteria in the U.S. Government Corporation Control Act that require the submission of business-type budgets to the chief executive.[34]

Focusing on local governments, especially in Pennsylvania, the Coalition to Improve Management in State and Local Government issued in 1992 the following guidelines with respect to local public authorities:

Whatever your role or concerns may be in respect to one or more public authorities, you need to bear in mind that ideally:

1. An authority is created only in order to perform income-generating functions that make it entirely or largely self-supporting; thus it requires commercial business-type financial operations which the creating local government is unable to carry out as a part of its regular operations.

2. The policies, programs, fees, and current and capital budgets of the authority are determined by a board appointed by the sponsoring jurisdiction.

3. Every board appoints an executive director or general manager who is responsible for the administration and operations of the authority.

4. The authority functions in cooperation with officials and appropriate departments of the city, township, borough, or county which creates it, or of a joint organ of two or more jurisdictions.

5. The authority functions in harmony with other local government units and in a context of effective intergovernmental and intersectoral cooperation.

6. Both formal and informal mechanisms are established for communication between the local government body and the authority board, and between the board and its executive director or general manager.

7. The authority demonstrates its effectiveness by announcing and achieving goals and operational outcomes which clearly convey to the parent local government and the public that it is efficient and effective.

Source: Coalition to Improve Management in State and Local Governments, "Standards for Local Public Authorities in Pennsylvania" (Pittsburgh: Carnegie Mellon University, 1992).

Some close observers of public authorities have called for more fundamental changes: the abolition of thousands of shell authorities; the dismantling of authorities created to take over functions normally supported by the regular budget; and amendment of outmoded state constitutions to give governors and legislatures more flexibility in borrowing funds. This last step alone would lead to elimination of many public authorities. None of this is likely to happen in the foreseeable future. Hit hard by recessions, cutbacks in federal aid, and voter resistance to bond referenda, state and local governments will continue to depend on public authorities for fiscal salvation. Judging by present trends, by the year 2000 some 45,000 to 50,000 public authorities and special districts may thrive and continue to raise controversial budget policy issues.

Points for Discussion

1. What are the major types of public enterprises in the United States, at all government levels? What accounts for their growth? What impact do they have on public sector expenditures, revenue, and debt?

2. What significant budgetary problems result from placing public enterprises off-budget? How would you solve them?

3. What are the major policy and budgetary controls over public enterprises in the United States? To what extent would you change them without sacrificing the autonomy and flexibility of public enterprises?

4. What are the pros and cons of having a unified budget incorporating all public enterprises? How far would you go in including loans and loan guarantees in the budget?

5. What changes, if any, would you recommend with regard to government-sponsored enterprises (GSEs)?

6. What changes, if any, would you recommend with regard to the U.S. Government Corporation Control Act of 1945?

7. What controls do you favor on federal loans and loan guarantees? In this connection, analyze the effectiveness of the Credit Reform Act of 1990.

8. With the advantage of hindsight, how might you have averted the collapse of the "thrifts" and the Farm Credit System?

9. How do you account for the continued proliferation of public authorities and special districts in state and local governments?

10. To what extent is it possible to reconcile the autonomy and accountability of public authorities?

11. Why do state and local governments maintain a hands-off policy with regard to public authorities?

12. To what extent should state and local governments follow the New York State model and the practices of New Jersey, Texas, Kentucky, California, and Wisconsin in controlling public authorities?

13. How far would you go in reducing the number of public authorities? How would you achieve your aims?

14. Would you recommend changing state constitutions to eliminate voter referenda on debt and other debt restrictions? Defend your position.

15. This chapter suggests that the number of state and local public authorities will increase rather than diminish. To what extent do you agree with this forecast?

16. "To ignore the budget effect of public enterprises is to lose control over fiscal policy." What are the pros and cons of this position?

CHAPTER 7

GETTING THE BUDGET AND ECONOMIC ACT TOGETHER
How Fiscal, Economic, and Monetary Policy Affect the Budget Process and the Economy

Fiscal policy drives the budget at all levels of government. It embodies a mix of taxes, expenditures, debt financing, and loans and loan guarantees. What that mix should be sparks the political debate on budgets. Fiscal policy affects not only governmental financing but the entire economy. By raising or lowering taxes and expenditures and by incurring debt, governments attempt to promote economic growth, maintain high levels of employment, control inflation, raise productivity, stimulate exports, and mitigate the effects of recession.

To achieve these economic goals, fiscal policy does not develop in a vacuum. It is shaped and molded by the ups and downs of the business cycle; the short- and long-term economic outlook; ideological biases; the stresses of a global economy that influences exports, imports, job creation, and the value of the dollar; and the monetary policies of the Federal Reserve Board, which determines the rise and fall of interest rates by controlling the money supply and the availability of credit (more later on this).

That fiscal policy and the budget process should become tools for managing the economy is a revolutionary development, not even sixty years old. Throughout the nineteenth century and up to the time of the Great Depression of the 1930s, fiscal policy was more narrow in scope. The primary emphasis was on financing wars, balancing the budget, and ensuring the economy, efficiency, legality, and propriety of expenditures.[1]

The abrupt change in the role of fiscal policy came in the 1930s with the Great Depression and the seminal writings of the British economist John Maynard Keynes. Both had the effect of upsetting the old comfortable doctrines of the limited role of budgeting.[2] Keynes argued persuasively that the lack of

145

demand and spending was the chief cause of the Depression. Because the private
sector failed to spend and invest sufficient funds to stimulate the economy, it was
up to governments to prime the pump. They could do this by borrowing funds
from the private sector and using the money for programs and projects that would
increase employment and consumption, and eventually lead to more private
investment in a growing economy. In this fashion governments would stimulate
the aggregate demands for goods and services. They would incur heavy deficits in
the process, but considering the benefits, the use of the national budget to offset
downward swings in the business cycle became an urgent issue for the first time,
deficits or no deficits.

Other weapons in the Keynesian armory included tax cuts in recessions, tax
increases and expenditure cuts in a booming economy, and the use of monetary
policy to control inflation. All are part of a "compensatory fiscal policy" designed
to correct weaknesses in the economy.

Roosevelt's New Deal exemplified the Keynesian approach, although Keynes
was not its theoretician, and many of its actions stemmed as much from pragmatic tinkering with the economy as from any deliberate design. What is significant is that the federal government set a precedent by assuming responsibility for
the national economy. This changed the nature of budgeting in national governments everywhere.[3]

In addition to all its other major functions, the budget process, especially at
the federal level, contends more than ever with the effect of the budget on the
economy and, conversely, that of the economy on the budget. Each component of
fiscal policy—spending, taxing, lending, and borrowing—undergoes careful
scrutiny to determine its specific effect on the economy and the economic goals of
the administration. The budget process thus carries a heavy burden in simultaneously addressing the intertwined issues of fiscal and economic policy while concentrating on the other facets of budgeting as well. This takes place in a political
climate where little consensus exists on budget and economic policy.

Within this framework, this chapter concentrates, in general terms, on the
linkages of fiscal and economic policy with the budget process. It then covers the
fiscal policies of the federal government, with particular emphasis on expenditure
and tax policy, attempts to control soaring deficits, and the role of monetary policy in this intricate relationship.

Moving to state and local governments, the chapter considers separately the
fiscal policies of these two levels of government and the latitude they have in controlling their own fiscal destinies in the shadow of the federal colossus.

The Budget Process and Fiscal, Economic, and Monetary Policies

The stakes are high in attempting to manage the economy through the major policy instruments of expenditures, taxes, credit, and monetary policy. Changes in
expenditures directly affect thousands of programs and projects, millions of beneficiaries of governmental largesse, and hundreds of interest groups, in every region
of the country. Equally sensitive is tax policy, which has a direct impact on the

income of employees, investors, pensioners, and private firms. The amount of governmental debt is another explosive issue. Should the budget be balanced? If so, how and when? How far should governments go in borrowing money to finance part of their expenditures? Every component of fiscal policy is related to every other component. The budget reflects the choices governments make among the major instruments of fiscal policy.

Effect of the Economy on the Budget

In the 1990s fiscal policy thus springs from estimates of both the effect of the economy on the budget and the proposed budget on the economy. How the national economy affects the budget is clear. A recession results in lower personal income and corporate profits, and hence in declining revenue, while expenditures for unemployment insurance and various welfare programs rise. In a severe recession the gap between revenues and expenditures widens to the point where chronic deficits occur. Conversely, as the economy recovers, taxes increase, expenditures decline, and deficits shrink. Even rare surpluses may emerge, usually at the state and local levels.

Government budgets are sensitive to inflation and interest rates as well as fluctuations of business cycles. Besides eroding the incomes of wage earners and pensioners, inflation drives up the cost of governmental goods, services, and benefits. This is especially true of entitlement programs such as social security and those pensions whose benefits vary with the cost of living.

Interest rates obviously affect debt service and the cost of borrowing money to fund capital projects and deficits. Several factors force interest rates up and down: extensive borrowing by governments, which puts pressure on interest rates; the rate of inflation; demands for credit by the private sector; and the monetary policies of the central bank (in the United States, the Federal Reserve Board [FRB]), which influence the movement of interest rates. High interest rates can slow down economic growth because of the heavy costs they impose on borrowers. Conversely, low interest rates can stimulate an otherwise stagnant economy.

On a global scale, still other pressures influence budget policy: favorable and unfavorable trade balances; the flight of jobs to low-wage countries; fluctuating rates of exchange of foreign currencies; foreign purchases of bonds issued by governments in the United States; foreign investments in the United States; and tariff and trade agreements. All leave their imprint on budget and economic plans.

Chapter 4 has underscored the effect of the economy on the budget by demonstrating the impact on revenues, expenditures, and deficits of just a 1 percent change in economic growth, unemployment, inflation, and interest rates.[4]

Impact of Budgets on the Economy

It is difficult enough to measure the effect of the economy on the budget. It is especially complex to gauge the impact of the budget on the economy. How do we know that a particular mix of fiscal policies will reduce unemployment, control inflation, encourage savings and investment, raise the aggregate demand for goods and services, and increase the utilization of productive capacity—in short, promote economic growth? What are the economic repercussions of specific budgetary actions? What is the precise linkage between budget policy and movements in the economy? How does fiscal policy influence the expectations and decisions of consumers and investors? Much economic theorizing, from Keynes to the present, centers on these questions, but no economic theory adequately explains the relationship between actions on the budget and developments in the economy.[5] Nor do the sharp divisions among economists help to clarify the relationship.

Other problems bedevil the efforts of decision makers to "fine-tune" the economy through fiscal policy. First, such unanticipated crises as wars; civil disturbances at home and abroad; oil price shocks; crop failures because of droughts, floods, and insect infestation; the rise or fall of food prices; and natural disasters may have a far more potent effect on the economy than the most finely crafted budgets. Second, fiscal and monetary policies may move in opposite directions, as was the case in the United States government from 1979 to 1982. During this period, fiscal policy encouraged expansion of the economy by cutting taxes and raising expenditures, while monetary policy, a reflection of the FRB's fear of inflation generated by governmental deficits, contracted the economy by driving up interest rates.[6] Third, policymakers may simply guess wrong in predicting economic developments or indulge in unwarranted rosy estimates about the state of the economy for temporary political gain. In the final analysis fiscal policy rests on economic assumptions about several key rates: unemployment, inflation, interest, and growth of the gross national domestic product. These assumptions also underpin revenue and expenditure estimates. If the assumptions go awry—and they frequently do—fiscal policy will miss its targets. For example, economists predicted neither the severity of the 1982–1983 recession nor the prolonged recession of 1990–1993, the most severe since the Great Depression. Nor was the strong recovery of 1994 foreseen. (The Budget Cycle Dating Committee of the National Bureau of Economic Research actually concluded in the fall of 1993 that the recession had begun in July 1990 and ended in March 1991. This offered little consolation to governments beset with shortfalls in revenue and deficits that persisted into 1993.)

Political Priorities' and Economic Theories' Influence on Fiscal Policy

Ultimately, noneconomic value judgments, political priorities affecting different economic sectors and income groups, and the economic theories that justify them shape fiscal policy. They determine levels of spending, the mix of governmental activities, the size and role of the public sector vis-à-vis the private sector, the proportion of spending for defense and for domestic programs, the nature of the tax structure, and the reliance on deficit spending. In budgeting, especially at the national level, the major political issues turn on jobs, inflation, tax burdens, and deficits. Political parties divide sharply on the fiscal policies best suited to cope with these problems.

The Keynesians. For support of their budget policies, political leaders lean on persuasive and congenial economic theories. From the 1930s until the end of the 1960s the followers of Keynes (the Keynesians and Neo-Keynesians), with their emphasis on demand management and compensatory fiscal policy, were especially influential in developing budget policy. Throughout the postwar period most governments outside of the communist bloc developed a Keynesian consensus in order to stimulate and stabilize the economy.[7]

Two statutes, albeit without teeth, actually enshrine the Keynesian consensus at the national level in the United States: the Employment Act of 1946 and the Full Employment and Balanced Growth Act of 1978 (the Humphrey–Hawkins Act). The first requires the United States "to use all practicable means consistent with its needs and obligations and other considerations of national policy" for the purpose of "promoting maximum employment, production, and purchasing power." The second enunciates a national policy of full employment, increased real income, balanced growth, a balanced budget, growth in productivity, and price stability. Relying primarily on the private sector, it sets as goals 3 percent unemployment and 3 percent inflation in five years and 0 percent inflation in ten years. It requires the president to report in the budget and in the annual economic report the extent to which the goals are met.[8] These goals still remain beyond reach.

Keynesian prescriptions proved to be "moderately successful" in the 1960s when several tax cuts pulled the economy out of recession.[9] In the 1970s, however, the United States experienced the worst of all possible worlds—stagflation (a stagnant economy and inflation)—primarily because of rising energy and food prices. With Keynesian theories increasingly challenged because of these developments, rival schools of economic thought put forward their own panaceas, which also left an imprint on fiscal policy. These were primarily the supply-siders, the school of rational expectations, the monetarists, and the mainline, or consensus, economists.

Supply-Siders and Others. The supply-siders, who were influential in the two Reagan administrations, argue that high tax rates should come down to unleash the productive forces of the economy and provide incentives to work, save, and invest. They blame tax policies for creating inflation and discouraging savings and investment. They reject fiscal policies focusing on the stimulation of aggregate demand. Their crown jewel was the massive tax cuts of 1982.

The small but marginally influential "school of rational expectations" disdains governmental intervention in the economy as ineffective. Since investors and consumers expect a fiscal stimulus in a recession, they discount it in advance and base their economic decisions on their own perceptions of self-interest. Consequently, when fiscal intervention comes, it has little effect. The market, and not the government, is the arbiter.[10]

The monetarists attribute inflation and slow economic growth to an excessive money supply, induced in part by large deficits. Hence, in order to maintain stable prices and lower interest rates, one thing the central bank, or Federal Reserve Board, must do is to expand the money supply slowly and steadily.[11]

Mainstream economists reject the extreme views of all schools and favor a pragmatic blend of demand management and fiscal and monetary policy. For a full discussion of the theories of the rival economic groups, consult the bibliography in the endnotes.

Whatever economic theories and noneconomic values motivate chief executives and legislators, their final decisions represent the most politically achievable combination of expenditures, taxes, and debt financing. A discussion of each component of fiscal policy follows.

Fiscal Policy in the Federal Government

Developing Expenditure Policies

Several dynamic forces influence federal outlays, which in 1993 approximated $1.4 trillion: the priorities accorded to defense and domestic programs; the uncontrollability of most expenditures because of mandatory entitlement programs, such as social security and Medicare, that are firmly imbedded in legislation; interest on the national debt; expenditure ceilings; the bailout of failed savings and loan institutions; the constraints imposed by large deficits; inflation; the loss of revenue through tax breaks, or the so-called tax expenditures; and the cumulative effect of thousands of decisions in the course of budget formulation. Table 7.1 registers the impact of these forces over a thirty-one-year period, 1962–1993.

What is especially striking is the growth of federal expenditures during war and peace. From $9.6 billion in 1940, outlays climbed inexorably to $106.8 billion in 1962 and to $1.4 trillion in 1993. For the rest of the 1990s all signs point to a budget that will reach $2 trillion by the year 2000 no matter what the president and Congress do. Even in terms of constant dollars (adjusting outlays for inflation), the trend has been relentlessly upward. As a result, the federal government consumes an ever-growing part of national resources in response to national needs and problems. In 1965 federal outlays represented 17.6 percent of GDP. By 1993 they hovered around 22.4 percent.

Unprecedented debt (over $4 trillion in 1993) and deficits, in particular, severely constrain the formulation of expenditure policy and limit budget options as never before. Congress and the president could remove their self-imposed shackles by a combination of tax increases and expenditure cuts. They have attempted this on several occasions.

Over a seventeen-year period from 1974 to 1990, legislators tried to rein in ever-increasing budgets. They approved the Congressional Budget Act of 1974; the Balanced Budget and Emergency Deficit Control Act of 1985 (the Gramm–Rudman–Hollings Act, also known as GRH); a sweeping amendment of GRH in 1987; and the Budget Enforcement Act of 1990 (BEA). Described in the chapter on legislative budgeting, these acts set automatic deficit and expenditure targets that were never met. Too little and too late, they were, at best, marginal attempts by the president and Congress to contain expenditures and raise revenues. In the face of the large-scale tax cuts and defense buildup in the 1980s, the virtual

TABLE 7.1

Outlays for major spending categories, fiscal years 1962–1993
(in billions of dollars)

	Discretionary spending	Entitlements and other mandatory spending	Deposit insurance	Net interest	Offsetting receipts	Total outlays
1962	74.9	32.3	−0.4	6.9	−6.8	106.8
1963	78.3	33.6	−0.4	7.7	−7.9	111.3
1964	82.8	35.7	−0.4	8.2	−7.7	118.5
1965	81.8	36.1	−0.4	8.6	−7.9	118.2
1966	94.1	39.9	−0.5	9.4	−8.4	134.5
1967	110.4	47.4	−0.4	10.3	−10.2	157.5
1968	122.1	56.1	−0.5	11.1	−10.6	178.1
1969	121.4	61.2	−0.7	12.7	−11.0	183.6
1970	124.6	68.7	−0.5	14.4	−11.5	195.6
1971	127.1	82.7	−0.4	14.8	−14.1	210.2
1972	133.1	96.8	−0.6	15.5	−14.1	230.7
1973	135.0	112.2	−0.8	17.3	−18.0	245.7
1974	142.5	127.1	−0.6	21.4	−21.2	269.4
1975	162.5	164.4	0.5	23.2	−18.3	323.3
1976	175.6	189.7	−0.6	26.7	−19.6	371.8
1977	197.1	206.6	−2.8	29.9	−21.5	409.2
1978	218.7	228.4	−1.0	35.5	−22.8	458.7
1979	240.0	248.2	−1.7	42.6	−25.6	503.5
1980	276.5	291.5	−0.4	52.5	−29.2	590.9
1981	308.2	340.6	−1.4	68.8	−37.9	678.2
1982	326.2	372.7	−2.2	85.0	−36.0	745.8
1983	353.4	411.6	−1.2	89.8	−45.3	808.4
1984	379.6	406.3	−0.9	111.1	−44.2	851.8
1985	416.2	450.0	−2.2	129.5	−47.1	946.4
1986	439.0	459.7	1.5	136.0	−45.9	990.3
1987	444.9	470.2	3.1	138.7	−53.0	1,003.9
1988	465.1	494.2	10.0	151.8	−57.0	1,064.1
1989	489.7	526.2	22.0	169.3	−63.9	1,143.2
1990	501.7	567.4	58.1	184.2	−58.8	1,252.7
1991	534.8	634.2	66.3	194.5	−106.0	1,323.8
1992	536.0	711.7	2.8	198.9	−67.1	1,380.9
1993	543.4	760.9	−28.0	198.9	−67.1	1,408.1

Source: Congressional Budget Office, *The Economic and Budget Outlook: Fiscal Years 1995–1999* (Washington, D.C., 1994), p. 92.

uncontrollability of entitlement programs, and a string of recessions, they had a negligible effect on steadily mounting deficits.

The presidential campaign of 1992 centered largely on the economy and the deficit. In 1993 the president and Congress, on a partisan basis, approved still another tax and expenditure package designed to reduce the deficit by $500 billion in five years. They capped discretionary expenditures; shaved expenditures for entitlement programs that were hitherto sacrosanct, especially social security, Medicare and Medicaid; imposed a broad-based energy tax; and raised taxes for affluent families and individuals. Whether the new target will be met is conjectural, given continued schisms on expenditure and revenue policy. Whether it should be met in view of its impact on a still-faltering economy remains a controversial issue.

Relatively Uncontrollable Expenditures. So large are mandatory expenditures that the range of discretion in budget decision making is severely constricted. From 1970 to 1981, the percentage of outlays labeled relatively uncontrollable by OMB jumped from 63 percent to 76.6 percent of all expenditures. In 1990 it reached 78.4 percent.[12] In order of magnitude, the major uncontrollable expenditures are for social security, interest on the national debt, Medicare, pensions, public assistance, the bailout of savings and loan institutions, farm price supports, contractual obligations, and unemployment compensation. In his last budget in January 1993, President Bush warned that "mandatory programs are taking over the budget."[13]

Discretionary Spending for Defense and Domestic Programs. Unlike mandatory programs, whose spending is driven by legislation, discretionary programs are funded directly by annual appropriation bills. This gives policymakers an opportunity to determine for at least one-fourth of the budget how far they want to go in continuing and supporting current activities and starting new ventures. Since the approval of the Budget Enforcement Act of 1990, discretionary programs have been divided into three categories—defense, international, and domestic—with an annual expenditure cap set for each category. In 1993 defense spending accounted for more than half of discretionary expenditures, although it was on a controversial downward path and likely to bear the brunt of future budget cuts. Discretionary domestic spending covers activities not encompassed by mandatory programs and is dwarfed by the latter. It represents only one-fourth of total domestic spending. International discretionary spending is fairly small, about $21 billion in 1993, and funds activities of the state department as well as international security, humanitarian, and financial programs. Much of the ongoing conflict over the budget will continue to focus on discretionary programs, with only marginal tinkering with mandatory programs.

Putting it all together, Table 7.2 highlights the role of discretionary and mandatory (i.e., uncontrollable) expenditures from 1994 to 2004 as estimated by the Congressional Budget Office, with the assumption that policies in effect in early 1993 would be continued.

TABLE 7.2

The budget outlook through 2004 (by fiscal year, in billions of dollars)

	1994	1995	1996	1997	1998	1999	2000	2001	2002	2003	2004
Revenues	1,251	1,338	1,411	1,479	1,556	1,630	1,706	1,783	1,868	1,958	2,054
Outlays											
Discretionary	543	541	547	547	547	564	582	600	619	638	658
Mandatory											
Social Security	318	335	352	370	388	408	429	450	473	497	523
Medicare	160	177	195	215	238	264	290	320	354	392	435
Medicaid	86	96	108	121	135	151	168	186	206	227	250
Civil Service and Military Retirement	62	65	67	70	73	78	81	85	89	92	96
Other	177	171	168	184	191	199	205	211	218	225	232
Subtotal	803	844	890	960	1,026	1,099	1,173	1,253	1,339	1,433	1,536
Deposit insurance	−5	−11	−14	−6	−4	−4	−3	−3	−2	−2	−2
Net interest	201	212	228	239	249	261	270	283	298	315	334
Offsetting receipts	−69	−77	−74	−78	−83	−86	−90	−94	−98	−102	−106
Total	1,474	1,509	1,577	1,661	1,736	1,834	1,931	2,039	2,156	2,282	2,419
Deficit	223	171	166	182	180	204	226	256	288	324	365

Source: Congressional Budget Office, *The Economic and Budget Outlook: Fiscal Years 1995–1999* (Washington, D.C., 1994), p. 29.

Note: Because of various technical distinctions and classifications, the table does not show a one-third/two-thirds split between discretionary and mandatory programs; the ratio, however, is still valid. Adding other major items brings uncontrollable expenditures to about 75 percent.

Inflation's Effect on Expenditures. Before the 1980s, inflation was largely responsible for automatic increases in federal expenditures. In the 1970s about half of budgetary increases were due to the effects of inflation on indexed programs and the purchase of supplies and services.[14] About 30 percent of all federal spending is indexed to cost-of-living adjustments, with social security the largest single factor.[15] With the onset of the 1991 recession inflation dropped precipitously, reaching an annual rate of less than 3 percent during 1993. This led to a significant decline in several categories of federal expenditures.

That Curious Hybrid: Tax Expenditures. Congress and the administration sometimes prefer to give tax breaks rather than grants and subsidies to favored individuals and groups in society. This has the effect of keeping expenditures down while still benefiting the recipients of governmental largesse. In budgetary accounting the tax advantages are counted as revenue losses and not as outlays. This curious hybrid, which is a cross between a tax benefit and an expenditure, is labeled "tax expenditures" and is defined in the Congressional Budget Act of 1974 as "revenue losses attributable to provisions of the federal tax laws which allow a special exclusion, exemption or deduction from gross income or which provide a special credit, a preferential rate of tax, or a deferral of liability."

Among the more important tax expenditures up to the end of 1992 were deductibility of mortgage interest on owner-occupied homes, deductibility of state and local income and property taxes, deductibility of charitable contributions, job credits, contributions for health insurance, pension contributions, accelerated depreciation, exclusion of interest on state and local tax-exempt bonds, and exclusion of costs of research and development on oil and gas exploration. The cost of tax expenditures is high; it resulted in an estimated revenue loss of nearly $400 billion in 1993.[16]

Shaping Tax Policy in the Federal Government

In absolute, relative, and per capita terms the federal government outtaxes all other governments in the United States, just as it outspends them. Of the total national tax yield in 1993, the federal government collected 62.5 percent, leaving state and local governments with 37.5 percent.

Personal and corporate income taxes generate the most revenue in the United States. In this area the federal government is virtually supreme, absorbing slightly over four-fifths of all personal income taxes (the biggest money-makers) and corporate income taxes. State and local government, however, collect most of the sales and gross receipts taxes and property taxes.

All taxes, including social insurance taxes, consumed an estimated 29.3 percent of GDP in 1993. The federal share was 18.3 percent, with state and local governments accounting for 11.0 percent.[17]

Who Pays the Taxes? In FY 1993 the federal government collected $1.2 trillion in taxes. Of this amount, personal income taxes accounted for 44.2 percent; social insurance taxes, 37.1 percent; corporation income taxes, 10.2 percent; excise taxes, 4.4 percent; and all other taxes (estate and gift taxes, customs duties, and miscellaneous receipts), 4.3 percent. As Table 7.3 shows, personal income taxes didn't become a significant factor in revenue collections until 1945, at the climax of World War II, when they sharply overshadowed social insurance taxes. Thereafter, they ranged from 39.5 percent to 48.2 percent of all taxes. In recent years they hovered around 45 percent.

The most striking shifts have occurred in corporation income taxes and social insurance taxes and contributions (payroll taxes for social security, unemployment insurance, Medicare, and retirement contributions). After reaching a high of 35.4 percent of all taxes in 1945, corporation income taxes steadily declined to a low of 6.2 percent in 1983, reflecting the 1981 tax breaks of the Reagan administration. The rationale for cuts in corporation taxes was the assumption that they would lead to more investment in plants and equipment and in capital formation generally. By 1992 corporation taxes accounted for about 9 percent of all revenue. What the federal government lost in corporation taxes it more than made up in social insurance taxes and contributions. From a relatively insignificant percent of

TABLE 7.3

Percentage composition of federal receipts by source
Selected years, 1940–1993

Year	Total	Personal income taxes	Corporation income taxes	Social insurance taxes and contributions	Excise taxes	Other
1940	100.0	13.6	18.3	27.3	30.2	10.7
1945	100.0	40.7	35.4	7.6	13.9	2.4
1950	100.0	39.9	26.5	11.0	19.1	3.4
1955	100.0	43.9	27.3	12.0	14.0	2.8
1960	100.0	44.0	23.2	15.9	12.6	4.2
1965	100.0	41.8	21.8	19.0	12.5	4.9
1970	100.0	46.9	17.0	23.0	8.1	4.9
1975	100.0	43.9	14.6	30.3	5.9	4.1
1980	100.0	47.2	12.5	30.5	4.7	5.1
1990	100.0	45.3	9.1	36.9	4.3	5.4
1991	100.0	44.4	9.3	37.8	4.0	4.7
1992	100.0	43.6	9.2	37.9	4.2	5.1
1993	100.0	44.2	10.2	37.1	4.4	4.3

Source: Executive Office of the President, Office of Management and Budget, *Budget of the United States Government, Historical Tables, Fiscal Year 1995* (Washington, D.C., 1994), pp. 23–24.

total taxes in 1945, social insurance taxes climbed to 36.1 percent in 1985 and about 38 percent in 1992. Personal income taxes and social insurance taxes affect individuals most directly. From 1990 to 1993 they accounted for approximately four-fifths of all taxes.

Evaluating the Federal Tax System. The tax structure of the United States government is the product of tax policies that evolved over the years in response to wars, the state of the economy, the Great Depression and recessions, the growth of the welfare state, the clash of interest groups seeking tax privileges, shifting fiscal and economic policies, and the ideological preferences of administrations and dominant legislative groups. Raising enough revenue to finance the budget is of course a chief concern of taxation. It is by no means, however, its sole purpose. Tax policy has also become an instrument for achieving economic and social goals. As part of its arsenal of economic tools, the federal government has used tax policy in attempts to combat recessions, control inflation, encourage savings, stimulate investment in plants and equipment, subsidize selected industries, relieve economic hardships, foster or discourage consumption, and redistribute income. The main vehicles used to further these ends have been changes in personal and corporate income taxes and social insurance contributions.

Ultimately, economic and noneconomic value judgments mold the tax system. Considering these assorted pressures, what are the criteria for evaluating the complex tax structure? If any consensus exists, it's that the tax system should be fair, efficient, and simple. These terms, however, are general and abstract. What appears fair to one group may be regarded as discriminatory by another. For many, issues of fairness and equity turn on the ability to pay. In this view, households with greater resources should pay more taxes and low-income households should pay fewer or no taxes. As incomes rise, taxes as a percent of income should also rise. Conversely, as incomes fall, taxes as a percent of income should also fall. Taxes meeting these criteria are termed "progressive." Their chief characteristics are stepped-up tax brackets, which in 1986, for the personal income tax, ranged from 11 percent to 50 percent. (In prior years the top rates had been 90 percent and 70 percent.) In 1987, the top marginal tax rate dropped to 31 percent, after major changes in the tax laws in 1986.

Taxes that bear little or no relation to ability to pay, such as sales, excise, payroll, and property taxes, are labeled "regressive." Regardless of income, everyone pays the same tax rate. This means that as incomes rise, the tax burden becomes a smaller percentage of income. It constitutes a higher percentage for low-income groups unless it is offset by tax credits and tax exemptions.

Tax equity also comes in at least two other forms: horizontal equity and vertical equity. A tax is horizontally equitable if individuals in similar economic circumstances pay the same taxes. Equal ability to pay should result in similar tax burdens. A tax is vertically equitable if the tax treatment of individuals in different income classes is proportionate. Each class of taxpayers pays taxes that remain at a consistent ratio to income in relation to income groups below it and above it. Still another aspect of equity is the relationship of taxes to the benefits received. The increasing acceptance of the view that some taxes and fees should reflect the benefits received accounts for the sharp increase of fees and charges in recent decades (e.g., bridge tolls, airport fees, and a variety of taxes at all governmental levels).

The efficiency criterion centers on the role of taxes in providing incentives to work, stimulating investment, and encouraging saving. Those who favor efficient taxes argue that taxes should not affect economic behavior. What individuals and corporations do should not be based on tax advantages, but on the perceived economic advantages of their decisions. For example, individuals should not invest in corporations, real estate, bonds, or other securities because of tax breaks, but because of the intrinsic merit of the investment. An efficient tax results in a better allocation of resources and does not distort economic decisions because of tax considerations, according to advocates of "economic efficiency." Whether tax policy results or even should result in behavioral neutrality remains a moot question.

Another concern is the relative simplicity and ease of administration of the tax system. The preferred system is one that is simple, understandable, predictable, and economical, with a high rate of compliance.

Ladd cautions us that it is not enough to label an individual tax "progressive" or "regressive." The burden of the entire tax system should be evaluated. Despite regressive taxes, the overall system can still be progressive because of the effect of other taxes. Conversely, a progressive income tax may not be sufficient to offset the regressive nature of sales, excise, payroll, and property taxes.[18]

Critiquing the Tax System. On the basis of these and other criteria, the taxpayers over the years have given low ratings to the overall system, with most dissatisfaction directed at income and property taxes.[19] The charges leveled against the federal tax system, particularly the personal income tax, run along these lines:

1. *The progressivity of the tax system has eroded.* The decline in the relative importance of the corporation income tax, the sharp rise in payroll taxes, and low marginal tax rates for affluent taxpayers have eroded the progressivity of the tax system. Between 1981 and 1990 the tax code gyrated more than in any other comparable period in recent U.S. history. Six major tax bills transformed the tax system: (1) the Economic Recovery Act of 1981 (ERTA), which led to massive tax cuts; (2) the Tax Equity and Fiscal Responsibility Act of 1982 (TEFRA), which sought to recoup some of the revenue lost by ERTA; (3) the Deficit Reduction Act of 1984 (DEFRA), which raised still more taxes to whittle down the deficit; (4) the Tax Reform Act of 1986 (TRA), which eliminated many tax loopholes for individuals and corporations, but lowered their top tax rates; (5) the Omnibus Budget Reconciliation Act of 1990 (OBRA), which, under the shadow of the deficit, boosted taxes again and cut expenditures; and (6) the Social Security Amendments of 1983, which raised payroll taxes and subjected 50 percent of social security benefits to the personal income tax. With the advent of the Clinton

administration in 1993, still further changes took place to cut the deficit and shift more of the tax burden to wealthier taxpayers and more affluent retirees.

At the end of twelve tumultuous years, the total federal effective tax rate (ETR) in 1991 (the percent of family income paid in federal taxes) was almost the same as it was in 1979: 23 percent. This average figure, however, masks a marked change in the distribution of taxes. The highest income group enjoyed a tax cut of about 5 percent. Other income groups experienced only negligible changes in their ETR. The overall tax system became less progressive as regressive payroll taxes overshadowed somewhat progressive income taxes.[20] Various studies stressed that the top 1 percent of taxpayers reaped most of the gains in income while low- and middle-income groups achieved only small gains or actually found that their income after taxes had declined.[21]

2. *The tax system is unfair and inequitable.* Because of available tax shelters, people with equal income do not necessarily pay equal taxes. Although the Tax Reform Act of 1986 closed some of the loopholes, the federal treasury continues to lose at least $400 billion a year because of tax exemptions, exclusions, abatements, and credits.

3. *The existing tax system does not produce enough revenue.* The federal tax system has not recovered from the largest tax cuts in history, in 1982. These cuts resulted in a loss of at least $1 trillion in revenue during the next eleven years.[22] Coupled with the defense buildup, the spiraling costs of entitlement programs, and the economic setbacks of recessions, the cuts triggered the largest deficits and debt in American history. Subsequent tax changes did little to stem the loss of revenue. Complicating the dilemma of policymakers, tax increases became politically dangerous in an era of tax revolts. Nor were taxpayers assuaged by the fact that combined federal, state, and local taxes in the United States represented the lowest share of GDP of the top twenty-three industrialized nations except Turkey.[23]

4. *The tax system is inefficient and motivates economic decisions.* Individual and corporate income taxes and the large number of tax preferences affect economic decisions by taxpayers. How they spend, invest, and save their money is determined as much by the tax effect as the economic advantages.[24] For example, the tax deductibility of interest encouraged private debt and the leveraged buyout of firms in the 1980s.

5. *Inflation increases taxes while it erodes real income.* Inflation increases taxes and decreases the real income of taxpayers in several respects. For example, taxes on capital gains and interest don't take into account the decreased value of the income because of inflation. On the other hand, debtors benefit from inflation because they repay their debt in cheaper dollars.

6. *The tax system penalizes savings.* Under specified conditions, earnings on savings such as pension and retirement funds, IRAs (individual retirement accounts), and tax-deferred annuities of various kinds are exempt from taxes. The income from other savings is fully taxable. Consequently, individuals who save the same amount of money may be taxed at different rates depending on the nature of their savings.[25]

7. *The corporation income tax is inequitable.* Two issues are involved: the level of corporate taxation and the charge of double taxation. First, critics assert that the tax law has shifted the tax burden from corporations to individuals. Hence, corporations don't pay their fair share. Second, the existing system, in effect, taxes corporate income twice; the corporations pay a tax on their profits and investors pay a tax on dividends received from corporations. Businesses, of course, have the option of shifting the corporate income tax, and, for that matter, any other business tax, to customers and consumers, thus raising prices. This move depends on market conditions. In a stagnant economy, owners, investors, and employees may absorb the tax burden. At best, the true burden of a tax on business is a "guesstimate."

8. *Taxes are still too high and reduce incentives to work, save, and invest.* This is still the central theme of supply-side economists and was strongly supported by the Reagan and Bush administrations. The Clinton administration found taxes too high for low- and middle-income taxpayers and too low for upper-income taxpayers.

9. *The tax code is so complex that many taxpayers can't understand it.* So complex is the income tax system that nearly half of all taxpayers require professional help to prepare their tax returns, and the rest spend a substantial amount of time on the annual tax exercise. This complexity leads to noncompliance and evasion of the tax code, with annual estimated revenue losses running over $100 billion.

Options for Tax Reform. This general critique of the tax system is but a bare bone summary of perceived defects in a tax code running into hundreds of pages, but it touches on the major problems. For virtually every problem, legislators, national administrations, economists, and interest groups have been quick to offer solutions. From 1964 to 1981 the federal government responded by cutting marginal tax rates; providing tax benefits to low-income groups; liberalizing depreciation allowances and investment tax credits; lowering taxes on capital gains for business; and effecting the unprecedented tax cuts of 1982 (for example, reducing the top rate from 70 to 50 percent, adjusting income tax brackets for inflation, and encouraging savings through IRAs and other financial investments). As far-reaching as some of these measures were, they still fell short of resolving the major tax problems. If anything, the 1982 tax cuts weakened the revenue structure and increased deficits and debt.

In a rare moment of consensus, Congress and the president eliminated some of the tax inequities by overhauling the tax structure completely in the Tax Reform Act of 1986 (TRA), the most sweeping changes in the tax law since the imposition of withholding taxes in World War II. The chief elements in the tax package were the elimination of most exclusions, deductions, and special benefits; sharp reduction in the number of tax brackets and a maximum ceiling of 31 percent on the income tax rate; some adjustment of taxable income for inflation; special tax benefits for the poor, the aged, and the blind; cuts in the top corporate tax rate to 34 percent; elimination, in whole or in part, of investment tax credits for business and less favorable depreciation allowances; treatment of capital gains like ordinary income; elimination of the tax deductibility of sales taxes; restrictions on the eligibility of municipal bonds for tax exemption of interest.

TRA was intended to be revenue neutral in the sense that it would produce the same amount of revenue as in previous years,[26] but it didn't go far enough. It perpetuated many of the inequities of the previous tax system and failed to cope with the growing deficit.

At the beginning of 1993 the new Clinton administration and Congress considered dozens of options for increasing federal revenue and overcoming long-standing defects in the tax code. Some would raise revenue from existing taxes by increasing tax rates, broadening the tax base, or extending the tax net to cover additional taxpayers. Some would tap new tax sources altogether, for example, consumption taxes and energy taxes. Still others would raise a variety of fees.

The following options commanded most attention:

1. *Raise additional revenue by restoring the progressivity of the personal income tax.* The Clinton administration proposed increasing the top tax rate from 31 percent to 36 percent for affluent couples with taxable incomes of $140,000 or more and individuals with taxable incomes of $115,000 or more. For those with incomes over $250,000 it proposed a surcharge of 10 percent, in effect raising the top rate to 39.6 percent. At the other end of the income scale, families with incomes below $20,000 would receive grants and credits to reduce or eliminate their taxes. All these measures were enacted in 1993.

2. *Impose a broad tax on all forms of energy to increase revenue still more and to promote conservation of resources.* The complex tax would be based on the energy content of gasoline, heating oil, natural gas, coal, electricity, hydroelectric power, and so on as measured in British thermal units (BTUs). From the start, this plan was doomed as much by its complexity as by the protests of industrial firms and regional interests that claimed they would be adversely affected. Instead, a modest increase of the transportation fuel tax of 4.3 cents per gallon proved to be more politically viable. Neither the president nor Congress advanced the proposal of Ross Perot during the presidential campaign to raise gasoline taxes by 50 cents per gallon over a five-year period, which would still leave them far below gasoline taxes in Europe.[27]

3. *Raise business taxes to compensate for the sharp decline in corporate income tax revenues, without injuring small businesses.* Under this plan the top corporate rate would climb from 34 percent to 36 percent. At the same time tax deductions for business meals, entertainment, lobbying, and club dues would be curbed. For small businesses, the administration floated such proposals as investment tax credits (many of which had been eliminated in 1986), a reduction in capital gains taxes, and tax breaks for investing in run-down urban areas.[28] Most of these were adopted.

4. *Initiate a national sales tax, or VAT (value added tax).* For years this has proved to be seductive, because of the vast amount of money it would raise, but politi-

cally dangerous. Though similar to a sales tax, VAT is collected differently. Instead of taxing the consumer at the retail level, the government imposes a tax at each stage of production and marketing on the value added to the product or service. Essentially, a company pays a sales tax on the difference between the raw materials and services it buys and the value of the finished product.[29] As Lester C. Thurow points out, a 14 percent VAT would raise enough money to replace the corporate income and payroll taxes. Alternatively, the revenue could be used to reduce the deficit and pay for the larger part of health care. In Western Europe 15 to 25 percent VATs are common.[30]

VAT comes under two attacks. First, like the sales tax, it is regressive. Second, it would drain the sales tax, a major source of revenue for state and local governments. The first problem can be overcome to a large extent by exemption of food and drugs and other items from VAT, and by income tax credits and exemptions for the poor. The second problem invites a political confrontation between the federal government on one hand and state and local governments on the other. Nearly all state policymakers are opposed to a federal retail sales tax, or a VAT, which would intrude on their ability to increase revenue generated by state retail taxes. Conservatives also fear that the largesse produced by VAT would increase government spending and fuel another round of inflation.[31]

5. *Tax consumption instead of income to encourage saving and investment.* Long favored by many economists, this is an idea whose time may never come. Under this concept the consumption tax would replace the income tax. Income would represent any source of funds: money earned, borrowed, or withdrawn from savings. Any money saved or invested would be deducted from the income. What's left would represent funds used for consumption and these would be taxed at progressive rates to penalize the high livers and favor the savers. Alice Rivlin, deputy director of OMB, sounded the epitaph on the consumption tax: While it has "great appeal," the "complexity and disruption" of changing existing tax systems is not worth the effort.[32]

6. *Adjust the capital gains tax.* After a profitable sale of an asset—a house, a stock, a bond, or a Stradivarius violin—the seller pays a tax on the capital gain that represents the difference between the purchase price and the selling price. How large should that tax be? Those who favor freeing old money for new investments regard capital gains as a stimulus to the economy and prefer to treat them tenderly. Until 1986 the top tax rate was 20 percent. Assuming an investor made a $10,000 profit, the tax was $2,000. The Tax Reform Act of 1986 made the tax rate the same as for ordinary income: 28 to 31 percent (33 percent under some circumstances). This was anathema to the Bush administration and supply-side economists, who claimed a lower tax rate would raise revenue because of more frequent sales of assets and would stimulate the economy. Economic studies are inconclusive on this score.[33] In 1993 Congress and the president agreed to keep the top capital gains tax rate at 28 percent.

Apart from rates, two other problems bedevil tax policy on capital gains. By passing on assets to their heirs after death, investors avoid a capital gains tax altogether.

The new base price of the asset is its value on the date of the inheritance. Any future capital gains are based on that price. An especially questionable feature of the capital gains tax is that it taxes both real gains and inflationary gains. Assume a collector bought a painting for $1,000 and some years later sold it for $5,000. The nominal gain of $4,000 would be taxed, but if inflation had increased 50 percent during that period the real gain would be $2,000. That is the amount that should be taxed according to those who favor indexing capital gains to inflation.

Still another way to make the capital gains tax more equitable is to provide incentives for long-term investments and penalize short-term speculation. This is the practice in Japan, where businesses have access to stable long-term capital commitments.

7. *Wipe out additional tax loopholes.* The Tax Reform Act of 1986 left the tax law still strewn with loopholes. Close some of the loopholes and some alluring revenue possibilities surface. It would be relatively easy to compile a list of "tax expenditures" of at least $300 billion, which could be used wipe out annual deficits and offset payments of interest on debt. In each case, however, the tax breaks or subsidies are intended to further social and economic policies or to protect favored groups. The supporters of these policies naturally stand ready to resist the onslaughts of budget balancers.

8. *Increase fees.* The fastest-growing source of revenue is user fees, charges, and special excise taxes. This is especially true at state and local levels, but the federal government is also adept in such forms of "revenue enhancement." The Highway and Airport Trust funds collect about $23 billion annually, primarily for highway, bridge, and airport construction. Customs duties and fees amount to about $17 billion and miscellaneous receipts covering a wide range of services bring in over $21 billion. As the federal government casts about for additional revenue, fees and charges loom large in every revenue package. For example, President Bush's last budget, of January 1993, proposed about $15 billion in additional fees over a five-year period. President Clinton's budget for the same period raised the ante to $25.8 billion.[34]

9. *Tax senior citizens.* The relative affluence of senior citizens has not escaped the attention of revenue seekers. At one time social security benefits were tax free. In 1983 half the benefits of retired couples earning over $32,000 were taxed. In the Clinton tax plan of 1993 the rate went up to 85 percent, designed to raise $32 billion in revenue over five years. Medicare benefits, which amount to about $10 billion annually, still remain a target for taxation despite a successful revolt by senior citizens against such levies in 1990. To highlight the disparity of income and wealth among different generations, the last Bush budget included a "generational accounts presentation." It contained the somber warning that "future generations are estimated to pay 79 percent more in taxes, net of social security and other benefits they receive, than the generation of people just born."[35] This was the rationale for taxing retired individuals with moderate or higher incomes and cutting the costs of programs designed for them.

These, then, are some of the major issues that surface in developing tax policy.

Of Deficits, Debt, and Balanced Budgets

The interplay of tax and expenditure policies has led to the largest deficit and debt in American history. By any measures, they are unprecedented in size and scope. Consequently, since the early 1980s fiscal policy centering on deficits and debt has become an overriding issue that influences nearly all decision making in Washington, D.C.

Deficits as such are neither new nor startling. In fact, they have been chronic since the Great Depression. In the sixty years from FY 1932 to FY 1992 the federal government ended fifty-two of those years with a deficit. A glance at Table 7.4 shows the string of deficits from 1962 to 1992, unbroken except for 1969, when the federal government sported a rare surplus of $3.2 billion. Compared with modern megadeficits, the deficits in the two decades after World War II were small and negligible. In the 1970s, in the wake of recessions, oil boycotts, and oil price shocks, they began to grow. By the 1980s annual deficits passed the $100 billion mark for the first time, and in 1991 and 1992 reached new highs of $269.5 billion and $290.2 billion, respectively. The triggering factors were tax cuts, an explosive growth in defense and entitlement programs, periodic recessions, and stagnant growth.

To fund these deficits the president and Congress went on an unparalleled borrowing spree. At first the debt grew slowly from 1940 to 1974. As Table 7.5 shows, it did not vault over the $500 billion barrier until 1975. By 1992 it had increased nearly eightfold, to over $4.3 trillion.

The debt and deficits were so large by historical standards that they dominated policymaking and budgeting during the 1980s and the first half of the 1990s. Especially distressing to those concerned about the size of the deficits was the fact that unbalanced budgets and mounting debt persisted in both bad and good times. While a case could be made for deficit financing to spur a recession-ridden and stagnant economy, it became difficult to justify deficits in periods of economic growth. In the early 1990s interest on the debt represented nearly 15 percent of the annual federal budget. This alone nipped new programs and policies in the bud. The critical question was not so much "Do we need it?" as "Can we afford it?"

What's Bad or Good About Deficits Anyway? To many economists, politicians, and policymakers and the public at large, the seemingly uncontrolled deficits and debt signify a government without fiscal discipline and an economy in jeopardy. By no means, however, do all economists and budgeteers agree on the effects of deficits—good and bad. There are so many conflicting claims and counterclaims that it is increasingly difficult to hammer out a consensus on fiscal policy. These are the major fears of those troubled by the explosion of deficits and debt:

1. *"Crowding out" the private sector.* The omnivorous demands of the public sector for borrowed funds crowd out the private sector from credit markets and thus limit the amount of funds available to the private sector for investment and capital formation. Personal savings are low to begin with, having dropped from an

TABLE 7.4

Revenues, outlays, and deficits, fiscal years 1962–1993
(in billions of dollars and as percent of GDP)

| | | | Deficit (−)/ | Percent of GDP | |
	Revenues	Outlays	Surplus	Revenues	Outlays
1962	99.7	106.8	−7.1	18.0	19.3
1963	106.6	111.3	−4.8	18.2	19.0
1964	112.6	118.5	−5.9	18.0	18.9
1965	116.8	118.2	−1.4	17.4	17.6
1966	130.8	134.5	−3.7	17.7	18.2
1967	148.8	157.5	−9.6	18.8	19.9
1968	153.0	178.1	−25.2	18.0	21.0
1969	186.9	183.6	3.2	20.2	19.8
1970	192.8	195.6	−2.8	19.6	19.9
1971	187.1	210.2	−23.0	17.8	20.0
1972	207.3	230.7	−23.4	18.1	20.1
1973	230.8	245.7	−14.9	18.1	19.2
1974	263.2	269.4	−6.1	18.8	19.2
1975	279.1	332.3	−53.2	18.5	22.0
1976	298.1	371.8	−73.7	17.7	22.1
1977	355.6	409.2	−53.7	18.5	21.3
1978	399.6	458.7	−59.2	18.5	21.3
1979	463.3	503.5	−40.2	19.1	20.7
1980	517.1	590.9	−73.8	19.6	22.3
1981	599.3	678.2	−79.0	20.2	22.9
1982	617.8	745.8	−128.0	19.8	23.9
1983	600.6	808.4	−207.8	18.1	24.4
1984	666.5	851.8	−185.4	18.0	23.0
1985	734.1	946.4	−212.3	18.5	23.8
1986	769.1	990.3	−221.2	18.2	23.5
1987	854.1	1,003.9	−149.8	19.2	22.5
1988	909.0	1,064.1	−155.2	18.9	22.1
1989	990.7	1,143.2	−152.5	19.2	22.1
1990	1,031.3	1,252.7	−221.4	18.9	22.9
1991	1,054.3	1,323.8	−269.5	18.6	23.3
1992	1,090.5	1,380.9	−290.4	18.4	23.2
1993	1,153.5	1,408.2	−254.7	18.3	22.4

Sources: OMB, Budget of the United States Government, Historical Tables, Fiscal Year 1995 (Washington, D.C., 1994), p. 17; Congressional Budget Office, The Economic and Budget Outlook: Fiscal Years 1995–1999 (Washington, D.C., 1994), p. 89.

Note: In 1991 the federal government shifted from GNP to GDP to conform to European and Japanese practices. GDP measures the production of goods and services in a country, excluding income paid or obtained from overseas. GNP includes income that residents receive from abroad, but deducts payment made overseas (see Glossary).

TABLE 7.5

Federal debt (by fiscal year, in billions of dollars)

	Debt held by the public	Debt held by government accounts*	Total gross debt	Debt subject to statutory limit	Debt held by the public as a percentage of GDP
1940	42.8	7.9	50.7	43.2	44.8
1941	48.2	9.3	57.5	49.5	42.9
1942	67.8	11.4	79.2	74.2	47.8
1943	127.8	14.9	142.6	140.5	72.8
1944	184.8	19.3	204.1	208.1	91.6
1945	235.2	24.9	260.1	268.7	110.9
1946	241.9	29.1	271.0	268.9	113.8
1947	224.3	32.8	257.1	255.8	100.6
1948	216.3	35.8	252.0	250.4	87.7
1949	214.3	38.3	252.6	251.0	81.6
1950	219.0	37.8	256.9	255.4	82.4
1951	214.3	41.0	255.3	253.3	68.4
1952	214.8	44.3	259.1	257.2	63.1
1953	218.4	47.6	266.0	264.2	60.0
1954	224.5	46.3	270.8	269.4	61.0
1955	226.6	47.8	274.4	272.3	58.9
1956	222.2	50.5	272.7	270.6	53.4
1957	219.3	52.9	272.3	269.1	50.0
1958	226.3	53.3	279.7	275.4	50.5
1959	234.7	52.8	287.5	282.4	48.9
1960	236.8	53.7	290.5	283.8	46.9
1961	238.4	54.3	292.6	286.3	46.1
1962	248.0	54.9	302.9	295.4	44.7
1963	254.0	56.3	310.3	302.9	43.5
1964	256.8	59.2	316.1	308.6	41.1
1965	260.8	61.5	322.3	314.1	38.9
1966	263.7	64.8	328.5	316.3	35.9
1967	266.6	73.8	340.4	323.1	33.6
1968	289.5	79.1	368.7	348.5	34.2
1969	278.1	87.7	365.8	356.1	30.0
1970	283.2	97.7	380.9	372.6	28.7
1971	303.0	105.1	408.2	398.7	28.8
1972	322.4	113.6	435.9	427.8	28.1
1973	340.9	125.4	466.3	458.3	26.8
1974	343.7	140.2	483.9	475.2	24.5
1975	394.7	147.2	541.9	534.2	26.1
1976	477.4	151.6	629.0	621.6	28.3
TQ	495.5	148.1	643.6	635.8	27.8
1977	549.1	157.3	706.4	700.0	28.6
1978	607.1	169.5	776.6	772.7	28.2
1979	639.8	189.2	828.9	827.6	26.3
1980	709.3	199.2	908.5	908.7	26.8

(continued)

TABLE 7.5 *(continued)*

Federal debt (by fiscal year, in billions of dollars)

	Debt held by the public	Debt held by government accounts*	Total gross debt	Debt subject to statutory limit	Debt held by the public as a percentage of GDP
1981	784.8	209.5	994.3	998.8	26.5
1982	919.2	217.6	1,136.8	1,142.9	29.4
1983	1,131.0	240.1	1,371.2	1,378.0	34.1
1984	1,300.0	264.2	1,564.1	1,573.0	35.2
1985	1,499.4	317.6	1,817.0	1,823.8	37.8
1986	1,736.2	383.9	2,120.1	2,111.0	41.2
1987	1,881.1	457.4	2,345.6	2,336.0	42.4
1988	2,050.3	550.5	2,600.8	2,586.9	42.6
1989	2,189.3	678.2	2,867.5	2,829.8	42.3
1990	2,410.4	796.0	3,206.3	3,161.2	44.1
1991	2,687.9	911.1	3,599.0	3,569.3	47.7
1992	2,998.6	1,004.0	4,002.7	3,972.6	51.1
1993	3,247.1	1,104.0	4,352.0	4,351.2	51.6

Sources: OMB, *Budget of the United States Government, Historical Tables, Fiscal Year 1995,* (Washington, D.C., 1994), p. 89; Congressional Budget Office, *Federal Debt and Interest Costs* (Washington, D.C., 1993); ————, *The Economic and Budget Outlook: 1995–1999,* p. 49.

* Treasury bonds, bills, and notes bought by trust funds such as the social security trust fund.

average of 8.2 percent of the net national product during the three decades preceding 1980 to an average of 2.6 percent from 1987 to 1989. Most of what's left is gobbled up by government borrowing. According to the Congressional Budget Office, increased savings and a reduction in the deficit equal to about 1 percent of GNP would increase living standards by the middle of the next century.[36]

2. *Raised interest and exchange rates.* Because of its extensive borrowing, the federal government drives up interest rates. This discourages investment and impedes economic growth. High interest rates increase the value of the dollar in relation to other currencies and thus hinder American exports, leading to trade deficits.[37]

3. *Intensified inflation.* The federal government follows three paths in financing deficits: (1) It borrows from the public, a practice leading to the "crowding out" phenomenon, (2) it borrows from federal trust funds, and (3) it relies on the Federal Reserve Board to buy part of its securities. The FRB pays for the securities by drawing on its own funds or "monetizing" the debt by printing money. These actions swell the money supply and may intensify inflation.[38]

4. *Foreign-held federal debt.* In 1992 foreigners held about $500 billion in federal debt, or about one-eighth of the total. Japan, the United Kingdom, and Germany were the chief creditors. An increasing share of the budget goes to service foreign debt. Some critics regard this as a loss of national patrimony.

5. *The debt is just the tip of the iceberg.* The federal government also faces trillions of dollars of unfunded liabilities, as in the case of social security benefits and implied guarantees of loans for housing, higher education, and agriculture.

6. *Limited budget options.* Large-scale borrowing results in allocating a larger portion of the budget to interest costs at the expense of operating programs and pressing needs. In a never-ending cycle, the built-in interest costs generate even more deficits.

There are analysts who take a less bleak view of deficits and debt. As they see it, deficits are neither good nor bad per se. At times they are essential, as in periods of recession. At times they are counterproductive, as in periods of high employment. In their view, it is far more important to manage deficits as a tool of fiscal policy than to bemoan their existence. This more benign outlook on deficits flows from the following considerations:

1. *Stimulation of the economy.* By cushioning the effect of a decline in economic activity, deficits serve to stimulate demand and eventually to revive the economy. In fact, deficit spending, coupled with lower interest rates, ended the recession of 1982–1983 and even more extensive spending might have terminated the recession of 1990–1993. No demonstrable economic damage results from deficits, at least in the United States. In fact, higher deficits in a stagnant economy may be the key to recovery and prosperity.[39]

2. *Unknown size of deficits.* We don't measure them correctly or account for them accurately. If we can't measure them, how can we know whether they're good or bad and what policies we should follow? The chief mistake is to measure deficits solely in terms of current, or nominal, dollars. If we take inflation into account, then the real value of the debt and deficits drops. In effect, the government is the winner and creditors, the losers. Second, the real debt is the market value of government securities, not the original value when they were issued. Third, budgetary practices unnecessarily inflate deficits. The federal government pays for highways, public buildings, telecommunications, and paper clips out of current appropriations. Were it to follow the policies of state and local governments by incorporating capital items in a capital budget and financing them by borrowing, it would be responsible solely for annual debt service. This would shave the amount of annual expenditures and decrease the deficit, but increase the overall debt.[40] Private corporations also follow this practice. The private sector allocates annual expenditures for capital facilities and equipment according to the life of the capital items. For a facility with a life of thirty years, the annual budget would show 1/30 of the cost.[41]

3. *Debt as a percentage of GDP.* Bald debt figures by themselves are not too revealing. What is significant is the ratio of the federal debt to GDP, which tells us whether we have the resources to sustain the debt. Using this criterion, the estimated debt of about $3.2 trillion held by the public in 1993 represented 51.6 percent of GDP. The gross debt was about $4.3 trillion, including the debt held by government trust funds. This ratio was higher than the ratios in effect during the thirty-four year period from 1957 to 1991, when percentages ranged from 29.5 percent (1974) to 50.5 percent (1958). Yet it was far lower than the ratios that prevailed after World War II, until 1956. In 1946, just after World War II, the percentage was 113.8, and there was no apparent alarm that the republic was sinking into bankruptcy.

4. *Look at the total public sector, not just the federal government.* While the federal government has been "in the red," state and local governments ran up surpluses (although decreasing ones) during much of the decade preceding 1990. If we combine federal, state, and local spending, as we should from an economic standpoint, then the net deficit would decline considerably. (The National Income Product Accounts, prepared by the federal government, does this routinely.)

5. *The doubtful relationship between deficits and economic performance.* From 1972 to 1981, Japan, Germany, and several other European countries had high deficits relative to the United States. Yet they had lower inflation, higher productivity, and steady economic growth. Whatever accounted for their performance, it did not appear to be affected by the size of the deficits or the growth of the public sector.[42] Some economists attribute the performance to a high national savings rate. While the United States had a deficit in 1992 that was one of the largest among industrialized countries, it had the capacity, because of its low taxes relative to GNP, to overcome it by raising taxes, according to the Organization for Economic Cooperation and Development.

The relationship between deficits and interest rates is also questionable. In the early 1990s the highest deficits in the United States were followed by historically low interest rates.

6. *Deficits are not a black hole into which funds sink irretrievably.* Creditors obviously benefit from deficits, because annual interest costs are income to them. Furthermore, deficits produce national assets such as roads, bridges, and waterways.

Options for Coping with Deficits. Few choices are as politically painful and marginally successful as options for cutting deficits. Among the alternatives advanced, three stand out:

1. A mix of expenditure cuts and revenue increases (the Congressional Budget Office in 1993 proposed 239 such policy changes).

2. Another five-year deficit reduction package such as the Clinton administration produced in 1993, following the deficit cuts mandated by the Gramm–Rudman–Hollings Act of 1985 and its later amendments and by the Budget Enforcement Act of 1990. All called for a phased reduction of the deficit.

3. A constitutional amendment requiring a balanced budget.

Even the most ardent advocates of deficit reduction do not favor cutbacks in one fell swoop. They fear that a sudden tightening of fiscal policy might jeopardize economic recovery. Furthermore, long-term policies that have produced the deficits over the years cannot be reversed by abrupt actions on revenues and expenditures in any one year. Hence, options for controlling deficits generally follow a multiyear strategy.

The one option that will not work is doing nothing on the assumption that economic growth will, in time, wipe out the deficits because of higher revenue and lower expenditures. Deficits are entrenched firmly in the budget structure because of uncontrollable costs and inadequate revenue; they will be chronic in good and bad times. Short of drastic changes in fiscal policy, as well as defense and domestic policy, deficits will not budge. Other proposed panaceas will not help much: neither expenditure freezes, nor automatic cuts (sequesters), nor multiyear deficit reduction targets.[43]

Proposal for a Constitutional Amendment for a Balanced Budget. Those who despair of reducing deficits through existing governmental decision-making systems, five-year plans, or formulas designed to produce automatic budget cuts tend to favor a constitutional amendment providing for an annual balanced budget. Two routes are available for the approval of an amendment and both have been taken: (1) a petition by two-thirds of all state legislatures (thirty-four of fifty states) for a constitutional convention to approve an amendment, and (2) the approval of an amendment by two-thirds of both houses of Congress subject to ratification by three-fourths of the state legislatures (thirty-eight states).

By 1984, thirty-six state legislatures—just two short of the required supermajority—had taken the first route.[44] At that point the bandwagon stalled. None of the eighteen other states took any action, as it slowly dawned on them that they might be affected by budget cutbacks. Furthermore, a national constitutional convention had not been tried since the creation of the republic, and fears of a runaway convention developed—one that would not only deal with budgeting, but would challenge other constitutional and legal norms as well.

Congress took the second route. It came close thrice to approving a constitutional amendment. In 1982 the Senate, by an overwhelming vote of 69–31, approved Senate Joint Resolution 58, a constitutional amendment providing for a balanced budget. The House of Representatives, however, turned it down (House Joint Resolution 350) when it approved the amendment by a majority vote (256–187), but failed by forty-six votes to achieve the two-thirds required for a constitutional amendment.[45] Conceivably, a switch of forty-six votes could have had the greatest impact on the federal budgeting system since the Budget and Accounting Act of 1921. In June 1992, H.J. Res. 290 fell only nine votes short of the two-thirds majority required to approve a constitutional amendment in the House of Representatives. The Senate could not muster enough votes for passage, either. In February and March of 1994, proponents of the amendment tried again, but lost by a narrow margin.[46]

Had the constitutional amendment prevailed, budgeting systems and policies would have been altered profoundly. Prior to each fiscal year Congress would adopt a statement of receipts and outlays, with outlays no greater than receipts. This would include all government receipts except borrowed funds, and all outlays except funds for the repayment of debt. Only an extraordinary majority of both houses of Congress, three-fifths of the members, could approve an unbalanced budget. (In times of war a simple majority would be sufficient.) As a guard against sharp tax increases, the amendment authorizes an increase in receipts no greater than the rate of increase in national income in the six- or twelve-month period prior to the beginning of the fiscal year. In effect, the size of government would be limited to the growth of the economy. A majority of all the members of both houses, however, could approve specific additional revenues, providing the president concurred. To increase the federal public debt limit, another extraordinary majority of three-fifths of Congress would be needed. In implementing the budget, Congress and the president would ensure that actual outlays not exceed approved outlays by the end of the fiscal year.[47]

The Pros of a Constitutional Amendment. The arguments in favor of an amendment to the Constitution to balance the budget range from simplistic ones (therein lies their appeal) to complex ones involving issues of public policy and philosophical values. Riding the crest of tax and expenditures limits in state and local governments, advocates of the amendment point to the forty-nine states with requirements for a balanced budget (Vermont is the exception). The nub of their argument is that if state governments can balance their budgets, so can the federal government. This position ignores two critical factors: (1) If states followed the same budgetary rules as the federal government, few of them would have balanced budgets.[48] (The discussion of state fiscal policy later in the chapter delves into this issue.) (2) The unique responsibilities of the federal government for national defense, economic growth, full employment, and price stability force the government to incur budget deficits deliberately.[49] Nevertheless, the amendment for a balanced budget is alluring because of the complexity of modern budgeting and the inability of governments so far to cope with deficits. As a former senior official of OMB put it:

> many people . . . have yearned for a simple rule that (1) would provide meaningful limits on the scope of public pursuits and (2) would hopefully assure effectiveness and efficiency in the government programs. Annual budget balance, balance in the budget over the business cycle, and the full employment concepts are all examples of such yearnings for a simple rule.[50]

On a more philosophical level, proponents of balanced budgets claim that a political bias in favor of deficit spending exists in democratic governments. To ensure their election, politicians prefer tax cuts to tax increases and increases in appropriations to retrenchment. As a result, the public sector continues to grow at the expense of the private sector and grows even faster than the economy. With no incentives to stem the growth of government, deficits will remain a perennial problem. Ordinary methods of control no longer suffice—neither central budget systems, the Congressional Budget Act of 1974, nor the deficit-reduction laws. Only a constitutional amendment that limits the size of the public sector would reverse present fiscal policy.[51]

The Cons of a Constitutional Amendment. Opponents of a balanced budget amendment raise at least eleven controversial issues.

1. *Still hard choices ahead.* Even with a balanced budget amendment, Congress and the president would have to make hard decisions about tax increases and spending cuts. The amendment is not a substitute for such choices.

2. *End of discretionary fiscal policy.* It would be difficult to put together a politically acceptable package to combat recessions because of the requirement for a supermajority. In effect, Congress would be hostage to the views of a minority of its members. This is a prescription for paralysis in decision making and for social conflict. Although Presidents Reagan and Bush were leading advocates of a balanced budget, they never proposed one in three terms in office.

3. *Difficulty of estimating revenues and expenditures.* The balanced budget approved by Congress would be based on several economic assumptions and forecasts of revenues and expenditures. These assumptions and forecasts, however, frequently prove to be grossly inaccurate and tend to be overly optimistic.[52]

4. *Delays in implementing the amendment.* Since it would take years for state legislatures to ratify it, the approval of an amendment by Congress would have only a minimal impact on current economic problems. In the foreseeable future Congress and the administration would still face deficits and the alternatives for dealing with them.

5. *Dubious wisdom of embodying transient economic policy in the Constitution.* In the 1980s it was fashionable to inveigh against excessive federal spending, especially in view of tax and spending limitations imposed by state governments. In the 1990s deficit reduction is the big issue. To place such transient economic policies in the Constitution may result in inflicting on future generations the doubtful wisdom of the past.

6. *Possibility of evading constitutional limitations.* A determined majority in Congress can get around limitations or any other rules by creating off-budget agencies, initiating a capital budget so as to lower current expenditures and increase borrowing, relying on one-time gimmicks to defer spending and raise revenues, or passing on more costs to state and local governments and the private sector.

7. *Problems of implementing a balanced budget.* In the course of the year the budget may be out of balance because of revenue shortfalls and expenditure increases. Yet the amendment is silent on how to cope with this frequent problem. One way is to delegate to the president the power to impound funds and to raise or lower taxes up to congressionally approved limits. If the past is a guide, it's unlikely that Congress will go along with such measures. A balanced budget, which is elusive to begin with, could thus become even more tenuous during its implementation. If Congress yields, however, the president would enhance his power to implement the budget.[53]

8. *The dominance of monetary policy.* With fiscal policy in the straitjacket of a constitutional amendment, the autonomous Federal Reserve Board would assume an increasingly important role in stabilizing the economy through control over the money supply, credit allocations, and interest rates.

9. *Delays in the courts.* Already shaped in part by litigation, the budget process would become even more litigious as various interest groups turned to the courts for interpretations of the application of the amendment.[54]

10. *No provision for erasing the previous debt of $4 trillion.* The amendment is silent on ways and means of achieving this political miracle.

11. *A prescription for fiscal paralysis.* Should the president submit a budget with, say, a $400 billion deficit, Congress would face the onus of raising taxes and cutting programs. Predictably, it would turn down the proposal and come up with one unacceptable to the president. Conversely, if Congress approves a budget calling for revenues of $1–2 trillion and the president vetoes the bill and recommends a $1 trillion ceiling, Congress would need a two-thirds majority to prevail. All the president needs is a vote of one-third plus 1 in either house and he determines tax policy. Such annual confrontations would spring directly from the constitutional amendment.[55]

Summing up these views, Alice M. Rivlin dismissed the proposed amendment:

> A balanced budget amendment does not deserve mention in a list of practical measures to address the deficit. It would enshrine the hope for budget balance in the Constitution without taking a single step toward facing the hard choices that are needed or enforcing those that are made. If the new administration and Congress agree on a balanced budget amendment, it is a sure sign that they have given up on action to eliminate the deficit on their watch.[56]

Coordinating Fiscal and Monetary Policies

Fiscal policies alone will not produce stable prices, low interest rates, economic growth, high employment, and a low dollar to stimulate exports. Such desirable goals also depend in large part on monetary policy, which influences interest rates, the supply of credit, the value of the dollar, and the amount of money in circulation. In the United States and other countries fiscal and monetary policies are the major economic levers. To work, both sets of policies must mesh closely. When they conflict, the economy suffers. For example, the relatively low deficits of the Carter administration in 1988 led the Federal Reserve Board, fearful of inflation, to raise interest rates to 20 percent, effectively throttling the economy. A more accommodating Board in 1993 kept short-term interest rates at about 3 percent, even in the face of the highest deficits in American history. Long-term rates (ten years or more), however, hovered around 6 percent.

Unlike other countries, the United States lacks a central decision-making point for developing coordinated fiscal and monetary policies. Fiscal policy (plus the budget policy that implements it) is the domain of the president's troika—OMB, the Treasury, and the Council of Economic Advisors—working in tandem with the powerful congressional fiscal committees. In 1993 President Clinton added a central economic council as part of the White House staff. Monetary policy, however, is the chief function of the autonomous Federal Reserve Board, the central bank of the United States. In Britain, France, Japan, and other countries, in contrast, the government holds the reins of both fiscal and monetary policy through its control of the central bank.

With these split responsibilities, tension inevitably develops between every administration and the FRB. Administrations generally prefer low interest rates and a low dollar to encourage investments and exports, not to mention the lower cost of servicing the government's debt. Constrained by deficits and limited in their ability to stimulate the economy by increasing expenditures, they look to the FRB to come up with a stimulative monetary policy, that is, low interest rates and an abundant supply of credit in the banks. But inflation is the primary concern of the FRB, and it uses all the instruments at its disposal to eliminate the threat. In the end, though, neither the administration nor the FRB can fine-tune the economy. Unpredictable lags occur between the approval of policies and their implementation. In the end it is the financial markets that determine interest rates and prices.

The FRB does, however, have powerful tools at its disposal. The Board, containing seven members appointed by the president and serving fourteen-year terms, sets interest rates indirectly by increasing or decreasing the money supply, raising or lowering reserves in banks, and setting interest rates for interbank loans. This is not the place to delve into the complexities of monetary policies, the mechanisms for implementing the policies, and the interlocking relations of fiscal, budget, and monetary policy. The bibliography contains useful references on these issues.[57]

Fiscal Policy in State Governments

After one of the deepest recessions since the 1930s, state governments emerged in 1992 with the following fiscal profile:

	Billions
Revenue from all sources, including $159 billion in federal aid and payments of some $10.9 billion from local governments	$741.9
General revenue (excluding revenue from state-owned liquor stores, utilities, and state-operated trust funds for retirement, etc.)	605.3
Expenditures from all sources (general expenditures: $611.9 billion)	700.9
Long-term debt	369.0

Source: U.S. Bureau of the Census, State Government Finances, 1992, Series GF/92-3 (Washington, D.C., 1993), Table 1.

Figure 7.1 highlights the sources of revenue and the expenditures by function.

The figures reflect the forces that have shaped the fiscal policies of the fifty states since World War II. They also result from the constraints under which state governments labor and which, unlike the federal government, severely limit their fiscal options. These are the major hurdles that confront state fiscal planners: federal economic and fiscal policy over which they have no control; stiff requirements for a balanced budget; tax and spending limits triggered by tax revolts;

FIGURE 7.1a GENERAL REVENUE OF STATE GOVERNMENTS, BY SOURCE: 1992

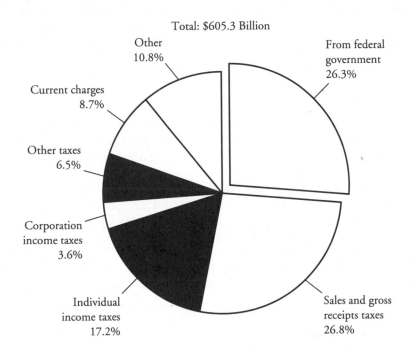

Total: $605.3 Billion

Other
10.8%

From federal
government
26.3%

Current charges
8.7%

Other taxes
6.5%

Corporation
income taxes
3.6%

Individual
income taxes
17.2%

Sales and gross
receipts taxes
26.8%

constitutional limits on borrowing; the drop in federal aid for state programs; federal mandates and court decisions that affect state spending; uncontrollable expenditures, especially for state aid to local governments; and earmarked funds. Juggling these interrelated problems makes state fiscal policy every bit as complex as federal policy, although the components and the emphasis may be different.

The Impact of Federal Economic, Fiscal, and Monetary Policy on the States

State fiscal policy does not stand alone. It is shaped and buffeted by federal economic, fiscal, and monetary policy. The states absorb the blows of recession and inflation and benefit from economic upturns. High interest rates raise the cost of borrowing. Changes in federal tax policy have a direct impact on state tax structures since many states follow federal definitions of taxable income and allowable deductions in tax returns. By eliminating deductions for state and local sales taxes and restricting the volume of tax-exempt bonds (as in 1986), the federal government directly affects state revenues and expenditures. Federal aid and expenditures impact sharply on state budgets and economies. Consequently, no budget planning at the state level can take place without a careful analysis of the national economy and federal fiscal and monetary policy. It's the economy that counts first and last.

FIGURE 7.1b GENERAL EXPENDITURE OF STATE GOVERNMENTS, BY FUNCTION: 1992

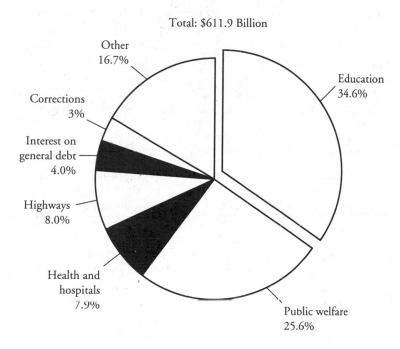

Total: $611.9 Billion

Other
16.7%

Education
34.6%

Corrections
3%

Interest on
general debt
4.0%

Highways
8.0%

Health and
hospitals
7.9%

Public welfare
25.6%

Source: U.S. Bureau of the Census, *State Government Finances,* 1992 (Washington, D.C., 1993), p. xiii.

Hammered by the economy for three consecutive years, the states ended fiscal years 1991, 1992, and 1993 with record low reserves: fiscal balances representing 1.1 percent, 0.3 percent, and 3 percent, respectively, of general fund expenditures. Year-end balances are the reserves states count on for unforeseen circumstances and for working capital to start a new fiscal year. As such, they represent a major benchmark of fiscal stress or health. A year-end balance of 5 percent is a bare bone minimum reserve. The 1982–1983 recession had inflicted similar damage, with balances plummeting to 2.9 percent and 1.5 percent.[58]

State spending dropped or virtually stood still during the recessions. In contrast to an average increase of 8.0 percent annually during the 1980s, general fund budgets increased by 5.1 percent in FY 1992 and 3.3 percent in FY 1993. In 1992 two-thirds of the states reduced previously enacted budgets by $4.5 billion, cut the size of their staffs, curbed welfare benefits and state aid to local governments, and imposed a variety of cuts across the board. Revenues increased modestly; up 6.5 percent in FY 1992 and 3.3 percent (projected) in FY 1993. Adjusted for inflation, the budgets in the early 1990s showed either no growth or a negative growth.[59] As the economy improved in 1994, somewhat increased revenue eased budget pressures marginally.

Only a review of the individual states can fully measure the impact of the economy and related social and economic pressures on budgets. For example, California experienced a deficit of $14.3 billion in 1991–1992, representing 25.3 percent of expenditures of $56.4 billion. Despite tax increases and unprecedented cuts in expenditures, the deficit still totaled $2.8 billion in 1993. Following closely was New York State with a deficit of $6.5 billion, accounting for 22 percent of the expenditure budget. Twenty-one states, most of them in the Northeast, ran up combined deficits of $35 billion in 1991–1992.[60] As the economy improved in 1994, revenues rose and deficits shrank somewhat.

The Balanced Budget Requirement

How can deficits develop when the constitutions and statutes of all but one state (Vermont) mandate a balanced budget? A good deal of myth making, especially among proponents of similar restrictions at the federal level, surrounds this requirement. Actually, the constitutional mandate is less of a fiscal barrier than meets the eye. Not all state funds are subject to the constraint of a balanced budget. It mainly applies to the general fund, which represents slightly more than half of total state spending. In many states it also covers federal funds, special funds, capital funds, and trust funds. Considering all these factors, the requirement for a balanced budget applies to 75 to 100 percent of the budget in thirty-six states, 50 to 75 percent in nine states, and 25 to 50 percent in three states.[61]

At what point should the budget be in balance? At the time the governor submits it? After the legislature enacts it? At the end of the fiscal year? In all phases of the budget cycle? The answers can be somewhat murky in view of the diversity of practices among the states. Forty-four states require the governor to submit a balanced budget. Thirty-seven compel the legislature to enact and the governor to sign a balanced budget. Budgets are required to be in balance at the end of the year in thirty-nine states. The evidence on this last point is not conclusive; what is clear is that thirteen of the thirty-nine states can end the year legally with deficits and carry over the deficits to the next year. Seven of the ten largest states have done this in recent years: California, New York, Illinois, Massachusetts, Michigan, Pennsylvania, and Texas.[62]

In thirty-six states governors (subject to various restrictions) can enforce a balanced budget by cutting spending with or without legislative approval. This power has been challenged in the courts with mixed results. Somewhat more influential are the symbolism and political appeal of a balanced budget to the public and the emphasis that bond-rating organizations place on a balanced budget.[63]

The requirement for a balanced budget is a mixed blessing for state governments. It disciplines the budget process, limits the size of deficits and debt, and forces reluctant decision makers to choose spending priorities. On the other hand, it fosters conservative spending and tax policies. In a recession, states are forced to raise taxes rather than cut them and reduce expenditures rather than increase them. The effect is to disrupt funding for operating programs and capital projects and, because of the uncertainty of funding, to inhibit financial planning.

Ballot Box Budgeting

The tax revolt that began in the 1970s led to tax and spending limits in twenty-four states by 1993. Distrustful of legislatures and governors, voters have resorted to initiatives and referenda to enforce their own brand of budgeting through the ballot box. At every turn the limits constrain fiscal policies in those states even further. The shackles imposed by the voters take such forms as limiting spending to a fixed percent of the prior year's expenditures; or to the percent increase in per capita income; or to the growth in the state's economy (GDP), the cost of living, and population. No state equals California in the intensity and frequency of tax revolts and in the resulting budget restrictions placed on the state government. Proposition 4 limits the growth of state expenditures to increases in the population and the inflation rate. Any revenue in excess of the limits is rebated to the taxpayers, who received $1.1 billion in 1988. As the 1991–1993 recession began, the flow stopped. Another proposition (98), approved by the voters in 1988, earmarks 40 percent of tax revenue for elementary and secondary schools and community colleges.[64] This was after Proposition 13 capped local real estate taxes, froze the taxes of "oldtimers," and raised taxes for new home owners. So much for horizontal equity.

That voters continue to take budget policy in their own hands in a fiscal crunch is evident from several key ballot initiatives decided in November 1993. In the state of Washington voters rejected a rollback in taxes, but nevertheless restricted spending growth to the rate of inflation and the increase in population. Oregonians turned down a constitutional amendment to establish a 5 percent sales tax. In Texas voters adopted a constitutional amendment that barred a state personal income tax without voter approval, while at the same time they authorized the state to borrow funds for the construction of prisons and health facilities. In Montana voters gathered enough signatures for a petition to suspend the implementation of legislation reforming the income tax system. Any changes would be subject to a voter referendum at the next election. These are but a few examples of "ballot box budgeting."

Constraints on Borrowing

Reflecting a distrust of legislatures that goes back to the nineteenth century, state constitutions are replete with controls over borrowing, especially for capital projects.[65] As Chapter 6 on "off-Budget budgets" demonstrates, the states have displayed considerable ingenuity in evading constitutional restrictions. At the end of FY 1992, long-term state debt stood at $369 billion. Nearly three-fourths of this debt can be attributed to public authorities.[66]

The Federal–State Fiscal Connection

Due to the fact that states count on federal aid for about one-fourth of their revenue, the uncertainties and complexities of federal financing touch every facet of the state budget process. After reaching new highs in the mid-1970s, federal aid declined sharply during the last years of the Carter administration and the early years of the Reagan administration. It did not pick up again until 1989 during the Bush administration, and then it reached new heights even after taking inflation into account. In FY 1993 estimated federal aid totaled $203.7 billion.[67] Increased federal aid, however, was targeted for individuals (for example, recipients of Medicaid) and not for most domestic programs.

Federal aid is not cost free. To obtain it states must, among other things, match federal money with their own revenue. For example, in 1992 Medicaid cost the states $44 billion, representing roughly a 57–43 percent federal–state split. Other major matching requirements cover welfare, transportation, and other health programs. Some federal mandates impose heavy costs on the states, running into billions of dollars, but provide no funds. Among them are requirements for assisting the disabled by providing equal access to service, employment, buildings, and transportation systems; water purification; elimination of environmental abuses; health care; and criminal justice.[68]

Federal and state court decisions turning on the rights of students, the ill, the mentally ill, prisoners, welfare recipients, and the homeless have also led to sharp increases in funding in a variety of programs. Chapter 12 explores the role of courts in budgeting.

Uncontrollable Expenditures: State Aid to Local Governments

The fiscal policy of state governments is circumscribed still further by so-called uncontrollable expenditures. Among the largest expenditures that remain uncontrollable in the absence of statutory changes are state aid to local governments. Approximately $201.3 billion spent for this purpose in 1992 accounted for about 29 percent of total state spending. Education, welfare, health, and transportation consume most state aid. Among the states the percent of the budget allocated to state aid ranges from 0.2 percent in Hawaii to 48.5 percent in California. Some caution should be used in interpreting these figures. In a state like Hawaii, which assumes functions normally performed by local governments, state aid will be negligible. In states with more decentralized programs, state aid becomes the largest single item in the budget. Still other factors influence the proportion of state aid in the budget: the local tax structure, which may make it unnecessary to lean on the state for more assistance; earmarked taxes that help local governments, but are not classified as state aid; full state funding of Medicaid and Aid to Families with Dependent Children (AFDC), which statistically fails to reflect state aid.

As sacrosanct as state aid is, it has not been entirely immune from cutbacks triggered by recent recessions. In 1991 fifteen states reduced state aid or granted additional sources of revenue to cities and counties. Bucking this trend, however, several states actually boosted local aid. From a practical and political standpoint other expenditures are virtually untouchable, even though no statutes mandate them. For example, states show little inclination to cut such discretionary programs as law enforcement and correction services.[69]

The Straitjacket of Earmarked Funds

The designation of specified revenues for specific purposes, or earmarking, is chronic among the states. Such earmarked funds curb budgetary discretion in all states, weaken budget control, freeze resources for particular purposes whether needed or not, create an inflexible revenue structure, and undermine the decision-making power of governors and legislatures. Supporters dismiss these contentions, arguing that special funds appeal to the voters, provide stability in programs, and assure a minimum level of support.

Leading all special funds in dollar amounts are highway trust funds that receive gasoline taxes and motor vehicle registration and license fees. These earmarked funds can only be used for highway and bridge construction and maintenance. While the highway trust fund is the largest earmarked fund, hundreds of other special funds exist. The taxes, fees, and charges that feed these funds can be committed only to specific programs such as education, unrestricted state aid to local governments, and mental health. Nearly 23 percent of state revenue—a formidable amount—is earmarked in this fashion. States vary in their earmarking practices. Alabama leads all the rest with nearly 80 percent of its taxes earmarked. At the other extreme, Alaska, Connecticut, Delaware, Hawaii, Louisiana, and Rhode Island freeze 10 percent or less of their revenue for specific purposes.[70] What is the impact of earmarking on the efficiency and effectiveness of state operations? No firm answers are available, because research along these lines has been negligible.

Developing Expenditure Policies amid a Sea of Constraints

These are the constraints that shape state fiscal policy. Hemmed in by such restrictions, the states attempt to forge expenditure policies that will be responsive to the needs of their residents. The wild card is the economy. For three decades, from 1947 to 1977, state expenditures flourished in a growing economy and even outpaced growth in federal expenditures. Then, under the quadruple blows of recession, inflation, tax revolts, and cuts in federal aid, the pendulum swung the other way.[71] As countermeasures, the states adopted a combination of expenditure cuts, tax increases, and debt financing to see them through the 1982–1983 and 1990–1993 recessions. No matter what they do states continue to face rising costs in Medicaid and corrections, which accounted for over 20 percent of state expenditures in 1992. Added to the costs of education (about 33 percent), these three functions consume most of the state budgets.[72] As Figure 7.2 shows, education, Medicaid, welfare (AFDC), and corrections accounted for nearly 64 percent of general fund appropriations for FY 1994. For the first time Medicaid outspent higher education.

Adjusting Tax Policies to Fiscal Constraints

States depend for their revenue primarily on sales and gross receipts taxes and personal and corporation income taxes. Forty states impose a personal income tax,

FIGURE 7.2 MAJOR COMPONENTS OF GENERAL FUND APPROPRIATIONS FOR FY 1994

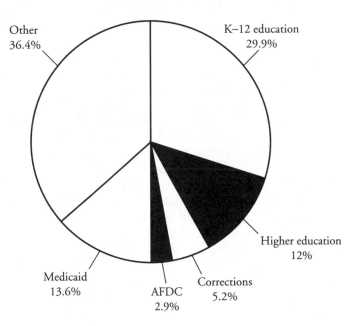

Other
36.4%

K–12 education
29.9%

Higher education
12%

Medicaid
13.6%

Corrections
5.2%

AFDC
2.9%

Source: National Conference of State Legislatures, *The Fiscal Letter,*
Nov./Dec. 1993.

forty-seven states a sales tax and a corporate income tax, and all states a variety of miscellaneous fees, charges, and taxes.[73] For each tax the tax rates and exemptions vary markedly among the states.

As Table 7.6 shows, sales taxes are the major producers of revenue, followed by personal and corporation income taxes.

While sales taxes remain the single largest generator of state revenue, they have declined relatively in importance in relation to income taxes. From 1957 to 1989 the ratio represented by income taxes more than doubled. "All other taxes" include cigarette, gasoline, and liquor taxes; revenue from lotteries; and fees and charges for licenses and services. Their overall percentage conceals the fact that fees and charges are the fastest-growing form of revenue. In FY 1993 over one-third of new revenue came from a wide variety of fees.[74]

How progressive, regressive, and equitable are state taxes? One test of progressivity is the balance in the tax system, that is, the relative proportion of revenue raised by each tax. If the sales and income taxes are roughly in balance, taxes may tend to be progressive. On the other hand, a state tax structure heavily dependent on sales, taxes may adversely affect low- and moderate-income taxpayers. As of 1992 the states tilted towards sales taxes. Nevertheless, this was a marked improvement over the 1970s, when the gap between sales and income taxes was greater.[75]

TABLE 7.6

Percentage distribution of state revenue by type of tax, selected years, 1957–1992

Year	Total taxes	Sales and gross receipts taxes	Personal and corporation income taxes	Property taxes	All other taxes, fees, charges
1957	100.0	58.1	17.5	3.3	21.1
1967	100.0	58.2	22.4	2.7	16.8
1972	100.0	55.5	29.1	2.1	13.3
1977	100.0	51.8	34.3	2.2	11.7
1979	100.0	51.0	35.8	2.0	11.2
1981	100.0	48.6	36.8	2.0	12.6
1982	100.0	48.4	36.7	1.9	12.9
1983	100.0	48.9	36.7	1.9	12.4
1984	100.0	48.7	37.8	2.0	11.5
1985	100.0	48.9	37.7	1.9	11.5
1986	100.0	49.3	37.6	1.9	11.2
1987	100.0	48.5	39.2	1.9	10.4
1988	100.0	49.3	38.6	1.9	10.3
1989	100.0	48.7	39.7	1.9	9.8
1990	100.0	48.9	39.2	1.9	9.9
1991	100.0	49.5	38.5	2.0	10.0
1992	100.0	49.5	38.4	2.0	10.0

Sources: Advisory Commission on Intergovernmental Relations, *Significant Features of Fiscal Federation,* vol. II, 1993 edition (Washington, D.C., 1993), Table 35; U.S. Bureau of the Census, *State Government Finances: 1992* (Washington, D.C., 1993), Table 10.

Still, in states largely dependent on high sales taxes, the tax system overall remained regressive.

Only seven states have high progressive income taxes: Massachusetts, Maryland, Wisconsin, New York, Minnesota, Oregon, and Hawaii. To ease the burden of taxes on the poor, a few states provide tax relief via sales tax credits and earned income tax credits. Countering this trend has been an increase in sales tax rates and a broadening of the sales tax base to include services and items hitherto exempt. The regressivity of the expanded sales tax has been offset somewhat by more progressive features of the income tax. According to Gold, "the combined effect of a higher sales tax and more progressive income tax was considerably less regressive than a simple sales tax increase."[76] This still leaves the states with a tax structure that, overall, remains regressive.

Given their needs, not all state governments tap their potential tax capacity fully or equally. Since 1962 the Advisory Commission on Intergovernmental Relations has used as a yardstick a Representative Tax System (RTS), which is intended to answer the following critical question: "What would be the total revenue of each of the 50 states if every state applied identical tax rates—national averages—to each of 26 commonly used tax bases?" RTS thus measures (1) the hypothetical tax capacity of a state and (2) its tax effort, or the extent to which it makes use of its capacity. On this basis only eighteen states in 1988 exceeded the national tax average for all states and, in relation to the others, made fuller use of their tax capacity.[77]

Not all budgeteers accept this approach; some prefer as a gauge the relationship of taxes to personal income, for example, the amount of taxes taken out of every $100 of income.

As a state fashions tax policy, it keeps a vigilant eye on other states lest lower tax rates elsewhere drive businesses and residents from the state. Interstate tax competition thus continues to remain a constraint on all states. As a result, state and local governments offer a cornucopia of concessions such as lower income tax rates, lower corporate income taxes, and a slew of tax abatements and exemptions. How seductive these tax breaks are is a moot question. While they may have some impact, the evidence is by no means conclusive that tax concessions affect decisions to locate or relocate firms. What counts, though, is that state and local officials think they do and shape the tax structure accordingly.[78]

Shaping Fiscal Policy in Local Governments

Figure 7.3 gives an overview of expenditures and revenues in cities and counties in 1991. It is important to stress that, unlike state governments, local governments have relatively little autonomy and flexibility in developing fiscal policy. State laws and constitutions prescribe the taxes they raise, restrict the funds they borrow, and impose limits on expenditures. Still other constraints concern the use of state and federal funds.

On top of these restrictions, local governments are inundated by a sea of state and federal mandates, many of them unfunded and most of them costly. Among hundreds of examples, several stand out: Montana's requirement that counties provide intensive juvenile detention facilities; Tennessee's new rules governing solid waste management; and Oregon's waste recycling program, which may cost counties $40 million.[79] Two especially critical factors are local dependence on federal and state grants and numerous "lid laws" that cap local revenues and expenditures. In 1990 local governments counted on intergovernmental grants for 37.2 percent of their total revenue of $512.3 billion from all sources. At the same time they were hemmed in by the following voter-imposed lids:[80]

Type of Lid	*Number of States*
Property tax rate limits	33
Property tax revenue limits	16
Revenue limits	3
Expenditure limits	3
Limits on assessment	6
Revenue rollbacks	7

FIGURE 7.3 EXPENDITURES AND REVENUE PATTERNS, CITIES AND COUNTIES, 1991

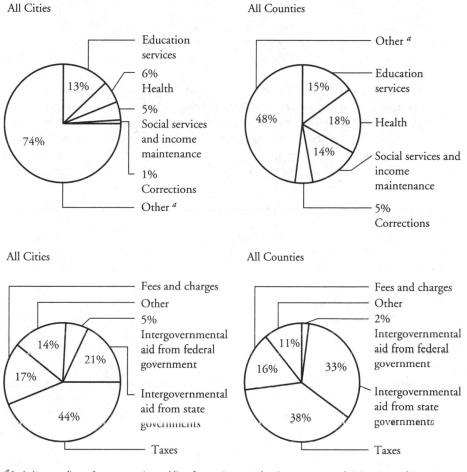

^{a} Includes expenditures for transportation, public safety, environment, housing, government administration, and interest.

Note: Percentages may not add to 100 due to rounding.

Source: U.S. General Accounting Office, *State and Local Finances* (Washington, D.C., 1993), pp. 62, 68.

Probably the best-known and most severe limits are Proposition 13 in California and Proposition 2½ in Massachusetts. Apart from their impact on the two states, they intensified the national debate on fiscal limits, triggered similar restrictions in other states, and brought new life to the movement to enact a constitutional amendment to balance the federal budget. Adopted by a 2–1 margin by voters in California in 1979, Proposition 13 reduced local property taxes in FY 1978–1979 by more than $7 billion. This represented 57 percent of all property taxes and 20 percent of all local revenue. In Massachusetts, Proposition 2½, an initiative law rather than a constitutional amendment, had a similar effect. It altered the tax structure and spending pattern in local governments and the division of responsibility for taxing and spending between state and local governments. Adopted in November 1980 because of voter disaffection with growing property taxes and local expenditures, Proposition 2½ forced local governments to reduce property taxes 15 percent each year until the tax rate reached 2.5 percent of full and fair market value. Only voter approval by a two-thirds vote in a referendum could override this limit.[81]

Not all federal and state restrictions on local programs are negative in effect. Some result in the maintenance of higher standards than would otherwise be the case. Nor can voter resistance to taxes and spending be dismissed as the populist whims of a mindless majority. It reflects an aversion to government and a choice to devote a larger proportion of income to personal consumption. To develop fair and defensible fiscal policies these attitudes must be recognized and confronted.

The Effect of Fiscal Constraints on Local Tax Structures

For local governments as a whole, the property tax is still a major producer of own-source revenue, despite the many attempts to whittle it down. In 1991 it accounted for 75.3 percent of all receipts, followed by general and selective sales taxes (14.9 percent), income taxes (5.5 percent), and other taxes and fees (4.3 percent). The overall figures, however, obscure the relative dependence of different levels of local government on property taxes. For cities, property taxes accounted for slightly more than half their revenue, and for counties, about three-fourths. But school districts and townships rely heavily on property taxes, which constituted well over 90 percent of their receipts.

Considering all sources of income, including state and federal aid, local taxes funded 39.6 percent of the budgets in 1991, followed by intergovernmental assistance amounting to 37.3 percent. The remaining 23.1 percent came from fees and charges.[82]

To aid hard-pressed local governments, especially large cities, state governments have authorized them to levy a variety of taxes, fees, and charges. In 1991 nearly 6,000 local governments in thirty states relied on general or selective sales taxes. In eleven states, local governments were permitted to tax personal income (this on top of federal and state personal income taxes). Large cities in Ohio, Michigan, and Pennsylvania, in particular, tapped this source of revenue. In four states local governments could also tax corporate income. While still small in relation to other sources of revenue, fees and charges for local service have increased dramatically in the wake of tax limitations and will continue to proliferate.[83]

With property taxes diminishing in importance, local governments increasingly turn to state governments for additional grants; broader authorization to levy nonproperty taxes; state takeover of welfare and judicial functions; and more extensive state participation in financing of major local programs such as elementary and secondary education, law enforcement and public safety, construction and maintenance of streets and highways, health, and welfare.

Fiscal Stress Unsettles Budgets

Between the economic blows of recessions; cutbacks in federal and state aid; external controls over taxing, spending, and borrowing; and an erosion of their tax base because of changing demographic and other social patterns, local governments in the United States, in the main, suffer from acute fiscal stress in performing their basic functions. This was especially true during the recessions of the early 1980s and 1990s. In 1991 the fifty counties with the largest budgets racked up deficits of over $760 million. For several years Bridgeport (Connecticut), Philadelphia, Scranton, and Yonkers (New York) teetered at the verge of bankruptcy. These cities, as well as ten other local governments in Pennsylvania and New York City, were monitored by state-appointed fiscal overseers. From 1992 to 1993 spending in the 688 largest cities inched up only 2 percent, less than the inflation rate of 3.3 percent. Revenues grew by only 0.8 percent. In the face of shortfalls, 40 percent of the cities cut services, capital construction, and staffs even more, and 40 percent also increased fees and taxes. Whatever reserves they had were dangerously depleted.

These were the ingredients of local fiscal policy as the last decade of the century began.[84]

* * *

This chapter has described how fiscal, economic, and monetary policies converge in the budget process and how they affect different levels of government. In this intricate relationship, the budget has more than ever become a tool to manage or influence national and regional economies. In the end, the major choices in fiscal policy are political, with the budget the battleground for competing tax, spending, and debt policies.

Points for Discussion

1. What are the main components of fiscal policy? What are the appropriate criteria for selecting a mix of taxes, expenditures, and debt financing?
2. How do you account for government's growing role in economic management? In what specific respects is the budget a tool of economic management? How effective is it? What are the chief economic theories that influence the role of the government in managing the economy through the budget?
3. In what specific ways does the economy affect the budget? Conversely, how does the budget affect the economy?
4. What role, if any, do state and local governments have in managing the economy? To what extent would you change their role?
5. What are the criteria for a fair and equitable tax policy? To what extent does the federal government have such a policy? The state governments? Local governments?
6. In what specific ways does federal fiscal policy influence the fiscal policy of state and local governments?

7. How much discretion do governments at all levels have in developing expenditure policies? How far would you go in expanding their discretion? How far would you go in controlling "uncontrollable expenditures?"
8. How do you account for the mushrooming deficits of the federal government? How effective are the deficit-reduction laws of the 1980s and the 1990s? How would you control deficits?
9. Budgeteers and economists differ on ways and means of measuring deficits. What are the major methods of measurement? Which ones do you favor and why?
10. What are the pros and cons of a federal balanced budget? What is your position?
11. To what extent do state governments balance their budgets? Should the federal government follow their model?
12. To what extent should the federal and state governments control the fiscal policies of local governments?
13. How would you relieve the fiscal stress of cities?
14. Analyze the deficit-reduction package of a government (federal, state, or local) in recent years. To what extent do you agree or disagree with the implicit or explicit fiscal policies in the proposal?
15. What are the main elements of monetary policy? How far would you go in restricting the autonomy of the Federal Reserve Board to formulate monetary policy? What steps can be taken to ensure the compatibility of fiscal and monetary policy?

CHAPTER 8

LEGISLATIVE BUDGETING
The Combat Zone

Once the head of government sends the executive budget to the legislative body, the scene of budgetary combat shifts to the legislative chambers. It is now up to the legislature to take on the mammoth task of analyzing, debating, supporting, attacking, and changing the executive budget. The end product of this complex decision-making process is a set of appropriation bills that may differ significantly from the original budget. In effect, a new budget is fashioned.

How does a legislative body achieve a consensus on the budget? Unlike the administration, which hammers out a budget under single and unified direction, the legislature is fragmented. It is divided by sharp partisan, economic, regional, ethnic, factional, social, and ideological differences. In contrast to the president and governors, who have broad national and statewide constituencies, the legislature represents more narrow constituencies. To what extent can it surmount internal schisms in the legislative halls to come up with a budget roughly acceptable to all factions? How far can it go in changing budgetary policies and allocations proposed by the administration? What limits, if any, exist in legislative budgeting? What are the appropriate budgetary functions of a legislative body? To what extent do legislatures carry out these functions?

No one answer to any of these questions holds for the 178 national legislative bodies in the countries represented in the United Nations in 1993, and the hundreds of thousands of subnational assemblies in states, provinces, regions, and local governments. Methods of coping with the executive budget vary with the political and legal systems and institutions in each country.

In the United States, legislative budgetary practices are in a class by themselves, and differ sharply from those followed by other legislative bodies. At the federal, state, and local levels legislatures possess a broad array of budgetary powers and, in many cases, have the resources to implement them. Consequently, they are more or less equal partners of the chief executive in budgeting. Still, differences persist among them in their relations with the executive. Of all American legislative bodies, Congress is the most freewheeling, and, in budgeting, is easily a match for the president. At the state level, legislatures increasingly enjoy parity with the governor in budget decision making, but the governors, with some exceptions, generally dominate the budget agenda. Among local governments budgeting is primarily an executive show, except in cities and counties with legally "weak" executives and strong legislative bodies.

To capture some of the diversity in legislative budget practices, this chapter focuses primarily on budgeting by Congress and state legislatures, touching briefly on budgetary practices in local legislative bodies. The intent is to highlight (1) the unique elements of legislative budgeting in the United States, and (2) the contributions that legislative systems can and do bring to budgeting.

Congressional Budgeting in the United States

In Congress the constitutional power of the purse is the keystone of legislative authority "underpinning all other legislative decisions and regulating the balance of influence between the legislative and executive branches of government."[1] And Congress wields that power to the point where it is the most independent and powerful legislative body in the world. The president proposes a budget, sets the framework for budget decision making, and uses his enormous prestige as chief executive and leader of his party to influence congressional action on the budget. But Congress can and does dispose of his budget, especially so when one party controls the executive branch, and another, one or both houses in Congress.

Ultimately, it is Congress that determines the level of revenue, expenditure, and debt. In thirteen appropriation acts covering some 5,000 programs, projects, and activities, Congress produces what is essentially a congressional budget. Through the appropriation bills and legislation authorizing programs, it acts on the president's budget by cutting it, increasing it, approving it, or shifting funds within it. Of course, the president is free to veto appropriation and other bills, subject to an override of the veto by an extraordinary majority of two-thirds of the members of Congress. Confronted, however, by thirteen large appropriation acts sent to him on a "take it or leave it" basis, the president frequently approves most of them because, from his perspective, the good may outweigh the bad. The president is in an especially acute dilemma when Congress approves only one omnibus spending bill, or continuing resolution, to authorize spending in the absence of a budget agreement, as it has on occasion. No wonder presidents yearn for the line-item veto powers enjoyed by most state governors, who can slash legislative appropriations (subject to a legislative override by super majorities).

Unlike state and local legislatures in the United States, Congress suffers no constitutional constraints in budgeting. It is under no obligation to approve a balanced budget. Its appropriation bills are not subject to line-item vetoes as is the case in many state governments, where the chief executive is free to accept changes he likes and to disapprove the rest. No tax and spending limits control the actions of Congress. No requirements for popular referenda on capital or other expenditures exist. Whatever constraints hamper congressional action on the budget are self-imposed, such as mandated and uncontrollable expenditures; the new budget process triggered by the Congressional Budget and Impoundment Control Act of 1974 (PL 93-344); the Balanced Budget and Emergency Deficit Control Act of 1985 (PL 99-177); the 1987 amendments to the 1985 legislation; the Budget Enforcement Act of 1990 (PL 101-508); the Reconciliation Act of 1993; the use of earmarked funds; and the creation of government corporations and other public authorities that are "off-budget," and exempt from the conventional budgetary process.

Congressional Budgeting versus Budgeting in the Executive Branch

In raising and spending money, Congress virtually matches every budget function performed by the Office of Management and Budget, the White House, the Council of Economic Advisers, and staff units in the treasury department and other agencies in the executive branch. Congress engages in policy development, budget analysis and formulation, revenue estimating, appropriating funds, raising taxes, monitoring the implementation of the budget, and overseeing and evaluating the activities of operating agencies. Unlike the executive branch, however, Congress works through a highly decentralized committee structure, with budgetary powers shared by and diffused among the committees: the fiscal committees (Appropriations, Finance/Ways and Means, and Budget in each house) and all the other committees.

All committees, not just the fiscal committees, participate in the budget process. Congress generally will not consider any appropriations unless the authorizing committees, such as the Agriculture Committee or the Banking Committee, have previously authorized programs and projects, either for specified periods of time or indefinitely, and set a ceiling on the amount of money the administration can spend (termed "budget authorization").

The Budget Committees in both houses establish overall levels of expenditures, revenue, loans and loan guarantees, and debt for the government as a whole and for each of twenty major functions. If Congress endorses these totals by resolution, all committees, in theory, must operate within this framework.

Once Congress approves authorizing legislation and overall expenditure levels, the way is clear to appropriate funds. In both houses the Appropriations Committees propose actual funding levels (budget authority), which may be less than but cannot exceed the ceilings in the authorizing legislation. They cannot, however, touch entitlement payments such as social security and Medicare. For these programs funds are appropriated almost automatically. Consequently, the Appropriations Committees have lost their once formidable powers.

The revenue-raising committees (the Ways and Means Committee in the House of Representatives and the Finance Committee in the Senate) act on all proposed taxes and other revenue. They also have jurisdiction over such entitlement programs as social security and Medicare, in effect combining responsibility for major expenditures and revenue measures.

Budgeting, then, is a complex three-stage process. The Budget Committees, with congressional approval, set expenditure, revenue and debt totals in the first place. The authorizing committees establish expenditure limits for individual programs and projects. Guided by these limits, the Appropriations Committees determine the appropriations or budget authority that should be allocated to the operating agencies. Once both houses reconcile their inevitable differences and concur on appropriation bills, a new congressional budget is launched subject to presidential approval or veto. On paper the process looks neat, orderly, and tidy. In practice, it is frequently disrupted by divisive partisan and ideological confrontations every step of the way.

Staffing for Congressional Budgeting

Beginning in a small way in 1946 with the passage of the Legislative Reorganization Act (PL 79-601), Congress has created an extensive legislative bureaucracy to assist it in carrying out its legislative functions, including budgeting. By 1992 over 38,000 employees were on the staffs of committees, individual legislators, the legislative leadership, and the congressional support agencies (the General Accounting Office, the Congressional Budget Office, the Congressional Research Service of the Library of Congress, and the Office of Technology Assessment).[2] Among the standing committees alone, both authorizing and fiscal committees, the staffs of the House of Representatives totaled 2,132 and those of the Senate about 1,000.[3] This includes both professional and clerical employees on the staffs of twenty-two standing committees in the House and sixteen in the Senate.[4] The majority members in each house control about two-thirds of these positions with roughly one-third allotted to the minority. Among the largest staffs are those of the fiscal committees, which in 1992 accounted for 21 percent of the total committee staff in the House of Representatives and about 20 percent in the Senate.[5]

In addition to committee staffs, the following central support offices serve Congress as a whole in budgeting and, in many cases, the fiscal committees in particular:

1. *The Congressional Budget Office,* which reviews the president's budget; develops fiscal, budgetary, and programmatic options to reduce deficits; analyzes economic, fiscal, and monetary trends; prepares multiyear projections of revenues and expenditures; monitors compliance with congressional resolutions on taxing and spending; alerts Congress to expenditures exceeding legislative limits; estimates the costs of proposed legislation; and analyzes urgent issues on an ad hoc basis.

2. *The staff of the Joint Committee on Taxation* (composed of representatives of the tax committees in both houses), which analyzes existing and proposed tax legislation.

3. *The staff of the Joint Economic Committee* (composed of ten senators and ten representatives), which reviews the president's annual Economic Report and

selected aspects of economic and monetary policy; international trade and finance; productivity and economic growth; intergovernmental policy; and investment, employment, and prices.

4. *The General Accounting Office,* which is the primary investigative and program evaluation arm of Congress for oversight of activities of the operating agencies. It is also the congressional monitor of budget implementation and the lead agency for improving accounting systems for control and information purposes.[6]

5. *The Congressional Research Service* of the Library of Congress, which conducts studies and develops data for the standing committees and individual members of Congress.

6. *The Office of Technology Assessment,* which alerts Congress to complex issues of science and technology and develops a range of policy options.

Other positions include the staffs of the congressional leadership, individual members of Congress, and the majority and minority caucuses in each house. While budgeting is not their primary concern, they inevitably are drawn into fiscal issues because budgeting dominates the development of policy as never before.

In this highly fragmented structure, tensions on budget policy develop not only between Congress and the president, but also between both houses and among congressional committees. How the 535 representatives and 100 senators, buttressed by their support staffs and agencies, resolve their internal struggles and strive to reach a consensus on budget decisions is what congressional budgeting is all about.

Five Cycles in Congressional Budgeting: Pre-1960 to 1992

To understand the current budget functions of Congress it is essential to review five distinct congressional cycles that left their impact on the budget process: the period up to the early 1960s, when the appropriation and tax committees were singularly influential in budget decisions; the decade stretching roughly between 1965 and 1974, when the powers of the appropriation committees eroded; the 1974–1985 period when the Congressional Budget and Control Act became operational; the period beginning in 1985 with congressional approval of the Balanced Budget and Emergency Deficit Control Act, which changed the Congressional Budget Act in several respects; and the six years from 1987 through 1992, when Congress and the president sought in vain to eliminate the burgeoning deficits, a practice that continued through 1993 and 1994.[7]

Cycle 1: Dominance of the Appropriations and Tax Committees until 1965. From the 1920s until the mid-1960s the Appropriations Committees and the tax committees dominated congressional budgeting. On the spending side, the Appropriations Committees embodied the congressional power of the purse. In terms of influence, the House Appropriations Committee overshadowed its counterpart in the Senate. This was due in part to the constitutional requirement that tax and appropriation bills originate in the House. As the roles of the two committees evolved over the years, the House committee became the guardian of the purse—the saver, the budget cutter. While also intent on expenditure control, the Senate Appropriations Committee became more of an appeals body, which frequently restored funds for programs and projects cut by the House committee. Differences between the two houses on levels of appropriations were usually resolved in joint conference committees. In his classic study, *The Power of the Purse,* Fenno documents the dynamics of legislative budgeting in the era ending in the mid-1960s.[8]

The target of the Appropriations Committees, especially in the House, was the president's budget. What they cherished most was their power to cut the budget. This they did in each of the sixteen years covered by the Fenno study. Rarely did they initiate additional appropriations on their own. Strong committee chairmen and ranking minority members unquestionably controlled the entire process. They assigned committee members to each of the thirteen subcommittees that handled the thirteen appropriation bills covering the programs of departments and agencies. Each of the subcommittees delved into the programs and projects of the agencies under its jurisdiction. Through this process subcommittee members became the most knowledgeable legislators in Congress with regard to the executive budget. Their principal tools of inquiry were numerous hearings with agency representatives, and staff analyses.

On the whole, members of the Appropriations Committees were a conservative lot. With no lack of advocates for program expansion in Congress, they saw themselves as bastions of economy and efficiency in a field of spenders. Not especially program oriented, they were less concerned with the effectiveness of programs than with the need to look for weak spots in departmental requests for funds. The burden of proof was on the agencies to justify any increases to suspicious subcommittees. Like their colleagues, the members of the subcommittees catered to the needs of their constituents and used their power to support pet programs. What won them laurels, however, was budget cutting.

The tax committees rarely harmonized their activities with those of the Appropriations Committees. Expenditure analysis proceeded in one direction and revenue analysis in another. Fiscal policy emerged by happenstance, not by explicit planning. For objective analysis of the implications of the various tax proposals and for the development of options, the revenue committees turned to the highly regarded staff of the Joint Taxation Committee, on which both the Ways and Means and Senate Finance Committees were represented.

Cycle 2: The Budget Wars of 1965 to 1974. In the decade covering roughly the period between 1965 and 1974, bridging the administrations of Presidents Johnson and Nixon, budgetary power shifted markedly from the fiscal committees to the authorizing committees and from the president to Congress. These changes grew out of the tensions sparked by the Great Society programs of the Johnson administration, the war in Vietnam, inflation, and recurring recessions. More than ever, the budget became the battleground for the selection of priorities, the allocation of funds, and the methods of financing the budget. The outcome of the struggle was an erosion of the powers of the relatively conservative fiscal committees; a corresponding growth in the influence of more liberal program advocates in the authorizing committees; the insulation of the greater part of public expenditures (entitlements) from the appropriations process; increasing congressional intervention in budget implementation, hitherto largely an executive prerogative; and the expansion and professionalization of legislative staffs.[9]

The new cycle in congressional budgeting began with the enlargement and liberalization of the House Appropriations Committee in the early 1970s. As part of a set of reforms, the Democratic Caucus in the House stripped the chairman of his power to appoint heads of subcommittees and elected them directly, favoring those of a liberal bent. The Caucus also permitted members of the Appropriations Committee to choose their own subcommittees instead of being appointed by the chairman and ranking minority members. With this breakdown of the seniority systems, advocates of program expansion and greater expenditures assumed control of the Appropriations Committees in both houses. Like the authorizing committees, the Appropriations Committees became spenders.[10]

The effect of these changes was to increase rather than cut the budget proposed by the president. During the 1960s, appropriations were generally lower than the president's budget requests. By the early 1970s the reverse was true. During this period bipartisan consensus, hitherto a prized value in the Appropriations Committees, weakened and acrimony intensified. Previously, minority reports and floor amendments to appropriations bills were infrequent; now they were commonplace.[11]

Especially significant was the removal of most public spending from the control of the Appropriations Committees and the revenue committees, which, as noted, also have jurisdiction over social security, other income maintenance programs, and health delivery systems financed by the federal government (e.g., Medicare). By 1992 only 40 percent of appropriations came under the aegis of the fiscal committees. The majority of expenditures consisted of entitlement programs and "backdoor spending," whereby agencies had continuing authority in substantive legislation to spend money, to enter into contracts, and to borrow funds.[12] In a dramatic shift of congressional power, the authorizing committees now controlled these expenditures because of their jurisdiction over the statutes that permitted them.

With these changes, the legislative budget process became even more fragmented. The president was clear as to his own priorities. In Congress, however, budgeting was splintered among the appropriations, tax, and authorizing committees. In contrast to the president's tight control over fiscal policy through the Office of Management and Budget, no congressional committee considered the budget as a whole. No comprehensive mechanism existed to develop program priorities and to coordinate fiscal and economic policies. Congressional actions still took place on a piecemeal basis and in a series of isolated and, at times, unrelated decisions. For detailed data, Congress looked to OMB and the operating agencies, because it lacked adequate staff resources to formulate comprehensive estimates of revenues, expenditures, and deficits and to develop alternatives to the president's fiscal policies.

In a continuing tug of war between congressional committees and between Congress and the president, it became increasingly difficult to achieve a consensus on fiscal policy. Congress failed to pass appropriations bills on time and regularly resorted to the expedient of continuing resolutions to fund agencies for varying periods of time. Uncontrollable expenditures (outside of the purview of the appropriations process) continued to soar. More and more frequently the president vetoed appropriations bills and by extraordinary majorities (over two-thirds) Congress more and more frequently overrode the vetoes. Deficits recurred and grew larger. Inflation dogged the economy.

For many years presidents had had the power to cut expenditures by freezing or "impounding" funds. A frustrated President Nixon began to exert this power not only to control expenditures, but to curtail or eliminate programs he disliked. As the conflict between the president and Congress intensified, Congress found no satisfactory way of dealing with impoundments of funds it had appropriated. For these assorted political, ideological, and institutional reasons fiscal discipline broke down. Congress now confronted a fractured budget process and its own impotence in competing with the president.

This cycle concluded with the 1974 budgetary revolution in Congress. Determined to put both its houses in order, Congress created a Joint Study Committee on Budget Control in 1972 and directed it to investigate "the procedures which should be adopted by the Congress for the purpose of improving congressional control of budget outlay and receipt totals, including procedures for establishing and maintaining an overall view of anticipated revenues for that year."[13]

Any misgivings in Congress about the need for drastic changes vanished as President Nixon in 1973 directly assaulted the congressional power of the purse by impounding some $18 billion of funds appropriated for water pollution control, transportation, housing, education, rural development, and other domestic programs. In some cases the impoundments followed on the heels of congressional overrides of presidential vetoes. This time President Nixon went too far.[14] By freezing funds appropriated by Congress he provoked a constitutional crisis.[15] The impoundment of funds was not new and virtually all presidents had resorted to it with some success.[16] What distinguished the impoundments of 1973 was their unprecedented size, scope, and severity and the ideological fervor and confrontational style with which President Nixon sought to dismantle the Great Society of the 1960s. Another irritant was President Nixon's unauthorized diversion of funds for the secret war in Cambodia.

State and local governments, which bore the brunt of the Nixon cuts, initiated over 100 law suits in federal courts challenging the constitutionality and legality of the impoundments. Some sixty cases were actually decided by the courts, with the decisions in the overwhelming majority of cases going against the Nixon administration.[17]

Confronted by such unprecedented challenges to its power of the purse, Congress counterattacked by adopting in large part the recommendations of the Joint Study Committee on Budget Control, which it had established in 1972.[18] In 1973 the Committee proposed sweeping changes in congressional budgeting. After extensive negotiations and modification of some of the proposals, Congress in June 1974 almost unanimously, on a bipartisan basis, approved the Congressional Budget and Impoundment Control Act of 1974 (PL 93-344). Beleaguered by the Watergate affair, a wounded President Nixon approved the legislation on July 12, 1974.

Cycle 3: The Congressional Budget Act of 1974. The Congressional Budget Act of 1974 is a landmark in legislative budgeting in the United States. In significance, scope, and potential impact it rivals the Budget and Accounting Act of 1921, which created the executive budget system in the federal government. It had the potential to alter profoundly the congressional budget system, in effect recapturing many of the budgetary powers given to the president since 1921. For the first time, the legislation provided a broad framework for looking at the budget as a whole; considering simultaneously expenditures, revenue, deficits, and debt; formulating fiscal and economic policy; controlling expenditures; developing independent sources of information to evaluate the president's budget; and controlling the president's implementation of the budget. It was almost too good to be true. The euphoria that followed the enactment of the legislation was striking. The supporters read their own interpretations into the act. Only upon its implementation did disagreement and acrimony surface.

The Budget Act of 1974 created several mechanisms, decision-making systems, informational requirements, and organizational structures that affected both congressional and executive budgeting: two budget committees; a concurrent resolution and reconciliation process for budget decision making; a new budget cycle; enlarged staff services for Congress; controls over "backdoor spending;" and new informational requirements imposed on the president. The Act was a new superstructure installed on the existing rickety framework. Schick's authoritative study, *Congress and Money,* provides an admirable account of the forces shaping the act and the substance of the Act.[19]

A central role for budget committees. To the existing constellation of the four fiscal committees, the legislation added two other standing committees—a Budget Committee in each house. The overriding purpose of the Budget Committees is to recommend at the outset of the budget process overall fiscal policy and broad national priorities, which, once endorsed by Congress, would guide the other committees in their spending and tax decisions. These take the form of targets for expenditures, revenues, and deficits or surpluses for the budget as a whole and expenditure ceilings for twenty functional categories such as national defense, health, and income security.

The vehicles for the recommendations of the Budget Committees and for decision making by Congress are two concurrent resolutions, which set the targets, and a reconciliation process, which is designed to ensure the compatibility of authorizing legislation and appropriation acts with the targets.

The framework for congressional budgeting: the first concurrent resolution.

In 1974 the budget process formally began in January (later defined as any time between the first Monday in January and the first Monday in February) when the president sent his budget to Congress for the fiscal year starting the following October. Prior to the 1974 act, the fiscal year started in July. With the growing complexity of the budget and the requirements imposed by the new budget system, Congress decided it needed more time to analyze the president's budget and to develop a congressional budget. No later than April 15, or roughly two and one-half months after the submission of the executive budget, the Budget Committees were required to report in each house the first concurrent resolution with recommendations on the following:

Total budget authority (appropriations) in the aggregate and for each of the twenty functions.

Total budget outlays (expenditures based on new and old budget authority) in the aggregate and for each of the twenty functions.

The level of revenue with recommended increases or decreases.

The proposed budget surplus or deficit based on the difference between outlays and revenues.

The level of debt with recommended increases or decreases.

The level of loan obligations and loan guarantees was added in 1985 and 1990 to control the credit activities of the federal government.

In reports accompanying the resolutions, the Budget Committees laid out the economic assumptions underlying their estimates; compared their estimates with those of the president and the Congressional Budget Office; included a five-year forecast of estimated revenues and expenditures based on current and recommended policies; and highlighted any changes in federal grants to state and local governments. Neither the first resolutions nor the reports were binding on the authorizing, appropriation, and tax-writing committees. Despite their tentative nature, however, if approved by Congress, they represented the first explicit expression of congressional priorities with regard to expenditures and taxation. They guided decision making in all committees and Congress as a whole. Furthermore, no house could act on appropriations bills until the first resolution passed (unless the house waived this requirement) since the entire new process would have been pointless if Congress had passed appropriations bills before determining priorities.

While formulating the first concurrent resolution in a short period of time, the Budget Committees depended heavily on analyses and estimates by the Congressional Budget Office and the other standing committees.

By May 15 (a date honored as much in the breach as in the observance) both houses were supposed to act on the first resolution in order to get the appropriation and revenue-raising processes under way. It is tough enough to reach a consensus on spending and taxing targets in each house. It is even tougher to get a meeting of the minds between the houses. When the Budget Committees of both houses differed in their proposed aggregates, as they customarily did, they attempted to resolve their conflicts through a conference committee. Once both houses adopted the recommendations of the conference committee, the first concurrent resolution was officially in effect. As a congressional resolution it did not require the president's approval. At this stage it represented the views of Congress as to proposed levels of spending, taxes, deficits, and debt. It did not actually authorize spending, appropriate funds, or raise revenue. That came later.

After both houses approved the totals, the Budget Committees allocated appropriate levels of budget authority and outlays to the Appropriations Committees. For example, if the first resolution authorized budget authority of $100 billion and budget outlays of $86 billion for the health function, it was up to the Appropriations Committees to come up with appropriations bills compatible with those figures. The Appropriations Committees in turn parceled out allocations to their subcommittees. As in the past, the parent Appropriations Committee and its subcommittees were free to recommend funding levels for specific agencies, programs, and projects. But they could not exceed the overall totals unless Congress concurred with the changes.

Since the Appropriations Committees generally could not act without legislation authorizing programs for specified periods of time and setting expenditures limits, they looked to the authorizing committees for quick decisions. To expedite the process, the 1974 act established a deadline of May 15 for reporting legislation authorizing new budget authority for new and continuing programs. In theory, then, the Appropriations Committees had all the tools they needed on May 15: authorizing legislation and aggregate functional spending totals.

To make certain that the committees stayed within the approved limits, even though they were nonbinding at this point, the Budget Committee followed a "score-keeping" procedure. Through the Congressional Budget Office they tracked all actions by the authorizing, spending, and taxing committees to determine compliance with the first concurrent resolution.

The second concurrent resolution. By September 15, only fifteen days away from the beginning of the fiscal year, Congress was required to adopt a second concurrent resolution. Unlike the first resolution, which was tentative, the second resolution was supposed to be firm and binding. In the four months following May 15, various significant events might have occurred. Economic assumptions might have changed. By July 15, in a midyear review, OMB updated the president's budget and, in the light of the latest data, reestimated spending, revenue, and deficit levels. CBO took a fresh look at all the data. Actions by committees and Congress as a whole might have differed significantly from the assumptions on which the first resolution was based. By September 10 Congress was expected to complete action on all the appropriation bills. The Budget Committees took all these developments into account in preparing the second resolution, with ceilings on expenditures and floors for revenue. Once Congress adopted the second resolution, no bills raising expenditures or lowering revenues could be approved without special congressional action. The authors of the Budget Act viewed the second resolution as the most critical part of the legislative budget process. It was intended to synthesize Congress's final decisions on fiscal policy and program priorities. It was to be the congressional budget. Confounding the reformers, it soon became a dead letter.

The reconciliation process. The reconciliation process harmonizes the totals in the resolutions with necessary changes in legislation raising or lowering expenditures, revenues, and debt. The resolutions normally have one set of overall figures that differ with those of authorizing legislation, appropriation acts, and tax legislation; it is therefore necessary to change the latter. On the basis of congressional decisions on the resolutions, the Budget Committees prepare reconciliation instructions directing authorizing and spending committees to draft legislation that would reduce or raise spending for programs under their jurisdiction. Similar directives go to the tax-writing committees. By no means do the Budget Committees act alone in formulating the instructions. They depend heavily on the advice, assistance, and recommendations of other committees. Furthermore, the reconciliation instructions deal with totals. It is up to the committees to translate the totals into specific legislative changes affecting programs and projects.

When the Budget Committees get the proposed statutory changes from the other committees, they package them in an omnibus reconciliation bill, which requires the president's approval. In 1981, for example, under pressure from newly elected President Reagan, Congress adopted the Omnibus Budget Reconciliation Act (OBRA) of 1981, which incorporated hundreds of legislative amendments that cut spending by $35 billion for FY 1982. Similar developments affecting revenues and expenditures occurred in later years.

In practice, the reconciliation process has come to follow the first concurrent resolution, and not the second as envisaged in the Budget Act; the statutory procedure proved to be too cumbersome and time consuming. The first resolution and the reconciliation bill became the chief decision-making processes in budgeting.

Controlling presidential impoundment of appropriated funds. Equally as significant as the new budget process were the constraints the Budget Act imposed on the president's flexibility to impound or delay the expenditure of funds appropriated by Congress. Prior to President Nixon's confrontation with Congress on the impoundment issue, the president had considerable latitude in implementing the budget. One of the main pillars of presidential authority in cutting expenditures was the Anti-Deficiency Act of 1905 as amended over the years.

The Budget Act of 1974 effectively superseded the Anti-Deficiency Act. Now the president must advise Congress if he proposes to rescind any part of an appropriation or defer the spending of funds approved by Congress. In either event, Congress can compel the president to release the funds. Should the president decide that any appropriations in whole or part are not needed, either for fiscal reasons or to attain the objectives of a program, he formally requests rescissions of budget authority (appropriations) from Congress. Unless both houses approve this step within forty-five legislative days, the president must make the funds available to the operating agencies. Should the president decide to delay the expenditures of appropriated funds for any part of the fiscal year, he must also notify Congress and justify the deferral. The deferral goes into effect unless either house turns it down.

Staffing the new congressional budget process. To the galaxy of existing staff services in Congress, the Budget Act added the Congressional Budget Office (CBO) and the staffs of the Budget Committees. It also expanded the oversight and evaluation functions of the General Accounting Office.

The upshot of these changes was that Congress now had its own independent sources of information and analysis. It no longer had to depend on OMB, CEA, or Treasury for economic, fiscal, and program data.

Congress's view of the Budget Act in 1974. At the time of its enactment, both conservatives and liberals were satisfied with the Budget Act of 1974. For conservatives it represented a means of expenditure control. For liberals the Act offered a mechanism to develop national priorities and to initiate defense cuts. For Congress as a whole the new budget system, though complex, appeared to give it parity in budgeting with the president and controls over executive implementation of the budget. The creation of the Budget Committees raised the specter of jurisdictional squabbles with other committees. Especially affected were the Appropriations Committees and the tax-writing committees. The Budget Committees took over some of the major traditional functions of the Appropriations Committees. New staff resources gave Congress the potential for developing its own independent budgetary data and strengthening its analytical capability without undue reliance on the administration.

Results of the Budget Act of 1974. Did the Act work? Did it meet the high hopes held out for it? A growing literature generated by budget watchers, legislators, and specialists on the workings of Congress has addressed itself to these questions.[20] In it one can find some muted optimism, skepticism, even cynicism, and grounds for despair.

In view of the original objectives of the Budget Act, it has indeed fallen far short of expectations, according to its critics. Uncontrollable expenditures remained essentially untouchable, apart from marginal changes and some minor controls over entitlements and other backdoor spending. Deficits soared with little prospect of balanced budgets in the foreseeable future. Congress still failed to act on most appropriations bills prior to the beginning of the fiscal year, resorting to continuing resolutions on spending. Even with the cuts of 1981 and later years, Congress exercised little restraint in spending and enthusiastically supported President Reagan's massive tax cuts and the defense buildup of the 1980s. The government was now embarked on an irreversible course of unprecedented deficits and national debt. There were shifts in priorities, with cutbacks in various domestic programs and increases in the defense budget. In the debate over priorities, conflict in a divisive Congress intensified. This was inevitable. From the start the Act had the potential for escalating conflict by forcing action on priorities and expenditure and revenue targets. After all, what is more politically painful than getting legislatures to go on record for spending totals and deficits?

Despite some hopeful beginnings, Congress consistently failed to meet its own deadlines for acting on budget resolutions.[21] That the Act worked as well as it did in the early years was due more to the willingness of the Budget Committees to defer to the proposals of the other committees than to any unusual fiscal discipline on the part of Congress. Furthermore, the late 1970s were relatively expansive years when it was easier to reach a consensus on the concurrent resolution, the reconciliation process, and appropriations bills. Beginning in 1980 as the economic crisis deepened, a highly partisan Congress could not readily agree on concurrent resolutions. By the mid-1980s the concurrent resolutions were more patchwork affairs hastily put together at the eleventh hour than a bonafide consensus on fiscal policy. At times the economic assumptions and expenditure and revenue estimates underlying the resolutions became exercises in fantasy.[22]

If the Act did not usher in a revolution in congressional budgeting, it still offered several important advantages, according to participants and observers. It focused attention on major problems, forced legislators to look at them closely, spelled out the consequences of alternative actions, and provided vastly improved and authoritative data for debate and decision making. In the view of proponents, Congress has never been better served than by the independent economic analysis, policy analysis, and program evaluation generated by CBO. By compelling Congress to look at the budget as a whole, the Budget Act disciplined the actions of individual legislators. No spending, revenue, or debt legislation could be enacted before the passage of the first concurrent resolution unless Congress breached this provision, as, unfortunately, it has on occasion. With the passage of the concurrent resolution, the Budget Committee had the means of orchestrating the actions of the other committees through CBO's score-keeping procedures.

The Act also had the effect of expanding the dialogue on fiscal issues between legislators and their constituents. It led to a better public awareness and understanding of the mysteries of deficits, debt priorities, and entitlement programs.

Legislators developed a keener insight into the effect of the budget on the economy and the impact of the economy on the budget.[23] The Budget Act also sharpened congressional understanding of the fact that the current budget is largely determined by past actions and future budgets by current decisions. The five-year projections of revenues and expenditures mandated by the Act pointed out the future fiscal implications of budgetary decisions made today.

Although rarely followed, the new timetable and fiscal ceilings were useful. The control of impoundments was a shining success. The reconciliation process offered an indirect way of controlling entitlements. Congress became aware of the implications of tax expenditures, loans, and loan guarantees.[24]

Even so, the gulf between good intentions and fiscal failure widened. Congress soon learned that though the Budget Act provides a unified structure for congressional budget making, it does not guarantee results. It gives Congress a process for building a coalition on fiscal policy and national priorities, but it cannot force a divided Congress to overcome its ideological, partisan, and economic differences. Without the political will, no decision-making process, no matter how brilliantly contrived, will work. Process is no substitute for consensus. Where consensus exists, there is little need for new processes, gimmicks, and magic formulas.

As Le Loup argues, "if budget reform has not been a smashing success neither has it been a failure . . . Procedures alone cannot change behavior; they can only facilitate policymaking when leadership and will exist."[25]

Members of Congress regularly deplored the flawed budget process. Yet, paradoxically, they were determined to preserve it at all costs as the "only game in town."[26] Nothing else seemed to give them equally effective means to control expenditures and to offset the budgetary powers of the president.

Cycle 4: The Balanced Budget and Emergency Deficit Control Act of 1985 (GRH I). By 1985 it was clear that the Budget Act of 1974 was not workable, given a government controlled by two parties and a divided and paralyzed Congress. Once again late appropriations, continuing resolutions on spending, breakdowns in the Act's timetable, and squabbles among committees became the order of the day. The president's budget was irrelevant and Congress was in disarray. What the president and Congress could not ignore, however, were the uncontrollable deficits and debt. Lacking a consensus on priorities and policies, they resorted once again to a mechanical process, the Balanced Budget and Emergency Deficit Control Act (GRH I), sponsored by Senators Gramm, Rudman, and Hollings and approved on December 18, 1985. The legislation changed the Congressional Budget Act in several significant ways and mandated a balanced budget by FY 1991. To get to a zero deficit in FY 1991, the new Act specified incremental reductions in the deficit each year, beginning with FY 1986. If the appropriations bills failed to achieve the deficit target in any one year, across-the-board spending cuts ("sequestrations") would be made to eliminate the excess deficit.[27]

The timetable for the reduction of deficits put teeth in the provisions of the Congressional Budget Act of 1974 that required Congress to approve the size of the deficit in the concurrent resolution. In at least five other major respects the Balanced Budget Act revised and tightened the 1974 legislation. First, it eliminated the second concurrent resolution altogether. Second, it advanced the date for congressional action on the concurrent resolution from May 15 to April 15. Third, it accelerated action on the reconciliation process by changing the deadline from September 25 to June 15. Fourth, it placed off-budget government corporations on budget. At the same time, as part of a political compromise, it removed two social security trust funds from the budget, thus eroding the unified budget. Fifth, it incorporated in the concurrent resolution loans and loan guarantees, in effect formalizing a credit budget.[28]

On the whole, conservatives supported the Balanced Budget Act. At last they appeared to have a mechanism for cutting spending, eliminating deficits, and improving the economy (acting on the assumption that lower deficits would reduce interest rates and inflation). Liberals anticipated that the Act would result in lower defense spending and force the president and Congress to increase taxes rather than cutting domestic programs as a means of curbing deficits.[29] These views were similar to the political postures they had adopted in approving the 1974 legislation. Regardless of any misgivings, such was the political appeal of a deficit-cutting mechanism that the Act swept through Congress easily. In the face of an outraged public, Congress had to do something, *anything* plausible.

But even supporters of the legislation had several reservations about it. Some regarded it as a simplistic means of dealing with deficits and fiscal policy. In fact, they feared that automatic cuts might derail the economy at a time when it needed the stimulation of expenditures. They also viewed the legislation as a confession of congressional impotence in budgeting. If it failed to reach agreement on the budget, Congress, in effect, would put the budget process on automatic pilot and let the president slash or sequester appropriations across the board, regardless of priorities. To some of the critics, the new process savored of political grandstanding. Members of Congress could court favor with their constituents by voting funds for programs, knowing full well that automatic cuts would follow if deficit targets were not met.[30] Senator Warren Rudman, one of the authors of GRH I, called it "a bad bill whose time had come."[31]

Senator Rudman was right. The bill turned out to be a paper tiger that was no better than the 1974 Act. Deficits continued to grow inexorably, even though Congress tried to minimize them by using dubious economic forecasts and resorting to accounting gimmicks. The prospect of reaching a zero deficit in FY 1991 turned out to be wishful thinking. The crisis came in 1987, when deficits exceeded the GRH I targets, triggering the sequestration process that would lead to large across-the-board cuts in domestic and defense expenditures. President Reagan and congressional leaders flinched at this prospect, and at a summit meeting gutted the GRH Act. They revised the Balanced Budget Act to cut the size of the deficit targets, changed the deadline for the elimination of deficits from 1991 to 1993, and provided for automatic cuts divided between defense and nondefense spending should deficits top the targets. They gave OMB the power to implement cuts on the basis of joint OMB–CBO estimates of revenues and expenditures.[32]

Once again, the budget process wheezed along on automatic pilot. As the impasse between the president and Congress continued on taxes and defense and domestic expenditures, a crash landing was inevitable.

Cycle 5: The Budget Enforcement Act of 1990 (BEA). When the crash came in 1990, President Bush and congressional leaders found they could not meet the GRH II target of $64 billion for FY 1991. The looming deficit was at least $110 billion greater than that amount. This meant deep across-the-board cuts (sequestrations) in domestic and defense programs. Unwilling to take such drastic measures, the president and the legislative leaders held a summit meeting and agreed to scuttle the GRH II deficit-reduction targets altogether and to substitute for them expenditure limits on discretionary programs (excluding social security and deposit insurance) over a five-year period, FY 1991–FY 1995. The Budget Enforcement Act of 1990 (PL 101-508) implemented the top-level agreement with these features:

1. A $500 billion reduction in the deficit was targeted for the five-year period ending in FY 1995. There were, however, no annual deficit targets.

2. Spending caps were set for discretionary programs for FY 1991–FY 1993, with separate limits set for defense, international, and domestic programs. For FY 1994 and FY 1995 an overall limit was set for all programs. Expenditures exceeding the limits could be "sequestered," or cut, by OMB, in effect giving the president line-item control. Caps could be adjusted depending on the state of the economy and international emergencies.

3. For new entitlement programs and revenue changes a pay-as-you-go procedure went into effect. Any increase in spending for entitlements must be offset by decreases in other entitlements (after adjusting for demographic trends and inflation). Any revenue increases must be offset by revenue decreases. These changes were intended to bring about "deficit-neutral" budgeting.

4. The president and Congress agreed on expenditure cuts and revenue increases. (The latter would haunt President Bush in his quest for a second term.)

5. Because of the political impasse, no priorities were changed. They were frozen by an impotent government.

Table 8.1 highlights the failure of GRH I and II to achieve any significant deficit reduction and shows the more "realistic" targets of BEA. Even these turned out to be overly optimistic.[33]

Congress and the administration quickly learned that the new formulas lent themselves to gamesmanship, just as was true of previous mechanical contrivances for cutting spending. When the deficit targets could not be met they were raised. To protect favorite discretionary programs, they were sometimes blended with entitlement programs. The payment of obligations was delayed to meet the deficit target. Congress and the president used the pretext of "emergencies" to trigger more spending. Unrealistic economic forecasts made it easy to play down deficits.[34]

TABLE 8.1

Budget Enforcement Act of 1990 and the Reconciliation Act of 1993
(in billions of dollars)

	Deficit Targets				
Fiscal year	1985 law (GRH I)	1987 law (GRH II)	1990 law (BEA)	Reconciliation Act 1994–1998	Actual deficit
1986	$171.9				$221.2
1987	144				149.8
1988	108	$144			156.2
1989	72	136			152.5
1990	36	100			221.4
1991	0	64	$327		269.5
1992		28	317		290.2
1993		0	236		254.7
1994			102		234.8e
1995			83		176.1e
(1994–1998)				$514*	

e = Estimate

*Deficit *reduction* target 1994–1998, enacted in 1993.

Sources: Congressional Research Service, "Congressional Budget Process Reform" (Washington, D.C., 1991), p. 5; Tax Foundation, *Facts and Figures on Government Finance,* 1992 edition (Washington, D.C., 1992), p. 89; ACIR, *Significant Features of Fiscal Federalism,* vol. II, 1993 edition (Washington, D.C., 1993), Table 5; Congressional Budget Office, *The Economic And Budget Outlook, Fiscal Years 1995–1999* (Washington, D.C., 1994), p. 25.

Those who defended BEA claimed that it was the first serious attempt to cut expenditures and that it made deficits smaller than they would otherwise have been. Nevertheless, Allen Schick castigated it as a seriously flawed deal: "Perhaps it was the best that two warring branches of government could do under the difficult circumstances that they faced a year ago . . . Both the Administration and Congress wanted to escape the budget impasse that had dominated policymaking for almost a decade, but neither side was willing to surrender any strategic positions." Schick stressed that the deficit crisis was as severe as it had been before the enactment of BEA. The impasse in budgeting continued by freezing priorities. Entitlements that represented 60 percent of expenditures were protected. Budgeting control applied only to discretionary programs, which totalled about 40 percent of federal spending.[35]

From 1993 on, the budget remained at the top of the political agenda. With President Clinton's election in 1992, one party controlled both the executive and legislative branches. Even so, a consensus on expenditures, taxes, deficits, and debt remained elusive. Finally, in 1993 Congress approved the Reconciliation Act for FY 1994 by a narrow margin. The Act established a new deficit-reduction target of $514 billion over a five-year period, maintained discretionary spending caps at or below FY 1993 levels for five years, and set in motion the largest tax increase in peacetime. The combined effect of the Reconciliation Act and the Budget Enforcement Act of 1990 was to fundamentally alter the budget process in Congress and the executive branch. As agencies prepared their budgets for FY 1995 and later years, they faced unprecedented ceilings on budget authority and outlays. Not only were they effectively barred from funding new programs except in unusual circumstances, but they found it difficult to sustain existing ones. Similarly, congressional committees discovered that their funding choices were severely limited. The outlook was for bitter controversy surrounding each annual budget. Whether the budget caps would continue and whether the political price of the fiscal straitjacket was too high became dominant issues in the Clinton administration.

Having failed to cope with deficits for twenty years, Congress in the early 1990s gave few indications that it had strengthened either its capacity to control fiscal policy or its political will to take on such "uncontrollable" programs as entitlements. Despite the new superstructures of congressional budgeting, the old legislative workways persisted. Alliances of congressional committees, interest groups, and administrators developed many of the political agendas. Variously termed "iron triangles" and "issue networks" (to use Heclo's memorable phrase), they left their imprint on policies and budgets even under the axe of deficit control.[36]

With all these changes culminating in BEA, Table 8.2 outlines the new budgetary calendar for Congress. Despite changing schedules and procedures Congress still avoided making such fundamental budgetary improvements that had been proposed during the last twenty years as the creation of a joint budget committee representing both houses; merger of the appropriations and authorizing committees; the consolidation and elimination of 135 subcommittees in the House of Representatives and 87 in the Senate; recapturing control over backdoor and uncontrollable spending; budget resolutions with more specific targets; nonpartisan forecasts of revenues and expenditures; a strengthened and more timely reconciliation procedure; and presidential rescissions subject to a mandatory congressional vote (in effect a line-item veto that has been proposed unsuccessfully in recent years).

Congressional Budgeting in the Shadow of the Congressional Budget Act, GRH, and BEA

The budgetary changes in 1974, 1985, 1987, 1990, and 1993 affected the policies and procedures of the fiscal committees and substantive committees in several significant ways. Despite the problems in formulating fiscal policy, the Budget Committees remain a formidable factor as brokers in establishing expenditure ceilings and allocating funds to the other committees for budget authority and outlays. The use of one concurrent resolution plus reconciliation procedures has become the heart of the congressional budgetary process.

TABLE 8.2
Budgetary calendar

Deadline	Event
Five days before president submits his budget to Congress	CBO issues sequestration preview report.
Between the first Monday in January and the first Monday in February	The president submits the budget to Congress.
Within six weeks after president submits budget to Congress	All committees submit their "views and estimates" reports to the Budget Committees.
By April 15	Congress adopts concurrent resolution on the budget. If budget resolution is not adopted by this date, Appropriations Committees will receive their allocations based on the amounts requested in the president's budget.
May 15	The House may act on appropriations even if a budget resolution has not yet been adopted.
June 15	Congress completes action on reconciliation legislation.
By June 30	The House completes action on appropriations; last date for triggering "within-session" discretionary sequester.

(continued)

Effect on Authorizing Committees. The authorizing committees continue to adopt proposed legislation, thus creating new programs and projects, extending or altering existing ones, specifying the duration of activities, and approving funding levels subject to later appropriations. In uncontrollable programs such as entitlement programs, they are dominant. Once they approve and Congress accepts spending authority for these programs, funds are provided more or less automatically, without the constraints of the appropriations process.

Since these committees control more than half of all expenditures, proposals surface from time to time to combine them with the Appropriations Committees.

TABLE 8.2 *(continued)*

Deadline	Event
July 1	First date that a "look-back" discretionary sequester can be triggered.
August 10	The president notifies Congress if and how he plans to exempt military uniformed personnel from sequestration.
August 15	CBO issues its sequestration update report.
August 20	OMB issues its sequestration update report.
September 30	Completion of reconciliation process if necessary.
September 30	Last date for triggering "look-back" discretionary sequester.
October 1	Appropriations enacted; next fiscal year begins.
Ten days after the end of the session of Congress	CBO issues its final sequestration report.
Fifteen days after the end of the session of Congress	OMB issues its final sequestration report; the president issues a sequestration order to all departments and agencies, which is effective immediately.

Source: Adapted from Stanley E. Collender, *The Guide to the Federal Budget, Fiscal 1993* (Washington, D.C.: Urban Institute Press, 1992), p. 34.

Effect on Appropriations Committees. In analyzing the president's budget and formulating a congressional budget, all roads still lead to the Appropriations Committees. To be sure, their once enormous powers have been whittled away by the Budget Committees and the authorizing committees, and they must operate within the boundaries set by the concurrent resolution and the reconciliation process. Nevertheless, only the Appropriations Committees, through their subcommittees, examine the president's budget in detail. If the Budget Committees engage in macrobudgeting, then microbudgeting is the strength of the Appropriations Committees. Despite all the changes in other stages of budgeting, the appropriations process has been relatively stable.[37] Furthermore, the emphasis on deficit reduction and expenditure ceilings has given the committees a new vitality.

The congressional budget recommended by the Appropriations Committees takes the form of thirteen appropriations bills (at times, one omnibus bill) accompanied by committee reports justifying the appropriations. Once both houses settle their differences and compromise on a final version of the appropriations acts, the bills go to the president for approval or veto. The committees also handle continuing resolutions to provide interim funding for agencies pending agreement on appropriations bills and supplemental appropriations. Each type of funding raises separate budgetary problems.

In appropriating funds recommended by the Appropriations Committees, Congress does not directly control expenditures by voting on the level of outlays. Rather, it provides budget authority, usually in the form of appropriations, which permits agencies to incur obligations for expenditures. For current operations, the budget authority is generally good for only the fiscal year (annual appropriations). For programs and projects that require a long lead time such as construction, research contracts, and subsidized housing, the budget authority is good for several years (multiyear appropriations). For entitlement programs, activities financed by trust funds (e.g., highway construction), and interest on the national debt, budget authority is permanent. At any one time, then, agencies have available for expenditure new budget authority and budget authority carried over from previous years. For example, of outlays of $1.5 trillion projected by the president for FY 1993, 21 percent represented expenditures from unspent budget authority enacted in prior years. Similarly, in recommending new budget authority of $1.5 trillion for the same year, the president indicated that the administration expected to use about 78 percent of that amount in one year. The rest would be tapped in future years.[38] Thus, to control expenditures it is necessary to control the budget authority sanctioning such expenditures.

The anatomy of major appropriations. Appropriations come in various forms, sizes, and shapes, as the following anatomical details suggest:

1. *Congress acts on less than half the appropriations.* For FY 1991 Congress appropriated about 37 percent of the required funds. The rest were permanent appropriations and other spending authority, which, under existing law, automatically provided budget authority without further action by Congress.

2. *Most appropriations are multiyear or indefinite.* Annual appropriations thus represent the smaller part of available budget authority.

3. *Use it or lose it.* When Congress provides budget authority for a specified period of time, agencies must use it or lose it. Any part of the appropriation that is not obligated lapses or expires, and cannot be used later. Congress may, however, come to the rescue by reappropriating funds that would otherwise expire and revert to the treasury.

4. *Ceilings on budget authority.* Budget authority conferred by the appropriations act is not a mandate to spend funds. It is a ceiling on obligations and expenditures. When the appropriations act provides a specific sum for programs and projects, it generally uses such statutory language as "not to exceed" the specified amount. In some cases, such as social security payments and interest on the national debt, circumstances may change rapidly. Hence, the legislation contains no ceiling, but indefinite authority.

To lighten the congressional workload in appropriating funds, several changes have been proposed: (1) advance budgeting requiring congressional approval one year in advance of the fiscal year; (2) biennial budgeting as practiced by some state governments; and (3) selective use of two-year appropriations.[39]

When Congress, in a divided government, reaches a stalemate on concurrent budget resolutions, appropriations bills, and authorization bills, as already noted, it increasingly relies on continuing resolutions to fund government on an interim basis. Consequently, continuing resolutions have become complex de facto appropriations. They include the duration of the resolution; the rate of expenditure; riders expressing legislative intent and restrictions; funds for programs whose authorization has expired; separate funding levels for different programs; and different expiration dates for appropriations. The procedure is messy and untidy, but it works at a time when it is difficult to achieve a political consensus through other available mechanisms.

Effect on Tax Committees. Despite the changes, the tax committees in both houses control the details of tax policy with the influence of the Budget Committees being limited to aggregate figures. They were key actors in the major tax cuts of 1981 and the tax reforms of 1986. At the same time, they continue to be responsible for legislation affecting social security, welfare, and Medicare, including payroll taxes.[40]

How State Legislatures Budget

Prior to the development of the executive budget system in state governments in the 1920s, state legislatures controlled the budget process. Beginning in a small way, the new system gradually challenged the primacy of the legislature in budgeting. With a statewide constituency, strong governors began to formulate budgets reflecting the needs of an urbanized society. They fought for the constitutional and legal machinery to back them up and, equally important, small, but strong, central budget staffs. If the decades preceding the late 1920s were the age of legislative ascendancy in budgeting, the period running roughly from the 1930s to the early 1970s was the time of executive hegemony.

During these later decades, even if legislatures were inclined to assert themselves, they were hemmed in by numerous legal constraints reflecting popular distrust. In many states they could meet only biennially, with the length of the session severely limited to several months. Unlike Congress, they had to act on a balanced budget submitted by the governor, although in some states they were under no compulsion to produce a balanced budget.

In many states the legislatures' power to change the executive budget was sharply circumscribed. The best they could do was to strike out items; any additions were subject to a gubernatorial veto. In some states only a supermajority (typically two-thirds of the members) could approve appropriation bills, thus giving unusual power to a minority of legislators. In nearly all states governors enjoyed an item veto power that presidents have long envied. Without turning down an entire appropriations bill, they could veto individual items. In various states this power extended even to appropriations language expressing legislative intent. As Abney and Lauth found, governors frequently used their item veto power for partisan, political purposes, and not as a major tool to implement fiscal policy. Of course, legislatures could attempt to override the item vetoes by extraordinary majorities, but more often than not, this was a losing battle.[41]

Still other fiscal straitjackets existed. In most states various funds were earmarked for special functions such as the design, construction, and maintenance of highways. This limited the budgetary flexibility of the legislature as well as the governor. Bond referenda and other constraints controlled funding for capital construction, although as Chapter 5 demonstrates, legislatures have developed considerable ingenuity and resilience in coping with them. In the wake of taxpayer revolts, nearly one-half of the states adopted tax and spending limits, beginning in the 1970s.[42] As in the federal government, uncontrollable costs represented the greater part of the budget. These costs included state grants to local governments for school districts and income maintenance programs.

Revitalized Legislatures Strengthen Their Budget Process

Beginning in the post–World War II period and extending into the 1980s, revitalized state legislatures increasingly insisted on parity with the governor in budgeting. At least three factors accounted for this turnabout. First, budgets grew dramatically and imposed new demands on legislative bodies. This was the time to assert the power of the purse or to confess impotence in the face of powerful executive budget systems that characterized most states. Nearly all legislatures opted for the strengthening of legislative budgeting. Second, the federal Legislative Reorganization Act of 1946, coupled with the expansion of congressional staffs, served as a model for beleaguered state legislatures. Third, two decisions by the United States Supreme Court, in 1962 and 1963, changed the basis for apportioning legislative seats to make legislative bodies more representative. This resulted in more equitable and responsive state legislatures eager to use the budget process to implement the policy goals of a wider constituency.[43]

On the march, resurgent state legislatures expanded and professionalized the staffs of their fiscal committees in the 1950s. Even before Congress established the Congressional Budget Office in 1974, legislatures in several states had created central staff agencies that served both houses. Similarly, staffing for authorizing committees, the legislative leadership, and individual members grew almost expo-nentially. By the 1970s state legislatures began to take more seriously their respon-sibility for oversight of the administration. From small beginnings, they built up staffs for program audits and evaluation in nearly all the states.

Gradually, legislatures sloughed off many of the shackles that constrained their actions. By the early 1990s twenty-nine states had annual rather than bien-nial fiscal years; eleven states had a combination of annual and biennial fiscal years; and only ten states had biennial fiscal years.[44] Even legislatures with bien-nial budgets found it necessary to meet annually to consider adjustments in the budget. Some twenty states dropped limits on the length of sessions and longer, virtually year-round sessions became the rule rather than the exception, especially in the larger states.[45] More confident, well-staffed, and better-paid legislatures increasingly overrode executive vetoes. Budgeting became a year-round responsi-bility, regardless of the length of session. After adjournment, various legislative committees and staff agencies engaged in fiscal planning and analysis and policy development. Though governors in most states still dominated the budget agenda, they increasingly had to reckon and compromise with well-led, well-informed, well-staffed, and assertive legislatures, especially in the larger states, that were participating more and more in the following functions:

Ratifying and/or formulating policies and programs.

Analyzing and formulating fiscal policy and budgets.

Appropriating funds and raising revenue.

Implementing the budget.

Overseeing the activities of the executive branch.

Organizational Structures for the Conduct of Budgetary Functions

State legislatures differ in their organizational structures and systems designed to perform budgetary functions. Like Congress, they operate through committees, but several major differences exist. On the whole they have fewer committees, and place far less reliance on subcommittees than does Congress, but much more emphasis on joint committees representing both houses. In contrast to the frag-mentation in decision making that is characteristic of Congress, state legislatures have developed mechanisms for unifying and coordinating fiscal policy and other substantive policies.

These trends are especially evident in the structure of fiscal committees. Most legislatures have separate appropriations and revenue committees, while a few leg-islatures combine them.

In sharp contrast to Congress, twenty-one state legislatures depend on joint legislative fiscal committees with equal representation of both houses to handle appropriations and revenue bills. These joint undertakings either exist side by side with the traditional fiscal committees or can supersede them, as in Texas and New Mexico. Among the especially effective joint committees responsible for all aspects of fiscal policy are the Joint Legislative Budget Committee in California and the Joint Committee on Finance in Wisconsin. While the separate fiscal committees formally act on appropriations and revenue bills, they are invariably swayed by the recommendations of the joint committees, which include members of the fiscal committees.[46]

In three states—Texas, New Mexico, and Colorado—the joint legislative committees virtually formulate a legislative budget. This is due in part to the still relatively weak executive budget system in those states. So influential are these joint committees (especially the Texas Legislative Budget Board) that they dominate the budget process.

In developing fiscal policy the state legislatures resort to various organizational mechanisms that hold a lesson or two for Congress. Where joint legislative fiscal committees exist, they recommend to both houses a coherent set of policies covering revenues, expenditures, and debt. It is a common practice in nearly all states for authorizing committees to refer most bills with fiscal implications to the appropriations committees. In this way the responsibility for expenditure decisions is centered in one committee in each house.

To coordinate tax and expenditure policy, revenue and appropriations committees hold joint meetings in many states, or at the very least, the chairmen of the committees try to reach a consensus. Where state legislatures merge their appropriations and revenue committees, they facilitate development of a unified fiscal policy. Other common means of coordinating the decisions of spending, tax, and authorizing committees are a vigorous legislative leadership, caucuses, interhouse conferences, steering committees, policy committees, joint hearings by fiscal committees, and extensive participation in decisions by the senior staff of the fiscal committees.[47]

To eliminate any uncertainty about the fiscal implications of legislation, forty-eight states attach fiscal notes to bills. As the term suggests, these notes estimate either the current and future costs or the revenue that would be generated by the bills.[48] For more significant bills they are often fairly extensive memoranda. Fiscal notes serve as a coordinating device by highlighting the budgetary impact of substantive legislation. For all their usefulness, these mechanisms, in the last analysis, are staff aids in preparing for the political caucuses where the binding decisions are made.

Burgeoning Legislative Staff Services

With aggressive legislatures determined to exercise their budgetary, policy-making, and oversight powers, a large and growing legislative bureaucracy has developed to assist them. So dramatic has been the staff explosion that as of 1988, the latest year for which accurate data were available, nearly 25,000 full-time professional, administrative, and clerical employees worked for the fifty state legislatures. During the legislative session they were augmented by over 8,800 aides.

From 1979 to 1989, full-time legislative staffing increased 45 percent.[49] This is a far cry from the meager staffing of state legislatures in the 1940s, which was reflected in the results of a pioneering study of the Committee on American State Legislatures of the American Political Science Association. In the early 1950s, this committee recommended minimal increases in staffing for fiscal analysis and policy research.[50]

Especially noteworthy is the size and quality of the full-time legislative staff. In size, New York, Texas, Pennsylvania, Florida, Illinois, and Michigan lead all the rest (the number of staffers ranging from 1,047 to 3,100). For many years California had the second largest legislative staff, after New York. In 1990 the voters in a referendum sharply reduced legislative funding by 35 percent. At least ten states manage to get along with fewer than 200 employees: Vermont, Wyoming, Delaware, North Dakota, South Dakota, New Hampshire, Maine, Idaho, Utah, and Nevada.

So varied is the array of legislative staff services that it almost defies generalization. The staff services can be partisan or nonpartisan; joint (both houses) or single-house; centralized or decentralized; part-time or full-time; presession, session, or post-session; or a combination of any of these. Each type of support service has numerous variations, and some large states such as New York, California, Illinois, Michigan, and Pennsylvania have every variety of professional staff services. For example, the Michigan legislature has two appropriations committees, two taxation committees, and two fiscal agencies. Illinois has two revenue committees, two appropriations committees, a Republican fiscal staff and the Joint Economic and Fiscal Commission.

In legislative budgeting, staff services in the following offices play a key role: fiscal committees, year-round legislative councils that serve the entire legislature, joint legislative budget committees, legislative auditors, standing committees, and program auditors. When policy issues are concerned, the staffs of authorizing committees advise the fiscal staffs on the budget implications of a piece of legislation. In nearly all state legislatures the staffs are responsible for the following components of budgeting:

Analyzing the governor's budget.

Developing alternatives to the executive budget and, in fifteen states, formulating a legislative budget.

Reviewing appropriations bills submitted by the governor or drafting bills on behalf of the legislature.

Forecasting revenues and expenditures.

Recommending fiscal policy.

Costing proposed legislation (composing fiscal notes).

Developing multiyear financial plans.

Analyzing the state's debt and estimating its capacity to undertake additional debt.

Analyzing programs, policies, and projects proposed by the governor.

Developing legislative policy options.

Evaluating the efficiency and effectiveness of programs and projects.

Planning legislative hearings on the budget and preparing staff papers for legislators.

Drafting committee reports.

Analyzing intergovernmental financing: federal grants to states and state aid to local governments.

Monitoring the implementation of the budget.

Reviewing administrative rules and regulations.

This is quite a portfolio of functions, for which the responsibility is mainly lodged in the fiscal committees, the joint legislative budget committees, and forty-four legislative audit agencies. While the strong suit of these staffs is objective analysis, they must be sensitive in a political milieu to partisan loyalties, affiliations, and problems. They must be aware of the interests and constituencies of legislative leaders, committee chairmen, and individual legislators. Without compromising their integrity and objectivity, sophisticated and experienced legislative staffers have learned how to highlight the political implications of issues for their bosses. Even strictly partisan staffs serve legislatures best by a broad analysis of the pros and cons of available options.

The fiscal staffs attempt to sort out the major public policy issues, get a sense of legislative priorities, and package recommendations for legislative decision. Throughout this process they facilitate the formulation of policy positions in each house, mediate differences with the second house, and bargain with the central budget office and other representatives of the governor. In various states they settle many issues at the staff level, leaving only difficult and politically sensitive problems for decision by legislative leaders and governors. Once decisions are made, the fiscal staffs translate them into legislation, appropriations bills, reports, and other fiscal documents. Reflecting on the skills and maturity of the fiscal staff, the chairman of an appropriations committee chortled, "We aren't outgunned by the Governor anymore. We can command our sources of information."[51]

In an age of advocacy and special interest groups, the legislative leadership also contends with alternative budgets prepared by "African-American caucuses," "Latino caucuses," environmental groups, business organizations, supporters of the poor, ill, and homeless, and so on. Some of these budgets are well prepared and it is up to the legislative staffs to analyze them and develop a defensible position for the leaders when necessary.

Analysis of the Governor's Budget

State legislatures get an early start in analyzing the governor's budgets. Contrary to congressional practices, the appropriations committees or joint legislative fiscal committees of some forty-one legislatures receive copies of agency budget requests before the governor submits the executive budget to the legislature. The central budget office and the fiscal committees frequently get them on more or less the same day.[52]

While constitutional and statutory deadlines generally set the date for the submission of the executive budget, various state legislatures and governors have informal arrangements for advance release of the budget. In some ten states, legislatures get it prior to the session; in fourteen, within a week of the session; and in ten, within two weeks. Because of the tight budget schedule and the relatively short legislative sessions, the early release of the budget requests and budgets expedites the entire decision-making process. It gives legislatures the necessary lead time to act on budget documents, appropriations bills, and revenue bills in advance of the fiscal year.[53]

The main burden of analyzing the budget and budget requests falls on the staffs of the fiscal committees and the joint legislative budget committees. Unlike the fragmented fiscal committees in Congress, these groups consider the entire budget: expenditures, revenues, debt, and the economic assumptions and forecasts underlying the estimates. In this respect they almost function like combined congressional appropriations, revenue, budget, and perhaps even authorizing committees because they review substantive bills with fiscal implications.

The quality of budget analysis by the fiscal staffs in many states is exceptionally high, and it is difficult to single out any one staff for special accolades. A list would include, among others, the fiscal staffs in Texas, New York, California, Florida, Michigan, Ohio, Louisiana, Illinois, Washington, Connecticut, and Pennsylvania. One of the most effective legislative agencies is the Office of the Legislative Analyst (OLA) in California, which serves as the staff of the Joint Legislative Budget Committee (composed of seven senators and seven assemblymen who sit on the fiscal committees). It has been a model for Congress in establishing the Congressional Budget Office and for other state legislatures.

Established in 1941 as a nonpartisan and objective fiscal research arm of the legislature, California's OLA scrutinizes every item in the proposed executive budget and appropriations bills, including funding levels for programs and projects, economic assumptions, fiscal policy, revenue estimates, bonding for capital construction, and, especially, new and controversial programs. Within five weeks of the submission of the governor's budget it produces a document, *Analysis of the Budget Bill,* that in size, weight, authority, and complexity rivals the executive budget. For every item proposed by the governor, the *Analysis* carries explicit recommendations, as well as an evaluation of the most urgent issues. OLA also assists the fiscal committees in acting on appropriations bills; conducts major studies of the efficiency and effectiveness of programs; analyzes all bills affecting costs and governmental operations; evaluates proposed initiatives to change the constitution (à la Proposition 13); and engages in policy and tax research.[54] Regrettably, OLA was an early victim of the legislative staff cuts of 1990 and lost 60 percent of its staff. In the same mindless lashing out at government, the voters refused to finance the Office of the Legislative Auditor despite thirty-seven years of effective fiscal and program analysis.[55]

Impetus of Appropriations Bills

The fiscal committees trigger action on the executive budget by sending to the legislature three key budget documents: proposed appropriations bills; committee reports explaining and justifying the proposed appropriations; and a record of legislative hearings on the budget. While all three documents shape fiscal decisions, the appropriations bills are obviously the most significant. Once approved by the legislature and the governor, they become the budget for the next fiscal year.

Before the 1970s, the most conspicuous omission in the appropriations process was the failure of nearly all legislative bodies to appropriate federal grants, which constitute the largest single source of state revenue (approximately 25 percent). Federal programs providing grants usually ignored the legislature and relied on the governor and state agencies to request, allocate, and administer grants. Most federal funding came from categorical grants, which prescribe in detail how the money should be spent and left few options for governors and legislatures. Under these circumstances, legislatures had little incentive to challenge the governor's nominal control of federal grants.

As block grants covering broad functions such as health and transportation superseded many categorical grants, governors rapidly acquired wide discretion and flexibility in allocating the funds. This was a political challenge legislatures could not ignore, because of the size of the grants and the impact on their constituents and pet programs. Over the objections of governors accustomed to executive prerogatives in grantsmanship, legislatures insisted on appropriating federal funds just as they appropriated other monies. In several states the controversy reached the courts with mixed results.

As matters stand now, some thirty-seven state legislatures appropriate federal funds with some degree of detail; seven legislatures provide automatic or open-ended appropriations, essentially leaving discretion with the governor; and six legislatures let the governors handle federal funds exclusively.[56]

In appropriating funds, nearly half of the state legislatures rely on what Congress rarely accomplishes—one omnibus appropriations bill. In this way all proposed expenditures are contained in one document, which lays out their interrelationships. The state legislatures of Wisconsin and California lead their counterparts in this respect. At the other extreme are the legislatures of Illinois with 150 to 200 appropriations bills, Oregon with 110, Mississippi with over 200, and Arkansas with over 400.[57]

In the event of a deadlock on appropriations between both houses or between the legislature and the governor, the new fiscal year may begin without an approved budget. This occurred in several deficit-ridden states in the late 1980s and early 1990s. In 1991 the New York State legislature set a dubious record by delaying action on appropriations bills for forty-eight days after the beginning of the fiscal year. Through continuing budget resolutions similar to those in Congress, the legislatures and governors in these cases kept the state governments financially afloat until they could settle their differences.

Legislative budgeting does not end with the approval of appropriations bills. No sooner are they passed than fast-moving events may render them obsolete. In such circumstances governors and legislatures rely on supplemental and deficiency appropriations. When revenue shortfalls become acute, as in 1991 and 1992, many states cut the appropriations they had approved earlier.[58]

Overseeing Implementation of Appropriations

State legislatures have as large a stake in the implementation of appropriations as in the formulation of the budget. So intertwined are legislative and executive responsibilities in budget implementation that they merit full exploration in Chapter 9.

Oversight of Administrative Activities

For years state legislatures gave lip service to oversight of administrative activities as a legislative prerogative no less sacrosanct than the power of the purse. In the 1960s they began to take this responsibility seriously. By the 1970s legislative oversight had become a boom industry and still shows no sign of faltering. Legislative oversight encompasses fiscal analysis as part of the appropriations process; post-audits cum program evaluation; investigations by standing and special committees; "sunset" reviews; a flow of information on the performance of programs and projects; and the review of administrative rules and regulations. In importance and usefulness, fiscal analysis and post-audits tower above all other oversight activities. While sunset reviews have been a recent fad, they have had relatively little impact.

The keystone of legislative oversight is the budget process; everything else is secondary. Through the fiscal staffs in each house and joint fiscal staffs, legislatures review the efficiency, effectiveness, and impact of programs and projects. Such periodic stock taking enables the legislature to cut or expand activities, change funding levels, revise substantive legislation, and spell out more explicitly legislative policies and intent.

For in-depth program audits and evaluations, legislatures have established a variety of agencies, with the United States General Accounting Office a model in many cases. Several publications of GAO have become the "bibles" of comprehensive auditing and evaluation, particularly "Standards for Auditing Governmental Organizations, Programs, Activities and Functions."

The growth of legislative program-audit units has been nothing short of phenomenal. In 1951 only eight state legislatures had such agencies. By the beginning of the 1980s, forty-four legislatures had at least one office with the primary responsibility for post-auditing. Some have more than one. Side by side with the legislative auditors are elected auditors in thirteen states and auditors appointed by the governor or jointly by the governor and legislative leaders in eleven states.[59] Operating agencies may lack funds, but they suffer no shortage of oversight.

As is true of strong central budget offices, the staffs of several fiscal committees conduct ad hoc program evaluations. Some examples are the Office of
the Legislative Analyst in California, the Office of Fiscal Affairs in New Jersey,
the Illinois Economic and Fiscal Commission, the Fiscal Agency in the lower
house of the Michigan Legislature, and the fiscal committees of the New York
State Assembly and Senate. Finally, standing committees periodically conduct
studies of programs in such areas as education, transportation, welfare, and law
enforcement. They rely either on their own staffs or central legislative research
agencies.

For thirty-six state legislatures the existing tools of oversight proved to be
insufficient. Following the lead of Colorado in 1976, thirty-five legislatures over
the next five years adopted sunset legislation along the lines recommended by
Common Cause, a public interest group. (A sunset law ends a program on a specified date unless the legislature renews it.) In addition, at least eight legislatures
incorporated sunset clauses in selected programs. The supporters of sunset review
hailed it as a process of forcing a systematic legislative evaluation of agencies and
programs instead of leaving it to chance and the whims of legislative auditors and
fiscal committees. By establishing a specific date for the termination of programs,
the sunset legislation compelled legislatures, or so they argued, to take a hard look
at programs and to decide whether to end, change, or continue them. Common
Cause found that sunset laws had contributed to governmental efficiency and
accountability.

Beginning in 1983, sunset review faded fast, and, supreme irony, the state of
Arkansas used its sunset provisions to phase out the sunset law! By 1992, the
number of states with sunset laws had dropped to twenty-eight. It became apparent that the alleged benefits were exaggerated; sunset review was a time-consuming and costly process that produced negligible results. It led to only some
insignificant regulatory and licensing agencies in the backwaters of administration
being terminated or merged with other agencies. Substantial programs were rarely
affected because of their strong constituencies.[60]

That sunset legislation should have swept through so many states underscores
the yearning for simple solutions to complex budgetary and policy problems.
Undoubtedly, other fads will follow.

Possible Next Steps in State Legislative Budgeting

State legislative budgeting has come a long way in the last forty years. In fact,
it is different than it was twenty or even ten years ago. Despite constitutional and
legal constraints, legislatures have developed budgetary mechanisms that Congress
would do well to emulate. Admittedly, no generalizations hold for all fifty state
legislatures. In some states the pace of budgetary improvement has been uneven.
Even so, in budgeting, policymaking, and oversight, "today's state legislatures in
general are more functional, accountable, independent, and representative,
and are equipped with greater information handling capacity than their predeces-

sors."[61] None of this guarantees better decisions, but legislatures are in a better position than ever to understand the options before them.

Some significant problems in legislative budgeting still need to be addressed: controls over public authorities and other off-budget agencies; more extensive participation in intergovernmental financing; the political will to tackle uncontrollable programs; joint legislative–executive development of revenue estimates; more extensive use of program auditing and evaluation; improved coordination of fragmented legislative agencies; and a reconsideration of "creative" bonding as a major means of financing capital construction.

A Quick Look at Local Legislative Budgeting

So wide are the variations in the powers and functions of about 39,000 local legislative bodies in the United States (excluding school and special districts) that any generalization about their roles in budgeting in county, city, town, and village government is hazardous. Some large local governments such as New York City, Philadelphia, Chicago, and Los Angeles have budgets larger than those of small state governments. At one extreme, New York City shoulders more functions than any other local government in the United States, among them higher education, welfare, hospital care, and housing. At the other extreme, many local governments perform only the basic functions of law enforcement, fire prevention and control, road maintenance, waste disposal, and sometimes water supply, leaving it to special districts (e.g., school, water, and utility districts), other levels of government, and public authorities to carry out the rest. Even more rudimentary are the functions of town and village governments.

In budgeting, as in other activities, local governments are constrained by the state. State constitutions and statutes prescribe their functions, the taxes they can impose, and their limits on expenditures and debt. More so than the states, local governments are dependent on intergovernmental grants. Many local legislative bodies combine legislative and administrative responsibilities; others function like state legislatures. Some are nonpartisan; others heavily partisan. Some are weak and under the thumb of the executive; some are strong. Except for several large cities and counties, very few local legislatures have staffs for fiscal analysis. Some have the capacity to analyze the major issues and to evaluate the performance of the executive; most lack it. Some understand budgeting and other aspects of financial management; others are befuddled. Some illustrate the worst in legislative budgeting; others the best. Only empirical studies can capture the diversity of practices in local legislative bodies and the dynamics of the small groups that influence budgetary decisions. Some noteworthy analyses exist, but hardly enough.

The legislative bodies in some 3,000 county governments illustrate these varied trends. In 77 percent of the counties, elected commissioners combine legislative and executive functions and share power with elected clerks, auditors, treasurers, and assessors. Without a chief executive, they analyze requests for funds; review budgets, often compiled by county clerks; query department heads at meetings of budget committees or the entire body; hold public hearings; and appropriate funds. About 18 percent of the counties, those that are relatively urbanized, follow a council–administrator model. The council appoints a county administrator or manager who prepares the budget and, with the aid of a budget staff, assists the council in formulating appropriations bills. Only 5 percent of the counties, representing, however, one-fifth of the population served by county governments, elect a council and a county executive. In these governments the council functions more like a state legislature, with responsibilities for appropriating funds and overseeing the administration. Staff resources, however, are minimal.

Somewhat similar patterns prevail among the more than 19,000 municipalities. They follow either a mayor–council or council–manager form of governance. In the case of the former, the mayor can be legally strong or weak. A strong mayor functions like a governor and prepares a budget for consideration by the legislative body. Some councils, in large cities such as Chicago and New York City, have fiscal committees with small staffs, hold public hearings, and attempt to analyze the executive budget. Where a "weak mayor" form of government exists, the mayor is first among his equals in the council, with some administrative responsibilities and the opportunity to appoint a few department heads. It is the council, however, that formulates the budget. In council-managed cities, the council appoints the city manager, who prepares the budget and defends it before the council. The city manager is accountable to the council for the administration of the budget, as well as for the management of all city agencies.

The nearly 17,000 towns function like traditional counties, with the town boards responsible for legislative and administrative activities. Relatively few town boards appoint town managers.[62]

Nearly all local legislative bodies fall short in their oversight of administrative activities.

Points for Discussion

1. Compare the budgetary powers of chief executives and legislative bodies in the United States. What are the major similarities and differences?
2. To what extent do you agree with the statement that the president proposes a budget and Congress disposes of it?
3. What are the limits, if any, of congressional budgetary powers?
4. What are the strengths and weaknesses of the Budget Act of 1974? What changes would you propose in the light of current developments, including the implementation of the Balanced Budget Act of 1985, the Budget Enforcement Act of 1990, and their subsequent amendments?
5. What are the major tools of congressional oversight? How would you strengthen them?
6. What are the major differences between the budgetary powers of Congress and the state legislatures?
7. What aspects of state legislative budgeting, if any, should be emulated by Congress? And the other way around?

8. How do you explain the changing role of state legislatures in budgeting vis-à-vis the governors?
9. What are the budgetary strengths and weaknesses of legislatures in local government? What changes would you propose?
10. Analyze federal or state appropriations bills, hearings of appropriations committees, and reports of appropriations committees to (a) consider their impact on the executive budget and (b) evaluate their role in budget decision making.
11. To what extent would you increase or decrease legislative staffing?
12. Consider congressional reforms proposed during the last twenty years. Which, if any, do you favor and why? Can you suggest other possible improvements?
13. How would you control back-door spending such as indefinite appropriations?
14. Would you favor revising sunset legislation? In what form? Why?
15. Analyze the budget process in a state with a strong legislature and weak governor (as in Texas and Florida) and in a state with a strong governor (e.g., Wisconsin and New York). What are the strengths and weaknesses of each system?

CHAPTER 9

IMPLEMENTING THE BUDGET
Converting Plans into "Real" Budgets*

Budgeting does not end with the passage of appropriations bills, which are but a major milestone in the budget process and the precursors of still more changes ahead. As finally approved, the appropriations bills often differ markedly from the original budget. In effect, a new budget emerges, one that incorporates changes in policies and funding levels for programs and projects. It is this budget that must be implemented at the start of the fiscal year.

Even the new budget is not static. For a variety of reasons, in the course of the year, spending agencies may get more or less money than approved in the original appropriations bills. First, in most governments the appropriations bill is neither a mandate to spend money nor an ironclad guarantee that agencies will get the funds appropriated for them. It is a ceiling on expenditures for a specified period of time. Second, as unforeseen problems and new conditions arise, the approved spending levels change, often drastically. In rapid succession administrations or legislatures may hold back funds, supplement funds, transfer funds, and provide emergency assistance. As a result, at the end of the fiscal year, the budget that has been actually implemented differs significantly from the budget proposed by the administration and the appropriations bills approved by the legislature. If there is a final form of the budget at all, it comes at the end of the year, when the process of implementation is complete. Only then can it be determined whether the budget is balanced or unbalanced.

In this dynamic process, the original budget is but a plan, a blueprint. So too are the appropriations bills. What counts is their actual implementation. And the devil is in the details.

Surprisingly, budgetary literature tends to minimize the significance of budget implementation and focuses mainly on budget formulation, policy development, and the approval of appropriations. It concentrates on the changes in base budgets

*A modified version of this chapter, with an international perspective, originally appeared in Donald Axelrod, "Budget Execution," in United Nations, *Government Budgeting in Developing Countries* (New York, 1986), pp. 82–98.

and increments and decrements *between* fiscal years, but overlooks the major adjustments *within* the fiscal year even though they alter budgetary outcomes significantly.[1] In some governments the changes within a fiscal year may be as great as, or even greater than, changes between fiscal years. For example, hit hard by the 1991–1993 recession, thirty-five states in 1992 reduced their budgets after legislatures had enacted appropriations. In 1991 twenty-nine states took this drastic action. Among them, Florida cut $558 million from approved appropriations; Georgia $540 million; Maryland $380 million; New York $407 million; and Pennsylvania $258 million.[2]

This chapter deals with the dynamics of budget implementation. It focuses on the major levers that control the budget in action: the allotment process, including transfers of funds and the use of supplemental, deficiency, and emergency appropriations; the preaudit of expenditures; cash management; and other control mechanisms. It analyzes the roles of central budget offices, operating agencies, and legislatures in budget implementation, and the tensions that spring up among them during this critical decision-making process.

The Allotment Process: Releasing Appropriated Funds

Once the legislature approves appropriations bills, the treasury does not automatically channel the funds to the spending agencies. In nearly all governments the central budget office apportions, or allots, the funds periodically (monthly, quarterly, or semiannually) or as needed. Except in many local governments, this practice is virtually universal in the United States and other countries. For example, in the United States government no funds are available for the spending agencies until the Office of Management and Budget apportions them, usually quarterly, for specific programs, projects, organizational subdivisions, and objects of expense in the agencies.[3] In turn, the agencies allot the funds to their constituent units. A similar pattern prevails among most state governments, where the central budget office generally allots funds quarterly to the operating departments. Only in a few states are funds allotted annually, semiannually, or on an as-needed basis.[4]

The Structure of the Allotment

Whatever form the apportionment, or allotment, takes depends on the structure of the appropriations bill. If the appropriations bill specifies a lump sum, then the allotment may be a lump sum, subject to restrictions imposed by the central budget office. Conversely, if the appropriation consists of numerous line items, the allotments follow the same classification. In the United States, Congress and forty-one state legislatures increasingly rely on lump sum appropriations for agencies, programs, and projects.[5]

A lump sum allotment presumably gives the spending agencies maximum flexibility and discretion in the use of funds, whereas allotments by line item would appear to tie their hands. In actual practice, various controls and explicit and implicit understandings limit the scope of discretion in the use of lump sum allotments: restrictions in the appropriation language; additional controls by the central budget office; nonstatutory expressions of legislative intent spelled out in committee reports, hearings, and debates; "gentlemen's agreements"; legislative vetoes; and the specific commitments agencies undertake in the justifications supporting their budget requests.[6]

The Rationale for Allotments

The authority to allot funds gives central budget offices a powerful tool. What spending agencies get depends not so much on the appropriations as on the amount of the appropriations parceled out by the central budget office. This process raises significant issues of public policy. On the surface, it appears to weaken the legislative power of the purse. It certainly curbs the discretion and flexibility of spending agencies in the use of appropriated funds. It leads to searching questions on the limits, if any, of an administration's power to allocate funds voted by a legislative body. Despite any misgivings, however, the allotment process is virtually universal. It enables administrations to do the following six things:

1. Adjust expenditure plans, policies, and priorities to take into account the legislature's action on the executive budget.
2. Control expenditures, thereby curbing deficiencies and deficits.
3. Cope with unforeseen developments.
4. Cope with changes in the economy.
5. Promote the efficiency and effectiveness of programs and projects.
6. Control the funding of new and untried programs and projects, and the phasing out of activities terminated or cut back by the legislature.

Adjusting Expenditure Plans in the Wake of Legislative Action on the Budget. After the legislature acts on appropriations bills, the original budget may be outmoded in several respects. Funding levels for some programs and projects may have changed. New programs and projects may have been added; others may have been deleted or changed. The economic assumptions on which the budget was based may no longer be tenable. The estimates of revenues and expenditures may be obsolete. Grants from other levels of government may not materialize at the levels hoped for. In a matter of weeks it becomes necessary to prepare a new spending plan, in effect a new budget, to reflect these changes before the new fiscal year begins.

Both the central budget office and the spending agencies participate in developing this new budget. The former updates economic, revenue, and expenditure projections to determine how much the administration can spend. The latter formulates new spending plans or operating budgets to reflect legislative changes and changes in the administration's policies. Once accepted by the central budget office, the revised spending plans serve as a basis for allotting funds.[7] For this reason, their importance cannot be exaggerated. In reviewing spending plans and requests for allotments, the central budget office determines whether the proposed plans are in line with the administration's priorities and policies and with legislative intent.

Since requests for allotments are, in effect, mini-operating budgets for a quarter, a half-year, or a year, they should, as should any informative budget, incorporate revised work programs that show activity by activity and project by project what and how much will be done and at what cost. Such data provide the rationale for allotting funds. They also serve as a yardstick to compare actual performance and costs with intended accomplishments. Increasingly, state governments in the United States require revised work programs as a basis for allotments.[8] In many governments, however, requests for allotments are mere mechanical exercises, in which proposed funding is not related to projected performance. Operating agencies and even central budget offices generally devote far more attention to the formulation of requests for appropriations than to the implementation of the budget through the allotment process.

The United States Office of Management and Budget controls apportionments in part through monthly reports on budget execution. Due no later than twenty days after the close of the month, the reports lay out available budget resources, obligations, outlays, unobligated balances, and the variances between apportionments, allotments, and actual experience. This would not be feasible without internal controls and accounting systems that are required by law "for preparing and supporting the budget requests of the agency; for providing financial information the president requires for formulating the budget; and for controlling the carrying out of the agency budget, i.e. budget execution."[9] To support the budget execution system, the U.S. Treasury Department provides current information on the fiscal activities of all agencies through its automated "star project."[10]

At the local level, mayors, city managers, and city councils employ several strategies to adjust the approved budget and revise allotments in the face of revenue shortfalls and unanticipated expenditures. Figure 9.1 shows how the International City Managers Association (ICMA) has synthesized some of these ploys.

Controlling Expenditures. Allotments serve in nearly all governments as a major means of controlling expenditures. Through a periodic release of funds, budget offices seek to avoid a premature exhaustion of appropriations before the fiscal year is over; keep the budget in balance; control deficits, if possible; and obviate the need for supplemental and deficiency appropriations. For example, the Anti-Deficiency Act of the United States Government authorizes the Office of Management and Budget to apportion funds so as to make certain that agencies do not incur obligations and expenditures in excess of appropriations and thus require supplemental and deficiency appropriations. To implement the policy, OMB may, with the approval of Congress, defer and rescind expenditures and cut expenditures automatically ("sequester" them) if they exceed deficit targets approved by the president and Congress.[11] Most state governors have similar powers to adjust the enacted budget, subject in some instances to legislative approval

FIGURE 9.1 HOW TO MANAGE CRISIS BUDGET ADJUSTMENTS

When a fiscal crunch is brought about by economic recession, officials often must revisit the budget and make cuts. Some of these cuts will be relatively painless; others will be immensely painful. The most difficult measures will involve cutting employees from the local government payroll. The following guidelines assume that cutting people from the organization is a last resort that most managers wish to avoid.

Review the budget to make sure the assumptions made when the budget was developed are still correct.

Is the budget basically sound? Are all of its revenue and expenditure figures on target? This exercise should always be undertaken at least once, six months into the budget year. It is important to adjust the budget so that any changes made are based on realistic numbers.

Make the necessary changes in expenditure or revenue figures.

Be sure these figures reflect the most current information on expenditures and revenues.

Calculate how much must be cut from the budget to balance it. Assign department heads and/or staff members with lead program responsibilities the following tasks:

- Separating discretionary expenditures, such as program monies, from nondiscretionary expenditures, such as salaries, utilities, and rents.

- Identifying nonessential programs and nonessential elements of essential programs. If the difference between an essential and a nonessential program is not obvious, draw up and issue guidelines on what makes a program essential.

- Examining essential programs to determine whether they can be provided in a less costly manner. To shift to less costly alternatives in a short period of time may not always be possible, so identify options that can be implemented quickly, where appropriate.

(For example, can the locality cooperate with a neighboring local government to provide a service jointly at a lower cost? Can the service be provided at a lower cost by contracting it out to a private provider? Some local governments ask tax-exempt organizations to pay a voluntary service fee in lieu of propery tax. If the community has such a program in place, might some tax-exempt organizations provide a service the city has been providing?)

- Examining the essential services to determine if a user fee could be instituted to offset the cost of providing a service. A user fee is most successful when the service is consumed in measurable units (for instance, a pound of garbage collected or an hour's use of a tennis court) and when the cost of assessing and collecting the fees would be less than the revenue gnerated by the fee.

- Suggesting three levels of cuts (if the budget is large enough to make this practical) and defending each program left uncut. Listening to the arguments made by department heads will help an official make his or her crucial decisions about community priorities.

If program cuts and adjustments are inadequate to make up the shortfall, identify jobs that can be cut.

First, determine which positions will be vacated through attrition. Which of these jobs can be eliminated?

Next, look at positions that are currently vacant. Can these be frozen, eliminated, or consolidated? Is it possible to take a critical element from the job description of a vacant position and add it to the job description of a current employee? Again, department heads

(continued)

FIGURE 9.1 *(continued)*

or staff members can make invaluable recom-mendations.

Finally, if a shortfall still exists, consider cutting personnel.

Look at any legal or labor union obstacles to layoffs. Again, closely examine community priorities to determine which employees should be let go.

Consider the problem from two perspectives: first, the importance or priority of the job being performed and, second, the quality of the employee's performance. In some cases, the best option may be to cut a position occupied by an employee; in others, it may be to lay off an employee because of below-average

performance. If the jurisdiction has excellent performers in lower-priority positions, administrators may wish to make these positions half-time instead of eliminating them entirely. Department heads and staff members with lead program responsibilities can be of great assistance in making these difficult decisions.

This feature box was written by Janice E. Tevanian and Craig R. Bagemihl of META, a consulting firm with offices in Arlington, Virginia, and Miami, Florida, that specializes in management systems, information technology, and environmental services.

Source: Joy Pierson, "Analyzing Services to Balance the Budget," ICMA, 1992.

and restrictions. For example, departments in Illinois submit a quarterly allotment plan to the governor through the Bureau of the Budget. In BOB's review the focus is on low-priority programs. Once questionable items are identified, the governor is free to impound the funds.

Under the broad umbrella of the allotment process, governments rely on the following mechanisms, among others, to control expenditures: monitoring revenues and expenditures, setting expenditure ceilings, encumbering appropriations, maintaining reserves, impounding funds, timing expenditures and obligations, clamping down on year-end spending sprees, accelerating expenditures, and tapping government-wide lump sums.

Monitoring revenues and expenditures. Central budget offices monitor revenues and expenditures closely on a monthly and, at times, weekly basis to determine whether actual experience is in line with the forecasts on which the budget and appropriations are based. An especially critical review takes place in the middle of the fiscal year, when it is possible to assess the results of budget implementation during the first half of the year and to develop firmer estimates for the rest of the year. The analysis focuses on shortfalls and longfalls in revenue; overspending and underspending; slippages in capital projects and major operating programs; the effect of these developments on the deficit position of the government; and the performance of agencies responsible for spending too much or too little. Analyses of this type influence subsequent allotments.

Midyear budget adjustments are common in many large cities, although they are not as much in the public eye as similar changes in the federal and state governments. On the whole, though, mayors have less flexibility than presidents and governors in switching funds among programs. No significant reallocation of moneys can take place within or between functions without the approval of the local legislative body. At best, mayors can transfer funds between objects of expense. Not all large cities allot funds to agencies. In fact, in 1990 only slightly more than one-fifth did. For budget adjustments, the mayor and council depend on monthly and quarterly expenditure reviews and on the use of "encumbrances" to freeze funds.[12]

In assessing expenditure trends, central budget offices frequently have to contend with agencies that spend at a rate that will soon deplete the appropriation. This may result from patent mismanagement or simply unforeseen developments. In the case of the former, the budget office may sharply cut back the allotment of funds. When uncontrollable factors make it necessary to spend more money than originally contemplated, it is necessary to tap other sources of funds.

Excessive spending attracts most attention, while little emphasis focuses on agencies that fail to spend much of their allotments and appropriations. That the latter can be a serious problem is evidenced by chronic underspending for various programs and projects at all levels of government. For example, in 1992 federal expenditures fell $66.1 billion short of estimates. Only about one-third ($21.4 billion) of the shortfall could be attributed to the economy. The rest resulted from policy changes and "technical" reasons (delays, management problems, and unforeseen difficulties).[13]

Failure to spend allotted funds reflects a variety of economic, technical, and fiscal factors and, in extreme cases, a breakdown in program and project management. Whatever the reasons (unless deliberately contrived to reduce deficits), underspending undermines the budget process no less than overspending. Hence, budget offices attempt to control both. Through the allotment process, they prod agencies to spend enough to meet their targets. This may surprise those who equate budgeting solely with cutting funding levels.

Setting expenditure ceilings. Regardless of the amount appropriated, the budget office frequently imposes a ceiling on expenditures and obligations. The ceiling may cover the entire agency or selected programs and projects. It may reflect a percentage cut across the board or selective cuts. It may cover overall expenditures or the separate components of expenditures, such as personal service, travel, and equipment. It may couple spending limits on staffing with controls over the filling of positions and vacancy freezes. Ceilings cannot be breached without the explicit sanction of the budget office. Only uncontrollable costs, by definition, are exempt from lids on expenditures (e.g., entitlement programs and interest payments). In recent years, the expenditure caps mandated by the U.S. Budget Enforcement Act of 1990 and the Reconciliation Act of 1993 represented the most ambitious use of expenditure ceilings in modern government.

State governors generally have a free hand in imposing cuts, except in fourteen states where some form of legislative approval is required (by the legislative leadership or a special fiscal committee).[14]

Encumbering appropriations. To make certain that agencies do not run out of funds to pay for contracts, salaries, and major acquisitions of equipment, central budget offices at all levels of government frequently encumber, or earmark (the terms are synonymous), parts of the appropriation or allotment. The encumbered funds locked up in this fashion can be used for no other purpose than that specified by the budget office. For example, if the appropriation includes $3 million for a new computer system, the budget office may encumber this amount. This effectively freezes the funds and prevents the agency from using the money for any other purpose.

Setting aside reserves for emergencies. As a hedge against emergencies and unanticipated contingencies, budget offices often set aside a specified percentage of an appropriation in an unallocated reserve. Only the budget office can release these unallocated funds. Thirty-four states have established rainy day funds to see them through shortfalls in revenue and deficits, for example, the Texas Economic Stabilization Fund, the Wisconsin Budget Stabilization Fund, the Utah Budget Reserve Account, and the Florida Working Capital Fund.[15] In the United States government, reserve funds have been used for flood control, disaster relief, outbreaks of animal and plant disease, and law enforcement.[16]

Impounding funds. The ultimate weapon in allotment control is the impoundment, rescission, and cuts of appropriated funds. As noted in Chapter 8 on legislative budgeting, the president and Congress can use these formidable powers only for discretionary programs. State governors have a much freer hand in this respect.

Timing expenditures and obligations. Another way to control expenditures is to delay the obligation and expenditure of funds by delaying contracts, programs, and projects. Revenue shortfalls frequently trigger such actions, which merely hold off the day of reckoning.

Clamping down on year-end spending sprees. In the last few months of the fiscal year, operating agencies in many governments go on a spending spree so as to use available funds before they lapse. To control this eleventh-hour splurge, budget offices at times allot funds more rigorously on a monthly basis. Such actions, however, are merely a fiscal Band-Aid; they are no substitute for a comprehensive annual spending plan, adjusted quarterly for changing conditions.

Accelerating expenditures. Allotments can be used to speed up as well as to delay expenditures. In combating recessions, Presidents Eisenhower and Kennedy ordered their budget offices to expedite the allotment of funds, especially for public works and income maintenance programs.[17]

Tapping government-wide lump sums. In addition to appropriating funds directly to the spending agencies, legislatures also appropriate government-wide lump sums for all agencies for salary adjustments, price increases, contributions to pension systems, emergencies, support for central maintenance services such as building management and computer systems, and fringe benefits such as health insurance programs. From these lump sums the central budget office allots to each agency its appropriate share. In effect, then, agencies get allotments from two or more sources: agency appropriations and government-wide appropriations.

Coping with Unforeseen Developments in the Current Budget. While implementing the budget, governments can almost count on unforeseen developments and crises. These have become the rule rather than the exception. Besides revenue shortfalls, governments are also buffeted by natural and manmade disasters, recessions, unexpected rises in workloads, legislative changes, price increases, wage settlements, expansion in the demand for services, judicial decisions, and civil disorder. When these occur, existing appropriations often turn out to be inadequate, despite stringent expenditure controls. One way out is to request supplemental and deficiency appropriations. For most governments, however, this is an undesirable last resort. Wherever possible, they prefer to reallocate existing funds within available appropriations instead of asking for "new" money. Through the allotment process they therefore reprogram and transfer existing funds and resort to available contingency and emergency funds.

Reprogramming existing funds. Within the same appropriation account (sometimes just a segment of a larger appropriation), agencies, with the approval of the central budget office, can shift funds among programs, activities, and object classes. In the federal government of the United States, the changes can be massive, especially in the Department of Defense, which in some years has reprogrammed some 50 percent of its appropriated funds.[18]

Transferring existing funds. Two types of transfers of appropriations can take place: between departments and within departments. In most governments in and out of the United States, financial laws and appropriations acts generally prohibit the transfer of appropriations between departments. Relatively few state governments in the United States permit this practice, and the nine that do, only under tight restrictions.[19] In rare instances Congress legislates such transfers. In the past, the process was open to abuse such as the wholesale transfer of funds by President Nixon during the war in Vietnam, a practice effectively stopped by the Congressional Budget Act of 1974.[20]

Most governments do allow the transfer of appropriations between programs, projects, activities, and object classes in the same department. The central budget office has broad powers to effect such transfers. At times, appropriations acts control the transfers by limiting them to specified percentages of the appropriation account, say, 5 to 20 percent; by setting dollar ceilings on transfers; or by prohibiting entirely the shift of funds between personal service and non–personal service object classes. On occasion, outraged by what it regards as excessive spending, the legislature may impose a lid on expenditures for consulting contracts, data processing services, travel, or the use of cars and airplanes. In 1992 forty-five governors could switch funds between programs in the same department. They could also transfer funds between object classes within a department. In eighteen states they require legislative approval for these actions.[21]

Coping with Changes in the Economy. Coupled with other measures, the allotment process can serve as a tool of economic management. In a period of economic contraction governments can, as noted, step up the allocation of funds for capital construction, acquisition of equipment, and income maintenance programs. Conversely, in an expanding or inflation-ridden economy, they can defer expenditures. The Ministry of Finance in Germany has unusual powers in this respect to use the process of budget implementation as a weapon in managing the economy. To combat inflation it can block expenditures, curb borrowing, and request higher taxes. To stimulate the economy, it can initiate additional expenditures, providing parliament doesn't object within a four-week period.[22]

Controlling the Efficiency and Effectiveness of Programs and Projects. Many governments have used the allotment process as a management tool as well as a mechanism for controlling expenditures. Agencies should, in theory, be allotted enough funds to run their programs and projects efficiently and effectively, but no more than that. But what constitutes enough? And how can central budget offices determine the efficiency and effectiveness of programs as a basis for allotting funds?

The kinds of controls the budget office exercises along these lines depend on the management systems in the government. A strong budget office with capability in management analysis, program evaluation, and project oversight frequently spots unnecessary delays in programs, administrative breakdowns, cost overruns, and slippages in attaining agency targets.

The allotment process enables the budget office to use a carrot and stick approach in dealing with such problems. It can hold up funds until questionable practices are corrected. Even well-run agencies, however, may experience difficulties because of factors beyond their control. The demand for services may exceed prior estimates and threaten to exhaust available funds before the end of the fiscal year. Under these conditions the budget office can supplement allotments.

Funding New Programs and Closing Down Programs and Projects Scheduled for Termination. Through allotments, central budget offices control the start-up of new programs and projects and the phaseout of others. When a new organization or program is launched, the budget office may have little basis for allocating funds. The tentative work programs, implementation schedules, and preliminary cost estimates that justified the original appropriation are essentially "guesstimates," and often unreliable. In the course of the year, however, the operating agency eventually develops a realistic work program and determines its actual cash requirements. By allotting funds on an as-needed basis, the budget office assists the agency in implementing new programs and projects.

When administrations and legislatures eliminate or cut programs and projects, the phaseout of these activities should be controlled as systematically as their original buildup. To avoid unnecessary disruptions, the central budget office attempts to manage a steady cutback in funds through allotment control. In the cutbacks of the early 1980s and early 1990s, however, frantic improvisation rather than a scheduled winding down of activities took place in many governments.

Supplemental and Deficiency Appropriations: "New" Money

When the allotment process fails to provide sufficient funds from existing appropriations, administrations and legislatures, at times reluctantly, count on supplements to the original appropriations to see them through. These changes take the form of supplemental and deficiency appropriations. Both types of appropriations provide funds either for unexpected developments or for known commitments on which accurate data were not available at the time of the passage of the original appropriations acts. On occasion, supplemental appropriations are deliberately contrived so as to reduce the size of the original appropriation and then quietly, without the glare of publicity, supplement them at a later date. It may also be possible to incorporate in the supplemental appropriations new programs that lacked sufficient support for funding in the first round of appropriations. Some legislators see a virtue in using supplemental appropriations as a tool of expenditure control. By cutting the size of the original appropriations, they shift to the agencies the burden of justifying additional funds.[23]

So routine have supplemental appropriations become that many governments (with the exception of the federal government) frequently provide a cushion in the financial plan to accommodate them. What the precise amounts will be results from hard bargaining between the administration and the legislature. Either the executive or the legislature in the United States can initiate supplemental and deficiency appropriations bills as revisions of the original budget bills. President Bush's last budget, in 1993, proposed $855 million in supplemental appropriations.[24] In the past the amounts were even more sizeable. From fiscal year 1975 to 1980 Congress approved over twenty-four supplemental appropriations, averaging about $20 billion annually.[25]

Some critics suggest that supplemental appropriations lead to fragmentation of the budgetary process. To take this view is to assume that the end product of budgeting is a comprehensive, coherent, and coordinated budget and set of appropriations bills, and that any deviations from them are aberrations. This chapter has emphasized that budgeting requires flexibility in responding to changing circumstances. Allotments, transfers, and supplemental appropriations are all parts of the adjustment mechanism.

The Effect of Budget Implementation on Operating Agencies

At first blush, budget implementation, especially through allotments and transfers, appears to hamper the discretion and flexibility of operating agencies. Nearly all agencies complain bitterly about control or even overcontrol by the central budget office because, in many cases, they can't commit funds, fill positions, purchase equipment, and send their employees on field trips without the explicit approval of that office. Closest to the scene of operations, they seek maximum flexibility in the use of funds without the interference of the budget staff. To what extent is it possible to reconcile the need for central control with the need for agency discretion in managing programs and projects?

No flat rule on flexibility in administering the budget holds for all agencies. Depending on circumstances, and relationships with the administration and the legislature, some agencies enjoy considerable latitude. Others are held by a tight rein. In general, though, operating agencies in many governments participate actively in the entire process of budget implementation. Far from being passive participants who are more acted upon than acting, they influence every phase of the process. Within the policies set by the central budget office, they formulate spending plans, initiate and amend allotments, propose changes in priorities, and collaborate actively with the budget office in expenditure control. Furthermore, with the power to sub-allot allocations from the central budget office, the agencies control expenditures throughout the entire organizational network. Without such decentralization in budget implementation, the central budget office would be swamped with detail.

In the United States the extent of decentralization in budget implementation varies with the political system, the political clout and managerial skills of an agency, and the management style of the administration. Agencies that have strong management systems and clearly control their programs, projects, and costs achieve considerable credibility with administrations and legislatures and, in general, gain more flexibility in controlling their funds.

When agencies abuse their discretion or fail to control their costs, the legislature and the administration are apt to impose additional controls on them. In appropriating funds, the legislature may shift from lump sums to inflexible line items. It may limit the agency's power to transfer funds and may insert restrictions on spending in the appropriations act. In addition, the central budget office may control allotments even more severely and limit agency discretion in sub-allotting and transferring funds.

In budget implementation, the rub comes when frustrated and possibly unsophisticated administrations impose line-item controls on spending on all agencies, the well-run and the mediocre alike. Agencies can tolerate expenditure ceilings, position controls, and other limits on expenditures, providing they can administer them and report the results of their actions to the central budget office. What they find discouraging and demeaning is the necessity to get prior approval on a case-by-case basis for thousands of items. Such overcontrol is unnecessarily time consuming and ultimately self-defeating. It has the unintended effect of discouraging agency participation in expenditure control and leading some agencies, as a consequence, to pad their budgets and request deficiency appropriations.[26] In the recent recessions, crude item-by-item controls were in effect in nearly all state and local governments.

Far from being inherently irreconcilable, central control and agency flexibility can be complementary. Within expenditure limits and policy guidelines established by the administration, the agency can still have broad discretion in implementing the budget. For such sharing of power to work, it is necessary to develop appropriate ground rules, standards, criteria, formulas, understandings, and comprehensive work programs.[27] For example, the development of a staffing pattern obviates the need for the approval of individual positions. The formulation of a costed work program makes it unnecessary to justify each separate item in budget implementation. The development of standards and criteria, however, is a difficult and time-consuming exercise. As a result, too many central budget offices and agencies tend to shun it and, in times of crisis, are apt to resort to "meat-ax" budgeting.

The Role of Legislatures in Budget Implementation

On the surface, executive flexibility during budget implementation appears to challenge legislative prerogatives. The moneys agencies actually get may be lower or higher than the appropriations. Legislative intent may be negated as funds are authorized but not spent, spent for unauthorized purposes, overspent despite legislative ceilings, or spent in violation of formal and informal expressions of legislative policy. How far can administrations go in budget implementation? What limits, if any, control their actions? To what extent should legislatures have a role in budget implementation? What kind of role? Or should they concentrate primarily on appropriations?

The controls exerted by legislatures on budget implementation vary with legal, political, and budgetary systems. In the United States, unfettered power by chief executives to manage expenditures has led to tensions and confrontations with legislatures at all levels of government. As a result, legislatures insist on participating in budget implementation just as they do in budget formulation. Inevitably, this involves them in the details of administration and upsets any tidy dichotomies of the respective roles of the chief executive and the legislature.

Congress and state legislatures in the United States exercise their growing power over budget implementation in a variety of ways, including control of allotments; prior approval of reprogramming (shifting funds between programs), transfers, and individual projects; approval of expenditures from emergency funds; oversight through reports on expenditures and revenues; changes in substantive legislation and appropriations acts; and in some states, such as California and Wisconsin, the use of budget directives to guide budget implementation.

Control of Allotments

As noted previously, the president is no longer free to impound appropriations or to delay apportioning funds from them. Congress can veto any proposed rescissions or deferrals of budget authority. Some automatic cuts, or "sequesters," of the approved budget can occur under GRH and BEA (see Chapter 8), but these are rare. With occasional exceptions, the impoundment of funds has not been a significant issue among state and local governments in the United States, although challenges in the courts have surfaced in recent years. Most state constitutions already give governors the power to veto items in an appropriation without the necessity of turning down the entire bill. Hence governors have less reason than presidents to freeze appropriations. In a recession-ridden economy, however, governors in the early 1990s tended to make more use of impoundments, subject to minimal legislative control.

Prior Approval of Reprogramming and Transfers

Through their committees and subcommittees (primarily appropriations committees) legislatures in many cases approve or reject executive proposals to reprogram, transfer, or, for certain projects, allocate appropriated funds. Formal action of this type rounds out the powers legislatures already exercise through informal consultation with operating agencies and central budget offices and through guidelines in appropriations acts and in reports of appropriations committees.[28] At the federal level agencies generally cannot reprogram funds without the explicit approval of subcommittees of the Appropriations Committees of both houses. This gives senior members of the subcommittees significant powers, which they exercise without needing to get the concurrence of the entire Congress.[29]

Fiscal committees in only about eighteen state legislatures have relatively limited power to prohibit gubernatorial transfers of funds.[30] Nevertheless, statutory guidelines frequently limit the governor's discretion.

Where legislatures have voice in budget implementation, they resort to a variety of means to authorize transfers. They either give exclusive power to a fiscal committee or share the power with the governor and other members of the administration on so-called control boards. For example, in New Mexico the Legislative Finance Committee monitors adjustments of the enacted budget. In Ohio the State Control Board, composed of legislative and executive representatives, approves transfers. In Hawaii legislative leaders have similar powers. In Georgia, the Fiscal Affairs Subcommittee of the General Assembly approves transfers between object classes and amendments to appropriations acts. In Wisconsin the Joint Finance Committee and the statutory Board of Government Operations (BOGO), representing both houses, authorize selected transfers. In Oregon an Emergency Board, composed solely of legislative representatives, can supplement funding for programs financed by federal and earmarked funds.

While the power of some state legislatures to authorize transfers in the course of budget implementation is gaining a foothold in some states and is impressive, it should not be exaggerated. In most states the administration controls transfers, subject only to the informal influence of legislative leaders.

Prior Approval or Veto of Projects and Programs

For some capital projects and programs Congress requires an unprecedented three-stage approval process. It is not enough to approve a project in the authorizing legislation and in the appropriations act. Before funds are allotted, the relevant committees insist on advance approval of such expenditures. For example, the General Services Administration cannot acquire, lease, purchase, or alter a public building valued over $500,000 without the specific authorization of the Committee of Public Works in both houses. As a result, both committees review some 100 plans and prospectuses annually. The Veterans Affairs Committees in both houses enjoy similar powers with regard to capital facilities for veterans.[31]

These are examples of the wide powers Congress has enjoyed over sixty years to veto the funding of projects and programs previously approved in appropriations acts. At least 120 statutes give Congress the legislative veto power—several estimates go even higher. While resisting presidential attempts to gain item veto power, Congress itself has persisted in using it in budget implementation. Congress was momentarily jolted in 1983, when the United States Supreme Court in *Immigration and Naturalization Service v. Chadha* ruled that the legislative veto was unconstitutional and represented an unwarranted congressional intrusion into the powers of the executive branch. Despite the cloud of unconstitutionality, however, Congress continues to exercise legislative vetoes, and presidents and operating agencies demur, but bow to the congressional power of the purse.[32]

Approving the Allotment of Emergency Funds

As noted, legislatures provide funds for emergencies either in the appropriations acts for the operating agencies or in a special government-wide appropriations bill. In either case, they participate extensively in the approval of allotments from such appropriations. In Congress, Appropriations Committees not only approve the use of reserve funds set aside for emergencies, but also commit themselves to replenish such funds in subsequent appropriations.[33] In about half the states, legislatures alone authorize allotments from emergency or contingency funds or share this power with the governor. Among the other states only gubernatorial approval is required.[34] As in the federal government, legislatures replenish allotted funds to keep emergency appropriations at a constant level.

Monitoring Other Adjustments in Spending

At the very least, legislatures require continuing reports from operating agencies and central budget offices on revenues, expenditures, allotments, transfers, and other adjustments in appropriations. They look to the staffs of their fiscal committees to analyze the data and to alert them to any significant deviations from appropriations acts or other expressions of legislative intent.

Basic Legislative Controls over Budget Implementation:
Appropriation Acts and Financial Laws

Transcending in importance all formal and informal mechanisms for controlling budget implementation is the overarching power of legislatures in the United States to limit executive actions through financial laws and appropriations. Just as

Congress empowered the president to allot funds in the Anti-Deficiency Act of 1906 (as revised), so it curbed the abuse of that power in the Congressional Budget and Impoundment Control Act of 1974. In the appropriations acts and other statutes, legislatures can contract or expand executive discretion to allot and shift funds, set standards and conditions for the use of funds, control the timing of expenditures, require prior approval of changes in funding levels, establish ceilings on expenditures, and lay out other expressions of legislative intent.

In any major legislative–executive confrontation on the implementation of appropriations bills in the United States, the legislature is bound to prevail, as presidents and several state governors have learned the hard way.

In a continuous loop, budget implementation follows budget formulation, but is also a prelude to the next round of budget formulation. How legislatures act on proposed budgets is determined in large part by their experience with the implementation of the current budget. Should executive actions elude their control, violate legislative intent, or prove to be grossly inefficient and ineffective, the legislature can take corrective measures in later appropriations acts and other statutes. As part of the checks and balances in American budgeting, these powers tend to make legislatures equal partners in budget implementation, just as they are in budget formulation. In recurring budget crises, this trend will intensify as the implementation of the budget becomes as significant as the formulation of the budget.

Nonetheless, the intervention of legislative bodies in such details of budget implementation as staffing levels, prior approval of projects, and shifts of funds appears to constitute an invasion of executive prerogatives. It appears to erode the traditional boundary between legislative policymaking and executive administration. Such dichotomies, however, may work out in theory, but rarely in practice. Without implementation, budget formulation is an empty exercise. What really counts in budget policy is its execution. To shut out legislative bodies from participation in budget implementation is to deny them a role in a major part of budget decision making. No American legislature will readily accept such limits on its powers.

The issue, then, is not whether legislatures in the United States should participate in budget implementation. Rather, it is the range of powers they should possess and the specific role they should play. In a fast-moving and fluid process influenced by political, legal, economic, personal, and social factors, each government will work out its own delicate balance of legislative–executive relationships in budget implementation.

Preauditing Expenditures, Internal Financial Controls, and Cash Management

Three other vital controls in budget implementation are the preaudit of expenditures, internal financial controls, and cash management. Though usually regarded as major instruments of financial management, these controls are essential in budget execution. The preaudit process, especially, is the watchdog of budget implementation. No payrolls are honored, no purchase orders endorsed, no claims paid, no grants made, and no contracts approved unless the office responsible for preauditing satisfies itself that the proposed expenditures comply with the pertinent statutes, appropriations, allotments, and informal understandings with the legislature. Through such checks the preaudit process enforces legislative and executive policies. Cash management serves another critical need, which is to make certain that enough money is on hand on time throughout the year to pay for budgeted expenses. With an empty treasury, even for short periods of time, a government is hardly in a position to implement any budgets and incurs still heavier costs by short-term borrowing to stay afloat. Internal controls, in the words of the U.S. Office of Management and Budget, "provide information on actual obligations, outlays, and budgetary resources and establish controls consistent with financial plans."[35]

The Preaudit Process: Guarding the Gate of the Treasury

In most governments two control points exist for the preauditing of expenditures: internal audits in the operating agencies and audits in a central control agency such as the office of the comptroller, auditor, or accountant.

At a minimum, internal audit units in the operating agencies preaudit all payrolls, vouchers, purchase orders, contracts, and other documents to check compliance with the financial laws, appropriations acts, and allotments by the central budget office. In particular, they review the availability of funds to pay for a proposed expenditure and the legality, accuracy, regularity, and propriety of the expenditure. Where they come across indications of fraud, waste, mismanagement, or cost overruns, they may "blow the whistle." They will not win any popularity contests within the agency, but they give the agency head the opportunity to take remedial measures before a central control agency or a legislative investigation ferrets out the transactions.

The failure of internal controls in New Jersey in 1989 highlights this issue. As a result of breakdowns of controls in the Department of Human Services and in the central accounting office, the Division of Developmental Disabilities overspent its budget by $32 million at a time when the state experienced a shortfall of $300 million in revenue. Even minimal preaudits could have averted this fiasco.[36]

From basic preaudits, the role of internal audit offices in some governments has evolved to the point where they analyze the utilization and costs of all resources, including staff, equipment, capital facilities, and supplies; the efficiency and economy of operations; the results achieved by programs and projects; and the adequacy of financial and performance reports. In the federal government, the Federal Managers Financial Integrity Act of 1982 established standards of internal financial and management controls for operating agencies, with the Executive Council on Integrity and Efficiency and the President's Council on Integrity and Efficiency responsible for oversight of the program.

Not all operating agencies in state and local governments have strong internal audit offices with such a broad range of functions. Nevertheless, this is the trend, and in several states, as in New York, it is mandated by law.[37]

In large national governments of countries such as the United States, Britain, France, and Germany, preauditing is primarily the responsibility of the operating agencies; a central control agency would be swamped by the large volume of transactions. In smaller governments, including state and local governments in the United States, a central control agency has the final responsibility for preauditing expenditures. State governments rely on a variety of organizations to do this. Some assign the function to elected comptrollers and auditors. Most state governments, however, have lodged preauditing in a central accounting office, which in several states is part of an umbrella agency such as a department of administration or department of finance.

Central control agencies act as guardians at the gate of the treasury. Whatever complies with the specific letter of law, the appropriations acts, and the allotments goes through, providing sufficient funds are available. Everything else is turned down. By law and practice, the central preaudit office does not concern itself with the need for and the efficiency and effectiveness of expenditures. That is the prerogative of the chief executive and the legislature.

Cash Management: Assuring the Availability of Needed Funds

Cash management focuses on both expenditures and revenues and seeks to avoid three dangers. One is a liquidity crisis, when governments run out of cash to meet known, let alone unforeseen, obligations. In this case, they look to lenders to bail them out temporarily at high interest cost. Another hazard is the failure to collect revenues owed to the government quickly and deposit them in the government's account. Still a third problem is the failure to invest funds that may not be needed for some days, weeks, or months. Temporarily idle cash balances draw no interest and hence represent a loss of potential revenue.

To manage cash, governments require the most current data that accounting systems can produce on expenditures, revenues, and especially on cash flow. The aim is to have enough, but just enough, cash on hand to cover liabilities and to invest idle funds temporarily in safe and profitable havens from which they can be drawn quickly as the need arises. For this purpose governments require timely reports on the status of all funds: revenues, expenditures, and obligations. For example, the U.S. Treasury Department prepares a daily cash report showing the operating balances of all funds. It is also necessary to forecast with some precision the cash needs of government for ensuing weeks and months. So large are the stakes that cash management is not a mere technical issue. In the course of the year over $1 trillion dollars flow through state and local governments and nearly $2.5 trillion through the federal government.[38]

Seasonality in Revenue Collections and Spending. Several policy and technical problems complicate cash management. One major issue is the uneven flow of revenues, which does not coincide with the flow of expenditures. What a delightful technocratic (and political) paradise it would be if just enough revenue poured in each month to cover the expenditures for that month. Unfortunately, revenues and expenditures fluctuate dramatically because of seasonal, statutory, and economic factors. At one time the government's exchequer may have cash in excess of its needs. On other occasions expenditures may top revenues by a wide margin, necessitating quick infusions of cash. Some of these developments are uncontrollable, as in the case of unexpected revenue shortfalls brought on by recession. Others are controllable, such as statutory timetables for expenditures and revenue collections. Controlling the ups and downs in the flow of funds to make maximum cash available when needed by depositing receipts quickly and investing idle funds wisely is what cash management is all about.[39]

The High Cost of Money: An Impetus for Cash Management. While cash management has been a perennial problem for all governments, it became an urgent issue in the late 1970s and early 1980s because of the high cost of money. With interest rates soaring to unprecedented heights, governments attempted to keep borrowing down to a minimum by managing available cash more effectively. Traditional budgetary and accounting tools, however, proved to be incapable of controlling the flow of cash. Other methods were needed. Recession brings a reverse twist. While interest rates are lower, the need to conserve funds and avoid borrowing is acute because of lowered revenues.

Reforming the Cash Management System. To improve cash management, federal, state, and local governments have initiated changes in systems, policies, and strategies. In the administrations of Presidents Carter, Reagan, and Bush, cash management became a prominent feature of the government's financial management improvement program. It still is. From 1980 to 1990 some noteworthy advances took place, culminating in the Cash Management Improvement Act of 1991. The aim of the federal government is to "convert to a maximum feasible extent an annual cash flow of more than $2 trillion to a fully electronic payment and collection system." Well on its way to accomplishing this goal, the government has been able to cut administrative costs and reduce borrowing. This is a far cry from the antiquated systems of the early 1980s, when over 500 separate financial systems could not control the flow of cash.[40]

At the national level, the establishment of the position of Chief Financial Officer (CFO) in twenty-three major agencies since 1990 has been a major impetus for improvements in cash management, internal audit controls, and financial systems designed to facilitate budget implementation. Under the leadership of OMB, which chairs a CFO Council, and with key roles played by Treasury and GAO, the CFOs concentrated on the following changes during the early 1990s:

1. *Accelerating the flow of receipts.* Various techniques are in effect to facilitate the deposit of revenue in a government's account as quickly as possible. Every day counts. Money on hand earns interest, makes it possible to repay short-term debt, and cuts down the amount of borrowing. The federal government and some of the states use a "lockbox" method whereby taxpayers send their payments to a designated post office box of a regional bank.

One problem is the cash collection system in federal agencies that collect miscellaneous receipts (e.g., duties, tariffs, loan repayments, and sales of goods and services). Despite pressures from Treasury and the Office of Management and Budget, some of the agencies fail to deposit the payments promptly in the appropriate banks. Part of the problem has been the lack of incentives for agencies to manage their cash resources efficiently; they get no rewards for superior performance or penalties for impeding the flow of revenue.

In 1984 Congress and the president took more aggressive action to expedite the collection and deposit of federal funds by including in the Deficit Reduction Act of 1984 (PL 98-369) broad authority for the secretary of the treasury in cash management. The secretary can prescribe the timing and methods for collecting funds and depositing them in the treasury. In a unique step, the Act authorizes the secretary to impose charges on agencies for noncompliance with the legislation. The charges could equal the opportunity cost lost to the general fund (the income the funds would have generated had they been invested at current interest rates).[41]

Still another collection system is the electronic Federal Tax Deposit System (FTD). In 1990, 5 million corporate taxpayers paid $880 billion to over 14,000 treasury tax and loan depositories. The FTD system is the government's largest collection mechanism. The treasury links the separate collection systems through a single worldwide network appropriately named Cash-Link. In theory, not a cent owed to the government should slip through this net.[42]

2. *Going after "deadbeats."* With a massive loan portfolio of some $840 billion ($210 billion in direct loans and $630 billion in guaranteed loans), the federal government has experienced a sharp increase in defaults on loans for housing, farms, higher education, and small business—all nontax debt. In 1991 it wrote off nearly $26 billion in loans and loan guarantees. To curb the government's risks, OMB has established several measures designed to provide early warnings of potential risks, to investigate lenders' qualifications more thoroughly, and to prepare more comprehensive reports on the status of loans. The government has also turned over the collection of overdue loans to private firms and conducted computer checks of defaults against tax refund files and federal payrolls.[43]

3. *Controlling disbursements.* Ideally, a government should pay vendors only when the bills are due—not sooner or later—unless the government benefits from substantial discounts. Premature payments deprive it of funds that could be invested or used for other purposes. Late payments are obviously unfair to the vendor. The same problem occurs in federal aid to state and local governments. Other levels of government should get the grants due to them at the right time, but no more and not earlier.

Because of the huge sums involved, the federal government has attacked these problems on several fronts. It has pressured agencies to centralize and schedule systematically the payment of bills. In attempting to control intergovernmental financing it now resorts to letters of credit for grants instead of sending the entire grant for one year to other levels of government. Under this system the appropriate federal agency sends a letter of credit to the grantee, authorizing it to draw specified amounts from the treasury through a commercial bank or a Federal Reserve Bank acting as its agent. This procedure reduces the amount of borrowing by the federal government and does away with a substantial fringe benefit for the recipients. Previously, the grantee (state and local governments and private recipients of grants) could deposit federal funds not immediately needed in a bank and draw interest on them. Now, through the letter of credit, it receives funds only as needed.

As a further step in streamlining the transfer of nearly $200 billion in funds annually between the federal and state governments, two penalties are now in effect: (1) The federal government pays interest to the states for late grants and (2), conversely, the states pay interest to the federal government for premature withdrawal of funds.[44]

President Reagan struck a blow on behalf of vendors by signing the Prompt Payment Act in 1982 (PL 97-177). The General Accounting Office had determined that agencies delayed the payment of a "high number of bills." This constituted a practice in cash management that was as poor as paying bills before their due date. Among other things, the legislation compels agencies to pay vendors interest on overdue payments. Reasonably effective, the act was responsible for the timely payment in 1990 of 88 percent of all vendors' bills.[45]

4. *Rescheduling receipts and expenditures.* To partly control the fluctuations in receipts and expenditures, several governments have resorted to a variety of measures: earlier payment of taxes; changes in the fiscal year so as to synchronize more closely the flows of receipts and expenditures; and revised dates for transfer payments to other levels of government. The latter is especially subject to manipulation to give the illusion of a balanced budget by shifting expenditures to another fiscal year.

5. *Strengthening data collection and forecasting methods.* Improved forecasting techniques coupled with comprehensive automated accounting and information systems form the "linchpin of an effective cash management program." Considering the many uncertainties, forecasting cash requirements week by week and month by month is far more complex than budgetary estimates of revenues and expenditures. It is necessary to look backward and forward at the same time. A retrospective look provides information on past patterns of cash flow, especially seasonal variations. A look ahead requires a careful review of prospective revenue collections and expenditures for debt service and operating and capital programs in each agency. Only after such evaluation is it possible to determine the optimal cash balances that should be retained for expenditures, the amounts that should be invested for specified periods, and the need for short-term loans to tide the government over. In short, what is needed is at least a monthly cash budget.[46]

6. *Mobilizing cash on hand.* Before looking elsewhere for help, governments attempt to pool all the cash they have on hand. To do this it is necessary to identify the free balances in all funds, not just the general fund, and to tap them as

needed. Two obstacles may prove to be formidable. First, statutory constraints in some governments make it impossible to commingle funds by shifting cash from one fund to another, even for temporary periods. This appears to be a self-defeating policy since the government is in effect borrowing from itself. Second, funds may be scattered among various banks, and, in the absence of a comprehensive central accounting system and central control of cash management, a government may have no current information on their status. Some state and local governments in the United States get around this problem by keeping their accounts in one or two banks.[47] However cash flow is monitored, some excellent software packages exist to facilitate the process.

7. *Resorting to short-term borrowing.* When all else fails in a budget crunch, the government often has no choice but to resort to "bridge financing," or short-term borrowing, until revenues, external grants, or the proceeds of bond issues arrive. For state and local governments in the United States, temporary borrowing may take the form of TANs (tax anticipation notes), RANs (revenue anticipation notes), or BANs (bond anticipation notes). Once the government receives the revenue, it repays the holders of the short-term notes. The need to resort to stopgap financing of this type may be predictable if governments, because of seasonal factors, don't have enough cash to pay for scheduled payments such as grants to other levels of government. In some instances, though, it is totally unexpected, as in the recessions of the early 1980s and 1990s.

8. *Investing idle cash balances.* Even cash-starved governments experience temporary periods of plenty when revenues exceed the funds that must be set aside to meet pending obligations. The strategies they follow in handling transient surpluses vary with institutional and legal arrangements and social and economic constraints in each government. As part of its cash management program, the federal government of the United States invests idle balances in the obligations of commercial financial institutions that administer Treasury and loan accounts. State governments have considerable leeway in managing their temporary cash balances, subject to various statutory and policy constraints to assure that their investments are safe, liquid (easy to sell at any time without penalty), and productive (yielding high interest). In most states the primary investments are securities of the United States Treasury. Other investments include high grade commercial paper, repurchase agreements (securities bought from banks and dealers who agree to repurchase them at a fixed price by a specified date), time deposits (savings accounts), and demand deposits (checking accounts).[48]

States face the problem of allocating idle funds between demand deposits that pay no interest and certificates of deposits and time deposits that do. The appropriate balance between the two is by no means obvious. In the United States, commercial banks provide a variety of services for state and local governments. They collect miscellaneous fees and taxes, accept deposits, clear checks, account for checks drawn from deposits in the banks, transfer funds, and process salary checks. Instead of collecting a fee for the services, most banks require the governments to maintain a minimum interest-free balance that can earn money for the banks. Nearly all state governments follow this practice.

By constitution, statute, or policy, states have fixed the responsibility for investment decisions in treasurers (elected or nonelected), comptrollers, boards, commissions, and advisory committees, with the central budget office having only a peripheral role. The pattern varies from state to state. Considering the revenue-producing potential of the decisions and their effect on state finances, the importance of these agencies cannot be overstated. Of all the states, Wisconsin probably has one of the most highly developed and sophisticated systems for investing funds. It has centralized all investments in the Wisconsin Investment Board, which manages the cash balances of all funds as well as the assets of the state retirement systems. Local governments are free to participate in the investment pool.[49]

Local governments in the United States follow investment practices and policies similar to those of the states, but they tend to place more funds than the states do in time and demand deposits. They also face more constraints in the choice of banks and are under pressure to keep their money in local banks as a stimulus to the local economy. To maximize the investment opportunities of local governments, some states have established statewide investment pools that offer diversified investments of varying maturity dates, economy of scale in management, and relatively high returns. Participation by local governments is voluntary, and they can deposit and withdraw funds daily. In general, smaller local governments tend to join the investment pool as a partial alternative to time and demand deposits. Larger local governments, however, have more options for alternative investments.[50]

Points for Discussion

1. What are the major objectives of budget implementation? Why is budget implementation equally as significant as budget formulation?

2. What are the major instruments of budget implementation? Assess each one and discuss its relative importance.

3. What limits, if any, should be placed on the executive's discretion in implementing the budget?

4. To what extent does executive control over budget implementation hamper the flexibility of operating agencies in managing their programs? What are the appropriate responsibilities of central budget offices and operating agencies in budget execution?

5. What role should legislatures play in budget execution? What are the strengths and weaknesses of present methods of control exercised by legislatures?

6. Should central budget offices allot funds to agencies periodically or on an as-needed basis? Defend your position.

7. In what specific ways are requests for apportionments and allotments minibudgets? Review and evaluate recent apportionments and allotments from federal, state, and local governments from this perspective.

8. Before requesting new funds from legislatures through supplemental and deficiency appropriations, what steps can a central budget office in the course of implementing the budget take to assure maximum utilization of existing funds?

9. In the event of a serious revenue shortfall, what policies and practices in budget implementation would you change?
10. In the event of serious underspending, what remedial steps would you take?
11. How effective is the federal Anti-Deficiency Act of 1906 (as revised) as an expenditure control tool? Would you recommend similar controls for state and local governments?
12. What are the major components of the preaudit process and why are they essential in budget implementation?
13. Why is cash management also a vital instrument of budget implementation? What are the desirable features of a comprehensive cash management system?
14. Obtain and evaluate examples of short-term borrowing by federal, state, or local governments.
15. What role should commercial banks play in governments' cash management?
16. Identify and evaluate some of the available software packages that assist local budgeteers in budget implementation.

CHAPTER 10

INFORMATION SYSTEMS CRITICAL TO BUDGETING
Accounting and Performance Measurement

Budgeting is no better than the supporting information systems that provide the essential data for planning, formulating, implementing, controlling, and evaluating budgets. These critical information systems are accounting and performance measurement. They constitute the data base of budgeting. Without them it is impossible to determine the cost, efficiency, and effectiveness of programs and projects or agency compliance with legislative appropriations. Such information is fundamental to budget decision making; more budgetary systems have foundered because of the lack of timely and reliable management and financial data than for any other reason.

The users of the information systems are legion. Operating agencies require them to plan, budget, manage, control, and evaluate their activities. The central staff agencies and the office of the chief executive depend on the data for policy development, the formulation of fiscal policy, budget implementation, and control of the performance of the executive branch. For the legislative branch, information systems are basic tools of oversight, policymaking, and legislative budgeting. The broad public and the multitude of special interest groups use the data to follow the costs and performance of government as a whole and of specific programs in particular. Bond-rating organizations, bond underwriters, and individual and institutional investors who buy government bonds count on data from the information systems to analyze the financial position of governments.[1]

In Figure 10.1, the General Accounting Office has portrayed in general terms the information requirements of operating agencies, Congress, the president, and the public for every phase of the management cycle: policy development (strategic

FIGURE 10.1 FEDERAL INFORMATION REQUIREMENTS PLANNING CHART

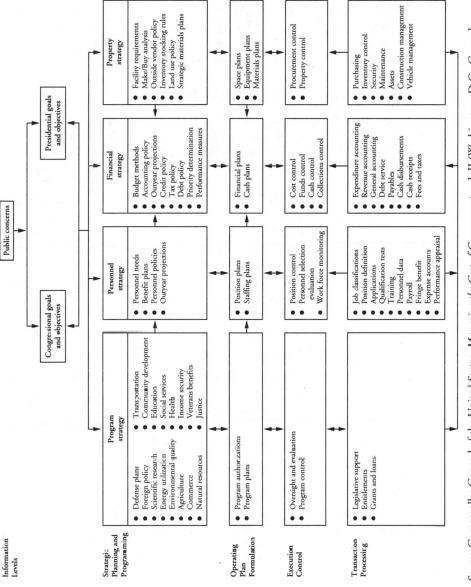

Source: Comptroller General of the United States, *Managing the Cost of Government*, vol. II (Washington, D.C.: General Accounting Office, 1985), p. 21.

planning and programming), budgeting, implementation of programs and budgets, accounting, and evaluation and auditing. To function, these interrelated management processes require a continuing flow of current and reliable accounting and performance data. This chapter covers the essential information systems.

Accounting Systems: The Bedrock of Budgeting

Accounting has a long history; it preceded organized and systematic budgeting by hundreds, if not thousands, of years. Limited at first to bookkeeping, accounting systems eventually became the source of key financial data. By the early twentieth century, accounting, linked with budgeting, had become an essential tool of budget control and accountability with regard to expenditures and revenues. At the federal level, the Budget and Accounting Act of 1921 and the Budget and Accounting Procedures Act of 1950 established the framework of fiscal control that continues to this very day. Similarly, in the 1920s state and local governments established basic budget and accounting systems in their constitutions and laws.

As accounting systems developed during the last twenty-five years, they provided the basis for comprehensive reporting that goes beyond budgeting alone. Such reports focus on the financial condition of governments and the results of governmental programs.

Accounting systems in government thus serve several purposes. Figure 10.2 provides a panoramic view of the role of accounting in budget formulation and implementation and revenue collection. While the chart is a snapshot of information requirements of the federal government for financial management, it applies to other governments as well. Underlying the entire structure are accounting systems for processing, recording, classifying, and reporting millions of financial transactions affecting expenditures, revenue, and debt. In providing such information the systems continuously measure the implementation of the current budget and accumulate data for the next. Essential for government as a whole and for individual agencies, accounting systems

> (1) signal when controls over funds and other resources have broken down, (2) alert managers when operations deviate from financial plans, (3) compare planned spending levels of obligations and costs incurred, (4) contrast planned work units with work actually done and (5) provide financial analysis needed to predict the consequences of alternative courses of action.[2]

No single method of classifying and reporting expenditures and revenues can serve all these purposes. Hence, governments have developed various interrelated accounting systems. Among them are budgeting, or appropriation, accounting; fund accounting; cash accounting; obligation (also termed encumbrance) accounting; accrual accounting; cost accounting; revenue accounting; and economic accounting (classifying accounts in economic terms for use in calculating national income accounts and the gross national product).

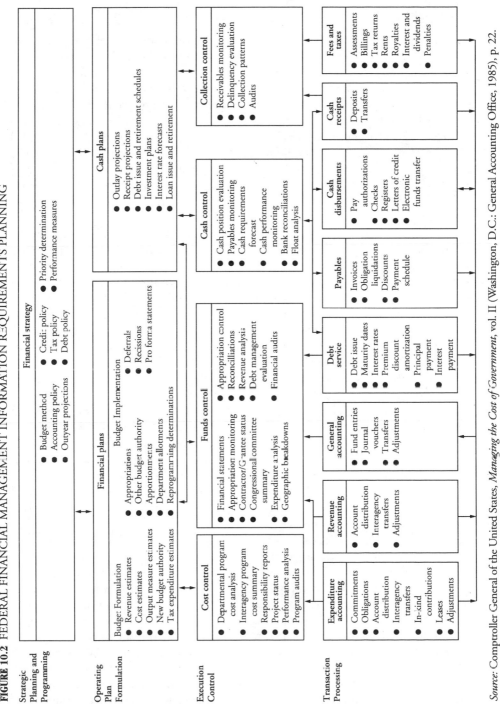

Source: Comptroller General of the United States, *Managing the Cost of Government,* vol. II (Washington, D.C.: General Accounting Office, 1985), p. 22.

Budgetary, or Appropriation, Accounting

A Prerequisite for Budget Formulation and Execution. Chief executives and legislative bodies determine the basic framework of the accounting system through the structure of the appropriations they approve.[3] The appropriations, not the budget documents submitted by the chief executive, are the legally adopted budget. As a minimum, therefore, the accounting system must mirror all the classifications in the appropriations and the allotments made from the appropriations. Through the appropriation acts, chief executives and legislatures control the *timing* of expenditures and revenues (the period covered); the *perspective* (funds, organizational units, and programs for which appropriations are made); the *basis* for accounting (cash and obligations); and *format* and *entity* (what's included and what's left out).[4] The accounting system must cover every one of these components.

In short, the chief executives and legislatures get whatever they want from the accounting system. Should they prefer to appropriate primarily by program and project rather than by organizational unit and object of expense, the government accountants have no choice but to account for expenditures on that basis. Should the appropriation act be studded with numerous line items covering objects of expense by organizational unit, the accounting system must, at a minimum, follow along and set up a record for each item. In practice, central and agency accounting offices supplement budget accounting systems with other classifications such as fund and accrual accounting, which are discussed below.

The appropriation acts that determine the accounting structure allocate monies by fund (the general fund or special fund); operating agency and agency subdivision; line item, such as staffing or other object of expense; program; and project. For example, of the fifty states in the United States, thirty-two appropriate monies by fund, thirty-six by agency, thirty-three by line item, and thirty-four by program.[5] None of these categories are mutually exclusive; an appropriation act can include one or more. For capital projects, states appropriate either funds for individual projects or a lump sum covering several projects. Each capital appropriation also fixes the time period in which the funds can be spent, say, one year, two or more years, or indefinitely.[6]

The flow of revenue follows a similar pattern, with tax and fee collections and other sources of revenue classified by fund.[7]

Every appropriation and every subsequent apportionment/allotment from that appropriation is translated into a separate budgetary account in the accounting system. It is this account that records and accumulates all the costs, commitments, liabilities, and obligations chargeable to the appropriation. Variously termed budgetary, or appropriation, accounting, this record shows the status of all appropriations: the amounts spent, the amounts committed, and the free balances available for expenditure. The data classified and summarized by the accounting system are crucial for budget formulation and implementation, expenditure control, cash management, and assurance of compliance with the terms of the appropriation bill. They provide the basis for political control and accountability by reporting revenues and expenditures and comparing actual results with the projected financial plan. Such budgetary accounts are essential for budgeting.

Beyond meeting the basic reporting requirements of administrations and legislatures, the budgetary accounting system makes it possible to control expenditures on a day-to-day basis. Before any claim, payroll, voucher, contract, or invoice can be approved for expenditure, it must first run the gamut of a preaudit either in the operating agency or the central accounting office to make certain that the proposed expenditure complies with the terms of the appropriation and the allotment and that money is available in the account to pay the bill. Through this method the chief executive and the legislature guard against unauthorized or excessive expenditures.

Budgetary Accounting and Fund Accounting Go Hand in Hand. The basic component in budgetary accounting and any other system of governmental accounting is the fund. Governments account for commitments, expenditures, and revenue for programs and projects mainly by fund. This contrasts sharply with the practices of private businesses which generally report the financial results of their operations as a single entity, regardless of the size of the firm. Only government corporations, public authorities, and self-financed revolving funds, with some exceptions, follow such commercial practices.

The fund, which is so central to governmental accounting, is "a fiscal and accounting entity with a self-balancing set of accounts for recording financial transactions generated by special activities."[8]

In contrast with the rest of the world, governments in the United States have a penchant for a bewildering array of funds, often created at the behest of advocacy groups to protect favored programs against budget cuts. The budget covers these funds and the accounting system records and reports all the transactions for each fund. A fund is a legal financial straitjacket. Pursuant to law, only certain types of revenue flow into the fund, and these can be used solely for restricted purposes. For example, most states have special highway funds that receive gasoline taxes for road construction and maintenance. This revenue cannot be used for any other purpose. What might be an impossible fiscal strain is eased by the fact that the largest fund in the United States is the general fund, which receives a substantial part, if not most, of the revenue (including loans) and finances most governmental activities.

At the federal level in the United States, the fund structure is fairly straightforward. Funds fall into two major categories: federal funds and trust funds. The federal funds include the general fund, which is the recipient of all revenue not earmarked by law for a specific purpose, and several other funds. The trust funds, earmarked for special purposes, encompass old-age, survivors, and disability insurance trust funds (social security); federal employees' retirement funds, the unemployment insurance trust fund; health insurance trust funds; and highway trust funds (earmarked for construction of the federally supported highway systems).

Each fund is backed up by its own accounting system. So large have trust funds become that they account for about 48 percent of all federal revenue.[9]

The fund structure of the federal government is sheer simplicity compared to the dazzling array of funds in state governments. The number of funds ranges from two in Delaware to nearly 4,000 in Hawaii. Between these extremes stand Wisconsin with 36, Massachusetts with 46, Illinois with about 200, California with 254, Connecticut with 296, Texas with 328, North Carolina with 500, Nebraska with 580, New York with 900, and Kansas with 1,209. On the average, about 23 percent of all state revenue in recent years has been earmarked for special activities. This represents a significant decline from 1954, when over half of all revenue was restricted.[10]

The earmarked special funds cover a variety of programs, projects, and activities, such as highway maintenance and construction, conservation, higher education, worker's compensation, retirement systems, reserves for contingencies, federal grants, transfer payments to local governments, and unemployment insurance. They include revolving funds, which finance intra-agency operations, and commercial-type funds, which cover the operations of public enterprises. Each of the special funds segregates resources for a specific purpose. Given this fiscal framework, all fifty state governments in the United States rely on fund accounting.

Local governments in the United States also have a maze of funds: the general fund, which finances in large part the basic municipal functions; special revenue funds dedicated to specific activities such as water and sewer systems and parks; debt service funds for the payment of principal and interest of long- and short-term debt; capital project funds; enterprise funds for business-type activities such as municipal utilities and toll bridges; trust funds, primarily for retirement systems; and revolving funds for interdepartmental operations such as central purchasing and car fleet management.[11]

Financial life is relatively simpler in other countries, which require only a few funds to account for governmental transactions. This is especially true of France and Britain and countries that follow their financial practices. Apart from trust funds for social security, health insurance, and retirement, which most governments have, the French treasury has but one universal fund for government receipts and expenditures. In Britain only three funds are used: the consolidated (general) fund, a contingency fund for unforeseen expenditures, and a public account (essentially trust funds). Except for some Latin American countries, Thailand, and Korea, which have a multiplicity of funds, most developing countries generally require ten or fewer funds.[12]

Fund structure poses some major problems for governments. To be sure, it serves the purpose of controlling the use of dedicated resources for restricted functions. However, the multiplicity of funds complicates budgeting and accounting. To understand the operations of government as a whole, it is essential to bring together reports of the operations of the general fund and statements for all other funds. Many governments report periodically the status of all funds and also combine the separate statements into one comprehensive statement. For example, the United States Treasury issues in January a "Combined Statement of Receipts, Expenditures and Balances of the United States Government" for the preceding fiscal year. This covers all appropriations and revenue accounts.

Recognizing and Measuring Expenditures and Revenues: Cash, Encumbrance/Obligation, and Accrual Accounting

This chapter has highlighted the thousands of budgetary accounts set up by governmental accounting offices in the wake of legislative action on appropriations and revenues. How does each account measure the costs of programs, organizational units, and objects of expense? How does it measure the revenue that pours into it? Cash, you say, thinking of your own check book, in which you enter your income and expenditures? Most governments would agree, for they keep their accounts on a cash basis. They recognize revenue and grants only when the cash comes in and expenditures only when they disburse checks and cash.[13] But there has been a gradual shift in recent years from cash accounting to other systems.

The Case for Cash Accounting. Cash accounting captures the flow of funds into and out of a budgetary account. It is simple, direct, and easy to understand. A government either has enough cash on hand to meet its obligations or it doesn't. It either incurs a cash deficit or achieves a surplus. If the revenue that comes in is not adequate to meet its needs, the government, short of cash, is forced to borrow funds. It is easy to identify the impact of cash transactions on the money supply and credit markets. Most countries budget on a cash basis and the U.S. budget remains essentially a cash budget. Political leaders and the public understand cash accounting. But cash accounting by itself doesn't tell the whole story. It highlights how much cash a government has in the bank, but not how much it owes.

Encumbrance/Obligation Accounting. Were a government to depend solely on cash accounting, it would soon invite unexpected financial crises. Accounting on a cash basis fails to give a complete picture of the funds available for expenditure. At the time an operating agency pays salaries and other bills, it also places purchase orders for goods and services and awards contracts for a variety of undertakings. These are obligations that the government must meet. To make certain that sufficient funds are set aside to pay for such commitments, governments frequently encumber, or earmark, part of the budgetary account. Without locking in sufficient funds for future payments in this fashion, agencies run the risk of prematurely depleting their appropriations or exceeding expenditure limits. To describe the status of an appropriations account accurately, then, it would be necessary to show the original appropriation or allotment, the expenditures and the obligations, and the unexpended and unencumbered balances. The free balances available for expenditure or commitment are the appropriation minus expenditures, obligations, and encumbrances to date. The following hypothetical table shows this relationship:

Cancer detection program, fiscal year 1993–94
Midyear report on status of appropriation account

	Millions
Appropriation or allotment	$10
Expenditures to date	4.5
Unliquidated obligations or encumbrances (not paid yet)	1.3
Unexpended balances	5.5
Unencumbered balances	4.2

On a cash basis, it would appear that the cancer detection program has a balance of $5.5 million available for expenditure. However, it is essential to reduce this figure by $1.3 million, the amount of the unliquidated encumbrances, to yield a free, or unencumbered, balance of $4.2 million. Only this amount can be spent during the rest of the year.

The encumbrance, or obligation, of funds through the budgetary accounting system is a major tool of budget execution and expenditure control in the governments of most states, the United States federal government, and most local governments.

Quite apart from purchase orders, contracts, and other commitments, state governments in the United States, as noted in Chapter 7, also encumber appropriations to control expenditures and to prevent overspending. For example, some governments treat payrolls for the entire year as an encumbrance and reserve part of the appropriation for such expenditures. Other blanket encumbrances may cover routine and predictable operations such as utility services, computer services, the feeding of institutionalized patients, and the scheduled replacement of the car fleet. Prior to the signing of a contract, the budget office may encumber the entire contractual amount. Encumbrances of this type are primarily budget devices to monitor and control the timing and volume of expenditures.

The Accrual Basis of Accounting, Pure or Modified. Invaluable as they are, cash cum encumbrance (obligation) accounting systems still do not reveal the full cost of programs and projects or the full amount of revenue owed to the government. An accounting system focusing solely on cash excludes obligations/commitments, which ultimately determine the cost of programs. But even including the status of obligations tells only part of the story. After all, obligations are not liabilities; they are simply funds set aside temporarily. They represent only a commitment to pay vendors at a later date, after an agency receives goods and services. Once these transactions are completed, the agency incurs liabilities to pay. How should an accounting system capture all these transactions to come up with the costs of programs?

In the interest of full disclosure of costs, professional bodies of accountants in the United States that set accounting standards for the private and public sectors have proposed that governmental accounting systems encompass all costs and liabilities. In this view, any cost incurred by a program or project, even if it's not yet paid, should be reflected in the accounting system. Similarly, it's not enough to recognize the collection of revenue in the accounting system. If the revenue is earned but not collected, it should be reflected in the system. These concepts are encompassed by what is termed accrual accounting and are in effect in the private sector. The Federal Accounting Standards Advisory Board (FASAB) defines accrual accounting as "The recognition of the financial effects of transactions, events and circumstances in the period[s] when [they] occur regardless of when the cash is received or paid."[14] Under this definition, expenditures accrue as soon as an agency receives goods and services, even though it pays no bills. Revenue accrues when the extent of taxpayer liability is known and taxes are demanded, before the end of the fiscal year, even though no taxes are yet paid. Accrual accounting differs from cash accounting in its timing:

> Under the cash method, financial transactions are recorded in accounts only at the time cash is received or paid. Materials purchased and used during the last week in December would be recorded in the month in which paid, probably in January. Under the accrual method, they would be recorded as a December cost; those used in January would be recorded as a January cost and so on. The accrual method makes it possible to obtain a more accurate total of costs for periods in which they are actually incurred than does the cash method. This in turn makes it possible to compare costs for such periods or to compute accurately the unit costs of performing work turned out by the employees each month.[15]

These oversimplified definitions barely hint at the complexity of accrual accounting. On the expenditure side, accrual accounting requires the recording of all costs, paid for or not, when the transaction takes place. Besides unpaid bills for goods, services, and contracts, governments accrue still other liabilities. They use equipment with a relatively short life. Should the cost of the equipment be depreciated each year in accordance with a fixed schedule as a legitimate part of program costs? Agencies draw supplies and materials from central stores. Should their value be included in the cost of a program? Employees incur sick leave, vacation, and pension benefits. These are bona fide liabilities. To what extent should budgets and accounting systems recognize them? All governments incur short- and long-term debt. How should the accounting system reflect these liabilities? Should they merely identify the principal and interest owed during the fiscal year or the entire amount due, possibly over the next thirty years? Tax refunds are ultimately due to taxpayers with overpayments. Should this liability be included as part of the accrued expenditures? A state government owes state aid for health, education, and welfare programs to local governments in one fiscal year. It prefers, however, to disburse the grants during the next fiscal year. Should the accounting system highlight these grants as liabilities during the first fiscal year? Even supporters of accrual accounting differ as to the costs that should be covered by its classification.

Seemingly, the concept of accrued expenditures and revenues is technical and complex and of concern only to accountants and budgeteers. Actually, it raises several major political and managerial issues. Budgets made on an accrual basis and not just on a cash cum obligations basis would change the nature of budgeting. Budgets ostensibly in balance on a cash basis would be thrown out of balance by adding to estimated cash expenditures unpaid liabilities for such items as transfer payments to other levels of government, tax refunds, governmental contributions to the pension system, and vendor bills. Small deficits (measured by cash expenditures) would become large deficits (measured by cash expenditures plus liabilities). For example, President Bush's proposed budget for FY 1993 estimated a deficit of $351.9 billion. Were all funds taken into account on an accrual basis, the deficit would have been projected at $523.3 billion. Had Congress learned earlier through the accrual process the full, though unpaid, cost of the savings and loan debacle, it might have moved more quickly to liquidate failed banks at enormous savings to the taxpayers.[16]

State governments display similar differences between expenditures determined on a cash basis and on an accrual basis. For example, on a cash basis the general fund of New York State was in balance during the 1988–1989 fiscal year. On an accrual basis, as shown in the Comptroller's Report, it had a deficit of $1.1 billion.[17]

The United States government adopts accrual accounting with a cool embrace. Considering the complexity, sophistication, and possible political disadvantages of accrual accounting, it is not surprising that relatively few countries have adopted it: France (partially), Sweden, Canada, Australia, New Zealand, and the United States. After some years of experimentation, the Netherlands and some other countries dropped it.[18] In the United States accrual accounting was a major recommendation of the two Hoover Commissions, the President's Commission on Budget Concepts in 1967, the American Institute of Certified Public Accountants, and the National Council on Governmental Accounting and its successor, the Government Accounting Standards Board. Largely at the instigation of the second Hoover Commission in 1955, Congress in 1956 (310 U.S.C. § 66a[c] [1956]) mandated accrual accounting for all executive agencies as follows:

> As soon as practicable after August 1, 1956 the head of each executive agency shall, in accordance with the principles and standards prescribed by the Comptroller General, cause the accounts of such agency to be maintained on an accrual basis to show the resources, liabilities, and costs of operations of such agency with a view to facilitating the preparation of cost-based budgets.

Neither the committee reports on the legislation nor the hearing preceding it defined the term "accrual basis." Congress left the definition up to the comptroller general despite the difficult conceptual issues posed by the application of accrual accounting to the federal government. It was enough for Congress that accrual accounting appeared to be a way of fully disclosing resources and costs.

Accrual accounting has thus been a statutory requirement for nearly forty years. Nevertheless, implementation of the legislation has been partial and fragmentary despite continuing pressure by the General Accounting Office, its firmest advocate. Mosher attributed the difficulties in implementing accrual concepts in budgeting in the federal government to the following obstacles:

> The first is political: the appropriation committees and subcommittees of Congress, particularly those involved in defense, have not been enthusiastic about accrual accounting, preferring to consider the simpler and traditional cash and obligation accounts. A second obstacle is administrative: accrual accounting is more difficult and costly than accounting on the basis of cash, which would have to be continued anyway. The third obstacle has to do with the tools of enforcement: the GAO has no feasible 'club in the closet' for those who do not live up to its rules.[19]

OMB and GAO continue to differ on the benefits of accrual accounting. OMB has adopted accrual concepts only partially in the budget process, combining cash and selected liabilities. In its accounting, GAO goes the whole way. While generally indifferent, Congress has begun to focus on unpaid, long-term liabilities.[20]

State and local governments move toward accrual accounting. The accounting guide for state and local governments in the United States has been Concepts Statement 1 (1987), issued by the Government Accounting Standards Board (GASB), the nationally recognized standard-setting agency. The main objective is to "determine whether current year revenues were sufficient to pay for current year services." For this purpose GASB recommends what it calls "modified accrual accounting." Using this approach, revenues will be recognized and recorded in the accounts when they are measurable, available, and collectible in the fiscal year. Thus, sales taxes and personal income taxes will accrue only when cash arrives, although some state and local governments that practice full-scale accrual accounting accrue them when the tax liability is known. On the expenditure side, GASB recommends that governments accrue liabilities such as purchases, salaries, vacations and sick leave, pensions, and debt service that are clearly payable in the fiscal year. This is a commonsense approach to accounting, combining cash revenues and expenditures and readily recognized liabilities to give a clear picture of a government's finances.

This approach appealed to state and local governments. Encouraged by wide acceptance of modified accrual accounting, GASB in May 1990 went one step further and adopted statement No. 11, which moves from modified accrual to accrual accounting in financial statements. Beginning on June 15, 1994, governments focused on total financial resources; recognized transactions when they took place, regardless of when cash was paid; and measured revenue when the government demanded it during the fiscal year, not when taxpayers remitted their checks. All this in the interest of full disclosure, which cash accounting alone does not make possible.[21]

As matters stand now, state governments in the United States generally follow modified accrual accounting. So do local governments, accounting for revenues when received, but recording accrued expenditures when they incur liabilities. In budgeting, the cash system still reigns supreme, but the accrual system is slowly making inroads. Some state and local governments have modified their budget presentation to show financial plans on a cash *and* accrual basis. Otherwise, budgeting and accounting would move in opposite directions.

Some reservations about accrual accounting. Despite its growing influence in the United States, the accrual system of accounting/budgeting does not lack critics. It is as difficult to estimate revenues, expenditures, and liabilities under an accrual system as it is under a cash system. Recognizing the problems of determining the precise amount of accrued expenditures, OMB settles for the best estimates it can develop. The United States Government accrues corporate taxes (based on corporate reports), but reports individual taxes on a cash basis. Any other approach would be beset by extraordinary methodological problems.

One of the reasons the Netherlands dropped accrual accounting was the difficulty of accruing revenues. Some estimates figured on an accrued basis were so rosy that they led to additional expenditures. When actual revenues fell significantly short of the accrued estimates, the government was forced to resort to increased deficit financing.[22] GASB attempts to get around such pitfalls by accruing taxes only when the government demands them from individual taxpayers.

Unless governments achieve a consensus on accrual accounting, they will bedevil the public with two sets of figures: the budget based on cash outlays, which may give an unduly optimistic picture; and the financial reports based on accrued revenues and expenditures, which may highlight sizeable deficits. The state of California, for one, recognizes this dilemma by pointing out in its budget that the "state's fiscal system is highly complex with many interrelationships between budgeting and accounting. Consequently, some of the changes in accounting that are necessary . . . impact the budget system and/or the governor's budget presentation. These interrelationships will result in . . . changes being accomplished over a number of years."[23]

Cost Accounting

For budget analysis and formulation, as well as program evaluation, it is essential to focus on the full cost of programs and projects. The costs include not only services and materials paid for out of appropriations and allotments targeted at specific programs and projects, but other resources as well. Among the costs that may not be reflected in the budget for a program or project are the following:

A portion of an agency's overhead

Requisitions from central stores and inventories

Services donated by other organizational units (in effect, from other appropriations)

The use of central services such as computers, reproducing facilities, and car fleets

The use of government-owned space

Fringe benefits

Depreciation of equipment

Consumption of resources paid for in the past or subject to future payment

Allocation of staff time to specific programs and projects[24]

Without such information, it is virtually impossible to evaluate the costs and benefits of programs and to develop cost-based budgets. Yet the cash cum obligation accounting system does not provide the data, because it is focused on individual appropriations and allotments and not on resources consumed by programs and projects. The accrual accounting system with its emphasis on liabilities helps, but not enough. In practice, accrual accounting rarely covers all costs of programs and projects, but concentrates instead on major unfunded liabilities and major resources that are acquired, though not paid for.

For a full accounting of the resources actually used it is necessary to turn to cost accounting, which is related to, but more comprehensive than, accrual accounting. But cost accounting is expensive; to capture all the relevant expenditure data on a regular basis, it is necessary to initiate a complex accounting system. Hundreds of thousands of documents must be coded by agency appropriation, duration, function (for example, health or education), subfunction, program, activity, project, fund, organizational unit, year, and objects of expense. These documents include purchase orders, invoices, vouchers, payrolls, requisitions, and contracts.

Because of the cost, governments and operating agencies have installed cost-accounting systems selectively for major programs and projects. At times, they resort to special studies rather than implementing full-blown cost-accounting systems. For example, in order to rationalize fees and charges for services, governments frequently conduct ad hoc analyses, which attempt to take into account all the related costs of activities. Even this is a major undertaking, involving analysis of depreciation, overhead, distribution of staff time, and the like. To determine whether commercial- or industrial-type work should be performed by government personnel or by contract with private firms, OMB requires agencies to conduct special comparative cost studies. These become a basis for deciding whether the government can procure products and services more economically from commercial sources.[25]

Providing Data for Economic Analysis and Planning

Governmental accounting systems provide essential data for economic analysis and planning in addition to facilitating budgeting and expenditure control. After all, governmental expenditures, revenue, and debt have a profound effect on the national economy. No aggregate data covering the entire economy can be developed without including such governmental transactions. For this purpose governments depend on accounting systems to provide information on (1) the economic character of expenditures, and (2) the government's segment of national income and product accounts (NIPA). Both categories are essential for the analysis of aggregate economic activity.

To bring out the economic character of expenditures, it is useful to segregate them by current and capital expenditures and, within each category, to subdivide them further into transfer payments, debt payments, and lending. Expenditures for education serve as an example to highlight these distinctions: Funds for a school building are an investment in capital formation; salaries and the purchase of supplies represent current expenditures; and transfer payments cover grants to other governments such as school districts. These components are subdivided in fine detail for purposes of analysis.[26]

Integrating Accounting Systems

Every accounting system is related to every other accounting system, although their concepts and bases may differ. Figure 10.3 sketches in broad strokes the relationships between the various classifications of accounts.

Limitations of Accounting Systems for Use in Budgeting, Management, and Financial Control

In 1989 the comptroller general of the United States found little in government accounting systems to cheer about:

> The government continues to rely on financial management systems that, despite improvement efforts over many years, are, frankly, second-rate. Decisionmakers at all levels of the federal government are not getting the financial information they need to help make policy and management decisions and to know the ultimate financial impact of those decisions. This information gap [in accounting] becomes especially critical as the government grapples with the deficit and is faced with difficult spending alternatives . . . the systems are antiquated and in a general state of disrepair. Hundreds of millions of dollars have been spent each year on uncoordinated efforts to upgrade these systems. In the meantime, costly as they are to operate and maintain, the old systems do not produce complete, timely, and reliable financial data.[27]

Critics have hurled similar jeremiads at the accounting systems of state and local governments in the United States and of various foreign governments. What's wrong with these systems anyway? What should be done about them? Who should decide?

At least ten gaps appear in the governmental accounting systems that are substantial enough to seriously impede budgetary processes. (Conversely, a flawed budget process may block improvements in accounting.) So far this chapter has

FIGURE 10.3 RELATIONSHIP OF ACCOUNTING SYSTEMS

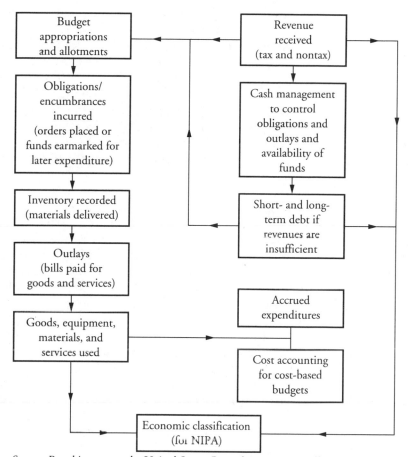

Sources: Based in part on the United States General Accounting Office, *Managing the Cost of Government,* vol. II (Washington, D.C., 1985), p. 17 and A. Premchand, *Government Budgeting and Expenditure Controls* (Washington, D.C.: International Monetary Fund, 1983), p. 388.

focused on four problems: the multiplicity of funds; the limitations of cash-based accounting systems; controversies about the application of accrual accounting; and the failure to fully cost programs and projects. In addition, six other major difficulties persist: the multiplicity of accounting systems and the lack of standardization among them; frayed linkages between budget and accounting systems; poor controls over expenditures, revenues, and debt; limited coverage of the accounting systems; conflicts with regard to the use of depreciation practices as in the private sector; and inadequate financial reporting.

Multiplicity of Accounting Systems

Every government faces the problem of selecting a focal point in its organization to collect, consolidate, maintain, and report accounting data. The options are decentralization of accounting systems among the operating agencies, centralization of accounting systems, and a combination of the two. Because of its sheer size, the federal government of the United States has decentralized accounting systems, not only to the departments, but to bureaus, divisions, and field offices within these departments. The treasury department is responsible for consolidating the data periodically to produce financial reports. This is the pattern in most national governments. On the other hand, state and local governments tend to centralize and integrate their accounting systems. Each organizational pattern has its drawbacks and advantages.

The federal government of the United States abounds in a multiplicity of accounting systems. Under the Accounting and Auditing Act of 1950 (31 USC 66a), each executive agency is required to operate accounting systems that provide data on obligations, accrued expenditures, applied costs, and outlays. Furthermore, the accounting systems must conform to principles and standards established by the comptroller general and must be approved by that official. In practice, the accounting systems are seriously fragmented and, in many cases, fail to follow uniform standards. Accounting systems of bureaus and divisions within individual agencies are not always integrated with departmental systems. In the 1980s "the government had over 500 financial systems, many of them antiquated, incompatible, or redundant, and many not in compliance with applicable accounting standards."[28] Many still lack GAO approval.

Concerned about the lack of uniform financial data for budgeting and accounting, the federal government took three major steps in 1990 and 1991:

1. Congress and the president approved the Chief Financial Officers Act of 1990 (CFO Act) that (a) establishes chief financial officers in governmental agencies to oversee and improve all aspects of financial management, and (b) creates two offices in OMB: an Office of Federal Financial Management (OFFM) headed by a comptroller, and the position of Deputy Director of Management.

2. In October 1990 the secretary of the treasury, the director of OMB, and the comptroller general (GAO) established the Federal Accounting Standards Advisory Board (FASAB) to develop and approve official accounting standards for the federal government.

3. In 1991 OMB developed a five-year plan to improve annual financial reporting in the agencies, to develop a standard financial database for OMB, the treasury, and the agencies, and to provide a uniform source of financial and budget information.[29]

Integrating Accounting and Budgeting Systems

State Governments Take the Lead. To a far larger extent than the federal government, many state governments have developed automated and integrated accounting systems fully compatible with budgetary systems and classifications. While accounting systems among the states are similar, they are not uniform, although they are moving in that direction. Nor do they necessarily use the same terminology, classification schemes, and reporting formats. Each state follows different techniques in budgeting and hence in accounting.

Within this framework, various state governments have initiated large-scale integrated accounting systems that serve budgeting requirements. For example, California launched CALSTAR (California State Accounting and Reporting System), which covers about 150 agencies and institutions and, among other things, provides data on program costs, revenue, and performance. With the computerized database on-line, the budget office, the accounting office, the legislature, and the operating agencies can tap into the system. The state of Washington has developed an automated accounting system that it labeled AFRS (Agency Financial Reporting System). AFRS will obviate the need for most decentralized accounting systems in the operating agencies, and provide data for budgeting and evaluation. Among other notable advances are changes in accounting systems in Texas, Florida, South Carolina, Virginia, and New York.[30]

Local Governments Have a Long Way to Go. Despite many improvements, most accounting systems in local governments of the United States barely serve budgetary requirements. However, Washington, D.C., Dayton, Ohio, and particularly New York City can show them how to link accounting and budgeting.

New York City's Integrated Financial Management Systems (IFMS), initiated in July 1977, is truly the "big apple" of local government accounting systems and leads all the rest in scope, complexity, and costs. IFMS was a direct outgrowth of New York City's financial crisis in 1975 and a breakdown in its accounting system. The city could not determine the size of its debt or the amount of cash in the banks. It was unable to reconcile accounting and budgetary data with regard to expenditures. So serious were the repercussions of the collapse of financial control that its effects have been compared to the stock market crash of 1929. Just as the crash led to more rigorous accounting standards for private corporations, so did the failures of New York City's accounting system lead to tougher standards for state and local government accounting throughout the United States.

In lieu of previous unreliable and fragmented systems, IFMS links budgeting, accounting, and other system components such as purchasing and payroll operations. A massive computerized database serves the entire system. Through a variety of mechanisms, IFMS enhances budget management and control. It signals, on an exception basis, deviations in revenue collections and expenditures from plans and forecasts. It tracks all changes in the implementation of the budget by agency, program, project, and fund. It also accounts for expenditures on an accrual basis.

After a good deal of trial and error and the expenditure of many millions of dollars, IFMS became fully operational some five years after the initial installation.[31]

Poor Controls over Revenues, Expenditures, and Debt

New York City was hardly the only government that was unable to control revenues, expenditures, and debt through its accounting system. Numerous GAO reports are replete with horror stories about the breakdown of accounting systems among federal agencies. For example, one bureau lost track of hundreds of millions of dollars of expenditures because of deficiencies in its automated accounting system. Another could not reconcile its records of advances to contractors and grantees with those of the recipients. In fact, the reports of both differed by more than 500 percent.[32] To budget under these conditions is to fly blind.

Limited Coverage of Public Sector Expenditures

Accounting systems reflect both the strengths and weaknesses of the budget process. If the budget encompasses expenditures from all resources—the general fund and special funds—then financial reports will present a complete picture of the use of total resources required to deliver services. Unfortunately, this is not the case at all levels of government. For example, some state governments do not budget or show in the budget document funds for such entities as public authorities, retirement systems and other trust funds, and, in a few instances, state colleges and universities.[33] GASB has attacked this problem by requiring reports on revenues and expenditures for all agencies for which elected officials have oversight responsibilities.

Conflicts with Regard to Depreciation Practices

One of the thorny issues in governmental accounting and budgeting is the depreciation of assets (equipment, buildings, and other facilities with a life of more than one year) over their useful lives. Taking depreciation into account, the value of assets consumed each year would be regarded as an operating expense like expenses for staff and supplies, and would be included in budgets and financial statements. After all, the wear and tear of government assets is as real a cost as any operating expenditure. Private firms systematically depreciate each year, in accordance with accounting and tax rules, the value of their plant, equipment, and buildings used that year. This constitutes part of the cost of doing business and is reflected in annual profit and loss statements. It is argued that federal, state, and local governments should do no less and adopt similar practices to account for the true cost of programs and projects. At present, only public authorities, enterprise funds, and revolving funds follow such policies, because they are income-producing entities.[34]

The adoption of depreciation practices would have major repercussions for budgeting and accounting. At present any asset purchased by the federal government, whether a typewriter or an aircraft carrier, is treated as current consumption, regardless of the length of its useful life. Were such assets depreciated each year, say, showing one-tenth of the cost rather than the purchase price, this would affect the calculation of expenditures, deficits, and surpluses.

Among the proponents of depreciation practices in the federal government have been the Department of the Treasury and the GAO. Both have joined forces in issuing prototype annual consolidated financial statements that include the cost of depreciation. They argue that financial reports of the government should reflect all costs and that depreciation is a major cost. Most governmental agencies, however, don't calculate the cost of depreciating buildings and equipment. Nevertheless, Treasury and GAO have assumed that buildings, structures, and facilities have a life of fifty years, ships and service craft 30 years, industrial plant equipment 20 years, and other depreciable assets 10 years. On this basis, depreciation may approximate 3 percent of total expenditures.[35]

State and local governments find little use for depreciation practices in budgeting and accounting except for public enterprises, revolving funds, and activities using cost-accounting systems. On the other hand, they favor the use of separate accounting records and separate reports for all fixed assets in order to (1) identify them; (2) evaluate their condition; (3) indicate their value, at least in terms of the original purchase price; and (4) use such data as a basis for replacing or rehabilitating obsolete equipment and buildings.[36]

A New Day for Financial Reporting

Nearly all governments issue monthly and annual financial reports that bring together in one place data on revenues, expenditures, obligations, balances, assets, and liabilities for the various funds. These are critical in determining the results of budget implementation; the current financial position; the extent of liquidity and solvency of governmental funds; accountability for the use of resources; fund balances; and the surplus, deficit, and debt position. In addition, the reports provide a basis for auditing. For example, in the United States government, the treasury, which is both banker and accountant for the central government, issues three critical reports: (1) a Daily Treasury Statement, which shows the cash balances in all funds and is used as a basis for investment decisions; (2) a Monthly Treasury Statement of Receipts and Outlays of the United States Government, which follows the budget structure and highlights deficits and/or surpluses for all funds; and (3) the United States Government Annual Report, which summarizes the government's financial position on a cash basis and the results of operations.

After years of inadequate, inaccurate, and incomplete reporting, governments at all levels are beginning to produce comprehensive and useful reports, thanks to the pressure of GASB, the FASAB (Federal Accounting Standards Advisory

Board), and bond-rating agencies. In GASB's codification of acceptable account-ing practices, financial reporting takes the form of a pyramid. At the apex of the pyramid are general purpose financial statements, which provide a summary view of all funds and account categories, with emphasis on the "big picture" and oper-ating results. One figure combines all funds. Further down the pyramid, reports highlight individual funds by type and compare budgeted and actual expenditures and revenues by fund. Finally, at the base of the pyramid are the details on rev-enue, expenditures by department and program, and debt.[37]

This is inadequate for some members of the financial community, who prefer one consolidated report, regardless of the number of funds, for these reasons: (1) Nothing is more significant than the financial position of government as a whole; (2) financial statements resembling those of private firms are simpler and more understandable than complex government reports; (3) the important figure is a "single number, net income," which summarizes operating performance for the year; (4) the multiplicity of funds reflected by the combined reports is confusing; and (5) consolidated reports present the best picture of the resources used.[38]

Relatively few governments issue consolidated reports of this nature; most prefer instead to use reports combining all funds. When they do consolidated reports, the reports have no official standing, as is true of Treasury's prototype reports. Treasury stresses that these reports do not compete with the budget of the federal government. Rather, they represent an attempt to provide

> useful information about the financial condition of the federal government as a
> whole . . . Consolidated financial statements of the United States government
> present a picture of the government's overall financial condition that is not avail-
> able elsewhere. For example, consolidated financial statements disclose the mag-
> nitude of the government's pension liabilities, public debt, and estimated losses
> on guarantee and insurance programs.[39]

Despite the enthusiasm of Treasury and GAO, consolidated reports in some governments may conceal more than they reveal. Rather than shedding light on financial transactions, they may misrepresent the fiscal condition of governments and confuse the users. Unlike commercial enterprises, which account for their diverse activities as a single entity, governments operate through separate funds, including trust funds. Both accounting and accountability take place on a fund basis. Each fund has its own objectives and restrictions and cannot be commin-gled with other funds. To consolidate the transactions of these separate funds into a single report is to "mix apples and oranges."

The risks of a consolidated report are fairly serious. For example, a consoli-dated report for a state government might show a substantial surplus. Yet the gen-eral fund may be in deficit while the earmarked highway fund may enjoy a large surplus. Legally, transfers between the two funds may not occur. Cash reports on a consolidated basis would also be misleading if they combined cash in operating accounts with cash in trust funds. The two pools of cash are not interchangeable. A consolidated financial statement masks management performance in administering individual funds and provides no information to the legislature on the implementation of appropriations for each fund. For these reasons, consolidated financial statements may make government look better than it actually is.[40]

Because of these factors, governments continue to issue combined reports. The challenge they face is to make the reports as meaningful and simple as possible.

Closing the Accounting Gap with GAAP, Computerized Systems, and Financial Management Improvement Programs

Governments have resorted to three major strategies to overcome their accounting problems and make accounting more relevant for budgeting: the adoption of GAAP (generally accepted accounting principles); the development of computerized systems that serve budgeting and accounting needs as cited above; and the initiation of systematic financial management improvement programs with a stress on improved budgeting and accounting systems. But who sets the standards for these changes?

Enter GAAP

In setting accounting standards, federal and state governments do not operate in a vacuum. Increasingly, they follow as guides the generally accepted accounting principles (GAAP) developed by authoritative nongovernmental bodies in which the various levels of government are represented. The principal ones are the National Council on Governmental Accounting (NCGA) sponsored by the Municipal Finance Officers Association; a successor body, the Government Accounting Standards Board (GASB), which is under the wing of a nonprofit organization, the Financial Accounting Foundation; and the American Institute of Certified Public Accountants. The Financial Accounting Foundation also sets accounting standards for the private sector. GAAP focuses primarily on state and local governments and represents a consensus as to uniform and minimal accounting and reporting standards and principles. As noted, the federal government looks to FASAB for the development of its accounting standards.

Undoubtedly, the most authoritative expression of GAAP for governments is NCGA's *Statement 1: Governmental Accounting and Financial Reporting Principles,* issued in 1979. In 1985 it was incorporated in large part in GASB's *Governmental Accounting and Financial Reporting Standards.* NCGA laid out these goals for accounting systems:

> A governmental accounting system must make it possible both: (a) to present fairly and with full disclosure the financial position and results of financial operations of the funds and account groups of the governmental unit in conformity with *generally accepted accounting principles;* and (b) to determine and demonstrate compliance with finance-related legal and contractual provisions.

These are the major features of GAAP, including the accrual or modified accrual basis of accounting:

1. *Recasting the government fund structure to reduce the number of special funds and to establish the following funds:*

   a. *Governmental:* general fund, special revenue funds (revenue legally restricted and earmarked for specified purposes), capital project funds (all resources for the acquisition or construction of major capital facilities), debt service funds (all resources to pay the principal and interest of long-term debt).

   b. *Proprietary:* enterprise funds (primarily to account for the operations of public enterprises) engaging in business-type activities, and internal service or revolving funds (accounting for intragovernmental operations or services provided to other governmental units on a cost-reimbursement basis).

   c. *Fiduciary funds:* funds held by government in a trustee capacity (e.g., pension funds).

2. *Accounting for fixed assets:* One accounting category, the General Fixed Assets Account Group (GFAAG), is used to account for fixed assets of general and special funds (other than proprietary funds) including infrastructures such as roads and bridges.

3. *Accounting for long-term debt:* A General Long-Term Debt Account Group (GLTDAG) includes long-term obligations such as general obligation debt and government long-term liability such as pension claims, judgments, and compensated absences.

4. *Developing accounting systems to provide a basis for budgetary control and to produce appropriate financial statements on the implementation of the budget.*

5. *Using common terminology and classifications in budgeting and accounting.*

6. *Financial reporting standards:* The preparation of general purpose financial statements (GPFS) classified by fund type and account group, detailed data on individual funds, and the publication of an annual financial report.

This skeletal summary hardly does justice to the many technical details, fine distinctions, and qualifications in GAAP. But it is clear that GAAP was a milestone and represented a challenge to traditional budgetary and accounting systems with its emphasis on a new fund structure; modified accrual accounting; and combined reporting for all funds, not just the general fund. The proponents of GAAP recognize that in many instances, constitutional and statutory provisions conflict with GAAP. For example, in many governments the general fund covers both operating and capital expenditures (including funds from bond issues). GAAP would account for capital outlays financed by borrowing through a Capital Projects Fund. GAAP also laid out a classification scheme that differs sharply from budgetary accounting, although it includes the latter.

GAAP Takes Hold. What might have been an issue of primary concern to accountants and budgeteers alone became, virtually overnight, a matter of public policy. The near bankruptcy of New York and other cities, the financial problems of several states, and the heavy deficits of the federal government led chief executives, legislators, and the financial community to look for salvation in GAAP, which promised full disclosure and accurate reporting of the accounts of all funds. This appeared to be one way to stave off future financial disasters.

Any wavering on the part of state and local governments with regard to accepting the accounting gospel according to GAAP quickly disappeared when the two main bond-rating organizations, Moody's and Standard & Poor's, insisted in the early 1980s on the use of GAAP as one of the criteria used in rating bond issues:

> All financial statements submitted to S&P either in connection with a rating request for a bond sale or for a review are expected to be prepared in accordance with Generally Accepted Accounting Principles (GAAP). Where legal requirements for recording transactions differ from GAAP, the accounting system employed should make provision for both, but in the preparation of general financial statements, GAAP must take precedence.[41]

To prove they meant what they said, both organizations in later years lowered the bond rating of several governments that continued to use the cash method of financial reporting. This naturally resulted in higher interest rates and reluctance on the part of investors to purchase the securities.

Under these pressures many state and local governments began to jump on the GAAP bandwagon. As of 1990, thirty-seven states prepared statewide financial statements à la GAAP. About one-third of this group implemented a modified accrual basis of accounting. At least ten began to develop their budgets in accordance with the GAAP format.[42] Of 3,600 local government entities (counties, cities, schools, colleges, utilities, and hospitals) reviewed by Standard & Poor's in the early 1980s, 61 percent used a modified accrual system and 35 percent an accrual system as a basis for accounting. Only 4 percent reported financial transactions on a cash basis.[43] This trend has accelerated.

Some Limitations of GAAP. Governments conforming with GAAP will continue to follow two tracks in accounting. The accounting system must still record and report transactions in accordance with the legally adopted budget. In addition, it also reports financial results in conformity with GAAP. And it is necessary to reconcile both sets of figures.

From the standpoint of users, the combined reports for all funds are so replete with data that they can overwhelm, rather than sharpen, understanding. Hence it is desirable to cut through the maze of figures and come up with selected financial and performance indicators and highlights that show significant trends at a glance. Increasingly, this is the approach in many governments.

Systematic Financial Management Improvement Programs

The development of comprehensive, integrated, and computerized budgeting accounting systems in accordance with GAAP cannot take place once and for all time. Nor can a single agency, no matter how highly placed, bring it about. What is needed is sustained effort for an indefinite period by a senior group representing the central staff and operating agencies of government. This approach turned out to be fairly effective in the federal government and in several state governments in the United States. In the federal government, the Joint Financial Management Improvement Program (JFMIP), the chief financial officers, OMB, and GAO are the catalysts for improving accounting and other aspects of financial management.

The Other Information System That Supports Budgeting: Performance Measurement

Cost data and financial reports by themselves don't tell the whole story. The missing link is performance measurement, which relates the results of programs and operations to costs. Such linkage has been the elusive goal of budget reform movements since the late 1940s. Nearly fifty years later, in the early 1990s, a consensus developed at all levels of government on the need to mesh accounting systems with systems measuring performance.

At the federal level the active proponents of such strengthened information systems are OMB, GAO, the chief financial officers, and the Joint Financial Management Improvement Program (JFMIP). OMB requires agencies to include performance measures, program data, financial data, and financial performance data in their annual financial statements. It has also initiated fifteen task forces to develop performance measures in areas of common concern to all agencies, such as property management, loan programs, and Medicare. Going further, the Clinton administration and Congress approved the Performance and Results Act of 1993, which requires five-year projections of expected results and annual reports on performance.

The new legislation formalizes and expands OMB and GAO programs in performance measurement. For example, GAO has stressed the need for agencies to articulate their missions and measurable objectives specifically, develop implementation plans to achieve their goals, measure progress, and report annually on their performance. The focus is on accountability for results and relating costs to results. Among the key measures GAO highlights are

input, such as dollars, staff, and materials;

workload or activity levels, such as the number of applications that are in process, usage rates, or inventory levels;

outputs or final products, such as the number of children vaccinated, number of tax returns processed, or miles of road built;

outcomes of products or services, such as the number of cases of childhood illnesses prevented or the percentage of taxes collected; and

efficiency, such as productivity measures or measures of the unit costs for producing a service (e.g., the staff hours it takes to process a Social Security claim or the cost to build a mile of highway).[44]

In 1991, in order to assess the status of performance measurement in the federal government, GAO surveyed 103 agencies covering 87 percent of all employees and 92 percent of total outlays. Nearly all agencies reported that they measured program inputs, work activity levels, quality and timeliness, and program outcomes. The problem was that most of these measures were internal and rarely reached agency heads, OMB, and Congress in summary form as a basis for policymaking. Only a few agencies used the performance measures to track their progress in attaining objectives and in achieving hoped-for results. Relatively few agencies linked the performance measures with financial statements.[45]

At the state and local levels GASB has spearheaded an equally aggressive approach to performance measurement. Since 1987, its *Concepts Statement No. 1, Objectives of Financial Reporting,* has emphasized the need to "assist in fulfilling government's duty to be publicly accountable . . . enable users to assess that accountability . . . and provide information to assist users in assessing the service efforts, costs and accomplishments of the governmental entity."[46] In the wake of *Concepts Statement No. 1,* GASB launched a major study to determine the state of the art in SEA (service efforts and accomplishments) and to ascertain whether SEA indicators were sufficiently developed to warrant their use in financial reporting.[47]

Completed in 1990, the study may turn out to be the most significant catalyst in the last fifty years to advance the use of performance measurement by state and local governments. For twelve major governmental functions (colleges and universities, economic development, elementary and secondary education, fire department programs, hospitals, mass transit, police department programs, public assistance programs, public health, road maintenance, sanitation collection and disposal, and waste and wastewater treatment) the survey group identified and developed the following indicators of service efforts and accomplishments:

1. *Input indicators.* These are designed to report the amount of resources, either financial or other (especially personnel), that have been used for a specific service or program. Input indicators are ordinarily presented in budget submissions and sometimes external management reports.

2. *Output indicators.* These report units produced or services provided by a service or program.

3. *Outcome indicators.* These are designed to report the results (including quality) of the service. Examples of outcome indicators are the change in students' test scores, the percentage of hypertensives treated who now have controlled blood pressure, and the value of property lost due to crime.

4. *Efficiency (and cost-effectiveness) indicators.* These are defined as indicators that measure the cost (whether in dollars or employee-hours) per unit of output or outcome. Examples are cost per million gallons of drinking water delivered to consumers, or cost per thousand gallons of effluent treated to a certain level of quality.

5. *Explanatory information.* This includes a variety of information about the environment and other factors that might affect an organization's performance on SEA indicators. Examples would be weather conditions for road maintenance, percentage of students with English as a second language for education, or quality of source water for water service.[48]

These indicators would make comparisons of current performance possible with that of previous years, with performance in similar jurisdictions, with technically developed standards or norms, with annual program targets, with performance in geographical areas in the same jurisdiction and on behalf of different client groups, and with performance in comparable private organizations.

How should SEA information be communicated and displayed? Since annual financial reports are "the primary accountability documents," nonfinancial information such as SEA indicators could be incorporated in the reports, as is done to some extent in Texas; Charlotte, North Carolina; and Dallas. Annual budgets could also highlight SEA indicators, as is done in many states and cities.[49] Both methods would strengthen the links between accounting and performance data.

To make certain that the SEA project would not be another academic exercise, in December 1992, the Government Accounting Standards Board (GASB) preliminarily accepted the concepts subject to a further round of hearings and investigation:

> Because users now recognize that information about SEA (in terms of outputs, outcome, and efficiency) is an essential part of the measurement of performance, financial reporting needs to be expanded to include those measures. Having considered the information users need for assessing accountability and making decisions, and the role of financial reporting in providing information to assess performances, the GASB believes that SEA information is an integral part of GPEFR [general purpose external financial reporting].[50]

GASB cautioned agencies against the use of oversimplified, single composite measures that are insufficient to assess performance. It emphasized that indicators cannot stand by themselves; they require explanation. Further investigation is needed to develop other indicators if necessary. In complex programs outcomes may be difficult to measure, so surrogate measures may have to do. SEA data cannot advise us whether program goals and objectives are still valid. Ultimately, this becomes a matter of value and political judgment. Continued testing is necessary to confirm the "understandability, reliability, relevance, timeliness, consistency and comparability of the measures."[51]

With these caveats, GASB started still another chapter in the fifty-year battle to root performance measurement in budgeting and accounting—a battle chronicled by Chapter 11, on budget reform.

Points for Discussion

1. In what specific ways do budget systems depend on accounting systems for essential data to formulate and implement budgets?
2. What are the major governmental accounting systems? To what extent are they interrelated? Which ones serve budgetary requirements best? Obtain and review examples of different accounting systems.
3. How do budgets and appropriation acts determine the structure of governmental accounting systems?

4. What are the strengths and weaknesses of budgetary/appropriation accounting systems?
5. Why is fund accounting critical, especially in the United States? How does it relate to budgetary accounting? What are some of the major problems of fund accounting and how would you correct them?
6. What are the major differences between cash, obligation/encumbrance, accrual, and modified accrual accounting? What are the chief advantages and disadvantages of each form of accounting? Which accounting systems facilitate budgeting?
7. What are the policy and political implications of accrual accounting for budgeting? Review and evaluate examples of budgets and accounting reports developed on an accrual basis.
8. How does cost accounting differ from other forms of accounting? Is it worth the cost to install a cost-accounting system?
9. To what extent would you follow the depreciation practices of private firms in costing governmental programs?
10. Of the ten major accounting problems discussed in this chapter, which ones are most significant? How would you solve them?
11. How far would you go in integrating separate accounting systems in government? Similarly, to what extent would you integrate budget and accounting systems? What critical factors determine the success or failure of integrated systems?
12. Which financial reports best serve the needs of budget decision makers, interest groups, citizens at large, and the financial community? How far would you go in consolidating or combining accounting data for separate funds? Review and evaluate financial reports from state and local governments.
13. What are the major components of GAAP? Which ones do you support and why? What has been the impact of GAAP on budgetary and accounting systems? To what extent do you agree with the position of Moody's and Standard & Poor's in requiring the use of GAAP as one of the conditions for higher bond ratings?
14. Ten states use GAAP for budgeting as well as accounting. How far would you go in recommending this practice for state and local governments generally?
15. To what extent would you recommend the merging of financial and nonfinancial data in one integrated information system? What are the main obstacles and problems? How would you overcome them?

CHAPTER 11

BUDGET REFORM
Elixir or Mirage?

Budget reform is in the air as never before. As deficits and debt soar, uncontrollable costs remain relatively untouchable, and accountability for expenditures becomes a sometime thing, frustrated voters, politicians, administrators, budgeteers, and academics continue a never-ending search for budget reforms that will solve these problems. This has been the story of budgeting in the twentieth century.

In the nineteenth century, when modern budgeting began (in Britain, France, Spain, and other European countries), budget systems remained fairly stable and static for nearly 100 years. The bitter political struggles that resulted in legislative primacy in taxing and spending had already taken place. Increasingly, governments were accountable to parliaments for expenditures. Though powerful, prime ministers and ministers of finance had to reckon with fractious legislators. In the United States, legislatures dominated relatively simple budget routines.

This seemingly comfortable state of affairs came to an end during the first two decades of the twentieth century as momentous changes occurred. In the wake of World War I and mounting social and economic problems, expenditures increased sharply. To control a growing government, budget staffs expanded in ministries of finance and in large operating agencies in Europe. In the United States the executive budget system took hold for the first time, starting in the 1920s.[1]

From these beginnings, wave after wave of budgetary reforms swept federal, state, and local governments in the United States and elsewhere during the next seventy-four years, and continue to this day. Every budgetary system in effect today bears the imprint of these changes and, in some respects, is the richer for them—in other respects, weaker. This chapter discusses the following fifteen major budget reforms and the legacy they left behind them:

1. The executive budget
2. Functional budgeting

3. Program and performance budgeting

4. Multiyear expenditure projections and budgets

5. Unified or comprehensive budgets

6. P.P.B.S. (Planning, Programming, Budgeting System)

7. Budgeting MBO style (management by objectives)

8. Productivity budgeting

9. ZBB (zero-based budgeting)

10. Target budgeting

11. Budgeting as a tool for economic management (covered in Chapter 7)

12. Legislative budgeting (see Chapter 8)

13. Gaining control of off-budget budgets (see Chapter 6)

14. Budgeting loans and loan guarantees (see Chapter 6)

15. Ballot box budgeting

The Basic Reform: The Executive Budget System

The earliest and most enduring budget reform in the United States is the executive budget system, wherein the chief executive is responsible for formulating and implementing the budget. So accustomed are we in the United States to executive budgets and powerful legislative bodies often eager to undo them, that it is difficult to recall that legislatures alone enjoyed primacy in financing government up to the 1920s. Presidents and governors had "little say over the estimates, appropriations, expenditures and policies of government bureaus and departments."[2] Their impotence in budgeting contrasted with the firm control over the budget exercised by prime ministers and members of their cabinets in parliamentary systems in Europe, especially those in Britain, France, and Germany.[3]

In the United States, by the turn of the twentieth century it had become clear that budgetary methods suitable to a rural economy could no longer cope with the changes brought about by the industrial and commercial revolution. Increasingly, activist governments embarked upon new and costly social, economic, and regulatory programs. Yet legislative bodies persisted in their old ways of doing business. They acted on fragmented and uncoordinated appropriations bills instead of a unified budget. The system, if it can be called that, placed little emphasis on expenditure control, accountability for results, efficiency and economy in governmental operations, or even a uniform classification of expenditures.[4]

The situation was anathema to the early reformers. Determined to make the chief executive the government leader in fact as well as in name, they hammered away on two themes: the need for an executive budget and the need for governmental reorganization, with the chief executive responsible for appointing and controlling the heads of nearly all agencies. The reformers were most explicit in their views of the proposed executive budget system. It should be a multifaceted tool for controlling expenditures, developing fiscal policy, managing resources, achieving economy and efficiency in governmental operations, formulating new policies, and facilitating accountability for results. They envisaged a budget classified by function, program, organizational unit, and object of expense. It should represent "a well-defined plan or prospectus of work to be financed in order that the government may make provision for the needs of the country."[5] So prescient were these proposals that in the 1990s few budgets or budget processes differ significantly in concept from the recommendations of the budget reformers of the first two decades of the twentieth century, led primarily by the New York Bureau of Municipal Research and President William H. Taft's Commission on Efficiency and Economy.[6]

Predictably, legislatures gave the various proposals for budgetary reform a chilly reception. Under mounting pressure, however, Congress finally approved the landmark Budget and Accounting Act of 1921 (42 Stat. 18, 1921), and most state legislatures, prodded by constitutional changes, had acceded to the new executive budget system by the end of the 1920s.[7]

Some of the early enthusiasm for the executive budget is evident in the euphoric comments of A. R. Hatton, who in 1915 edited a volume on "Public Budgets" in *The Annals of the American Academy of Political and Social Science:*

> It may be made one of the most potent instruments of democracy . . . The budget provides a means through which citizens may assure themselves that their effort which has been devoted to common ends is not used for private gain, is not misused, or frittered away, but is applied to the accomplishment of those purposes which the community approved and is made to produce the maximum results for the efforts expended.[8]

Though revolutionary at the time, the newly developed executive budget system was quickly labeled traditional and conventional by impatient critics in the 1920s and in later years. It failed to live up to their expectations. In most instances governments in the United States classified budgets and appropriations by fund, organizational unit, line items, and objects of expense. The emphasis was on line-item expenditure control, with little attention to the performance of programs and projects. One early critic was Lent D. Upson, who in 1924 urged governments to present in the budget, for each activity, a complete picture of what they hoped to accomplish and the means of accomplishing it. Anticipating what later would be the main thrust of program budgeting and PPBS, Upson, citing health agencies as an example, complained that budgets

> do not state the practical minimum death rate, the cost in dollars to secure that minimum and the plan for accomplishing that ideal . . . The budget should be expressed in terms of work to be accomplished as well as in material things to be purchased . . . The budget should be supplemented by an operations audit that will measure the effectiveness of expenditures as thoroughly as financial audits measure the legality of expenditures.[9]

Upson's charges were but the opening gun in a salvo of criticism attacking the executive budget system during the next seventy years. The critique of the budget process may be summed up as follows: It focused on inputs (money, staff, and materials) instead of on outputs or results. Lacking a program orientation (following Upson's theme), it did not pinpoint the objectives, costs, and accomplishments of programs. Born in an era of distrust of government, it was primarily an instrument to control expenditures. As such it was negative and ill suited to the positive development of programs in a welfare state.

Reformers cited still more weaknesses. Budgeting focused on marginal changes in line items instead of on periodic reviews of the efficiency and effectiveness of all governmental programs. If any linkage existed between budgets and long-range plans and policies, it was not readily apparent. The budget process often ignored the future program and fiscal impact of current decisions. Few significant issues were studied in any depth as part of the budget process. The lack of adequate performance indicators and performance measurement systems made it difficult to analyze the efficiency and effectiveness of programs and projects. As a result, the traditional executive budget system, contrary to expectations, became less than an adequate mechanism for the rational and efficient allocation of funds.

Much of the criticism was justified, as we will note. Some of it was wide of the mark. For example, the fact that a budget appears in traditional format with expenditures lined out by organizational unit and object of expense does not necessarily signify the absence of program planning, development, and evaluation. In fact, during the 1930s, 1940s, and 1950s, the federal and state governments embarked on a variety of social and economic programs, with the budget offices often at the center of program development. Yet the budget decisions arrived at after intensive analysis were translated into the familiar line-item format. To use the parlance associated later with PPBS, budget offices "cross-walked," or reclassified program costs into the more widely accepted categories of organizational unit and objects of expense. This is still the case in many governments, where legislatures are more comfortable with traditional and less controversial classifications of expenditures.

The traditional system is a potent means of control and resource management. This was the case in the 1920s and, with even more urgency, is the case in the 1990s, when several critics charge that the budget is out of control. By focusing on objects of expense, the traditional budget guards against loose estimates of program costs. It makes agencies accountable for the resources entrusted to them.

The political appeal of the traditional budget is irresistible. A program cut is visible, stirs up a vocal constituency, and invites a political fallout. A cut in allocations for personal service, supplies, and travel may be just as damaging to a program, but the impact is not readily apparent.

For these assorted reasons, the traditional budget will survive as the bedrock of budgeting and as a chief instrument of expenditure control. Other changes add important new dimensions to the conventional budget, but do not supplant it.

Over the years, several budget reforms followed on the heels of the traditional budget. All aimed to inject more rationality, objectivity, and accountability into the budget process. Some reforms were modest but useful accretions to the system. Others were launched with a good deal of hoopla, gimmickry, and rhetorical

overkill. Each major reform had its claque of proponents who promised a technocratic utopia, and a covey of opponents who pronounced the reform dead before
it had barely gotten off the ground. Each proposed change was a creature of its
times and yet, in several respects, was similar to every other reform. Still, differences in emphasis, approach, and rhetoric were evident. None of the changes
would have shocked the early reformers, who had recommended or anticipated
nearly all of them. Beginning in the 1940s, the first of the reforms to surface was
functional budgeting.

Functional Budgeting: Focusing on the Costs of Broad Goals

Functional budgeting is an attempt to group expenditures by the broad purposes
or functions of government, regardless of organizational unit or object of expense.
With this classification, decision makers would at least roughly know the costs of
such functions as health, education, transportation, and welfare and be in a position to weigh relative priorities in very general terms. Using this approach, the
United States Bureau of the Budget developed an informal system in the 1940s to
display government costs by broad functions. Reasonably satisfied with the
results, it adopted in 1948 a comprehensive functional classification of budget
authority and outlays with the following rationale:

> By grouping together items which are functionally related, regardless of the
> agency which is responsible, this type of classification provides for the Congress
> and the public a useful summary of what the government is doing, or expects to
> do, and in general focuses upon the ultimate purpose which the government pro-
> grams are designed to serve.[10]

During the 1950s, state governments in the United States and governments
elsewhere in the world began to present costs by major function. At present, this
is virtually a universal practice, with the number of functions ranging from six to
about twenty. By giving such a global view of expenditures, governments reached
what appeared to be a happy compromise between traditional budgeting, which
focused on inputs, and the complexities of program budgeting, which requires the
costing of hundreds of programs.

Providing Additional Information by Subdividing Functions

Presidents presented their budgetary proposals within a framework of broad
functions until the 1960s, when rising expenditures, the implementation of new
programs, and the adoption of the unified budget made it desirable to break
down functions into subfunctions for a more comprehensive analysis of governmental costs.[11] Thus the function "natural resources and environment" was
divided into five subfunctions: pollution control and abatement, water resources,
conservation and land management, recreational resources, and other resources.
Each subfunction in turn comprised several programs (more on this later). The
subfunction was a bridge between the major function and individual programs.[12]

Converting Functional Classifications into an Instrument of Control

For nearly three decades, the functional presentation was used primarily to highlight expenditures trends and to serve as a rough guide to an administration's priorities. With the passage of the Congressional Budget Act of 1974 (PL 93-344), it became an instrument of control. The Act, as noted in Chapter 8, requires Congress to establish by resolution targets for outlays and budget authority for each of the major functions. In the budget presentation, the president must follow this as well. For the 1993–1994 fiscal year, Congress and the president used the following seventeen functions and four broad categories of expenditure to classify appropriations and outlays:

National defense

International affairs

General science, space, and technology

Energy

National resources and environment

Agriculture

Commerce and housing credit

Transportation

Community and regional development

Education, training, employment, and social services

Health

Medicare

Income security

Social security

Veterans benefits and services

Administration of justice

General government

General purpose fiscal assistance

Interest

Allowances

Undistributed offsetting receipts[13]

The functional structure is not static. The Congressional Budget Act also requires the General Accounting Office, in cooperation with the Office of Management and Budget, the secretary of the treasury, and the Congressional Budget Office to "develop, establish, maintain and publish standards, terminology, definitions, classifications, and codes for federal fiscal, budgetary and program related data and information." Since 1975 these offices have been instrumental in revising the integrated structure of functions, subfunctions, and programs to serve the needs of Congress and the executive branch.[14]

Functional Classifications in Other Governments

State governments in the United States take somewhat different approaches in developing functional classifications. Notwithstanding differences in terminology, the categories are similar. For example, the state of New Jersey classifies appropriations and expenditures by eight statewide programs, which are akin to functions: public safety and criminal justice; physical and mental health; education and cultural and intellectual development; community development and environmental management; economic planning, development, and security; transportation services; government direction, management, and control; and special government services. Within each category the budget includes a further breakdown by broad programs virtually tantamount to subfunctions, followed by specific departmental programs.[15]

As variations of functional classifications, several states emphasize broad themes in highlighting budget priorities. For example, Oregon has developed some 270 "benchmarks" under broad categories such as children and families, education and workforce preparation, health and health care, physically livable communities, socially livable communities, clean natural environment, and government efficiency. Each benchmark lays out quantitative goals for the next two decades. Thus one benchmark, health care access, aims at giving 99 percent of Oregonians access to basic health care by 1995. Another, with regard to stream quality, would reduce the miles of rivers and streams not meeting federal and state water-quality standards from 1,100 in 1992 to 75 in the year 2000. Each benchmark is linked to costed programs in the operating agencies.[16]

Coining still another phrase for a related approach, Ohio has formulated what it calls "the new paradigm budget." The new paradigm is a "new way of providing state services oriented toward cost effective and community-based service delivery systems." One paradigm (among a total of eight) is "family and children: early intervention and coordination." The Ohio budget lays out the funds for nine programs (e.g., Head Start and day care) designed to achieve the goals of the paradigm.[17]

Nearly all other countries summarize expenditures by broad function, supplementing classifications by organizational units, objects of expense, and economic categories.[18] The United Nations has urged the use of combined functional and economic classifications in budgeting to highlight the costs of the major purposes of government and the economic nature of the costs (e.g., capital and current costs, subsidies, transfer payments, and interest).[19]

Functional Budgeting Canadian Style: "Envelope Budgeting"

After some years of experimentation with various budget reforms, the government of Canada developed in 1979 and modified in 1986 "envelope budgeting" to control a runaway budget. Part of a larger decision-making system called Policy and Expenditure Management System (PEMS), envelope budgeting is functional budgeting. All government programs are assigned to one of ten functions, or spending envelopes. Each envelope has an expenditure ceiling that is approved by the cabinet and cannot be changed without the consent of the cabinet. To get additional funds ministers have the latitude to cut existing programs, including some uncontrollable programs, and, again with cabinet approval, to draw on a small policy reserve set aside for contingencies. Envelope budgeting takes place within a rolling five-year expenditure plan. Thus, in 1993 the cabinet updated the five-year envelope for FY 1993–1994 to 1997–1998.[20]

* * *

Functional budgeting represented the first major shift from traditional budgeting by object of expense and organizational unit. By focusing on costs of the major purposes of government, it facilitated the debate on budget priorities. It also served as a bridge to budgeting by programs and led to a new hierarchical method of classifying and analyzing costs: by function, subfunction, program, subprogram, and activity.

The Rise of Program and Performance Budgeting

A product of the early 1950s, program and performance budgeting endures in every corner of the world, contrary to frequent obituaries written by chroniclers of budgetary developments. It has proved to be the hardiest budget reform and continues to flourish with each passing year, often under different labels and acronyms. While some writers quibble about the differences between program and performance budgets, they are one and the same thing.[21] An early definition by the United States Bureau of the Budget is still apt:

A performance budget is one which presents the purposes and objectives for which funds are required, the costs of the programs proposed for achieving these objectives, and quantitative data measuring the accomplishments and work performed under each program.[22]

The focus in budgeting, then, is on results to be attained and the work to be done rather than on organizational units and objects of expense alone. This was not a new idea. From 1907 to the 1940s, several federal and local budget offices in the United States engaged in program and performance budgeting to varying degree, without always explicitly billing it as such or reflecting it in the budget document.[23] The reform, however, made no headway until 1949, when the Hoover Commission on the Organization of the Executive Branch of the Government popularized the concepts and techniques of program and performance budgeting and launched a widespread movement to implement them.

The commission was highly critical of the then-existing budgetary system in the federal government, which not only classified expenditures largely by object of expense and organization, but was so fragmented that the costs of any one program were spread among several line items and rarely identified. The result was that it was difficult, except for insiders, to identify programs and to determine program costs.[24]

Prodded by the Hoover Commission, the federal government mandated the implementation of program and performance budgeting by statute. The Budget and Accounting Procedures Act of 1950 (64 Stat. 832) required the head of each agency, in consultation with the director of the Bureau of the Budget, to support "budget justifications by information on performance and program cost by organizational unit." Amendments to the National Security Act in 1949 required the Department of Defense to install performance budgeting in the three services (63 Stat. 578).

The United States budget for the 1950–1951 fiscal year was the first to show the effects of program and performance budgeting. Agencies buttressed about 90 percent of all proposed expenditures with schedules laying out program and performance costs, specifying the major purposes to be served, and summarizing in a work program the work to be done to achieve the given objectives. Congress began in a small way to appropriate funds by program and activity rather than by object of expense alone. Nevertheless, the second Hoover Commission was unhappy with these small beginnings and in 1955 urged the full-scale implementation of program budgeting.[25]

Though conceptually simple, program and performance budgeting proved to be a very time-consuming and often frustrating undertaking as governments at all levels, following the lead of the federal government, attempted to implement the following components of the "new reform":[26]

1. Identifying programs and program costs, such as rehabilitation of the physically and emotionally handicapped, correctional services, and highway safety.

2. Breaking down the programs into smaller units such as subprograms, activities, and cost centers. Thus, a cancer control program might include as subprograms case finding, medical care and treatment, and public education. Case finding could be further subdivided into activities such as X-ray screening and laboratory testing. This three-part program structure led to semantical confusion and endless wrangling as to the meaning of program, subprogram, and activity. It was also necessary to distinguish programs from functions and subfunctions. Thus, cancer control could be part of a subfunction such as preventing, controlling, and treating chronic disease. In turn, the subfunctions could be part of the broader function of health services.

3. Developing units of measurement for the work to be done for each activity, for example, the number of X rays, the number of laboratory tests, the number of miles of roads maintained, the number of surgeries to correct physical handicaps, or the number of prisoners counseled. Some units of measurement are relatively easy to identify in quantifiable programs. In more complex areas such as education, mental health, and law enforcement, the development of performance measures is more difficult, but still doable.

4. Measuring the work to be done for each activity and the time and cost required to accomplish this work. Without a work-measurement system and an

accounting system that accumulates costs by programs, this relatively simple step cannot be implemented.

5. Developing unit times and unit costs for each activity, such as the time and cost of maintaining a mile of road. Is historical experience sufficient to determine unit costs or times? Or should standard times and costs based on detailed methods studies be developed?

6. Summarizing all the data in a work program for each activity: work to be done, units of measurement, unit time and cost, and total time and cost. The cost includes not only personal service, but other objects of expense as well.

7. Using the work program for each activity or cost center to develop the agency budget.

8. Appropriating funds by program.

9. Reporting and comparing actual performance and cost with projected performance and cost. Such variance analysis is integral to program and performance budgeting because it sheds light on the efficiency and effectiveness of programs.

10. Using quarterly performance reports in budget implementation as a basis for allocating funds to agencies.

11. Determining the extent to which the achievement of the targets for each activity led to the attainment of the short- and long-term program goals such as reducing the incidence of various types of disease or the number of highway accidents, injuries, and fatalities. These are measures of effectiveness, quality, results.

Examples of Program and Performance Budgeting

Several examples illustrate the approach taken by governments in installing program and performance budgets. In 1972 some states endorsed a model budget for state highway maintenance as a basis for program development and resource allocation.[27] Some twenty years later, the model is still used. As Table 11.1 shows, the costs of the ten major activities comprising highway maintenance are based on a detailed work program including units of measurement and objects of expense.

In an even more ambitious effort beginning in the 1980s, the Michigan Department of Mental Health relied on program and performance budgeting in developing its budget estimates. For each of its major programs (inpatient services, residential services, outpatient services, etc.) it classified patients on the basis of behavior: good to superior functioning, mild impairment in functioning, moderate impairment in functioning, major impairment in functioning, and those requiring total supervision. For each group the department formulated standard definitions and an appropriate treatment such as sustenance, rehabilitation, crisis resolution, sustenance adjustment, and prevention. Through its management information system, the department tracked the services and the cost of the services given to the various patients. On this basis it was able to develop key

TABLE 11.1

Model of program and performance budgeting for highway maintenance

A: State maintenance performance budget summary for top management

		Work program		Object of expenditure			
Code	Maintenance activity	In work units	In man-days	Labor	Equipment	Materials	Contractual services, etc.	Total budget
	Roadway Surface							
101	Patch with premix	3,500 tons mix	2,800	$67,200	$11,200	$ 21,000	—	$ 99,400
102	Level with premix	32,000 tons mix	2,090	50,200	43,900	192,000	—	286,100
103	Deep patch with premix or full-depth replacement	7,000 tons mix	1,285	30,800	36,200	42,000	—	109,000

B: State maintenance performance budget summaries for legislature and executive

Object of expenditure (in thousands of dollars)

Maintenance activity group	Labor	Equipment	Materials	Contractual services, etc.	Total budget	Expenditure percentage
Roadway surfaces	1,415	1,022	1,260	321	4,018	26
Shoulders and side approaches	208	189	221	—	618	4
Drainage	391	170	210	—	771	5
Roadside	1,100	510	398	—	2,008	13
Major structures	307	67	90	—	464	3
Snow and ice control	602	1,300	1,648	—	3,550	23
Traffic services	996	390	774	—	2,160	14
Extraordinary maintenance	63	61	28	—	152	1
Service functions and overheads	1,057	226	97	160	1,540	10
Betterment	91	45	13	—	149	1
State Maintenance Budget	6,230	3,980	4,739	481	15,430	100
Expenditure percentage	40	26	31	3	100	

Source: Roy Jorgensen Associates, Performance Budget Systems for Highway Maintenance Management (Washington, D.C.: Highway Research Board, 1972), p. 27.

performance data used for both program development and budgeting, such as client days of care, client hours of service, staff hours per client, and cost per patient day for the various types of treatment. These became the building blocks of the department's budget.[28]

Program and Performance Budgeting in the 1990s

Because of technical and political problems, it takes a quantum leap to move from traditional budgeting to program and performance budgeting. As a sine qua non, it is essential to develop the supporting systems discussed in Chapter 10: budgetary accounting, cost accounting, and work and performance measurement systems. Furthermore, a key aspect of program and performance budgeting is the concept of a contract. Under this approach, an administrator gets a lump sum in return for a commitment to turn out specified levels of performance. This proved to be a sticking point for legislators who, in the interest of control, preferred line-item appropriations rather than lump sums.

Accustomed to the old rules of the game, budgeteers and politicians were disquieted by program and performance budgeting. Much of the behind-the-scenes information would now be out in the open. It was asking too much of them to take a stand on operating targets, estimated workload, and performance standards. This might leave the decision makers in an exposed and vulnerable position in contrast with the safe haven and obscurity of budgets classified by organizational units and objects of expense.

Given these conditions, governments at first faltered in implementing program and performance budgeting and instituted it, if at all, on a piecemeal basis. The momentum, however, has picked up dramatically in recent years.

Program and Performance Budgeting in the Federal Government. Now program and performance budgeting is firmly entrenched in the federal government, with budgets identifying programs and activities, showing their total costs, and breaking down these costs by organizational unit and object of expense. The budget also includes key workload factors. As long advocated by proponents of program and performance budgeting, the appropriations act is a broad lump sum that blends funds for activities as well as for major objects of expense. Now the administration and Congress can have it both ways. In decision making they can use data on program and performance as well as on objects of expense.[29]

State Governments Jump on the Bandwagon. Similarly, program and performance budgeting pervades the budget process in most state governments in the United States. Robert D. Lee, Jr., who has monitored state budget developments for more than twenty years, found dramatic advances from 1970 to 1990. Table 11.2 highlights the growing impact of program and performance budgeting.

Visits to state governments and reviews of their budget documents demonstrate vividly the inroads of program and performance budgeting. From Califor-

TABLE 11.2

Program information in budget requests and revisions

Type of information	Percent of states providing information	
	1970	1990
Program effectiveness measures in budget requests	24	95
Productivity measures in requests	29	86
Effectiveness measures revised to reflect changed funding levels	13	49
Productivity measures revised to reflect changed funding levels	22	51

Program information in budget documents

Effectiveness measures	29	65
Productivity measures	45	77
Future year projections of effectiveness measures	2	26
Future year projections of productivity measures	8	37

Source: Robert D. Lee, Jr., "Developments in State Budgeting; Trends of Two Decades," *Public Administration Review* (May/June 1991), p. 256.

nia to New York, from Minnesota to Texas, the same trends are apparent: an emphasis on the goals and objectives of programs and subprograms, workload and costs, measures of efficiency and effectiveness, and work programs linked to budget requests.

To be sure, some critics cavil, pointing out that much of this information is for show rather than for use.[30] They question whether the data reflect the use of analytical techniques and influence budget decisions. They stress the difficulty of linking cost and performance. Some of these reservations are appropriate. Far more empirical work than has been done is needed to gauge the impact of program budgeting on funding state operations.

Program and Performance Budgeting in Local Governments. In the United States, local governments were among the first to practice program and performance budgeting. They are still at it. Of the 451 municipalities with a population ranging from 25,000 to 1 million that responded to a questionnaire on management practices in 1988, over three-fourths claimed they were using program and performance budgeting.[31]

Program and Performance Budgeting in Other Countries. Influenced by practices in the United States and the United Nations publication, *A Manual for Programme and Performance Budgeting,* nearly fifty countries installed variants of

program and performance budgeting in the 1960s, followed by even more countries in the next thirty years. Among the developed countries, Sweden, Britain,
Canada, and France were the leaders, although no country implemented a full-
scale version of program budgeting. What they achieved, however, apparently had
some impact on budget decision making.[32]

Developing countries adopted program budgeting enthusiastically. It appeared
to be a way of translating long-term objectives in their development plans into
operating targets in the annual budget. The UN encouraged them in this undertaking by pointing out that program budgeting "involves establishing appropriate
relationships between long- and short-range plans and that segment of the plans
that is proposed to be carried out in the annual budget."[33] Nearly all Latin
American countries, several Asian countries, and some African countries introduced versions of program budgeting. The most ambitious efforts took place in
Brazil, the Philippines, India, and Malaysia.[34]

Despite some success, "the history of performance budgeting [among developing countries] is one of high hopes and disappointing achievements." Central budget offices and legislative bodies rely only infrequently on performance budgets in
making decisions, preferring the traditional line-item budget. Performance measures are incomplete and inadequate. Old line-accounting systems don't always
accumulate costs by programs and activities. Most developing countries have dual
budgets (an operating budget and a capital budget) with different classification systems so that it is difficult to apply common program structures to both. Few links
exist between performance budgets and medium-term development plans.[35]

*   *   *

Notwithstanding many setbacks, governments everywhere continue to install
elements of program and performance budgeting on a piecemeal basis. If a reform
has proved to be so enduring, it must offer governments a means, even if not fully
realized, to rationalize and control expenditures, plan and cost programs, evaluate
performance, and stimulate further improvements in financial management. This
continues to be the strength of program and performance budgeting. As Dean
pointed out,

> Ideas take time to penetrate. Performance budgeting contained some good ideas
> and they are still penetrating. It seems over optimistic that performance budget-
> ing will experience a further upsurge of enthusiasm given its care-worn image,
> but sooner or later a similar set of concepts will be applied to the public sector.
> When that happens, performance budgeting will have laid an important founda-
> tion for their development.[36]

Peering beyond the Horizon: Multiyear Budget Projections and Budgets

An annual budget carries the burden of past policy, budgetary, and legislative
decisions, leaving little room for maneuvering. Hence, in any one year, the over-

whelming proportion of expenditures is uncontrollable. Whether uncontrollability results from legislative mandates, the reluctance to tamper with discretionary programs, or fixed charges such as interest on debt and retirement contributions, the effect is to reduce sharply the range of executive and legislative discretion. At best, then, short of a crisis, chief executives and legislative bodies can only nip at the margins of the budget. To break out of this fiscal straitjacket and to make decisions with an eye to the future, governments have initiated two significant budgetary reforms: (1) multiyear projections of expenditures and revenue and (2) multiyear budgets.

The Growing Use of Five-Year Budget Projections

In an insufficiently recognized budget reform, five-year projections of expenditures and revenue are now a standard practice in governments in the United States and most parts of the world. Their aim is to estimate the future effect of current budget decisions. Before initiating, expanding, or deleting programs and projects, decision makers would, in theory, understand the fiscal implications of their policies during each of the next five years: the impact on revenues, expenditures, deficits, and debt. A longer-term perspective could serve as a brake on expenditures by highlighting the limited funds available now and in the future under the current revenue structure and current expenditure commitments. It might also introduce more candor into budgeting by compelling chief executives and legislators to look beyond the current fiscal year. To sell a new program, administrations, whether cannily or in sheer ignorance, at times propose a small startup appropriation for the next fiscal year. In later years expenditures may soar as the program takes off. A five-year projection might spell out the fiscal consequences in advance.

Multiyear Budget Projections in the Federal Government. Multiyear projections of revenue and expenditures began in 1961, when the United States Bureau of Budget laid out in the budget document for the first time estimated receipts and outlays for a ten-year period. The figures were in rough aggregate form, with no breakdown by function or program, no year-by-year analysis, and no discussion of the economic assumptions underlying the numbers. Behind the scenes, however, the budget office used more detailed data for planning purposes, including three levels of projections: low, medium, and high.[37]

Congress later mandated a similar approach in two major pieces of legislation. In 1970 the Legislative Reorganization Act (PL 91-510, Section 221) called for five-year projections of budget authority and outlays for legislative proposals by the executive branch that would initiate or expand major programs. In 1974 Congress went further in the Congressional Budget and Impoundment Control Act of 1974 (PL 93-344), which required three sets of projections: (1) budget projections by the president for four fiscal years beyond the next budget year, (2) five-year projections by the Budget Committees of Congress to accompany the concurrent resolution, and (3) similar projections by the Congressional Budget Office after the beginning of each fiscal year. The projections were not intended to be statements of future policies or decisions, but estimates of the future effect of current policies and commitments in the light of various fiscal and economic assumptions.

In the early 1980s, the Reagan administration relied on long-range forecasts to sell the president's program of lower taxes, cuts in domestic spending, sharp increases in military spending, and a balanced budget.[38] To reorder the administration's priorities over a five-year period, OMB issued the following instructions with regard to the preparation of the 1983–1984 budget:

> The multi-year budget planning system . . . enables the President to evaluate the long-term consequences of proposed program or tax policy initiatives and to make decisions in that context. Each agency, including off-budget Federal entities, will prepare and submit materials containing estimates covering agency programs beyond the budget year [BY + 4] [current budget year plus the four following— Ed.]. These estimates will be used to update amounts contained in the multi-year budget planning system base, and to establish revised planning ceilings.[39]

The administration's forecasts turned out to be unreliable, inaccurate, and overly rosy. As the prospect of a balanced budget receded, President Reagan turned against multiyear projects altogether. Terming the forecasts "worthless" and the statutory requirement for them "idiotic," he claimed at a news conference in 1985 that "I pay no attention to them" and "there isn't any economist in the world who can do that and accurately tell you what you're going to need down the road."[40] However, President Reagan was virtually alone in urging their abandonment.

State Governments Peer into Their Budgetary Future. To get to a better grip on expenditures, multiyear projections of revenues and expenditures have become a standard practice in most state governments. They take various forms. In some states they are an integral part of the budgetary process, as in Pennsylvania, Hawaii, Ohio, Texas, and Wisconsin. In other states such as New Jersey, they serve as background data for the preparation of the annual budget. A minority of states, typified by New York, require by law the annual preparation of projections in a separate document, apart from the regular budget process.[41]

Other Countries' Use of Multiyear Projections. Nearly all industrialized countries prepare multiyear expenditure and revenue projections as part of their budgeting and planning processes. Most of the forecasts are rolling five-year estimates and hence are changed annually. Projections vary in their comprehensiveness and specificity. At one extreme, Britain and Germany develop detailed projections for major functions and programs and specify the assumptions on which the estimates rest. At the other, Japan prefers highly aggregated totals so as not to tip its hand on policy decisions. As in the United States, the driving force behind multiyear forecasts is primarily the need for expenditure control and deficit reduction.[42]

The Growing Use of Multiyear Budgets

As significant as multiyear projections of revenues and expenditures are, they are not decisions. They are merely estimates that guide, but do not bind, decision makers. Multiyear budgeting, however, is budget decision making that covers expenditure requirements for two or more years. Several factors prompt the growing use of multiyear budgets. For one, budget priorities cannot be shifted in one year. It may take several years to achieve the aims of new administrations. Second, advance budgeting provides stability in financing programs and projects. Third, multiyear budgets are a means of expenditure control and deficit reduction. They deliberately provide limited resources for the next few years to agencies so as to avoid the annual battle of adding increments to the budget. Fourth, budget targets set in advance discourage piecemeal decisions. Finally, multiyear budgets lighten the budgetary workload of administrations and legislative bodies by spreading decisions over several years.

For these assorted reasons, no annual budget exists in pure form anywhere. Of the fifty state governments in the United States, twenty-one, or over two-fifths, practice variations of biennial budgeting. However, their practices differ. The budgets and the appropriations may both be biennial, or the budget may be biennial, but appropriations annual. The states with biennial budgets generally adjust their budgets in the off years. In capital budgeting the time horizon is longer for most states. In most states capital budgets run up to twelve years with four- or five-year budgets heavily favored. The annual or biennial budget, however, determines the slice of the capital budget that will be funded during the coming fiscal year.[43] Local governments follow similar practices in capital budgeting.

The federal government breaches the annual budget in several ways: entitlement programs, which indefinitely mandate payments for individuals meeting statutory requirements; transfer payments to state and local governments that are based on statutory formulas; contract authority, which authorizes agencies to contract for goods and services in advance of an actual appropriation; multiyear appropriations; borrowing authority authorizing obligations and expenditures; permanent appropriations, which authorize expenditures up to amounts specified by legislation; forward funding, which obligates funds in one fiscal year for programs that are to operate in subsequent fiscal years; carryover provisions, which in a limited number of programs allow officials to carry over into the next year funds approved for the previous fiscal year; and advance appropriations for selected construction programs such as airport construction, mass transportation, and urban renewal programs. In addition, in 1986 Congress enacted still another form of multiyear budgeting, termed "milestone budgeting," which allows Congress to approve up to five years of funding in advance for selected weapons systems. The appropriations would be based on the achievement of targets, or "milestones," during the multiyear period.[44]

With the passage of the Balanced Budget and Emergency Deficit Control Act of 1985 (PL 99-177) and its later changes, Congress and the president expanded multiyear budgeting. The Act mandates a phased annual reduction in deficits until a balanced budget is reached. The Budget Enforcement Act of 1990 and the Reconciliation Act of 1993 set expenditure ceilings over a five-year period, again with the aim of cutting the deficit, as Chapter 8 points out.

Still other variations of multiyear budgeting continue to emerge. In 1977 the Congressional Budget Office suggested that Congress consider such alternatives as the use of three-to-five-year rolling budget targets, biennial budgeting, staggered two-year budgeting (enacting roughly half the budget each year), and selective two-year appropriations for programs whose needs can be forecast relatively easily.[45] Hardly a year goes by without a revival of these or similar proposals. Such an approach, in Niskanen's words, would "institutionalize a concern about future costs."[46]

Budgets That Tell the Whole Story: Unified, or Comprehensive, Budgets

Another major goal of budgetary reform has been a unified, or comprehensive, budget covering all funds, receipts, and expenditures in the public sector. This is yet another means of strengthening control over the public purse and enforcing accountability. In addition, it provides a complete picture of cash flow in the government, the size of the surplus or deficit, and borrowing needs. But the goal remains elusive in most governments.

The federal government of the United States came close to a unified budget in 1969, when it implemented the recommendations of the President's Commission on Budget Concepts and combined the so-called administrative budget, covering the activities of departments and agencies, with the budgets of trust funds. The trust funds (those held "in trust" by the government) include social security, Medicare, unemployment insurance, and federal aid to highways and airports. Prior to 1969, they were off-budget.[47] The immediate result of their inclusion was that the budget became more comprehensive and receipts and expenditures rose dramatically. Over the years, however, the unified budget eroded. Initially, the growth of off-budget budgets of government corporations subverted the process. Then, in 1985 the Balanced Budget and Emergency Deficit Control Act, as previously noted, pulled the social security system out of the budget, but folded in government corporations.

State governments in the United States have been slower to combine all receipts and expenditures in one budget. Most of them exclude from budget totals either funds for public authorities or special funds or some taxes collected by the state and distributed to local governments. Under the stimulus of GAAP (generally accepted accounting principles), which recommends the inclusion of all funds in the budget, they now include the overall data in their financial reports, if not in their budgets.[48]

The Budget "Happening" of All Time: PPBS

The advent of PPBS (Planning, Programming, Budgeting System) in the mid-1960s was the greatest budget "happening" in the United States since the creation of the executive budget system. Started in Washington, D.C., PPBS soon spread to the states, local governments, and other countries. Practitioners, scholars, and foreign officials trekked to Washington, D.C., to observe first-hand the latest revelation in budgeting. In a few short years the spate of academic literature on the subject reached monumental proportions. Yet by 1971 the system that had started with a bang died without a whimper, only to be resurrected in various guises during the next twenty years. At this point it is useful to understand the attraction of PPBS, the reasons for its rapid rise and fall, and its resurrection.

Conceptually, PPBS was exciting. It seemed to combine in one system long- and medium-term planning of policies; programming of expected performance and costs over a five-year period; and annual budgeting. None of the components of the system were, of course, new. Weaving them together into a comprehensive system was a new approach. The entire system focused on alternative means and costs of achieving the purposes and objectives of governmental programs in the light of an explicit analysis of needs. Backed up by an array of analytical tools such as systems analysis, cost–benefit analysis, and cost–effectiveness analysis, the system promised to achieve greater rationality and efficiency in the allocation of funds. Despite this allure, PPBS might have remained an ambitious blueprint were it not implemented in 1961 by the Department of Defense, under the leadership of Secretary Robert McNamara, in "the first attempt to establish a decision process based upon the systems approach on a wide scale in a large and significant segment of the total governmental establishment."[49] What worked in Defense was, in the opinion of the Johnson administration, good enough for the rest of the federal establishment.

This is not the place to analyze the budgeting system in Defense or to weigh the quality of budgetary decisions that resulted from the McNamara system and later modifications of that system, which persisted into the 1990s.[50] Curiously, though, few objective evaluations exist of what PPBS accomplished or failed to accomplish in Defense.[51] For better or worse, the defense budget increased until the cuts of the 1990s after the end of the cold war. This had the effect of muffling any criticism of McNamara's decisions in the military establishment, the centralization of decisions in the secretary's office, or his decision-making style. What was important was that the decision-making system captivated President Johnson.

Prior to adoption of PPBS, the president and the Bureau of the Budget had become increasingly dissatisfied with the information furnished by domestic agencies in support of the Great Society programs and other ventures dear to the president. As the flood of domestic legislation crested, actual costs outran all estimates. At the same time, the costs of the war in Vietnam were becoming ominously high. With resources limited, it became difficult to sort out priorities, determine how well the domestic programs were doing, look for relationships between results and costs, seek more acceptable alternatives to existing programs, and project for several years ahead the impact of current decisions. Especially disturbing was the lack of in-depth analysis of programs and budgets within agencies and among agencies that worked in closely related fields such as income maintenance.[52]

For a panacea the president turned to the McNamara budgeting system and, with only slight modifications, in 1965 directed all domestic agencies to put it into effect simultaneously. With typical Johnsonian hyperbole, the president announced in August 1965 that he was introducing "a very revolutionary system of planning and programming and budgeting throughout the vast Federal government, so through the tools of modern management the full promise of the finer life can be brought to every American at the lowest possible cost."[53]

PPBS Takes Off in 1965

Promptly dubbed the Planning, Programming, Budgeting System (PPBS), the system announced by the president was implemented in detailed directives by the Bureau of the Budget.[54] These were the components of the system:

1. *Three-way program structure.* This consisted of program category, program subcategory, and program elements. The program structure encompassed the activities of all agencies and was focused on purposes, outputs, and results rather than on means to ends. For example, in February 1966 the purpose-oriented program categories of the Department of Housing and Urban Development were decent housing for all Americans, improved land use for community development, effective urban transport, support for state and local administration of community development activities, and management of departmental programs and resources. The category (purpose) "decent housing for all Americans" was divided into eight program subcategories with narrower objectives, of which one was to "conserve and improve housing stock." This in turn comprised four program elements, or major activities: rehabilitation through insured financing, rehabilitation through direct loans, rehabilitation through grants, and property improvements through short-term loans.

As part of the system, it was necessary to identify and cost each of the three program levels. This was no mean feat. Most governmental programs have more than one purpose. Yet PPBS required that the appropriate share of costs be allocated to each purpose. More than just another way of classifying governmental programs and costs, the program structure was intended to be a decision-making tool. It was designed to facilitate debate and choice with regard to appropriate goals, objectives, scope and nature of activities, results, the effectiveness and efficiency of operations, and the search for suitable alternatives. It was a breathtaking blueprint.

2. *Program memoranda (PM).* At the outset, PPBS required a zero-based review of each program category. Agencies submitted for each category a program memorandum (PM), which covered purposes and objectives, urgent program issues, costs and effectiveness of alternatives considered, the rationale for the agency's preferred option, anticipated accomplishments for the next several years, and evidence of the analytical techniques used to buttress the agency's choice. So enormous and complex was the task that the Bureau of the Budget early in the game caved in under agency pressure and requested PMs only for major issues.

3. *Special analytical studies (SAS)*. The agency, in consultation with the Bureau of the Budget, initiated a limited number of special analytical studies for particularly complex problems such as airport user charges, highway safety programs, vocational rehabilitation, and infant mortality. On occasion, a selected SAS termed a "presidential memorandum" went to the president for decision.

4. *Multiyear program and financial plan (MYPFP)*. Capping the entire exercise was the MYPFP, the end product of the extensive analyses in each agency. This was the programming part of PPBS. It was essentially a rolling multiyear budget that, on the basis of assorted economic and programmatic assumptions, projected outputs, costs, and required financing for the past year, the current year, the upcoming budget year, and the four out years for each program category. Outputs were quantitative measures of the services produced by program elements, such as the number of workers trained, the number of physically handicapped individuals employed, or the number of B-52 squadrons activated. Agencies were encouraged to supplement these measures with more meaningful gauges of achievement and effectiveness. The MYPFPs carried forward the fiscal and programmatic implications of past and present decisions.

Table 11.3 shows, in highly simplified form, the skeletal structure of MYPFPs, vintage 1965. In practice, the tables went farther and classified outputs and costs by programs controlled by statutory formulas, such as social security (the uncontrollable programs); programs controlled by workload; programs at the mercy of market forces, such as agricultural price supports and interest on debt (more uncontrollables); programs requiring legislation; programs honoring presidential commitments; and programs limited to levels of appropriations approved by Congress, such as construction grants and foreign assistance. All this in twenty-five copies sent to the Bureau of the Budget!

5. *Change in budget cycle*. The budget cycle was altered to incorporate consideration of the PMs, the SASs, and the MYPFPs. Two separate budgetary tracks were now in effect: the conventional budget requests and the documentation supporting PPBS. Both reached the central budget office at the same time in a blitz of paper. After the president submitted the budget to Congress, agencies changed their MYPFPs once again to reflect presidential decisions.

The Very Model of Budget Rationality

In almost every respect PPBS mimicked the McNamara system, except for the use of different acronyms. It looked like the very model of rationality by embodying these concepts:

Allocating resources to purposes and objectives on the basis of in-depth economic and programmatic analysis.

Focusing openly and explicitly on the ends and objectives of governmental programs over a medium-term period.

Sharpening objectives and quantifying them where possible.

TABLE 11.3

Example of multiyear program and financial plan covering outputs and costs

Manpower training outputs, FY 1965–1971

	FY						
	65	66	67	68	69	70	71
I. Manpower Development Assistance							
A.							
B. Manpower Training							
1.							
2. On-the-job-training (No. of workers trained—000)	XX	XX	XX	XX	XX	XX	XX

Costs, FY 1965–1971

	FY ($ rounded to tenths of millions)						
	65	66	67	68	69	70	71
I. Manpower Development Assistance							
A.							
B. Manpower Training							
1.							
2. On-the-job-training	XX	XX	XX	XX	XX	XX	XX

Totals and subtotals should be shown for program categories and subcategories.

Source: Executive Office of the President, Bureau of the Budget, Supplement to Bulletin No. 66-3, "Planning-Programming-Budgeting" (Washington, D.C., February 21, 1966).

Comparing the costs and benefits of alternative paths to agreed-upon objectives.

Selectively analyzing urgent programmatic and budgetary issues.

Developing performance indicators to measure the effectiveness and efficiency of programs.

Emphasizing the results, outcomes, and outputs of programs and their full costs.

Developing a program structure, regardless of organizational lines, as a framework for analysis.

Measuring the relationship between resources and outputs.

Evaluating existing programs from scratch.

Forcing competition and trade-offs among programs, regardless of past policies, to pick the best mix of programs designed to attain specific objectives.

Expanding choices by decision makers by offering them options.

Laying out the long-range as well as the immediate effects of past and current budgetary decisions.

Making forward planning respectable again and linking planning with multiyear and annual budgets.

Building a relevant database.

Forcing earlier decisions prior to budget making.

"Cross-walking" between program costs and appropriations accounts (reclassifying program costs to show the costs of objects of expense and the costs of the appropriate organizational units). This was a bow to the traditional budget still required by Congress.

Focusing on the costs and benefits of programs in terms of their impacts on segments of the population.

This was heady brew. Of course PPBS was not new; the concepts go back to the budget reformers in the early part of the twentieth century. Much of it can't be distinguished from program and performance budgeting, except for (1) the multiyear planning dimension, which was never fully implemented in program budgeting; (2) the attempt to allocate costs to the achievement of purposes; and (3) the emphasis on policy development and program evaluation. PPBS systematized multiyear budget forecasts already in effect. It incorporated true zero-based budgeting, not the misnamed ZBB of the Carter administration. It emphasized more than before analytical techniques that had long been in use, such as cost–benefit analysis, cost–effectiveness analysis, and systems analysis. Truly new aspects were the integration of the components into a formal system, the emphasis on PPBS in decision making, the packaging of the system, and the hoopla and exaggerated claims that attended its arrival.[55]

State and Local Governments Climb on the PPBS Bandwagon

State and local governments in the United States soon climbed on the fast-moving bandwagon. In fact, New York State took pride in initiating PPBS in 1964, a year before President Johnson made it official doctrine in the federal government.[56] The states followed different patterns in adapting PPBS to their requirements. For example, Pennsylvania and New York hewed closest to the federal model and even went beyond it in providing policy guidance to agencies and emphasizing long-range planning rather than just multiyear forecasting and budgeting.[57] In contrast, states such as Wisconsin and California rejected a total systems approach. Wisconsin's strategy was to go slowly and to develop a four-level program structure (program, subprogram, activity, and subactivity) that the legislature would support and incorporate in the appropriation acts. It also concentrated on the development of management information and accounting systems that would support program budgeting. For each program, it developed over the years specific objectives and a variety of performance indicators focusing on outputs and results. Whenever possible, it attempted to identify the resources necessary to produce specific results. It engaged in selective analysis of major policy issues and, through trial and error, attempted to relate state planning to budgeting. Policy positions adopted by the governor were made public. With this evolutionary approach, Wisconsin found less need for the paperwork and paraphernalia of PPBS associated with New York State, Pennsylvania, and the federal government.[58] California followed variants of this approach.

Not all local governments in the United States moved as quickly as the states to initiate PPBS. In the late 1960s, about 31 percent of the cities and 26 percent of the counties had incorporated some of the components of PPBS in their decision-making systems. Philadelphia and New York City represented opposite extremes in their approach to PPBS. Philadelphia instituted the entire apparatus of PPBS, lock, stock, and barrel. New York City followed a more selective approach when it came to the conclusion that little was to be gained in concentrating on program structures and performance measures, absent any meaningful data. It focused instead on the major issues confronting the city and conducted a series of studies on the efficiency and effectiveness of crime prevention, air pollution control, refuse disposal, and industrial development, to give but a few examples.[59]

Taking Stock of PPBS in the United States

In 1971 President Nixon's OMB sent shockwaves through the federal bureaucracy and other levels of government, when it dismissed PPBS only four years after its implementation by revising budget instructions as follows:

> Agencies are no longer required to submit with their budget submissions the multi-year program and financing plans, program memoranda, and special analytical studies or the schedules that reconcile information classified according to their program and appropriation structures.[60]

Several states and local governments also backed away from PPBS after only a few years of experience with it. For example, in 1970 New York State discarded PPBS in favor of PAR (Program Analysis and Review), an approach rather than a system, which emphasized issue analysis and a slow agency-by-agency development of performance measures and multiyear projections of outputs, costs, and personnel requirements.[61]

The action by OMB brought to a climax the steady drumfire of criticism that began shortly after the advent of PPBS. To be sure, PPBS didn't lack articulate defenders, and they entered the fray with enthusiasm. The critique took two main paths. One centered on the tactical and pragmatic problems in implementing so ambitious a reform as PPBS. The other, more serious, found PPBS conceptually flawed from the start and an unrealistic, if not naive, mechanism for budgetary decision making in a political milieu. What is astonishing in looking back at the debate is the speed with which opponents and proponents rushed into print with instant judgments when PPBS had barely gotten under way. We have noted how long it takes to implement program and performance budgeting. For a more ambitious system like PPBS, the time span is even greater.

The Pragmatic Critique of PPBS. Many of the problems of PPBS in the federal government stemmed from its simultaneous introduction across the board in agencies that were ill prepared to implement it. Few departments had the expertise that Defense had developed in program budgeting since the 1950s and in inaugurating the McNamara system in 1961. Some cautious voices urged a selective, go-slow approach. Nevertheless, the Johnson administration and the Bureau of the Budget persuaded themselves of the value of the "shock effect" of an instant PPBS. To hard-pressed agencies struggling with the new system, the Bureau of the Budget offered only general guidance and instructions. Despite its title, PPBS was not a single system for the government as a whole. Each agency had to develop its own version of PPBS in the light of its own policies, programs, objectives, administrative capacity, and bureaucratic environment. Relatively few agency heads appreciated the value of a PPBS approach as a means of planning, budgeting, and monitoring their own programs. Of sixteen agencies reviewed by GAO and BOB in 1969, only three departments had made substantial progress in implementing PPBS. To most agencies PPBS was a budget office "show," which they went through the motions of accepting because of presidential pressures.[62]

Belying all claims of an integrated system, the Bureau of the Budget and the operating agencies superimposed PPBS on long-standing budgetary procedures. In addition to preparing their conventional budget requests and justifications, agencies now had to present requests in the PPBS format. Even more disheartening, the budget examination staffs in the Bureau of the Budget and in most agencies had little to do with PPBS. As in the past, they reviewed the cost and performance of operating programs as a basis for budgetary recommendations. Newly recruited staffs, with economists and planners predominant, dealt with budget requests PPBS-style. They had little voice in budgetary decisions. Professional jealousies and competition between the two staffs shed more heat than light on the budget process.[63]

Under the PPBS banner, proponents resumed the battle of program structures that had been won in the 1950s, when justification of budget requests by program had become common. This time, however, the program structure focused on the missions, objectives, purposes, and outputs of programs. Structuring programs along these lines resulted in unceasing debate reminiscent of the medieval concerns about the number of angels that could dance on the head of a pin. Most major governmental programs have multiple objectives and outputs. In a family-planning program, the objectives can be limitation in family size, reduction in poverty, and decrease in infant mortality. A highway transportation program has such objectives as decreases in accidents and deaths, economical movement of people and goods, quick access by law enforcement agencies, and road networks compatible with environmental and aesthetic values. All of these objectives are valid. But how does one develop a program and subprogram around each objective and allocate costs to it? How does one define meaningful outputs and objectives? How does one quantify them? To what extent are they quantifiable?

The stress on program structure by purpose led to extreme views on both sides of the issue. On the one hand, Carlson claimed that the program structure is the "unifying concept" and "the explicit framework for decision making." At the opposite pole, Wildavsky charged that "fixation on program structure is the most pernicious aspect of PPBS" and that it is a "sham that piles up meaningless data under vague categories."[64]

Because of the sudden imposition of PPBS, agencies in many cases lacked the data required by the system: performance indicators and program costs in PPBS format. Without adequate supporting management control and accounting systems, several agencies floundered. Some cost allocations were arbitrary. It was difficult to pin down the efficiency and effectiveness of programs. Multiyear program and financial plans often became just wish lists.

The heart of PPBS was policy and program analysis. At times the heart beat faintly. Good data and analysts were in short supply, although rapid recruitment made up for the latter deficiency. Agencies made only spotty progress in identifying and quantifying problems, partly because of the scarcity of relevant data and partly because of the limitations of quantification. Some critics feared that the stress on mathematical and economic tools "leads to underestimation of those aspects of problems which are not quantifiable and to resulting distortions of conclusions."[65] In short, "if you can't count it, it doesn't count." With a few shining exceptions, many of the early PPBS studies were disappointing and superficial. Nevertheless, several agencies turned out impressive and influential studies, among them Health, Education, and Welfare; Housing and Urban Development; Transportation; and the Office of Economic Opportunity.[66] Very early in the game, the Bureau of the Budget gave up the pretense of analyzing all programs de novo. This resulted in a more thoughtful consideration of fewer issues.

PPBS was not useful in dealing with the largest segments of governmental expenditures: entitlement programs, transfer payments to state and local governments, tax expenditures, and off-budget expenditures. Nearly all of these were uncontrollable programs that had been frozen in legislation.

Congress greeted PPBS with something less than enthusiasm. By itself this was not new. Congress had opposed every major budgetary reform for more than fifty years prior to PPBS. Regardless of the PPBS format, Congress insisted on the traditional budgetary presentation and on preserving the existing appropriation structure. Committee review continued to focus on organizational units and objects of expense with a dash of program analysis.[67]

The Political Critique of PPBS. The acid test of PPBS, or, for that matter, any other budgetary reform is its effect on decision making. Absent any discernible improvements in resource allocations, it seems nothing short of folly to incur the heavy administrative and political costs of implementing so complex a system as PPBS. Wildavsky and others argue that PPBS was doomed from the start, and that its proponents were incredibly naive in expecting any positive results. Far from being a neutral instrument for "better budgeting," it was riddled with political values that ran counter to the customary modes of bargaining, negotiation, compromise, and conflict resolution. By changing the basis for allocating funds, PPBS intensified tensions among competing groups. By allegedly looking at all programs from scratch instead of at manageable incremental slices, it resumed the political battles of yesteryear. In theory, everything was up for grabs. By laying out explicit objectives, outputs, and alternatives instead of bland generalities on which everyone could agree, it escalated conflict instead of containing it. The multiyear program and financial plans added an impossible "burden of calculation" to an already choked budgetary process. Budgeting was not comprehensive à la PPBS, but sequential, repetitive, and fragmentary. So counterproductive was PPBS that it impeded budgetary decision making instead of expediting it. Consequently, it had little effect on decisions.[68]

Wildavsky wrote an epitaph for PPBS: "I have not been able to find a single example of successful implementation of PPB . . . PPB deserved to die because it was an irrational mode of analysis that leads to suppression rather than correction of error." He regarded the few examples of successful PPBS studies as rare exceptions, arguing, "no one knows how to do program budgeting." To ask agencies to engage in program budgeting is to ask them to come up with better policies. What passed for program budgeting PPBS-style was a "vast amount of inchoate information characterized by premature quantification of irrelevant items." Wildavsky was all for policy analysis and the search for alternative programs that work, but only if detached from the trappings of PPBS.[69]

Unlike Wildavsky, who wanted to rescue policy analysis from PPBS, Schick preferred to extricate PPBS from the stifling embrace of the budget process. He regards the budget process as fundamentally "anti-analytic" because of its preoccupation with day-to-day budgetary routines. PPBS failed as a "change agent because it did not succeed in penetrating these vital budgetary routines." For analysis to succeed it should be dislodged from budgeting.[70]

A More Balanced View of PPBS in the Federal Government. The Wildavsky and Schick positions caricature what happened to PPBS. They direct their barbs mainly at a paradigm of PPBS that existed only in the minds of some of its naive advocates, who did not fully understand governmental decision making, let alone budgeting. These early proponents oversold and misrepresented an elaborate structure resting on an "oversimplified view of the world, of the society, and of government." They promised a technocratic utopia of rationality and efficiency in budgetary allocations. They overstressed the need for clear, specific, and quantified objectives of governmental programs. They appreciated neither the complexity of the process nor the political fallout from being overly specific about some objectives. Nor did it occur to them that it was possible to develop useful options without getting bogged down in a complex program structure.[71] In many of their analyses they failed to consider the lack of theoretical links between the inputs and the direct outputs and consequences of governmental programs. They minimized and overlooked the many problems of implementation. Having developed alternatives and recommendations, they looked for instant feedback and decisions from political decision makers who preferred to keep their options open until the very last moment for political "horse-trading." The early zealots of PPBS were indeed easy targets for phrasemakers.

Much of the criticism of PPBS came in the early years, when some budget watchers looked for instant results. Not finding them, they pronounced the system dead. Even then they were wide of the mark. In acting on the 1970–1971 budget, President Johnson benefited from presentations in PPBS form by the Bureau of the Budget, which in many difficult areas laid out possible alternatives and their immediate and long-range impact. Mosher, a more balanced observer, noted that "there can be no question that PPBS has influenced a great many budgetary decisions: within the agencies; in the Office of Management and Budget; in the determinations of the President; and in some of the committees of Congress." Mosher cites numerous examples of studies that influenced the decision-making process.[72] Similar testimony came from other close observers.

Taking Stock of PPBS in State and Local Governments

State and local governments ran into similar problems and issues in implementing PPBS. Analysts who followed these developments brought back good and bad news. The good news was the increased use of analysis in budgeting, the development of alternatives, the tentative use of performance indicators, and the explicit formulation of policy guidelines in some states. The bad news was the crude quality of multiyear projections, the chasm between planning and budgeting, the reliance on traditional budgetary routines for most decisions, the difficulty of developing measures of the impact of programs, the indifference of legislative bodies, a tedious preoccupation with program structures, shaky support by top management, and the difficulty of dealing with special funds and intergovernmental grants.[73]

The Legacy of PPBS: "PPBS Is Dead! Long Live PPB!"

The legacy left by PPBS is a rich one. Contrary to the dire predictions based on premature judgments, anecdotage, and scanty evidence, PPBS is alive and well in the 1990s and thriving under various guises. In the federal government, a once reluctant Congress took it to its bosom with the passage of the Congressional Budget and Impoundment Control Act of 1974 (PL 93-344). The embrace was total: multiyear projections; budget classifications by mission, function, and program; the use of sophisticated analytical techniques; searching analyses by the Congressional Budget Office and the General Accounting Office; the development of performance indicators; and the improvement of accounting and information systems.

With admirable prescience, Dwight Waldo had predicted these developments more than a decade earlier: "It [PPBS] leaves even where it is formally disestablished, a residue of techniques and altered perspectives; its impact will come to have been permanent."[74]

The impact of PPBS is now pervasive throughout the federal bureaucracy and Congress. The PPBS approach has strengthened and institutionalized program analysis, multiyear planning, rolling multiyear budgets, and the search for alternatives to existing programs and policies. It has resulted in a better quality of budget analysis, a greater number of in-depth studies, more extensive use of performance indicators, and a sharper focus on the objectives and outcomes of governmental programs.[75]

The same trends are apparent in state government. Virtually all states used aspects of PPBS in budgeting in the late 1980s and early 1990s, with an emphasis on program structures, highly selective program analysis, outputs, the development of alternative programs, multiyear perspectives, the formulation of performance indicators, and the strengthening of supporting accounting and other information systems.[76] Several states still follow variations of the comprehensive PPBS model, among them Pennsylvania, Texas, Hawaii, Michigan, and North Carolina.

Hailed as a "new budgeting process in 1992" by the executive and legislative budget offices, the Texas Strategic Planning System, covering a six-year period, combines missions, program analysis, agency goals and objectives, the resources necessary to achieve approved objectives, and the monitoring of performance. Figure 11.1 portrays the attempted integration of plans and budgets.

Since the 1960s Pennsylvania has linked its budgets with a multiyear Commonwealth Program Plan. For FY 1993–1994 it focused on six major programs: protection of persons and property, intellectual development and education, health and human services, economic development, transportation and communications, and recreation and cultural enrichment. Each of these major programs or purposes was divided into program categories and program subcategories with performance and costs laid out for a five-year period. Reminiscent of the program memorandum (PM) of the federal PPBS, the budget highlighted program revisions necessitating changes in funding levels.[77]

PPBS came to the federal government in a period of affluence, when the emphasis in analysis was on justifying expenditures for new and expanded programs. Those states that practice variants of PPBS in the economic and budgetary crunch of the 1990s are concerned with the effects of reductions and cutbacks in programs and on the fiscal burdens of local governments. They focus on program performance and productivity. Once shut out of PPBS, state legislatures now take an active role, as in Hawaii, Texas, and New York, in implementing elements of the system. Program analysts are entrenched as never before in the legislative bureaucracy.

MBO (Management by Objectives) Comes to Budgeting

After the Nixon administration dismantled PPB as a formal system in June 1971, it nevertheless continued to stress multiyear program planning, analysis, and evaluation.[78] About two years later, in April 1973, it left its own unique imprint on the budget process: the use of MBO techniques.

The MBO–budget connection was intended to be a rough-and-ready, pragmatic approach to problems of resource allocation. Unlike PPBS, it was not a

FIGURE 11.1 TEXAS STRATEGIC PLANNING TEMPLATE

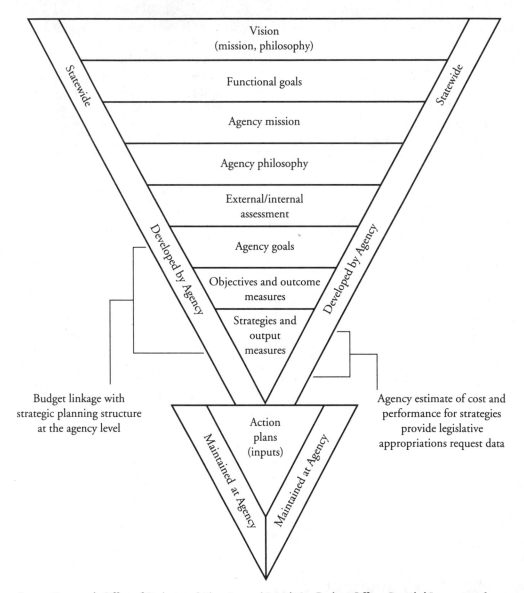

Source: Governor's Office of Budget and Planning and Legislative Budget Office, *Detailed Instructions for Preparing and Submitting Requests for Legislative Appropriations for the Biennism Beginning Sept. 1, 1993* (Austin, Tex., 1992), p. 2.

system. The focus was on selective targets and the costs of meeting them, with controls instituted along the way to measure performance. Because MBO had been in varying degree part of the management process in most agencies, no new and formidable procedures à la PPBS were needed. It was an "uncomplicated result-oriented approach" that, seemingly with little effort, could be tied to the regular budget process. MBO called more for a change in orientation than a change in systems.[79]

MBO lingered on for about two years, during the last months of the Nixon administration and the early months of the Ford administration. It had some minimal impact on budgetary decisions for fiscal years 1974–1975 and 1975–1976. Then it "evaporated to become part of the climate of management albeit a part whose specific influence is limited and incapable of precise measurement."[80]

The linkage between MBO and budgeting had some ripple effect among state and local governments, which already tended to use MBO techniques as part of the management system. Relatively few governments formally integrated MBO with budgeting, but with the current emphasis on budgeting for results and performance evaluation, MBO, under new names and acronyms, is wedded to the budget process more than ever.

Budgeting for Productivity Improvement

Since 1962, the federal government has incorporated productivity measurement in the budget process, following an earlier emphasis on work measurement. Productivity measurement has been a major preoccupation of the Joint Financial Management Improvement Program, which over the years has hammered away on the usefulness of productivity data in setting meaningful management goals, justifying funds for staffing and capital equipment, analyzing manpower utilization, spotting opportunities for management improvement and economies, strengthening accountability, and projecting future resource requirements on the basis of estimated outputs. From the beginning, however, it also cautioned the central staff agencies in the federal government, especially OMB, that the process should include incentives for superior performance, and that productivity measurement should not become just another means of cutting budgets.[81] At this point, the productivity measurement umbrella covers the majority of federal employees and is still a useful budgetary tool in analyzing staffing needs and utilization.

In recent years most state governments and many large cities have stressed the use of productivity data in budgeting.[82] With labor costs accounting for about 80 percent of operating budgets, this is a long overdue development.

The Myth and Reality of Zero-Based Budgeting (ZBB)

On February 14, 1977, the Carter administration unveiled ZBB with the ballyhoo and hyperbole reminiscent of PPBS in the Johnson days. No longer would budgeting focus solely on new and expanded programs. All budget requests for both ongoing and new programs would be reviewed from scratch. They would compete on an equal footing. Unnecessary and obsolete activities would be terminated and funds redeployed to essential programs. For each activity alternative funding levels would be developed to control expenditures but still get the job done. The president cited his success in Georgia, where he

> devised a procedure whereby the future budgets would start from scratch—at zero. It meant chopping the state government up into individual functions, and analyzing each service delivery system annually regardless of whether it was fifty years old or a brand new proposal for a future program.[83]

The Carter Blueprint for ZBB

Shortly after the new administration assumed office, OMB issued detailed instructions for the implementation of ZBB that almost rivaled PPBS in the complexity of paperwork imposed on the agencies.[84] One major difference, however, was that ZBB was from the start an integral part of the budget process, and not a parallel system. In fact, it was to be "the sole basis for the preparation of budget requests." The basic building block of ZBB was the decision unit. This could be a program, an organizational entity, an activity, or a cost center. It was to be low enough in the hierarchy to identify meaningful and discrete programs and activities, but not too low. Otherwise excessive paperwork and review might result. Conversely, it could not be too high in the bureaucracy, or broad decision units would impede rather than facilitate analysis.

For each decision unit, managers had to prepare decision packages based on four different funding levels (with variations permitted):

1. *Minimum level,* below which the program and activity would not be viable
2. *Current, or maintenance, level,* carrying forward existing services without any major policy changes
3. *Intermediate level,* somewhere between the minimum and current levels
4. *Enhancement, or improvement, level,* which called for additional funding for increased outputs and services.

OMB directed the operating agencies to include in the decision packages the following: objectives, which should be explicit statements of intended output, preferably but not necessarily quantified; performance measures to gauge the efficiency, effectiveness, and workload of the decision unit; the actual measurement of accomplishments; resource requirements for the budget year and four subsequent years; and other program information. In effect, four budgets would be prepared, one for each funding level.

At this point a top-down and bottom-up decision-making process would begin. Top management would provide policy guidelines in setting objectives for lower-level managers. The latter would consider alternative methods of accomplishing their objectives and the effect of different funding levels on their performance. On this basis they would rank the decision packages in priority order. As the ranked decision packages moved up the hierarchy, they would be reviewed at higher levels and deleted, revised, or supplemented. To facilitate analysis by top management, the individual decision packages would be consolidated and recast "in a broader frame of reference to focus on significant program alternatives or issues." These, too, would be ranked and would form the basis for budget requests.

This was essentially the Carter blueprint for ZBB, beginning with the 1978–1979 fiscal year. OMB attached to its instructions several exhibits that illustrate the process. Among them is Table 11.4, which exemplifies a decision package for personal income tax services based on the minimum level of funding. It is one of four decision packages for the program, the others reflecting minimum, intermediate, and enhanced funding levels.

The Critics Deal Unkindly with ZBB

Predictably, after three years of experience with the new budget system, the president and OMB were pleased with their handiwork. They pointed to savings that had been achieved by comparing programs, developing priorities, and forcing trade-offs between activities. OMB, in particular, found the priority ranking of decision units helpful and claimed ZBB facilitated an across-the-board analysis of similar or related programs in different agencies.[85]

Budgeteers, program managers, and budget watchers, however, gave ZBB mixed reviews, most of them negative. If there was any consensus, it was that zero-based review of programs was not feasible on a broad scale and on a regular basis and that, in any event, it did not even take place. Budget analysis focused on incremental inputs and outputs at marginally different levels of expenditure. ZBB had little effect on developing alternatives to existing activities. The current service level for each activity, or the so-called core, was the starting point of analysis. Using that as a base, operating agencies often developed decision packages by allocating arbitrary percentages of the base. For example, the Department of Agriculture used four "bands," each representing a different percentage of the core: minimum, reduced, current, and increased. The General Accounting Office found little evidence of adequate analysis as a basis for developing the decision packages. The use of percentage allocations was an easy way out.[86]

The ranking of packages in priority order turned out to be a frustrating exercise with little impact on decisions. Each agency attempted to develop appropriate criteria to rank its array of decision packages. But performance data were often inadequate. Goals and objectives were at times ambiguous or multiple in nature, making it difficult to link specific packages to the attainment of objectives. Directors of agencies found it difficult to rank and understand consolidated decision packages. Since entitlement programs are in the main uncontrollable, few agencies attempted to rank them or to develop decision packages with alternative levels of performance.[87]

The workload was onerous. One agency experienced a 300 percent increase in budget documentation, with 90,000 pieces of paper prepared for 478 decision

TABLE 11.4

Minimum level decision package, Department of Revenue, Tax Bureau, Tax Service

Activity: Department staff will conduct 2,700 training sessions for the VTA (Volunteer Tax Assistance) program and 1,125 sessions in 40 major cities for the PI (Practitioner Institutes) program. The MUT (Materials for Understanding Taxes) program will be eliminated.

Resource requirements	19PY	19CY	19BY	Planning estimates			
				19BY+1	19BY+2	19BY+3	19BY+4
Funds ($000)							
Budget authority	1,017	1,571	1,227	1,246	1,272	1,291	1,322
outlays	1,006	1,569	1,221	1,242	1,268	1,287	1,318
Positions (end of year)							
Full-time permanent	35	49	38				
Total	56	81	59				
VTA program	(25)	(53)	(48)				
PI program	(25)	(22)	(11)				
MUT program	(6)	(6)	(0)				

Short-term objectives:

VTA Program. To train 27,000 volunteers, so that 57,000 volunteers will be available to provide services by the end of the budget year.

PI Program. To provide training services to 45,000 practitioners annually.

MUT Program. To eliminate this program.

(continued)

TABLE 11.4 (*continued*)

Workload measures (000)	193Y-1	19BY	19CY	19BY
VTA training sessions conducted	1.3	1.3	3.0	2.7
VTA volunteers trained	20	20	30	27
Practitioner institutes conducted	2.5	2.5	2.25	1.125
Practitioner participants trained	75	75	90	45
MUT: Student publication orders	4,680	4,680	4,680	0

Impact on major objectives: The program will be operating at the lowest levels at which the decision unit can make meaningful contributions toward fulfilling its objectives.

VTA Program. By the end of four years (19BY + 3) the program will have trained at total of 215,000 volunteers, of which 105,000 are expected to be available to provide services. The volunteers should be able to serve 35% of the target population by this date. The objective of serving 40% of the target population will not be met until the end of the six years (19BY + 5).

PI Program. Tax practitioners will be able to receive updated training in tax legislation only once every ten years on the average.

MUT Program. Individual states and school systems must rely on their own resources to deal with basic tax instruction. As a result, most senior level secondary school students will not receive basic instruction on tax law and how to complete the tax forms.

Basis for minimum level: The VTA program must be maintained near the existing levels in the short run in order to meet legislatively mandated performance levels. After the major objective has been reached (40% of target population), it may be possible to reduce the level of activity and still maintain coverage at 40%.

The Practitioner Institutes (PI) program should not be eliminated altogether because it would have a negative impact in five to ten years on their understanding of tax laws. However, the number of PI programs may be reduced in half and still insure that tax practitioners in the greatest need will receive instruction. Other forms of instruction are available through university courses and Department of Revenue publications.

The MUT program for secondary school students may be eliminated since their tax responsibilities will not be substantial in the short run and the students will have other opportunities to learn about tax requirements in future years.

Source: Executive Office of the President, Office of Management and Budget, Circular A-115, "Zero-Base Budgeting" (Washington, D.C., May 5, 1978).

packages representing 75 decision units. Prior to the advent of ZBB, about 22,500 pages had proved to be sufficient. Health, Education, and Welfare developed 1,200 decision packages covering 350 decision units. And these represented consolidated packages for a summit review. By themselves, these figures, though impressive, are not conclusive. What counts is the impact on the budget process. On this score, ZBB fell far short of expectations. It resulted in little visible evidence of reallocation of funds or reordering of priorities. It increased processing costs with few commensurate budgetary benefits. In general, agencies in most cases continued to get increments at or above the current service level. In its wake ZBB left a confused, threatened, and frustrated group of administrators and agency budget officials. GAO reported that "ZBB's first two years have created little change in the Federal budget process, generated only limited optimism for the system and shown little success in the agencies we studied."[88]

ZBB fared no better in subsequent years. GAO therefore proposed a more flexible approach: a streamlining of the process and a sharp reduction of the paperwork. Instead of annual reviews of all decision packages, it suggested a selective analysis on a scheduled basis of a limited number of programs. Other proposals included fewer decision packages and limits on ranking; a close link between ZBB and planning and evaluation processes; stepped-up analytical capacity; reconciliation of decision packages with the program and activity structure used in the budget to avoid "crosswalks"; and less rigidity in OMB's instructions, so that each agency could develop a custom-tailored ZBB process.[89]

Beginning in 1981, the Reagan administration took this approach, with some modifications, as it saw in the "decremental" features of ZBB a handy tool for cost reduction. For political reasons it abandoned the ZBB label associated with President Carter. It retained decision units, coinciding with the agency program and organizational structure, as the basis for budget requests. For each decision unit, agencies were required to develop three funding options (including decrements) and to rank them by priority. More importantly, they were expected to come up with enough decrements to cut their budget ceiling by a percentage prescribed by OMB.[90] With minor modifications, this is still the stance of the federal government. In preparing their budget requests, the departments, on a selective basis, are expected to specify three levels of budget authority and outlays ("reduced," "current policy," and "agency request") and to rank programs in order of priority.[91]

State Governments' Use of ZBB: A Tool of Cutback Management

Many, but not all, state governments adopted ZBB with alacrity as they saw in it a means of coping with the fiscal crises of the late 1970s and early 1980s. By 1979 variations of ZBB had rooted themselves in some twenty-four states. As in the federal government, ZBB, stripped of its pretensions, came down to incremental and decremental budgeting with favored choices, centering on 90, 100, 105, and 110 percent of the base budget. Each alternative budget was ranked more or less subjectively. Budget analysis focused on the outputs and results of each level of expenditures.[92]

Above all, ZBB was a tool for cost cutting. To stay within their resources and obviate, if possible, the need for tax increases, most states imposed expenditure ceilings on the agencies. Sometimes called "target budgeting" (as in Michigan, Utah, and Washington), the ceilings represented a fixed percentage of current levels of expenditures. In more than half the states formally committed to ZBB, the target, or the minimum level, ranged upward of 90 percent of the base budget. In general, states allowed agencies to request funds above the arbitrary ceiling. This served as a safety valve for highly pressured agencies, and also as a means of spotting worthwhile programs that might otherwise be pushed aside by the budget crunch. A common practice was to rank in priority order requests for funding above the target.[93]

ZBB fitted in cozily with existing budgetary systems, and challenged none of them. Whether states practiced program or traditional budgeting, it had a place. Unlike other budgetary reforms to which state legislatures were indifferent if not hostile, ZBB, in whole or part, was either initiated or actively supported by the legislatures in several states.[94]

Hatry and Schick concluded that few significant changes in budgetary outcomes resulted from ZBB. While the emphasis on alternative budgets provided more data to central budget offices to evaluate the cost and performance of activities, only minor shifts in resources occurred between agencies. Most reallocations of funds took place within individual agencies. As in the federal government, ZBB had a negligible impact on mandatory, or uncontrollable, expenditures. Priority rankings were based largely on subjective judgments, and not on program evaluation or any serious attempt to relate the level of services to costs. In cutting expenditures, budget offices concentrated more on objects of expense than on program alternatives. The data supporting the decision packages of ZBB were sparse and fragmentary. Contrary to the pure model of ZBB, little reordering of priorities or competition for resources occurred on a government-wide basis.[95]

Among the state governments, Georgia had been a leader in implementing ZBB. The claimed advantages of ZBB in Georgia during Jimmy Carter's term as governor turned out to be grossly exaggerated. Such reallocation of resources as occurred took place because of a governmental reorganization, and not because of more than 10,000 decision packages of questionable quality that few had time to review. Minmier, who had followed developments in Georgia closely, put it bluntly:

> There has not been a single verifiable instance where the new budgetary system has caused a shifting of financial resources other than during reorganization. In view of the increased effort required in preparing a zero-base budget, it is understandable why many budget analysts feel they are conducting an exercise in futility.[96]

ZBB in Other Countries: Few Attempt Alternative Budgeting

Save for the Philippines, Canada, and Greece, alternative budgeting has not influenced budgetary systems in other countries. The government in Canada, within the framework of envelope budgeting, developed three alternative budgets—A, B, and X—beginning in 1977. The "A" budget represents the cost of maintaining programs at their present levels and completing capital projects under contract. The "B" budget constitutes the enhancement level, and comes into play if additional funds are available. It covers the cost of expanding existing programs, adding new ones, and starting capital projects. "X" is the recession budget. It shows the amount that would be spent if the current level of expenditures were reduced by approximately 10 percent by deleting marginal projects and activities and cutting back various departmental programs.

If funds permit, the government leans to the "B" budget. Otherwise it looks to the "X" budget for possible cuts. Even the "A" budget is not immutable if studies suggest the desirability of reducing or shifting resources within it. Proposed new projects and programs undergo a zero-based review in the PPBS style. In general, the budget combines components of the three funding levels.

After modest beginnings, the Canadian system of alternative budgeting ran into some familiar problems: a mass of paperwork at lower levels and difficulties in consolidating decision packages for review by senior management; the need to reconcile decision-making units with the traditional budget format; difficulties in spelling out alternative levels of service; the complexity of the ranking process; and less than adequate program analysis.[97]

The Tenuous Roots of ZBB in American Cities

Toward the end of the 1970s, budget directors of only thirty-five American cities with a population of over 50,000 reported they were using or had used the ZBB approach. Others indicated that ZBB had not as yet taken root in their jurisdictions, but most of them supported alternative budgeting. Especially appealing to pro-ZBB budget officers, mayors, and local legislative bodies was the use of minimum levels in budgeting and the opportunity this approach gave them to cut and/or reallocate resources.[98]

ZBB: Alternative Budgeting

In the end, ZBB amounts to alternative budgeting, and not to a zero-based review of programs. As alternative budgeting, ZBB (despite the unfortunate label) has merit and, in fact, is not new. It is the very essence of budgeting. Every administration at every level of government systematically or informally assesses the effect of varying budget scenarios before arriving at a decision. It analyzes alternative ways of conducting and funding activities and attempts to sort them out in rough order of priority. For example, during the Eisenhower administration in the 1950s, agencies supplemented their budget requests by showing the effect of funding levels 5 to 10 percent higher or lower than estimates.[99]

Long before ZBB became a slogan in the Carter administration, Verne Lewis laid out the theoretical framework for alternative budgeting in a memorable article in 1952. Citing the lack of an allocation theory due to "no absolute standards of value," Lewis argued that "budget analysis is basically a comparison of the relative uses of funds." To facilitate the analysis, he suggested that agencies submit alternative budgets representing 80, 90, 100, and 120 percent of the base budget. It would then be possible to determine the marginal benefits of the varying allocations. In this way alternative budgeting becomes a tool for decrements or increments, depending on fiscal policy.[100]

Analyses of this type, devoid of ZBB rhetoric, are in general use in nearly all governments in the United States. Several examples highlight this trend. Oregon focuses on spending alternatives. It begins with a base budget that represents 80 percent of the current service level. Termed the "reduced-level budget," it is an austerity budget. Even with changes, the total request for programs financed by the general fund cannot exceed 90 percent of the current service level. For major policy decisions that result in adding or reducing funds, decision packages become vehicles for budgeting.

In Ohio the starting point for budget decision making is the "core budget level" (CBL) for state programs. This is not a minimum or maximum level of funding, but rather the base level, reflecting a continuation of current policy. What is different is that the Office of Budget and Management determines the CBL, based on a review of revenue estimates. Any requests for funding above the CBL must be supported by supplemental justifications. Similarly, Colorado focuses on a base representing current appropriations. To adjust this base, agencies separately request "continuation budget increases or decreases." To effect major program changes the agencies prepare "decision item adjustments," which may result in expanding, refinancing, reducing, or eliminating base funding.[101]

Target Budgeting

In developing alternative budgets, agencies begin with a ceiling, or target, established by the president, governor, or mayor. This is "top-down budgeting," which avoids a frustrating exercise whereby agencies "prepare detailed estimates that add up to an unacceptable total" or propose "policies which the executive will not approve."[102]

While target budgeting is obviously not new, it has become a fashionable phrase. For nearly fifty years, OMB, in behalf of the president, has set tentative budget targets for federal agencies, based on a preliminary review of budget needs and on overall budget totals acceptable to the president. Agencies that wish to exceed the target are requested to prepare alternative budgets. Currently, targets are in effect for all discretionary spending.

As Lewis points out, this flexible system has several advantages over ZBB:

> Like ZBB, targets are established by the chief executive prior to preparation of detailed proposals. Unlike ZBB, however, the targets are not fixed percentages of the prior year budget or other arbitrary amounts. Instead, targets can be tailor-made for each situation after review of agency skeleton estimates and program

issues. Targets can be set at, below or above the current level as appropriate. The target setters can take into account changes in price levels, work loads, legislation, executive policy and other factors that impact the budgetary scene. The aim in setting the targets is to reflect the best judgment at the time of the chief executive and his budget staff.[103]

Dollar ceilings, or targets, prevail in most state governments, especially in an era of austerity. In 1990 nearly half of the states specified dollar ceilings; 60 percent, policy ceilings to expand or retard specific programs; and 61 percent, ceilings based on the current level of services.[104] The same trend was apparent in large cities in the early 1990s.[105]

Budgeting As an Instrument for Economic Management

In the aftermath of the Great Depression and World War II, national budgeting has become a major instrument for managing the economy through a combination of fiscal and monetary policies. Chapter 7 covers these issues in detail. But no discussion of major budgetary reforms would be complete without emphasizing as a major reform the role of the budget process as a tool of economic management.

Legislative Budget Systems: Also a Major Reform

To give a full accounting of budget reforms, we should also stress that the strengthened legislative budget system (discussed in Chapter 8), despite some failings, ranks among the major budgetary reforms, especially in the United States.

Getting a Grip on Off-Budget Budgets

Now that off-budget budgets have become a formidable part of total public expenditures, all levels of government are attempting to subject them to greater control and accountability. This is true of government corporations, special districts, public authorities, and government-sponsored enterprises (GSEs). Successful attempts to rein in these autonomous bodies may represent one of the major budget reforms of our day. Chapter 6 deals with this issue.

Budgeting Loans and Loan Guarantees

Since the 1930s, especially at the federal level, loans and loan guarantees have become a major means of achieving public objectives. As significant as outright expenditures, they eluded budget controls until the early 1980s. Finally, in 1990, the Federal Credit Reform Act placed the cost of credit programs on a budgetary basis equivalent to other federal spending. Representing many billions of dollars, the credit budget is now an integral part of the federal budget (see Chapter 6).

Ballot-Box Budgeting

No discussion of budget reforms, the good and the bad, would be complete without reference to populist attempts to reform the budget via the ballot box. A spokesman for still more tax and spending limits in California put it this way in 1992: "The people believe it is time to take our destiny in our own hands. In order to restore accountability to our government, we find it necessary to reform the budget process."[106]

It is this fervor that resulted in the many tax and spending limits now embedded in constitutions and statutes, a plethora of earmarked funds, and controls over borrowing. Still more are in the works and may be implemented before the year 2000. At the federal level, the same populist movement has embraced the balanced budget and item veto power for the president.

If most of the reforms discussed in this chapter represent "rational" budgeting, then populist budgeting smacks more of a search for simple formulas designed to cope with fiscal complexity. Therein lies its appeal and its dangers.

The Impact of Budget Reforms: Some Conclusions

Do these fifteen budgetary reforms make a difference? This depends on the yardsticks used to measure the impact of the reforms. Among the measures prized by the reformers are expenditure control, allocative efficiency (targeting funds for justifiable programs and projects), improvements in the efficiency and effectiveness of programs and projects, strengthened accountability, and, above all, the impact of reforms on budget decisions. For Schick, the last point is the overriding test. "Did the innovation alter the basis for making budget decisions? Only if the answer is 'yes' can an innovation be considered successful."[107]

Some Critics Blast Budget Reforms

On the basis of this criterion, several influential commentators on the budget scene score the reforms as failures because they find little evidence of their utility in decision making. Some find the reforms flawed at the core because they run counter to political and administrative decision-making styles. The leading proponents of this view were Wildavsky in the United States and Tarschys in Sweden, who claimed that incrementalism rather than comprehensive and rational budgeting is the dominant form of budgeting in nearly all political systems. The focus is on marginal changes in last year's budget with regard to both revenue and expenditures—in short, on increments and, in recent years, on decrements. This results not from political perversity, but from necessity.[108]

Wildavsky's eloquent explanation and defense of incrementalism has become almost conventional wisdom, at least to students and academicians, if not practitioners. His argument generally runs along these lines: The starting point in budgeting is the base budget, which brings forward all the accumulated political decisions of the past, including mandatory and uncontrollable expenditures. To review this budget from scratch annually is to invite large-scale political warfare. It is therefore essential to contain conflict and to reach a consensus by concentrating on relatively few manageable and politically feasible issues, namely the increments. This may be an untidy and fragmentary approach, but it works. It facilitates political calculations by limiting the number of choices. It brings to the surface, sequentially and repetitively, familiar and controllable issues. It enables participants in budget bargaining to determine whether they are getting their fair share of the gain or the pain. With the rules of the game understood by all players, incrementalism promotes stability in the budget process. In contrast, comprehensive and zero-based budgeting would result in confusion and disarray as an unmanageable number of centers of political influence and interest groups vied for public funds.[109]

Hence Wildavsky challenges would-be reformers who fail to understand "the political implications of budgetary reform":

> The tradition of reform in America is a noble one not easily to be denied. But in this case it is doomed to failure because it is aimed at the wrong target. If the present budgetary process is rightly or wrongly deemed unsatisfactory then one must alter in some respects the political system of which the budget is but an expression.[110]

This led Wildavsky to a defense of the traditional line-item budget, which has survived because it is a mechanism for incremental choices. In his view no better tools exist to control expenditures and enforce accountability than line items and increments and decrements. Despite the add-ons in the budget process, such as economic management, program planning and evaluation, and management planning, control remains the dominant feature.[111]

Going farther, Schick despairs of budgeting altogether, traditional or reformed. No longer can the budget process perform its most basic functions, especially control of expenditures. In fact, "the budget is out of control" at the federal level and no amount of innovation can set it right. Control is the very "bedrock of budgeting." Everything else is secondary. As evidence of lack of control, Schick cites uncontrollable expenditures, mounting deficits, budgetary decisions made outside of the budget process, expenditures that exceed estimates, unstable budgets that shift with the vagaries of the economy, and the resort to off-budget practices. He says this crisis

> has brought budgetary innovation to a virtual halt. For the first time in more than a century, no single concept or approach commands widespread support or convincingly promises better results. From the emergence of modern budgeting in nineteenth century Europe until the recent zero-based budgeting debacle in the United States, there was an abiding confidence that the methods by which public funds were spent could be made more rational. Nowadays, however, budgetmakers and scholars alike appear to be paralyzed by the intractability of problems facing government.[112]

Hence, in 1986, Schick pronounced his epitaph on budgetary reform:

The age of budgetary reform has passed. From executive budgeting early in this century through planning, programming and budgeting (PPB) in the 1960s and zero based budgeting (ZBB) in the 1970s, the practice and literature of budgeting were repeatedly stirred by efforts to improve the process. Now, however, the cupboard of budgeting innovation appears to be bare; little on the horizon is comparable in scope and ambition to the major reforms that dominated budgeting in previous decades.[113]

Focusing directly on the federal government, in 1990 Schick warned that "the capacity to govern depends on the capacity to budget." That capacity had withered. Then, in a biting indictment he detailed the failings of the "deceitful" and "gimmicky" budget process.[114]

The Practitioners Ignore the Critics of Budget Reform

We now have something of a paradox. Despite the epitaphs on reform, federal, state, and local governments in the United States, at an accelerated rate and in varying degree, have synthesized virtually all the elements of budget reform in their management systems. The same trend is apparent in other countries. Both the practitioners and the Wildavsky–Schick–Tarschys school can't be right. Who is?

Upon close examination, much of the critique of budget reforms does not hold up. It either caricatures the reforms, as was done in the case of ZBB and PPBS; pronounces the reforms unworkable absent instant success; or looks for a cause-and-effect relationship between the reforms and budget decisions, ignoring the complexity of factors that shape the decisions. Fundamentally, the critique rests on two crumbling pillars: the theory of incrementalism and the irrelevance of budgetary reform in decision making (the politics vs. rationality issue).

Incrementalism As an Explanation of Budget Decisions

Plausible as the theory of incrementalism is, it has come under increasing attack as but a partial and imperfect explanation of the budget process. What are increments (or decrements): a combination of increases and decreases, some new programs or projects, selected cutbacks, several policy shifts? If the theory holds that decision makers merely prefer to deal with a limited number of increments at any one time, rather than a flash flood of new initiatives, it seems to add a note of common sense to our understanding of the dynamics of budgeting. But even this is a shaky generalization when one considers the spate of budgetary changes during the New Deal period, the Great Society era, and the early years of the Reagan administration; the ambitious agenda of the Clinton administration in 1993 and the Mitterand administration in France; at the state level, during the Rockefeller years in New York; and severe budget cuts in all states in the 1980s and 1990s. To call these changes mere increments is to overlook the nature of drastic policy shifts. Or do crises and strong personalities temporarily overcome the incremental bias in budgeting?

Even without crises, the theory of incrementalism fails to explain the changes in the composition of the budget over a five-to-ten-year period. The differences between the beginning and end of the period can be dramatic. Going beyond just marginal adjustments of base budgets, the changes reflect new departures, reordering of priorities, and important shifts of allocations. Also, as Chapter 9 on budget implementation indicates, budgetary changes within the year can be as significant as changes between years. The incrementalists overlook these major developments. The proponents of the theory of incrementalism also fail to spell out what constitutes an increment. Is it a marginal change of 1 percent, 5 percent, 50 percent? A significant percentage change can constitute a major policy shift that can hardly be termed an incremental adjustment.[115]

Finally, the theory of incrementalism turns out to be a creature of its times, the relatively prosperous 1960s and 1970s, when fair shares of increments and protection of the base budget appeared to be realistic expectations, at least in the perception of participants. Confident that this relatively stable state of affairs would persist, several analysts, on the basis of some empirical studies, developed theories about determinants of expenditures. They claimed these enabled them to forecast expenditures with a negligible margin of error. But, as Premchand reminds us, "after more than three decades of effort, there is as yet no comprehensive theory of public expenditures and their determinants." Too many unpredictable ideological, technical, and economic factors get in the way.[116]

As an explanation of budget decision making, incrementalism, with its emphasis on predictable outcomes, was swamped by an era of austerity, uncontrollable expenditures because of entitlement programs, large deficits, expenditure ceilings, cutbacks in base budgets, and changes in fiscal policy.[117]

Budget Reforms and Political Decision Making: On a Collision Course?

What should we make of the charges that budget reforms are not sufficiently sensitive to the political nature of resource allocations and that they are irrelevant unless they influence budgetary decisions? The impact of budgetary reforms can only be determined on a case-by-case basis. Yet budgetary literature is singularly bereft of such vital data. (This serious omission, however, does not inhibit unsupported generalizations.) Furthermore, it is difficult to trace the influence of rational analysis on budgetary decisions. Numerous pressures and factors obviously shape the final decisions, including the data generated by reformed budgetary systems. Even if politicians reject recommendations flowing out of such systems, this does not signify a system breakdown. The important issues and options surface. The significant data are there. Decision makers are aware of the consequences of the road taken or not taken. If they come to the conclusion that political values transcend the value of efficiency, they still will have meaningfully utilized a system that defines problems, offers a range of choices, and reduces uncertainty. In this sense the process works. Budget reforms in effect today constitute "politically responsive, research oriented, and information-sensitive governmental decision systems." They make possible an interaction of political bargaining and analytic processes, and facilitate, without guaranteeing, informed political decisions.[118]

As Charles L. Schultze, former director of OMB and former chair of the Council of Economic Advisers, put it with regard to PPBS, "[It] is not a mechanical substitute for good judgment, political wisdom and leadership."[119]

* * *

We now come full circle to the issues raised in a classic article by V. O. Key, Jr., in 1940. Key found American budgeting literature "singularly arid" in dealing with "the most significant aspect of public budgeting, i.e., the allocation of expenditures among different purposes so as to achieve the greatest return." No budgetary theory enabled governments to deal with the basic question, "On what basis shall it be decided to allocate X dollars to activity A instead of activity B?" Ultimately, the question comes down to "value preferences between ends lacking a common denominator." In looking for an approach to "the practical working out of the issue," Key suggested "the canalizing of decisions through the governmental machinery so as to place alternatives in juxtaposition and compel consideration of relative values."[120]

This is precisely what budgetary reforms seek to achieve.

Points for Discussion

1. Of all the budget reforms cited in the chapter, which are the most significant and why?
2. What are the common elements among budgetary reforms? What are the major differences?
3. How do you explain the persistence of the traditional line-item budget?
4. What are the pros and cons of multiyear budgeting? Analyze the Budget Enforcement Act of 1990 and the Reconciliation Act of 1993 as major examples of multiyear budgeting.
5. How do you account for the fact that program and performance budgeting, though conceptually simple, requires thirty to forty years for full implementation?
6. What are the strengths and weaknesses of program and performance budgeting? How far would you go in recommending its use at the federal, state, and local levels of government?
7. What are the major differences between program and performance budgeting and PPBS?
8. What are the pros and cons of PPBS? How do you account for its rise and fall? What legacy did PPBS leave for governments?
9. To what extent would you recommend the use of Canadian-style "envelope budgeting" in the United States?
10. What are the lasting effects of MBO (management by objectives) and productivity measurement as budget reforms? To what extent are they similar to or different from other budget reforms?

11. Is ZBB (zero-based budgeting) a fraud? Defend your position. How far would you go in implementing full-scale, "true," ZBB?
12. From the start, ZBB apparently turned out to be alternative budgeting. To what extent do you agree with Lewis on this reform? How useful is alternative budgeting as practiced by governments in and out of the United States? How useful is it as a tool of decrementalism?
13. Discuss the relationship between alternative budgeting and target budgeting.
14. To what extent do you agree with Wildavsky and Schick that budget reforms are dead or irrelevant? How do you account for the fact that governments persist in applying these reforms in budgeting despite the sharp criticism of some academicians?
15. Discuss Key's view on the lack of a theory in budgeting and his suggestions for getting around this problem. To what extent are the various budget reforms compatible with his views?
16. Review recent budget documents of federal, state, and local governments and evaluate the impact of budget reforms on these documents.
17. Explain the impact of populist, or ballot-box, budgeting on budget systems.

CHAPTER 12

THE JUDICIAL POWER OF THE PURSE
How Courts Control Budgets[1]

No longer is budget decision making the sole prerogative of chief executives and legislatures in the United States. Since the early 1950s, federal and state courts have participated in budgeting on an unprecedented scale. Through their decisions and orders they have intervened in every phase of the budget process at all levels of government. Hundreds of court decisions affect budget formulation and implementation, capital construction, the issuance of bonds, intergovernmental grants, legislative–executive relations in budgeting, taxation, and the financing of public authorities.

Few aspects of budgeting are beyond the reach of the courts. Their decisions determine not only funding levels, but standards of service, staffing patterns, salaries and wages, and even executive and legislative budget procedures. Not content with decisions alone, courts in many cases devise remedies and oversee the implementation of their orders by appointing monitors, committees, special masters, and, at times, receivers to administer programs.[2]

While judicial decrees affect nearly all government programs, their most profound impact has been on programs and policies in mental health and retardation, correctional services for adult and youthful offenders, education, welfare, and environmental protection. In many states, court orders have drastically altered the financing and operation of these programs and sharply increased state budgets. Even the threat of a court challenge can result in significant programmatic and budgetary changes.

From a fiscal standpoint the impact of court decisions is dramatic. As Figure 12.1 demonstrates, court orders drove nearly 30 percent of the Texas budget in 1991, primarily for elementary and secondary education and for corrections (approximately $10 billion in a $34 billion budget financed by general revenue).

FIGURE 12.1 RESTRICTIONS ON THE TEXAS BUDGET

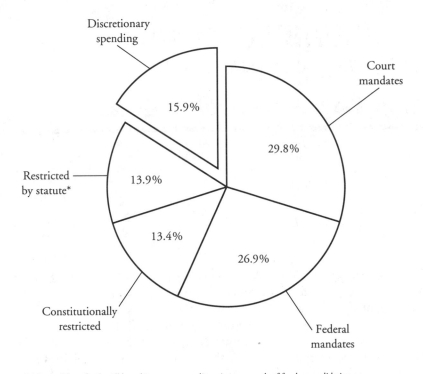

Discretionary spending — 15.9%

Court mandates — 29.8%

Restricted by statute* — 13.9%

13.4%

Constitutionally restricted

26.9%

Federal mandates

* Many of these funds will be subject to greater discretion as a result of funds consolidation.

Source: State of Texas, Office of the Governor, Governor's Revenue Task Force, 1991, *Working for Texas*, (Austin, 1993), p. 7.

In 1990 the Division of Management and Budget of the State of Michigan estimated that court decisions might raise the cost of Medicaid by $53 million; corrections by over $100 million; the retirement system by $185 million; the local judicial system by $500 million to $1 billion; mental health programs by $21 million; and education "hundreds of millions." This is but a rough sample of cases in various stages of litigation.[3]

These developments occur even though courts have no direct role in the budget process. Their point of entry is litigation initiated by an aggrieved plaintiff. In seeking the protection of the courts, plaintiffs typically assert that existing programs deprive them of individual rights guaranteed by federal and state constitutions and laws. In much of the litigation, they invoke the protection of the Eighth Amendment of the United States Constitution, which prohibits "cruel and unusual punishment," and the Fourteenth Amendment, which guarantees equal protection of the laws and due process in all issues affecting life, liberty, and property. (Similar clauses exist in the constitutions of state governments.) When the courts provide relief by ordering modification of programs and policies, they generally (with some exceptions) ignore the impact on budgets. In fact, state governments cannot plead lack of funds as a basis for noncompliance with decisions. As one federal judge put it, "the decisions of the courts are legion that cost burden is not a defense to the deprivation of individual rights."[4]

Determining the Allocation of Resources for Programs

By the end of the 1970s many states had overhauled their programs and capital facilities and sharply expanded their appropriations for mental health, mental retardation, correctional services, education, and welfare. This was due to the direct and indirect effect of a string of landmark court decisions that continued into the 1990s. A few examples extracted from hundreds of decisions will illustrate the impact of the courts on budget formulation.

Appropriations for the Mentally Ill and Mentally Retarded

Beginning in the 1970s, several precedent-setting decisions, originally in Alabama and then in other states, had a direct impact on programs for the mentally ill and mentally retarded. For example, in *Wyatt v. Stickney*, Judge Frank Johnson, Jr., of the federal district court in Alabama ordered the Mental Health Board in 1971 to provide within six months the required level of care for the mentally ill in a large institution. When it became clear that the state had failed to comply with the decision, Judge Johnson issued a broad decree affecting all mental hospitals and prescribing "minimum constitutional standards." In an appendix to the decision, he laid down the standards, which included the amount of square feet of space per patient, provisions for privacy, furniture per patient, toilet and washing facilities, individual treatment plans, and staffing ratios that provided for every 250 patients two psychiatrists, four other physicians, twelve registered nurses, seven social workers (with two having an M.S.W. degree), and other categories of professional and paraprofessional personnel. In effect, Judge Johnson had revised the mental health budget of the state of Alabama.[5]

The court made it clear that the lack of funds, staff, and facilities was no defense and, in the event of failure to comply with its decree, threatened the state as follows:

> In the event, though, that the Legislature fails to satisfy its well-defined obligation, and the Mental Health Board, because of the lack of funding or any other legally insufficient reason, fails to implement fully the standards herein ordered, it will be necessary for the Court to take affirmative steps, including appointing a master, to ensure that proper funding is realized and that adequate treatment is available for the mentally ill of Alabama.

The state did not appeal this decision to the federal circuit court or the United States Supreme Court. Instead it sharply increased budgets for mental health programs.

Following the lead of Alabama, the federal court in Minnesota in 1977 agreed that compliance with its decree with regard to programs for the mentally retarded would cost the state an additional $10 to $12 million a year. Nonetheless, it issued the by now familiar dictum, "If Minnesota chooses to operate hospitals for the mentally retarded, the operation must meet minimal constitutional standards, and that operation may not be permitted to yield to financial considerations."[6]

Going beyond the rulings in Alabama and other states, the federal courts in New York State, over more than a ten-year period beginning in 1973, controlled the programs and budgets for the mentally retarded. The courts mandated a drastic shift from institutionalization to community care, larger state and local budgets, and implementation of revised standards for the care and treatment of patients. In 1975, the court approved a consent decree covering staffing ratios, the level of service, the rate of deinstitutionalization, and space standards. These were embodied in some thirty-five standards for the mentally ill and forty-nine standards for the mentally retarded.[7] Reluctant because of the heavy fiscal implications, the governor nonetheless signed the decree. The budgets for mental health programs rose sharply in succeeding years.[8]

When Michigan failed to implement a consent decree governing the rights of mental patients, the United States Department of Justice in 1990 filed a complaint in the federal district court, charging constitutional violations. In a settlement approved by the court, the state agreed to raise the budget for three mental hospitals by at least $11 million annually.[9]

Appropriations for Correctional Services

Several landmark court decisions have led to a restructuring of prison systems for adult and youthful offenders, and a sharp increase in operating and capital budgets for correctional services in many states and cities.[10] In virtually every case the plaintiffs attacked the conditions of confinement as "cruel and inhuman punishment," proscribed by the Eighth Amendment of the United States Constitution.

As in the cases affecting the mentally ill and the mentally retarded, the court made short shrift of state pleas about the lack of funds for prisons. In a ruling reminiscent of the decision in the Minnesota case with regard to mentally retarded individuals, the court warned the state of Arkansas,

> Let there be no mistake in the matter; the obligation of the Respondents to eliminate existing unconstitutionalities does not depend upon what the Legislature may do or upon what the Governor may do, or indeed, upon what Respondents may be able to accomplish. If Arkansas is going to operate a penitentiary system, it is going to have to be a system that is countenanced by the Constitution of the United States.[11]

Similar rulings raised capital and operating costs for corrections in at least fourteen states and many cities and counties. Texas stands out as a major example of the consequences of court mandates. Twenty years of legal battles began in 1971 when a convict, David Ruiz, with the support of the United States Department of Justice, complained about prison conditions that were "so oppressive as to produce deprivation psychosis."[12] When the state stalled in effecting improvements, the federal district court in 1980 seized control of the Texas prison system and its 50,000 inmates. It did not relinquish control until 1992, when the state raised $1.1 billion to construct 25,300 additional cells.[13]

Tennessee also experienced court supervision of its prison system beginning in 1982. Only after it had spent $340 million to build six new prisons, with 7,000 beds and improved medical care for inmates, did the federal district court turn back the prisons to the state in 1993.[14]

In states and elsewhere in the United States, court intervention does not end with a decision or a decree. Through special masters, review panels, and human rights committees, the courts monitor the implementation of their orders until they are satisfied that the states have complied fully.

Appropriations for Education

Decisions by federal and state courts have affected all levels of education and have had a far-reaching impact on state and local education budgets. Even when plaintiffs have lost lawsuits, the litigation process itself has served as a catalyst to initiate changes in policies and budgets.[15] Litigation in education has covered such broad issues as racial segregation in schools; discriminatory practices in the allocation of resources to schools and universities with large minority groups; the education of physically handicapped children; state and local financing of elementary and secondary education; and the distribution of state aid to parochial schools and school districts. In terms of their fiscal effect, judicial decisions on desegregation, handicapped children, and school financing have been the most significant.

Through interpretations of the Fourteenth Amendment, the federal Rehabilitation Act of 1973, and the federal Education of All Handicapped Children Act of 1975, federal courts have compelled school districts to establish programs appropriate for handicapped children. While expressing concern about the fiscal effects of their decisions, federal judges have nonetheless issued decrees for individualized programs that cost state and local governments and school districts billions of dollars.[16]

The courts have been especially active in adjudicating issues relating to elementary and secondary education and in raising appropriations for education. Between 1971 and 1992 plaintiffs in twenty-three states charged that funding for K–12 education was inequitable and discriminatory. In eleven states the courts concurred with this view and overturned school funding systems.[17] Once started, the momentum for change in school financing has never let up.

Most of the controversy turns on the support of elementary and secondary education, which represent the largest single component of state and local government budgets. To finance these programs, local governments and school districts rely heavily on local property taxes, augmented by state and federal grants. The effect has been that school districts with a substantial local tax base (because of affluent individual and corporate taxpayers) spend more for education than those with skimpy tax resources. While the states have attempted to equalize opportunities for children in all school districts by granting relatively more funds to poorer districts, sharp disparities between districts in expenditures per pupil persisted. Beginning in 1971, this method of financing education was attacked as a violation of the equal protection clauses in both the United States Constitution and state constitutions.

At least forty lawsuits took this position over the next twenty years. One far-reaching decision in New Jersey may capture the flavor of the litigation. In *Robinson v. Cahill* the supreme court of New Jersey categorically outlawed existing methods of funding public schools, which, in its view, violated not only the equal protection clauses, but also the requirement in the state constitution for a "thorough and efficient system of elementary and secondary education."[18] In 1973 it ordered the state to finance a "system of education out of state revenues raised by levies imposed uniformly on taxpayers of the same class." Dissatisfied with the sluggish pace of change, the court in subsequent decisions took a series of drastic actions. It imposed deadlines on the state to come up with appropriate legislation and ordered provisional relief for poor school districts. In 1975 it enjoined the state from distributing aid to school districts altogether and did not lift the injunction until 1976, when the legislature passed the state's first personal income tax to fund public education equitably. Still dissatisfied, the court in 1990 ordered the state to equalize spending between rich and poor districts.[19] This led to a nearly $1-billion increase in state aid in 1991–1992 and infuriated voters in suburban school districts, which received less assistance than they had in the past.

The courts exerted similar pressure in the other states, as well. For example, in California, extended litigation began with *Serrano v. Priest* in 1971, when the highest state court ruled categorically with regard to existing formulas for financing elementary and secondary education,

> This funding scheme invidiously discriminates against the poor because it makes the quality of a child's education a function of the wealth of his parents and neighbors. Recognizing as we must that the right to an education in our public schools is a fundamental interest which cannot be conditional on wealth we can discern no compelling state purpose necessitating the present method of financing.[20]

Confronted with dramatic educational disparities in Texas, where the poorest school district spent $2,337 per student and the wealthiest, $56,791 per student, the state supreme court imposed a June 1993 deadline on the state to close the gap in spending. Otherwise it threatened to shut off state aid for schools altogether. The governor and legislature barely met the deadline by approving an additional $1.2 billion in state education aid and giving wealthy school districts several options for sharing their largesse with needier districts.[21]

Beginning in 1987, the federal courts adopted even tougher measures in Kansas City, Missouri, to wipe out the last vestiges of segregation in the school system. The federal district court ordered the creation of magnet schools, a sharp increase in operating and capital budgets, and a 25 percent jump in property taxes to pay for the new program, without a voter referendum. Despite the last unprecedented step, the United States Supreme Court in 1990 upheld this decision.[22]

Welfare Costs

Several decisions, primarily by federal courts, have had a direct impact on federal, state, and local welfare costs and on the management of welfare programs. The rulings deal with such issues as residency requirements for welfare; the attempts of states to place a ceiling on welfare and medical costs; eligibility for food stamps; the funding of abortions; the adequacy of procedures for denying benefits; and state welfare administration. In many of the cases, the plaintiffs invoked the equal protection and due process clauses of the United States Constitution. In others, they challenged the legality of state and local actions. No clear trend is apparent in decisions by the federal courts. In some cases, they gave more weight to constitutional guarantees than to costs. In others, the reverse was true.[23]

As Medicaid costs soared, the states tried to rein them in by cutting reimbursement rates for health care providers. In *Wilder v. Virginia Hospital Association,* the United States Supreme Court in 1990, for the first time, gave the providers the right to sue the state administrators in the courts with regard to the reasonableness of the rates. Predictably, this gave the federal courts a new role in setting health care rates in the various states. Once the floodgates were open, the suits poured in. A few examples among many demonstrate the fiscal results of the court actions. In Pennsylvania a federal judge ordered the state to increase reimbursement rates for hospitals up to 35 percent, raising state costs by some $30 million. In New York City the U.S. Court of Appeals in 1990 required the state to pay the 20 percent co-payment for beneficiaries of Medicaid who were also eligible for Medicare. Similar rulings in the state of Washington led to increased rates for hospitals. In 1993, when privately owned nursing homes in Kansas balked at reimbursement rates, the federal district court gave them the relief they sought. In at least ten other states similar suits led to significant increases in state budgets.[24]

Determining the Size of State and Local Government Payrolls

Both federal and state courts have intervened in virtually every aspect of personnel administration, including pay levels, minimum wages, overtime pay, collective bargaining, position classification, alleged inequity in salaries for women, and pension benefits. For example, in *Garcia v. San Antonio Metropolitan Transportation*

Authority the United States Supreme Court, by a 5–4 vote, decided in 1985 that the Fair Labor Standards Act controlled overtime pay and minimum wages of employees of state and local governments.[25] When rough estimates indicated that the ruling might cost state and local governments up to an additional $4 billion annually, primarily for overtime pay, Congress tried to soften the blow by approving PL 99-150. Nevertheless, the court decision and the legislation led to a plethora of law suits, and imposed on state and local governments a series of complex regulations with regard to overtime, minimum wages, work periods, and record keeping.[26]

The flavor of the litigation that affected the management of state and local governments can be sensed by several examples. In *Gilligan v. Emporia* (1993), a federal circuit court of appeal ruled in Kansas that employees of the Emporia Water and Sewer Departments who were on call were not entitled to overtime pay. Also in 1993, the United States Supreme Court gave state and local governments in Texas more flexibility in granting employees time off in lieu of overtime pay. A federal court in Nebraska took a different stance. Under the Fair Labor Standards Act (FSLA), salaried executive, professional, and administrative employees are exempt from the overtime provisions. Nevertheless, the court ruled that if any of these employees could be docked for absenteeism, they could not be regarded as salaried employees and hence were eligible for overtime pay. This opened the states to more liability for overtime compensation.[27]

In another significant case, the American Federation of State, County, and Municipal Employees (AFSCME) claimed in 1982 that the state of Washington discriminated against women employees in violation of the federal Civil Rights Act. On the whole, it argued, women received less pay than men in jobs of comparable worth. The federal district court found that this was indeed the case. Faced with an estimated cost of $400 million in back pay for approximately 15,000 employees, the state appealed to the federal court of appeals. Reversing the previous decision, the court of appeals supported the state's policy of basing compensation on practices in the marketplace rather than on complex theories of comparable worth. Nevertheless, the state and the union reached agreement on a $404-million pay package for jobs held primarily by women, that would be phased in from 1986 to 1991.[28]

Faced with a revenue shortfall in 1992, the state of Nevada deferred for three months a 4 percent salary increase approved by the legislature. The Nevada Supreme Court, however, ruled that the governor and the State Board of Examiners lacked the constitutional and statutory authority to delay the pay increase.[29]

Monitoring Budget Implementation

The courts have been equally active in monitoring the implementation of the budget at all levels of government in the United States. In this context they have grappled with such issues as the power of presidents and governors to impound funds appropriated by the legislature; the use of legislative vetoes by Congress and state legislatures to turn down expenditures previously approved in appropriations acts; the start-up of construction projects for which funds were appropriated, but which might conflict with other legislation; and the need for administrations to comply with nonbinding expressions of legislative intent.

In an unparalleled intervention in budget implementation, the federal courts, beginning in 1971 reviewed the impoundment of funds by the Nixon administration from 1969 to 1973, in what would eventually be some 100 cases. Prior to 1971, no federal courts had dealt with the issue.[30] Except in two or three cases, the federal courts made short shrift of the administration's arguments. All cases but one were decided by federal district and circuit courts (courts of appeal). In the case that reached the Supreme Court, the Court, like the lower courts, ordered the administration to allot to the states funds for water pollution control appropriated by Congress.[31]

Similar issues came to a head in at least four states, and for the first time, governors encountered serious challenges to the exercise of their powers to allot appropriated funds. For example, confronted by a projected deficit of $145.4 million in FY 1980–1981, the secretary of administration of the state of Wisconsin, among other cutbacks, withheld from local governments 4.4 percent of an appropriation of $57.3 million for property tax relief. The supreme court of the state ruled that no statutory authority existed for this move and that a state government is merely a "conduit for transferring funds appropriated for property tax relief to local governments."[32]

Turning Down Capital Projects That Conflict with Other Legislation

Even when funds were appropriated for major construction projects, the courts, on occasion, have prevented the implementation of the projects because of conflict with other legislation. They have stopped or terminated the construction of dams, power plants, prisons, and highways because the projects ran afoul of statutory standards for the protection of the environment, protection of endangered species, and preservation of historic sites.

One illustrative case is *Sierra Club et al. v. U.S. Army Corps of Engineers et al.* After ten years of litigation, a federal appeals court in 1985 finally barred the construction of the Westway, a controversial multibillion dollar highway project in New York City. The court's ruling was based in large part on the failure of the Army Corps of Engineers to prepare an acceptable environmental impact statement as required by other statutes. The court was especially critical of the inadequate analyses by the Corps of the impact of the project on the survival of striped bass in the Hudson River.[33]

Refereeing the Distribution of Intergovernmental Grants

State and local governments depend on federal grants as a major source of revenue. Local governments also count heavily on state assistance. The funds go directly to the governments for numerous programs and projects and to individual beneficiaries, as in welfare programs. In the distribution of the grants, sharp conflicts have arisen between grantors, beneficiaries, and would-be beneficiaries. In hundreds of cases the adversaries have turned to the courts for relief. The result has been the development of a formidable body of case law that encompasses virtually every aspect of intergovernmental financing.

In adjudicating the issues, the courts interpret the statutes authorizing the grants; determine in some instances the constitutionality of the grants; and look for compliance with across-the-board, or "cross-cutting," statutory provisions that affect all grants regardless of source. These requirements include standards for civil rights, antidiscrimination in employment, environmental protection, flood control, survival of endangered species, facilities for the disabled, and preservation of historic sites.[34]

Ruling on Voter Referenda on Budgetary Policy

Public referenda on bond issues for capital construction and on changes in fiscal policy are an integral part of the budget process in state and local governments in the United States. Such ultimate expressions of democratic rule would appear to be beyond the reach of the courts. Yet on occasion, state courts, on constitutional grounds, have removed measures from the ballot, blocked their use, ignored referenda, and even nullified referenda after voter approval.

Several cases in New Jersey, Florida, California, and New York illustrate the courts' power to reject the results of public referenda. In 1978 the voters in New Jersey approved a $100 million bond issue for a variety of public works projects. Nevertheless, the state supreme court ruled in 1979 that the referendum was unconstitutional, because the state constitution required bond issues to be devoted to a single purpose (for example, transportation) and not multiple purposes.[35] In Florida, the highest court removed from the ballot in 1984 a measure that would have limited tax increases in state and local governments and would have required a referendum on revenues in excess of the proposed ceilings. Some $2 billion was involved. The court found that, contrary to the state constitution, the measure was not devoted to a single subject and was so broad as to be ambiguous.[36]

Going farther, the supreme court in California refused to give the voters an opportunity to act on an initiative calling for a balanced federal budget. Under the terms of the initiative, the legislature would be compelled to petition Congress for a constitutional convention that would adopt an amendment to the United States Constitution mandating a balanced budget. Legislators who refused to approve the petition would forfeit their salaries and other benefits. The court ruled that such compulsion on the legislature was unconstitutional because the state constitution envisaged that the legislature would use its best judgment on issues of public policy.[37]

In New York State, the court of appeals ignored the explicit wishes of the voters, expressed in a referendum. Nothing could be clearer than state voter rejection of a $500 million bond issue for prison construction in 1981. Nevertheless, the governor and the legislature authorized a public authority, the Urban Development Corporation, to sell bonds in order to finance prison construction. When a group of voters challenged this step, they were turned down because, according to the court of appeals, they had no standing to sue and, in any event, had waited too long to file a complaint. In no way did the court decision even pretend to delve into the issues raised by the plaintiffs.[38]

Other states have followed New York in creating public authorities and giving them the power to sell bonds whether or not the voters approve. As noted in Chapter 6, nearly all state courts, with a few shining exceptions, have blessed this strategy to evade the constitution.[39]

Ruling on the Constitutionality and Legality of Taxes

Under federal and state constitutions in the United States, governments have concurrent taxing powers. The result is that nearly all levels of government impose income, corporation, sales, excise, gross receipts, and energy taxes and a variety of user fees. In hundreds of cases over the years, taxpayers have challenged the constitutionality and legality of many of the taxes. In the process federal and state courts have made some far-reaching decisions affecting the taxing powers of all governments.

In view of the plethora of judicial decisions, it is difficult to draw broad generalizations. One can, however, discern several trends. For example, federal courts have been vigilant regarding the commerce, supremacy, and equal protection clauses in the United States Constitution in settling interstate conflicts on taxation and preventing states from imposing unfair tax burdens on nonresidents. Thus the United States Supreme Court found unconstitutional a commuter tax levied in a few states against nonresidents.[40] It declared invalid under the supremacy and commerce clauses a tax by Louisiana on natural gas distributed by pipeline companies to other states.[41] On the other hand, the Supreme Court approved a severance tax on coal by Montana even though about 90 percent of the coal was shipped outside of the state. In the case at issue it found that residents and nonresidents had similar tax burdens.[42] The Supreme Court also upheld a West Virginia wholesale gross receipts tax, which, the plaintiff charged, interfered with interstate commerce.[43] But it refused to go along with a state tax in Hawaii that discriminated against products of other states in favor of local products.[44]

For years the states have sought to collect sales taxes on mail order purchases. Nationally, this would yield nearly $4 billion in additional revenue. In 1992 the United States Supreme Court dashed their hopes by turning down a statute in North Dakota requiring mail order companies to collect some $6.6 million in sales taxes annually in behalf of the state. The court found that the legislation imposed an unconstitutional burden on interstate commerce.[45] On the other hand, in 1989 the Court approved a 5 percent tax imposed by Illinois on interstate telephone calls originating or terminating in that state and charged to an

Illinois address. Since the burden fell equally on state residents and out-of-state callers, it did not discriminate against interstate commerce, according to the court.[46]

Another tax issue centered on discriminatory practices in seventeen states where the states exempted pensions of retired state and local employees from income taxes, but taxed the pensions of federal retirees. Not only did the Supreme Court find this policy unconstitutional, but in 1993 required the states to refund the illegal taxes. Some $2 billion in refunds was at stake.[47]

One of the major decisions of the Supreme Court affecting state and local finance was *South Carolina v. Baker* in 1988. That decision discarded a century-old doctrine of reciprocal immunity whereby the federal government didn't tax interest on municipal bonds and the states didn't tax interest on U.S. Treasury bonds and notes. For the first time the Court ruled that interest on unregistered state and local bonds is subject to federal taxation.[48] Alarmed by the shattering of a precedent that had governed federal–state relations, the National Governors' Association called on Congress to amend the constitution to exempt state and local bonds from federal taxation. No such action was taken, however.

In 1992 the Supreme Court had the last word on California's Proposition 13, which had triggered a national tax revolt by sharply reducing and capping local property taxes in 1979. One result of the proposition was that differing tax rates could be applied to identical properties, depending on the time of purchase. While this policy may not be desirable, the Court found it to be a "rational" system, because it does not discriminate against any class of citizens.[49] The ruling spurred more efforts to limit taxes in other states.

Overseeing the Budget Process

The courts have intervened in the budget process itself by ruling on the requirement that governors submit balanced budgets, the reduction of federal deficits, the format of the executive budget, the scope and format of appropriations bills, the exercise of item veto powers by the governors, and, as noted above, the implementation of the budget. Several cases illustrate the extent of judicial intervention.

Federal courts first dealt with the issue of balanced budgets on the federal level after the passage of the Balanced Budget and Emergency Deficit Control Act of 1985 (PL 99-177). Among other things, the Act, as noted in Chapter 8, mandated a phased reduction of federal deficits over a five-year period until the budget was balanced. In a decision supported by the Supreme Court, a three-judge district court in 1986 excluded the comptroller general from the deficit reduction process, on the ground that his participation would breach the separation of legislative and executive powers.[50]

Like forty-nine other governors (Vermont is the exception), the governor of New York State must submit a balanced budget based on estimated revenues and expenditures. According to a plaintiff, the governor went too far in 1980 when he included estimated proceeds from tax and revenue anticipation notes in his financial plan. These figures were too "iffy," the plaintiff charged. The highest state court, the court of appeals, nevertheless approved the estimates, so long as they were not "dishonest." Only in the latter case could they be labeled unconstitutional.[51] It is something of a novel role for courts to scrutinize estimates for evidence of questionable manipulation. In another case, the same court ruled that the constitution required the governor to submit a balanced budget, but it did not compel him to keep the budget in balance during the fiscal year. Therefore, he could not withhold funds in the course of budget implementation by citing the need to maintain a balanced budget.[52]

Local budgets also came under the courts' scrutiny. In 1988, New York State's court of appeals voided Nassau County's budget, which had been approved by the county legislative body and the county executive. The court found that the budget was illegal because it did not take into account a $90 million surplus squirreled away for property tax relief. This step violated the county charter, according to the court. A vigorous dissent argued that the court was setting a "destabilizing and sweeping precedent" and that the accuracy of budget estimates should be left to the executive and legislative branches of government.[53]

Ruling on the Scope and Format of Appropriations Bills

An especially thorny problem in executive–legislative relationships is the format of the appropriations bill. This is not a mere technical issue: The form of the appropriations bill determines the extent of legislative and executive control of the budget. In the interest of tight legislative control, should the appropriations bill be itemized, as is required by constitutions in many states? If so, what is the meaning of itemization? Does the growing use of lump sums in appropriations bills erode legislative powers?

In two telling decisions the New York State Court of Appeals, still the most active in the country on budget issues, rejected attacks on lump sum appropriations. In *Hidley v. Rockefeller,* the court asserted that critics are on weak ground in attacking lump sum appropriations as skimpy and inadequate. Appropriations bills don't stand by themselves. They should be read together with the executive budget, which runs to nearly 1,000 pages and is crammed with detailed information on expenditures and revenues. While budgets and appropriations acts are not exempt from "judicial scrutiny and review," the degree of itemization is a political issue that should be negotiated by the legislative and executive branches.

Ruling on Costly Tort Suits against Governments

A series of court decisions has led to an explosion of civil liability suits against federal, state, and local governments for torts (or civil wrongs) committed by the governments or their employees. Several federal laws and court decisions in particular have subjected state and local governments to suits for money damages brought by individuals in federal courts. As a result, the scope of liability has broadened, monetary awards with a serious impact on budgets have escalated, and insurance rates have become so costly as to be prohibitive for many local governments.[54]

This is a far cry from the days when the federal and state governments as sovereign bodies enjoyed immunity from tort suits, and local governments benefited from limited immunity. Several key court cases and legislation have chipped away at that immunity. As matters stand now, federal officials individually are immune from suits for common-law torts, provided they (1) act within the scope of their official duties, and (2) do not violate the constitutional rights of citizens. However, the Tort Claims Act of 1970 (28 U.S.C. 2674) authorizes individuals to sue the federal government for money damages arising out of common-law torts.[55]

In general, state governments may not be sued without their consent. The courts have so ruled because of the states' sovereign immunity under the Eleventh Amendment of the Constitution.[56] In self-denying legislation, however, nearly all state governments have waived their immunity in whole or part and virtually invited the financial burden of expanded tort liability.[57] As if this weren't enough, several decisions by the United States Supreme Court have eroded the protection of the Eleventh Amendment. For example, a 5–4 majority of the Court found the states liable for monetary damages for the cleanup of hazardous waste.[58]

Local governments are practically defenseless against tort suits as a result of several critical Court decisions such as (1) *Monell v. the Department of Social Services of the City of New York,* which stripped local governments of any sovereign immunity against civil litigation by injured parties; and (2) *Owen v. City of Independence, Missouri,* which held local governments responsible for violations of the United States Constitution and federal statutes.[59]

Beginning in 1984, state and local governments turned to Congress and state legislatures for relief. Since 1989 at least twenty-one states have approved legislation limiting state and local tort liability, such as caps on damage awards and expansion of the scope of government immunity.[60] Federal actions, however, are still unpredictable.

Should the Judicial Power of the Purse Be Curbed?

Whether chief executives and legislatures like it or not, they now share budget-making powers with the courts. Decrying this trend, critics of judicial activism claim that the courts are usurping the policymaking and budgeting prerogatives of executives and legislatures.[61] Not content with responding to grievances, the courts, in the view of the critics, have moved into problem solving, thus encroaching on the powers of executives and legislatures.[62] It is one thing to protect procedural safeguards such as due process. It is another to force new substantive policy requirements on governments.[63] The effect of decisions by an "imperial judiciary" has been to erode budgeting as a tool of popular control and to curb the authority and discretion of elected administrators.[64]

The courts, however, have no lack of defenders. Supporters see them as the only means of protecting the constitutional rights of individuals. They argue that intolerable conditions and urgent needs bring plaintiffs to the courts. The courts neither encourage nor initiate such litigation. Frequently, the question before the courts is not "Who should do it?" but whether anything should be done at all.[65] When the courts act, they exercise their authority reluctantly, because no other remedies exist.

As advocates of judicial activism see it, the courts generally intervene on three grounds: the failure of officials to comply with the constitutions and laws, the reluctance of elected officials to act on unpopular measures, and the need to interpret broad and ambiguous statutory measures. Anthony Lewis put the nub of the issue this way in 1991:

> People complain about interventionist judges. But few stop to consider why it happens. The fault lies not in our judges but in ourselves—in the way American democracy now works, or rather does not work . . . That we have to look to judges to focus our minds on pollution and decayed hospitals and overcrowded prisons is not a happy fact. But it will go on—it must go on—until we regain the ability to decide such issues for ourselves.[66]

In the light of the strong views held by the proponents and opponents of judicial activism, what are the prospects of limiting the judicial power of the purse? Neither conservative nor liberal courts demonstrate any discernible self-restraint in this regard when constitutional issues are at stake. If anything, federal and state governments are inviting more rather than less judicial intervention by rewriting constitutions and statutes to set tax and expenditure limits and mandate balanced budgets. What they fail to achieve by political consensus they hope to gain by new statutory formulas. This opens the way for still more court rulings as litigants challenge or seek interpretations of the legal provisions.

In the foreseeable future, then, the courts will continue to participate in budget decision making in the United States. Policymakers and budgeteers at all levels of government must reckon with the impact of judicial decrees. This has important implications for the process of budget formulation and implementation. No planning and funding of major programs and projects can take place without an eye to actual and potential litigation. Straussman and Thurmaier see something of a paradox in this development.

> Rights-based budgeting drives out discretion since court decisions mortgage future budgetary increments. This is anathema to budgeteers who thrive on trade-offs and jealously guard any residue of flexibility that can be garnered in a process increasingly prone toward formula-based decisions . . . Where is the paradox? The resolution of constitutional rights cases may lead to spending decisions that would not occur in the absence of litigation. When this happens budgetary discretion is circumscribed. Yet, it is precisely this erosion of discretion that may be necessary to provide the budgetary support for rights protection. It is in this sense that the courts have become silent partners in the budgetary process.[67]

To accommodate their "silent partners," budgeteers and administrators find that skills in fiscal, program, policy, and management analysis are not enough. Still another arrow belongs in their quiver: legal analysis. Nearly all budget offices now recognize this fact of budgetary life.

Points for Discussion

1. To what extent are courts involved in every phase of budgeting? How do you explain their expanded role?
2. To what extent do you concur or disagree with judicial decisions that assert that lack of funds is no excuse for changing major programs and projects?
3. In what significant ways have courts changed policies and programs and increased budgets in such functions as mental health, programs for the mentally retarded, correctional services, education, and welfare? Which major court decisions do you support? Which ones do you oppose? Why?
4. What major aspects of budget implementation have been changed by court decrees? What is your position on these decisions?
5. What are the major arguments for and against judicial activism? Where do you stand?
6. To what extent do you support Anthony Lewis's position?
7. Assuming you think the courts have gone too far, how would you limit their role in budgeting? Do you agree or disagree with the conclusion in the chapter that the courts will continue to participate in budget decision making?
8. Analyze a judicial decision rendered in the last five years and ascertain its effect on state and local budgets.
9. What are the pros and cons of court control over boards of education and correction departments?
10. What are the forms of day-to-day control exercised by the courts? How effective are they?

CHAPTER 13

REINVENTING GOVERNMENT FOR THE YEAR 2000
The Sixty-Year Battle to Improve Management via the Budget Process

Apparently, no improvement in government budgeting or management can take place without having a trendy term or a memorable acronym to describe it. In the early 1990s the catchy phrase was "reinventing government," taken from the popular book *Reinventing Government: How the Entrepreneurial Spirit Is Transforming the Public Sector*, by David Osborne and Ted Gaebler.[1] As the Clinton administration assumed office in 1993, it seized upon the slogan to initiate a sweeping six-month investigation of the federal government.

Headed by Vice President Al Gore, the National Performance Review, with "reinvention teams" including representatives of OMB and the treasury department, probed all promising nooks and crannies of the federal bureaucracy and its organizational structure and systems. The outcome of the effort was a report with a catchy title: *From Red Tape to Results: Creating a Government that Works Better and Costs Less* (Sept. 1992). Promising some $108 billion in savings between FY 1995 and FY 1999 and a cut of 252,000 jobs (nearly 12 percent of the federal workforce), the report laid out far-reaching changes in governmental organization, programs, and policies; the consolidation and elimination of offices and streamlining of operating systems; changes in procurement policies; expanded privatization of activities; decentralization of services; elimination of red tape; simplification of regulations; and modernization of computer systems—all embedded in over 800 recommendations.[2]

Some two-thirds of the recommendations could be enacted by the stroke of a pen via an executive order, according to the report. The remaining proposals—the toughest part—required legislative approval. The president made it clear that the "reinventions" were an integral part of his strategy to trim the budget deficit.

The question of whether the recommendations were sound and doable and the savings real or inflated can be left for another day. (CBO expressed some doubt on the latter by sharply whittling down estimated savings.[3]) What is significant is that the enthusiastic proponents of "reinventing government" overlooked the fact that OMB and other central staff agencies have been reinventing government for more than sixty years under the umbrella of such mundane phrases as "management improvement" and "administrative improvement."

From the earliest days of budgeting, management improvement programs have been an integral part of the budget process. No other decision-making system has the leverage to pressure departments to improve program management.[4] As used here, "management improvement" encompasses the efficiency, economy, effectiveness, productivity, impact, and results of governmental activities.[5] The budget process focuses systematically on all of these issues. In fact, no other system offers as many opportunities to identify administrative failings and to take corrective action. If exercised, the power of the purse can be a formidable weapon for altering organizational structures, operating systems, programs, and policies.

Three major developments fostered the symbiotic relationship between budgeting and management improvement. First, the landmark Budget and Accounting Act of 1921 lodged responsibility for government-wide administrative improvements in the Bureau of the Budget (BOB), the precursor of OMB.[6] Second, the influential Brownlow Committee Report of 1937, which was instrumental in shaping the Executive Office of the President (EOP), argued that BOB was the logical staff agency for stimulating management improvement.[7] Third, after Congress in 1939 approved the creation of EOP with BOB as one of its major constituent units, President Roosevelt issued Executive Order 8248, which gave BOB a broad charter for management improvements.[8]

With this charter, BOB institutionalized its management functions in a Division of Administrative Management. So creative and influential were the activities of this division that they stimulated management improvement among federal agencies, state governments, and municipalities and also served as a model for other countries. From the start, systematic management improvement programs were more or less intertwined with the budget process, setting a pattern that, with some ups and downs, persisted into the 1990s.

In the nearly six decades that followed the creation of the Administrative Management Division, the role of budget offices in management improvement changed continuously, depending on the management values, styles, political pressures, and priorities of presidents, governors, mayors, and budget directors. From the 1940s through the 1950s, the stress was on operational efficiency, with policy development and program evaluation being secondary factors. In the 1960s the focus was on the effectiveness of the programs of the Great Society and the capacity of federal, state, and local governments to coordinate and conduct intergovernmental activities. As a result, program evaluation, policy coordination, and governmental reorganization dominated the agenda for management improvement.[9] In the wake of the recessions of the early 1980s and early 1990s, revenue shortfalls, deficits, and debt haunted the budget process. Once again, the emphasis in management improvement shifted to efficiency, cost reduction, productivity, automation, tight financial management, the elimination of waste, and the eradication of red tape.

As a result of these developments, central budget offices in the federal and state governments and large cities and counties of the United States conduct, in varying degree, the following management activities:

1. Promoting management improvement programs in operating agencies.

2. Monitoring the results of such programs.

3. Conducting surveys of urgent organizational, systems, and policy problems.

4. Developing organizational plans and plans of operation.

5. Evaluating the efficiency and effectiveness of programs and projects.

6. Participating in the development of new programs and policies.

7. Developing methods of measuring work and productivity.

8. Participating with the operating agencies in establishing performance standards and performance measurement systems.

9. Analyzing staff utilization.

10. Fostering and monitoring the use of computer and telecommunication systems.

11. Furthering the development of management information systems.

12. Eliminating unnecessary paperwork.

13. Participating in the solution of intergovernmental problems.

14. Reducing the burden of unnecessary regulations affecting private businesses, individuals, and other governmental levels (primarily an OMB function).

15. Reducing the cost of administrative support activities such as the management of space, travel, vehicles, printing and reproduction, procurement, and office machines and equipment.

16. Identifying governmental activities that should be farmed out to the private sector (privatization).

17. Improving financial management in collaboration with comptrollers' and treasurers' offices (especially accounting systems, cash management, and debt management).

18. Assisting agencies in policy implementation and the delivery of program services.

No one budget office can possibly conduct this formidable array of activities by itself. To be effective, it must work closely with the operating departments and with other central staff agencies such as offices of comptrollers, accountants, auditors, administrative services, and personnel management. Above all, it depends on the management capability of the operating departments, for, in the last analysis, management improvement is the responsibility of each agency. At best, central budget offices can stimulate, goad, and even inspire agencies to strengthen their programs, operating systems, and organizational structures. They can suggest priorities and orchestrate government-wide efforts to improve management. They can persuade agency heads to establish strong offices of management and program analysis. In the end, they can use the power of the purse to effect necessary changes, on the theory that nothing stimulates the imagination like a budget cut. Ultimately, however, a management improvement program is no better than the combined efforts of individual agencies.

Over the years, chief executives and legislatures have wavered in their support of sustained efforts to improve management. Except for momentary political gains as they rail against "waste and inefficiency," they find that voters soon lose interest in the technical details of restructuring organizations and systems. For that matter, so do they. And a perennial task for all budget offices is to devise ways to keep chief executives interested and supportive in the face of the visibility and glamor of new policies and programs.

On occasion, under the pressure of deficits, political leaders become impatient with the slow pace of change. Hence, they frequently launch comprehensive, one-time, across-the-board studies of the government, such as the Gore National Performance Review; President Reagan's Grace Commission (the President's Private Sector Survey on Cost Control—PPSSCC), which produced over 2,000 recommendations (many of them controversial) estimated to save $424 billion; the two Hoover Commissions of 1947–1949 (President Truman) and 1953–1955 (President Eisenhower); clones of the Hoover Commission in many states; Iowa's Committee on Government Spending Reform in 1991; Montana's Futures Project in 1990; and South Carolina's Commission on Government Restructuring in 1991.[10]

At times, legislatures, budget watchers, and academics question whether a central budget office, bogged down in nonstop routines and pressures, is an appropriate catalyst for management improvement. Consequently, from time to time they propose the creation of new offices, divorced from the budget process and focusing exclusively on strengthening governmental organizations, systems, and programs.

These are some of the issues that surface as each administration develops its own approach to management improvement. The Roosevelt and Truman administrations fostered systematic management improvement programs. The Eisenhower administration, however, preferred to focus on the solution of ad hoc problems. The Kennedy administration emphasized the use of productivity measurement in budgeting. The Johnson administration launched a "war on waste" to cut the costs of the Great Society programs while intensifying the evaluation of programs. The Nixon administration highlighted the importance of management by reorganizing BOB into an Office of Management and Budget (OMB), and focused on critical problems. The short-lived Ford administration dealt selectively with management problems. The Carter administration initiated extensive program evaluations as part of a government-wide management improvement program. Under the banner of "Reform '88," the Reagan administration mounted an attack on "waste and inefficiency" and concentrated on improving financial management. Running from 1982 to 1988, Reform '88 was the largest sustained management effort since the days of F.D.R. and Harry Truman.

Beset by unprecedented deficits, the Bush and Clinton administrations, in a manner reminiscent of the Roosevelt and Truman administrations, once again emphasized management improvements. The centerpiece of the Bush presidency in this respect was the passage of the Chief Financial Officers Act of 1990, which, among other things, established the Office of Deputy Director for Management in OMB; created, also in OMB, the Office of Federal Financial Management, headed by a controller, to oversee accounting, cash management, and credit standards and systems; and set up in twenty-three major agencies chief financial officers to strengthen all facets of financial management. The administration also breathed new life into the President's Council on Management Improvement, which had been established in 1984, with the mission of identifying and implementing new opportunities for management improvement; and the President's Council on Integrity and Efficiency, designed to combat fraud and waste in federal programs since 1981, primarily through the offices of inspectors general in the operating agencies.[11]

In submitting its last budget, in 1992, the Bush administration applauded these steps, as well as the appointment of joint OMB–agency "SWAT" teams and review teams to solve critical problems in at least fourteen agencies; major systems changes; quality improvement and performance measurement; improved accounting, reporting, and auditing practices; and the elimination of costly "high risk areas" in forty agencies.[12]

The Clinton administration embraced all of these measures with enthusiasm and added still more: the National Performance Review, followed up by detailed surveys in individual agencies, and the passage of the Government Performance and Results Act of 1993, which "requires federal agencies to develop five-year strategic plans with measurable long-term goals, annual performance plans and annual performance reports, comparing goals set to those actually achieved."[13]

How successful were the management improvement programs in producing more efficient, economical, and effective programs and projects? To what extent has it been possible to employ the budget process to effect management improvements? Those who have followed the shifting fortunes of management improvement programs over a sixty-year span have given them mixed reviews—mainly negative—along these lines.

1. *The "golden" days of the 1940s and 1950s have been betrayed.* Since the Roosevelt and Truman administrations, budget directors and the White House staff have not fully understood the potential of the budget process to improve management.[14] Nor have they given it high priority. Once presidents learned to use OMB as their managerial arm, the good old days would return. In 1993 the Clinton administration appeared to be on the verge of returning to the old faith.

2. *The gains of management improvement programs are minimal.* This echoes previous criticisms. The Comptroller General in 1990, while applauding several improvements, still voiced some troubling reservations:

We found that the prospects for OMB's long-term success in providing management leadership remain constrained by its long-standing inability to establish a stable institutional management capacity and effective relationships between OMB's management and budget staffs, and among OMB, the agencies, and Congress . . . We concluded that several operational and organizational adjustments could help OMB achieve a stable management framework. These changes involved (1) focusing its limited resources on agency programs and activities most in need of attention; (2) having the budget divisions oversee management improvement efforts; (3) having the management staff work with the budget examiners to help review problem areas and analyze agency action plans; and (4) establishing a systematic process built into the budget review cycle for evaluating key agency-specific and crosscutting management issues that affect program effectiveness.[15]

3. *Budget directors and their deputies come and go and so do management improvement programs.* Other critics argue that management improvement programs have failed not because of lack of effort, but because of the turnover of budget directors and their assistants responsible for directing management efforts. With presidential blessings, over a dozen budget directors have launched such programs only to leave after their projects had barely sunk fragile roots.[16] Now that management improvement has a strong institutional base, as a result of the creation of the statutory Office of the Deputy Director of OMB for Management, it may prove to be more durable.

4. *Budget examination drives out management analysis and program evaluation.* In OMB and the operating agencies, specialized units typically headed management improvement programs. They had, however, little effect on budgetary decisions, which were the domain of budget examination units during the late 1970s and the 1980s.[17]

5. *The budget process is inhospitable to management improvement.* So complex and detailed has budgeting become and so driven is it by inexorable timetables, that it cannot accommodate a careful consideration of management issues.[18]

6. *Operating agencies lack incentives to implement management improvements.* Unless agencies clearly benefit from proposed management improvements, they will resist them. If the change enhances OMB control over the agency, it is especially objectionable.[19] Yet the support of operating agencies is a prerequisite for any strong management improvement program.

7. *Management improvement programs can succeed only if they are directed by a special office in the White House.* Picking up the theme that management improvement programs get mired in the swamps of the budget process, several presidential advisers and legislative committees and the National Academy of Public Administration have urged the creation in the White House of a special office that would concentrate solely on management.[20]

8. *OMB should still be the sole resource for management improvement programs.* After the 1940s and 1950s, it is argued that OMB is no longer the sole resource for centrally directed management improvement efforts. By the 1970s, GAO had

overshadowed it in program evaluation, and in the early 1980s had begun broad management studies of agencies.[21] Largely at the instigation of OMB and GAO, the operating agencies have over the years built up staff units responsible for management audits and program evaluation. To strengthen internal financial and management control, Congress in 1978 approved the Inspector General Act (PL 95-452), which established the offices of inspectors general, initially in twelve agencies and later in eighteen (seventeen statutory). Their primary mission is to ferret out inefficiency, waste, fraud, and abuse in the activities of their agencies.[22] Later came the Chief Financial Officers Act of 1990.

9. *The resolution of major management problems depends on outside investigative bodies like the Hoover, Grace, and Gore Commissions.* The first Hoover Commission was relatively successful. Few results flowed from the work of the Grace Commission, which raised many controversial policy issues. The full results of the Gore Commission are not yet known.

Despite the strength of these formidable critiques of management improvement programs and the role of OMB as the chief architect of such efforts, presidents and budget directors persist in ignoring them. Under different labels and with varying emphases, they have continued to resurrect systematic management improvement programs. Contrary to the recommendations of trusted advisers, presidents have continued to hold OMB responsible for the central direction of management activities.

Part of the dilemma results from the expectations of the critics. Management improvements do not occur by fiat or in dramatic and easily documented happenings. They result from thousands of actions, large and small, over time, to improve policies, operating systems, and organizational structures. None of these changes takes place once and for all. No perfect end state exists. The pace of change is uneven, cyclical, and even suffers reversals.[23] As conditions change and new problems arise, further adjustments and new solutions are needed. Hence, management improvement must necessarily be an unceasing and dynamic process. For these reasons a central staff agency, close to the president and armed with the power of the purse, is in a unique position to exercise continuing pressures on the operating departments. With a government-wide perspective, such an agency can deal with management problems to which departments assign low priority or are reluctant to handle. Its role will continue to be a difficult one, however. With budgeting increasingly dominated by political demands, administrative management too often becomes a low-priority function in the budget office, except in times of fiscal crisis.

The Legacy of Federal Management Improvement Programs

Despite their weaknesses, federal management improvement programs have produced noteworthy results during the last sixty years:

1. *Restructuring agencies and strengthening operating systems.* The battle to improve governmental structures and delivery systems is a never-ending one, with systems

"becoming obsolete or falling into disrepair faster than we know how to fix them."[24] That is why one-time studies, no matter how ambitious, can be only temporary palliatives. There is no substitute for unremitting pressure to adjust organizations and systems to the current and the long-term needs of society.

2. *Measuring and improving productivity.* Productivity improvement has been a stop-and-go affair. After a promising start in 1970, federal productivity measurement covered more than two-thirds of all federal civilian employees by 1975, and most agencies reported steady gains in productivity. Thereafter the program languished until 1988, when, under the aegis of Reform '88, the Reagan administration introduced PIP (Productivity Improvement Program). PIP was designed, among other things, to achieve an average annual productivity increase of 3 percent. The goal remained elusive; during the first year productivity increased by 1.6 percent, only to drop in later years. Since the program was not tied closely to the budget process, agencies didn't take it too seriously.[25] With the implementation of the Performance and Results Act of 1993, productivity improvement once again may become a priority.

3. *Intensifying program evaluation as an integral part of management improvement.* In budgeting, the linkage between program evaluation and budget formulation is now accepted as conventional wisdom. Nevertheless, during the 1980s GAO found a significant decline in the capacity to evaluate programs and in the availability of data on programs. Staffs assigned to evaluation studies were slashed, and agencies made greater use of outside consultants.[26]

4. *Stressing automatic data processing (ADP) and telecommunications as vital elements of management improvement programs.* OMB and the General Service Administration have had a key role in these developments and have been responsible for developing government-wide plans for modernizing ADP and telecommunications.[27] However, as late as 1992, GAO discovered major flaws in government information systems.

> Over the past several years, we have evaluated numerous attempts to modernize government information systems; among the major problems we found were large cost increases, long development delays, and systems that do not meet users' needs. In many cases, these development shortcomings occurred because of inadequate detailed planning to identify current and future user needs and a premature commitment to a specific design that did not consider alternative solutions or how well each would satisfy users' needs. These problems are not new. Both the Commission on Government Procurement in 1972 and the Blue Ribbon Defense Panel in 1986 produced similar findings.[28]

Considering the costs of ADP and telecommunications investments, which run into hundreds of billions of dollars annually for hardware, software, and staff, the importance of information systems planning as an integral part of management improvement programs cannot be overstressed. At present, responsibility for coordinating government-wide programs for managing, procuring, and utilizing ADP, telecommunications, and office information equipment is split between

OMB and the Information Resources Management Service of GSA (General Services Administration). Whether OMB alone should carry on these activities because of their linkage to the budget process may be a leading management issue of the 1990s.

5. *Reducing the paperwork burden on the private sector and governments.* In this effort OMB has been the lead agency and has had a modicum of success, although the paperwork burden has increased about 4 percent annually.[29]

6. *Cutting administrative costs.* In FY 1986, OMB set as a target a 10 percent reduction in administrative costs, which would result in an estimated savings of $594 million annually.[30] Whether these savings materialized is a moot question. Administrative overhead continued to be fair game for the Bush and Clinton administrations.

Management Improvement Programs in State and Local Governments

In virtually every respect, state and local governments in the United States parallel the experience of the federal government in conducting management improvement programs as an integral part of the budget process. Beginning in the late 1940s and early 1950s, several state budget officers established management analysis units modeled after BOB. Among the early leaders were the Organizational and Cost Control Division of the California Department of Finance, the Administrative Management Unit of the New York State Division of the Budget, and the Organization and Management Bureau of the Connecticut Division of the Budget.

By the 1970s nearly all state governments had central management-analysis units.[31] The organizational patterns vary, but in most cases, the central budget office carries the main responsibility for stimulating management improvement among the agencies. In some states, such as Wisconsin, Minnesota, and California, an umbrella organization, either a department of administration or a department of finance, centralizes all or nearly all government-wide staff services, including budgeting and management analysis. Among other variations are the Office of Management and Productivity in the governor's office in New York State and the Office of Inspector General in Florida, which work closely with the budget offices. In many states, major departments have also established management-analysis units, frequently at the urging of the budget office.

Because of the recessions of 1982–1983 and 1990–1993, cuts in federal grants, and ceilings on taxes and expenditures, state governments emphasized even more strongly the need for management capability. As a result, the management improvement activities in most states include comprehensive management surveys; organizational and systems studies; program analysis and evaluation; productivity improvement; performance measurement; the development of computer systems, including management information systems; privatization; and improvements in financial management.[32] All of these activities are closely linked with budgeting.[33] Nearly all projects designed to improve management are ad hoc in nature and are triggered by crises, recessions, shortcomings in services, or budget cuts. Few state governments engage in comprehensive, systematic, government-wide management improvement programs. Among the exceptions are New York, Wisconsin, Minnesota, Texas, Oregon, the state of Washington, North Carolina, Connecticut, Kansas, South Carolina, and Georgia.[34]

Through their central budget offices, special statewide commissions, or a combination of the two, the states have launched management reforms on a scale not known since the 1950s and 1960s. The common themes are productivity improvement, as in Texas, Georgia, Florida, and Minnesota; stepped-up program evaluation, as in California, Maryland, and Oregon; performance measurement in most states; strategic planning tied in with budgeting, as in Florida, Minnesota, Missouri, Kentucky, Illinois, and Utah; privatization, as in Massachusetts, Michigan, and fifteen other states; reform of management systems, as in Arizona, Arkansas, Ohio, and Oklahoma; consolidation of human service programs, as in Louisiana, Florida, and Michigan; and restructuring of state government, as in New Mexico and Colorado.[35]

In these unprecedented efforts, several state budget offices took the lead, among them the Michigan Department of Management and Budget, the Georgia Office of Planning and Budget (especially the Management Review Division), the California Department of Finance, the South Dakota Bureau of Finance and Management, the New York State Division of the Budget (in collaboration with the Governor's Office of Management and Productivity), Iowa's Department of Management, and Connecticut's Office of Planning and Management.[36] In addition, from 1988 to 1992, thirty-five states set up commissions with wide-ranging mandates to restructure governmental organizations, policies, and systems. Among them were Alabama's Management Improvement Program, Colorado's Commission on Governmental Productivity, Georgia's Commission on Effectiveness and Economy, Maine's Restructuring Commission, New Jersey's Management Review Commission, and Washington's Commission for Efficiency and Accountability in Government.[37]

This is not the place to detail the numerous improvements and savings accomplished by the states. What is clear is that they were significant and quantifiable achievements, and not just political ploys. The recession of the early 1990s triggered many of the changes; once the economy recovers, it remains to be seen whether sustained efforts to improve management will continue. In such efforts, the central budget office can be the lead agency, but as Donald C. Stone warns the states,

> If an OMB or a budget division is primarily concerned with budgeting and related functions, a subordinate administrative management staff will not likely be able to perform many of the services identified above [management services], unless its director has equal status within the organization as the director of the budget review staff.[38]

Management Improvement Strategies in Local Government

Given the diversity of local governments in the United States, it is difficult to generalize about linkages between budgeting and management improvement at the local level. At one extreme, many municipalities maintained in the 1990s ongoing programs of management improvement. At the other extreme, some local political systems thwarted any attempts at management improvement. In general, though, one can find reasonable ground for optimism, as municipalities in the 1980s began to use such management tools as management analysis, program evaluation, productivity and performance measurement, and ADP on a large scale. Nearly all local governments integrated management improvement programs with the budget process.[39]

Impressive as the gains in the 1980s were, they don't equal the surge of management improvements in the early 1990s, largely induced by the "great recession." A major catalyst has been the Coalition to Improve Management in State and Local Government, which since 1984 has forged an alliance of organizations representing state and local governments. At the local level, four associations have worked with municipalities in meshing policy development, planning, work programming, and budgeting and in improving delivery systems: the National Association of Counties (NACO), the National League of Cities (NLC), the U.S. Conference of Mayors (USCM), and the International City Managers Association (ICMA). Some of the guides issued by the Coalition from 1987 to 1993 illustrate the thrust of their efforts: *County Executive's Management and Productivity Program: How to Do It; The Mayor's Executive Management Program: How to Succeed; Cities and Counties: Implementing an Executive Management Improvement Program;* and *Managing Public Authorities.* Still others are in the works. In addition to publishing such guides, the Coalition consults, does troubleshooting, holds workshops, and identifies sources of technical information and assistance.[40]

Success stories abound throughout the country (failures too!), with or without the help of the Coalition. For example, under the leadership of the Office of Management and Productivity of the County of Allegany, Pennsylvania, some thirty-seven departments have integrated mission development, goal setting, work planning, budgeting, and performance measurement. The project proved to be successful enough to induce 130 municipalities in Allegany County to participate in a similar undertaking.[41]

None of the changes are without flaws. Too many budget decisions are made without reference to performance data. At times, information overload chokes the system. Some powerful agencies flout the requirements for performance measurement or don't use the available data. The measurement of the outcomes of programs still remains an arcane art in some places. City managers and councils may simply ignore performance data. Management changes are slow in coming.[42] In appraising these developments, a long-term view is helpful. It took twenty years for local governments to get to this point. With available management tools, it may take another twenty years (say, until 2010) to effect management improvements that really count.

A Quick Tour of Management Improvement around the World

Faced with stagnant economies and revenue shortfalls, governments throughout the world have implemented management and budget reforms, with a heavy emphasis on performance indicators and performance measurement. With parliamentary forms of government, they encounter fewer obstacles than in the United States in effecting changes. Among the countries with improved management practices are Britain, Australia, New Zealand, Canada, and Sweden.

In Britain the government links performance measures, budgets, and management changes in the annual Public Expenditure White Paper. For example, the paper covering 1988–1989 through 1990–1991 included over 1,800 measures of the results of programs. Presumably, a record of poor results would identify the need for management improvements. Australia follows a similar approach, but with more of an emphasis on targets of workload and efficiency. In Canada, performance measurement, management changes, and budgeting proceed on separate paths and meet more by happenstance than by design.

In contrast, Sweden is far more systematic and uses a carrot-and-stick approach. The emphasis is on linking performance measurement and three-year budgets. When an agency provides comprehensive performance measures and is clearly intent on correcting its management failings, it receives a good deal of flexibility in allocating budgeted funds over a three-year period. Sluggish agencies go through an annual budget cycle. In the first two years of the three-year cycle, agencies favored with flexibility must submit reports on the outcomes of their programs. Should favorable results continue, another three-year budget with built-in flexibility follows.[43]

New Zealand has proved to be far more adventurous in implementing management reforms. It restructured agencies to separate policy development from service delivery. To strengthen accountability for results, it changed its budgets from line items to "output categories." For each output, it specified agreed-upon quantities, qualities, and timing. In effect, the budget is now a contract, which is similar to the concept of program budgeting. Outputs are priced and annual reports compare actual results with planned results laid out in appropriation bills. Agencies break the contract (the annual performance agreement) at their own peril. The government distinguishes between outputs and outcomes. Managers are accountable for outputs, not outcomes, and the latter reflect political decisions and external influences. In this administrative culture, officials stress that "doing things right is an administrative function; doing the right thing is a political function." Thus, outputs alone become the basis for budgeting, accountability, and management changes.[44]

A major resource for program audits, and hence management improvements, is the office of independent auditor-general, or comptroller general (à la GAO in Washington), in both developed and developing countries. (In France, Germany, Austria, Italy, and several other countries, a judicial body—a court of accounts—serves as the independent auditor.)[45] Among the more notable and influential offices engaged in audits of the effectiveness and efficiency of programs and projects are the National Audit Office of Britain; the National Audit Board of Sweden; the Court of Accounts of Germany; the Auditors General in Malaysia, Thailand, Australia, New Zealand, and India; and the Comptroller General in Canada. Program audits by these offices have an obvious impact on budget decisions.

*   *   *

Linking management improvement with budgeting is an ongoing battle everywhere. All too often chief executives and legislatures are indifferent to what appear to be lackluster management improvement programs. Such programs rarely become the centerpiece of a political agenda. Management fads come and go. So urgent, however, is the need to judge the efficiency, effectiveness, and results of programs and projects in an era of fiscal stress that management improvement in one form or another will continue to be an integral part of budgeting.

Points for Discussion

1. What are the major components of management improvement programs in governments? What are the most appropriate strategies to accomplish management improvements: the budget process or other means?
2. What are the pros and cons of integrating management improvement programs with the budget process?
3. How do you account for the results of management improvement programs in the federal government over a sixty-year period? What changes would you propose?
4. In lieu of relying on the central budget office as the spearhead for management improvement, several critics have recommended such alternatives as a management unit in the office of the chief executive, a separate agency, or more reliance on sweeping one-time studies by groups like the Hoover, Grace, or Gore Commissions. Which approach do you favor and why?
5. In view of changes in administration, political pressures, and varying management styles of chief executives and budget directors, what can be done to provide stability in management improvement programs?
6. Compare management improvement programs among federal, state, and local governments. What are the major differences and similarities?
7. How do you account for the current emphasis on performance measurement as an integral part of management improvement programs?
8. In what respects can practices in New Zealand serve as a model for management practices in the United States?
9. Aside from central budget offices, what other offices at different levels of government engage in management improvement programs? How would you harmonize their efforts?
10. Management improvement seems to flourish in a time of fiscal stress. How can you keep it alive in a period of relative affluence? Should you?

APPENDIX
Budget's Own Language: A Glossary of Selected Budget, Accounting, and Economic Terms Used in the Federal Budget Process

Budget Terms and Definitions

activity A specific and distinguishable line of work performed by one or more organizational components of a governmental unit for the purpose of discharging a function or subfunction for which the government unit is responsible. For example, food inspection is an activity performed in the discharge of the health function.

advance appropriation Budget authority, provided in an appropriation act, that is first available in a fiscal year beyond the fiscal year for which the appropriation act is enacted. The amount is not included in the budget totals of the year for which the appropriation bill is enacted, but rather in those for the fiscal years in which the amount will become available for obligation.

advance funding Budget authority provided in an appropriation act to obligate and disburse (outlay), in the current fiscal year, funds from a succeeding year's appropriation. The funds so obligated increase the budget authority for the fiscal year during which they are obligated, and decrease it for the succeeding fiscal year. Advance funding is a means to avoid making supplemental requests late in the fiscal year for certain entitlement programs, in cases where the appropriations for the current year prove to be insufficient.

agency There is no single definition of the term agency. Any given definition usually relates to specific legislation. Generally, executive agency means any executive branch department, independent commission, board, bureau, office, or other establishment of the federal government, including independent regulatory commissions and boards.

allotment An authorization by the head (or other authorized employee) of an agency to his subordinates to incur obligations within a specified amount. The amount allotted by an agency cannot exceed the amount apportioned by the Office of Management and Budget.

apportionment The action by which OMB distributes amounts available for obligation, including budgetary reserves established pursuant to law, in an appropriation or fund account. An apportionment divides amounts available for obligation by specific time periods (usually quarters), activities, projects, objects, or a combination thereof. The amounts so apportioned limit the amount of obligations that may be incurred. In apportioning any account, some funds may be reserved to provide for contingencies or to effect savings, pursuant to the Antideficiency Act. Funds, including Antideficiency Act reserves, may also be proposed for deferral or rescission, pursuant to the Impoundment Control Act of 1974.

The apportionment process is intended to (1) prevent the obligation of amounts available within an appropriation or fund account in a manner that would require deficiency or supplemental appropriations and (2) achieve the most effective and economical use of amounts made available for obligation.

appropriation act A statute under the jurisdiction of the House or Senate Committees on Appropriations that provides budget authority. Enactment generally follows adoption of authorizing legislation unless the authorization itself provides the budget authority. Currently, thirteen regular appropriations acts are enacted annually. When necessary, Congress may enact supplemental or continuing appropriations.

authorization A substantive law that sets up or continues a federal program or agency. Authorizing legislation is normally a prerequisite for appropriations. For some programs, the authorizing legislation itself provides the authority to incur obligations and make payments.

authorizing committee A standing committee of the House or Senate with legislative jurisdiction over the subject matter of those laws, or parts of laws, that set up or continue the legal operations of federal programs or agencies. An authorizing committee also has jurisdiction in those instances where back-door authority is provided in the substantive legislation.

back-door authority Budget authority provided in legislation outside the normal (Appropriations Committees) appropriations process. The most common forms of back-door authority are authority to borrow (also called borrowing authority or authority to spend debt receipts), contract authority, and entitlement authority, for which budget authority is not provided in advance by appropriation acts. In other cases (e.g., interest on the public debt), a permanent appropriation is provided that becomes available without any current action by Congress.

balanced budget A budget in which receipts are equal to or greater than outlays.

baseline An estimate of spending, revenue, the deficit or surplus, and the public debt expected during a fiscal year under current laws and policy. For the purposes of the Budget Enforcement Act, the baseline is defined as the projection of current-year levels of new budget authority, outlays, revenues, and the surplus or deficit into the budget year and out years, and is based on laws enacted through the applicable date. *See also* **CBO baseline.**

bases of budgeting Methods for calculating budget figures. Not all methods are mutually exclusive. For example, the federal budget includes both net and gross figures and reports both obligations and cash or cash equivalent spending. As a general rule, budget receipts and outlays are on a cash equivalent basis. However, interest on public issues of public debt is recorded on an accrual basis.

biennial budget A budget covering a period of two years. The federal government has an annual budget, but biennial budget proposals have been made. The two-year period can apply to the budget presented to Congress by the president, to the budget resolution adopted by Congress, or to appropriations measures.

budget amendment A revision to a pending budget request, which the president submits to Congress before it completes appropriations action.

budgetary reserves Portions of budgetary resources set aside (withheld through apportionment) by OMB by authority of the Antideficiency Act (31 U.S.C. 1512) solely to provide for contingencies or effect savings. Such savings are made possible through changes in requirements or through greater efficiency of operations. Budgetary resources may also be set aside if specifically provided for by particular appropriation acts or other laws.

budget authority Authority provided by law to enter into financial obligations that will result in immediate or future outlays involving federal government funds. Budget authority includes the credit subsidy cost for direct loan and loan guarantee programs, but does not include authority to insure or guarantee the repayment of indebtedness incurred by another person or government. The basic forms of budget authority include (1) appropriations, (2) borrowing authority, (3) contract authority, and (4) authority to obligate and expend offsetting receipts and collections. Budget authority may be classified by its duration (one-year, multiple-year, or no-year), by the timing of the legislation providing the authority (current or permanent), by the manner of determining the amount available (definite or indefinite), or by its availability for new obligations.

budget estimates Estimates of budget authority, outlays, receipts, or other budget measures that cover the current, budget, and future years, as reflected in the president's budget and budget updates.

Budget Preparation System (BPS) A computer system used by OMB to collect and process much of the information required to prepare the budget.

budget updates Amendments to, or revisions in, budget authority requested, estimated outlays, and estimated receipts for the ensuing fiscal year. The president is required by the Congressional Budget and Impoundment Control Act of 1974 [P.L.

93-344, 31 U.S.C. 11(g)] to transmit such statements to Congress by April 10 and July 15 of each year; however, the president may also submit budget updates at other times during the fiscal year.

capital budget A budget that segregates capital investments from the operating budget's expenditures. In such a budget, the capital investments that are excluded from the operating budget do not count toward calculating the operating budget's surplus or deficit at the time the investment is made. States that use capital budgets normally finance the capital investment from borrowing and then charge amortization (interest and debt repayment) to the operating budget.

CBO baseline The Congressional Budget Office's baseline for the upcoming fiscal year. This baseline shows the pattern of federal government revenues and expenditures for the next five years if current policies continue. It appears in CBO's annual report to the Budget Committees on the economic and budget outlook for the upcoming year. The CBO baseline is revised, as necessary, once the president's budget is released. It is also modified as necessary to conform to new legislative requirements, such as those imposed by the Gramm–Rudman–Hollings Act and the Budget Enforcement Act.

collections Amounts received by the federal government during the fiscal year. Collections are classified into two major categories: (1) governmental receipts (also called budget receipts) and (2) offsetting collections. Governmental receipts consist of receipts from taxes, duties, social insurance premiums, court fines, compulsory licenses, and deposits of earnings by the Federal Reserve System. Gifts and contributions (as distinguished from payments for services or cost-sharing deposits by state and local governments) are also counted as governmental receipts. Governmental receipts do not include offsetting receipts, which are treated as offsets to outlays. Total governmental receipts include those specifically designated as off-budget by provisions of law. Total government receipts are compared with total outlays in calculating the budget surplus or deficit.

commitment An administrative reservation of an allotment or of other funds in anticipation of their obligation.

concurrent resolution on the budget A resolution passed by both houses of Congress, but not requiring the signature of the president, that sets forth or revises the Congressional budget for the United States government for a fiscal year.

Congressional budget The budget as set forth by Congress in a concurrent resolution on the budget. By law, the resolution establishes, for the fiscal year beginning on October 1 of the year of the resolution, planning levels for the two following fiscal years and appropriate levels for the following:

- Total federal revenues.
- The appropriation level of total budget outlays and of total new budget authority.
- New budget authority, budget outlays, direct loan obligations, and primary loan guarantee commitments in total and for each major functional category.

- Social security outlays and revenues.
- The surplus or deficit in the budget.
- The public debt—debt subject to statutory limits.

continuing appropriation/resolution Legislation that may be enacted to provide budget authority for federal agencies and/or specific activities to continue in operation when Congress and the president have not completed action on appropriations by the beginning of the fiscal year. Until regular appropriations are enacted, continuing appropriations may take their place. Continuing appropriations are usually passed in the legislative form of joint resolutions. A continuing resolution may be enacted for the full year, up to a specified date, or until regular appropriations are enacted. A continuing resolution usually specifies a maximum rate at which the obligations may be incurred, based on levels specified in the resolution. The resolution may state that obligations may not exceed the current rate or must be the lower of the amounts provided in the appropriations bills passed in the House or Senate. If enacted to cover the entire fiscal year, the resolution will usually specify amounts provided for each appropriation account.

controllability The ability of Congress and the president to increase and decrease budget outlays or budget authority in the year in question, generally the current or budget year. "Relatively uncontrollable" refers to spending that the federal government cannot increase or decrease without changing existing substantive law. For example, outlays in any one year are considered to be relatively uncontrollable when the program level is determined by existing statute or by contract or other obligations.

cost-based budgeting Budgeting in terms of costs to be incurred, that is, the resources to be consumed in carrying out a program, regardless of when the funds to acquire the resources were obligated or paid, and without regard to the source of funds (e.g., appropriation). For example, inventory items become costs when they are withdrawn from inventory, and the cost of buildings is distributed over time through periodic depreciation charges, rather than in a lump sum when the buildings are acquired.

cross-walk Any procedure for expressing the relationship between budgetary data from one system of classification to another, such as between appropriation accounts and authorizing legislation or between the budget functional structure and the congressional committee spending jurisdictions.

current services estimates Estimates submitted by the president of the levels of budget authority and outlays for the ensuing fiscal year, based on the continuation of existing levels of service. These estimates reflect the anticipated costs of continuing federal programs and activities at present levels without policy changes. Such estimates ignore all new presidential or Congressional initiatives, including reductions, that are not yet law.

With his proposed budget each year, the president must transmit current services estimates and the economic assumptions on which they are based. Current services estimates are also included in the "Mid-Session Review of the Budget."

debt, federal There are three basic tabulations of federal debt: (1) gross federal debt, (2) debt held by the public, and (3) debt subject to statutory limit.

debt management Operations of the United States Treasury Department that determine the composition of the federal debt. Debt management involves determining the amounts, maturities, other terms and conditions, and schedule of offerings of federal debt securities and raising new cash to finance the government's operations. The objective of debt management is to raise the money necessary for the government's operations at the least cost to taxpayers, and in a manner that will minimize the effect of government operations on financial markets and the economy.

debt service Payment of interest and principal on borrowed funds. The term may also be used to refer to payment of interest alone.

deferral of budget authority Temporary withholding or delaying of the obligation or expenditure of budget authority, or any other type of executive action that effectively precludes the obligation or expenditure of budget authority. Budget authority may be deferred to provide for contingencies, to achieve savings or greater efficiency in the operations of the government, or as otherwise specifically provided by law. Budget authority may not be deferred in order to effect a policy in lieu of one established by law or for any other reason.

Deferrals may be proposed by agencies, but must be communicated to Congress by the president in a special message. Deferred budget authority may not be withheld from obligation unless an act is passed to approve the deferral and the act is presented to the president. Additionally, unless Congress has approved a deferral, budget authority whose availability expires at the end of the fiscal year must be made available with sufficient time remaining in the fiscal year to obligate that budget authority before the end of the fiscal year.

deficiency appropriation An appropriation made to an expired account to cover obligations that have been incurred in excess of available funds. Deficiency appropriations are rare, because obligating in excess of available funds is generally prohibited by law. Deficiency appropriation is sometimes erroneously used as a synonym for supplemental appropriation.

deficit The amount by which the government's budget outlays exceed its budget receipts for a given period, usually a fiscal year. For purposes of defining deficits under Gramm–Rudman–Hollings as amended by the Budget Enforcement Act, this amount excludes off-budget activities such as the outlays and receipts of the Postal Service and social security. The total deficit is the amount by which the government's on-budget and off-budget outlays exceed the sum of its on-budget and off-budget receipts for a given period, usually a fiscal year.

deficit financing A situation in which the federal government's excess of outlays over receipts for a given period is financed primarily by borrowing from the public.

discretionary A term that usually modifies either "spending," "appropriation," or "amount." "Discretionary spending" refers to outlays controllable through the congressional appropriation process.

earmarking (1) Dedicating collections by law for a specific purpose or program. Earmarked collections comprise trust-fund receipt accounts, special-fund receipt accounts, and offsetting collections credited to appropriation accounts. These collections may be classified as budget receipts, proprietary receipts, or reimbursements to appropriations. (2) Dedicating appropriations for a particular purpose. Legislative language may designate any portion of a lump-sum amount for particular purposes.

entitlements Legislation (entitlement authority) that requires the payment of benefits (or entitlements) to any person or unit of government that meets the eligibility requirements established by such law. Authorizations for entitlements constitute a binding obligation on the part of the federal government, and eligible recipients have legal recourse if the obligation is not fulfilled. Budget authority for such payments is not necessarily provided in advance, and thus entitlement legislation requires the subsequent enactment of appropriations unless the existing appropriation is permanent. Examples of entitlement programs are social security benefits and veterans' compensation or pensions.

fiscal policy Federal government policies with respect to taxes, spending, and debt management that are intended to promote the nation's macroeconomic goals, particularly with respect to employment, gross domestic product, price level stability, equilibrium in the balance of payments, the exchange rate, the current account, and the national savings/investment balance. The budget process is a major vehicle for determining and implementing federal fiscal policy.

fiscal year Any yearly accounting period, regardless of its relationship to a calendar year. The fiscal year for the federal government begins on October 1 of each year and ends on September 30 of the following year; it is designated by the calendar year in which it ends. For example, fiscal year 1990 began October 1, 1989, and ended September 30, 1990. (Prior to fiscal year 1977, the federal fiscal year began on July 1 and ended on June 30.)

full funding Provides budgetary resources to cover the total cost of a program or project at the time it is undertaken. Full funding differs from incremental funding, where budget authority is provided or recorded for only a portion of total estimated obligations expected to be incurred during a single fiscal year. Full funding is generally discussed in terms of multiyear programs, whether or not obligations for the entire program are made in the first year.

functional classification A system of classifying budget resources so that budget authority, outlays, receipts, and tax expenditures can be related to the national needs being addressed. Each concurrent resolution on the budget allocates these budgetary resources—except receipts and tax expenditures—among the various functions in the budget. Each budget account is generally placed in the single budget function (for example, national defense or health) that best reflects its major purpose, an important national need. A function may be divided into two or more subfunctions, depending upon the complexity of the national need addressed.

government-sponsored enterprises Privately owned and operated enterprises established and chartered by the federal government to perform specific functions under the supervision of a government agency. Because they are private corporations, they are excluded from the budget totals.

grant A federal financial assistance award making payment in cash or in kind for a specified purpose. The federal government is not expected to have substantial involvement with the state or local government or other recipient while the contemplated activity is being performed. The term "grants" frequently has a broader meaning and may include grants to nongovernmental recipients, whereas the term "grants-in-aid" is commonly restricted to grants to states and local governments. The two major forms of federal grants-in-aid are block grants and categorical grants.

Block grants are given primarily to general-purpose governmental units in accordance with a statutory formula. Such grants can be used for a variety of activities within a broad functional area. Examples of federal block-grant programs are the Omnibus Crime Control and Safe Street Act of 1968, the Housing and Community Development Act of 1974, and the grants to states for social services under Title XX of the Social Security Act.

Categorical grants can be used only for a specific program. They may be formula or project grants. Formula grants allocate federal funds to states or their subdivisions in accordance with a distribution formula prescribed by law or administrative regulation. Project grants provide federal funding for fixed or known periods for specific projects or the delivery of specific services or products.

impoundment Any action or inaction by an officer or employee of the United States Government that precludes the obligation or expenditure of budget authority provided by Congress.

incremental funding The provision (or recording) of budgetary resources for a program or project, based on obligations estimated to be incurred within a fiscal year, when such budgetary resources will cover only a portion of the obligations to be incurred in completing the program or projects as programmed. This differs from full funding, where budgetary resources are provided or recorded for the total estimated obligations for a program or project in the initial year of funding.

line item In executive budgeting, a particular expenditure, such as program, subprogram, or travel costs and equipment. In congressional budgeting, it usually refers to assumptions about particular programs or accounts implicit but not explicit in the budget resolution. In appropriations acts, it usually refers to an individual account or part of an account for which a specific amount is available.

line-item veto A power (not presently granted to the president) to disapprove—in the same manner allowed under article I, section 7 of the Constitution—one or both of the following: (1) particular items of expenditure or (2) budget accounts indicated in the budget. Granting the president a line-item veto would require a constitutional change or a series of legislative and statutory changes. The line-item veto exists at the state level in forms that vary from state to state.

loan guarantee A loan guarantee is an agreement by which the government pledges to pay part or all of the loan principal and interest to a lender or holder of a security, in the event of default by a third-party borrower. If it becomes necessary for the government to pay part or all of the loan principal or interest, the payment is a direct outlay. Otherwise, the guarantee does not directly affect federal budget outlays.

loan insurance A type of loan guarantee whereby a government agency operates a program of pooled risks, pledging the use of accumulated insurance premiums to secure a lender against default on the part of the borrower.

means of financing Ways in which a budget deficit is financed or a budget surplus is used. A budget deficit may be financed by treasury (or agency) borrowing, by reducing treasury cash balances, by allowing unpaid liabilities to increase, or by certain equivalent transactions. Conversely, a budget surplus may be used to repay borrowings or to build up cash balances.

mission budgeting A budget approach that focuses on purpose rather than input and directs attention to an agency's success in meeting its responsibilities. By grouping programs and activities according to an agency's mission or end purposes, mission budgeting makes it easier to identify similar programs. At the highest level in the budget structure, mission represents basic end-purpose responsibilities assigned to an agency. Descending levels in the budget structure then focus more sharply on the specific components of the mission and the programs needed to satisfy it. Line items, the supporting activities necessary to satisfy the mission, are at the lowest levels in the budget structure.

mixed-ownership government corporation A federally chartered enterprise or business activity designated by statute (31 U.S.C. 856) as a mixed-ownership government corporation. Mixed-ownership government corporations are subject to audits by the General Accounting Office as required by the Government Corporation Control Act, as amended (31 U.S.C. 857). They are also required to submit annual business-type budget statements to the treasury and to the Office of Management and Budget.

multiyear budget planning A process (such as the one used to develop the president's budget and the Congressional budget) designed to ensure that the long-range consequences of budget decisions are identified and reflected in the budget totals. The president's (or executive) budget includes multiyear planning estimates for budget authority, outlays, and receipts for four years beyond the budget year. The Congressional budget process considers estimates covering a three-year period. However, under the Budget Enforcement Act, Congressional budgets cover a five-year period. This process provides a structure for the review and analysis of long-term program and tax policy choices.

object classification A uniform classification identifying the transactions of the federal government by the nature of the goods or services purchased (such as personnel compensation, supplies and materials, and equipment), without regard to the agency involved or the purpose of the programs for which they are used.

obligational authority The sum of (a) budget authority provided for a given fiscal year, (b) balances of amounts brought forward from prior years that remain available for obligation, and (c) amounts authorized to be credited to a specific fund or account during that year, including transfers between funds or accounts.

obligation-based budgeting A system wherein financial transactions involving the use of funds are recorded in the accounts primarily when obligations are incurred, regardless of when the resources acquired are to be consumed.

obligations incurred Amounts of orders placed, contracts awarded, services received, and similar transactions during a given period that will require payments during the same or a future period. Such amounts will include outlays for which obligations had not been previously recorded and will reflect adjustments for differences between obligations previously recorded and actual outlays to liquidate those obligations.

off-budget The term refers to the status of transactions of the government (either federal funds or trust funds) that belong on-budget according to budget concepts but that are required by law to be excluded from the budget. The budget documents routinely report the on-budget and off-budget amounts separately and then add them together to arrive at the consolidated government totals.

outlays The issuance of checks, disbursement of cash, or electronic transfer of funds made to liquidate a federal obligation. Outlays also occur when interest on the treasury debt held by the public accrues, and when the government issues bonds, notes, debentures, monetary credits, or other cash-equivalent instruments in order to liquidate obligations. Also, under credit reform, the credit subsidy cost is recorded as an outlay when a direct or guaranteed loan is disbursed. Outlays during a fiscal year may be for payment of obligations incurred in prior years (prior-year obligations) or in the same year. Outlays, therefore, flow in part from unexpended balances of prior-year budgetary resources and in part from budgetary resources provided for the year in which the money is spent.

program Generally defined as an organized set of activities directed toward a common purpose, or goal, undertaken or proposed by an agency in order to carry out its responsibilities. In practice, however, the term program has many uses and thus does not have a well-defined, standard meaning in the legislative process: It is used to describe an agency's mission, programs, functions, activities, services, projects, and processes.

program evaluation In general, the process of assessing program alternatives, including research and results, and the options for meeting program objectives and future expectations. Specifically, program evaluation is the process of appraising the manner and extent to which programs

- Achieve their stated objectives.
- Meet the performance perceptions and expectations of responsible federal officials and other interested groups.
- Produce other significant effects of either a desirable or undesirable character.

projections Estimates of budget authority, outlays, receipts, or other budget amounts extending several years into the future. Projections are generally intended to indicate the budgetary implications of existing or proposed programs and legislation. Projections may include alternative program and policy strategies and ranges of possible budget amounts. Projections usually are not firm estimates of what will occur in future years, nor are they intended to be recommendations for future budget decisions.

reappropriation Statutory action to continue the availability, whether for the same or different purposes, of all or part of the unobligated portion of budget authority that has expired or would otherwise expire. Reappropriations are counted as budget authority in the first year for which the availability is extended.

reconciliation A process Congress uses to reconcile amounts determined by tax, spending, credit, and debt legislation for a given fiscal year with levels set in the concurrent resolution on the budget for the year. Section 310 of the Congressional Budget and Impoundment Control Act of 1974 (2 U.S.C. 641) provides that the resolution may direct committees to determine and recommend changes to laws, bills, and resolutions as required to conform to totals for budget authority, revenues, and the public debt. Such changes are incorporated into either a reconciliation resolution or a reconciliation bill.

reprogramming Shifting funds within an appropriation or fund account to use them for different purposes than those contemplated at the time of appropriation (e.g., obligating budgetary resources for a different object class from the one originally planned). While a transfer of funds involves shifting funds from one account to another, reprogramming involves shifting funds within an account. Reprogramming is generally preceded by consultation between federal agencies and the appropriate congressional committees. It often involves formal notification and opportunity for congressional committees to state their approval or disapproval.

rescission Legislation enacted by Congress that cancels the availability of budgetary resources previously provided by law before the authority would otherwise lapse.

sequestration (Budget Enforcement Act term) The cancellation, in accordance with the Budget Enforcement Act, of budgetary resources provided by discretionary appropriations or direct spending law. The Budget Enforcement Act created three types of sequestration: discretionary spending sequestration, pay-as-you-go sequestration, and deficit-reduction sequestration.

spending committees The standing committees of the House and Senate with jurisdiction over legislation that permits the obligation of funds. For most programs, the House and Senate Appropriations Committees are the spending committees. For other programs, the authorizing legislation itself permits the obligation of funds (back-door authority). When this is the case, the authorizing committees are then the committees with spending responsibility.

subfunction Subdivisions of a budget function. For example, health care services and health research are subfunctions of the function "health."

subsidy Generally, a payment or benefit made by the federal government for which there is no current charge. Subsidies are designed to support the conduct of an economic enterprise or activity, such as ship operations. They may also refer to provisions in the tax laws that provide certain tax expenditures and to the provisions of loans, goods, and services to the public at prices lower than market value, such as interest subsidies.

substantive law Statutory public law other than appropriation law; sometimes referred to as basic law. Substantive law usually authorizes the executive branch, in broad general terms, to carry out a program of work. Annual determination as to the amount of the work to be done is usually thereafter embodied in an appropriation law.

supplemental appropriation An act appropriating funds in addition to those in an annual appropriations act. Supplemental appropriations provide additional budget authority beyond the original estimates for programs or activities (including new programs authorized after the date of the original appropriations act) in cases where the need for funds is too urgent to be postponed until enactment of the next regular appropriations bills. Supplements may sometimes include items not appropriated in the regular bills for lack of timely authorization.

tax expenditure A revenue loss attributable to a provision of the federal tax laws that (1) allows a special exclusion, exemption, or deduction from gross income or (2) provides a special credit, preferential tax rate, or deferral of tax liability. Tax expenditures are subsidies provided through the tax system. Rather than transferring funds from the government to the private sector, the Treasury Department forgoes some of the receipts that it would have collected, and the beneficiary taxpayers pay lower taxes than they would have had to pay. Examples include tax expenditures for child care and the exclusion of fringe benefits from taxation.

transfer of funds When specifically authorized in law, all or part of the budget authority in one account may be transferred to another account. Depending upon the nature of the transfer, these charges and credits will be treated as either expenditure transfers or nonexpenditure transfers.

unified budget Under budget concepts set forth in the *Report of the President's Commission on Budget Concepts,* a comprehensive budget in which receipts and outlays from federal and trust funds are consolidated. When these fund groups are consolidated to display budget totals, transactions that are outlays of one fund group for payment to the other fund group (that is, interfund transactions) are deducted to avoid double counting. The unified budget should, as conceived by the President's Commission, be comprehensive of the full range of federal activities. However, by law, budget authority, outlays, and receipts of off-budget programs (currently only the U.S. Postal Service and social security) are excluded from the current budget, but data relating to off-budget programs are displayed in the budget documents.

user fee A fee charged to users for goods or services provided by the federal government. User fees generally apply to federal activities that provide special benefits to identifiable recipients above and beyond what is normally available to the public. User fees are normally related to the cost of the goods or services provided. They may be paid into the general fund or, under specific statutory authority, may be made available to an agency carrying out the activity. An example is a fee for entering a national park.

wholly owned government corporation A federally chartered enterprise or business activity designated by statute as a wholly owned government corporation. Each such corporation is required to submit an annual business-type statement to the Office of Management and Budget and is subject to a financial audit by the General Accounting Office, pursuant to the Government Corporation Control Act of 1945. The Pension Benefit Guaranty Corporation is an example of a wholly owned government corporation.

Accounting Terms and Definitions

account A separate financial reporting unit for budget, management, and/or accounting purposes. All budgetary transactions are recorded in accounts, but not all accounts are budgetary in nature (that is, some accounts do not directly affect the budget, but are used purely for accounting purposes). Budget (and off-budget) accounts are used to record all transactions within the budget (or off-budget), whereas other accounts (such as deposit funds, credit financing, and foreign currency accounts) are used for accounting purposes connected with funds that are nonbudgetary in nature.

accounting systems The total structure of records and procedures that record, classify, and report information on the financial position and operations of a governmental unit or any of its funds, balanced account groups, and organizational components.

accrual basis for accounting The basis of accounting under which revenues are recorded when earned and expenditures are recorded when goods are received or services performed, even though the receipt of the revenue or the payment of the expenditure may take place, in whole or part, in another accounting period.

appropriation account/fund account A summary account established in the treasury for each appropriation and/or fund showing transactions in such accounts. Each such account provides the framework for establishing a set of balanced accounts on the books of the agency concerned.

assets Any item of economic value owned by a governmental unit. The item may be physical in nature (tangible) or a right to ownership (intangible) that is expressed in terms of cost or some other value.

cash basis of accounting The basis of accounting whereby revenues are recorded when received in cash and expenditures (outlays) are recorded when paid, without regard to the accounting period to which the transactions apply.

contingent liability An existing condition, situation, or set of circumstances involving uncertainty as to a possible loss to an agency that will ultimately be resolved when one or more future events occur or fail to occur. For the purpose of federal credit programs, a contingent liability is a conditional commitment that may become an actual liability because of a future event beyond the control of the government. Contingent liabilities include such items as loan guarantees and bank deposit insurance.

depreciation The systematic and rational allocation of the costs of equipment and buildings (having a life of more than one year) over their useful lives. To match costs with related revenues in measuring income or determining the costs of carrying out program activities, depreciation reflects the use of the asset(s) during specific operating periods.

fund accounting The legal requirement for federal agencies to establish accounts for segregating revenues and other resources, together with all related liabilities, obligations, and reserves, for the purpose of carrying on specific activities or attaining certain objectives in accordance with special regulations, restrictions, or limitations. Fund accounting, in a broad sense, is required in the federal government to demonstrate agency compliance with requirements of existing legislation for which federal funds have been appropriated or otherwise authorized.

internal control The plan of organization and all of the coordinate methods and measures adopted within a federal agency to safeguard the agency's assets, check the accuracy and reliability of its accounting data, promote operational efficiency, and encourage adherence to prescribed managerial policies.

liabilities Amounts owed for items received, services rendered, expenses incurred, assets acquired, construction performed (regardless of whether invoices have been received), and amounts received but as yet unearned.

Economic Terms and Definitions

ability to pay The principle that the tax burden should be distributed according to a person's income. It is based on the assumption that as a person's income increases, the person can and should contribute a larger percentage of his/her income to support government activities. The progressive federal income tax is based on this principle.

aggregate demand Total purchases of a country's output of goods and services by consumers, businesses, government, and foreigners during a given period.

balance of payments A statistical record of economic transactions between one country, for example, the United States, and the rest of the world. The balance of payments accounts normally distinguish among transactions involving goods, services, short-term capital, and long-term capital.

business cycles The recurrent phases of expansion and contraction in overall business activity, evidenced by fluctuations in measures of aggregate economic activity, notably real gross domestic product. Although business cycles are recurrent, both the duration and the magnitude of individual cycles vary greatly.

constant dollar A dollar value adjusted for changes in prices. Constant dollars are derived by dividing current dollar amounts by an appropriate price index, a process generally known as deflating. The result is a constant dollar series as it would presumably exist if prices and transactions were the same in all subsequent years as the base year. Any changes in such a series would reflect only changes in the real volume of goods and services. Constant dollar figures are commonly used for computing the gross domestic and national product and its components and for estimating total budget outlays.

Consumer Price Index (CPI) A measure of the price level of a fixed "market basket" of goods and services relative to the value of that same basket in a designated base period. Measures for two population groups are currently published, CPI-U and CPI-W. CPI-U is based on a market basket determined by expenditure patterns of all urban households, while the market basket for CPI-W is determined by expenditure patterns of only urban wage-earner and clerical-worker families. The urban wage-earner and clerical-worker population consists of clerical workers, sales workers, craft workers, operatives, service workers, and laborers. Both indexes are published monthly by the Bureau of Labor Statistics. The CPI is used to adjust for inflation the income payments of social security beneficiaries and payments made by other programs.

cost–benefit analysis An analytic technique that compares the costs and benefits of investments, programs, or policy actions in order to determine which alternative or alternatives maximize net benefits. Cost–benefit analysis attempts to consider all costs and benefits, regardless of whether they are reflected in market transactions. The costs and benefits included depend upon the scope of the analysis, for example, private or social, local, state, or national. Net benefits of an alternative are determined by subtracting the present value of costs from the present value of benefits.

cost–effectiveness analysis An analytic technique used to choose the most efficient method, that is, the lowest-cost method, for achieving a given investment program or policy result. The scope of this analysis is more limited than that of cost–benefit analysis, which does not take the program or policy result as a given.

countercyclical policy Policy aimed at reducing the size and duration of swings in economic activity in order to keep economic growth closer to a pace consistent with low inflation and high employment. It includes monetary and fiscal policies affecting the level of interest rates, money supply, taxes, and government spending.

crowding out Most commonly refers to the displacement of private investment expenditures by increases in public expenditures financed by sales of federal government securities. The extent of the displacement depends on such factors as the responsiveness of private savings and investment to changes in interest rates and the degree to which the Federal Reserve monetizes the increase in public debt.

current-account balance The net revenues that arise from a country's international sales and purchases of goods and services, net international transfers (public or private gifts or donations), and net factor income (primarily capital income from foreign-located property owned by residents less capital income from domestic property owned by nonresidents). The current-account balance differs from net exports in that the former includes international transfers and net factor income.

current dollar The dollar value of a good or service in terms of prices current at the time the good or service is sold. This contrasts with the value of the good or service measured in constant dollars.

cyclical deficit The part of the budget deficit that results from cyclical factors rather than from underlying fiscal policy. The cyclical deficit reflects the fact that when GDP falls, revenues automatically fall and outlays automatically rise. By definition, the cyclical deficit is zero when the economy is operating at potential GDP. Compare with standardized-employment deficit.

discount rate One of the following:

(1) The interest rate that a commercial bank pays when it borrows from a Federal Reserve bank. The discount rate is one of the tools of monetary policy used by the Federal Reserve System. The Federal Reserve customarily raises or lowers the discount rate to signal a shift toward restraining or easing its money and credit policy. (*See also* **monetary policy.**)

(2) The interest rate used to determine the present value of a future stream of receipts and outlays, or, in cost–benefit analysis, of benefits and costs. This use of the term is completely distinct from that in monetary policy, and the interest rates involved are generally not those charged by Federal Reserve banks.

domestic demand Total purchases of goods and services, regardless of origin, by U.S. consumers, businesses, and governments during a given period. Domestic demand equals gross domestic product minus net exports.

economic growth An increase in a nation's productive capacity leading to an increase in the production of goods and services. Economic growth is usually measured by the annual rate of increase in real (constant dollars) gross domestic/national product.

GNP gap The difference between the economy's output of goods and services and its potential output at full employment—that is, the difference between actual GNP (gross national product) and potential GNP.

gross domestic product (GDP) The value of all final goods and services produced within the borders of the United States in a given period of time, whether produced by residents or nonresidents.

gross national product (GNP) The market value of all final goods and services produced by labor and property supplied by residents of the United States in a given period of time. Depreciation charges and other allowances for business and institutional consumption of fixed capital goods are subtracted from GNP to derive net national product. GNP comprises the purchases of final goods and services by persons and governments, gross private domestic investment (including the change in business inventories), and net exports (exports less imports). The GNP can be expressed in current or constant dollars.

high-employment budget The estimated receipts, outlays, and surplus or deficit that would occur if the U.S. economy were operating at a specified low level of unemployment (traditionally defined as a certain unemployment rate of the civilian labor force).

implicit price deflator (GDP deflator) For a particular year, the ratio of the gross domestic product's (GDP) current dollar value to its constant dollar value. The deflator is implicit because the constant dollar value for total GDP is calculated independently (as the sum of parts that have been individually adjusted to constant dollar terms). For this reason, the value of the deflator is affected by shifts in current dollar expenditure patterns among categories.

investment Physical investment is the current product set aside during a given period to be used for future production; in other words, an addition to the stock of capital goods. According to the national income and produce accounts, private domestic investment consists of investment in residential and nonresidential struc-tures, producers' durable equipment, and the change in business inventories. Financial investment is the purchase of a financial security. Investment in human capital is spending on education, training, health services, and other activities that increase the productivity of the work force. Investment in human capital is not treated as investment in the national income and product accounts.

macroeconomics The branch of economics concerned with aggregate economic analysis as opposed to the analysis of individual economic units, markets, or industries. For example, macroeconomics includes the study of the general price level, national output or income, and total employment, rather than the prices of individual commodities or particular incomes and the employment of individual firms.

microeconomics The branch of economics concerned with analysis of individual economic units, markets, or industries as opposed to aggregates. For example, microeconomics deals with the division of total output among industries, products, and firms; with the allocation of resources among competing uses; and with the determination for relative prices of particular goods.

monetary policy The strategy of influencing movements of the money supply and interest rates to affect output and inflation. An "easy" monetary policy suggests faster money growth and initially lower short-term interest rates in an attempt to increase aggregate demand, but it may lead to a higher rate of inflation. A "tight" monetary policy suggests slower money growth and higher interest rates in the near term in an attempt to reduce inflationary pressure by reducing aggregate demand. The Federal Reserve System conducts monetary policy in the United States.

national income and product accounts Accounts prepared and published by the Department of Commerce that provide detailed quarterly and annual data on aggregate economic activity within the United States. These accounts depict in dollar terms the composition and use of the nation's output and the distribution of national income to different recipients. With a few exceptions, the output that is measured is the output acquired in market transactions by the final users. The accounts make it possible to measure aggregate output and income and trace trends and fluctuations in economic activity.

national savings Total saving by all sectors of the economy: personal saving, business saving (corporate after-tax profits not paid as dividends), and government saving (budget surplus or deficit—indicating dissaving—of all government entities). National saving represents all income not consumed, publicly or privately, during a given period.

net national saving National saving less depreciation of physical capital.

present value The worth of a future stream of returns or costs in terms of money paid immediately (or at some designated date). A dollar available at some date in the future is worth less than a dollar available today because the latter could be invested at interest in the interim. In calculating present value, prevailing interest rates provide the basis for converting future amounts into their "money now" equivalents.

producer price indexes A set of price measures for producers of commodities in the manufacturing, agriculture, forestry, fishing, mining, gas and electricity, and public utilities sectors. These indexes can be organized by either commodity or stage of processing and are published monthly by the Bureau of Labor Statistics. Changes from one month to another are usually expressed as either monthly or annualized percentage rates of change.

stabilization The maintenance of high-level economic activity with an absence of severe cyclical fluctuations. Stability is usually measured by an absence of fluctuations in production, employment, and prices, three aspects of economic activity that tend to fluctuate in a cyclical fashion.

stagflation The simultaneous existence of high unemployment and high inflation.

standardized-employment budget A budget that removes the influence of economic fluctuations by calculating the level of receipts and expenditures that would occur under current law if economic activity were equal to some estimate of the economy's high-employment potential.

standardized-employment deficit The level of the federal government budget deficit that would occur under current law if the economy were operating at potential GDP. It provides a measure of underlying fiscal policy by removing the influence of cyclical factors from the budget deficit. Compare with cyclical deficit.

technical and economic assumptions Assumptions about factors affecting estimations of future outlays and receipts that are not a direct function of legislation. Economic assumptions involve such factors as the future inflation and interest rates. Technical assumptions involve all other nonpolicy factors. For example, in the Medicare program, estimations regarding demography, hospitalization versus outpatient treatment, and morbidity all affect estimations of future outlays.

transfer payment In the national income and product accounts, a payment made by the federal government or a business firm to an individual or organization for which no current or future goods or services are required in return. Government transfer payments include social security benefits, unemployment insurance benefits, government retirement benefits, and welfare payments. Transfer payments by business firms consist mainly of gifts to nonprofit institutions.

Sources: Adapted from United States General Accounting Office (GAO), *A Glossary of Terms Used in the Federal Budget Process* (Washington, D.C., 1993); United States Congressional Budget Office, *The Economic and Budget Outlook: Fiscal Years 1994–1998* (Washington, D.C., 1993); GAO, *A Glossary of Terms in the Federal Budget Process and Related Accounting, Economic and Tax Terms* (Washington, D.C., 1981).

NOTES

Chapter 1

1. Allen Schick, *The Capacity to Budget* (Washington, D.C.: Urban Institute, 1990).
2. Executive Office of the President, Office of Management and Budget (OMB), *Budget of the United States Government, Historical Tables, Fiscal Year 1995* (Washington, D.C., 1994), Tables 15.2 and 15.3, pp. 238–239. The ratio of governmental expenditures to GDP is no more than a limited rough index. In constant dollars (adjusting for inflation) outlays don't increase as fast as they do in current dollars.
3. Ibid., Tables 1, 6, 7, 8, 9; Tax Foundation, *Facts and Figures on Government Finance, 1992 Edition* (Washington, D.C., 1992), p. 34.
4. OMB, Historical Tables, Table 15.1, p. 237.
5. Ibid., Table 10.
6. Ibid.; U.S. Bureau of the Census, *State Government Finance: 1992* (Washington, D.C., 1993); Tax Foundation, *Facts and Figures on Government Finance, 1992 Edition*, pp. 306–307.
7. ACIR, *Significant Features*, Table 5; Congressional Budget Office (CBO), *The Economic and Budget Outlook* (Washington, D.C., 1993), p. xiii.
8. OMB, *Historical Tables*, Table 15.6, p. 242; National Governors' Association and National Association of State Budget Officers, *The Fiscal Survey of States* (Washington, D.C., 1992), p. 36.
9. ACIR, *Significant Features*, Table 92.
10. Roy Bahl, *Financing State and Local Government in the 1980s* (New York: Oxford Univ. Press, 1984), pp. 17–21.
11. For a pioneering analysis of the dependence of the federal government on third parties, see Frederick C. Mosher, "The Changing Responsibilities and Tactics of the Federal Government," *Public Administration Review* 39 (Nov./Dec. 1980), pp. 542–548.
12. United States General Accounting Office (GAO), *Federal Aid to State and Local Governments,* (Washington, D.C., 1991), pp. 28–30; ACIR, *Significant Features*, p. 5.
13. For an exploration of these issues, see Alice M. Rivlin, *Reviving the American Dream* (Washington, D.C.: Brookings Institution, 1992).
14. For an articulate and skeptical view of planning, see Naomi Caiden and Aaron Wildavsky, *Planning and Budgeting in Poor Countries* (New York: John Wiley & Sons, 1974), pp. 264–291.
15. *PA Times,* Sept. 1, 1993, p. 1.
16. See, for example, Aaron Wildavsky, *The Politics of the Budget Process,* 3d ed. (Boston: Little, Brown & Co., 1979).

17. Ibid. Later, in the face of fiscal cuts in the early 1990s, Wildavsky tended to minimize the role of incrementalism.
18. OMB, *Budget of the United States Government, Fiscal Year 1993* (Washington, D.C., 1992), pp. 1–15.
19. Caiden and Wildavsky, *Poor Countries,* chapters 2–3.

Chapter 2

1. Advisory Commission on Intergovernmental Relations (ACIR), *Significant Features of Fiscal Federalism, 1993 Edition,* Vol. 1 (Washington, D.C., 1993), Table 2.
2. *New York Times,* July 18, 1991, p. B12.
3. For example, see Donald Axelrod, "The Budgetary System of the Arab Republic of Egypt," (Unpublished Report for United Nations, Oct. 1979); Siegmar Kunas, "The Budget of the Federal Republic of Germany," *Public Budgeting and Finance* 2 (Autumn 1982), pp. 47–51.
4. State of Wisconsin, Department of Administration, *Manual for Preparation of the Executive Operating and Capital Budgets, 1993–1995 Biennium* (Madison, April 1992).
5. Robert D. Lee, Jr., "Developments in State Budgeting: Trends of Two Decades," *Public Administration Review* 51 (May/June, 1991), p. 255.
6. State of Oregon, Executive Department, *1993–95 Biennium Budget Instructions* (Salem, 1992).
7. United States General Accounting Office (GAO), *Budget Formulation: Many Approaches Work But Some Improvements Are Needed,* (Washington, D.C., February 29, 1980), pp. 7–9.
8. Joint Financial Management Improvement Program, *Financial Handbook for Federal Executives and Managers* (Washington, D.C., August 1991), pp. 7–8.
9. GAO, *Budget Formulation,* p. 85.
10. Philip G. Joyce and Daniel R. Mullins, "The Changing Fiscal Structure of the State and Local Public Sector," *Public Administration Review* 51 (May/June 1991), pp. 240–253.
11. Charles H. Levine, "Hard Questions for Hard Times" in Charles H. Levine, ed., *Managing Fiscal Stress: The Crisis in the Public Sector* (Chatham, N.J.: Chatham House Publishers, Inc., 1980), pp. 4–11.
12. *Financial Handbook,* p. 9.
13. United States Congress, Congressional Budget Office, *The Economic and Budget Outlook: An Update* (Washington, D.C., September 1982), p. 92; A. Premchand, "Inflation Budgeting" in International Monetary Fund, *Seminar on Budgeting and Expenditure Control* (Washington, D.C., 1982), pp. 77–80.
14. United States General Accounting Office, *Consistent and Uniform Treatment of Inflation Needed in Program Cost Estimates Provided to the Congress* (Washington, D.C., March 1978), pp. i–iv; National Association of State Budget Officers, *Budgetary Process,* (Washington, D.C., 1992) p. 12; Premchand, "Inflation Budgeting," pp. 76–78; Executive Office of the President, Office of Management and Budget (OMB), Circular No. A-11, "Preparation and Submission of Budget Estimates" (Washington, D.C., 1992).
15. For example, see State of Kansas, Division of the Budget, *The Governor's Economic and Demographic Report, 1992–1993* (Topeka, Kansas, 1993); State of Oregon, Executive Department, *Statewide Initiatives* (Salem, 1992); Commonwealth of Pennsylvania, *Governor's Executive Budget, 1993–94* (Harrisburg, 1993); State of Texas, Governor's

Office of Budget and Planning and Legislative Budget Office, *Detailed Instructions for Preparing and Submitting Reports for Legislative Appropriations* (Austin, 1992); Ohio Office of Budget and Management, *Guidance for Preparation of Executive Budget 1994–95* (Columbus, 1992).

16. Gloria A. Grizzle, "Does Budget Format Really Govern the Actions of Budgetmakers?," Public Budgeting and Finance 6 (Spring 1986), pp. 60–72.

17. President's Commission on Budget Concepts, Report (Washington, D.C., 1967), pp. 24–26.

18. Elmer B. Staats, "Financial Management Improvements: An Agenda for Federal Managers," Public Budgeting and Finance 1 (Spring 1981), p. 46.

19. Council of State Governments, Project Committee of State Accounting Project, "Budgeting Accounting Relationships" (Lexington, Ky., 1982).

20. State of California, Governor's Budget 1992–93, (Sacramento, 1992), Appendix 7; State of New York, Executive Budget for the Fiscal Year April 1, 1993 to March 31, 1994 (Albany, N.Y., 1993), pp. xiv–xviii.

21. Richard Goode, Government Finance in Developing Countries (Washington, D.C.: The Brookings Institution, 1984), p. 28.

22. OMB, "Preparation and Submission of Budget Estimates, 1992."

23. Staats, "Financial Management Improvements," p. 46.

24. Allen Schick, "Controlling Nonconventional Expenditure" 27, Public Budgeting and Finance 6, No. 1, pp. 3–17.

25. Grizzle, "Does Budget Format Really Govern the Actions of Budgetmakers?"; State of California, Statutes of 1979 (SB14), Chapter 503 and Memorandum (Sacramento, 1979); State of California, Department of Finance, "Program Base Analysis Requirements of the 1982–83 Governor's Budget," (Sacramento, March 2, 1981).

Chapter 3

1. Joint Financial Management Improvement Program (JFMIP), 1992 Report on Financial Management Improvement (Washington, D.C., 1993).

2. United States General Accounting Office (GAO), Budget Formulation: Many Approaches Work But Some Improvements are Needed, (Washington, D.C., February 29, 1980), p. 37.

3. Ibid., p. 111.

4. Ibid., p. 142.

5. Joint Financial Management Improvement Program (JFMIP), Operating Budgets: A Practical Approach (Washington, D.C., November 1975), pp. 1–2.

6. Executive Office of the President, Office of Management and Budget (OMB), Budget of the United States Government, Fiscal Year 1993, Appendix one-140.

7. Tax Foundation, Facts and Figures on Government Finance, 1992 Edition (Washington, D.C., 1992), pp. 23–24.

8. OMB, Circular No. A-11, "Preparation and Submission of Budget Estimates" (Washington D.C., 1992), p. 28.

9. JFMIP, Operating Budgets, p. 8.

10. GAO, Budget Formulation, pp. 1–2.

11. PA Times, September 1, 1993, p. 1.

12. This summary synthesizes various budget practices in several federal agencies; the states of California, New York, Wisconsin, Oregon, Washington, Texas, Ohio, North

Carolina, Pennsylvania, and Illinois; and the governments of Britain, France, Sweden, Brazil, and Mexico.

13. Aaron Wildavsky, *The Politics of the Budgetary Process,* Third Edition (Boston: Little, Brown & Co., 1979), pp. 63–126.

14. OMB, "Preparation and Submission of Budget Estimates," p. 23.

15. State of New Jersey, *Budget Fiscal Year 1992–93* (Trenton, 1992), p. D-161.

16. Howard F. Miller, "A Public Accounting: Behind the State Budget," *Public Budgeting and Finance* 1 (Winter 1981), p. 70.

17. This is certainly the case in the states of Wisconsin, Texas, and New Jersey, which have comprehensive and open budget processes.

Chapter 4

1. Joint Financial Management Improvement Program (JFMIP), *Financial Handbook for Federal Executives and Managers* (Washington, D.C., 1991), pp. 4–5.

2. For a comprehensive analysis of the evolution of OMB see Larry Berman, *The Office of Management and Budget and the Presidency, 1921–1979* (Princeton, N. J.: Princeton Univ. Press, 1979); Fritz Morstein Marx, "The Bureau of the Budget: Its Evolution and Present Role," *The American Political Science Review* XXXIX (August 1945), pp. 653–684 and XXXIX (October 1945), pp. 869–898; Frederick C. Mosher, *A Tale of Two Agencies* (Baton Rouge, La.: Louisana State Univ. Press, 1984); Allen Schick, *The Capacity to Budget* (Washington, D.C.: Urban Institute, 1990).

3. National Association of State Budget Officers, "Principles for State Executive Budget Offices" (Lexington, Ky.: The Council of State Governments, 1973), pp. 3–4.

4. Based on a survey of six states and correspondence with twenty states in 1991 and 1992.

5. Theodore Poister and Gregory Streib, "Management Tools in Municipal Government Trends over the Past Decade," *Public Administration Review* (May/June 1989), pp. 240–248.

6. Berman, *The Office of Management and Budget and the Presidency,* p. 91.

7. Mosher, *A Tale of Two Agencies,* p. 26.

8. Hugh Heclo, "OMB and the Presidency—the Problem of 'Neutral Competence'" *Public Interest* (Winter 1975), p. 85.

9. Ibid., p. 81.

10. Ibid., p. 83.

11. Ibid., p. 91; Allen Schick, "The President's Budget Problem," *Public Budgeting and Finance* 1 (Winter 1981), p. 63.

12. Mosher, *A Tale of Two Agencies,* p. 130.

13. Ibid., p. 131.

14. Dale McComber, "A Public Accounting: An OMB Retrospective," *Public Budgeting and Finance* 1 (Spring 1981), p. 81; Allen Schick, "The Budget Bureau That Was: Thoughts on the Rise, Decline and Future of a Presidential Agency," *Law and Contemporary Problems* XXXV (Summer 1970), pp. 519–539; Larry Berman, "OMB and the Hazards of Presidential Staff Work," *Public Administration Review* 38 (November/December 1974), pp. 520–24; Samuel Stafford, "Political OMB Cuts Agencies to Size," *Government Executive* (August 1974), pp. 20–22.

15. Mosher, *A Tale of Two Agencies,* p. 135.

16. Heclo, "OMB and the Presidency," p. 88.

17. McComber, "A Public Accounting," p. 81.

18. Mosher, *A Tale of Two Agencies,* p. 135; Berman, "OMB and the Hazards of Presidential Staff Work," p. 523.

19. New York State Budget Division, "Fiscal Guidelines for 1988–89" (Albany, N.Y., 1988).

20. Mosher, *A Tale of Two Agencies,* pp. 120–121.

21. Congressional Budget Office (CBO), *The Economic and Budget Outlook: Fiscal Years 1994–1998* (Washington, D.C., 1993), p. 110; ———, *The Economic and Budget Outlook: Fiscal Years 1995–1999,* (Washington, D.C., 1994), p. 76.

22. CBO, *The Economic and Budget Outlook: Fiscal Years 1994–1998* (Washington, D.C., 1993), pp. 1–22.

23. Ibid., p. 109.

24. William J. Shkurti, "A User's Guide to State Revenue Forecasting," *Public Budgeting and Finance* (Spring 1990), pp. 79–80.

25. Congressional Budget Office, *A Review of the Accuracy of Treasury Revenue Forecasts, 1963–1978* (Washington, D.C., 1981), pp. 1–2.

26. United States General Accounting Office, *1991 Budget Estimates* (Washington, D.C., 1992), p. 4.

27. National Governors' Association and National Association of State Budget Officers, *The Fiscal Survey of States* (Washington, D.C., 1992), p. 7.

28. Ibid., pp. 48–49.

29. *City and State,* April 24, 1989; *State Budget and Tax News,* May 21, 1992.

30. *Barron's,* December 2, 1991, pp. 8–17; *State Policy Reports,* July 1991, June 1990; *New York Times,* Dec. 7, 1993, p. B1; July 12, 1989, p. B1; *Governing,* January 1989, p. 118.

31. William Greider, *The Education of David Stockman and Other Americans* (New York: E. P. Dutton, 1981), p. x. The book is an amplified version of "The Education of David Stockman," *Atlantic Monthly* CCXLVII (December 1981), pp. 27–54. For a personal and colorful account of Stockman's years as budget director, see David A. Stockman, *The Triumph of Politics* (New York: Avon Books, 1987).

32. Greider, *Education of David Stockman,* pp. 37–54.

33. *Barron's,* February 14, 1994, p. 10.

34. *Governing,* January 1989, p. 47.

35. Greider, *Education of David Stockman,* p. 123.

36. Richard P. Nathan, "OMB—One Year Later." (Paper delivered at the annual meeting of the American Political Science Association, Chicago, Sept. 10, 1971, citing comments by Kermit Gordon, former Director of the U.S. Bureau of the Budget, at the Pollak Lectures at Harvard University in 1965.)

37. United Nations, *A Manual for Government Accounting* (New York, 1970), pp. 17–21; International Monetary Fund, *A Manual on Government Financial Statistics,* draft, (Washington, D.C., 1974), pp. 191–3, 208–9.

38. State of Wisconsin, Department of Administration, *Executive Budget Policy Issue Papers, 1993–94 Biennium* (Madison, 1993).

39. For example, see North Carolina, Office of State Budget and Management, *Post-Legislative Summary of Appropriations, 1993–1994* (Raleigh, 1993); State of Florida, Office of the Governor, *1993 1994 Biennial Budget, 1992 Amendment* (Tallahassee, 1991).

40. For example, see State of Wisconsin, Department of Administration, *Annual Fiscal Report for Year Ending June 30, 1991* (Madison, 1991).

41. See Chapter 11.

Chapter 5

1. United States General Accounting Office (GAO), *Pros and Cons of a Separate Capital Budget for the Federal Government* (Washington, D.C., 1983), pp. 32, 33, 35.
2. United States Department of Commerce, Bureau of the Census, *Governmental Finances in 1990–91* (Washington, D.C., October 1991) p. 13.
3. GAO, Separate Capital Budget, p. 33.
4. Government Finance Research Center of the Municipal Officers Association, *Building Prosperity: Financing Public Infrastructure for Economic Development* (Washington, D.C., 1983), p. 118.
5. National Association of State Budget Officers (NASBO), *Capital Budgeting in the States: Paths to Success* (Washington, D.C., 1992).
6. Executive Office of the President, Office of Management and Budget, (OMB) *Budget of the United States Government FY 1993,* (Washington, D.C., 1992), part 3, p. 35.
7. GAO, *Separate Capital Budget,* p. 32.
8. Advisory Commission on Intergovernmental Relations (ACIR), *Significant Features of Fiscal Federalism,* Vol. 2 (Washington, D.C., 1993), Tables 24, 29.
9. NASBO, *Capital Budgeting in the States.*
10. GAO, *Separate Capital Budget,* p. 2.
11. Ibid.
12. United States General Accounting Office (GAO), *Budget Issues: Budgeting Practices in West Germany, France, Sweden and Great Britain* (Washington, D.C., 1986).
13. D.A.F. Auld, *Budget Reform: Should There Be a Capital Budget for the Public Sector?* (Toronto: C. D. Howe Institute, 1984), p. 1.
14. National Council on Public Works Improvement (NCPWI), *Fragile Foundations: A Report on America's Public Works* (Washington, D.C., 1988); Committee for Economic Development, Research and Policy Committee, *Strengthening the Federal Budget Process: A Requirement for Effective Fiscal Control* (New York, 1983), pp. 42–43; United States General Accounting Office (GAO), *Federal Capital Budgeting, A Collection of Haphazard Practices* (Washington, D.C., 1981), pp. 3–4; Pat Choate and Susan Walter, *America in Ruins: Beyond the Public Works Pork Barrel* (Washington, D.C.: The Council of State Planning Agencies, 1981), p. 3.
15. GAO, *Separate Capital Budget,* p. 36.
16. United States General Accounting Office, *Capital Investment* (Washington, D.C., 1992).
17. Maynard, S. Comiez, *A Capital Budget Statement for the United States Government* (Washington, D.C.: The Brookings Institution, 1966), pp. 13, 30–33.
18. NCPWI, *Fragile Foundations.*
19. United States General Accounting Office, (GAO), *Capital Budgeting Information* (Washington, D.C., 1989).
20. Otis L. Graham, *Toward A Planned Society: From Roosevelt to Nixon* (New York: Oxford Univ. Press, 1976), p. 14.
21. State of Hawaii, *State Capital Improvements* (Honolulu: Legislative Auditor, updated since 1968 version appeared).
22. NASBO, *Capital Budgeting,* p. 6.
23. California Office of Legislative Analysis, *Analysis of the 1990–91 Budget Bill* (Sacramento, 1990), p. 1, 202.
24. Harry P. Hatry, Anne P. Millar, and James Evans, *Capital Investments: Priority Setting Process in Local Governments* (Washington, D.C.: The Urban Institute, 1982).

25. Illinois Department of Commerce and Community Affairs, *Capital Improvement Planning and Budgeting* (Springfield, 1988), pp. 9, 34.
26. Robert L. Bland and Samuel Nunn, "The Impact of Capital Spending on Municipal Operating Budgets" *Public Budgeting and Finance* (Summer 1992), pp. 33–37.
27. GAO, *Capital Budgeting.*
28. State of Hawaii, *State Capital Improvements,* p. 16.
29. National Council on Public Works Improvement, *The Nation's Public Works: Defining the Issues* (Washington, D.C., 1986).
30. Alan W. Steiss, *Local Government Finance: Capital Facilities Planning and Debt Administration* (Lexington, Mass.: Lexington Books, 1975), p. 88; United States General Accounting Office (GAO), *Effective Planning and Budgeting Practices Can Help Arrest the Nation's Deteriorating Public Infrastructure* (Washington, D.C., 1982), p. 43.
31. See Robert Haveman, *The Economics of the Public Sector* (New York: John Wiley & Sons, 1970); Robert Dorfman, ed., *Measuring Benefits of Government Investments* (Washington, D.C.: The Brookings Institution, 1965); A. R. Prest and Ralph Turvey, "Cost Benefit Analysis: A Survey," *Economic Journal* (1965), pp. 683–735; Harley H. Hinrich and Graeme M. Taylor, ed., *Program Budgeting and Benefit–Cost Analysis* (Pacific Palisades, Calif.: Goodyear Publishing Co., 1969); Roland N. McKean, *Public Spending* (New York: McGraw Hill, 1968); Otto Eckstein, *Water Resource Development* (Cambridge, Mass.: Harvard Univ. Press, 1958).
32. Raymond E. Mikesell, *The Rate of Discount for Evaluating Public Projects* (Washington, D.C.: American Enterprise Institute, 1977), p. 5.
33. United States General Accounting Office (GAO), *Civil Agencies Make Limited Use of Cost–Benefit Analysis in Support of Budget Requests* (Washington, D.C., 1975), pp. 1–7.
34. Mikesell, *The Rate of Discount.*
35. Charles K. Coe, "Life-Cycle Costing by State Governments," *Public Administration Review* (Sept./Oct. 1981), pp. 564–66.
36. United States General Accounting Office, *Greater Use of Value Engineering* (Washington, D.C., 1985).
37. State of Texas, Governor's Budget and Planning Office and the Legislative Budget Office, *Detailed Instructions for Preparing and Submitting Requests for Legislative Appropriations For the Biennium Beginning September 1991* (Austin, 1990).
38. State of Hawaii, *State Capital Improvements,* p. 4.
39. NASBO, *Capital Budgeting,* pp. 53–62.
40. Department of Commerce, Bureau of the Census, *Governmental Finances,* Series GF, No. 5 (Washington, D.C., various years).
41. Bernard Jump, Jr., "Meeting State and Local Financing Needs in the 1980s: Can the Municipal Debt Market Do Its Share," *Public Budgeting and Finance* 2 (Winter 1982), pp. 58–60; GAO, *Federal Capital Budgeting,* pp. 87–89.
42. OMB, *Budget of the United States Government, FY 1993,* part 3, pp. 8–28.
43. *South Carolina v. Baker,* (1988).
44. Donald Axelrod, *Shadow Government* (New York: John Wiley & Sons, 1992), p. 19.
45. Robert P. Inman, "Anatomy of a Fiscal Crisis," *Business Review* (Federal Reserve Bank of Philadelphia), (Sept./Oct. 1983), pp. 15–22; Twentieth Century Fund (Report of the Task Force on the Municipal Bond Market), *Building a Broader Market* (New York: McGraw-Hill, 1976), pp. 56–59; State of New York, "Official Statement, 1979, Tax and Revenue Anticipation Notes" (Albany, May 9, 1979); Axelrod, *Shadow Government,* pp. 63–72.

46. Public Securities Association, *Fundamentals of Municipal Bonds,* (New York, 1981), pp. 115–124.

47. Advisory Commission on Intergovernmental Relations, *Understanding the Market for State and Local Debt,* M104 (Washington, D.C., 1981), pp. 46–53.

48. Merl M. Hackbart and James S. Leigland, "State Debt Management Policy," *Public Budgeting and Finance* (Spring 1990), pp. 37–54.

49. John E. Petersen and Wesley C. Hough, *Creative Capital Financing for State and Local Governments* (Chicago: Municipal Finance Officers Association, 1983), p. 140; GAO, *Effective Planning and Budgeting Practices,* pp. 29–34.

50. Axelrod, *Shadow Government,* Chapter 5.

51. Ibid., Chapter 2.

52. Ibid., pp. 44–49.

53. Twentieth Century Fund, *The Rating Game,* (New York: Twentieth Century Fund, 1974) pp. 8–11, 51–54; Public Securities Association, *Fundamentals of Municipal Bonds,* p. 40.

54. James Leigland and Merl Hackbart, "Case Studies in State Debt Management" (unpublished paper, June 2, 1989).

55. NASBO, *Capital Budgeting,* p. 7.

Chapter 6

1. The major studies are several definitive articles on government corporations and Government-Sponsored Enterprises by Harold Seidman; Annmarie Hauck Walsh, *The Public's Business* (Cambridge, Mass.: MIT Press, 1978); Diana B. Henriques, *The Machinery of Greed* (Lexington, Mass.: Lexington Books, 1980); James T. Bennett and Thomas J. DiLorenzo, *Underground Government: The Off-Budget Public Sector* (Washington, D.C.: CATO Institute, 1983); Donald Axelrod, *Shadow Government* (New York: Wiley & Sons, 1992).

2. Executive Office of the President, Office of Management and Budget (OMB), *Budget of the United States Government, Fiscal Year 1994,* (Washington, D.C., 1992), p. 148.

3. Ibid., Appendix One-148.

4. OMB, *Budget of the United States Government, Fiscal Year 1994,* p. 51.

5. Ibid., p. 56; *New York Times,* February 21, 1994, p. B6.

6. Axelrod, *Shadow Government,* p. 27.

7. OMB, *Budget of the United States Government, Fiscal Year 1985,* "Special Analysis F, Federal Credit Programs", pp. F1–2.

8. Harold Seidman, "Nonprofit Intermediaries: Symptom or Cure?" in Harold Orlans, ed., *Nonprofit Organizations* (New York: Praeger, 1980), pp. 41–43.

9. National Academy of Public Administration (NAPA), *Report on Government Corporations* (Washington, D.C., 1981), pp. 9–12.

10. Ibid., pp. iii–iv.

11. OMB, *Budget of the U.S. Government, FY 1994,* pp. 49–51; Congressional Budget Office (CBO), *Credit Reform* (Washington, D.C., 1989); CBO, *Budgeting for Administrative Costs Under Credit Programs* (Washington, D.C., 1992), p. 1.

12. CBO, *Budgeting Treatment of Deposit Insurers* (Washington, D.C., 1991).

13. CBO, *Government Sponsored Enterprises* (Washington, D.C., 1991), pp. xxi–xxv.

14. OMB, *Budget of the U.S. Government, FY 1994,* p. 51.

15. CBO, *Government Sponsored Enterprises,* p. 2.

16. Ibid., pp. 2–4.
17. Ibid., p. 2.
18. United States General Accounting Office (GAO), *Regulatory Proposal for Government Sponsored Enterprises* (Washington, D.C., 1991), p. 3.
19. CBO, *Government Sponsored Enterprises,* p. xviii.
20. Thomas H. Stanton, "Increasing the Accountability of Government–Sponsored Enterprises: Next Steps," *Public Administration Review* (Nov./Dec. 1991), p. 574; CBO, *Government Sponsored Enterprises,* pp. xxxix, 242–243; GAO, *Regulatory Proposal,* p. 4; Harold Seidman, "Government Sponsored Enterprises," *Public Budgeting and Finance* (Autumn 1989), pp. 76–88.
21. Axelrod, *Shadow Government,* p. iii.
22. United States Bureau of the Census, *1992 Census of Governments,* vol. 1 (Washington, D.C., 1993); ———, *Preliminary Report,* "Government Units in 1992" (Washington, D.C., 1992).
23. Annmarie Walsh, "Forward," in Xenia W. Duisin, *Government Corporations, Special Districts and Public Authorities: Their Organization and Management: A Selected Annotated Bibliography* (New York: Institute of Public Administration, 1985).
24. Axelrod, *Shadow Government,* p. 15.
25. Ibid., p. 15.
26. Ibid., p. 15–16.
27. Ibid., p. iii.
28. Bennett and DiLorenzo, *Underground Government,* p. 59.
29. Axelrod, *Shadow Government,* p. 17.
30. Ibid., p. 39.
31. Ibid., p. 39.
32. Ibid., Chapter 13.
33. Bennett and DiLorenzo, *Underground Government,* pp. 103–106.
34. Axelrod, *Shadow Government,* pp. 316–317.

Chapter 7

1. Allen Schick, "Introduction," in Allen Schick, ed., *Making Economic Policy in Congress* (Washington, D.C.: American Enterprise Institute, 1983), pp. 1–2; A. Premchand, *Government Budgeting and Expenditure Control* (Washington, D.C.: International Monetary Fund, 1983), p. 3.
2. The centerpiece of John Maynard Keynes theories is *The General Theory of Employment, Interest and Money* (New York: Harcourt Brace, 1936).
3. Schick, "Introduction," *Making Economic Policy.*
4. Based on Congressional Budget Office (CBO), *The Economic and Budget Outlook: Fiscal Years 1994–1998* (Washington, D.C., 1993), p. 110; ———, *The Economic and Budget Outlook: Fiscal Years 1995–1999,* p. 76.
5. Lance T. LeLoup, "Congress and the Dilemma of Economic Policy," in Schick, *Making Economic Policy,* p. 31.
6. Alice M. Rivlin, "Overview," in Alice M. Rivlin, ed., *Economic Choices, 1984* (Washington, D.C.: The Brookings Institution, 1984), p. 5.
7. Isabel V. Sawhill, "The Program for Economic Recovery," in John L. Palmer and Isabel V. Sawhill, *The Reagan Experiment* (Washington, D.C.: The Urban Institute, 1982), p. 35; CBO, *Closing of Fiscal Policy Loop: A Long-Run Analysis* (Washington, D.C.,

1977), pp. 1–2; Samuel Brittan, *The Role and Limits of Governments* (London: Maurice Temple Smith Ltd., 1983), p. 14.

8. Le Loup, "Dilemma of Economic Policy," pp. 17–21.

9. Robert D. Reischauer, "Getting, Using and Misusing Economic Information," in Schick, *Making Economic Policy,* p. 40.

10. CBO, *Understanding Fiscal Policy* (Washington, D.C., 1978), p. 37.

11. John W. Ellwood, "Budget Control in a Redistributive Environment" in Schick, *Making Economic Policy,* p. 90; J. Howard McClure and Thomas D. Willett, "Understanding the Supply-siders," in William C. Stubblebine and Thomas D. Willett, *Reaganomics: A Midterm Report* (San Francisco: Institute of Contemporary Studies, 1983), pp. 61–62; David G. Raboy, ed., *Essays in Supply-side Economics* (Washington, D.C.: Institute for Research on the Economics of Taxation, 1982). Among the theoretical fountainheads of supply-side economics are Victor A. Canto, Douglas H. Jones, and Arthur B. Laffer, *Foundations of Supply-Side Economics: Theory and Evidence* (New York: Academic Press, 1983); Paul Craig Roberts, *The Supply-Side Revolution* (Cambridge, Mass.: Harvard Univ. Press, 1984); George Gilder, *Wealth and Poverty* (New York: Basic Books, 1981); Arthur Laffer and Jan P. Seymour, *The Economics of the Tax Revolt* (New York: Harcourt Brace Jovanovich, 1979); David G. Tuerck, "Rational Expectations and Supply Side Economics: Match or Mismatch," in David G. Raboy, ed., *Research on the Economics of Taxation* (Washington, D.C.: Institute for Research on Economics of Taxation, 1982), pp. 65–92. For a conservative, though balanced, review of economic policy in various administrations see Herbert Stein, *Presidential Economics: The Making of Economic Policy From Roosevelt to Reagan and Beyond* (New York: Simon & Schuster, 1984).

12. Tax Foundation, *Facts and Figures on Government Finance, 1992 Edition* (Washington, D.C., 1992), p. 105.

13. Executive Office of the President, Office of Management and Budget, *Budget of the United States Government, Fiscal Year 1993* (Washington, D.C., 1993), Part one, p. 15.

14. CBO, *Economic and Budget Outlook 1994–1998,* pp. 41–45.

15. United States General Accounting Office (GAO), *An Analysis of the Effects of Indexing for Inflation on Federal Expenditures* (Washington, D.C., 1979), pp. i–ii; CBO, *An Analysis of the President's Budgetary Proposals for Fiscal Year 1983* (Washington, D.C., 1982), p. 57.

16. OMB, *Budget of the United States Government, Fiscal Year 1993,* Part two, pp. 39–40.

17. OMB, *Budget of the United States Government Historical Tables Fiscal Year 1995* (Washington, D.C., 1994), p. 237; Advisory Commission on Intergovernmental Relations, (ACIR) *Significant Features of Fiscal Federalism,* 1993 edition, vol. 2, (Washington, D.C., 1993), Tables 25, 31, 47, 51, 59.

18. Helen F. Ladd, "The Meaning of Balance for State–Local Tax Systems, in Steven D. Gold, ed., *The Unfinished Agenda for State Tax Reform* (Denver: National Conference of State Legislatures, 1988).

19. ACIR, *Changing Public Attitudes on Government and Taxes* (Washington, D.C., 1992).

20. CBO, *Economic and Budget Outlook 1994–1998,* pp. 66–68.

21. Cited in *New York Times,* Dec. 8, 1992, p. D1.

22. Howard E. Shuman, *Politics and the Budget,* Second edition (New York: Prentice Hall, 1988), p. 245.

23. Organization for Economic Cooperation and Development (OECD), *Revenue Statistics of OECD Member Countries, 1965–1992* (Paris, 1991).

24. CBO, *Economic and Budget Outlook: Fiscal Years 1994–1998,* p. 337.

25. Henry J. Aaron and Harvey Galper, *Assessing Tax Reform* (Washington, D.C.: The Brookings Institution, 1985), pp. 8, 10, 75.

26. Timothy J. Conlan, Margaret T. Wrightson, and David R. Bean, *Taxing Choices* (Washington, D.C.: Congressional Quarterly Press, 1990), pp. 2–6.

27. *New York Times,* May 28, 1993, p. A12.

28. Ibid; Feb. 18, 1993, p. A1.

29. CBO, *Effects of Adopting A Value Added Tax* (Washington, D.C., 1992).

30. *New York Times,* June 8, 1993, p. A21.

31. GAO, *Tax Policy* (Washington, D.C., 1990).

32. *New York Times,* November 3, 1993.

33. CBO, *How Capital Gains Tax Rates Affect Revenue,* (Washington, D.C., 1988).

34. OMB, *Budget of the United States Government, Fiscal Year 1994,* (Washington, D.C., 1993), Part two, pp. 1–12 (the Bush Budget); ———, p. 17 (the Clinton Budget).

35. Ibid., Part II, p. 7.

36. CBO, *The Federal Deficit: Does It Measure the Government's Effect on National Savings?* (Washington, D.C., 1990), pp. 1, 8.

37. Benjamin M. Friedman, *Day of Reckoning* (New York: Random House, 1988), p. 10.

38. GAO, *An Analysis of Fiscal and Monetary Policies* (Washington, D.C., 1982), p. 23.

39. Robert Eisner, *How Real is the Federal Deficit?* (New York: Free Press, 1986).

40. Ibid.

41. Ibid.; Tom Wicker, "Policy and Perception," *New York Times,* May 27, 1986; Robert Eisner, "Deficit Madness," *New York Times,* July 14, 1984, p. 23. According to Eisner the failure to measure deficits correctly distorts decision making in fiscal policy.

42. CBO, *Balancing the Federal Budget and Limiting Spending: Constitutional and Statutory Approaches* (Washington, D.C., 1982), p. 9.

43. CBO, *Reducing the Deficit* (Washington, D.C., 1993).

44. GAO, *Budget Deficit* (Washington, D.C., 1990).

45. CBO, *Balancing the Federal Budget,* pp. 1–3.

46. CBO, *Reducing the Deficit,* p. 7; *New York Times,* Feb. 25, 1994, p. A14.

47. CBO, *Balancing the Federal Budget,* pp. 69–72.

48. GAO, *Balanced Budget Requirements* (Washington, D.C., 1993).

49. CBO, *Reducing the Deficit,* p. 8.

50. Samuel M. Cohn, "Needed Disciplines in Federal Budget Policy," *Tax Review* (January 1977), p. 1.

51. Aaron Wildavsky, *How to Limit Government Spending* (Berkeley: Univ. of Calif. Press, 1982); James Buchanan and Richard E. Wagner, *Democracy in Deficit: The Political Legacy of Lord Keynes* (New York: Academic Press, 1977); Edmond R. Tufts, *Political Control of the Economy* (Princeton, N.J.: Princeton Univ. Press, 1980); Aaron Wildavsky, "Constitutional Expenditures Limitation and Congressional Budget Reform," in Rudolph G. Penner, *The Congressional Budget Process After Five Years* (Washington, D.C.: American Enterprise Institute, 1981), pp. 87–100.

52. CBO, *Economic and Budget Outlook* 1994–1998, p. 7.

53. Ibid., p. 87.

54. Louis Fisher, "The Effects of a Balanced Budget Amendment on Political Institutions," *Journal of Law and Politics,* vol. IX (1989), pp. 96–100.

55. Ibid., p. 93.

56. *Public Administration Times,* Oct. 1, 1992, p. 6.

57. CBO, *The Budgetary Status of the Federal Reserve System* (Washington, D.C., 1985); Don Fair, "The Independence of Central Banks," *The Banker,* vol. 129 (October

1979), pp. 33–41; "Central Banking Arrangements in Selected European Countries," *International Currency Review*, vol. 12 (1980); CBO, *Economic and Budget Outlook 1994–1998*, pp. 76–81; William Greider, *Secrets of the Temple* (New York: Simon & Schuster, 1987); Bank for International Settlements, *Eight European Central Banks* (New York: Praeger, 1963); Sherman J. Maisel, *Managing the Dollars* (New York: W. W. Norton & Co., 1983), pp. 34–39.

58. National Governors' Association and the National Association of State Budget Officers (NASBO), *The Fiscal Survey of States*, (Washington, D.C., 1992), p. 23; ———, 1993; National Conference of State Legislatures, The Fiscal Letter, Nov./Dec. 1993.

59. Ibid., pp. 7–8, 11.

60. James Savage, "California's Structure Deficit Crisis," *Public Budgeting and Finance* (Summer 1992), pp. 82–95.

61. NASBO, "State Balanced Budget Requirements: Provisions and Practice" (Washington, D.C., 1992).

62. Ibid.; GAO, *Balanced Budget Requirements*.

63. GAO, *Balanced Budget Requirements*, pp. 21–23.

64. ACIR, *Significant Features of Fiscal Federalism*, 1993 edition, vol. 1, (Washington, D.C., 1993), Table 6; "NASBO News," Nov. 1993.

65. Donald Axelrod, *Shadow Government* (New York: Wiley, 1992), pp. 36–37.

66. United States Bureau of the Census, *State Government Finances: 1992* (Washington, D.C., 1993), Table 1.

67. Steven D. Gold and Jennifer McCormick, "Trends in Federal Aid to States Since 1989" (Albany, N.Y.: Rockefeller Institute of Government, State Univ. of New York, 1993).

68. American Heritage Foundation, *How Washington Boosts State-Local Budget Deficits* (Washington, D.C., 1990); *New York Times*, March 24, 1992, p. A.

69. ACIR, *Significant Features*, 1993, Table 41, pp. 212, 219; Center for the Study of the States, *State Policies Affecting Cities and Counties in 1991* (Albany, N.Y.: Rockefeller Institute of Government, State Univ. of New York, 1992).

70. Ronald K. Snell, "Earmarking State Tax Revenues," *Intergovernmental Perspective* (Fall, 1990), pp. 12–16; Steven D. Gold, Brenda Erickson, and Michelle Kissell, *Earmarking State Taxes* (Denver: National Conference of State Legislatures, 1987).

71. Jane Roberts, Jerry Fensterman, and Donald Lief, "States, Localities Continue to Adopt Strategic Policies," *Intergovernmental Perspective*, vol. 1 (Winter 1985), p. 19.

72. ACIR, *Significant Features*, 1993, Table 73, 99; National Conference of State Legislatures, *State Budget Actions 1992* (Denver, 1992).

73. Center for the Study of the States, *State Tax Reform in 1991: An Overview* (Albany, N.Y.: Rockefeller Institute of Government, 1992).

74. "NASBO News," July 1992.

75. Center for the Study of the States, *State Tax Reform*, p. 27.

76. Ibid., p. vii.

77. Carol E. Cohen, "State Fiscal Capacity and Effort: The 1988 Representative Tax System Estimates," *Intergovernmental Perspective* (Fall 1990), pp. 17–22.

78. Hal Hovey, "State and Local Tax Policy: Looking Ahead," *Intergovernmental Perspective* (Fall 1990), p. 7.

79. Gold and McCormick, "Trends in Federal Aid," pp. 24–25.

80. ACIR, *Significant Features*, 1993, vol. 1, table 7.

81. James P. Piffner, "Budgeting and the People's Reforms," *Public Administration Review*, vol. 40 (March/April 1980), p. 198; Jerry McCaffrey and John H. Bowman,

"Participatory Democracy and Budgeting," *Public Administration Review,* vol. 38 (November/December 1978), pp. 530–533; Anita A. Summers, "Proposition 13 and Its Aftermath," *Business Review* (March/April 1979); John M. Greine and Harry P. Hatry, "Coping with Cutbacks: Initial Agency Level Response in 17 Local Governments to Massachusetts' Proposition 2 1/2" (Washington, D.C.: Urban Institute, 1982).

82. ACIR, *Significant Features,* 1993, vol. 2, Table 60.

83. Tax Foundation, *Facts and Figures on Governmental Finance, 1992 Edition* (Washington, D.C., 1992), pp. 34–312.

84. *City and State,* April 1991; *Public Administration Times,* Feb. 1, 1992; *New York Times,* July 9, 1993, summarizing a fiscal survey by the National League of Cities.

Chapter 8

1. Richard F. Fenno, Jr., *The Power of the Purse* (Boston: Little, Brown, 1966), p. xiii.

2. United States Office of Personnel Management, *Federal Civilian Workforce Statistics, Employment and Trends as of January 1993* (Washington, D.C., February 1993). See also, Norman J. Ornstein, Thomas E. Mann, and Michael J. Malbin, *Vital Statistics on Congress 1991–92 edition* (Washington, D.C.: American Enterprise Institute, 1992), p. 120.

3. Congressional Research Service, *Congressional Committee Staff and Funding,* May 26, 1993 (Washington, D.C.).

4. Ibid.

5. Ibid.

6. Frederick C. Mosher, *The GAO: The Quest for Accountability in American Government* (Boulder, Colo.: Westview Press, 1979).

7. For an authoritative account of congressional cycles in policymaking, budgeting, and oversight see James L. Sundquist, *The Decline and Resurgence of Congress* (Washington, D.C.: The Brookings Institution, 1981).

8. For a general account of these developments see Fenno, *The Power of the Purse.* Lance T. Le Loup, "Appropriations Politics in Congress," *Public Budgeting and Finance* 4 (Winter 1984), pp. 78–98, summarizes the major themes of Fenno's work and relates them to congressional budget practices of the early 1980s.

9. Le Loup, "Appropriations Politics," pp. 78–79.

10. Howard E. Shuman, *Politics and The Budget,* (Englewood Cliffs, N.J.: Prentice Hall, 1992), pp. 184–186.

11. Dennis S. Ippolito, "Reform, Congress and the President" in W. Thomas Wander, F. Ted Hebert, and Gary W. Copeland, eds., *Congressional Budgeting: Politics, Process and Powers* (Baltimore: John Hopkins Univ. Press, 1984), p. 137.

12. Lance T. Le Loup, *The Fiscal Congress: Legislative Control of the Budget* (Westport, Conn.: Greenwood Press, 1980), p. 18.

13. United States Congress, House of Representatives, Committee on the Budget, *The Congressional Budget Process: A General Explanation* (Washington, D.C.: USGPO, 1982), p. 5. PL 92-599 authorized the study.

14. Allen Schick, *Congress and Money: Budgeting, Spending and Taxing* (Washington, D.C.: The Urban Institute, 1980), pp. 39–45, 55–60; Stanley E. Collender, *The Guide to the Federal Budget, Fiscal 1985 Edition* (Washington, D.C.: The Urban Institute Press, 1984), pp. 12–15; Wander, "The Politics of Congressional Budget Reform," in

Wander et al., *Congressional Budgeting*, pp. 12–13; Roger H. Davidson and Walter J. Oleszek, *Congress and Its Members*, 4th ed. (Washington, D.C.: Congressional Quarterly, Inc., 1994), p. 32.

15. Schick, *Congress and Money*, pp. 44–48.

16. "Impounding Funds," *Harvard Law Review* 86 (June 1973), pp. 1505–1535; Nile Stanton, "History and Practice of Executive Impoundment of Appropriated Funds," *Nebraska Law Review* 53, no. 1 (1974), pp. 3–4.

17. Sally Weintraub, "The Impoundment Question—An Overview," *Brooklyn Law Review* 40 (Fall 1973); Louis Fisher, *Court Cases on Impoundment of Funds: A Public Policy Analysis* (Washington, D.C.: Congressional Research Service, 1974).

18. United States Congress, Joint Study Committee on Budget Control, *Recommendations for Improving Congressional Control over Budgetary Outlays and Receipt Totals* (Washington, D.C.: USGPO, April 1973).

19. The description of the Budget Act of 1974 that follows is based in part on Schick, *Congress and Money*, pp. 55–60; Committee on the Budget, *The Congressional Budget Process*, pp. 6–21; and Collender, *Guide to the Federal Budget*, pp. 15–21.

20. Among several noteworthy accounts of the congressional budget process are the following: Lawrence C. Dodd and Bruce I. Oppenheimer, *Congress Reconsidered*, 3rd ed. (Washington, D.C.: Congressional Quarterly Press, 1985); Joel Haveman, *Congress and the Budget* (Bloomington: Indiana Univ. Press, 1978); Dennis S. Ippolito, *Congressional Spending* (Ithaca, N.Y.: Cornell Univ. Press and the Twentieth Century Fund, 1981); Le Loup, *The Fiscal Congress;* Thomas E. Mann and Norman J. Ornstein, eds., *The New Congress*, 2nd ed. (Washington, D.C.: American Enterprise Institute, 1981); Rudolph G. Penner, ed., *The Congressional Budget Process After Five Years* (Washington, D.C.: American Enterprise Institute, 1981); Schick, *Congress and Money;* James L. Sundquist, *The Decline and Resurgence of Congress* (Washington, D.C.: The Brookings Institution, 1981); Wander et al., *Congressional Budgeting*.

21. F. Ted Hebert, "Congressional Budgeting, 1971–1983: Continuity and Change," in Wander et al., *Congressional Budgeting*, p. 33.

22. Daniel P. Moynihan, "'Budget Process' Is an Oxymoron," *New York Times*, March 20, 1985, p. A. 27.

23. United States Senate, Committee on the Budget, *Can Congress Control the Power of the Purse?*, Hearings, 95th Congress, 2nd Sess., Jan. 17–19, 1978, (Washington, D.C.: USGPO, 1978).

24. Shuman, *Politics and the Budget*, pp. 294–295, 298–299.

25. Lance T. Le Loup, "The Impact of Budget Reform on the Senate," in Wander et al., *Congressional Budgeting*, p. 99.

26. Roger H. Davidson, "The Congressional Budget: How Much Change? How Much Reform?" in Wander et al., *Congressional Budgeting*, p. 164.

27. United States Congress, Congressional Budget Office (CBO), *Reducing the Deficit: Spending and Revenue Options* (Washington, D.C., March 1986), pp. 8–10.

28. Balanced Budget and Emergency Deficit Control Act of 1985, Secs. 30–301.

29. Lance T. Le Loup, Barbara Luck Graham, and Stacey Barwick, "Deficit Politics and Constitutional Government: The Impact of Gramm–Rudman–Hollings," *Public Budgeting and Finance* 7 (Spring 1987), p. 87.

30. Peter T. Kilborn, "Future for Budget Law: A Political Balancing Act," *New York Times*, December 13, 1985, p. B8; Tom Wicker, "Risky Abracadabra," *New York Times*, October 11, 1985, p. A35.

31. Shuman, *Politics and the Budget*, p. 282.

32. Shuman, *Politics and the Budget,* p. 127; Rudolph G. Penner and Alan J. Abramson, *Broken Purse Strings* (Washington, D.C.: Urban Institute, 1988); Joseph White and Aaron Wildavsky, *The Deficit and the Public Interest* (Berkeley: Univ. of California Press, 1991), p. 522.

33. Robert Keith, "Budget Enforcement in 1992" (Washington, D.C.: Congressional Research Service, 1993); Richard Doyle and Jerry McCaffery "The Budget Enforcement Act of 1991," *Public Budgeting and Finance* 12 (Spring 1992).

34. Philip G. Joyce, "The Budget Enforcement Act, Its Survival," *Public Budgeting and Finance* 12 (Spring 1992); Doyle and McCaffery, "The Budget Enforcement Act," p. 37.

35. Allen Schick, Statement Before Task Force on Budget Process, Committee on the Budget, House of Representatives, Oct. 10, 1991 (Washington, D.C.: USGPO, 1991), pp. 55–64.

36. *New York Times,* April 11, 1993, p. 26; for a discussion of "iron triangles" and "issue networks" see Hugh Heclo, "Issue Network and the Executive Establishment" in A. King, ed., *The New American Political System* (Washington, D.C.: American Enterprise Institute, 1978); J. Kingdon, *Agendas, Alternatives and Public Policies* (Boston: Little, Brown & Co., 1984).

37. Le Loup, "Appropriations Politics," pp. 80–81.

38. Executive Office of the President, Office of Management and Budget (OMB), *The Budget for Fiscal Year 1993* (Washington, D.C., 1992), Appendix One, p. 142.

39. CBO, *Advance Budgeting: A Report to the Congress* (Washington, D.C., 1977); OMB, *A Study of the Feasibility of Submitting the President's Budget and Enacting Budget Authority in Advance of the Current Timetable* (Washington, D.C., January 1977); United States General Accounting Office (GAO), *Biennial Budgeting: Summary of the Major Issues* (Washington, D.C., April 1984), pp. 1–7.

40. Schick, *Congress and Money,* pp. 485–562.

41. Glen Abney and Thomas P. Lauth, "The Line-Item Veto in the States: An Instrument for Fiscal Restraint or an Instrument of Partisanship?", *Public Administration Review* (May/June, 1989), pp. 372–377; Barbara Yondorf and B.J. Summers, *Legislative Budget Procedures in the 50 States* (Denver: National Conference of State Legislatures, 1983), pp. 5, 66–67.

42. Advisory Commission on Intergovernmental Relations (ACIR), *Significant Features of Fiscal Finances,* vol. 1 (Washington, D.C., 1992).

43. Herbert Sydney Duncombe and Florence Heffron, "Legislative Budgeting," in Jack Rabin and Thomas D. Lynch, eds., *Handbook on Public Budgeting and Financial Management* (New York: Marcel Dekker, 1983), p. 434; Alan Balutis and Daron K. Butler, eds., *The Political Pursestrings: the Role of the Legislature in the Budgetary Process* (New York: Sage Publications, 1975), p. 20. The two landmark court cases were *Baker v. Carr* 369 U.S. 186 (1962) and *Gray v. Sanders* 372 U.S. 368 (1963).

44. ACIR, *Significant Features,* 1993 edition, vol. 1, table 2.

45. William T. Pound, "The State Legislatures" in *The Book of the States, 1984–1985* (Lexington, Ky.: The Council of State Governments, 1984), p. 79.

46. Tony Hutchison, *The Legislative Role in Revenue and Demographic Forecasting* (Denver: National Conference of State Legislatures, 1987).

47. Council of State Governments, *Book of the States, 1992-93* (Lexington, Ky., 1992), p. 177; Yondorf and Summers, *Legislative Budget Procedures.*

48. Yondorf and Summers, *Legislative Budget Procedures,* p. 103.

49. National Conference of State Legislatures, *Staff Size in State Legislatures,* (Denver, 1988).

50. Belle Zeller, ed., *American State Legislatures* (New York: Crowell, 1954).
51. John Marchi, Chairman of the Assembly Ways and Means Committee, New York State Legislature, cited by the *Albany [New York] Times Union,* February 24, 1985, p. 1.
52. Yondorf and Summers, *Legislative Budget Procedures,* p. 28.
53. Ibid., pp. 30–33.
54. Based on interviews in 1991 with A. Alan Post; see also Naomi Caiden, "An Interview with A. Alan Post, Legislative Analyst for the State of California, 1950–1977," *Public Budgeting and Finance* 4 (Autumn 1984), pp. 75–90; D.J. Doubleday, *Legislative Review of the Budget in California* (Berkeley: Institute of Governmental Studies, Univ. of California, 1967).
55. *New York Times,* Dec. 6, 1992, p. 31.
56. Yondorf and Summers, *Legislative Budget Procedures,* pp. 76–77.
57. Yondorf and Summers, *Legislative Budget Procedures,* p. 42.
58. Anthony M. Hutchinson, Arturo Perez, and Ronald Snell, *State Budget Actions 1992,* (Denver: National Conference of State Legislatures, 1992).
59. Richard E. Brown and Ralph Craft, "Auditing and Public Administration: The Unrealized Partnership," *Public Administration Review* 40 (May/June 1980), pp. 259–261; Kay T. Pohlman "State Financial Administration," in *The Book of the States, 1984–1985,* pp. 236–239.
60. *Book of the States, 1992–93,* pp. 201–204; ACIR, "State Legislatures," in *The Question of State Government Capability,* p. 116; Common Cause, *The Status of Sunset in the States* (Washington, D.C., 1982); Edwin Margolies, Richard Hurley, and William Berry, *Sunset Laws: A Critical Analysis and New Approach* (Albany: New York State Temporary Commission on Management and Productivity in the Public Sector, undated but probably 1977); New York State Legislature, Senate Research Service, *Sunset . . . It's Not all Rosy* (Albany, 1977).
61. ACIR, "State Legislatures," p. 123.
62. David Merriman, *The Control of Municipal Budgets* (New York: Greenwood Press, 1987); International City Managers Association, *The Municipal Yearbook, 1992* (Washington, D.C., 1992); Duncombe and Heffron, "Legislative Budgeting," pp. 447–448; H.S. Duncombe, *Modern County Government* (Washington, D.C.: National Association of Counties, 1977); S.W. Torrence, *Grassroots Governments: The County in American Politics* (Washington, D.C.: Robert B. Luce, 1974); Frederick O.R. Hayes et al., *Linkages: Improving Financial Management in Local Government* (Washington, D.C.: Urban Institute, 1982), pp. 23–43.

Chapter 9

1. Ronald B. Hoskins, "Within Year Appropriation Changes in Georgia State Government" (Ph.D. dissertation, Univ. of Georgia, 1983), pp. 31, 42, 51
2. National Governors' Association, National Association of State Budget Officers, *The Fiscal Survey of States* (Washington, D.C., 1992), p. 11.
3. Joint Financial Management Improvement Program (JFMIP), *Financial Handbook for Non-financial Executives in the Federal Government* (Washington, D.C., 1992).
4. Advisory Commission on Intergovernmental Relations (ACIR), *Significant Features of Fiscal Federalism, 1992,* vol. 1 (Washington, D.C., 1992).
5. National Conference of State Legislatures (NCSL), *Legislative Authority Over the Enacted Budget* (Denver, 1992), pp. 10–11.

6. Ibid., pp. 7–9.

7. Hoskins, "Within Year Appropriation Changes," p. 87.

8. Based on a survey of state budget offices in 1992.

9. Executive Office of the President, Office of Management and Budget (OMB), *Instructions on Budget Execution, Circular A-34* (Washington, D.C., Aug. 26, 1985, as amended), part III, 31.1.

10. JFMIP, *1991 Report* (Washington, D.C., 1992), p. 9.

11. See Chapter 8 on Legislative Budgeting for a discussion of rescissions, deferrals, and sequesters.

12. John P. Forrester and Daniel R. Mullins, "Rebudgeting: The Serial Nature of Municipal Budgeting Processes," *Public Administration Review* (Sept./Oct. 1992), pp. 467–472.

13. United States Congress, Congressional Budget Office (CBO), *The Economic and Budget Outlook: Fiscal Years 1994–1998* (Washington, D.C., 1993), p. 108.

14. NCSL, *Legislative Authority* (Denver, 1992), pp. 19–23.

15. ACIR, *Significant Features, 1992*, vol. 1.

16. Bernard T. Pitsvada, "Federal Budget Execution," *Public Budgeting and Finance* 3 (Summer 1983), pp. 92–93.

17. Louis Fisher, *Presidential Spending Power* (Princeton, NJ: Princeton Univ. Press, 1975), p. 56.

18. Ibid.

19. NCSL, *Legislative Authority*, pp. 25–29.

20. Fisher, *Presidential Spending Power*, p. 106.

21. NCSL, *Legislative Authority*, pp. 25–31.

22. F.A. Piduch, "Adapting the Budget During the Execution Phase to Changed Budgeting and Accounting Procedures" (Berlin: German Foundation for International Development, 1979), pp. 88–89.

23. Fisher, *Presidential Spending Power*, pp. 103–104, 232–38; Dennis S. Ippolito, *Congressional Spending* (Ithaca: Cornell Univ. Press, 1981), p. 164.

24. OMB, Budget of the United States Government, Fiscal Year 1993, appendix 1, p. 1154.

25. Ippolito, *Congressional Spending*, p. 164.

26. Fisher, *Presidential Spending Power*, p. 261.

27. Pitsvada, "Federal Budget Execution," p. 102.

28. Ibid., pp. 96–97.

29. Fisher, *Presidential Spending Power*, pp. 88–89.

30. NCSL, *Legislative Authority*, p. 38.

31. United States General Accounting Office (GAO), *Farsighted Planning and Budgeting Needed for Public Buildings Program* (Washington, D.C., 1980), pp. 3–6; CBO, *The Federal Buildings Program: Authorization and Budgetary Alternatives* (Washington, D.C., 1983), pp. xii, 3.

32. Martin Tolchin, "In Spite of the Court, the Legislative Veto Lives On," *New York Times*, December 21, 1983. The landmark decision on legislative vetoes was *Immigration and Naturalization Service v. Jagdish Rai Chadha*, 454 U.S. 912, 17 L. ed. 2d 80, 102 S.Ct. 971. Apropos of this decision and legislative vetoes, Tolchin quotes Louis Fisher: "Are they unconstitutional? By the court's definition they are; will this change the behavior between committees and agencies? Probably not."

33. Pitsvada, "Federal Budget Execution," p. 91.

34. ACIR, *Significant Features,* 1992.

35. OMB, *Instructions on Budget Execution,* Part III.

36. "People: Overspending Official Spurs New Jersey Law," *Governing,* July 1989, p. 68.

37. New York State Division of the Budget, "Internal Control Implementation, Certification and Reporting," *Budget Policy and Reporting Manual* (Albany, N.Y., 1989).

38. JFMIP, *1991 Report;* David A. Wismer, "Approach to Cash Flow Forecasting," *Journal of Cash Management* 5 (Jan./Feb. 1985), pp. 12–16; Ronald W. Forbes, "State and Local Government Cash Management Practices," in John E. Petersen and Catherine L. Spain, eds., *Essays in Public Finance and Financial Management* (Chatham, N.J.: Chatham House Publishers, 1978).

39. John E. Petersen, *Financial Planning for State Government* (Washington, D.C.: Council of State Planning Agencies, 1977), p. 35; Frank M. Patitucci and Michael H. Lichtenstein, *Improving Cash Management in Local Government: A Comprehensive Approach* (Washington, D.C.: Municipal Finance Officers Association, 1977), p. 4.

40. JFMIP, *1991 Report.*

41. JFMIP, *News Bulletin* (Winter issue 1984), p. 6.

42. JFMIP, *1991 Report.*

43. OMB, Budget of the United States Government, Fiscal Year 1993, appendix 1, Ch. 3; JFMIP, *Annual Report 1992;* JFMIP, *Annual Report 1986.*

44. JFMIP, *Annual Report 1991.*

45. Ibid.

46. ACIR, *Understanding State and Local Cash Management* (Washington, D.C., 1977), pp. 17–18.

47. Forbes, "State and Local Government Cash Management Practices," p. 55.

48. Merlin M. Hackbart and Robert S. Johnson, *State Cash Balance Management Policy* (Lexington, Ky.; Council of State Governments, 1975), pp. 6–8.

49. Council of State Governments, *Investing State Funds: The Wisconsin Investment Board* (Lexington, Ky., 1976).

50. ACIR, *Understanding State and Local Cash Management,* p. 5; Forbes, "State and Local Government Cash Management Practices," pp. 56–58.

Chapter 10

1. Comptroller General of the United States, *Managing the Cost of Government,* vol. II (Washington, D.C.: General Accounting Office, 1985), pp. 24–25; Relmond P. Van Daniker and Kay T. Pohlman, *Preferred Accounting Practices for State Government* (Lexington, Ky.: Council of State Governments, 1983), p. 161; Barry Anderson, "Budget Accounting," *Public Budgeting and Finance* 9 (Autumn 1989), p. 95.

2. Elmer B. Staats, "The Effect of Poor Information on Management Decisions," *Proceedings of the Ninth Financial Management Conference: A New Decade–The Outlook for Financial Management* (Washington, D.C.: Joint Financial Management Improvement Program, 1980), p. 27.

3. Comptroller General, *Cost of Government,* vol. II, p. 46.

4. Van Daniker and Pohlman, *Preferred Accounting Practices,* p. 133.

5. Ibid., appendix M.

6. Ibid., p. 145.

7. Ibid., appendix M.

8. Government Accounting Standards Board (GASB), *Concepts Statement 1* (Norwalk, Conn., 1987).

9. United States General Accounting Office (GAO), *Budget Issues: Earmarking in the Federal Government* (Washington, D.C., 1990).

10. Ronald K. Snell, "Earmarking State Tax Revenue," *Intergovernmental Perspective* 16 (Fall 1990); Relmond P. Van Daniker and Kay T. Pohlman, *Inventory of Current State Government Accounting and Reporting Practices* (Lexington, Ky.: Council of State Governments, 1980), pp. 4–5.

11. Ernest Enke, "Municipal Accounting," in J. Richard Aronson and Eli Schwartz, eds., *Management Policies in Local Government Finance* (Washington, D.C.: International City Managers Association, 1975), pp. 288–90.

12. A. Premchand, *Government Budgeting and Expenditure Controls,* (Washington, D.C.: International Monetary Fund, 1983).

13. Van Daniker and Pohlman, *Inventory,* p. 17.

14. Federal Accounting Standards Advisory Board, *Statement of Recommended Accounting Standards No. 1,* exposure draft (Washington, D.C., 1991), p. 5.

15. GAO, *Frequently Asked Questions About Accrual Accounting in the Federal Government* (Washington, D.C., 1980), p. 3.

16. Executive Office of the President, Office of Management and Budget (OMB), *Budget of the United States Government, Fiscal Year 1993* (Washington, D.C., 1992), part 3, p. 58; F. Stevens Redburn, "How Should Government Measure Spending? The Uses of Accrual Accounting," *Public Administration Review* (May/June 1993), pp. 232–233.

17. State of New York, *Executive Budget April 1, 1988 to March 31, 1989* (Albany) New York State Division of the Budget, 1988), pp. M5, M6; State of New York, *Comprehensive Annual Financial Report of the Comptroller, 1989* (Albany, 1989), p. 7.

18. Premchand, *Government Budgeting,* p. 393.

19. Frederick C. Mosher, *The GAO: The Quest for Accountability in American Government* (Boulder, Colo.: Westview Press, 1979), pp. 220–221.

20. Ron Points, "Recent Development in Accounting and Financial Management in the United States," in A. Premchand, ed., *Government Financial Management* (Washington, D.C.: International Monetary Fund, 1990), pp. 334–336.

21. Martin Ives, "25 Years of State and Local Governmental Financial Reporting—An Accounting Standards Perspective," *Government Accountants Journal* (Fall 1992), pp. 1–5.

22. Premchand, *Government Budgeting,* p. 392.

23. State of California, *Governor's Budget 1992–93* (Sacramento, Calif., 1992), appendix 14.

24. Comptroller General, *Cost of Government,* vol. II, pp. 5, 27–28.

25. Joint Financial Management Improvement Program (JFMIP), *Financial Handbook* (Washington, D.C., 1991), pp. 52–53.

26. The OECD and United Nations systems of national accounts treat governmental transactions on an accrual basis for accounting, but not for budgeting. See United Nations, *A Manual for Government Accounting* (New York, 1970), pp. 11–12, 19; United Nations, *Government Accounting in Economic Development Management* (New York, 1977), p. 11; OMB, *Budget of the United States Government, FY 1987, Special Analyses,* special analysis B, "Federal Transactions in the National Income and Product Accounts" (Washington, D.C., 1986).

27. Charles A. Bowsher, "Federal Financial Management Forum" (Washington, D.C., GAO, Sept. 22, 1989).

28. JFMIP, *1991 Report on Financial Management Improvements* (Washington, D.C., 1991), p. 9.
29. Ibid., pp. 5–9.
30. State of California, *Governor's Budget 1992–93*, p. 131; Charles A. Bowsher, "Federal Financial Reform" (Washington, D.C.: GAO, 1988).
31. Letter from Martin Ives, Vice Chairman, Government Accounting Standards Board, March 19, 1993.
32. Comptroller General, *Cost of Government,* vol. II, p. 11.
33. Van Daniker and Pohlman, *Preferred Accounting Practices,* pp. 77–78, 83, appendix M.
34. Ibid., pp. 165–166.
35. Statements of the secretary of the treasury and General Accounting Office in Department of the Treasury, *Consolidated Financial Statements,* various years.
36. Van Daniker and Pohlman, *Preferred Accounting Practices,* p. 165.
37. GASB, *Governmental Accounting and Financial Reporting Standards* (Stamford, Conn.: Financial Accounting Standards Board, 1985).
38. Van Daniker and Pohlman, *Preferred Accounting Practices,* pp. 165–166.
39. Department of the Treasury, *Consolidated Financial Statements, FY 1983* (Washington, D.C., 1983).
40. Robert N. Anthony, *Financial Accounting in Non-Business Organizations* (Stamford, Conn.: Financial Accounting Standards Board, 1978), p. 10.
41. Standard and Poor's Corporation, "Municipal Accounting and Financial Reporting" (press release, Dec. 4, 1979) and "Policy Statement," May 9, 1980.
42. For example, see New York State Legislative Commission on Economy and Efficiency in Government, *Accounting and Financial Reporting Reform in New York State* (Albany, N.Y., 1980), exhibit I, pp. 1–2; Oregon Revised Statutes, Public Financial Administration, section 291.040, pp. 1205–1206; State of California, Statutes of 1984, chapter 1286; The Accounting, Financial Reporting and Budget Accountability Reform Act, chapter 405, Laws of New York State 1981; *Public Administrative Times,* Feb. 1990, supplement.
43. Standard and Poor's, "Credit Comment," reprinted from *Credit Week,* July 26, 1982.
44. GAO, *Program Performance Measures* (Washington, D.C., 1992), p. 2.
45. Ibid., pp. 5–9.
46. GASB, *Concepts Statements No. 1,* Objectives of Financial Reporting (Stamford, Conn., 1987).
47. Harry P. Hatry, James R. Fountain, Jr., Jonathan M. Sullivan, and Lorraine Kremer, eds. *Service Efforts and Accomplishments Reporting: Its Time Has Come* (Norwalk, Conn.: GASB, 1990), pp. 4–5.
48. Ibid., p. 10.
49. Ibid., pp. 24–26, 30.
50. GASB, *Preliminary Views of GASB on Concepts Relating to Service Efforts and Accomplishments Reporting* (Norwalk, Conn., 1992), p. 11.
51. Ibid., pp. 15–19.

Chapter 11

1. A. Premchand, *Government Budgeting and Expenditure Controls,* (Washington, D.C.: International Monetary Fund, 1983), p. 320.

2. Morton Keller, *Affairs of State: Public Life in Late Nineteenth Century America* (Cambridge, Mass.: Harvard Univ. Press, 1977), p. 297, cited by New York State Division of the Budget, *The Executive Budget in New York State: A Half-Century Perspective* (Albany, 1981), p. 8. Keller emphasizes this point with regard to presidents, and Robert Kerker, the chief author of the New York State study, applies it to governors as well.

3. See A. Premchand, "Government Budgetary Reform: An Overview," *Public Budgeting and Finance* 1 (Summer 1981), p. 75.

4. United States Commission on Efficiency and Economy, *The Need for a National Budget,* House Document No. 654, 62d Congress, 2nd Session, June 1912; "Message of the President Transmitting the Report," in Albert C. Hyde and Jay M. Shafritz, eds., *Government Budgeting: Theory, Process, Politics* (Oak Park, Ill.: Moore Publishing, 1978), pp. 4–5.

5. Ibid., p. 5.

6. Jane S. Dahlberg, *The New York Bureau of Municipal Research: Pioneer in Government Administration* (New York: New York Univ. Press, 1966), pp. 174–5, 208.

7. New York State Budget Division, *The Executive Budget in New York State,* pp. 7–39.

8. Cited by Lent D. Upson, "Half-Time Budget Methods," *Annals of the American Academy of Political and Social Science* CXIII (May 1924), p. 69.

9. Ibid., pp. 73–74.

10. Executive Office of the President, Bureau of the Budget (BOB), *The Budget of the United States Government, Fiscal Year 1947–48,* p. 1353, cited by Thomas J. Cuny, *The Functional Classification of the Budget* (Executive Office of the President, Office of Management and Budget, November 1975), p. 1.

11. Cuny, *Functional Classification,* pp. 2–5.

12. Executive Office of the President, Office of Management and Budget (OMB), *Budget of the United States Government, Fiscal Year 1993* (Washington, D.C., 1992), appendix 1–8.

13. Ibid., appendix 1–6.

14. United States General Accounting Office (GAO), *Progress in Implementing Program and Budget Information for Congressional Use* (Washington, D.C., August 30, 1976), pp. 1–13.

15. State of New Jersey, Division of the Budget and Accounting, *Budget, Fiscal Year 1992–1993* (Trenton, 1992), B–9.

16. Oregon Progress Board, *Oregon Benchmarks* (Salem, 1993).

17. State of Ohio, Office of the Governor, *The New Paradigm Budget, Fiscal Years 1994–1995* (Columbus, 1993).

18. Wenceslas Baudhillart and Robert Poinsart, *Twenty Years of Budgetary Reform: A Tentative International Stocktaking* (Brussels: International Institute of Administrative Science, 1982), pp. 12, 38.

19. United Nations, *Classification of the Functions of Government* (New York, 1980), pp. iii, 52.

20. Dan A. Cothran, "Entrepreneurial Budgeting: An Early Reform," *Public Administration Review* (Sept./Oct. 1993), pp. 467–468; David A. Goode, "Envelope Budgeting: the Canadian Experience" (Paper presented at the annual meeting of the American Society for Public Administration, New York City, April 16–19, 1983); Jerry McCaffrey, "Canada's Envelope Budget: A Strategic Management System," *Public Administration*

Review 44 (July/August 1984), pp. 316–320; L. R. Jones and Marilynne Musso, "Envelope Budgeting" (Eugene, Oreg.: Univ. of Oregon, Department of Planning, Public Policy and Management, November 1982), pp. 9–16.

21. For example, see Frederick C. Mosher, *Program Budgeting: Theory and Practice* (Chicago: Public Administration Service, 1954), p. 79.

22. BOB, *Work Measurement in Performance Budgeting and Management Improvement* (Washington, D.C., 1950).

23. Ralph S. Roberts, "USDA's Pioneering Performance Budget," in Hyde and Shafritz, *Government Budgeting*, pp. 106–11; Donald C. Kull, "Budget Administration in the TVA," *Public Administration Review* 9 (Winter 1949); Catheryn Seckler-Hudson, "Performance Budgeting in Government," Advanced Management (March 1953), pp. 5–9, 30–32; Premchand, *Government Budgeting*, pp. 321–322. A landmark study, which in large part laid the foundations for performance budgeting, is Clarence E. Ridley and Herbert A. Simon, *Measuring Municipal Activities: A Survey of Suggested Criteria for Appraising Administration,* 2nd ed. (Chicago: The International City Managers' Association, 1943).

24. United States Commission on Organization of the Executive Branch of the Government, *Budgeting and Accounting Report* (Washington, D.C., 1949), pp. 1–17, 77, 84; Seckler-Hudson, "Performance Budgeting in Government," pp. 81–82; UN, *A Manual of Programme and Performance Budgeting* (New York, 1965), p. 5.

25. United States Commission on Organization of the Executive Branch of the Government, *Budgeting and Accounting: A Report to Congress* (Washington, D.C., 1955), pp. 11–15, 17–27. See also United States Commission on Organization of the Executive Branch of the Government, *Task Force Report on Budgeting and Accounting,* (Washington, D.C., June 1955).

26. Based in part on Daniel Klepak, "Installing a Performance Budget," *Management Forum* (American Society for Public Administration, 1956 [no month indicated]); Daniel Klepak, "Performance Budgeting for Hospitals and Institutions" (Chicago: Municipal Finance Officers Association, 1956).

27. Roy Jorgensen Associates, *Performance Budgeting System for Highway Maintenance Management, National Cooperative Highway Research Program Report* (Washington, D.C.: Highway Research Board, National Academy of Sciences, 1972), p. 23.

28. State of Michigan, Department of Mental Health, *Fourth Annual Program Policy Guidelines, Fiscal Year 1980–81* (Lansing, May 1979), pp. 6–42; see also Oregon Executive Department, Budget and Management Division, *Statewide Initiative, Performance Measurement* (Salem, 1992).

29. OMB, *Budget of the United States Government, Fiscal Year 1993, Appendix;* ———, Circular A–11, "Preparation and Submission of Budget Estimates" (Washington, D.C., 1992).

30. For an example of such early criticism, see Allen Schick, *Zero-Base '80, Status of Zero-Base Budgeting in United States* (Washington, D.C.: National Association of State Budget Officers, December 1979).

31. Theodore Poister and Gregory Streib, "Management Tools in Municipal Government: Trends Over the Past Decade," *Public Administration Review* (May/June 1989), pp. 240–248.

32. UN, *Programme and Performance Budgeting;* Baudrillart and Poinsart, *Twenty Years of Budgetary Reform;* Premchand, *Government Budgeting*, pp. 321–325, 339–343.

33. UN, *Programme and Performance Budgeting*, p. 5.

34. Peter N. Dean, *Assessing the Performance Budget Experiment in Four Developing Countries* (Glasgow: Univ. of Strathclyde, June 1985), pp. 9, 12.

35. Ibid., p. 2, 31–35.

36. Ibid., p. 35.

37. United States House of Representatives, Budget Committee, 96th Congress, 1st Session, *Second Concurrent Resolution on FY 1980 Budget, A Multi-Year Perspective* (Washington, D.C., 1979), p. 5; OMB, "The OMB Long Range Projection System," (Washington, D.C., December 12, 1975).

38. David E. Rosenbaum, "Budget Forecasts? Pay No Attention," *New York Times,* January 12, 1985, p. 5.

39. OMB, Circular No. A–11 (Revised), "Preparation and Submission of Budget Estimates," July 8, 1982, p. 39.

40. Rosenbaum, "Budget Forecasts?"

41. Based on visits to and a review of budget documents of various states.

42. Premchand, *Government Budgeting,* pp. 205–225; United Kingdom, The Treasury, *The Presentation of Expenditure Plans in Selected Countries,* Doc. 196 (London: HMSO, February 1978), pp. 37–56; Federal Republic of Germany, *Financial Plan 1979–1983* (Bonn: Ministry of Finance, 1979), pp. 1–3, 6; Premchand, "Government Budgetary Reform," p. 81; Baudrillart and Poinsart, *Twenty Years of Budgetary Reform,* pp. 18–20, 34–35; Siegmar Kunas, "The Budget of the Federal Republic of Germany," *Public Budgeting and Finance* 2 (Autumn 1982), p. 48; Joseph C. Campbell, *Contemporary Japanese Budget Policies* (Berkeley: Univ. of California Press, 1977), pp. 214–215.

43. Advisory Commission on Intergovernmental Relations, *Significant Features of Fiscal Federalism,* 1992 edition (Washington, D.C., 1992), table 2.

44. United States Congress, Congressional Budget Office (CBO), *Advance Budgeting* (Washington, D.C., 1977), pp. 24–25, 37, 75–84, Congressional Budget Office, *Assessing the Effectiveness of Milestone Budgeting* (Washington, D.C., 1987).

45. CBO, *Advance Budgeting,* pp. 30–31; ———, *Reducing the Deficit: Spending and Revenue Options,* (Washington, D.C., 1983).

46. William A. Niskanen, *Structural Reform of the Federal Budget Process* (Washington, D.C.: American Enterprise Institute, 1973), p. 47.

47. Henry Wickwar, "Budgets One and Many," *Public Administration Review* 44 (March/April 1984), p. 101; Niskanen, *Structural Reform of the Federal Budget Process,* p. 8; Jesse Burkhead, *Government Budgeting* (New York: John Wiley & Sons, 1956), pp. 118–119; *President's Commission on Budgets Concepts, Staff Papers and Other Materials Reviewed by the President's Commission* (Washington, D.C., October 1967), pp. 161–163.

48. See Chapter 10.

49. Robert J. Mowitz, *The Design of Public Decision Systems* (Baltimore, Md.: Univ. Park Press, 1980), p. 9.

50. For an analysis of PPBS in Defense, see Frederick C. Mosher, "New Integrated Systems for Planning, Programming and Budgeting, United States of America" (Prepared for XVth International Congress of Administrative Sciences, 1971); Charles J. Hitch and Roland N. McKean, *Economists of Defense in the Nuclear Age* (Cambridge, Mass.: Harvard Univ. Press, 1970), pp. 23–39; David Novick, ed., *Program Budgeting* (Cambridge, Mass.: Harvard Univ. Press, 1965), pp. 82–93. For an analysis of the current version of PPBS in Defense, see L. R. Jones, "Policy

Development Planning and Resource Allocation in the Department of Defense," *Public Budgeting and Finance* (Fall 1991), pp. 16–21.

51. Frederick C. Mosher, "Limitations and Problems of PPBS in the States," *Public Administration Review* 29 (March/April 1969), p. 160; Mowitz, *The Design of Public Decision Systems,* p. 20.

52. Mosher, "New Integrated Systems for Planning, Programming and Budgeting."

53. Cited by Mowitz, *The Design of Public Decision Systems,* p. 9.

54. BOB, Bulletin No. 66-3, "Planning–Programming–Budgeting," October 12, 1965; ———, Supplement to Bulletin No. 66-3, February 21, 1966; ———, Bulletin No. 68-9, Supplement No. 1, July 17, 1968.

55. Mosher, "Limitations and Problems of PPBS," p. 160.

56. State of New York, Division of the Budget and the Office of Planning Coordination, *Guidelines for Planning, Programming, Budgeting* (Albany, 1968).

57. Robert J. Mowitz, *The Design and Implementation of Pennsylvania's Planning, Programming, Budgeting System* (College Park, Pa.: Pennsylvania State Univ., undated), pp. 16, 23. Commonwealth of Pennsylvania, *Program Policy Guidelines* (Harrisburg: Governor's Office, 1976).

58. Paul F. Brown, "An Operational Model for a PPB System" (Lexington, Ky.: National Association of State Budget Officers, 1970); "PPBS—The Wisconsin Experience" (Madison: Wisconsin State Department of Administration, undated).

59. Richard E. Winne, *Results of Survey of Local Government Budgeting, Program Planning, Analysis and Evaluation Efforts* (Washington, D.C.: The Urban Institute, March 1972), pp. 1, 47–53; Carter F. Bales, "Implementing PPBS in New York City" (Chicago, Ill.: Municipal Finance Officers Association, 1969).

60. OMB, Circular No. A-11, "Preparation and Submission of Budget Estimates," June 21, 1971.

61. State of New York, Executive Department, Division of the Budget, *Guidelines for Program Analysis and Review,* (Albany, June 8, 1970).

62. K. E. Marvin and A. M. Rouse, "The Status of PPB in Federal Agencies: A Comparative Perspective," in United States Congress, Joint Economic Committee, *Analysis and Evaluation of Public Expenditures: The PPB System* (Washington, D.C., 1969), p. 814; Carl W. Tiller, "The Demise of PPBS," *Federal Accountant* 2 (June 1972), p. 9; Allen Schick, "A Death in The Bureaucracy: The Demise of Federal PPB," *Public Administration Review* 33 (March/April 1973).

63. Edwin L. Harper, Fred A. Kramer, and Andrew M. Rouse, "Implementation and Use of PPB in Sixteen Federal Agencies," *Public Administration Review* 29 (November/ December 1969), p. 624; Mosher, "New Integrated System for Planning, Programming and Budgeting."

64. William A. Carlson, "Programme Structure: A Framework for Decision Making," in Λ. K. Prawiraatmadya, D. Joon Chien, P. S. Sundram, eds., *Integrated Approach to Budgeting,* vol. 1 (Kuala Lampur, Malaysia: Asian Centre for Development Administration, January 1977), pp. 80–81; Aaron Wildavsky, "Rescuing Policy Analysis from PPBS," *Public Administration Review* 29 (March/April 1969), pp. 4–5.

65. Mosher, "New Integrated Systems for Planning, Programming and Budgeting."

66. Ibid.

67. Mosher, "Limitations and Problems of PPBS," p. 161.

68. For a colorful statement of these views see Wildavsky, *The Politics of the Budgetary Process,* 3rd ed., Chs. 4–6 and also Wildavsky, "Rescuing Policy Analysis from PPBS." For a classic explanation of the incremental mode of decision making see

Charles E. Lindblom, "The Science of Muddling Through," *Public Administration Review* 19 (Spring 1959), pp. 79–88.

69. Wildavsky, "Rescuing Policy Analysis from PPBS," pp. 193–195.

70. Schick, "A Death in the Bureaucracy," pp. 144–152.

71. Mosher, "Limitations and Problems of PPBS," pp. 160, 162–163.

72. Mosher, "New Integrated Systems for Planning, Programming and Budgeting."

73. George Washington Univ., State-Local Finances Project, *Implementing PPB in State, City and County: A Report on the 5-5-5 Project* (Washington, D.C., 1969); Haldi Associates, Inc., *A Survey of Budgeting Reform in Five States* (Lexington, Ky.: Council of State Governments, 1973); James Ramsey and Merlin M. Hackbart, *Innovations in State Budgeting* (Lexington, Ky.: Center for Public Affairs, Univ. of Kentucky, 1978).

74. Dwight Waldo, "Developments in Public Administration," *Annals of the American Academy of Political Science* (November 1972), p. 232, cited by John A. Worthley, "PPB: Dead or Alive," *Public Administration Review* 34 (July/August 1974), pp. 392–394.

75. Tiller, "The Demise of PPBS," pp. 12–13.

76. Robert D. Lee, "Developments in State Budgeting: Trends of Two Decades of Public Administration Review 5 (May/June 1991)," pp. 257–259.

77. Commonwealth of Pennsylvania, *1993–94 Governor's Executive Budget* (Harrisburg, 1993).

78. Stanley B. Botner, "PPB Under Nixon," *Public Administration Review* 32 (May/June 1972), pp. 254–55.

79. Chester A. Newland, "Policy/Program Objectives and Federal Management: the Search for Government Effectiveness," *Public Administration Review* 36 (January/February 1976), p. 20.

80. Richard Rose, "Implementation and Evaporation: The Record of MBO," *Public Administration Review* 37 (January/February 1977), p. 70.

81. Joint Financial Management Improvement Program, *Annual Report to the President and Congress, Productivity Programs in the Federal Government*, vol. 1 (Washington, D.C., July 1976), pp. 3–4, 76, 94–95.

82. Lee, "Developments In State Budgeting," p. 256; Poister and Streib, "Management Tools in Municipal Government," p. 245; State and Local Governments Research Program, *The Status of Productivity Measurement in State Governments: An Initial Examination* (Washington, D.C.: Urban Institute, 1975); "Measuring a Government's Productivity in the State of Washington," *Public Productivity Review* 1 (March 1976), p. 139; State of Wisconsin, Department of Administration, "Productivity in Wisconsin" (Madison, undated); H. P. Hatry and D. M. Fisk, *Improving Productivity: Productivity Measurement in Local Government* (Washington, D.C.: Urban Institute, 1971), pp. 35–46.

83. Jimmy Carter, *Why Not the Best?* (Nashville, Tenn.: Broadman Press, 1975), p. 127.

84. OMB, "Zero-Based Budgeting," OMB Bulletin No. 77–9, April 19, 1977 and ———, Circular No. A–115, May 5, 1978.

85. OMB, *Budget of the United States Government, Fiscal Year 1981, Special Analyses* (Washington, D.C., 1980), pp. 347–348; ———, *The Budget of the United States Government, Fiscal Year 1982*, pp. 312–319.

86. GAO, *Budget Formulation: Many Approaches Work But Some Improvements Are Needed* (Washington, D.C., February 19, 1980), pp. 72–74; Jerome A. Miles, "Fundamentals of Budgeting and ZBB," in Thomas D. Lynch, ed., *Contemporary Public Budgeting* (New Brunswick, N.J.: Transaction Books, 1981), p. 76.

87. Allen Schick, "The Road from ZBB," *Public Administration Review* 39 (March/April 1978), pp. 177–180; Miles, "Fundamentals of Budgeting and ZBB," p. 26; Murray Comarow, "Interview with James T. McIntyre, Jr., Director of OMB," *The Bureaucrat* (Summer 1978), pp. 40–44; Regina Herzlinger, "Zero-based Budgeting in the Federal Government," *Sloan Management Review* (Winter 1979), pp. 3–14.

88. GAO, *Streamlining Zero-base Budgeting Will Benefit Decisionmaking,* (Washington, D.C., September 25, 1979), p. 31.

89. GAO, *Budget Formulation,* pp. 76–79; ———, *Streamlining Zero-base Budgeting,* p. 47–49.

90. OMB, Circular No. A–11 (Revised), "Preparation and Submission of Budget Estimates," July 8, 1982, pp. 31–33.

91. OMB, Circular No. A–11, July 1992, Exhibits 15A and 15B.

92. Erick Kuntz, "Memorandum on ZBB" (New York State Division of the Budget, July 11, 1982). The National Association of State Budget Officers found that ZBB had spread to ten states in 1976 and to nearly 24 in 1979.

93. Schick, *Zero-Base '80,* pp. 27–29, 30–31.

94. Ibid.

95. Allen Schick and Harry Hatry, "Zero-Based Budgeting: The Manager's Budget," *Public Budgeting and Finance* 2, No. 1, pp. 72–87.

96. George S. Minmier, *An Evaluation of the Zero–base Budgeting Systems in Governmental Institutions* (Atlanta, Ga.: School of Business Administration, Univ. of Georgia, 1975), pp. 131, 157.

97. Government of the Philippines, Ministry of the Budget, *Zero-Base Budgeting Handbook* (Manila, Undated); John C. Strick, "Zero-based Budgeting: An Innovation or Rediscovery of Old Concepts?" *Canadian Tax Journal* 28 (January/February 1980), pp. 43–52; A. W. Johnson, "Planning, Programming and Budgeting in Canada," *Public Administration Review* (January/February 1973), pp. 23–31.

98. Perry Moore, "Zero-based Budgeting in American Cities," *Public Administration Review* (May/June 1980), pp. 253–258.

99. Thomas H. Hammond and Jack H. Knott, *A Zero-Based Look at Zero-base Budgeting,* (New Brunswick, N.J.: Transaction Books, 1980), p. 102.

100. Verne B. Lewis, "Toward a Theory of Budgeting," in Allen Schick, ed., *Perspectives on Budgeting* (Washington, D.C.: American Society for Public Administration, 1981), pp. 28–45.

101. Based on correspondence, telephone calls, visits, and a review of documents of various states in 1993.

102. Verne B. Lewis, "Reflections on Budget Systems," *Public Budgeting and Finance* (Spring 1988), p. 15.

103. Ibid., p. 116.

104. Lee, "Developments in State Budgeting," p. 255.

105. Irene S. Rubin, "Budgeting for Our Times: Target Base Budgeting," *Public Budgeting and Finance* (Fall 1991), pp. 6–9.

106. State Policy Reports, (Alexandria, Va., Sept. 1992).

107. Allen Schick, "Budgetary Innovations," in *Budgeting and Expenditure Control,* p. 91.

108. Daniel Tarschys, "From Expansion to Restraint: Recent Developments in Budgeting," *Public Budgeting and Finance* 6 (Autumn 1986), pp. 25–37.

109. Wildavsky, *The Politics of the Budgetary Process,* 3rd edition, pp. 6–62.

110. Aaron Wildavsky, "Political Implications of Budgetary Reform," in Schick, *Perspectives on Budgeting,* p. 72.

111. Aaron Wildavsky, "A Budget for all Seasons? Why the Traditional Budget Lasts," *Public Administration Review* 38 (November/December 1978), pp. 501–505.
112. Schick, "Budgetary Innovations," pp. 95, 100–106.
113. Allen Schick, "Macro-Budgetary Adaptations for Fiscal Stress in Industrialized Democracies, *Public Administration Review* 46 (March/April 1986), p. 124.
114. Allen Schick, *The Capacity to Budget* (Washington, D.C.: Urban Institute Press, 1990).
115. John J. Bailey and Robert J. O'Connor, "Operationalizing Incrementalism: Measuring the Muddle," *Public Administration Review* 31 (January/February 1971), pp. 60–66.
116. A. Premchand, "Government Budget Reforms: Agenda for the 1980's," *Public Budgeting and Finance* 1 (Autumn 1981), p. 20.
117. Eventually, Wildavsky accepted this verdict. See Aaron Wildavsky, *The New Politics of the Budget Process* (New York: Scott Foresman and Little, Brown & Co.: 1988).
118. Mowitz, *Design of Public Decisions,* pp. 56–59.
119. Cited in Lewis, "Reflections," p. 17.
120. V. O. Key, Jr., "The Lack of a Budgetary Theory," in Hyde and Shafritz, eds., *Government Budgeting,* pp. 18–23.

Chapter 12

1. The chapter title is taken in part from Gerald E. Frug, "The Judicial Power of the Purse," *University of Pennsylvania Law Review* 126 (April 1978), pp. 715–793.
2. George E. Hale, "Federal Courts and the State Budgetary Process," *Administration and Society* 11 (November 1979), p. 358; Linda Harriman and Jeffrey D. Straussman, "Do Judges Determine Budget Decisions? Federal Court Decisions on Prison Reform and State Spending for Corrections," *Public Administration Review* 43 (July/August 1983), p. 343; Jeffrey D. Straussman and Kurt Thurmaier, "Budgeting Rights: The Case of Jail Litigation," *Public Budgeting and Finance* (Summer 1989), pp. 30–42).
3. State of Michigan, Division of Management and Budget, "The Judicial Impact on the Michigan Budget" (Lansing, 1990).
4. *Benjamin v. Malcolm,* 495 F. Supp. 1357 (1980), cited in Harriman and Straussman, "Do Judges Determine Budget Decisions?" p. 350. See also *Gates v. Collier,* 390 F. Supp. 482 (1975) *aff'd* 525 F.2d 965 (1976) for a vigorous restatement of this position. Cooper argues, however, that in a significant number of cases, courts have been mindful of costs. See Philip J. Cooper, "Conflict or Constructive Tension: The Changing Relationships of Judges and Administrators," *Public Administration Review* 45 (November 1985), pp. 644–645.
5. 334 F. Supp. 1341 (1971); *Wyatt v. Stickney,* 344 F. Supp. 373 (1972).
6. *Patricia Welsch et al. v. Vera Likens et al.,* 550 F.2d 1122 (1977).
7. *New York State Association for Retarded Children and Patricia Parisi et al. v. Nelson A Rockefeller,* 337 F. Supp. 752–769 (1973); *New York State Association for Retarded Children Inc. and Patricia Parisi et al. v. Governor Hugh Carey,* 393 F. Supp. 715 (1975), "Final Judgment and Consent decree." Several later decisions involved the same parties.
8. State of New York, *Executive Budget,* various fiscal years from 1975–1976 through 1993–1994 (Albany: Budget Division); Helen Bloom, "Facing the Fiscal Dilemma,"

in Valeria Bradley and Gary Clarke, eds., *Paper Victories and Hard Realties: The Imple-mentation of the Legal and Constitutional Rights of the Mentally Disabled* (Washington, D.C.: Health Policy Center of Georgetown Univ. 1976), pp. 85–91; Michael S. Lottman, "Paper Victories and Hard Realties" in Bradley and Clarke, *Paper Victories,* pp. 94–95.

9. *U.S.A. v. State of Michigan* (1990), cited in "The Judicial Impact on the Michigan Budget."

10. Hale, "Federal Courts and the State Budgetary Process," pp. 358–359; Harriman and Straussman, "Do Judges Determine Budget Decisions?" p. 344.

11. *Holt v. Sarver,* 309 F. Supp. 362 (E.D. Ark. 1970) *aff'd* 442 F.2d 304 (1971).

12. *David R. Ruiz et al. and United States of America v. W. J. Estelle,* 666 F.2d 854 (5th Cir. 1982).

13. *New York Times,* December 13, 1992, p. 42.

14. *New York Times,* May 16, 1993, p. 19; *Scotty Grubbs et al. v. Christine Bradley et al.,* 821 F. Supp. 496 (M.D. Tenn. 1993).

15. Richard A. L. Gambitta, "Litigation, Judicial Deference and Policy Change," *Law and Policy Quarterly* 3 (April 1980), pp. 141–142.

16. For a discussion of the budgetary impact of cases affecting handicapped children see R. Shep Melnick, "The Politics of Partnership," *Public Administration Review* 45 (November 1985), pp. 657–658.

17. *PA Times,* Feb. 1, 1994, p. 8; Michael W. Kirst, "The New Politics of State Education Finance," *Phi Delta Kappan* (February 1979), pp. 427–436; Hale, "Federal Courts and the State Budgetary Process," p. 361.

18. Lawyers' Committee for Civil Rights Under Law, School Finance Project, *Update on State-wide School Finance Cases* (Washington, D.C., April 1980); State of New York, Attorney General, *Reply Brief for Defendants–Appellants in Board of Education, Levit-town Union Free School District et al. v. Nyquist* (Albany, April 30, 1982), Appendices A and B; *New York Times,* June 8, 1990, p. B2.

19. The first case was adjudicated in the Superior Court in *Robinson v. Cahill,* 119 N.J. Super. 40 (Law Div. 1972). The Supreme Court affirmed the decisions and took additional actions in *Robinson I,* 62 N.J. 473 (1973); *Robinson II,* 63 N.J. 196 (1973); *Robinson IV,* 67 N.J. 333 (1975); and *Robinson V,* 70 N.J. 155 (1976); *Abbott, et al. v. F.G. Burke, Commissioner of Education, et al.,* 119 N.J. 287 (1990). See also *Board of Education, Levittown et al. v. Nyquist et al.,* 94 Misc. 2d 466 (1978), *aff'd* 408 NYS 2d 606 (1978); 57 N.Y. 2d 27, 453 NYS 2d 643 (1982).

20. *Serrano v. Priest,* 18 Calif. 3d 728, *cert. denied,* 432 U.S. 907 (1977).

21. *New York Times,* Dec. 4, 1992, p. A26; *NASBO News,* July 1993; *Carrollton-Farmers Branch Independent School District, et al. v. Edgewood Independent School District et al.,* 826 S.W.2d 489 (1992). For examples of developments in other states see *Rose et al. v. The Council for Better Education,* 790 S.W.2d 186 (Kentucky 1989); *Helena Elemen-tary School District et al. v. The State of Montana et al.,* 236 Mont. 44, 784 P.2d 412 (1990).

22. *Missouri v. Jenkins,* 485 U.S. 495 (1990).

23. Frug, "The Judicial Power of the Purse," pp. 774–780.

24. *Wilder v. Virginia Hospital Association,* 58 U.S. L.W. 4795 (1990); *Multicare Medical Center et al. v. State of Washington et al.,* 768 F. Supp. 1349 (W.D. Wash. 1991); *U. of Michigan Hospital et al. v. Otis R. Bowen,* 812 F.2d 1005 (6th Cir. 1987); *Temple University v. John F. White, Jr. et al.,* 729 F. Supp. 1093 (E.D. Pa. 1990); *New York*

City Health and Hospitals Corporation v. Perales, (2d Cir. 1992); *Kansas Health Care Assoc. v. Kansas Dept. of Social and Rehabilitation Services,* 958 F.2d 1018 (10th Cir. 1992).

25. Charles Wise and Rosemary O'Leary, "Is Federalism Dead Or Alive in the Supreme Court?" *Public Administration Review* (Nov./Dec. 1992), p. 565; 469 U.S. 528 (1985).

26. Wise and O'Leary, "Is Federalism Dead?", pp. 568–569.

27. *Gilligan v. Emporia,* 986 F.2d 410 (10th Cir. 1993); *Moreau v. Klevenhagen,* 113 U.S. 1905 (1993); *William C. McDonnel et al. v. City of Omaha,* 999 F.2d 293 (8th Cir. 1993); *NASBO News,* May 1993, ———, Nov. 1991.

28. *American Federation of State, County, Municipal Employees (AFSCME) v. State of Washington,* 578 F. Supp. 846 (W.D. Wash. 1983), reversed *AFSCME v. State of Washington,* 770 F.2d 1401 (1985); Michael Graham, "Comparable Worth: Judicial, Legislative and Administrative Developments" (Paper presented at the National Conference of the American Society for Public Administration, Anaheim, Calif., April 13–16, 1986).

29. *State of Nevada Employees Association v. Controller of the State of Nevada,* 824 P.2d 276 (1992).

30. Louis Fisher, *Court Cases on Impoundment of Funds: A Policy Analysis* (Washington, D.C.: Congressional Research Service, 1974), p. i.

31. *Train v. City of New York,* 420 U.S. 35 (1975); Fisher, *Court Cases on Impoundment,* pp. 80–90.

32. *City of Milwaukee et al. v. Kenneth E. Lindner, Secretary of Department of Administration, et al.,* No. 80–1643–OA (1980).

33. *Sierra Club et al. v. U.S. Army Corps of Engineers et al.,* 771 F.2d 409 (1985); *New York Times,* Sept. 12, 1983, pp. A1, B5.

34. George D. Brown, "The Courts and Grant Reform: A Time for Action," *Intergovernmental Perspective* 7 (Fall 1981), pp. 6–14.

35. *New Jersey Association on Correction v. Lan, Secretary of State of New Jersey,* 403 A.2d 437, 80 N.J. 199 (1979).

36. *Fine v. Firestone,* 448 Fla. 984 (1984); *Public Administration Times,* March 1, 1985.

37. *American Federation of Labor–Congress of Industrial Organization et al. v. Lewis K. Uhler, Secretary of State,* 686 P.2d 609, 36 Cal. 3d 687, 206 Cal. Rptr. 89 (1984).

38. *New York State Coalition for Criminal Justice v. Coughlin,* 479 NYS 850 (1984).

39. Donald Axelrod, *Shadow Government* (New York: John Wiley & Sons, 1992), pp. 118–142.

40. For example, see *Austin et al. v. State of New Hampshire et al.,* 420 U.S. 656 (1975).

41. *Maryland v. Louisiana,* 49 L.W. 4562 (1981).

42. *Commonwealth Edison v. Montana,* 49 L.W. 4957 (1981), cited in *Intergovernmental Perspective* 9 (Winter 1982), p. 21.

43. *Armco Inc. v. Hardesty,* 467 U.S. 638 (1984).

44. *Bacchus Imports Ltd. et al. v. H. H. Dias, Director of Taxation of the State of Hawaii,* 464 U.S. 1015 (1983).

45. *Quill Corporation v. North Dakota,* 112 U.S. 1904 (1992).

46. *Goldberg v. Sweet, Director of the Illinois Department of Revenues,* and *GTE Sprint Communications v. Sweet,* 488 U.S. 252 (1989).

47. *Davis v. Michigan Department of Treasury,* 489 U.S. 803 (1989); *Harper et al. v. Virginia Department of Taxation,* 113 U.S. 2510 (1993).

48. *South Carolina v. Baker,* 486 U.S. 1062 (1988); Wise and O'Leary, "Is Federalism Dead?", p. 567.

49. *Nordlinger v. Hahn,* 112 U.S. 2326 (1992); *NASBO News,* July 1992.
50. *Bowsher v. Syner,* 106 U.S. 3181, 92 LE 2d 583 (1986).
51. *Wein v. Carey,* 393 N.Y.2d 959 (Ct. App. 1977); Donald Axelrod, *A Budget Quartet* (New York: St. Martin's Press, 1989), p. 76.
52. *Oneida v. Berle,* 427 N.Y. 2d 407 (Ct. App. 1980).
53. *Korn v. Gulotta,* 72 N.Y.2d 363, 534 N.Y.2d 108 (Ct. App. 1988).
54. Kenneth O. Eikenberry, "Governmental Tort Litigation and the Balance of Power," *Public Administration Review* 45 (November 1985), pp. 742–745; Wise and O'Leary, "Is Federalism Dead?", pp. 564–565.
55. Charles R. Wise, "Liability of Federal Officials: An Analysis of Alternatives," *Public Administration Review* 45 (November 1985), pp. 746–747.
56. Ibid., p. 750.
57. Eikenberry, "Governmental Tort," p. 742.
58. *Pennsylvania v. Union Gas Co.,* 491 U.S. 1 (1989).
59. 436 U.S. 658 (1978) and 445 U.S. 622 (1980).
60. *Public Administration Times,* Nov. 3, 1989, p. 3.
61. Raoul Berger, "The Supreme Court as a Legislature: A Dissent," *Cornell Law Review* 64 (August 1979), pp. 998–1000; ———, *Government by Judiciary* (Cambridge, Mass.: Harvard Univ. Press, 1977).
62. Donald L. Horowitz, *The Courts and Social Policy* (Washington, D.C.: The Brookings Institution, 1977), pp. 7–11.
63. Nathan Glazer, "Should Judges Administer Social Services?" *The Public Interest* 5 (Winter 1978), pp. 64–80.
64. Ibid.; Nathan Glazer, "Towards An Imperial Judiciary," *The Public Interest* 41 (Fall 1975), pp. 104–123.
65. Lloyd L. Weinreb, "Judicial Activism," *New York Times,* February 3, 1982, p. A27.
66. Anthony Lewis, "Why Judges Act," *New York Times,* May 13, 1991, p. A15.
67. Straussman and Thurmaier, "Budgeting Rights," p. 41.

Chapter 13

1. (Reading, Mass.: Addison-Wesley, 1992.)
2. *New York Times,* Sept. 1, 1993, p. A6; Sept. 8, 1993, p. A1; *Public Administration Times,* Oct. 1, 1993, p. 1; ———, Nov. 1, 1993, p. 11.
3. *New York Times,* Nov. 17, 1993, p. A22.
4. George P. Shultz and Kenneth Dam, *Policy Making Beyond the Headlines* (New York: W. W. Norton, 1978), p. 421, cited in Donald Haider, "Presidential Management Initiatives: A Ford Legacy to Executive Management Improvement," *Public Administration Review* 39 (May/June 1979), p. 256.
5. Some rough-and-ready definitions. *Efficiency* is the production of more outputs at the same cost or the production of the same outputs at lower costs. *Economy* covers savings in operations through efficiency, policy changes, and other means. *Effectiveness* is the extent to which the objectives of governmental programs are met. *Productivity* is the relationship between resources (inputs) and outputs and hence is a measure of efficiency. *Impact* is the measure of the effect of programs and projects, good and bad, on the social, economic, and environmental conditions that led to the implementation of the programs and projects in the first place. *Results* are a broad measure that covers all the other measures: efficiency, economy, productivity, effectiveness, and impact.

6. 42 Stat. 20 (1921).

7. United States Government, *Report of the Committee with Studies of Administrative Management in the Federal Government* (Washington, D.C., 1937), p. 20.

8. Executive Order 8248 was issued on September 9, 1939, and is cited in Larry Berman, *The Office of Management and Budget and the Presidency, 1921–1979* (Princeton, N.J.: Princeton Univ. Press, 1979), pp. 13–14.

9. Haider, "Presidential Management Initiatives," pp. 251–52.

10. United States General Accounting Office (GAO), *Compendium of GAO's Views on the Cost Saving Proposals of the Grace Commission,* vol. II (Washington, D.C., 1986), p. 2; National Governors' Association, *An Action Agenda to Redesign State Government* (Washington, D.C., 1993); United States Commission on Organization of the Executive Branch of the Government, *Report to Congress* (1947–1949 and 1953–1955); President's Private Sector Survey on Cost Control, *Report to the President* (Washington, D.C., 1986); Ronald C. Moe, "A New Hoover Commission: A Timely Idea or Misdirected Nostalgia?" *Public Administration Review* 42 (May/June 1982), p. 272; Congressional Budget Office (CBO) and GAO, *Analysis of the Grace Commission's Major Proposals for Cost Control, A Joint Study* (Washington, D.C., 1984), pp. 1–2; Charles T. Goodsell, "The Grace Commission: Seeking Efficiency for the Whole People," *Public Administration Review* 44 (May/June 1984), pp. 197–202.

11. Joint Financial Management Improvement Program (JFMIP), *Report on Financial Management Improvements* (Washington, D.C., 1991), p. 5.

12. Executive Office of the President, Office of Management and Budget, *Budget of the United States Government, FY 1993,* Part One, 307–333.

13. *Public Administration Times,* Sept. 1, 1993, p. 1.

14. The National Academy of Public Administration, *The President and Executive Management* (Washington, D.C., 1976), cited in Haider, "Presidential Management Initiatives," p. 256.

15. "OMB Leadership," statement of Charles A. Bowsher, Comptroller General, before Senate Committee on Government Affairs, Oct. 4, 1992.

16. Haider, "Presidential Management Initiatives," p. 256.

17. National Academy of Public Administration, "Strengthening OMB's Role in Improving the Management of the Federal Government" (Washington, D.C., 1981).

18. Haider, "Presidential Management Initiatives," pp. 256–257.

19. Ibid., p. 257.

20. Berman, *OMB and the Presidency,* pp. 58–64, 85, 107; Ronald C. Moe, "The HUD Scandal and the Case for an Office of Federal Management," *Public Administration Review* (July/Aug., 1991), p. 302.

21. Roger L. Sperry, "Auditing, Evaluation and Management Improvement—The Canadian Experience," *GAO Review* (Spring 1983), p. 26.

22. GAO, *Improving Interior's Auditing and Investigating Activities* (Washington, D.C., 1979), pp. 2–3; *Compendium,* vol. II, p. 44; *Government Computer News,* April 11, 1986, p. 68.

23. Thomas J. Anton, "Intergovernmental Change in the United States," in T. C. Miller, ed., *Public Sector Performance* (Baltimore: The Johns Hopkins Univ. Press, 1984), pp. 16–17.

24. OMB, *Management of the U.S. Government, Fiscal Year 1986* (Washington, D.C., 1985), p. 9.

25. GAO, *OMB's Management Leadership* (Washington, D.C., 1989), pp. 45–46.

26. GAO, *Program Evaluation Issues* (Washington, D.C.: 1989).

27. OMB, *Management of the U.S. Government,* pp. 48, 58.

28. GAO, *Strategic Information Planning,* (Washington, D.C., 1992), pp. 1, 6.

29. GAO, *Paperwork Burden Change in Recent Years* (Washington, D.C.: 1989).

30. OMB, *Management of the U.S. Government,* pp. 43–44.

31. State and Local Government Research Program, *The Status of Productivity Measurement in State Government: An Initial Examination* (Washington, D.C.: The Urban Institute, 1975), p. 1.

32. Stanley J. Botner, "The Use of Budgeting/Management Tools by State Government," *Public Administration Review* 45 (September/October 1985).

33. National Association of State Budget Officers (NASBO), "State Budget Management and Productivity Improvement Projects," *Quarterly Bulletin,* various issues.

34. *NASBO News,* Sept., 1991, Sept. 1991, Sept. 1993.

35. NASBO, *Restructuring and Innovations in State Management: Some Recent Examples* (Washington, D.C., 1993).

36. Ibid.; *NASBO News,* July 1992.

37. NASBO *Restructuring and Innovations,* pp. 54–55.

38. Donald C. Stone, "Orchestrating Governors' Executive Management," *State Government* (Spring 1985), p. 37.

39. Theodore Poister and Gregory Streib, "Management Tools in Municipal Government; Trends Over the Past Decade," *Public Administration Review* (May/June 1989), pp. 240–248.

40. Claire Daehnick, "Management Improvement Strategies," *Public Administration Review* (May/June 1991), pp. 271–272.

41. Ibid., p. 273.

42. CBO, *Using Performance Measures in the Federal Budget Process* (Washington, D.C., 1993), p. 14–17.

43. Ibid., pp. 20–21; Allen Schick, "Budgeting for Results: Recent Developments in Five Industrialized Countries," *Public Administration Review* (Jan./Feb., 1990), pp. 26–34.

44. JFMIP, *News,* Winter 1992.

45. Donald Axelrod, "Performance Audit for Development," in United Nations, *Public Auditing Techniques for Performance Improvement* (New York, 1980), pp. 61–82; Ernst Heuer, "Organizational Audit," Ibid., pp. 44–45.

SELECT BIBLIOGRAPHY

Henry J. Aaron and Harvey Galper, *Assessing Tax Reform* (Washington, D.C.: The Brookings Institution, 1985).

Richard Aronson and John Hilley, *Financing State and Local Governments,* 4th ed. (Washington, D.C.: The Brookings Institution, 1986).

Roy Bahl, *Financing State and Local Government in the 1980s* (New York: Oxford Univ. Press, 1984).

James T. Bennett and Thomas J. DiLorenzo, *Underground Government: The Off-Budget Public Sector* (Washington, D.C.: The CATO Institute, 1983).

Larry Berman, *The Office of Management and Budget and the Presidency, 1921–1979* (Princeton, N.J.: Princeton Univ. Press, 1979).

James H. Bowhay and Virginia D. Thrall, *State Legislative Appropriations Process* (Lexington, Ky.: National Conference of State Legislatures and Council of State Governments, 1975).

Jess Burkhead, *Government Budgeting* (New York: John Wiley & Sons, 1956).

Edward J. Clynch and Thomas P. Lauth, eds., *Governors, Legislatures and Budgets* (Westport, Conn.: Greenwood Press, 1981).

Timothy J. Conlan, Margaret T. Wrightson, and David R. Bean, *Taxing Choices* (Washington, D.C.: Congressional Quarterly Press, 1990).

Robert Eisner, *How Real Is the Federal Deficit?* (New York: Free Press, 1986).

Richard F. Fenno, Jr., *The Power of the Purse* (Boston: Little, Brown, 1966).

Louis Fisher, *Presidential Spending Power* (Princeton, N.J.: Princeton Univ. Press, 1975).

Benjamin M. Friedman, *Day of Reckoning* (New York: Random House, 1988).

Gerald E. Frug, "The Judicial Power of the Purse," *University of Pennsylvania Law Review* 126 (April 1978), pp. 715–793.

Steven D. Gold, *Unfinished Agenda for State Tax Reform,* (Washington, D.C.: National Conference of State Legislatures, 1988).

———, *Reforming State–Local Relations: A Practical Guide* (Washington, D.C.: National Conference of State Legislatures, 1989).

Richard Goode, *Government Finance in Developing Countries* (Washington, D.C.: The Brookings Institution, 1984).

William Greider, *The Education of David Stockman and Other Americans* (New York: E. P. Dutton, 1981).

Diana B. Henriques, *The Machinery of Greed* (Lexington, Mass.: Lexington Books, 1981).

Donald L. Horowitz, *The Courts and Social Policy* (Washington, D.C.: The Brookings Institution, 1977).

Dennis S. Ippolito, *Congressional Spending* (Ithaca, N.Y.: Cornell Univ. Press, 1981).

Daphne A. Kenyon and John Kincaid, eds., *Competition Among State and Local Governments* (Washington, D.C.: Urban Institute Press, 1991).

John J. Kirlin, *The Political Economy of Fiscal Limits* (Lexington, Mass.: Lexington Books, 1982).

Helen F. Ladd and John Yinger, *America's Ailing Cities: Fiscal Health and the Design of Urban Policy* (Baltimore: Johns Hopkins Univ. Press, 1989).

Lance Le Loup, *Budgetary Politics,* 3rd ed., (Brunswick, Ohio: King's Court, 1986).

Charles H. Levine, ed., *Managing Fiscal Stress—The Crisis in the Public Sector* (Chatham, N.J.: Chatham House Publishers, 1980).

Frederick C. Mosher, *A Tale of Two Agencies* (Baton Rouge: Louisiana State Univ. Press, 1984).

———, *Program Budgeting: Theory and Practice* (Chicago: Public Administration Service, 1954).

———, *The GAO: The Quest for Accountability in American Government* (Boulder, Colo.: Westview Press, 1979).

Robert J. Mowitz, *The Design of Public Decision Systems* (Baltimore: University Park Press, 1980).

Walter R. Oleszek, *Congressional Procedures and the Policy Process* (Washington, D.C.: Congressional Quarterly Press, 1989).

Joseph A. Pechman, *Federal Tax Policy,* 50th ed., (Washington, D.C.: The Brookings Institution, 1987).

A. Premchand, *Government Budgeting and Expenditure Controls* (Washington, D.C.: International Monetary Fund, 1983).

A. Premchand and Jesse Burkhead, eds., *Comparative International Budgeting and Finance* (New Brunswick, N.J.: Transaction Books, 1984).

Michael D. Reagan and John G. Sanzone, *The New Federalism,* 2nd ed. (New York: Oxford Univ. Press, 1981).

Alice M. Rivlin, ed., *Economic Choices, 1984* (Washington, D.C.: The Brookings Institution, 1984).

———, *Reviving the American Dream* (Washington, D.C.: The Brookings Institution, 1992).

Allen Schick, *Budgetary Innovations in the States* (Washington, D.C.: The Brookings Institution, 1971).

———, *Congress and Money: Budgeting, Spending and Taxing* (Washington, D.C.: The Urban Institute, 1980).

———, ed., *Making Economic Policy in Congress* (Washington, D.C.: American Enterprise Institute, 1983).

———, *The Capacity to Budget* (Washington, D.C.: The Urban Institute, 1990).

Howard E. Shuman, *Politics and the Budget,* 2nd ed. (Englewood Cliffs, N.J.: Prentice Hall, 1988).

David A. Stockman, *The Triumph of Politics* (New York: Avon Books, 1987).

United Nations, *A Manual for Programme and Performance Budgeting* (New York, 1965).

———, *Report on Budget Management Techniques in Selected Developed Countries* (New York, 1978).

United States Comptroller General, *Managing the Cost of Government,* vols. I and II (Washington, D.C.: General Accounting Office, 1985).

United States General Accounting Office, *Budget Formulation: Many Approaches Work But Some Improvements Are Needed* (Washington, D.C., 1980).

Relmond P. Van Daniker and Kay T. Pohlman, *Preferred Accounting Practices for State Governments* (Lexington, Ky.: Council of State Governments, 1983).

Annmarie Hauck Walsh, *The Public's Business* (Cambridge, Mass.: MIT Press, 1978).

W. Thomas Wander, F. Ted Herbert, and Gary W. Copeland, eds., *Congressional Budgeting: Politics, Process and Powers* (Baltimore: Johns Hopkins Univ. Press, 1984).

Aaron Wildavsky, *The Politics of the Budgetary Process,* 3rd ed. (Boston: Little, Brown, 1979).

———, *The New Politics of the Budgetary Process* (Glenview, Ill.: Scott, Foresman, 1988).

Deil S. Wright, *Understanding Intergovernmental Relations* (Duxbury, Mass.: Duxbury Press, 1981).

Barbara Yondorf and B. J. Summers, *Legislative Budget Procedures in the 50 States* (Denver, Colo.: National Conference of State Legislatures, 1983).

INDEX